TRANSLATOR AND SENIOR EDITOR:
Rabbi Israel V. Berman

MANAGING EDITOR:
Baruch Goldberg

EDITOR:
Rabbi Moshe Sober

ASSOCIATE EDITOR:
Dr. Jeffrey M. Green

COPY EDITORS:
Alec Israel
Michael Plotkin

BOOK DESIGNER:
Ben Gasner

GRAPHIC ARTIST:
Michael Etkin

TECHNICAL STAFF:
Moshe Greenvald
Meir Hanegbi
Yona Ratzon

Random House Staff

PRODUCTION MANAGER:
Kathy Rosenbloom

ART DIRECTOR:
Bernard Klein

CHIEF COPY EDITOR:
Amy Edelman

THE TALMUD

THE STEINSALTZ EDITION

VOLUME VIII

TRACTATE KETUBOT

PART II

VOLUME VIII
TRACTATE KETUBOT
PART II

RANDOM HOUSE
NEW YORK

THE TALMUD

תלמוד בבלי

THE STEINSALTZ EDITION

Commentary by Rabbi Adin Steinsaltz (Even Yisrael)

Published in the United States by Random House, Inc., New York, and simultaneously in Canada by Random House of Canada Limited, Toronto.

Library of Congress Cataloging-in-Publication Data

(Revised for vol. 8)
The Talmud = [Talmud Bavli]
English, Hebrew, and Aramaic.
Accompanied by a reference guide.
Includes bibliographical references.
Contents: v. 8- Tractate Bava metzia— —
v. 7 Tractate Ketubot
1. Talmud—Commentaries. I. Steinsaltz, Adin.
BM499.5.E4 1989 296.1'250521 89-42911
ISBN 0-394-57665-9 (guide)
ISBN 0-394-57666-7 (v. 1)
ISBN 0-679-41632-3 (v. 8)

Manufactured in the United State of America
24689753
First American Edition

In memory of
Hedi Steinberg

The Steinsaltz Talmud in English

The English edition of the Steinsaltz Talmud is a translation and adaptation of the Hebrew edition. It includes most of the additions and improvements that characterize the Hebrew version, but it has been adapted and expanded especially for the English reader. This edition has been designed to meet the needs of advanced students capable of studying from standard Talmud editions, as well as of beginners, who know little or no Hebrew and have had no prior training in studying the Talmud.

The overall structure of the page is similar to that of the traditional pages in the standard printed editions. The text is placed in the center of the page, and alongside it are the main auxiliary commentaries. At the bottom of the page and in the margins are additions and supplements.

The original Hebrew-Aramaic text, which is framed in the center of each page, is exactly the same as that in the traditional Talmud (although material that was removed by non-Jewish censors has been restored on the basis of manuscripts and old printed editions). The main innovation is that this Hebrew-Aramaic text has been completely vocalized and punctuated, and all the terms usually abbreviated have been fully spelled out. In order to retain the connection with the page numbers of the standard editions, these are indicated at the head of every page.

We have placed a *Literal Translation* on the right-hand side of the page, and its punctuation has been introduced into the Talmud text, further helping the student to orientate himself. The *Literal Translation* is intended to help the student to learn the meaning of specific Hebrew and Aramaic words. By comparing the original text with this translation, the reader develops an understanding of the Talmudic text and can follow the words and sentences in the original. Occasionally, however, it has not been possible

to present an exact literal translation of the original text, because it is so different in structure from English. Therefore we have added certain auxiliary words, which are indicated in square brackets. In other cases it would make no sense to offer a literal translation of a Talmudic idiom, so we have provided a close English equivalent of the original meaning, while a note, marked "lit.," explaining the literal meaning of the words, appears in parentheses. Our purpose in presenting this literal translation was to give the student an appreciation of the terse and enigmatic nature of the Talmud itself, before the arguments are opened up by interpretation.

Nevertheless, no one can study the Talmud without the assistance of commentaries. The main aid to understanding the Talmud provided by this edition is the *Translation and Commentary,* appearing on the left side of the page. This is Rabbi Adin Steinsaltz's highly regarded Hebrew interpretation of the Talmud, translated into English, adapted and expanded.

This commentary is not merely an explanation of difficult passages. It is an integrated exposition of the entire text. It includes a full translation of the Talmud text, combined with explanatory remarks. Where the translation in the commentary reflects the literal translation, it has been set off in bold type. It has also been given the same reference numbers that are found both in the original text and in the literal translation. Moreover, each section of the commentary begins with a few words of the Hebrew-Aramaic text. These reference numbers and paragraph headings allow the reader to move from one part of the page to another with ease.

There are some slight variations between the literal translation and the words in bold face appearing in the *Translation and Commentary.* These variations are meant to enhance understanding, for a juxtaposition of the literal translation and the sometimes freer translation in the commentary will give the reader a firmer grasp of the meaning.

The expanded *Translation and Commentary* in the left-hand column is intended to provide a conceptual understanding of the arguments of the Talmud, their form, content, context, and significance. The commentary also brings out the logic of the questions asked by the Sages and the assumptions they made.

Rashi's traditional commentary has been included in the right-hand column, under the *Literal Translation.* We have left this commentary in the traditional "Rashi script," but all quotations of the Talmud text appear in standard square type, the abbreviated expressions have all been printed in full, and Rashi's commentary is fully punctuated.

Since the *Translation and Commentary* cannot remain cogent and still encompass all the complex issues that arise in the Talmudic discussion, we have included a number of other features, which are also found in Rabbi Steinsaltz's Hebrew edition.

At the bottom of the page, under the *Translation and Commentary,* is the *Notes* section, containing additional material on issues raised in the text. These notes deepen understanding of the Talmud in various ways. Some provide a deeper and more profound analysis of the issues discussed in the text, with regard to individual points and to the development of the entire discussion. Others explain Halakhic concepts and the terms of Talmudic discourse.

The *Notes* contain brief summaries of the opinions of many of the major commentators on the Talmud, from the period after the completion of the Talmud to the present. Frequently the *Notes* offer interpretations different from that presented in the commentary, illustrating the richness and depth of Rabbinic thought.

The *Halakhah* section appears below the *Notes.* This provides references to the authoritative legal decisions reached over the centuries by the Rabbis in their discussions of the matters dealt with in the Talmud. It explains what reasons led to these Halakhic decisions and the close connection between the Halakhah today and the Talmud and its various interpreters. It should be noted that the summary of the Halakhah presented here is not meant to serve as a reference source for actual religious practice but to introduce the reader to Halakhic conclusions drawn from the Talmudic text.

English commentary and expanded translation of the text, making it readable and comprehensible

Hebrew/Aramaic text of the Talmud, fully vocalized, and punctuated

Literal translation of the Talmud text into English

Marginal notes provide essential background information

Hebrew commentary of Rashi, the classic explanation that accompanies all editions of the Talmud

Numbers link the three main sections of the page and allow readers to refer rapidly from one to the other

Notes highlight points of interest in the text and expand the discussion by quoting other classical commentaries

REALIA

קַלְתָּהּ **Her basket.** The source of this word is the Greek κάλαθος, kalathos, and it means a basket with a narrow base.

Illustration from a Greek drawing depicting such a basket of fruit.

CONCEPTS

פֵּאָה ***Pe'ah.*** **One of the presents left for the poor** (מַתְּנוֹת עֲנִיִּים). The Torah forbids harvesting "the corners of your field," so that the produce left standing may be harvested and kept by the poor (Leviticus 19:9).

The Torah did not specify a minimum amount of produce to be left as *pe'ah*. But the Sages stipulated that it must be at least one-sixtieth of the crop.

Pe'ah is set aside only from crops that ripen at one time and are harvested at one time. The poor are allowed to use their own initiative to reap the *pe'ah* left in the fields. But the owner of an orchard must see to it that each of the poor gets a fixed share of the *pe'ah* from places that are difficult to reach. The poor come to collect *pe'ah* three times a day. The laws of *pe'ah* are discussed in detail in tractate *Pe'ah*.

TRANSLATION AND COMMENTARY

[1]**and her husband threw her a bill of divorce into her lap or into her basket**, which she was carrying on her head, [2]would you say **here, too,** that **she would not be divorced?** Surely we know that the law is that she *is* divorced in such a case, as the Mishnah (*Gittin* 77a) states explicitly!

אֲמַר לֵיהּ [3]Rav Ashi **said** in reply **to** Ravina: The woman's **basket is** considered to be **at rest, and it is she who walks beneath it.** Thus the basket is considered to be a "stationary courtyard," and the woman acquires whatever is thrown into it.

MISHNAH הָיָה רוֹכֵב [4]**If a person was riding on an animal and he saw an ownerless object** lying on the ground, **and he said to another person** standing nearby, **"Give** that object **to me,"** [5]if **the other person took** the ownerless object **and said, "I have acquired it for myself,"** [6]he has **acquired it** by lifting it up, even though he was not the first to see it, and the rider has no claim to it. [7]But **if, after he gave** the object **to** the rider, the person who picked it up **said, "I acquired** the object **first,"** [8]**he** in fact **said nothing.** His words are of no effect, and the rider may keep it. Since the person walking showed no intention of acquiring the object when he originally picked it up, he is not now believed when he claims that he acquired it first. Indeed, even if we maintain that when a person picks up an ownerless object on behalf of someone else, the latter does *not* acquire it automatically, here, by *giving* the object to the rider, he makes a gift of it to the rider.

LITERAL TRANSLATION

in a public thoroughfare [1]and [her husband] threw her a bill of divorce into her lap or into her basket, [2]here, too, would she not be divorced?

[3]He said to him: Her basket is at rest, and it is she who walks beneath it.

MISHNAH [4][If a person] was riding on an animal and he saw a found object, and he said to another person, "Give it to me," [5][and the other person] took it and said, "I have acquired it," [6]he has acquired it. [7]If, after he gave it to him, he said, "I acquired it first," [8]he said nothing.

GEMARA [9]We have learned there: "Someone who gathered *pe'ah* and said, 'Behold this is for so-and-so the poor man,' [10]Rabbi Eliezer says:

בִּרְשׁוּת הָרַבִּים [1]וְזָרַק לָהּ גֵּט לְתוֹךְ חֵיקָהּ אוֹ לְתוֹךְ קַלְתָּהּ — [2]הָכָא נַמִי דְּלָא מִגָּרְשָׁה?

[3]אֲמַר לֵיהּ: קַלְתָּהּ מֵינָח נַיְיחָא, וְאִיהִי דְּקָא מְסַגְּיָא מִתּוּתָהּ.

מִשְׁנָה [4]הָיָה רוֹכֵב עַל גַּבֵּי בְהֵמָה וְרָאָה אֶת הַמְּצִיאָה, וְאָמַר לַחֲבֵירוֹ "תְּנָה לִי", [5]נְטָלָהּ וְאָמַר, "אֲנִי זָכִיתִי בָּהּ", [6]זָכָה בָּהּ. [7]אִם, מִשֶּׁנְּתָנָהּ לוֹ, אָמַר, "אֲנִי זָכִיתִי בָּהּ תְּחִלָּה", [8]לֹא אָמַר כְּלוּם.

גְּמָרָא [9]תְּנַן הָתָם: "מִי שֶׁלִּיקֵּט אֶת הַפֵּאָה וְאָמַר, 'הֲרֵי זוֹ לִפְלוֹנִי עָנִי', [10]רַבִּי אֱלִיעֶזֶר

RASHI

קלתה — סל שעל ראשה, שנותנת בה כלי מלאכתה וטווי שלה. הכי נמי דלא הוי גיטא — והאנן תנן במסכת גיטין (עז,א): זרק לה גיטה לתוך חיקה או לתוך קלתה — הרי זו מגורשת!

משנה לא אמר כלום — דאפילו אמרינן המגביה מציאה לחבירו לא קנה חבירו, כיון דיהבה ליה — קנייה ממה נפשך. אי קנייה קמא דלא מתכוין להקנות לחבירו — הא יהבה ניהליה במתנה. ואי לא קנייה קמא משום דלא היה מתכוין לקנות — הויא ליה הפקר עד דמטא לידיה דהאי, וקנייה האי במאי דעקרה מידיה דקמא לשם קנייה.

גמרא מי שליקט את הפאה — אדם בעלמא שאינו בעל שדה. דאי בבעל שדה — לא אמר רבי אליעזר זכה. דליכא למימר "מגו דזכי לנפשיה", דאפילו הוא עני מוזהר הוא שלא ללקט פאה משדה שלו, כדאמר בשחיטת חולין (קלא,ב): "לא תלקט לעני" — להזהיר עני על שלו.

GEMARA תְּנַן הָתָם [9]**We have learned elsewhere** in a Mishnah in tractate *Pe'ah* (4:9): **"Someone who gathered *pe'ah*** — produce which by Torah law [Leviticus 23:22] is left unharvested in the corner of a field by the owner of the field, to be gleaned by the poor — **and said, 'Behold, this** *pe'ah* which I have gleaned **is** intended **for so-and-so the poor man,'** [10]**Rabbi Eliezer says:** The person who gathered the *pe'ah* **has acquired it**

NOTES

מִי שֶׁלִּיקֵּט אֶת הַפֵּאָה **If a person gathered *pe'ah*.** According to *Rashi*, the Mishnah must be referring to someone other than the owner of the field. By Torah law the owner of a field is required to separate part of his field as *pe'ah*, even if he himself is poor, and he may not take the *pe'ah* for himself. Therefore the "since" (מִגּוֹ) argument

HALAKHAH

קַלְתָּהּ **A woman's basket.** "If a man throws a bill of divorce into a container that his wife is holding, she thereby acquires the bill of divorce and the divorce takes effect." (*Shulḥan Arukh, Even HaEzer* 139:10.)

הַמְלַקֵּט פֵּאָה עֲבוּר אַחֵר **A person who gathered *pe'ah* for someone else.** "If a poor person, who is himself entitled to collect *pe'ah*, gathered *pe'ah* for another poor person, and said, 'This *pe'ah* is for X, the poor person,' he acquires the *pe'ah* on behalf of that other poor person. But if the person who collected the *peah* was wealthy, he does not acquire the *pe'ah* on behalf of the poor person. He must give it instead to the first poor person who appears in the field," following the opinion of the Sages, as explained by Rabbi Yehoshua ben Levi. (*Rambam, Sefer Zeraim, Hilkhot Mattenot Aniyyim* 2:19.)

On the outer margin of the page, factual information clarifying the meaning of the Talmudic discussion is presented. Entries under the heading *Language* explain unusual terms, often borrowed from Greek, Latin, or Persian. *Sages* gives brief biographies of the major figures whose opinions are presented in the Talmud. *Terminology* explains the terms used in the Talmudic discussion. *Concepts* gives information about fundamental Halakhic principles. *Background* provides historical, geographical, and other information needed to understand the text. *Realia* explains the artifacts mentioned in the text. These notes are sometimes accompanied by illustrations.

The best way of studying the Talmud is the way in which the Talmud itself evolved - a combination of frontal teaching and continuous interaction between teacher and pupil, and between pupils themselves.

This edition is meant for a broad spectrum of users, from those who have considerable prior background and who know how to study the Talmud from any standard edition to those who have never studied the Talmud and do not even know Hebrew.

The division of the page into various sections is designed to enable students of every kind to derive the greatest possible benefit from it.

For those who know how to study the Talmud, the book is intended to be a written Gemara lesson, so that, either alone, with partners, or in groups, they can have the sense of studying with a teacher who explains the difficult passages and deepens their understanding both of the development of the dialectic and also of the various approaches that have been taken by the Rabbis over the centuries in interpreting the material. A student of this kind can start with the Hebrew-Aramaic text, examine Rashi's commentary, and pass on from there to the expanded commentary. Afterwards the student can turn to the Notes section. Study of the *Halakhah* section will clarify the conclusions reached in the course of establishing the Halakhah, and the other items in the margins will be helpful whenever the need arises to clarify a concept or a word or to understand the background of the discussion.

For those who do not possess sufficient knowledge to be able to use a standard edition of the Talmud, but who know how to read Hebrew, a different method is proposed. Such students can begin by reading the Hebrew-Aramaic text and comparing it immediately to the *Literal Translation*. They can then move over to the *Translation and Commentary*, which refers both to the original text and to the *Literal Translation*. Such students would also do well to read through the *Notes* and choose those that explain matters at greater length. They will benefit, too, from the terms explained in the side margins.

The beginner who does not know Hebrew well enough to grapple with the original can start with the *Translation and Commentary*. The inclusion of a translation within the commentary permits the student to ignore the *Literal Translation*, since the commentary includes both the Talmudic text and an interpretation of it. The beginner can also benefit from the *Notes*, and it is important for him to go over the marginal notes on the concepts to improve his awareness of the juridical background and the methods of study characteristic of this text.

Apart from its use as study material, this book can also be useful to those well versed in the Talmud, as a source of additional knowledge in various areas, both for understanding the historical and archeological background and also for an explanation of words and concepts. The general reader, too, who might not plan to study the book from beginning to end, can find a great deal of interesting material in it regarding both the spiritual world of Judaism, practical Jewish law, and the life and customs of the Jewish people during the thousand years (500 B.C.E.–500 C.E.) of the Talmudic period.

THE TALMUD

THE STEINSALTZ EDITION

VOLUME VIII

TRACTATE KETUBOT

PART II

Introduction to Chapter Two

הָאִשָּׁה שֶׁנִּתְאַרְמְלָה

The laws of evidence clearly define the boundaries of valid testimony. Only Jewish males who have reached the age of majority, and who are not related to either of the litigants, and who are not related to each other may testify in court. In general, no one may incriminate himself ("a person may not present himself as an evildoer"), and a person's testimony about himself is not accepted. However, an admission in a monetary matter is accepted as incontrovertible evidence.

Nevertheless, there are areas in which — whether by Torah law or by Rabbinic ordinance — a court may rely on evidence that does not satisfy the aforementioned conditions. The reasons for this are varied. Sometimes evidence is viewed as "the mere revealing of a matter," i.e., the announcement of a fact which by its nature will in any case ultimately be revealed and publicized. Occasionally the Sages relied on imperfect testimony because the legal problem at hand was essentially related only to a Rabbinic ordinance, and they ruled that in such a matter perfect testimony was not necessary. Moreover, and this is the main subject under discussion in this chapter, there are cases in which the evidence is a composite of several statements, so that we must either accept it as a whole, with all its components, or reject it completely. In such cases — for example, when we apply the principle that "the mouth that forbade is the mouth that permitted" — we rely on a declaration which would not have been accepted if it had been made in isolation from the rest of the declaration.

This chapter also discusses a number of other Halakhic issues, both in ritual law

(lineage, the priesthood, ritual purity and impurity) and in civil law (the authentication of promissory notes, the payment of debts). In some instances, judges may accept evidence that is flawed in one way or another, and the limits within which such testimony is regarded as reliable are defined. One of the central topics of the chapter is the status of a woman who was captured by non-Jews and later released. The Sages assume that captive women are usually raped by their captors. Since a priest's wife who has been raped is forbidden to her husband, and any woman who willingly or not has had sexual relations with a non-Jew is forbidden to marry a priest, all former captive women are forbidden to priests. However, since this prohibition is based on doubt, the Sages accept imperfect evidence that no rape took place in order to permit women who were once held captive to marry or remain married to priests.

These are the main problems discussed in this chapter, although several other subjects are clarified incidentally during the discussion of the central topics.

TRANSLATION AND COMMENTARY

MISHNAH This Mishnah continues the subject of the latter part of the first chapter of our tractate: how to deal with a case of divorce that involves a dispute between the husband and the wife regarding the amount of the wife's ketubah settlement. In the cases discussed in the first chapter, Rabban Gamliel and Rabbi Yehoshua disagreed about the law in cases where neither party can prove its claim. Rabbi Yehoshua applied the general legal principle that in monetary matters the burden of proof falls on the plaintiff (in this case, the wife). Hence the husband need pay only the smaller sum, unless the wife can prove that she is entitled to more. Rabban Gamliel, by contrast, placed the burden of proof on the husband. According to his viewpoint, the wife's claim is accepted without proof, in spite of the general legal principle cited by Rabbi Yehoshua, because in the cases discussed in the first chapter the wife's arguments are inherently more credible than the husband's.

In this Mishnah we consider two extreme cases in which Rabban Gamliel and Rabbi Yehoshua are in agreement. In the first case, Rabban Gamliel agrees with Rabbi Yehoshua's argument that the burden of proof is on the plaintiff, because in this case the wife's claim is not significantly more credible than the husband's. Hence he need pay only the smaller sum, unless she can prove that she is entitled to more. In the second case, involving a dispute not directly related to divorce and ketubot, Rabbi Yehoshua agrees with Rabban Gamliel's view that a plaintiff's argument may sometimes be credible enough to override the general legal principle that he must prove his claim. However, before agreeing to place the burden of proof on the defendant, Rabbi Yehoshua demands a degree of credibility far greater than that accepted by Rabban Gamliel in the first chapter.

הָאִשָּׁה שֶׁנִּתְאַרְמְלָה [1]**If a widowed or divorced woman** comes to court to obtain her ketubah,

הָאִשָּׁה

[1]שֶׁנִּתְאַרְמְלָה אוֹ שֶׁנִּתְגָּרְשָׁה,

LITERAL TRANSLATION

MISHNAH [1][If] a woman was widowed or was divorced,

RASHI

משנה האשה שנתארמלה או נתגרשה — ותובעת כתובתה.

NOTES

הָאִשָּׁה שֶׁנִּתְאַרְמְלָה **If a woman was widowed.** The second chapter of tractate *Ketubot* is a direct continuation of the first. Familiarity with a number of basic concepts introduced in the first chapter is necessary in order to understand the second chapter. The following is a review of some of this information.

When a man marries, he automatically assumes certain financial obligations toward his wife. In general, these obligations are fixed by law and cannot be altered. Among them is the requirement that the husband pay his wife, in the event of their divorce, a sum of money from his own property, above and beyond whatever the wife brought into the marriage as her dowry. If the marriage is ended by the death of the husband, a similar obligation falls on the husband's estate. This sum of money consists of two parts: the basic ketubah settlement (עִיקַּר כְּתוּבָּה) which is fixed by law, and an optional additional sum (תּוֹסֶפֶת כְּתוּבָּה) which the husband may choose to write into the ketubah at the time of marriage.

The term "ketubah" itself has several meanings, depending on the context. It can be used to refer to the fixed, basic ketubah settlement mentioned above, or to the totality of the husband's obligations toward his wife, or to the actual document attesting his obligations that the husband gives his wife at the wedding ceremony. In one place in our tractate (below, 47b), it is even used to refer to the property the wife brought into the marriage as a dowry. It is important to note that, in spite of the etymology of the word "ketubah" (which comes from the root כתב, meaning "to write"), the ketubah was by no means universally recorded in writing. The main reason for writing a ketubah was to enable the husband to give his wife an optional additional sum, beyond the basic ketubah settlement (*Tosafot*). In places where it was not customary for the husband to give his wife this additional sum of money, no ketubah document was written at all, since all its standard provisions are fixed by law. Today, however, the universal custom is to write a ketubah.

The basic ketubah settlement — i.e., the minimum sum of money that the husband must pay from his own property if he divorces his wife, or that his estate must pay if he dies — is fixed at 200 zuz for a woman who was a virgin at the time of marriage. There is a Tannaitic dispute about whether this basic settlement for virgins has the status of Torah law or is a Rabbinic enactment (see above, 10a; below, 56a-b). All agree, however, that the Torah did not institute any basic ketubah settlement for divorcees or widows, or for other women who were not virgins at the time of marriage. Nevertheless, the Rabbis instituted that such women should receive a basic ketubah settlement of 100 zuz (a maneh).

הָאִשָּׁה שֶׁנִּתְאַרְמְלָה **If a woman was widowed.** The amount of the settlement to which a divorcee or widow is entitled depends on whether she was a virgin at the time of her marriage (see previous note). Normally, the woman's status and the amount of the settlement to which she is entitled are recorded in the ketubah document drawn up at the time of marriage. But in certain unusual circumstances, the woman's status at the time of her marriage may not be clear at the time of her divorce. The husband

[1] הִיא אוֹמֶרֶת: "בְּתוּלָה נְשָׂאתַנִי", [2] וְהוּא אוֹמֵר: "לֹא כִּי, [3] אֶלָּא אַלְמָנָה נְשָׂאתִיךְ",

LITERAL TRANSLATION

[1] [and] she says: "[When] you married me, [I was] a virgin," [2] and he says: "Not so, [3] but [when] I married you, [you were] a widow,"

RASHI

והוא אומר – המתגרשה קאי. ולאלמנה היורשין אומרים לה: אלמנה נשאך אבינו, ואין לך אלא מנה. ושטר הכתובה אבד.

TRANSLATION AND COMMENTARY

[1] **and says:** "I am entitled to the full 200 zuz, because **I was a virgin when you married me,"** [2] and her ex-husband **says: "That is not true.** You are entitled to only 100 zuz, [3] because **when I married you, you were already a widow,"** then, if the ketubah document is not available, either because it has been lost or because the locality is one in which it is not customary to write ketubah documents, the Mishnah rules that the husband's claim is accepted unless the wife can prove that she was a virgin at the time of their marriage. The Mishnah's reasoning is that in a case such as this we must follow the general legal principle that the burden of proof falls on the plaintiff — the wife. But in order to prove her claim, the wife need not bring direct proof that she was a virgin at the time of the marriage. It is sufficient for her to demonstrate that at her wedding ceremony she was treated in the

NOTES

and wife may disagree as to whether the wife was a virgin at the time of their marriage. If the wife was in fact a virgin at that time, she would be entitled to the higher sum of 200 zuz; if she was not, she would be entitled to only 100 zuz (or perhaps to nothing at all, if a fraudulent claim was discovered).

Such disputes are discussed in the Mishnayot in the second half of the first chapter of our tractate, and here in the first Mishnah of the second chapter. Clearly, it is quite difficult in such cases to prove what the woman's status was at the time of marriage. Hence the discussion in the Mishnah revolves around the procedure to be followed when neither side brings real proof and the court is forced to rule on the basis of legal presumptions and prima facie credibility.

Generally in such cases Rabban Gamliel accepts the wife's assertions and requires the husband to prove that she was not a virgin when they married. Rabban Gamliel accepts the wife's claim even though the onus is normally on the plaintiff to prove his or her claim, and in these cases the woman is the plaintiff demanding money. Rabban Gamliel believes the wife because several factors support her claim: (1) In the cases described in the first chapter, the wife is in a position to know the facts, whereas her husband can only conjecture. Thus we have a situation (called "certain and perhaps") in which the plaintiff says: "I am certain you owe me money," and the defendant says: "Perhaps I do, but perhaps I do not." In such situations, the plaintiff's claim appears much more credible than the defendant's. (2) Every woman is born a virgin, and this establishes a legal presumption (חֲזָקָה) that she has remained a virgin until proven otherwise. (3) In some of the cases discussed in the first chapter, the woman's claim is disadvantageous to her in some way, and it would have been to her advantage to have made a different claim. Her claim is therefore supported by the argument called *miggo,* according to which a claimant is unlikely to put forward a disadvantageous argument that is not based on fact. While this argument does not necessarily prove that she is telling the truth, it does lend a certain credence to her claim. In view of these considerations, Rabban Gamliel rules that the husband must pay the higher amount of 200 zuz, unless he can prove that his wife was not in fact a virgin at the time of their marriage.

Rabbi Yehoshua, by contrast, rejects Rabban Gamliel's arguments and applies the normal legal principle that in any monetary claim the burden of proof rests on the plaintiff. Thus in this case the woman, who wishes to be awarded a larger sum, must conclusively prove her claim; it is not sufficient for her to present arguments that have only a limited degree of credibility.

It should be noted that Rabban Gamliel agrees that none of the arguments he advances is in itself sufficient to compel the husband to pay the larger sum. It is only a combination of the "certain and perhaps" argument with one of the other two arguments that gives the wife's claim sufficient weight to overcome the standard legal presumption in favor of the defendant. Rabbi Yehoshua, however, rejects this reasoning, and refuses to accept even a combination of these arguments in place of conclusive proof.

הָאִשָּׁה שֶׁנִּתְאַרְמְלָה אוֹ שֶׁנִּתְגָּרְשָׁה If a woman was widowed or was divorced. In general, the ketubah laws are the same for widows and for divorcees. In both cases, the woman is entitled to the same financial arrangements. The only difference is that, in the case of a divorcee, the woman is paid by her ex-husband (and if there is a dispute, she must sue him in court), whereas in the case of a widow the husband's role is assumed by his heirs. The Jerusalem Talmud notes, however, that the situation of a widow does not appear to fit the case described in our Mishnah. For the Gemara below (16a) explains that we are referring to a case of "certain and certain," where the wife claims with certainty that she was a virgin when she married and the husband claims with equal certainty that she was a widow. Clearly such claims are possible in a case of divorce, but when a widow sues her late husband's heirs, how can they be certain that she was already a widow at the time of her marriage to their father?

The Rishonim explain that our Mishnah is applying a principle called "we advance the claims on behalf of orphans." Under Talmudic law, when a plaintiff sues an heir on the basis of an obligation assumed by the latter's father, we consider the defendant to have made, with certainty, any claim that the father could have made, even if the heir in fact presented no argument at all. The purpose of this regulation is to protect heirs from baseless lawsuits against which they cannot defend themselves because they have no personal knowledge of the matters in dispute. Thus, in our case, the Mishnah is teaching us that if the husband has died and his widow is demanding

TRANSLATION AND COMMENTARY

way virgins are customarily treated. [1]Thus, **if there are witnesses that** at her wedding ceremony **she went out** to meet her bridegroom **with a *hinuma*** (an adornment worn on a virgin bride's head; see below, 17b), [2]**and the hair of her head was loose,** she is considered to have proved her case, and **her ketubah is 200 zuz.** In Talmudic times, only virgin brides used to wear a *hinuma* on their heads and let their hair hang down loose below it. Widows, by contrast, would not wear a *hinuma* or let their hair down. Thus, if the wife can bring witnesses to testify that this practice was followed at her wedding ceremony, she is considered to have proved her case, and her husband must pay her the 200 zuz she is demanding (unless he can prove that she really was a widow when they married). [3]**Rabbi Yoḥanan ben Berokah says: The distribution of parched grain** at a wedding **is also proof** that the bride is a virgin. In the place where Rabbi Yoḥanan

[1]אִם יֵשׁ עֵדִים שֶׁיָּצָאת בְּהִינוּמָא [2]וְרֹאשָׁהּ פָּרוּעַ, כְּתוּבָּתָהּ מָאתַיִם. [3]רַבִּי יוֹחָנָן בֶּן בְּרוֹקָה אוֹמֵר: אַף חִילּוּק קְלָיוֹת רְאָיָה.

LITERAL TRANSLATION

[1]if there are witnesses that she went out with a *hinuma* [2]and [the hair of] her head was loose, her ketubah is two hundred [zuz]. [3]Rabbi Yoḥanan ben Berokah says: The distribution of parched grain is also proof.

RASHI

אם יש עדים – על נשואיה שיצאת מבית אביה לבית בעלה. **בהינומא** – בגמרא מפרש. **וראשה פרוע** – *איצטייבליד״ה = שערה על כתפיה, כך היו נוהגין להוציא את הבתולות מבית אביהן לבית החתונה. **אף חילוק קליות** – רגילים היו לחלק קליות להתינוקות בנישואי הבתולות. **קליות** – כשהשבולין לחין מייבשין אותן בתנור והן קליות ומתוקין לעולם.

NOTES

her ketubah settlement when the ketubah document is not available, we act as if the husband's heirs have claimed that she was a widow when she married, and the onus is on her to prove that she was a virgin at the time.

It is possible to explain the entire passage in this way, with the claims attributed to the husband actually being made by the court in place of the husband's heirs. But for the sake of simplicity, we have assumed throughout the commentary that we are dealing with a case of divorce, and that the husband himself made the claims attributed to him.

אִם יֵשׁ עֵדִים If there are witnesses. Normally, when a person is required to prove a claim, he must bring two witnesses. In the case discussed here, however, the standards of proof are less stringent. Thus the Mishnah rules (below, 28a) that one of the two witnesses who testify that they saw the woman go out with a *hinuma* on her head at her wedding may be a man who was a minor at the time, even though we do not normally accept testimony about events recalled from childhood. The Gemara explains that the probabilities are in any case strongly in the woman's favor, since most women are indeed virgins when they marry. Hence we only require some corroboration to satisfy ourselves that this is a normal case, and for this purpose inferior testimony is adequate.

שֶׁיָּצָאת בְּהִינוּמָא That she went out with a *hinuma.* The Rishonim ask: Since the first Mishnah in tractate *Ketubot* (above, 2a) ruled that virgins should marry on Wednesday and widows on Thursday, why can witnesses not be brought to testify about the day of the week on which the wedding ceremony was held?

Ra'ah cites the Jerusalem Talmud which explains that the day of the wedding ceremony can prove nothing about virginity, because there are many circumstances under which the rule about virgins marrying on Wednesday is relaxed.

Rashba adds that even when virgins were careful to marry only on Wednesday, widows were not particular about marrying on Thursday. The Gemara (above, 5a) gives two reasons why widows often preferred to marry on Thursday rather than on Wednesday. First, although Wednesday night is propitious, Thursday night is even more propitious; and second, when a man marries a widow, he takes only two days off from work (the day of the ceremony and the next day), and so it is best to hold the wedding as close as possible to Shabbat, in order to gain a third day of celebration. Clearly, neither of these considerations is very compelling, and many widows preferred to marry on Wednesday. Thus, even if witnesses were to testify that the wedding took place on Wednesday, this would still not prove that the bride was not a widow.

שֶׁיָּצָאת בְּהִינוּמָא That she went out with a *hinuma.* The Jerusalem Talmud asks: What if the woman was actually a virgin but legally a widow (e.g., if her first husband died before the marriage was consummated)? In such a case, the amount of the ketubah depends on her legal status, whereas the wedding customs may reflect her bridal status. The Jerusalem Talmud answers that the custom of distinguishing between a virgin and a widow at the wedding ceremony was adhered to very strictly, and a widow would not wear a *hinuma,* even if she was in fact a virgin.

The Jerusalem Talmud also asks about the related case concerning a virgin whose hymen was ruptured through injury. In such a case, the wedding customs would almost certainly have followed the practice for virgins. The Jerusalem Talmud gives two answers to this question: (1) Our Mishnah may reflect the viewpoint of Rabbi Meir, who maintains that a woman who ruptured her hymen in this way is legally a virgin. (2) Even if our Mishnah follows the viewpoint of the Sages who disagree with Rabbi Meir, such injuries are quite rare and we need not concern ourselves with them. Hence, if the woman proves that she was treated as a virgin at her wedding, we consider this to be sufficient corroboration of her claim; if the husband wishes to claim otherwise, the burden of proof rests on him.

כְּתוּבָּתָהּ מָאתַיִם Her ketubah is two hundred zuz.

HALAKHAH

אִם יֵשׁ עֵדִים שֶׁיָּצָאת בְּהִינוּמָא If there are witnesses that she went out with a *hinuma.* "If a woman claims that she

BACKGROUND

אִם יֵשׁ עֵדִים If there are witnesses. Naturally, if the wife brings witnesses who know that she was presumed a virgin when she married (such as witnesses who saw the ketubah and can testify that she was described in that document as a virgin), this is proof of her claim. But the Sages added that even indirect evidence submitted by witnesses that, at her wedding, the bride was treated as it is customary to treat a virgin, also constitutes adequate proof. For it is explained below in the Gemara that, as most women are virgins when they marry, it is assumed that a woman who advances this claim is speaking truthfully. Therefore indirect proof of this kind is sufficient.

LANGUAGE

הִינוּמָא *Hinuma.* Scholars disagree about the etymology and meaning of this word. Many maintain that it is derived from the Greek ὑμέναιος, *hymenaios,* meaning "bridal song," and by extension "marriage" in general. *Rabbenu Ḥananel,* cited by *Arukh,* seems to derive *hinuma* from the Greek ἔννομος, *ennomos,* meaning "lawful." Still others associate *hinuma* with the Greek ὑμήν, *hymen,* which means both "hymen" and "thin veil."

LANGUAGE (RASHI)

איצטייבליד״ה* (correct reading: אישייבלידא). From the Old French *esjevelede,* meaning "with uncovered hair."

SAGES

רַבִּי יוֹחָנָן בֶּן בְּרוֹקָה Rabbi Yoḥanan ben Berokah. A Tanna of the third and fourth generations, Rabbi Yoḥanan ben Berokah was one of the Sages who took part in the Great Assembly known as "Kerem beYavneh" ("the Vineyard in Yavneh") after the destruction of the Second Temple, and he was a disciple of Rabbi Yehoshua. Rabbi Yoḥanan ben Berokah's Halakhic teachings are found in the Mishnah and in Baraitot, and Aggadic teachings are also reported in his name. Little is known of his private

life other than that he had a son who became one of the great Sages of the following generation, and who is always called Rabbi Yishmael the son of Rabbi Yoḥanan ben Berokah.

SAGES

רַבִּי יְהוֹשֻׁעַ Rabbi Yehoshua. This is Rabbi Yehoshua ben Ḥananyah the Levite, one of the leading Sages of the generation following the destruction of the Second Temple. Rabbi Yehoshua had served in the Temple as a singer, and, after the destruction, he was one of the students who went to Yavneh with their outstanding teacher, Rabban Yoḥanan ben Zakkai. Unlike his colleague, Rabbi Eliezer, Rabbi Yehoshua maintained the Halakhic viewpoint of his teacher and of Bet Hillel.

Although Rabbi Yehoshua played an important part in the leadership of the people (he was apparently a senior judge), he earned a meager living from hard and unremunerative work. After renewing his close ties with the House of the Nasi (the president of the Sanhedrin), he was apparently supported by Rabban Gamliel, who used to give him the tithe belonging to the Levites.

Rabbi Yehoshua was famous among both Jews and non-Jews as an extraordinary scholar, possessing wide knowledge not only of Torah but also of secular subjects. He was a celebrated preacher.

Continuing the method of his teacher, Rabban Yoḥanan ben Zakkai, Rabbi Yehoshua was a moderate person and tried to deter the people from ferment which would lead to rebellion against the Roman regime. For a while he had close relations with the emperor's court, and was highly regarded there, as he had been sent to Rome as a member of several national delegations.

Although Rabbi Yehoshua was modest and humble, he was very firm in maintaining his opinions and principles and did not make concessions even when difficult personal controversies developed. However, in other matters he accepted authority,

[1]וּמוֹדֶה רַבִּי יְהוֹשֻׁעַ בְּאוֹמֵר לַחֲבֵירוֹ: [2]"שָׂדֶה זוֹ שֶׁל אָבִיךָ הָיְתָה, וּלְקַחְתִּיהָ הֵימֶנּוּ",

LITERAL TRANSLATION

[1] And Rabbi Yehoshua agrees that if someone says to his fellow: [2] "This field was your father's, and I bought it from him,"

RASHI

ומודה רבי יהושע — מפרש בגמרא: היכא קאי ומאי מודה.

TRANSLATION AND COMMENTARY

ben Berokah lived, it was customary to distribute parched grain among the children attending a wedding ceremony, if the bride was a virgin. But if the bride was a widow, this custom was not practiced. Thus, according to Rabbi Yoḥanan ben Berokah, if the wife can prove that parched grain was distributed at her wedding, she is entitled to receive the 200 zuz she is demanding.

וּמוֹדֶה רַבִּי יְהוֹשֻׁעַ [1] The Mishnah now considers a case involving a dispute (related only indirectly to divorce and ketubot) in which Rabbi Yehoshua agrees with the assertion made by Rabban Gamliel that a plaintiff's argument may sometimes be so credible that the burden of proof falls on the defendant and not on the plaintiff. **Rabbi Yehoshua agrees that if someone** who is in possession of a field **says to another person:** [2] **"This field** originally **belonged to your father, and I bought it from him,"** then the person in possession

NOTES

Throughout this Mishnah, it is assumed that the woman is entitled to a ketubah payment of some kind. The only question is whether she is entitled to the 200 zuz awarded to a virgin or the 100 zuz awarded to a widow. This issue is discussed by the Gemara below (16b): Normally, when a woman demands her ketubah payment, she presents a ketubah document supporting her claim. But if the woman discussed in our Mishnah had had such a document, it would have proved conclusively whether or not she was a virgin at the time of her marriage, and no dispute would have arisen. Clearly, then, we are dealing with a case where the woman did not present a ketubah document. But the rule is that any creditor holding a promissory note cannot collect unless he presents the note. Once he has been paid, he must tear it up, so that it cannot be used to collect a second time. Why, then, is the woman entitled to any payment at all if she does not present her ketubah document?

The Gemara gives two possible explanations. Either the woman had a document and lost it, or she never had a written document because she married in a place where the custom was not to write a ketubah document but rather to rely on the fact that most of the ketubah obligations are in any case fixed by law. And according to both explanations, when the husband pays the ketubah, the wife writes him a receipt so that he can prove he has already paid, should she attempt to collect a second time.

שָׂדֶה זוֹ שֶׁל אָבִיךָ הָיְתָה This field was your father's. Certain general principles of Talmudic jurisprudence underlie this case. In any monetary dispute it is normally the plaintiff who must prove his case, and in the absence of proof the claim against the defendant is dismissed. (Indeed, according to the Halakhah, which follows Rav Naḥman [above, 12b], the defendant need not even respond to the plaintiff with a definite counterclaim.) Hence, in every case it is important to determine who is the plaintiff and who is the defendant.

In a dispute over movable property, the person in actual possession is usually considered the defendant, because we presume that he obtained possession of the property legally, until proven otherwise. Our Mishnah, however, is dealing with a case of real estate, and here the law is somewhat different. Real estate is considered to be in the possession of the last uncontested owner, until proven otherwise. Thus, in a dispute over ownership of real estate between the last known owner and a person in possession who claims to have bought it, the party in possession is considered the plaintiff, and the known owner is considered the defendant. Actual possession is of little significance, unless we do not know who the previous owner was, for then we assume that the person in possession owned the property all along, and we consider him to be the defendant.

In the case in our Mishnah, we did not initially know who the previous owner was. Hence, the person in possession was considered the defendant, and the person who claimed to have inherited the field from his father was required to prove his claim. But once the man in possession admitted that the field did indeed originally belong to the claimant's father, the claimant automatically inherited his father's rights and became the defendant, and the burden of proof reverted to the man in possession, who had become the plaintiff. Nevertheless, in the first clause, where there are no witnesses, the man in possession is believed, because the "mouth that forbade" argument constitutes satisfactory proof; but in the second clause, where there are witnesses and the "mouth that forbade" argument does not apply, he is not believed.

HALAKHAH

was a virgin when she married and is therefore entitled to a ketubah of 200 zuz, and her husband (in the case of divorcee) or his heir (in the case of a widow) claims that she was not a virgin and is entitled to only 100 zuz, and the *ketubah* document is not available (because it has been lost or because this is a place where it is not customary to draw up a written ketubah), if the woman produces witnesses who can testify that the customs associated with virgins were followed at her wedding, she is entitled to 200 zuz. But if she cannot produce such witnesses, her husband need pay her only 100 zuz, but he must take an oath that he does not owe her the additional 100," following the Mishnah. (*Rambam, Sefer Nashim, Hilkhot Ishut* 16:25; *Shulḥan Arukh, Even HaEzer* 96:15.)

[1]שֶׁהוּא נֶאֱמָן, [16A] [2]שֶׁהַפֶּה שֶׁאָסַר הוּא הַפֶּה שֶׁהִתִּיר. [3]וְאִם יֵשׁ עֵדִים שֶׁהִיא שֶׁל אָבִיו, [4]וְהוּא אוֹמֵר: ״לְקַחְתִּיהָ הֵימֶנּוּ״, [5]אֵינוֹ נֶאֱמָן.

LITERAL TRANSLATION

[1]that he is believed, [16A] [2]because the mouth that forbade is the mouth that permitted. [3]But if there are witnesses that it was his father's, [4]and he says: "I bought it from him," [5]he is not believed.

RASHI

שהפה שאסר — זה אינו יודע שהיתה של אביו, אלא על פיו של זה, ומה שאסר — הרי התיר.

TRANSLATION AND COMMENTARY

[1]**is believed** without proof. The person in possession of the field is considered the plaintiff here, since by his own admission the field originally belonged to the other person's father, and no evidence exists that the father ever sold it. Nevertheless, in this case we do not apply the normal rule that the plaintiff must prove his claim in order to be awarded money by the court. We accept without further proof his claim that he bought the field, unless the other person can produce evidence that the field belongs to him.

[16A] [2]The Mishnah explains: Rabbi Yehoshua normally requires the plaintiff to submit convincing evidence, and not just a more credible argument than the defendant's. In this case, however, even Rabbi Yehoshua accepts the possessor's claim without proof, **because** it has a very high degree of credibility, illustrated by the Mishnah with the metaphor. **"The mouth that forbade is the mouth that permitted."** In other words, in a situation where we would have no reason to think that a problem existed if a certain statement had not been made, and that same statement includes a solution to the problem, we view the statement as a single unit and consider the problem solved. We must not divide the statement in two, accepting the problem but ignoring the solution. Thus, in the case in our Mishnah, if the person in possession of the field had said nothing, he would have been considered the defendant, and the other person — the plaintiff — would have had to prove that the field belonged to him, which he was apparently unable to do. It was the admission of the person in possession ("this field was your father's") that created the claim to the field. But the admission of the person in possession was combined with the claim that he had purchased the field ("and I bought it from him") as a single statement. Therefore, the court cannot rely on the statement of the person in possession without accepting it in its entirety. Hence he is believed, and the burden of proof falls on the other person. [3]**But,** notes the Mishnah, the claimant need not prove that the person at present in possession of the field did not buy it. It is sufficient **if there are witnesses** who testify **that** the field originally **belonged to his father.** As soon as the claimant provides independent evidence that the field originally belonged to his father, the person in possession becomes the plaintiff and must prove that he acquired the field legally. According to Talmudic law, if we know that real estate was owned in the past by someone other than the person in possession of it at present, that present possession is not in itself sufficient to create a presumption of ownership. Hence, where there is independent evidence that the field belonged to the claimant's father, the claimant no longer needs to rely on the possessor's admission, and the burden of proof falls on the man in possession. [4]He is now the plaintiff, and if he continues to **say: "I bought** this field **from** your father," without bringing proof, [5]**he is not believed.** Since the person in possession is considered the plaintiff, his claim that he bought the field must be proved, in accordance with the normal legal principle that the burden of proof falls on the plaintiff.

NOTES

הַפֶּה שֶׁאָסַר הוּא הַפֶּה שֶׁהִתִּיר **The mouth that forbade is the mouth that permitted.** This expression appears in several other places in the Mishnah, notably *Ketubot* 2:5 (below, 22a) and *Demai* 6:11, and it describes a situation in which we would have no reason to imagine that a problem existed were it not for a certain statement, and included in the statement is a solution to the problem. In every instance except the one brought in our Mishnah, the problem concerns a ritual matter. Only in our Mishnah is this expression applied to a monetary question.

The other Mishnah in this chapter in which the expression is used (below, 22a) deals with a divorcee who wishes to remarry. Normally, a divorcee is required to produce a bill of divorce. In the case there, however, her claim to be a divorcee is believed solely on the basis of her own declaration. Since we did not know that she had ever been married until she came forward and stated that she had been married and divorced, we have no right to accept only one part of her statement, confirming the problem but rejecting the solution, because "the mouth that forbade [i.e., that raised a doubt about her status] is the mouth that permitted." Commenting on this Mishnah, the Gemara explains that the idea could have been derived from a verse in the Torah, but is so logical that it does not need Scriptural support.

In our Mishnah, where the expression "the mouth that forbade" is applied to a monetary case, the reasoning behind it is not quite so self-evident. It is clear from the Gemara (below) that in a monetary case "the mouth that forbade" is in fact a form of *miggo* argument, in which a

and generally had a humorous, realistic temperament, accepting life with joy. All the Sages of the following generation were his students, and in most of the controversies with the Sages of his own generation, the Halakhah followed his view, and his system became the path taken by the Halakhah. Ḥananyah, his nephew, was his outstanding student.

LITERAL TRANSLATION

GEMARA [1]The reason is that there are witnesses. [2]But [if] there are no witnesses, [3]the husband is believed. [4]Shall we say that [the Mishnah] taught an anonymous [ruling] that is not in accordance with Rabban Gamliel? [5]For if Rabban Gamliel, [6]surely he said: She is believed!

גמרא [1]טַעְמָא דְּאִיכָּא עֵדִים. [2]הָא לֵיכָּא עֵדִים, [3]בַּעַל מְהֵימָן. [4]לֵימָא תְּנַן סְתָמָא דְּלָא כְּרַבָּן גַּמְלִיאֵל? [5]דְּאִי רַבָּן גַּמְלִיאֵל, [6]הָא אֲמַר: אִיהִי מְהֵימְנָא!

RASHI

גמרא טעמא דאיכא עדים – דיצאתה בהינומא. **הבעל מהימן** – ולא אמרינן: הואיל ומספקא לן על יום נישואיה אם בתולה היתה אם בעולה – העמד אותה על חזקתה של קודם לכן, ומתחלה בתולה היתה. **היא נאמנת** – דאזיל בתר חזקה דגופא.

TRANSLATION AND COMMENTARY

GEMARA טַעְמָא דְּאִיכָּא עֵדִים [1]The Gemara begins its analysis of the Mishnah by considering the first half of the Mishnah, in which the wife claims to have been a virgin at the time of her marriage and maintains that she is therefore entitled to a ketubah of 200 zuz; but the husband claims that she was a widow, and is therefore entitled to a ketubah of only 100 zuz. The Mishnah rules that if the wife can produce witnesses to testify that she was treated as a virgin at her wedding, she is believed. The Gemara observes: **The reason** why we believe her **is because there are witnesses** who support her claim. [2]**But** the implication is that in a case **where there are no witnesses,** [3]**the husband's** claim **is believed,** in accordance with the general principle that the burden of proof always falls on the plaintiff, and in this case the wife is the plaintiff since she is claiming her ketubah from her ex-husband, the defendant. Now, in a dispute between a husband and a wife regarding the wife's virginity at the time of their marriage, the wife's claim is intrinsically more credible. Hence it would appear that the author of this Mishnah applies the general principle that the burden of proof falls upon the plaintiff, even when the plaintiff is the wife and has a more credible claim than the defendant's. Now, the question of whether this general principle applies to a dispute of this kind about the virginity of a bride is itself the subject of a difference of opinion between Rabban Gamliel and Rabbi Yehoshua. Rabbi Yehoshua applies the general principle and places the burden of proof on the wife, whereas Rabban Gamliel accepts the wife's claim without proof and places the burden of proof on the husband. Thus it would appear that our Mishnah follows Rabbi Yehoshua. But the Mishnah does not qualify its ruling by stating that it represents the opinion of a particular Tanna. It issued the ruling anonymously, and this normally means that the Halakhah was decided in favor of this viewpoint. [4]**Shall we say,** asks the Gemara, **that the Mishnah** indeed **taught an anonymous ruling that is** in accordance with the viewpoint of Rabbi Yehoshua and **not in accordance with** that of **Rabban Gamliel,** and that the Halakhah follows Rabbi Yehoshua? [5]**For if** the Mishnah agreed with **Rabban Gamliel,** [6]**surely** it would have placed the burden of proof on the husband, in accordance with the viewpoint of Rabban Gamliel, who **said** that in cases such as this the wife **is believed!**

NOTES

claim is believed because the claimant could have made a better claim but refrained from doing so. Thus, in the case in our Mishnah, the person in possession could have denied that the field had ever belonged to the other person's father, and he would then have been allowed to keep the field since the other person had no proof of ownership. Instead, the person in possession chose to admit that the field had once belonged to the other person's father, and to claim that he himself had bought it from the father. Thus, by refraining from making a better claim, the person in possession lent credence to the claim he did make. It is not clear, however, whether "the mouth that forbade" is simply a synonym for *miggo* or a special kind of *miggo*.

There are two main schools of thought among the Rishonim regarding the relationship between "the mouth that forbade" and *miggo*. *Tosafot* and others explain that "the mouth that forbade" is simply the standard *miggo*. According to this explanation, Rabbi Yehoshua would have agreed with Rabban Gamliel in the first chapter if the woman had presented a valid *miggo*. The reason he rejected the *miggo* arguments the woman did present is that they were flawed. *Rashi* and other Rishonim explain that Rabbi Yehoshua would not have been satisfied with an ordinary *miggo* in the cases described in the first chapter. The reason he accepted the *miggo* in our Mishnah is because "the mouth that forbade" is an especially powerful *miggo*, and is accepted even where an ordinary *miggo* is not.

הָא לֵיכָּא עֵדִים בַּעַל מְהֵימָן But if there are no witnesses, the husband is believed. When the wife cannot prove that she was treated like a virgin at her wedding, her husband, as the defendant, is given the benefit of the doubt and pays only the 100 zuz that are not in dispute. From the language of the Gemara, it would appear that the husband's claim that his wife was a widow when he married her is believed without any substantiation at all (*Ra'ah*).

HALAKHAH

הָא לֵיכָּא עֵדִים בַּעַל מְהֵימָן But if there are no witnesses, the husband is believed. "If the husband claims that his wife was a widow when he married her, and his wife claims that she was a virgin, and neither can bring any

TERMINOLOGY

טַעְמָא דְ...הָא.... The reason is X; but if.... Sometimes the Talmud raises an objection based on precise analysis of the details mentioned in a source, asserting that the law is applicable only under specific circumstances, and that under other circumstances the law would be different.

SAGES

רַבָּן גַּמְלִיאֵל Rabban Gamliel II (of Yavneh). Rabban Gamliel was president of the Sanhedrin and one of the most important Tannaim in the period following the destruction of the Second Temple. His father, Rabban Shimon ben Gamliel (the Elder) had also been president of the Sanhedrin, and one of the leaders of the nation during the rebellion against Rome. Rabban Gamliel was brought to Yavneh by Rabban Yoḥanan ben Zakkai after the destruction of the Temple, so that he became known as Rabban Gamliel of Yavneh. After Rabban Yoḥanan ben Zakkai's death, Rabban Gamliel presided over the Sanhedrin.
During Rabban Gamliel's presidency, Yavneh became an important spiritual center. The greatest of the Sages gathered around Rabban Gamliel: Rabbi Eliezer (Rabban Gamliel's brother-inlaw), Rabbi Yehoshua, Rabbi Akiva, Rabbi Elazar ben Azaryah, and others.
Rabban Gamliel wished to create a spiritual center for the Jews which would unite the entire people, as the Temple had done until that time. For this reason he strove to enhance the honor and the central authority of the Sanhedrin and its president. His strict and vigorous leadership eventually led his colleagues to remove him from his post for a short period, replacing him with Rabbi Elazar ben Azaryah. However, since all knew that his motives and actions were for the good of the people and were not based on personal ambition, they soon restored him to his position.
We do not possess many Halakhic rulings explicitly given in the name of Rabban

TRANSLATION AND COMMENTARY

אֲפִילּוּ תֵּימָא רַבָּן גַּמְלִיאֵל [1]The Gemara answers: **You may even say** that our Mishnah **is in accordance with Rabban Gamliel,** because the case discussed in our Mishnah lies outside the dispute between Rabban Gamliel and Rabbi Yehoshua. [2]For **Rabban Gamliel stated his opinion** that the woman's enhanced credibility overrides this principle **only in the cases** discussed in the first chapter of our tractate, which were cases of **"certain and perhaps,"** where the wife's claim was certain and the husband's was doubtful. [3]**But** the case discussed **here** in our Mishnah is **a case of "certain and certain,"** not "certain and perhaps." In our Mishnah the woman declares with certainty that she was a virgin when she married, and the man states with equal certainty that she was a widow. [4]Hence, in this particular case Rabban Gamliel **does not** disagree with

[1]אֲפִילּוּ תֵּימָא רַבָּן גַּמְלִיאֵל. [2]עַד כָּאן לָא קָאָמַר רַבָּן גַּמְלִיאֵל הָתָם אֶלָּא בְּבָרִי וְשֶׁמָּא, [3]אֲבָל הָכָא, בְּבָרִי וּבָרִי, [4]לָא אֲמַר.

LITERAL TRANSLATION

[1]You may even say [that it is in accordance with] Rabban Gamliel. [2]Rabban Gamliel only said [this] there in [a case of] "certain and perhaps," [3]but here, in [a case of] "certain and certain," [4]he did not say [it].

RASHI

בברי ושמא — גבי משארסתני נאנסתי, היא טוענת ברי לי הוא, והוא אינו טוען אלא שמא עד שלא ארסתיך. דהא אינו יודע מתי נאנסה.

Gamliel. However, in his time, and under his influence, some of the most important decisions in the history of Jewish spiritual life were made. These included the decision to follow the School of Hillel; the rejection of the Halakhic system of Rabbi Eliezer; and the establishment of fixed formulae for prayers. In those Halakhic decisions attributed to Rabban Gamliel, we find an uncompromising approach to the Halakhah, and in reaching his conclusions he was faithful to his principles. We know that two of his sons were Sages: Rabban Shimon ben Gamliel, who served as president of the Sanhedrin after him, and Rabbi Ḥanina ben Gamliel.

TERMINOLOGY

עַד כָּאן לָא קָאָמַר פְּלוֹנִי הָתָם...אֲבָל הָכָא... Rabbi X only stated [his opinion] there...but here.... Sometimes the Talmud rejects the comparison of statements made by the same scholar, or of statements made by different scholars, by stating: "Rabbi X stated his opinion only in case A, but in case B, which differs from case A, he would not have maintained this opinion...."

NOTES

But this presents a difficulty. By Torah law, when a defendant admits that he owes money, but insists that he owes less than is being claimed, he is believed only if he takes an oath called "the oath of partial admission" (described in greater detail below, 18a). In our case, since the wife claims 200 zuz and the husband admits owing 100 and denies owing the other 100, why should the husband be believed unconditionally? He should be required to take an oath.

There is a dispute among the Rishonim on this matter. *Rambam* rules that the husband is not in fact believed unless he takes a Torah oath regarding his "partial admission." Most Rishonim, however, are of the opinion that the husband is believed without an oath. *Ra'avad* points out that, by Torah law, oaths are never imposed if a dispute involves real estate. Therefore, no Torah oath can be applied to the ketubah, since it is a debt that is secured by a lien on real estate. *Ritva* and other Rishonim argue, on the basis of the Jerusalem Talmud, that the oath of partial admission applies only when a defendant arbitrarily divides a single debt in two, admitting part and denying part. In our case, by contrast, the division is not arbitrary. The first 100 zuz are an obligation that the husband cannot possibly deny, whereas the second 100 zuz can be regarded as a separate obligation which he denies completely.

Maggid Mishneh distinguishes between a case in which the wife never had a written ketubah, and therefore the husband cannot deny his obligation to pay at least 100 zuz (as *Ritva* argued), and a case in which the wife lost her ketubah. In the latter case, since the husband could have claimed that he had already paid the entire ketubah, his admission should be subject to the oath. *Tur,* however, rejects this distinction.

Maggid Mishneh suggests that *Rambam* does not disagree with the other Rishonim's interpretation of the Gemara. He, too, agrees that in Talmudic times the husband was believed without an oath, because the ketubah was secured by a lien on real estate. After the completion of the Talmud, however, the Geonim decreed that the ketubah should be collected from movable property as well as from real estate. Hence, the ketubah is no longer considered a matter of real estate, and the Torah oath regarding partial admission is applicable. *Derishah* objects to this distinction, arguing that even after the decree of the Geonim, the ketubah still creates a lien on the husband's real estate. *Meiri* explains that where the ketubah is secured by a document, it is still considered a real-estate matter, even after the decree of the Geonim, and is still exempt from the oath of partial admission. But we are dealing here with a woman who lost, or never had, her ketubah document, and in such a case the ketubah is no longer considered a matter of real estate.

Even those Rishonim who disagree with *Rambam*, arguing that the Torah oath of partial admission does not apply, agree that in practice the husband is not believed unless he takes a special Rabbinic oath called *heset*, which applies to any defendant against whom a serious claim is made, even where by Torah law the defendant is believed without an oath. The reason our Gemara did not mention this oath is that it was instituted only in Amoraic times, after the completion of the Mishnah.

HALAKHAH

proof, the husband is believed and need pay only 100 zuz. He must, however, take an oath that he does not owe the other 100 zuz. According to *Rambam,* the oath he is required to take is one oath enjoined by Torah law, because he admitted part of his wife's claim. According to *Ra'avad,* however, he is not required to take a Torah oath, since a ketubah establishes a lien on his real estate and the law is that no oath need be taken concerning a dispute involving real estate; but he must take the Rabbinic oath called *heset*, which applies to most monetary claims.

"*Maggid Mishneh* notes that a person who admits part of a claim takes an oath only if he had the option of denying the entire claim. Hence, *Maggid Mishneh* distinguishes between (1) a ketubah lost by a woman in a place where it was customary to write a ketubah — where the husband could have denied the entire claim if he had wished, by saying that the ketubah had been paid — and (2) a place where it was not customary to write a ketubah, and where the husband is not believed if he claims to have paid, unless he has a receipt. In the former case the oath is authorized by Torah law, whereas in the latter it is merely a Rabbinic *heset* oath." (*Rambam, Sefer Nashim, Hilkhot Ishut* 16:25; *Shulḥan Arukh, Even HaEzer* 96:15.)

LANGUAGE

וּדְקָאָרֵי לָהּ מַאי קָאָרֵי לָהּ And he who asked this, why did he ask it? This expression of astonishment is found often in the Talmud when the answer to a question is so obvious that one wonders why the question was asked in the first place. The etymology of this expression is not clear. Some authorities suggest that the root of the word אָרֵי is ארה, which means "to toss." Thus the expression means: "What was the Sage who tossed this idea to us trying to teach us?" *Arukh* cites a Geonic tradition that the root of the word אָרֵי is ער, which means "to stir up." Thus the expression means: "Why did the Sage who stirred up this idea do so?" Others explain the words of the Geonim a little differently, deriving the word אָרֵי from ארא, which means "to grasp." Thus the expression means: "What did the Sage who grasped this idea understand?"

¹וּדְקָאָרֵי לָהּ, מַאי קָאָרֵי לָהּ? ²הָא בָּרִי וּבָרִי הוּא! ³כֵּיוָן דְּרוֹב נָשִׁים בְּתוּלוֹת נִישָּׂאוֹת, ⁴כִּי בָּרִי וְשֶׁמָּא דָּמֵי. ⁵וְהָכִי נַמִי מִסְתַּבְּרָא, ⁶מִדְּקָתָנֵי: "וּמוֹדֶה רַבִּי יְהוֹשֻׁעַ".

LITERAL TRANSLATION

[1] And he who asked this, why did he ask it? [2] Surely it is [a case of] "certain and certain"! [3] Since most women are married [as] virgins, [4] it is like [a case of] "certain and perhaps." [5] And this also stands to reason, [6] since [the Mishnah] taught: "And Rabbi Yehoshua agrees."

RASHI

ודקארי לה – למימר סתמא דלא כרבן גמליאל. **מאי קארי לה** – ומאי עלה בדעתו לאפוקי מדרבן גמליאל, הא לא דמיא לה! **כיון דרוב נשים בתולות נישאות** – קרובה טענתה להיות אמת יותר משלו, וכברי ושמא דמיא. **והכי נמי מסתברא** – דרבן גמליאל מודה בה דבעל מהימן.

TRANSLATION AND COMMENTARY

Rabbi Yehoshua and believe the woman, even though her claim is more credible than the defendant's. In a case such as ours, Rabban Gamliel would probably agree that the burden of proof should fall on the plaintiff — the wife — in accordance with the general principle. Therefore the first half of our Mishnah may represent the opinion of both Sages, and in no way reflects a decision in favor of Rabbi Yehoshua.

וּדְקָאָרֵי לָהּ [1] This reply to the Gemara's question is convincing. It is clear that the first half of our Mishnah is dealing with a case in which Rabban Gamliel would agree with Rabbi Yehoshua's argument that the defendant should be believed in the absence of proof, even if the plaintiff's arguments are more credible. And the objection raised from the first chapter is groundless, because all the cases in the first chapter were cases of "certain and perhaps," whereas our Mishnah is dealing with a case of "certain and certain." **But,** objects the Gemara, since the solution to this objection is so obvious, **why did** the Amora **who asked this** question **ask it** in the first place? How could he compare the "certain and perhaps" cases in the first chapter with the case discussed in our Mishnah? [2] **Surely it is** obvious that our Mishnah is dealing with **a case of "certain and certain,"** concerning which Rabban Gamliel and Rabbi Yehoshua agree!

כֵּיוָן דְּרוֹב נָשִׁים [3] The Gemara replies that the Amora who asked the question reasoned as follows: The woman claims to have been a virgin when she married, whereas her ex-husband insists that she was a widow. Her claim is intrinsically more credible than his, **since most women** are, in fact, **virgins when they marry.** Therefore the case in our Mishnah should be considered an instance of "certain and perhaps." And just as, in a case of "certain and perhaps," Rabban Gamliel places the burden of proof on the defendant because he considers the plaintiff's claim to be more plausible, [4] so too in our case should the burden of proof fall on the husband (according to Rabban Gamliel), as our case **is considered like a case of "certain and perhaps."** Since the Mishnah does not rule in this way, the Amora who asked the question felt justified in inferring that the Mishnah was ruling against Rabban Gamliel and in favor of Rabbi Yehoshua.

וְהָכִי נַמִי מִסְתַּבְּרָא [5] We have seen that the Amora who asked the question had a logical argument to support his assumption. The Gemara now goes on to bring independent proof that Rabban Gamliel would not, in fact, have disagreed with the ruling of the first clause of our Mishnah. **This also stands to reason,** i.e., additional support can be brought for the argument that the case in our Mishnah is not subject to any dispute between Rabbi Yehoshua and Rabban Gamliel, even though the wife's claim is more plausible than the husband's, and may perhaps be comparable to a case of "certain and perhaps." [6] Support can be brought **from** the following clause, **which is taught** in the second part of **the Mishnah: "And Rabbi Yehoshua agrees** with Rabban Gamliel in a case where 'the mouth that forbade is the mouth that permitted.'"

NOTES

וְהָכִי נַמִי מִסְתַּבְּרָא And this also stands to reason. Normally, this expression indicates that the Gemara is about to bring independent support for the answer just given. In this case, the previous question was: "Did the Sage who asked this question not know that Rabban Gamliel disagrees only in a case of 'certain and perhaps'?" And the answer was: "Since most women are virgins when they marry, the credibility of the woman's claim is equivalent to 'certain and perhaps.'" Thus, if the phrase is to be understood in the normal manner, it must mean: "There is independent support for the idea that a statistical majority is equivalent to 'certain and perhaps.'" Some Rishonim, notably *Ramban* and *Ba'al HaMa'or*, do indeed explain the passage this way (see next note).

Many Rishonim, however, including *Rashi,* explain that the Gemara is not bringing support for the answer to the last question, but rather for the answer to the question before that: "Does the Mishnah's anonymous ruling not appear to favor Rabbi Yehoshua? No, because Rabban Gamliel agrees with Rabbi Yehoshua in a case of 'certain and certain.'" According to this explanation (followed by our commentary), the Gemara is bringing independent support for the idea that Rabban Gamliel agrees with Rabbi Yehoshua in the case described in our Mishnah (see also next note).

אִי אָמְרַתְּ בִּשְׁלָמָא אַיְירִי רַבָּן גַּמְלִיאֵל בְּמוֹדֶה, ²שַׁפִּיר. ³אֶלָּא אִי אָמְרַתְּ לָא אַיְירִי רַבָּן גַּמְלִיאֵל בְּמוֹדֶה, ⁴רַבִּי יְהוֹשֻׁעַ לְמַאן מוֹדֶה?
⁵מִי סָבְרַתְּ רַבִּי יְהוֹשֻׁעַ אַהַאי

LITERAL TRANSLATION

¹Granted if you say [that] Rabban Gamliel is dealing with [a case where] he agrees, ²it is well. ³But if you say [that] Rabban Gamliel is not dealing with [a case where] he agrees, ⁴with whom does Rabbi Yehoshua agree?
⁵Do you think [that] Rabbi Yehoshua is referring to this

TRANSLATION AND COMMENTARY

אִי אָמְרַתְּ ¹The Gemara now explains how the statement of Rabbi Yehoshua in the second clause of our Mishnah supports the argument that Rabban Gamliel agrees with the first clausc. **If you say that** the first clause **is dealing with a case where Rabban Gamliel agrees** with Rabbi Yehoshua, ²**there is no problem.** For if Rabban Gamliel accepts the ruling of the first clause, the Mishnah is in effect citing a case in which Rabban Gamliel agrees with Rabbi Yehoshua's argument, and it is reasonable for the Mishnah to balance this ruling with a case in which Rabbi Yehoshua agrees with Rabban Gamliel.[3] **But if you say that** the first clause reflects the view of Rabbi Yehoshua alone, and **does not deal with a case where** Rabban Gamliel **agrees** with Rabbi Yehoshua, ⁴**with whom does Rabbi Yehoshua agree** in the second clause of the Mishnah? Both clauses reflect the view of Rabbi Yehoshua, and Rabban Gamliel's dissenting view is nowhere introduced!

מִי סָבְרַתְּ ⁵The Gemara immediately dismisses this argument: **Do you think that Rabbi Yehoshua was** necessarily **referring to** a Mishnah in **this chapter** when he said that he was in agreement with Rabban Gamliel?

RASHI

אי אמרת בשלמא איירי רבן גמליאל במודה – דהך רישא הודאה הוא דקא מודה רבן גמליאל לרבי יהושע, ואמר: אף על גב דפליגנא עלך בברי ושמא – מודינא לך בברי וברי – היינו דשייך למיתני בתריה ורבי יהושע מודה לרבן גמליאל בהאומר לחברו שדה זו כו׳. דאף על גב דפליגנא בפרק קמא במשארסתני נאנסתי, דאף על גב דאיכא למימר מגו לא מהימנא, מודינא בהאי מגו. דאי בעי שתיק ולא אמר ליה של אביך היתה, כי אמר ליה נמי לקמתיה הימנו – מהימן, כדלקמן. **אלא אי אמרת לא איירי** – רישא במודה רבן גמליאל, מאי ״מודה רבי יהושע״? מאי שייך למיתנייה הכא, ואהיכא קאי?

NOTES

אִי אָמְרַתְּ בִּשְׁלָמָא אַיְירִי רַבָּן גַּמְלִיאֵל בְּמוֹדֶה Granted if you say that Rabban Gamliel is dealing with a case where he agrees. Our commentary follows *Rashi* and most other Rishonim (*Rabbenu Ḥananel, Rambam,* and others), who explain that the Gemara is bringing support for the idea that Rabban Gamliel agrees with Rabbi Yehoshua in the case described in our Mishnah (see previous note) by means of a stylistic argument: If the first clause of our Mishnah is dealing with a case where Rabban Gamliel agrees with Rabbi Yehoshua, then it is reasonable to think that the second clause is considering a case where Rabbi Yehoshua agrees with Rabban Gamliel. But if the first clause reflects Rabbi Yehoshua's view alone, and Rabban Gamliel's view is not mentioned or implied anywhere in the Mishnah, what does the second clause mean when it says that "Rabbi Yehoshua agrees"? With whom is he agreeing?

Some Rishonim had difficulty with this explanation. The Mishnah should perhaps be interpreted as saying: "Rabbi Yehoshua disagrees with Rabban Gamliel in the first clause, but agrees with him in the second" (*Tosafot*). If it is sufficient for Rabban Gamliel's view to be implied, it is just as logical to claim that he disagrees with the first clause as to claim that he agrees. Conversely, if it is stylistically important to mention Rabban Gamliel in the first clause, as a parallel to mentioning Rabbi Yehoshua in the second clause, he should have been mentioned explicitly, just as Rabbi Yehoshua was mentioned explicitly (*Ramban*).

Ritva answers that the subject of the previous Mishnayot in the first chapter was the dispute between Rabban Gamliel and Rabbi Yehoshua about the credibility of the conflicting claims of the wife and the husband. Hence, when the Mishnah cites another similar case, but without mentioning the Tannaitic dispute, it is reasonable to explain it as one in which the two Tannaim agree. In the second clause, however, where an apparently unrelated case is considered, it is important to state explicitly that Rabbi Yehoshua agrees with Rabban Gamliel.

שַׁפִּיר It is well. *Rashi* explains that Rabbi Yehoshua should be understood as saying the following to Rabban Gamliel: We disagreed about two matters — "certain and perhaps," and *miggo.* Just as you agreed with me in a case of "certain and certain," because it is not the same as a case of "certain and perhaps," I now agree with you in a casc of "the mouth that forbade," because it is not the same as the *miggo* arguments of the first chapter.

Some Rishonim object to this explanation, because at this stage the Gemara has not yct suggested that Rabbi Yehoshua's admission refers to the *miggo* arguments of the first chapter. Our commentary follows *Ra'ah* and *Ritva,* who explain that the entire discussion revolves around "certain and perhaps," and Rabbi Yehoshua is really saying the following to Rabban Gamliel: Just as you agreed with me that, in the absence of proof in a case of "certain and certain," the defendant is believed, because his claim is stronger than in the case of "certain and perhaps," I now agree with you that, in the absence of proof in a case of "the mouth that forbade," the plaintiff is believed, because his claim is much stronger than in the case of "certain and perhaps."

פִּירְקִין קָאֵי? [1]אַמִּגּוֹ קָאֵי, וְאַפִּירְקִין קַמָּא קָאֵי. [2]אַהֵיָּיא?

LITERAL TRANSLATION

chapter? [1]He is referring to *miggo*, and he is referring to the first chapter.

[2]To which [case is he referring]?

RASHI

אמגו קאי – אפלוגתא דאיכא למימר בה מגו בפרק קמא קאי, וקאמר: אף על גב דפליגנא במגו דהתם – במגו דהכא מודינא, כדלקמן. **אהייא** – איכא מגו.

TRANSLATION AND COMMENTARY

[1]**He was referring to** a related disagreement he had with Rabban Gamliel **in the first chapter.** The reason Rabbi Yehoshua agrees to place the burden of proof on the defendant in the second clause of our Mishnah is because the plaintiff's claim is supported by the argument called "the mouth that forbade is the mouth that permitted." This is actually a special kind of *miggo* argument, in which we accept a person's claim because if he had wished to lie he could have made a more advantageous claim. But, as the Gemara will explain below, in at least one case in the first chapter — where the wife's claim was "certain" and her husband's was uncertain ("perhaps"), and Rabban Gamliel disagreed with Rabbi Yehoshua — the wife's claim was supported by a *miggo* argument, yet Rabbi Yehoshua refused to accept Rabban Gamliel's viewpoint and to place the burden of proof on the husband. Thus we see that Rabbi Yehoshua did not consider a *miggo* argument to be grounds for placing the burden of proof on the defendant. On the other hand, our Mishnah tells us that Rabbi Yehoshua does accept Rabban Gamliel's viewpoint if the plaintiff is supported by the special type of *miggo* called "the mouth that forbade is the mouth that permitted." Thus we see that Rabbi Yehoshua disagrees with Rabban Gamliel about a regular *miggo,* but agrees with him where the *miggo* is one based on the principle of "the mouth that forbade is the mouth that permitted." It is therefore possible that our entire Mishnah here at the beginning of the second chapter reflects the viewpoint of Rabbi Yehoshua alone. In the first clause, Rabbi Yehoshua states that the woman is not believed even in a case that is the equivalent of "certain and perhaps." According to this interpretation, Rabban Gamliel would have disagreed with this ruling, but the Mishnah is concerned only with the viewpoint of Rabbi Yehoshua. In the second clause, Rabbi Yehoshua notes that although he disagrees with Rabban Gamliel over a case in the first chapter where the plaintiff's claim is supported by an ordinary *miggo,* he agrees with Rabban Gamliel if the plaintiff's claim is supported by the *miggo* known as "the mouth that forbade is the mouth that permitted." Thus we see that it is possible to interpret the Mishnah in a way that does not assume that Rabban Gamliel would necessarily agree with Rabbi Yehoshua regarding the first clause, and that it is not possible to disprove this interpretation by citing the fact that Rabbi Yehoshua agrees with Rabban Gamliel in the second clause.

אַהֵיָּיא [2]The Gemara stated, above, that in at least one of the cases in the first chapter of *Ketubot* in which Rabban Gamliel disagreed with Rabbi Yehoshua, the wife's claim was supported by a *miggo,* and Rabbi Yehoshua nevertheless refused to believe her, even though her claim was "certain" and her husband's was uncertain ("perhaps"). Moreover, according to one explanation offered by the Gemara, Rabbi Yehoshua was referring to this case when he said that he would agree with Rabban Gamliel's reasoning if the *miggo* were of "the mouth that forbade was the mouth that permitted" kind. The Gemara now asks: **To which case could** Rabbi Yehoshua **have been referring?** Which of the cases in the first chapter involved a *miggo?*

NOTES

מִגּוֹ *Miggo*. Throughout this passage, the Gemara frequently refers to the important legal argument called *miggo* (lit., "from the midst of," or "since"), which a party to a monetary dispute can use to support his claim. *Miggo* applies whenever a litigant could have made a claim more advantageous to himself than the one he actually made, but refrained from doing so. In such a case, we tend to give credence to the claim he actually made.

Most commentators agree that the strength of the *miggo* argument is the enhanced credibility of the litigant's claim. Indeed, *miggo* is sometimes described in the Gemara as מַה לִּי לְשַׁקֵּר — "What reason do I have for lying?" For if the litigant had wanted to lie, he would presumably have put forward the most advantageous claim available to him. And *since* (hence the name given to this argument) he did not do so, the most likely explanation is that the claimant is telling the truth. Nevertheless, certain Aḥaronim (*Kovetz Shiurim*) have suggested a different explanation of the *miggo* argument. According to this view, when a litigant refrains from using an advantageous argument and instead employs a weaker one, the weaker argument assumes all the force of the strong argument "from whose midst" it arose.

While *miggo* does lend a degree of credence to a litigant's claim, it is not a compelling proof, and is subject to many restrictions in practice. Among them are: (1) The advantageous argument must be freely available to the litigant; there must be no legal or psychological barrier against its use. (2) *Miggo* is of no value at all if it clashes with the testimony of witnesses. (3) The stronger claim must be stronger in every way; a *miggo* claim is not accepted if it would have been disadvantageous in some other way, or if it would not have been sufficient to win the case. (4) According to many Rishonim, *miggo* can be used only to support the claim of a defendant, but a plaintiff cannot override the legal presumption in favor of a defendant with a mere *miggo*.

One of the weak points in the rationale of the *miggo*

TERMINOLOGY

אַהָאי פִּירְקִין קָאֵי Is referring to this chapter. Usually the Gemara attempts to understand a given phrase in a single clause of the Mishnah as referring to that Mishnah, or, in any event, to the previous Mishnah in the same chapter. However, the division of the text of the Mishnah into individual Mishnayot is not always clear, and it was occasionally done in arbitrary fashion by copyists and printers. Moreover, although the division of the text into chapters is an ancient tradition and better founded than the division into Mishnayot, it is not always uniform in all manuscripts and editions of the Mishnah. Sometimes the division between one chapter and another does not derive from any essential difference in the content of the two chapters, and therefore it may happen that comments appearing in one chapter relate to what was said in the earlier chapter.

אַהֵיָּיא To which case is he referring? Sometimes, when a concluding sentence in a Mishnah, a Baraita, or an Amoraic statement refers to or differs from an earlier statement in the same source, it is not clear to which of the previous statements it is referring. In such cases, the Talmud may ask: "To which statement does this sentence refer?"

CONCEPTS

מִגּוֹ *Miggo* (lit., "from the midst of," "since"). An important legal argument, used to support the claim of one of the parties in a dispute. If one of the litigants could have made a claim more advantageous to himself than he actually did, we assume he was telling the truth. The *miggo* argument may be expressed in the following way: "Since he could have made a better claim (for had he wanted to lie, he would presumably have put forward a claim more advantageous to himself), we assume that he is telling the truth." For he could say: מַה לִּי לְשַׁקֵּר — "What reason do I have for lying?" There are, however, certain limitations governing the application of this

TRANSLATION AND COMMENTARY

אִילֵּימָא אַהָא [1] The Gemara now systematically examines the various differences of opinion between Rabban Gamliel and Rabbi Yehoshua, working backwards from the last one, which appears in the next-to-last Mishnah in the first chapter. The Gemara suggests: Perhaps **you may say** that Rabbi Yehoshua was referring **to the following** Mishnah (above, 13a): **"If an unmarried woman was pregnant**, and people **asked her:** [2] **'What is the nature of this embryo?** Who is the father of the unborn child?' [3] And she answered: 'I was made pregnant **by a man called So-and-so, and he is a priest** [or some other fit person],' [4] in such a case **Rabban Gamliel and Rabbi Eliezer say:** The woman **is believed.** Her claim that the father of her unborn child is a fit person is accepted, and she remains fit to marry into the priesthood. [5] **But Rabbi Yehoshua** disagrees, and **says: We do not accept what she says.** If she cannot prove her claim that the father of her unborn child is someone who leaves her fit to marry into the priesthood, we must presume that she became pregnant from a *mamzer* — the offspring of an incestuous or adulterous relationship, who is forbidden to marry a Jewish woman of unblemished ancestry."

הָתָם מַאי מִגּוֹ אִיכָּא [6] The Gemara asks: **There,** in the Mishnah just quoted, **what *miggo* is there?** The argument between Rabban Gamliel and Rabbi Yehoshua in that Mishnah relates to claims of "certain" and "perhaps" and to other arguments, but not to *miggo*. For a person to make use of the *miggo* argument, he must have had some other, more advantageous claim, which he refrained from presenting. This lends credence to the argument actually presented, since the person seems to be telling the truth. But what other claim could this woman have presented that would have been more advantageous to her than saying that she had had intercourse with a priest? Could she have denied that she had had intercourse? [7] **Surely her stomach is between her teeth!** She is obviously pregnant, and must have had intercourse with someone!

אֶלָּא אַהָא [8] **Rather,** suggests the Gemara, let us say that Rabbi Yehoshua was referring **to the following** Mishnah from the first chapter (above, 13a), and that the woman's claim there is supported by a *miggo* argument: [9] **"If an unmarried woman was seen talking with a certain** unidentified **man,** [10] and people **asked her: 'What kind of person is this man?** Is he someone who would render you unfit to marry into the priesthood if you had sexual relations with him?' [11] And she replied: **'His name is So-and-so, and he is a priest** [or some other fit person],' in such a case the Tannaim disagree about whether the woman is to be believed. [12] **Rabban Gamliel and Rabbi Eliezer say:** The woman **is believed** with regard to her claim that the

LITERAL TRANSLATION

[1] If we say to the following: "[If] she was pregnant, and they said to her: [2] 'What is the nature of this embryo?' [3] [And she said: 'It is] from a man [called] So-and-so, and he is a priest,' [4] Rabban Gamliel and Rabbi Eliezer say: She is believed. [5] Rabbi Yehoshua says: We do not live from her mouth."

[6] There, what *miggo* is there? [7] Behold, her stomach is between her teeth!

[8] Rather, to the following. [9] "[If] they saw her talking with someone, [10] and they said to her: 'What is the nature of this man?' [11] [And she said: 'He is] a man [called] So-and-so, and he is a priest,' [12] Rabban Gamliel and Rabbi Eliezer say:

אִילֵּימָא אַהָא: "הָיְתָה [1] מְעוּבֶּרֶת, וְאָמְרוּ לָהּ: [2] 'מַה טִּיבוֹ שֶׁל עוֹבָּר זֶה?' [3] 'מֵאִישׁ פְּלוֹנִי, וְכֹהֵן הוּא', [4] רַבָּן גַּמְלִיאֵל וְרַבִּי אֱלִיעֶזֶר אוֹמְרִים: נֶאֱמֶנֶת. [5] רַבִּי יְהוֹשֻׁעַ אוֹמֵר: לֹא מִפִּיהָ אָנוּ חַיִּין". [6] הָתָם מַאי מִגּוֹ אִיכָּא? [7] הֲרֵי כְּרֵיסָהּ בֵּין שִׁינֶּיהָ! [8] אֶלָּא אַהָא: [9] "רָאוּהָ מְדַבֶּרֶת עִם אֶחָד, [10] וְאָמְרוּ לָהּ: 'מַה טִּיבוֹ שֶׁל אִישׁ זֶה?' [11] 'אִישׁ פְּלוֹנִי, וְכֹהֵן הוּא', [12] רַבָּן גַּמְלִיאֵל וְרַבִּי אֱלִיעֶזֶר אוֹמְרִים:

RASHI

הרי כריסה בין שיניה — ואינה יכולה לומר לא נבעלתי.

NOTES

argument is the possibility that a litigant may have refrained from making a stronger claim, not because of a scrupulous concern for the truth, but simply because he had become flustered or confused in the course of the litigation. However, there is a special sort of *miggo*, called מִגּוֹ דְּאִי בָּעֵי שָׁתִיק — "since he could have remained silent if he had wished." In this situation, the litigant could have won the case without saying a word, since the other party had no case, but instead he chose to present an argument, asking the court to believe it. In such a case it is very unlikely that the litigant presented his argument out of confusion, and we consider it very credible indeed. According to some Rishonim, "the mouth that forbade" of our Mishnah, which even Rabbi Yehoshua accepts, is in fact this "silent *miggo*." But even those Rishonim who reject this explanation agree that some of the restrictions that apply to a regular *miggo* do not apply to a *miggo* where the litigant could have remained silent.

principle; for example, אֵין מִגּוֹ בְּמָקוֹם עֵדִים — "There is no *miggo* where there are witnesses." In other words, *miggo* is inadmissible where witnesses contradict the litigant's claim. The principle of *miggo* is the subject of profound legal analysis in the Talmud and its commentaries.

SAGES

רַבִּי אֱלִיעֶזֶר Rabbi Eliezer. When the name "Rabbi Eliezer" occurs in the Talmud without a patronymic, it refers to Rabbi Eliezer ben Hyrcanus (also known as Rabbi Eliezer the Great), who was one of the leading scholars in the period after the destruction of the Second Temple.

Rabbi Eliezer was born to a wealthy family of Levites who traced their descent to Moses. Rabbi Eliezer began studying Torah late in life, but quickly became an outstanding and beloved disciple of Rabban Yohanan ben Zakkai. Indeed, Rabban Yohanan remarked that "if all the Sages of Israel were on one side of the scale and Eliezer ben Hyrcanus on the other, he would outweigh them all."

Rabbi Eliezer was known for his remarkable memory, and was famed for faithfully reporting and following the traditions of others without altering them. He himself leaned toward the views of Bet Shammai, even though he studied with Rabban Yohanan ben Zakkai, who was a follower of Bet Hillel. Rabbi Eliezer's principal opponent, Rabbi Yehoshua ben Hananyah, generally followed the views of Bet Hillel, and many basic Halakhic disputes between these scholars are reported in the Mishnah.

Because of his staunch and unflinching adherence to tradition, Rabbi Eliezer was unwilling to accede to the majority view where his own views were based on tradition. Indeed, Rabbi Eliezer's conduct generated so much tension among the Sages that his own brother-in-law, Rabban Gamliel, eventually placed him under a ban, to prevent controversy from proliferating. This ban was

נֶאֱמֶנֶת. [1]רַבִּי יְהוֹשֻׁעַ אוֹמֵר: לֹא מִפִּיהָ אָנוּ חַיִּין".

[2]הָתָם מַאי מִגּוֹ אִיכָּא? [3]הָנִיחָא לְזֵעִירִי, דַּאֲמַר: מַאי "מְדַבֶּרֶת"? [4]נִסְתְּרָה. [5]מִגּוֹ דְּאִי בָּעֲיָא, אָמְרָה: "לֹא נִבְעַלְתִּי", [6]וְקָאָמְרָה: "נִבְעַלְתִּי", [7]מְהֵימְנָא. [8]אֶלָּא לְרַב אַסִי, דַּאֲמַר: [9]מַאי "מְדַבֶּרֶת"? [10]נִבְעֶלֶת, [11]מַאי מִגּוֹ אִיכָּא?

[12]וְאֶלָּא אַהָא: [13]"הִיא אוֹמֶרֶת: 'מוּכַּת עֵץ אֲנִי', [14]וְהוּא אוֹמֵר: 'לֹא כִּי, אֶלָּא דְּרוּסַת אִישׁ אַתְּ', [15]רַבָּן גַּמְלִיאֵל וְרַבִּי אֱלִיעֶזֶר

LITERAL TRANSLATION

She is believed. [1]Rabbi Yehoshua says: We do not live from her mouth."

[2]There, what *miggo* is there?

[3]This is well according to Ze'iri, who said: What is [meant by] "talking"? [4]She secluded herself [with him]. [5]Since, if she had wished, she could have said: "I did not have intercourse," [6]and she said: "I did have intercourse," [7]she is believed. [8]But according to Rav Assi, who said: [9]What is [meant by] "talking"?, [10]she had intercourse, [11]what *miggo* is there?

[12]But rather, to the following: [13]"[If] she says: 'I was injured by a stick,' [14]and he says: 'Not so, but rather, you had intercourse with a man (lit., "you are one trodden by a man"),' [15]Rabban Gamliel and Rabbi Eliezer

TRANSLATION AND COMMENTARY

man with whom she was seen is a fit person, and she remains fit to marry into the priesthood. [1]**But Rabbi Yehoshua** disagrees and **says: We do not accept what she says."**

הָתָם מַאי מִגּוֹ אִיכָּא [2]Again the Gemara refutes the argument, asking: **There,** in the Mishnah just quoted, **what *miggo* is there?** There are two alternative interpretations of this Mishnah. According to one, *miggo* may indeed be a factor, but according to the other, the argument between Rabban Gamliel and Rabbi Yehoshua relates to claims of "certain" and "perhaps" and to other arguments, but not to *miggo*. [3]The Gemara explains: **This is satisfactory according to Ze'iri's** interpretation. **For** Ze'iri **said:** When the Mishnah says that the woman was seen "talking" with a man, it is clearly using a euphemism for some sort of immoral behavior. **What** exactly **does it mean** by this euphemism? [4]It means that the woman was seen **secluding herself with** this man, thereby raising the suspicion that she might have had intercourse with him. According to Ze'iri, Rabbi Yehoshua maintains that the woman is rendered unfit to marry into the priesthood, even though nobody actually saw her engaging in intercourse. According to this interpretation, when the woman admits to having had intercourse and insists that the man was a priest, her claim is supported by a *miggo,* [5]**since, if she had wished, she could have said: "I did not have intercourse** at all." [6]Instead **she said: "I did have intercourse,** but the man was a priest." Hence she is unlikely to have fabricated her claim, [7]and **she is believed.** Thus, from the fact that Rabbi Yehoshua rejects her claim, it follows that Rabbi Yehoshua does not consider *miggo* sufficient grounds to place the burden of proof on the defendant, and this could indeed be the case of *miggo* to which Rabbi Yehoshua was referring in our Mishnah. [8]**But,** notes the Gemara, this argument is valid only according to the interpretation of Ze'iri. It is not valid **according to Rav Assi, who said:** [9]**What does** the Mishnah **mean by** the euphemism **"talking"?** [10]It means that **she** was seen **having intercourse** with this man. According to Rav Assi, the woman is only rendered unfit to marry into the priesthood if she definitely had intercourse, but if she was only seen secluding herself, even Rabbi Yehoshua would agree that she remains fit to marry a priest. According to this interpretation, the argument between Rabban Gamliel and Rabbi Yehoshua concerns a case where the woman definitely had intercourse but insists that her partner was a priest. This dispute relates to claims of "certain" and "perhaps" and to other arguments, but not to *miggo.* [11]For **what *miggo* is there** in this case? Since the woman was seen having intercourse, what possible claim could she have made that would have been better than saying she had intercourse with a priest?

וְאֶלָּא אַהָא [12]**Rather,** suggests the Gemara, let us say that Rabbi Yehoshua was referring **to the following** Mishnah from the first chapter (above, 13a), and that the woman's claim there is supported by a *miggo* argument. That Mishnah deals with a case where the wife admits that she was not a virgin at the time of the marriage, but insists that she did not lose her virginity through intercourse. The husband has no way of knowing the facts, but he suspects her of having had intercourse. The Mishnah says: **"If** a man marries a woman under the assumption that she is a virgin, and later, when he finds out that she was not a virgin at the time of the marriage, [13]**she says** to him: **'I was injured by a stick,** and as a result my hymen was ruptured,' [14]**and** the husband **says:** 'This is **not so.** In fact **you had intercourse with a man,'** in such a case the Tannaim disagree as to whether or not to believe the woman. [15]**Rabban Gamliel and Rabbi Eliezer**

RASHI

וקאמרה נבעלתי — ולכשר נבעלתי, מהימנא.

lifted only after Rabbi Eliezer's death.
All the Sages of the next generation were Rabbi Eliezer's students. Most prominent among them was Rabbi Akiva. Rabbi Eliezer's son, Hyrcanus, was also a Sage.

SAGES

זְעִירִי Ze'iri. A Babylonian Amora of the second generation. See *Ketubot,* Part I, p. 174.

רַב אַסִי Rav Assi. A Babylonian Amora of the first generation, Rav Assi was one of the Sages of Hutzal, near Neharde'a. When Rav arrived in Babylonia he met Rav Kahana and Rav Assi, who were already eminent scholars. On several occasions Rav Assi disagrees with Rav, and Rav takes heed of his words and acts accordingly. Rav Assi reports several teachings in the name of Rav. He was also a colleague of Shmuel. Once, Rav, Shmuel, and Rav Assi met at a festive banquet, and each scholar deferred to the others at the entrance. Rav's and Shmuel's students, in particular Rav Yehudah and Rav Huna, were also students of Rav Assi, and transmit teachings in his name. This Rav Assi is often confused with Rabbi Assi, who was one of the leaders of the third generation of Amoraim in Eretz Israel, and a colleague of Rabbi Ammi.

אוֹמְרִים: נֶאֱמֶנֶת. [1]וְרַבִּי יְהוֹשֻׁעַ אוֹמֵר: לֹא מִפִּיהָ אָנוּ חַיִּין״. [2]הָתָם מַאי מִגּוֹ אִיכָּא? [3]בִּשְׁלָמָא לְרַבִּי אֶלְעָזָר, [4]דְּאָמַר: בְּמָנֶה וְלֹא כְלוּם. [5]מִגּוֹ דְּאִי בָּעֲיָא אָמְרָה: ״מוּכַּת עֵץ אֲנִי תַּחְתֶּיךָ״, [6]וְאִית לָהּ מָאתַיִם, [7]וְקָאָמְרָה: ״מֵעִיקָּרָא״, [8]דְּלֵית לָהּ אֶלָּא מָנֶה, [9]מְהֵימְנָא. [10]אֶלָּא לְרַבִּי יוֹחָנָן, [11]דְּאָמַר: בְּמָאתַיִם וּמָנֶה, [12]מַאי מִגּוֹ אִיכָּא?

LITERAL TRANSLATION

say: She is believed. [1]And Rabbi Yehoshua says: We do not live from her mouth."

[2]There, what *miggo* is there? [3]It is well according to Rabbi Elazar, [4]who said: [Their claims are] about a maneh and nothing. [5]Since, if she had wished, she could have said: "I was injured by a stick [when I was already] betrothed to (lit., 'under') you," [6]and she would have had two hundred [dinarim], [7]but she said: "From the outset," [8]where she has only a maneh, [9]she is believed. [10]But according to Rabbi Yoḥanan, [11]who said: [Their claims are] about two hundred [dinarim] and a maneh, [12]what *miggo* is there?

RASHI

בשלמא לרבי אלעזר דאמר — בפרק קמא טענתייהו במנה ולא כלום. מוכת עץ שלא הכיר בה — אינה יכולה לתובעו אלא מנה, והוא אומר: דרוסת איש את, ואין ליך כלום. איכא מגו, דאי בעיא אמרה מוכת עץ אני תחתיך. **אלא לרבי יוחנן** — דאמר: טענתייהו במאתים ומנה, שהיא תובעתו מאתים — ליכא מידי בין תחתיו למעיקרא, מאי מגו איכא?

TRANSLATION AND COMMENTARY

say: She is believed. [1]**And Rabbi Yehoshua says: We do not accept what she** says."

הָתָם מַאי מִגּוֹ אִיכָּא [2]Again the Gemara asks: **There,** in the Mishnah just quoted, **what *miggo* is there?** There are two alternative interpretations of this Mishnah as well. According to one, *miggo* may indeed be a factor; but according to the other, the argument between Rabban Gamliel and Rabbi Yehoshua relates to claims of "certain" and "perhaps" and to other arguments, but not to *miggo*. [3]The Gemara explains: **There is no problem according to Rabbi Elazar's** interpretation, because according to him *miggo* may be a factor. [4]For Rabbi Elazar **said: The** conflicting **claims** of the husband and the wife **are about a maneh and nothing.** The wife demands a ketubah settlement of a maneh (100 zuz), and her husband does not want to give her anything. According to Rabbi Elazar, there is no difference in the amount of the ketubah paid to a woman who lost her virginity through intercourse and a woman who lost her virginity in some other way. In both cases, she is entitled to only a maneh. The only difference is when the wife deceived her husband and falsely claimed to be a virgin. If she in fact lost her virginity through intercourse, she forfeits her ketubah altogether, as a penalty for her deceit; whereas if she lost it in some other way, she does not. Hence in our case, even if the woman was injured by a stick, as she claimed, she would still not be entitled to the full ketubah of 200 zuz to which a virgin is entitled, but only to the maneh awarded to a non-virgin. But if she lost her virginity through intercourse, she is not entitled to a ketubah settlement at all, because she deceived her husband by claiming to be a virgin when she was not. According to this interpretation, when the wife admits to having lost her virginity but insists that it was not through intercourse, [5]her claim is supported by a *miggo*, **since, if she had wished, she could have said: "I was injured by a stick when I was already betrothed to you."** The critical moment in determining the virginity of the woman is the first stage of marriage, betrothal (אֵירוּסִין), not full marriage (נִשּׂוּאִין), when the marriage is consummated. If the woman had in fact been a virgin at the time of betrothal, but was injured by a stick before her marriage was consummated, [6]**she would have** been entitled to **two hundred dinarim,** the sum guaranteed to virgin brides. [7]**But** instead **she said:** "I had already lost my virginity **from the outset,** before my betrothal, but I lost it through an injury, not through intercourse." [8]Hence **she is entitled to only a maneh.** [9]And since she is unlikely to have fabricated her claim, **she is believed.** But Rabbi Yehoshua rejects her claim, showing that he does not consider *miggo* sufficient grounds for placing the burden of proof on the defendant, and this could indeed be the case of *miggo* to which Rabbi Yehoshua was referring in our Mishnah. [10]**But,** notes the Gemara, this argument is valid only according to the interpretation of Rabbi Elazar. It is not valid **according to** the interpretation of **Rabbi Yoḥanan,** [11]**who said that they disagree about two hundred zuz and a maneh:** The wife demands the higher amount of 200 zuz to which a virgin is entitled, whereas her husband is prepared to give her only the maneh of a non-virgin. According to Rabbi Yoḥanan, a woman who lost her virginity through an accident remains a virgin in the eyes of the law and is entitled to the higher ketubah of 200 zuz, regardless of whether she lost her virginity before or after her betrothal. According to this interpretation, the argument between Rabban Gamliel and Rabbi Yehoshua relates to claims of "certain" and "perhaps" and to other arguments, but not to *miggo*. [12]For **what *miggo* is there** in this case? Since the wife definitely had a ruptured hymen when she married, what possible claim could she have made that would have been better than the one she did state — that

SAGES

רַבִּי אֶלְעָזָר Rabbi Elazar. Rabbi Elazar ben Pedat was one of the greatest of the Palestinian Amoraim. He came originally from Babylonia and studied there with Rav and Shmuel. But it seems that he immigrated to Eretz Israel as a young man and married there. In Eretz Israel he became the main disciple of Rabbi Yoḥanan. The spiritual affinity between Rabbi Elazar and Rabbi Yoḥanan was so great that occasionally an objection is raised to an argument presented in the name of one of them because it conflicts with the other's teachings, since they are assumed to have adopted the same approach to Halakhah.

Rabbi Elazar venerated his teacher, Rabbi Yoḥanan, and in time the bond between them grew so strong that Rabbi Yoḥanan said of him: "Have you seen the son of Pedat, who sits and expounds the Torah like Moses from the very mouth of the Almighty?"

Rabbi Elazar was a priest. He was very poor for most of his life, and his material situation apparently did not improve until his later years, when he was one of the leaders of the nation.

After Rabbi Yoḥanan's death, Rabbi Elazar was one of the most important scholars in Eretz Israel. He was also one of the Sages who participated in setting the Hebrew calendar, and he would send Halakhic rulings from Eretz Israel to Babylonia, where they were regarded as authoritative and binding.

Many stories are told of Rabbi Elazar's great love for the Torah, and he is presented as the model of a person entirely immersed in the study of Torah.

Because of his greatness, he was known as מָרָא דְאַרְעָא דְיִשְׂרָאֵל — "Master of Eretz Israel." Almost all of the Amoraim of the third generation in Eretz Israel were his students. His son, Rabbi Pedat, was also a Sage.

רַבִּי יוֹחָנָן Rabbi Yoḥanan This is Rabbi Yoḥanan bar Nappaḥa, one of the greatest Amoraim, whose teachings are of primary importance both in the Babylonian and in

[1]אֶלָּא אַהָא: [2]״הַנּוֹשֵׂא אֶת הָאִשָּׁה וְלֹא מָצָא לָהּ בְּתוּלִים, [3]הִיא אוֹמֶרֶת: ׳מִשֶּׁאֵרַסְתַּנִי נֶאֱנַסְתִּי, [4]וְנִסְתַּחֲפָה שָׂדֵהוּ׳, [5]וְהוּא אוֹמֵר: ׳לֹא כִּי, [6]אֶלָּא עַד שֶׁלֹּא אֵירַסְתִּיךְ׳, [7]רַבָּן גַּמְלִיאֵל וְרַבִּי אֱלִיעֶזֶר אוֹמְרִים: נֶאֱמֶנֶת. [8]וְרַבִּי יְהוֹשֻׁעַ אוֹמֵר: לֹא מִפִּיהָ אָנוּ חַיִּין״.

[9]דְּמִגּוֹ דְּאִי בָּעֲיָא אָמְרָה: [10]״מוּכַּת עֵץ אֲנִי תַּחְתֶּיךָ״, [11]דְּלָא קָא פָּסְלָה נַפְשָׁהּ מִכְּהוּנָּה, [12]וְקָאָמְרָה: ״נֶאֱנַסְתִּי״, [13]דְּקָא פָּסְלָה נַפְשָׁהּ מִכְּהוּנָּה, [14]מִשּׁוּם הָכִי קָאָמַר רַבָּן גַּמְלִיאֵל דִּמְהֵימְנָא.

[15]וְקָאָמַר רַבִּי יְהוֹשֻׁעַ לְרַבָּן גַּמְלִיאֵל: [16]בְּהַאי מִגּוֹ דְּהָכָא,

LITERAL TRANSLATION

[1]Rather, to this: [2]"[If] someone married a woman and did not find in her [signs of] virginity, [3][and] she says: 'After you betrothed me I was raped, [4]and your (lit., "his") field has been flooded,' [5]and he says: 'Not so, [6]but rather [it happened] before I betrothed you,' [7]Rabban Gamliel and Rabbi Eliezer say: She is believed. [8]And Rabbi Yehoshua says: We do not live from her mouth."

[9]For since, if she had wished, she could have said: [10]"I was injured by a stick [when I was already] betrothed to you," [11]by which she would not have disqualified herself from the priesthood, [12]but she said: "I was raped," [13]by which she does disqualify herself from the priesthood, [14]for this [reason] Rabban Gamliel says that she is believed.

[15]And Rabbi Yehoshua says to Rabban Gamliel: [16]About this *miggo* here,

TRANSLATION AND COMMENTARY

she was legally still a virgin because she was injured by a stick?

אֶלָּא אַהָא [1]**Rather,** concludes the Gemara, the only possible case to which Rabbi Yehoshua could have been referring is **the following** Mishnah from the first chapter (above, 12b), in which the woman's claim is indeed supported by a *miggo* argument. That Mishnah deals with a case where a wife admits to having lost her virginity through intercourse, but insists that it was the result of rape. [2]**If** a man **marries a woman** under the assumption that she is a virgin, **but** when they engage in their first act of intercourse he **discovers that she is not a virgin,** [3]**and** the woman **says:** 'It is true that I was not a virgin, for **after you betrothed me, I was raped;** [4]**but** since it happened after you betrothed me, and since **it was your misfortune** that I was raped, I am still entitled to receive the full ketubah,' [5]**and** the husband **says: 'Not so;** [6]I am not required to pay you your ketubah, because **you may have lost your virginity before I betrothed you,** and if so, you are not entitled to the ketubah of a virgin, for I married you under the mistaken assumption that you were a virgin,' [7]in such a case **Rabban Gamliel and Rabbi Eliezer say:** The woman **is believed,** and is entitled to her ketubah, [8]whereas **Rabbi Yehoshua says: We do not accept what she says** and do not accept her claim."

דְּמִגּוֹ דְּאִי בָּעֲיָא אָמְרָה [9]The dispute in this Mishnah relates to claims of "certain" and "perhaps" and to other arguments, but also to *miggo.* **For** when the woman admitted to having been raped, but insisted that the assault had occurred after her betrothal, her claim was supported by a *miggo,* **since if she had wished she could have said:** [10]**"I was injured by a stick when I was already betrothed to you,"** in which case she would still have been entitled to the full ketubah of a virgin, as explained above. [11]Moreover, **she would not have disqualified herself from the priesthood,** since a woman who has lost her virginity through injury is permitted to marry a priest. [12]**But** in fact **she said: "I was raped,"** [13]thereby **disqualifying herself from the priesthood.** A priest is forbidden to marry a woman who has had intercourse with a man forbidden to her, even if she was raped, and for a married woman this includes all men other than her husband. Hence a married (or even betrothed) woman who was raped is not permitted to marry a priest. It is therefore clear that the woman's claim is to her disadvantage, and is thus unlikely to have been fabricated. [14]**For this reason Rabban Gamliel says that she is believed.**

וְקָאָמַר רַבִּי יְהוֹשֻׁעַ [15]Rabbi Yehoshua, on the other hand, rejected the woman's claim, in spite of the *miggo.* Thus it follows that Rabbi Yehoshua does not consider *miggo* sufficient grounds for placing the burden of proof on the defendant, and if in our Mishnah Rabbi Yehoshua was referring to a case of *miggo,* as one interpretation of the Gemara suggested, this must be the case it had in mind. According to that interpretation, our entire Mishnah reflects the viewpoint of Rabbi Yehoshua. In the first clause, Rabbi Yehoshua restates his disagreement with Rabban Gamliel regarding claims of "certain" and "perhaps"; **but** in the second clause, **Rabbi Yehoshua** considers the question of *miggo,* and **says to Rabban Gamliel:** [16]**I agree with you about the** "mouth that forbade is the mouth that permitted" ***miggo* here** in the second chapter,

RASHI

משארסתני – אירע לי ונסתחפה שדהו, ואית לי מאתים. **וקאמרה** – מוכת עץ אני מעיקרא, ולא תבעה אלא מנה – מהימנא.

the Jerusalem Talmud. He lived in Tiberias and survived to a great age. Almost nothing is known of his family origins. He became an orphan at an early age and, although his family apparently had considerable property, he spent most of his wealth in his strong desire to study Torah constantly, so that he actually became poor. He was just old enough to study under Rabbi Yehudah HaNasi, the editor of the Mishnah. But most of his Torah knowledge was derived from Rabbi Yehudah HaNasi's students, from Ḥizkiyah ben Ḥiyya and from Rabbi Oshaya, from Rabbi Ḥanina and from Rabbi Yannai, who greatly praised him. In time he became the head of a yeshivah in Tiberias, marking the beginning of a period during which his fame and influence constantly increased. For a long time Rabbi Yoḥanan was the leading Rabbinic scholar of the entire Jewish world, not only in Eretz Israel but also in Babylonia, whose Sages respected him greatly. Many of them came to Eretz Israel and became his outstanding students. He was a master of both Halakhah and Aggadah. His teachings in both areas are found in many places, and serve as the basis for both of the Talmuds. In recognition of his intellectual and spiritual greatness, the Halakhah is decided according to his opinion in almost every case, even when Rav or Shmuel, the great Amoraim of Babylonia (whom he himself regarded as his superiors), disagree with him. Only when he disagrees with his teachers in Eretz Israel (such as Rabbi Yannai and Rabbi Yehoshua ben Levi) does the Halakhah not follow his opinion.

Rabbi Yoḥanan was renowned for being handsome, and much was said in praise of his good looks. By nature he was excitable, so that occasionally he was too severe with his friends and students, but immediately afterwards was stricken with remorse. We know that his life was full of suffering. Ten of his sons died in his lifetime. There is a Geonic tradition that one of

TRANSLATION AND COMMENTARY

[1] even though **I disagree with you about the** standard ***miggo* there,** in the case of rape discussed in the first chapter.

מִכְּדִי הַאי מִגּוֹ [2] Throughout the preceding passage, the Gemara has assumed that "the mouth that forbade is the mouth that permitted" is an especially effective type of *miggo*. The Gemara now explains why it is so effective. The Gemara asks: **Since** an ordinary *miggo*, like those in the first chapter, **is a *miggo*, and** the "mouth that forbade" argument **is** also **a *miggo*,** [3] **what is the difference between this *miggo* and that *miggo*?** Why is the "mouth that forbade" argument so much more effective than other forms of *miggo*?

הָכָא [4] The Gemara answers with a metaphor: **Here,** in the case of the field mentioned in our Mishnah, which is a case of "the mouth that forbade," **there is no slaughtered ox before you** requiring an explanation as to how it was slaughtered, [5] whereas **there,** in the case of rape described in the first chapter, which is a case of an ordinary *miggo*, **there is a slaughtered ox before you.** In other words, in the case of the field in our Mishnah, there is no evidence that would lead us to suspect that the person in possession of the field is not its legal owner. It is only his admission that the field once belonged to the claimant's father that creates a doubt. Hence his statement must be taken as a whole, and he must be believed when he states that he bought the field. But in the case of rape discussed in the first chapter, there is real evidence that the woman lost her virginity, and she must account for it. Hence, even though her statement is supported by a *miggo* and appears credible, it is not a substitute for proof, and is not sufficient according to Rabbi Yehoshua.

מוֹדֵינָא לָךְ. [1] בְּהַהוּא מִגּוֹ דְּהָתָם, פָּלֵיגְנָא עִילָּוָךְ. [2] מִכְּדִי הַאי מִגּוֹ וְהַאי מִגּוֹ, [3] מַאי שְׁנָא הַאי מִגּוֹ מֵהַאי מִגּוֹ? [4] הָכָא, אֵין שׁוֹר שָׁחוּט לְפָנֶיךָ. [5] הָתָם, הֲרֵי שׁוֹר שָׁחוּט לְפָנֶיךָ.

LITERAL TRANSLATION

I agree with you. [1] About that *miggo* there, I disagree with you.

[2] Now since this is a *miggo* and that is a *miggo*, [3] what is the difference between this *miggo* and that *miggo*?

[4] Here, there is no slaughtered ox before you. [5] There, there is a slaughtered ox before you.

RASHI

הכא — גבי שדה אין שור שחוט לפניך, שיעלה על לב בעליו לתבוע מי שחטו. כלומר, אם שתק זה — לא היו לו עוררים. הלכך, אי לאו דדבר פשוט הוא שלקחה הימנו — לא היה אומר לו של אביך היתה. הלכך אמרינן מגו. אבל גבי לא מצא לה בתולים — שור שחוט לפניך, בתולים שלא מצא לה הם הסיתוהו לבא לבית דין, ואף על פי שיש לה להשיב טענה טובה מזו — לא אמרינן מגו, דדלמא לא אסקה אדעתה. אי נמי, איערומי קא מערמא.

his sons, Rabbi Matena, an Amora of Babylonia, did not pre-decease him. The death of Rabbi Yoḥanan's student, friend, and brother-in-law, Resh Lakish, for which he considered himself responsible, brought his own death closer.

Rabbi Yoḥanan had many students. In fact, all the Amoraim of Eretz Israel in succeeding generations were his students and imbibed his teachings — so much so that he is said to be the author of the Jerusalem Talmud. His greatest students were his brother-in-law Resh Lakish, Rabbi Elazar, Rabbi Ḥiyya bar Abba, Rabbi Abbahu, Rabbi Yose bar Ḥanina, Rabbi Ammi, and Rabbi Assi.

NOTES

בְּהַהוּא מִגּוֹ דְּהָתָם פָּלֵיגְנָא עִילָּוָךְ **About that *miggo* there, I disagree with you.** Our commentary follows *Rashi*, who explains that Rabbi Yehoshua is aware of the *miggo* arguments of the first chapter. Nevertheless, he refuses to believe the woman because he maintains that *miggo* — even when combined with a legal presumption and a plea of "certain and perhaps" — is not sufficient to override the general principle that the burden of proof falls on the plaintiff, unless the *miggo* is the special *miggo* called "the mouth that forbade."

The Rishonim object: For a *miggo* to be a valid support for a weaker claim, the stronger claim must be sufficient to enable the litigant to win the case; otherwise, the "weaker" claim will in fact prove stronger. But in all the cases in the first chapter, the woman would not have been believed, according to Rabbi Yehoshua, even if she had made the "better" claim, since Rabbi Yehoshua requires her to submit real proof, and not merely a reasonable claim. Hence, the *miggo* arguments of the first chapter would be invalid, according to Rabbi Yehoshua.

Most Rishonim agree that the *miggo* arguments of the first chapter are indeed defective. According to *Tosafot*, this is why Rabbi Yehoshua rejected them (see next note). Other Rishonim explain that, although the *miggo* arguments of the first chapter are defective, they are effective in conjunction with the "certain and perhaps" argument (*Rashba* and others).

הֲרֵי שׁוֹר שָׁחוּט לְפָנֶיךָ **There is a slaughtered ox before you.** The Gemara uses this metaphor to illustrate why the argument of "the mouth that forbade is the mouth that permitted" is more credible than the *miggo* arguments of the first chapter. The Gemara informs us that, in the *miggo* arguments of the first chapter, there was "a slaughtered ox before us," whereas in our chapter there was no such "ox." Unfortunately, the Gemara does not explain what the "ox" metaphor means, and the Rishonim offer several widely differing explanations.

Our commentary follows *Rashi*, who explains that the "mouth that forbade" argument is in fact identical with "the silent *miggo*," which applies when a claimant could have won his case without saying a word, but instead chose to present a claim. *Rashi* explains the Gemara's metaphor as follows: If a person finds his ox lying dead with its throat cut, he immediately looks for the killer, but if he is not aware that his ox is dead, he does not look for a killer. Likewise, in the case of an ordinary *miggo*, as in the first chapter, the manifest state of affairs creates a dispute that must be adjudicated in court. Hence, even if one of the claimants has a *miggo*, because he used an argument that was less advantageous than another he might have employed, we do not accept this as proof that the claimant is scrupulously honest — he had to make an argument of some kind, and may have had some personal reason for making the weaker claim. In our Mishnah, on the other hand, there were no facts to be adjudicated in court until one of the claimants made a statement of his own

TRANSLATION AND COMMENTARY

וְכֵיוָן דְּרוֹב נָשִׁים בְּתוּלוֹת נִישָּׂאוֹת [1]The Gemara now considers another aspect of our Mishnah. The Mishnah stated that the woman must prove that she was a virgin bride by producing witnesses able to testify about the customs followed at her wedding. **But since most women are virgins when they marry,** as mentioned above, the woman's claim is plausible. [2]Hence the Gemara asks: Even **if witnesses do not come** to testify to the customs followed at the wedding, [3]**what of it?** The woman's claim should still be believed, because this is in fact the usual case, and the burden of proof should fall on the husband.

אָמַר רָבִינָא [4]**Ravina said** in reply: We do not believe her, because the logic of her claim is flawed, **since,** although **it is possible to say** that **most women are virgins when they marry,** [5]a significant **minority are**

[1]וְכֵיוָן דְּרוֹב נָשִׁים בְּתוּלוֹת נִישָּׂאוֹת, [2]כִּי לָא אָתוּ עֵדִים, [3]מַאי הָוֵי? [4]אָמַר רָבִינָא: מִשּׁוּם דְּאִיכָּא לְמֵימַר: רוֹב נָשִׁים בְּתוּלוֹת נִישָּׂאוֹת, [5]וּמִיעוּט אַלְמָנוֹת,

LITERAL TRANSLATION

[1]But since most women are married [as] virgins, [2]if witnesses did not come, [3]what of it? [4]Ravina said: Because it is possible to say: Most women are married [as] virgins, [5]and a minority [as] widows,

RASHI

וכיון שרוב נשים – קושיא היא.

SAGES

רָבִינָא **Ravina.** A Babylonian Amora of the fifth and sixth generations, Ravina apparently came from Mata Meḥasya, though some authorities claim that he came from Eretz Israel. He was among Rava's students. The Gemara records Halakhic discussions between the two and, more frequently, between Ravina and various other students of Rava. Although Ravina was older than Rav Ashi, he accepted him as his teacher and became his student and colleague. Ravina was apparently also actively involved in the editing of the Babylonian Talmud, which was accomplished by Rav Ashi. We have little information about his private life, though the Talmud implies that he had children. Rav Ashi's sons were students of Ravina. He also had many other students, the most important of whom was Ravina the Younger (רָבִינָא זוּטֵי), his sister's son, who completed the main task of the final editing of the Talmud.

NOTES

accord. Hence, we believe that statement, for if it were not true, the claimant would not have created problems for himself by making it.

The greatest difficulty with *Rashi*'s explanation is that he is forced to explain our Mishnah as referring to a case where the son was not aware that the field had been owned by his father, until the person in possession informed him. But most Rishonim agree that the Mishnah is also referring to a case where the son sued the person in possession, but lacked proof until the latter admitted that the field had originally belonged to the plaintiff's father. This, however, would leave the person in possession with a regular *miggo* but not a silent one. *Ritva* suggests that even if the son did originate the suit, the person in possession could still have remained silent, because the claim would be entirely baseless and would be dismissed out of hand in court.

Tosafot and *Rosh* explain that the "mouth that forbade" argument is simply an ordinary *miggo,* whereas the *miggo* arguments of the first chapter are defective. According to this explanation, a dead ox is a problem that cannot be explained away. Similarly, the problem in the first chapter of the woman's lack of virginity is not adequately addressed by her defective *miggo.* In our Mishnah, by contrast, there is no dead ox, and the *miggo* is quite convincing.

Some Rishonim have a different version of this metaphor, according to which there *is* "a slaughtered ox" in the case of the field in our Mishnah, and there is *not* in the *miggo* arguments of the first chapter. *Ramban* and others explain that "a slaughtered ox before you" refers to a matter that has been fully clarified and can no longer be disputed by reasonable people. In our Mishnah, for example, the person in possession of the field has a solid argument, and there can be little doubt that he is telling the truth. In the first chapter, by contrast, there is no really compelling argument.

Ba'al HaMa'or notes that the metaphor refers not merely to a dead ox, but to a *slaughtered* one. In tractate *Ḥullin,* the Gemara declares that a dead animal is presumed to be non-kosher unless it can be proved that it was slaughtered in accordance with Jewish law. But once we know it was slaughtered in accordance with Jewish law, this presumption ceases to be valid. Similarly, in our Mishnah, the person in possession of the field has presented an argument so compelling that it is equivalent to proving that an ox was slaughtered properly. Hence we can no longer presume that the field belongs to the other person. In the first chapter, by contrast, the woman's argument is not so compelling, and the legal presumption in favor of the defendant remains in force.

וְכֵיוָן דְּרוֹב נָשִׁים **But since most women.** The Gemara's assertion — that the woman should be believed without witnesses on the basis of a statistical majority alone — appears to assume that a statistical majority is considered sufficient proof to compel a defendant to pay money. The Rishonim note that this assumption is the subject of a difference of opinion between Rav and Shmuel in the following case (*Bava Batra* 92a): If a person buys an ox to use for farm work, but gives no indication at the time of the purchase whether he wants the ox for work or for meat, and the ox turns out to be dangerously ill-tempered, so that it cannot safely be kept alive and has to be slaughtered for meat, Rav is of the opinion that the buyer can demand his money back, because most oxen are bought for farm work, whereas Shmuel maintains that a statistical majority, although accepted as proof in ritual matters, is not sufficient to compel a defendant to pay money.

Many Rishonim (*Tosafot, Rashba, Ritva*) explain that our Gemara's question was addressed to Rav, and would not have been asked according to Shmuel. This explanation presents difficulties, because it implies that our Gemara follows Rav, whereas the Halakhah follows Shmuel. It finds support, however, in the passage in *Bava Batra* in which the Gemara cites the question and answer in our passage as an objection against Rav and as his response to it.

A further difficulty is posed by a parallel passage that appears later on in our chapter (28a). There the Mishnah rules that the witnesses whom the woman must bring to prove she was treated as a virgin at her wedding need not meet the regular standards of testimony. The Gemara explains that this is because the statistical majority supporting the woman's claim is already considered proof, so that only minimal corroboration is needed. Apparently, that passage also maintains that a statistical majority can

TRANSLATION AND COMMENTARY

widows. [1]Moreover, the two groups are not at all alike, for **whenever a virgin marries,** [2]**the marriage attracts attention,** whereas in the case of the minority of brides — those who are widows — their status is less widely known. [16B] [3]It follows, therefore, that **since there was no publicity** to the effect that **this woman** was a virgin when she married, [4]the statistical **majority** supporting her claim **is flawed,** and it is quite likely that she was, in fact, a widow.

אִי כָּל הַנִּשֵּׂאת בְּתוּלָה [5]The Gemara now objects to Ravina's use of the word "whenever." **If** Ravina is right, and ***whenever*** **a woman marries as a virgin** the marriage **receives publicity,** then there is no room for doubt. If people did not hear about it, it could not have happened. But if so, why does the Mishnah rule that the woman must produce witnesses to testify that she was treated as a virgin? [6]Even **if witnesses do come** forward to support her claim, **what of it?** [7]These witnesses are clearly **liars,** since we know for certain that she was not a virgin!

אֶלָּא אֲמַר רָבִינָא [8]In the light of this objection, **Ravina** amended his explanation slightly, **saying:** Although it is true that most women are virgins when they marry, a significant minority are widows. [9]Moreover, **most** (though not all) **women who are married as virgins** attract notice and **receive publicity** when they marry.

[1]וְכָל הַנִּשֵּׂאת בְּתוּלָה, [2]יֵשׁ לָהּ קוֹל, [16B] [3]וְזוֹ, הוֹאִיל וְאֵין לָהּ קוֹל, [4]אִיתְרַע לָהּ רוּבָּא.
[5]אִי כָּל הַנִּשֵּׂאת בְּתוּלָה יֵשׁ לָהּ קוֹל, [6]כִּי אָתוּ עֵדִים, מַאי הָוֵי? [7]הָנָךְ סָהֲדֵי שַׁקָּרֵי נִינְהוּ!
[8]אֶלָּא אֲמַר רָבִינָא: [9]רוֹב הַנִּשֵּׂאת בְּתוּלָה יֵשׁ לָהּ קוֹל,

LITERAL TRANSLATION

[1]and whoever is married [as] a virgin, [2]is talked about (lit., "has a voice"), [16B] [3]and [with regard to] this woman, [4]since she is not talked about, the majority has become flawed.

[5]If whoever is married [as] a virgin is talked about, [6]when witnesses come, what of it? [7]These witnesses are liars!

[8]Rather, Ravina said: [9]A majority of those who are married as virgins are talked about,

RASHI

יש לה קול — והרבה יודעים שיצאה בהינומא. **וזו הואיל ואין לה קול** — שאין מעיד עליה שיצאתה בהינומא. **כי אתו עדים מאי הוי** — כיון דחזקה דיש לה קול, הרבה היו יודעין.

BACKGROUND

וְכָל הַנִּשֵּׂאת בְּתוּלָה יֵשׁ לָהּ קוֹל And whoever is married as a virgin is talked about. This assumption is based on the fact that a second marriage (of a widow or of a divorcee) is usually celebrated modestly, and the marriage is not widely publicized. By contrast, a woman who marries for the first time is usually treated to a large and impressive wedding ceremony, to which her family are sure to invite their close friends. Therefore the marriage of a virgin has a "voice"; it is publicized, for many people know of it, and it is difficult to believe that there would be no witnesses to it.

NOTES

serve as proof in monetary cases such as the one in our Mishnah, but it would be difficult to argue that it too follows Rav's view against the Halakhah. *Tosafot* explains that this passage can even represent the viewpoint of Shmuel, since the combination of a statistical majority and deficient testimony is enough to compel a defendant to pay money, even according to Shmuel.

Some Rishonim, however, distinguish between the statistical majority in the passages in *Ketubot* and that in the dispute between Rav and Shmuel in *Bava Batra*. In our passage, the woman has another argument to support her claim — the legal presumption that she was born a virgin and remained so until it was proved otherwise. Thus the woman has both a statistical majority and a legal presumption supporting her claim, and even Shmuel would agree that this is sufficient to compel a defendant to pay (*Ba'al HaMa'or, Tosefot Rid*).

The Jerusalem Talmud asks our Gemara's question about statistical majorities, and answers that our Mishnah maintains (like Shmuel) that statistical majorities are not sufficient to compel a defendant to pay. This would seem to support *Tosafot*'s explanation that our Gemara's question is only pertinent according to Rav (*Ramban*). But *Meiri* attempts to reconcile the Jerusalem Talmud with *Ba'al HaMa'or*'s explanation.

הָנָךְ סָהֲדֵי שַׁקָּרֵי These witnesses are liars. The Gemara suggests that the witnesses should be considered liars because their testimony is not confirmed by public knowledge. The Rishonim ask: Since mere rumor is never considered to be equal to the valid testimony of two witnesses, why should the Gemara dismiss the witnesses as liars, merely because there is no rumor that the woman was a virgin?

Ritva explains that testimony is more reliable than a rumor only when the rumor conflicts with it. For the rumor could be false, and there is no reason to accept it over the testimony of witnesses. In our case, however, the problem is that there is no rumor when there should be one. A false rumor may be the work of an unscrupulous person, but there is no satisfactory explanation for the absence of a rumor. Hence we must question the validity of the testimony. *Shittah Mekubbetzet* adds that if the witnesses had really known that the woman was a virgin, they themselves would have caused the matter to become public knowledge.

The Rishonim ask another question: Why should the testimony of the witnesses that the woman was a virgin itself not be considered a rumor? *Rashi* explains that a matter of public knowledge is normally known by many people. Thus, if only two witnesses can be found to corroborate the woman's claim, this arouses suspicion. *Rashbam* (*Bava Batra* 92b) distinguishes between an explicit rumor that the woman was known to be a virgin, and indirect evidence that she was treated as a virgin. If the woman was a virgin, there should be a rumor to that effect. The witnesses do not know that the woman was a virgin; they testify only that she wore a *hinuma*. Thus, although their testimony may be satisfactory indirect evidence that the woman was a virgin, it does not amount to an explicit rumor.

According to this latter explanation, *Ḥatam Sofer* suggests an alternative solution to our first question. The witnesses might have been believed had their testimony directly contradicted the rumor, since testimony is more reliable than rumor. But since they admit that they too do not know whether she was a virgin, and their testimony concerning the *hinuma* conflicts with the lack of a rumor

¹וְזוֹ, הוֹאִיל וְאֵין לָהּ קוֹל, ²אִיתְרַע לָהּ רוּבָּא.

³״אִם יֵשׁ עֵדִים שֶׁיָּצְתָה בְּהִינוּמָא, וכו׳״. ⁴וְלֵיחוּשׁ דִּלְמָא מַפְּקָא עֵדִים בְּהַאי בֵּי דִינָא וְגָבְיָא, ⁵וַהֲדַר מַפְּקָא לָהּ לִכְתוּבָּה בְּהַאי בֵּי דִינָא וְגָבְיָא בָּהּ!

⁶אָמַר רַבִּי אַבָּהוּ: ⁷זֹאת אוֹמֶרֶת: כּוֹתְבִין שׁוֹבֵר.

LITERAL TRANSLATION

[1] and [with regard to] this woman, since she is not talked about, [2] the majority has become flawed.

[3] "If there are witnesses that she went out with a *hinuma*, etc." [4] But let us be concerned [that] perhaps she may produce witnesses in this court and collect, [5] and return [and] produce a ketubah in that court and collect with it!

[6] Rabbi Abbahu said: [7] This implies (lit., "says"): We write a receipt.

TRANSLATION AND COMMENTARY

[1] It follows that **since there was no publicity** to the effect that **this woman** was a virgin when she married, [2] the statistical **majority** supporting her claim **is flawed,** and it is quite likely that she was, in fact, a widow. Therefore she must produce witnesses to testify that she was treated as a virgin at her wedding.

אִם יֵשׁ עֵדִים [3] The Gemara now considers the next clause of the Mishnah: **"If there are witnesses** who testify **that,** at her wedding ceremony, **she went out with a *hinuma*** and the hair of her head was loose, we take this as evidence that she was treated as a virgin, and her ketubah is 200 zuz." The Gemara objects: Normally, when a woman claims her ketubah, she produces a ketubah document which explicitly states the sum to which she is entitled, and after the ketubah has been paid, the document is torn up. Clearly, in this case the woman did not produce her ketubah for some reason — perhaps because it was lost. Yet we still accepted her claim, provided that she could bring acceptable alternative proof. [4] **But** it is wrong to allow a creditor to collect a debt without tearing up the promissory note — even when the debtor admits that he has not yet paid. **We should be concerned that** this woman **may perhaps produce witnesses in this court and collect,** [5] in accordance with the law stated in our Mishnah, and later recover the lost ketubah **and proceed** to a second court, **and produce the ketubah in that court and collect with it** a second time. The husband will not be believed if he claims to have already paid, because the document is still intact. Instead, the woman should be told to produce her ketubah, and if she cannot do so, she should forfeit her claim, just like any other creditor.

אָמַר רַבִּי אַבָּהוּ [6] **Rabbi Abbahu said** in reply: [7] Our Mishnah **is implying** that **we** generally **write a receipt.** When the man pays the woman her ketubah in accordance with the law of our Mishnah, she writes him a receipt. And if she later produces her ketubah, her husband can prove that he has already paid by producing his receipt. Ordinarily, the burden of proof falls on the creditor, not on the debtor. Accordingly, it is the responsibility of the creditor to take care of the promissory note that proves he is owed money, whereas the debtor is not required to keep a receipt, as he does not need to prove anything. However, in a case where the creditor claims to have lost the promissory note and the debtor admits the debt, there is a dispute among the Sages as to whether we require the debtor to pay, and we order the creditor to write a receipt, or whether we permit the debtor to withhold payment until the note has been returned.

RASHI

דלמא מפקא עדים — עדי הינומא. **כותבין שובר** — שכשיפרע לה כתובתה תכתוב לו שקבלה כתובתה, ויהיה בידו לזכות. **זאת אומרת** — ולא כמאן דאמר אין כותבין, בבבא בתרא.

NOTES

about her virginity, we must assume that there was some error, and that the woman did not in fact wear a *hinuma*, or that she wore a *hinuma* even though she was not entitled to do so.

כּוֹתְבִין שׁוֹבֵר We write a receipt. Ordinarily, the burden of proof falls on the creditor, not the debtor. Accordingly, it is the responsibility of the creditor to take care of the promissory note that proves he is owed money. However, when the creditor claims to have lost the promissory note and the debtor admits the debt, there is a dispute among the Tannaim and the Amoraim as to whether we require the debtor to pay and order the creditor to write a receipt, or whether we permit the debtor to delay payment until the note is returned (*Bava Batra* 171b). Rav and Shmuel rule in favor of Rabbi Yehudah, who maintains that it is not fair to expect the debtor to pay and accept a receipt. For if the receipt is ever lost, and the creditor produces his note, the debtor may be forced to pay again. Thus the debtor will be forced to keep the receipt for an unlimited period, and this is an unreasonable demand. Rabbi Yoḥanan and Resh Lakish, however, rule in favor of Rabbi Yose, who maintains that the debtor must pay and accept

HALAKHAH

כּוֹתְבִין שׁוֹבֵר We write a receipt. "If a debtor comes to pay his debt, and the creditor claims that he has lost the promissory note, the debtor cannot refuse to pay the debt until the document is found. Rather, he must pay the debt,

SAGES

רַבִּי אַבָּהוּ Rabbi Abbahu. A Palestinian Amora of the third generation, Rabbi Abbahu was the most important of Rabbi Yoḥanan's disciples. He was the head of a yeshivah and a judge in Caesarea, as well as the representative of the Jewish people to the Romans. He also transmitted teachings in the name of Resh Lakish, Rabbi Elazar, Rabbi Yose bar Ḥanina, and others. Rabbi Zera was a student and colleague of his. His other colleagues were: Rabbi Ḥiyya bar Abba, and Rabbi Ammi and Rabbi Assi, the heads of the Tiberias Yeshivah. Among his students were Rabbi Yonah, Rabbi Yose, and Rabbi Yirmeyah. Sages gathered around him, and they became known as the Rabbis of Caesarea. He was prolific in Aggadah and was an excellent preacher. He spoke Greek well, and taught that language to his daughter. His father-in-law was Rabbi Taḥlifa of Caesarea, and his sons were the Sages Ḥanina, Avimi, and Zera.

CONCEPTS

שׁוֹבֵר Receipt. The Hebrew root שבר means "to break," and the word שׁוֹבֵר from this root means precisely a document meant to break, i.e., to nullify the validity of another document. A receipt in which the lender declares that he has received payment for his debt is thus a שׁוֹבֵר, in that it nullifies the original promissory note or other form of monetary obligation.

In a place where it is customary to rely upon a שׁוֹבֵר, the recipient is obliged to retain it for a long time, to forestall any possibility of his being required to pay the debt twice.

TRANSLATION AND COMMENTARY

According to Rabbi Abbahu, our Mishnah rules in favor of the view that we do write receipts. Hence, in a case where the husband admits that he has not yet paid the ketubah, but claims that he owes only 100 zuz, we order him to accept a receipt and pay the 100 zuz to which he admits — or 200, if the woman can prove she was treated as a virgin at her wedding.

רַב פַּפָּא אָמַר [1]**Rav Pappa said:** It is possible that our Mishnah maintains that ordinarily we do not write a receipt, but that in our Mishnah **we are dealing with a place where they do not write a ketubah** at all. In most places the custom was to detail the ketubah obligations in a written document, but in some places, when a husband divorced his wife, he would simply pay the sum fixed by law, without need for a written document. Thus, the reason why our Mishnah is not concerned about the woman producing a document in another court may be because she never had a written ketubah in the first place. But in a place where the custom is to write a ketubah, the husband is not required to pay at all until the wife produces her ketubah, since the law is that we do not write a receipt.

וְאִיכָּא דְּמַתְנֵי לָהּ אַבָּרַיְיתָא [2]The Gemara notes: **There are some** versions of this dispute between Rabbi Abbahu and Rav Pappa **which teach** the issue **in connection with the following Baraita,** which explains

[1]רַב פַּפָּא אָמַר: בְּמָקוֹם שֶׁאֵין כּוֹתְבִין כְּתוּבָּה עָסְקִינַן.
[2]וְאִיכָּא דְּמַתְנֵי לָהּ אַבָּרַיְיתָא:

LITERAL TRANSLATION

[1]Rav Pappa said: We are dealing with a place where they do not write a ketubah.

[2]And there are [some] who teach it [as referring] to the [following] Baraita:

RASHI

רב פפא אמר – לעולם אין כותבין, דנמצא זה צריך לשמור שוברו מן העכברים. ומי שיש לו שטר על חברו – או יביא השטר ויחזירנו, או לא יטול כלום. ומתניתין במקום שאין כותבין כתובה, אלא סומכין על תנאי בית דין שתקנו לבתולה מאתים ולאלמנה מנה, דליכא למיחש לדלמא הדרה ומפקא לה. **דמתני לה** – לדרבי אבהו ולדרב פפא.

NOTES

a receipt, because it would be unfair to expect the creditor to remain unpaid. The Halakhah follows the latter opinion.

Later on in the passage, Abaye asks why the School of Rabbi Yose prefers to be unfair to the debtor rather than to the creditor, and Rava responds by citing a verse (Proverbs 22:7): "The borrower is the slave of the lender." From this verse we learn that in general the lender's convenience is favored over the borrower's (like that of a master over that of a slave), because the lender did the borrower a favor by lending him the money. The Rishonim note that Rava's reasoning applies only to a person who borrowed money, not to a ketubah or any other debt that was not created through a loan. Nevertheless, the Rishonim explain that the Sages did not make any distinction between different kinds of debts, and in every case insisted that the debtor pay and accept a receipt (*Tosafot, Rashba*).

בְּמָקוֹם שֶׁאֵין כּוֹתְבִין כְּתוּבָּה With a place where they do not write a ketubah. Most of the obligations of the ketubah are fixed by law and cannot be changed. In particular, the basic ketubah settlement, which is set at 200 zuz for a virgin and 100 for a non-virgin, may not be reduced, even with the wife's consent. In general, it is not necessary to write a promissory note for an obligation such as a ketubah, which is fixed by law, because the person obligated cannot in any case deny his obligation, or even claim to have paid already without proof. Hence there were some places where it was not customary to write a ketubah. In many places, however, it was customary for the husband to add an additional optional sum — called an "additional ketubah" (תּוֹסֶפֶת כְּתוּבָּה) — above and beyond the obligatory 200 (or 100) zuz, and this is the main reason why the ketubah was written down (*Tosafot, Bava Metzia 17a*). Today the universal custom is to write a ketubah.

In a place where it was customary not to write a ketubah, the woman was entitled only to the basic ketubah settlement (*Rambam, Hilkhot Ishut* 16:22). If the husband wished to give her an "additional ketubah," he had to ignore the local custom and write a ketubah. According to some authorities, the same is true in a place where it was

HALAKHAH

and the creditor must give him a receipt. If the debtor suspects that the creditor is hiding the document, he may demand that a ban of excommunication be imposed on 'a person who hides his document,' and if the debtor is certain that the creditor is hiding the document, he can refuse to pay until the creditor takes an oath that he is not hiding it. If the creditor admits that he has the document in his possession, but claims that it is not available at the moment (e.g., it is stored in another town), the debtor can refuse to pay until the document is produced." (*Rambam, Sefer Mishpatim, Hilkhot Malveh VeLoveh* 23:16; *Shulhan Arukh, Ḥoshen Mishpat* 54:2-3.)

בְּמָקוֹם שֶׁאֵין כּוֹתְבִין כְּתוּבָּה With a place where they do not write a ketubah. "If the woman claimed that she was a virgin and the man claimed that she was a widow, and if she can prove that she was treated as a virgin at her wedding, she is entitled to 200 zuz, following the Mishnah. But this applies only in a place where it is not customary to write a ketubah (or even in a place where it *is* customary to write a ketubah, if she claims that the ketubah was lost and the husband admits that he has not yet paid — *Maggid Mishneh*). But in a place where it is customary to write a ketubah, she does not collect anything without producing her ketubah." (*Rambam, Sefer Nashim, Hilkhot Ishut* 16:25; *Shulhan Arukh, Even HaEzer* 96:15.)

BACKGROUND

כּוֹס שֶׁל בְּשׂוֹרָה **The cup of good tidings.** This cup of wine was apparently passed around after a newly married woman had intercourse and her virginity was confirmed. Since it was used to inform others of the new wife's status, it was called "the cup of good tidings."

TRANSLATION AND COMMENTARY

the law of our Mishnah in greater detail, rather than in connection with our Mishnah itself: [1] **"If a woman lost her ketubah** document, [2] **or concealed it** somewhere in her house and can no longer find it, [3] **or her ketubah was burnt,** and she claims to have been married as a virgin, but her husband claims that she was a widow, the woman can bring proof of another kind. If she can prove that she was treated as a virgin at her wedding, she is believed. [4] For example, **if people danced before her** [5] **or played before her,** [6] **or passed before her the cup of good tidings** [7] **or the cloth of virginity** — [8] **if she has witnesses** who can attest **to any one of these** customs, [9] she has proved her claim, and **her ketubah is two hundred zuz."** The Gemara explains below that special songs were sung when the guests danced at a virgin's wedding, and the dancers used to entertain the couple in special ways. Since these practices were not performed when widows remarried, they are considered proof of a bride's virginity. The "cloth of virginity" refers to the case described in Deuteronomy 22:17, in which a bride is accused of not being a virgin, and her father disproves the accusation by displaying "the (bloodstained) cloth of virginity." The "cup of good tidings" is explained below.

וְלֵיחוּשׁ [10] According to this version, the Gemara's initial question concerned this Baraita: Why do we not order the woman to produce her ketubah? Why does the Baraita accept alternative proof? **We should be concerned that** this woman **may produce witnesses in this court and collect,** in accordance with the law of the Baraita, [11] **and** later **produce her ketubah in** another **court and collect with it** a second time. The husband will not be believed if he claims to have paid already, because the document is still intact. Rather, the woman should be told to produce her ketubah, and if she cannot do so, she should forfeit her claim!

אָמַר רַבִּי אַבָּהוּ [12] According to this version, **Rabbi Abbahu said** in reply: [13] The Baraita **is implying** that in a case like this **we write a receipt.** According to Rabbi Abbahu, the Baraita is ruling in favor of the view that in a case where the husband admits that he has not yet paid the ketubah, we order him to pay it and to accept a receipt, so that if the woman later produces her ketubah and again demands payment, he can prove that he has already paid.

[1] ״אִיבְּדָה כְּתוּבָּתָהּ, [2] הִטְמִינָה כְּתוּבָּתָהּ, [3] נִשְׂרְפָה כְּתוּבָּתָהּ, [4] רָקְדוּ לְפָנֶיהָ, [5] שִׂחֲקוּ לְפָנֶיהָ, [6] הֶעֱבִירוּ לְפָנֶיהָ כּוֹס שֶׁל בְּשׂוֹרָה [7] אוֹ מַפָּה שֶׁל בְּתוּלִים — [8] אִם יֵשׁ לָהּ עֵדִים בְּאֶחָד מִכָּל אֵלּוּ, [9] כְּתוּבָּתָהּ מָאתַיִם״. [10] וְלֵיחוּשׁ דִּלְמָא מַפְּקָא עֵדִים בְּהַאי בֵּי דִינָא וְגָבְיָא, [11] וַהֲדַר מַפְּקָא לִכְתוּבָּתָהּ בְּהַאי בֵּי דִינָא וְגָבְיָא בָּהּ!

[12] אָמַר רַבִּי אַבָּהוּ: [13] זֹאת אוֹמֶרֶת: כּוֹתְבִין שׁוֹבֵר.

LITERAL TRANSLATION

[1] "[If] she lost her ketubah, [2] [or] concealed her ketubah, [3] [or] her ketubah was burnt, [4] [then if people] danced before her, [5] [or] played before her, [6] [or] passed before her the cup of [good] tidings [7] or the cloth of virginity — [8] if she has witnesses about one of all these, [9] her ketubah is two hundred [zuz]."

[10] But let us be concerned [that] perhaps she may produce witnesses in this court and collect, [11] and return [and] produce her ketubah in that court and collect with it!

[12] Rabbi Abbahu says: [13] This implies: We write a receipt.

RASHI

הטמינה כתובתה — והיא תובעת מאתים, והוא אומר אלמנה נשאתיך. **רקדו לפניה** — אם יש עדים שרקדו לפניה ביום נישואיה. **כוס של בשורה** — המבשר עליה סימני בתולות. ולקמן מפרש מאי היא.

NOTES

customary to write a ketubah, if the woman lost her ketubah and wished to be paid in return for a receipt (in accordance with Rabbi Abbahu's opinion). Here too she would only be entitled to the basic ketubah settlement (*Maharshal*). Many authorities, however, rule that the woman is entitled to the "additional ketubah" as well (*Mordekhai; Haggahot Mordekhai* in the name of the Geonim).

אִיבְּדָה... הִטְמִינָה... נִשְׂרְפָה **She lost... she concealed... was burnt.** *Shittah Mekubbetzet* objects: Normally a Baraita is written in the style called לֹא זוֹ אַף זוֹ ("not only this, but also that"), in which the clauses are arranged in the order of increasing novelty. It would appear that the order of our Baraita should have been: "Burnt, lost, concealed," to reflect the increasing novelty of forcing the husband to pay in return for a receipt, without receiving the ketubah back. Not only do we make him pay if the ketubah was burnt, we even do so if it was merely lost and may still be recovered, and even if it was hidden somewhere in the house.

Shittah Mekubbetzet explains that the order of the Baraita reflects a different issue: That we believe the woman when she claims to have been a virgin, on the basis of the customs followed at her wedding. If the woman is lying, the only way to refute her claim of virginity is to recover the lost ketubah. Nevertheless, not only do we believe her if the ketubah was lost — when there is a real danger of the ketubah being rediscovered, and she is therefore afraid to lie — but we even do so if the ketubah was hidden, and she can be confident that no one will find it, or even when it was burnt, in which case she can be *certain* it will never be recovered and knows that her claim can never be refuted.

TRANSLATION AND COMMENTARY

רַב פַּפָּא אָמַר [1]According to this version, **Rav Pappa said:** It is possible that the Baraita maintains that we do not write a receipt, [2]and that **we are dealing with a place where they do not write a ketubah** at all. According to Rav Pappa, the reason why the Baraita was not concerned that the woman might produce a document in another court was because the woman did not have a written ketubah in the first place. But where the custom is to write a ketubah, the husband is not required to pay at all until the wife produces her ketubah, since the law is that we do not write a receipt.

[1]רַב פַּפָּא אָמַר: [2]בְּמָקוֹם שֶׁאֵין כּוֹתְבִין כְּתוּבָּה עָסְקִינַן.
[3]וְהָא ״אִיבְּדָה כְּתוּבָּתָהּ״ קָתָנֵי!
[4]דִּכְתַב לָהּ אִיהוּ.
[5]סוֹף סוֹף מַפְּקָא לָהּ וְגָבְיָא בָּהּ!
[6]מַאי ״אִיבְּדָה״? [7]אִיבְּדָה בָּאוּר.

LITERAL TRANSLATION

[1]Rav Pappa said: [2]We are dealing with a place where they do not write a ketubah.
[3]But surely it teaches: "[If] she lost her ketubah"!
[4]Where he did write one for her.
[5]Ultimately she can produce it and collect with it!
[6]What [does] "she lost" [mean]? [7]She lost it in a fire.

וְהָא אִיבְּדָה כְּתוּבָּתָהּ קָתָנֵי [3]Before comparing the two versions of the difference of opinion between Rabbi Abbahu and Rav Pappa, the Gemara clarifies a few points concerning the second version. According to this version, Rav Pappa explains the Baraita as referring to a place where it was not customary to write ketubot. **But surely,** objects the Gemara, **the Baraita teaches: "If she lost her ketubah."** Clearly we are dealing with a case where the woman had a ketubah, which she lost. How, then, can Rav Pappa claim that the Baraita was referring to a place where it was not customary to write such documents?

דִּכְתַב לָהּ אִיהוּ [4]The Gemara answers: According to Rav Pappa, the Baraita is referring to a case **where** the husband decided to **write** a ketubah **for** his wife, even though local custom did not require this. Later, the woman lost her ketubah, and argued with her husband that she had been a virgin when she married.

סוֹף סוֹף [5]The Gemara objects to this explanation: How does this solve our original problem — that it is unfair to force the husband to pay if the woman does not tear up her ketubah, because she might use it to collect twice? **Ultimately,** if the woman finds her lost ketubah, **she can** still **produce it and collect with it!** Therefore, since we are assuming that receipts are not written, the husband should not be required to pay.

מַאי אִיבְּדָה [6]The Gemara answers: According to Rav Pappa, we must explain the word *ibbedah* (אִיבְּדָה) in the Baraita as "destroyed" rather than "lost" (the word has both meanings in Hebrew). According to this explanation, **what does** the Baraita **mean** when it says that **"she lost"** her ketubah? [7]It means that witnesses saw that it **was destroyed** completely — **in a fire,** for example. Hence there is no further cause for concern that she may recover her ketubah and use it to collect a second time.

NOTES

דִּכְתַב לָהּ אִיהוּ **Where he did write one for her.** Rav Pappa's answer and the subsequent question and answer of the Gemara are difficult to understand. Rav Pappa's position is that the Baraita is referring to a place where it is not customary to write a ketubah, whereas in a place where it is customary to write a ketubah the husband need not pay unless the woman produces her ketubah. But if Rav Pappa concedes that the Baraita is referring to a case where the husband did in fact write a ketubah, what difference does it make if the normal custom in the place was to write a ketubah or not? The husband should be permitted to withhold payment until the ketubah is returned.

Several Rishonim (*Ramban, Rashba, Ritva*) cite *Ra'avad,* who explains that the Baraita is referring to a case where the husband cannot prove that he wrote a ketubah. The woman admits that he did so, but claims it was lost. The husband does not believe that the ketubah was lost, and suspects her of hiding it. Therefore, in a place where it is not customary to write a ketubah, we believe that she lost the ketubah, because her claim is supported by a *miggo,* since she could have denied that he ever wrote it. But in a place where it is customary to write a ketubah, she has no *miggo,* and we do not believe her.

According to this explanation, the Gemara's next objection — "Ultimately she will be able to produce the ketubah and collect with it" — is difficult to understand. We have already established that we believe her claim that the ketubah was lost. Why, then, should we be concerned that she might produce the ketubah? *Ramban* explains that our concern is that she may find the lost ketubah and produce it. Hence the Gemara is forced to explain that she claimed that the ketubah was irretrievably destroyed.

According to this explanation, the Gemara's conclusion — that the woman can collect only if there are witnesses that the ketubah was burnt — is difficult to understand. Why should she not be believed without witnesses when she claims that the ketubah was burnt? She has a *miggo,* since she could have claimed that a ketubah was never written. *Rashba* explains that at this stage in the discussion the Gemara is aware that the *miggo* is flawed, because the woman may prefer to claim that the ketubah was lost or burnt, rather than to deny its existence, for the husband might produce the witnesses who signed the ketubah.

LITERAL TRANSLATION

[1] If so, this is [the same as] "it was burnt"! [2] Moreover, [3] what is there to say [about] "she concealed"? [4] And furthermore, [5] why do I [need] "she lost"?

[6] Rather, [7] any [case where] she lost [it] is as if she concealed [it] in front of us, [8] and we do not give [the ketubah money] to her unless witnesses say [that] her ketubah was burnt.

[1] אִי הָכִי, הַיְינוּ ״נִשְׂרְפָה״! [2] וְעוֹד, [3] ״הִטְמִינָה״ מַאי אִיכָּא לְמֵימַר? [4] וְתוּ, [5] ״אִיבְּדָה״ לָמָּה לִי?

[6] אֶלָּא, [7] כָּל אִיבְּדָה כִּי הִטְמִינָה בְּפָנֵינוּ דָּמֵי, [8] וְלָא יָהֲבִינַן לַהּ עַד דְּאָמְרִי עֵדִים נִשְׂרְפָה כְּתוּבָּתָהּ.

TRANSLATION AND COMMENTARY

אִי הָכִי [1] The Gemara now raises a series of objections to this explanation: The Baraita says that the woman "lost her ketubah, or concealed it, or her ketubah was burnt." But **if** the Baraita means by the word "lost" that her ketubah was destroyed in a fire, **this is the same as** saying that "her ketubah **was burnt."** Why does the Baraita repeat itself in this way? [2] **Moreover,** continues the Gemara, even if we accept that the word "lost" means "destroyed in a fire," [3] **what can we say about** the clause that reads: **"She concealed** her ketubah"? The word "concealed" cannot be explained away as meaning "destroyed." Clearly, we are dealing with a case where the woman had a ketubah to conceal. How, then, can we solve our original problem — that the court cannot force the husband to pay if the woman does not tear up her ketubah, because she can produce it and use it to collect a second time — since our assumption is that receipts are not written? [4] **And furthermore,** continues the Gemara, if the word "lost" means "destroyed in a fire," [5] **why does** the Baraita **need** to mention the case where **"she lost** her ketubah"? Surely it teaches us nothing that we cannot learn from the later clause, which says: "It was burnt"!

אֶלָּא [6] **Rather,** says the Gemara, we must explain the Baraita differently, if it is to be interpreted as referring to a place where it was not customary to write a ketubah but the husband chose to write one anyway. The Baraita reads: "If she lost her ketubah, or concealed her ketubah, or her ketubah was burnt — if people danced before her, etc." A period must be inserted in the Baraita after the words "concealed her ketubah," and the clauses in the Baraita must be understood as follows: [7] In **any case where she** claims to have **lost** her ketubah, we do not believe her, and it **is as if she concealed** her ketubah **in front of us.** Even if she produces witnesses that she was a virgin, and even if her husband admits to owing the money, we do not make him pay, because of the possibility that she may produce her ketubah later and collect a second time, since it is not the practice to write receipts. [8] **We give her the ketubah money only if witnesses say that her ketubah was burnt.** In such a case, if witnesses testify that they danced before her, etc., she is entitled to the full 200 zuz.

RASHI

אלא — הכי קאמר: כל אבידה כמי שהטמינה בפנינו דמי, ולא גביא. והכי קתני: אבדה כתובתה, הטמינה כתובתה, נשרפה כתובתה, אם רקדו לפניה וכו׳. והכי פירושה: אמרה אבד שטר כתובתה — הרי היא כמו שהטמינה כתובתה בפנינו כדי להוציא ולגבות פעם שניה, ואינה גובה כלום, אלא אם כן תביא השטר. ואם אמרה נשרפה, ויש עדים שנשרפה, דהשתא ליכא למיחש למידי — תביא עדים שרקדו לפניה, שזהו סימן לבתולה, ותגבה מאתים.

NOTES

וְתוּ אִיבְּדָה לָמָּה לִי **And furthermore, why do I need "she lost"?** Ostensibly, this objection is the same as the Gemara's first objection, which was: "If the Baraita means by the word 'lost' that her ketubah was destroyed in a fire, this is the same as saying that 'her ketubah was burnt,' so why does the Baraita repeat itself?" Indeed, *Ritva* attributes this question to a scribal error.

Other Rishonim attempt to argue that there is a difference between the two objections. *Tosafot* explains that we could have answered the first objection by understanding the expression "she lost" as a sort of introduction: "She lost her ketubah by, for example, burning it in a fire." However, this would still not explain why we need such an introduction.

עַד דְּאָמְרִי עֵדִים נִשְׂרְפָה כְּתוּבָּתָהּ **Unless witnesses say that her ketubah was burnt.** Our translation and commentary follow *Rashi*'s version of the Gemara, according to which the Gemara's conclusion is that the woman is believed only if she can produce witnesses to testify that the ketubah was burnt. The Rishonim object: The Gemara is explaining how the Baraita would be interpreted by Rav Pappa, who maintains that it is referring to a place where it is not customary to write a ketubah, whereas in a place where it *is* customary to write a ketubah, the husband need not pay unless the woman produces her ketubah. But if we are referring to a case where the husband chose to write a ketubah, and witnesses testify that it was burnt, what difference does it make if the normal custom in the place was to write a ketubah or not? The husband should be required to pay in any case, since the woman cannot possibly recover her ketubah and collect a second time.

Tosafot and *Rosh* explain that in a place where it is customary to write a ketubah, the husband is required to write his wife another ketubah if the first one is destroyed. But if the husband went out of his way to write a ketubah in a place where it was not customary to do so, there is no reason to suspect that, he wrote a second one. *Rashba* explains that, according to the Gemara's conclusion, Rav Pappa no longer understands the Baraita as referring

1מַאן דְּמַתְנֵי לָהּ אַבָּרַיְיתָא, 2כָּל שֶׁכֵּן אַמַּתְנִיתִין. 3וּמַאן דְּמַתְנֵי לָהּ אַמַּתְנִיתִין אֲבָל אַבָּרַיְיתָא לָא, 4כִּי קוּשְׁיָא.

5״אִם יֵשׁ עֵדִים, כו׳״. 6וְלֵיחוּשׁ דִּלְמָא מַפְּקָא עֵדֵי הִינוּמָא בְּהַאי בֵּי דִינָא וְגָבְיָא, 7וַהֲדַר מַפְּקָא עֵדֵי הִינּוּמָא בְּבֵי דִינָא אַחֲרִינָא וְגָבְיָא!

8בְּמָקוֹם דְּלָא אֶפְשָׁר, 9וַדַּאי כָּתְבִינַן שׁוֹבֵר.

LITERAL TRANSLATION

1The one who teaches this [as referring] to the Baraita, 2how much more so [does he apply it] to our Mishnah. 3But the one who teaches it [as referring] to our Mishnah does not [apply it] to the Baraita, 4in accordance with the difficulty.

5"If there are witnesses, etc." 6But let us be concerned [that] perhaps she may produce witnesses of *hinuma* in this court and collect, 7and return [and] produce witnesses of *hinuma* in another court and collect!

8In a place where it is not possible [in another way], 9we certainly write a receipt.

TRANSLATION AND COMMENTARY

מַאן דְּמַתְנֵי לָהּ אַבָּרַיְיתָא 1Having clarified the second version of Rav Pappa's statement, the Gemara now compares the two versions of the difference of opinion between Rabbi Abbahu and Rav Pappa. The second version, **which teaches** that Rabbi Abbahu and Rav Pappa disagreed **about the Baraita,** 2would concede that their dispute **applies all the more so to our Mishnah,** because the Mishnah can easily be explained either as referring to a place where ketubot are not written, or as ruling in favor of the view that receipts *are* written. 3**But the** version **that teaches** that Rabbi Abbahu and Rav Pappa disagreed **about our Mishnah would not** accept that their dispute **applies to the Baraita,** 4**because of the difficulty** raised in relation to Rav Pappa's explanation. Even though we were able to explain that the Baraita was referring to a case where the husband chose to write a ketubah and the woman then burnt it, this explanation was rather forced. Clearly, the simplest explanation of the Baraita is that it is ruling in favor of the view that receipts are written; and according to the first version, even Rav Pappa would admit that this is true of the Baraita (although he would still argue that the Mishnah is referring to a place where it was not customary to write a ketubah).

אִם יֵשׁ עֵדִים 5In the light of the previous discussion, the Gemara again considers the ruling of our Mishnah that **"if there are witnesses** that the woman wore a ***hinuma*** at her wedding, she is entitled to a ketubah of 200 zuz." According to Rav Pappa, the Mishnah follows the view that receipts are not written, and is referring to a place where it was not customary to write a ketubah. The Gemara raises an objection to this explanation: How can the Baraita order the husband to pay without any kind of documentation? 6**We should surely be concerned that** this woman **may perhaps produce witnesses in this court** that she wore a ***hinuma*** at her wedding, **and collect** her ketubah in accordance with the law of the Mishnah, 7**and** later **produce** other **witnesses in another court** that she wore a ***hinuma*** at her wedding, **and collect** her ketubah again. The husband will not be believed if he claims to have paid already, because the woman can collect without a document, on the basis of oral testimony.

בְּמָקוֹם דְּלָא אֶפְשָׁר 8The Gemara answers: **In a place where it is not possible** to solve this problem **in any other way,** 9**we definitely require a written receipt,** even according to the view that receipts are not normally written. Thus, according to everyone, in the case in our Mishnah the wife must give her husband a receipt. According to Rabbi Abbahu, this is because the Halakhah is that receipts are always written.

RASHI

מאן דמתני לה — לדרבי אבהו ורב פפא אברייתא. **כל שכן אמתניתין** — דכיון דאברייתא דקתני בהדיא אבדה כתובתה גביא, ועלה קאמר רב פפא דלא גביא. ומתרץ לה דהכא קתני: אבדה כתובתה הרי היא כמו שהטמינה, וכשנשרפה הוא דקא גביא, ולעולם אין כותבין שובר, כל שכן דאמתניתין איכא למיתני פלוגתא דרב פפא אדרבי אבהו, למימר דבמקום שאין כותבין כתובה עסקינן. **ומאן דמתני** — פלוגתא דרב פפא ודרבי אבהו אמתניתין. **אבל אברייתא לא** — מתני ליה, דודאי שמעינן מינה דכותבין שובר, דהא במקום שכותבין כתובה עסקינן. **כי קושיין** — דקתני אבדה כתובתה. ולא ניחא לשנויי שינויא דחיקא, למימר אבדה כתובתה כהטמינה כתובתה קאמר. **כיון דלא אפשר** — כגון במקום שאין כותבין כתובה, וגובות על פי עדים, ויש לחוש שמא תלך לבית דין אחר ותביא עדים אחרים ותגבה פעם שניה — ודאי כתבינן שובר.

NOTES

specifically to a place where it is not customary to write a ketubah, and insists only that the Baraita cannot be used to prove that in general we do write receipts, because it refers to the unusual situation in which the ketubah was burnt.

בְּמָקוֹם דְּלָא אֶפְשָׁר In a place where it is not possible in another way. According to the Gemara's conclusion, Rav Pappa and Rabbi Abbahu agree that, in the case discussed in the Mishnah, the husband pays the ketubah in return for a receipt. They disagree, however, as to whether this can serve as a precedent for documented debts in which a creditor loses his document, or whether we write receipts only for obligations that are fixed by law and that are not supported by any written document (*Ramban*).

LITERAL TRANSLATION

[1] "They passed before her the cup of [good] tidings." [2] What is "the cup of [good] tidings"? [3] Rav Adda bar Ahavah said: [4] We pass a cup of wine of terumah before her, [5] as if to say: This [woman] was fit to eat terumah.

[6] Rav Pappa objected to this: [7] But does a widow not eat terumah?

[8] Rather, Rav Pappa said: [9] This [woman] is first, [10] like terumah is first.

[11] It was taught: [12] "Rabbi Yehudah says: We pass a barrel of wine before her."

[13] Rav Adda bar Ahavah said: [14] [For] a virgin, we pass a closed one before her; [15] [for] one who has engaged in intercourse, we pass an open one before her.

[1] "הֶעֱבִירוּ לְפָנֶיהָ כּוֹס שֶׁל בְּשׂוֹרָה". [2] מַאי "כּוֹס שֶׁל בְּשׂוֹרָה"?

[3] אָמַר רַב אַדָּא בַּר אַהֲבָה: [4] כּוֹס יַיִן שֶׁל תְּרוּמָה מַעֲבִירִין לְפָנֶיהָ, [5] כְּלוֹמַר: רְאוּיָה הָיְתָה זוֹ לֶאֱכוֹל בִּתְרוּמָה.

[6] מַתְקִיף לַהּ רַב פַּפָּא: [7] אַטּוּ אַלְמָנָה מִי לָא אָכְלָה בִּתְרוּמָה?

[8] אֶלָּא אָמַר רַב פַּפָּא: [9] זוֹ רֵאשִׁית, [10] כִּתְרוּמָה רֵאשִׁית.

[11] תַּנְיָא: [12] "רַבִּי יְהוּדָה אוֹמֵר: חָבִית שֶׁל יַיִן מַעֲבִירִין לְפָנֶיהָ".

[13] אָמַר רַב אַדָּא בַּר אַהֲבָה: [14] בְּתוּלָה, מַעֲבִירִין לְפָנֶיהָ סְתוּמָה; [15] בְּעוּלָה, מַעֲבִירִין לְפָנֶיהָ פְּתוּחָה.

RASHI

ראויה היתה זו לאכול בתרומה — אי נישאת לכהן, דבתולה שלמה נמלאת ולא בעולה, שתפסל לכהן מחמת זנות. מתקיף לה רב פפא — ומה זו עדות ללא נישאת אלמנה? אטו — אי נישאת כשהיא אלמנה לכהן הדיוט, מי לא אכלה בתרומה? זו ראשית — בעילתה ראשית.

TRANSLATION AND COMMENTARY

According to Rav Pappa, this is because the Mishnah is referring to a place where ketubot are not written; but in any other situation, we would not require the debtor to pay unless the creditor produces the promissory note.

הֶעֱבִירוּ לְפָנֶיהָ [1] The Gemara now explains one of the terms appearing in the Baraita cited in the previous passage. The Baraita states that if the woman can prove that at her wedding the guests **"passed before her the cup of good tidings,"** this is taken as evidence that she was a virgin then, and she is entitled to the full 200 zuz. [2] The Gemara asks: **What is this "cup of good tidings,"** and how does it indicate that the woman was a virgin?

אָמַר רַב אַדָּא בַּר אַהֲבָה [3] **Rav Adda bar Ahavah said** in reply: The "cup of good tidings" is in fact a cup of wine that was set aside as terumah — the portion of produce that may be consumed only by priests and by members of their immediate households. [4] **We** symbolically **pass a cup of terumah wine before** a virgin bride, [5] **as if to say: This woman was fit to** marry a priest and to **eat terumah.** An unmarried woman who has had intercourse is generally disqualified from marrying a priest. Thus the cup of terumah wine implies that this woman has not had intercourse, and is still a virgin.

מַתְקִיף לַהּ רַב פַּפָּא [6] **Rav Pappa objected to this** explanation: [7] **Does a widow not eat terumah?** While it is true that an unmarried woman who has had intercourse is disqualified from marrying a priest, it does not follow that only virgins are qualified. A widow who has never had extramarital relations is also permitted to marry a priest and to eat terumah!

אֶלָּא אָמַר רַב פַּפָּא [8] **Rather, Rav Pappa said:** The "cup of good tidings" is indeed a cup of terumah wine, but we do not pass it before her to suggest that she was fit to marry a priest. [9] Rather, the symbolism is that **this** woman **is first** (i.e., marrying for the first time), [10] **like terumah, which is called "first"** in the Torah (Numbers 18:12).

תַּנְיָא [11] The Gemara now cites another Baraita describing a slightly different custom: **It was taught** in a Baraita: [12] **"Rabbi Yehudah says: We pass a barrel of wine before her."** This is taken as evidence that the woman was a virgin, and is entitled to a ketubah of 200 zuz.

אָמַר רַב אַדָּא בַּר אַהֲבָה [13] The Gemara now explains how the barrel indicates that the woman was a virgin: **Rav Adda bar Ahavah said:** [14] **For a virgin, we pass a closed** barrel of wine **before her,** symbolizing her virginity. [15] **For** a woman **who has** already **engaged in intercourse** — whether during a previous marriage

SAGES

רַב אַדָּא בַּר אַהֲבָה **Rav Adda bar Ahavah.** A famous Babylonian Amora of the first and second generations. He was born (or was circumcised) on the day Rabbi Yehudah HaNasi died. Rav Adda was a disciple of Rav, and transmitted several teachings in his name. Among his colleagues were Rav Huna, Rav Ḥisda, and Rav Naḥman. Many teachings are transmitted in his name in the Talmud. He was renowned for his piety, righteousness, and modesty, and lived to an advanced age.

BACKGROUND

כִּתְרוּמָה רֵאשִׁית **Like terumah is first.** The Torah requires the separation of various gifts and tithes from produce grown in Eretz Israel. It is universally agreed that the Torah requires such gifts at least from grain, wine, and oil. Although some of these gifts are given while still in the field, or while the produce is still growing, once the produce has been harvested, the first gift is terumah, which is given to the priests. In the Torah, and also in the Prophets (see, for example, Jeremiah 2:3), terumah is therefore called the "first" gift.

חָבִית שֶׁל יַיִן **A barrel of wine.** To bring in a full cask of wine was regarded as a mark of honor for a guest in the Talmudic period, and as an expression of great happiness. By bringing an entire cask rather than some smaller container of wine, the host showed generosity and the wish to make his guests happy. The bringing of a cask of wine to a wedding banquet was therefore meant to express joy and honor, but the manner of bringing the cask was also used to hint at the essence of that celebration.

NOTES

The Rishonim explain that this line of the Gemara can be properly understood only in the light of a passage in tractate *Bava Metzia* (17a), in which the Gemara establishes that when a person demands payment of an obligation fixed by law (such as a ketubah in a place where it is not customary to write one), the onus is on the obligated person to prove that he has already paid, because "there can be no arguments against an obligation fixed by law" (*Tosafot, Ritva*).

Shittah Mekubbetzet notes that the Gemara's answer — that even Rav Pappa would agree that in this case we write a receipt — applies only where the husband died and his widow demanded her ketubah payment from his heirs. But in a case of divorce, it is also possible to mark the bill of divorce in such a way that it can no longer be used to collect the ketubah.

LITERAL TRANSLATION

[1]Why? [2]Let us pass [it] before a virgin, [3]and before one who has engaged in intercourse let us not pass anything!

[4]Sometimes she may seize two hundred [zuz] [5]and say: "I was a virgin, [6]and the fact (lit., 'this') that they did not pass [it] before me [7]was because they were unavoidably prevented."

[8]Our Rabbis taught: "How do we dance before the bride? [9]Bet Shammai say: [17A] [10][Each] bride as she is.

[1]אַמַּאי? [2]נִיעֲבַר קַמֵּי בְּתוּלָה, [3]וְקַמֵּי בְּעוּלָה לָא נִיעֲבַר כְּלָל! [4]זִימְנִין דְּתָפְסָה מָאתַיִם, [5]וְאָמְרָה: ״אֲנָא בְּתוּלָה הֲוַאי, [6]וְהַאי דְּלָא עֲבָרוּ קַמָּאי [7]אִתְנוּסֵי הוּא דְּאִתְנִיסוּ״. [8]תָּנוּ רַבָּנַן: ״כֵּיצַד מְרַקְּדִין לִפְנֵי הַכַּלָּה? [9]בֵּית שַׁמַּאי אוֹמְרִים: [17A] [10]כַּלָּה כְּמוֹת שֶׁהִיא.

RASHI

זימנין דתפסה מאתים – בלא בית דין. וכי בעינן לאפוקי מינה, משום דאין עדים שהעבירו לפניה, אמרה: איתנוסי הוא דאיתניסו. שיכורים היו מאונס יין המשתה. הלכך, השתא אתו עדים שהעבירו לפניה פתוחה – ותו ליכא מידי. **כיצד מרקדים** – מה אומרים לפניה. **כמות שהיא** – לפי יופיה וחשיבותה מקלסין אותה.

TRANSLATION AND COMMENTARY

or in any other circumstances — **we pass an open** barrel **before her,** symbolizing her lost virginity.

אַמַּאי [1]The Gemara asks: **Why** do we need to publicize the non-virgin's lost virginity so blatantly? [2]**Let us pass** a closed barrel **before a virgin,** [3]**and not pass anything before** a woman **who has** already **engaged in intercourse,** thus distinguishing between the two in a more sensitive manner.

זִימְנִין דְּתָפְסָה מָאתַיִם [4]The Gemara answers: An open barrel passed before a woman is positive evidence that she is not a virgin. The absence of a barrel, however, is less conclusive, and this can **sometimes** lead to problems. For example, a widow **may seize two hundred zuz** [5]**and say: "I was a virgin."** Normally the burden of proof falls on the woman, as our Mishnah ruled; but if she seizes 200 zuz, and her husband sues her to return part of it, she becomes the defendant, and the burden of proof falls on the husband. Now, if the husband can produce positive evidence that his wife was not a virgin, he will win his case, but if he can only show that at the wedding they failed to pass the customary barrel before her, [6]she can reply **that they did not pass** the barrel **before her** [7]because **they were prevented by** some **unavoidable circumstance.** Therefore we pass an open barrel before a non-virgin, so that there will be positive evidence for people to remember.

תָּנוּ רַבָּנַן [8]The Baraita cited in the previous passage mentioned that it was customary to dance before a virgin bride. **Our Rabbis taught** the following Baraita, which explains how this was done: **"How do we dance before a bride?** What song do the dancers sing while they dance? [9]**Bet Shammai say:** [17A] [10]They sing the praises of **each bride as she is.** The dancers sing about the qualities with which the bride is

NOTES

אִתְנוּסֵי הוּא דְּאִתְנִיסוּ They were unavoidably prevented. Since the woman could make this claim and seize the ketubah money dishonestly, it is better to have positive evidence (which the husband can produce) that the woman was a widow, than to rely on the absence of evidence that she was a virgin. The Rishonim ask: The Mishnah and the Gemara mention several different wedding customs that applied exclusively to virgins (such as the *hinuma* and the parched grain described in the Mishnah, the "cup of good tidings" described above, and the aromatic oils described below, 17b), but the open barrel is the only one that has a version reserved for widows. What if a woman were to seize 200 zuz and claim that she was a virgin, in a place where the custom was for virgins to wear a *hinuma,* and to argue that she was unavoidably prevented from wearing the *hinuma* for some reason?

Ramban notes that *Rashi* explains that the "unavoidable circumstance" in our Gemara which prevented the celebrants from carrying around the barrel was drunkenness. Accordingly, he explains that the customs reserved for virgins were carried out so scrupulously that a woman would not be believed if she were to claim that they were omitted in her case. Only in the case of the barrel is it possible that the celebrants were too drunk to carry it around. But all the other customs took place earlier, during the ceremony, when the celebrants were unlikely to be drunk.

Tosafot explains, along similar lines, that the "unavoidable circumstance" in our Gemara refers to the barrel being too heavy to lift. This, too, applies only to the barrel custom, but not to the others.

כֵּיצַד מְרַקְּדִין לִפְנֵי הַכַּלָּה How do we dance before the bride? The bridegroom is not mentioned in this Baraita, even though it is clear from many sources that it is no less important to entertain the bridegroom than it is to entertain the bride. Our commentary follows *Maharam Schiff,* who explains that this Baraita is explaining the previous Baraita, which referred to a special dance that was performed only for virgins. Presumably, other forms of entertainment were intended for the groom.

כַּלָּה כְּמוֹת שֶׁהִיא Each bride as she is. The basic position of Bet Shammai is clear — that the dancers must not utter falsehoods while praising the bride. The Rishonim disagree, however, as to what exactly Bet Shammai wish the dancers to say. Our commentary follows *Rashi* and most Rishonim, who explain that the dancers praise the good qualities of the bride. *Tosafot* explains that if the bride has some obvious blemish, the dancers say nothing. Alternatively, they sing about something of which she has reason to be proud. *Ri Migash* adds that if the bride is very ugly, the dancers find something entirely different to sing about, e.g., her family or her intelligence.

Some Rishonim cite a Geonic tradition that disagrees with this explanation. According to this view, Bet Shammai

TRANSLATION AND COMMENTARY

endowed, avoiding anything negative. [1] **But Bet Hillel say:** We treat every bride as if she is beautiful, and sing before her: **'A beautiful and graceful bride.'** [2] **Bet Shammai said to Bet Hillel:** How do we act in **a case where** the bride **is lame or blind?** [3] **Do we sing of her as: 'A beautiful and graceful bride'?** [4] **But** surely we cannot act in this way, because **the Torah** forbids us to lie, as the verse (Exodus 23:7) **states: 'Keep far from a false matter'!** [5] **Bet Hillel said to Bet Shammai** in reply: **According to your argument, if a person makes a bad purchase in the marketplace,** [6] **should someone** who sees him after the purchase **praise it to him or criticize it to him?** [7] Clearly even **you would agree** that **he should praise it to him,** rather than distress the buyer unnecessarily by pointing out the unfortunate truth. Similarly, if you pointedly avoid referring to a bride's defects, you will remind her of them and cause the couple distress. In such cases it is better to praise the bride greatly." [8] The Baraita concludes: **"From here** — by following the reasoning expressed by Bet Hillel in this case — **the Rabbis said: A person's disposition toward people should always be congenial."**

[1] וּבֵית הִלֵּל אוֹמְרִים: 'כַּלָּה נָאָה וַחֲסוּדָה'. [2] אָמְרוּ לָהֶן בֵּית שַׁמַּאי לְבֵית הִלֵּל: הֲרֵי שֶׁהָיְתָה חִיגֶּרֶת אוֹ סוּמָא, [3] אוֹמְרִים לָהּ: 'כַּלָּה נָאָה וַחֲסוּדָה'? [4] וְהַתּוֹרָה אָמְרָה: 'מִדְּבַר שֶׁקֶר תִּרְחָק'! [5] אָמְרוּ לָהֶם בֵּית הִלֵּל לְבֵית שַׁמַּאי: לְדִבְרֵיכֶם, מִי שֶׁלָּקַח מִקָּח רַע מִן הַשּׁוּק, [6] יְשַׁבְּחֶנּוּ בְּעֵינָיו אוֹ יְגַנֶּנּוּ בְּעֵינָיו? [7] הֱוֵי אוֹמֵר: יְשַׁבְּחֶנּוּ בְּעֵינָיו. [8] מִכָּאן אָמְרוּ חֲכָמִים: לְעוֹלָם תְּהֵא דַּעְתּוֹ שֶׁל אָדָם מְעוֹרֶבֶת עִם הַבְּרִיּוֹת".

LITERAL TRANSLATION

[1] But Bet Hillel say: 'A beautiful and graceful bride.' [2] Bet Shammai said to Bet Hillel: If she was lame or blind, [3] do we say about her: 'A beautiful and graceful bride'? [4] But the Torah states: 'Keep far from a false matter'! [5] Bet Hillel said to Bet Shammai: According to your words, [if] someone has bought a bad purchase from the marketplace, [6] should one praise it in his eyes or criticize it in his eyes? [7] You must say: He should praise it in his eyes. [8] From here the Sages said: A person's disposition toward people should always be congenial."

RASHI

חסודה — חוט של חסד משוך עליה. **מכאן אמרו** — מדברי בית הלל שאמרו ישבחנה. **תהא דעתו של אדם מעוררבת עם הבריות** — לעשות לאיש ואיש כרצונו.

BACKGROUND

מִדְּבַר שֶׁקֶר תִּרְחָק "Keep far from a false matter." Bet Shammai made use of this verse rather than the explicit injunction, "you shall not lie" (Leviticus 19:11), because the verse in Leviticus refers to telling a lie for the purpose of fraud and extorting money on false pretences, while the expression, "keep far from a false matter," shows that not only open and direct lies are forbidden, but also that one should avoid saying anything that is deliberately misleading.

לְעוֹלָם תְּהֵא דַּעְתּוֹ שֶׁל אָדָם מְעוֹרֶבֶת עִם הַבְּרִיּוֹת A person's disposition toward people should always be congenial. This is a warning that everyone, even Torah scholars, must be involved with other people, must make every effort to understand them, and must be able to live an amicable social life. This injunction is necessary because sometimes, in one's desire to be severe with oneself in word and in deed, one may distance oneself from society and become unable to associate with other people. In this context it is explained that polite words, though they are sometimes not the absolute truth, are part of the structure of social relations.

NOTES

are of the opinion that the words of the dancers' song are: "The bride [regardless of whether she is pretty or ugly] is as she is," in other words, as she was created by God (*Ritva, Shittah Mekubbetzet*).

נָאָה וַחֲסוּדָה Beautiful and graceful. *Ḥatam Sofer* notes that the word חֲסוּדָה is sometimes used to mean "a generous person," and "beautiful" can also refer to moral qualities. He explains that Bet Hillel purposely selected words that had a number of meanings, to avoid a blatant falsehood. Nevertheless Bet Shammai objected, because the words in context clearly mean "beautiful and graceful," and refer to the bride's physical rather than moral qualities.

Rashi notes that the word "graceful" need not be entirely false, even in its physical sense, as the term sometimes reflects a subjective evaluation whereby a plain-looking woman is seen as quite attractive (*Megillah* 13a).

מִי שֶׁלָּקַח מִקָּח רַע If someone has bought a bad purchase. It is proper and polite to praise an object that a person has purchased, so as not to distress him (*Likkutei Geonim*). *Rashash* points out that Bet Hillel are not referring to a person who seeks advice on whether to buy a piece of merchandise. In such a case, it is the adviser's duty to tell the buyer the truth, however unpleasant. They are referring to a case where the buyer has already made his purchase, so that criticizing the merchandise would serve no constructive purpose, and would only cause the buyer unnecessary anguish.

יְשַׁבְּחֶנּוּ בְּעֵינָיו אוֹ יְגַנֶּנּוּ בְּעֵינָיו Should one praise it in his eyes or criticize it in his eyes? *Ritva* notes that in general it is permitted to tell a white lie in order to prevent unwarranted embarrassment to oneself (*Bava Metzia* 23b) or to someone else (*Yevamot* 65b). What, then, is the reasoning of Bet Shammai? *Tosafot* explains that it is one thing to tell a white lie when confronted with an embarrassing situation, and quite another for the Rabbis to institute a practice that legitimizes prevarication on a regular basis.

לְעוֹלָם תְּהֵא דַּעְתּוֹ שֶׁל אָדָם מְעוֹרֶבֶת עִם הַבְּרִיּוֹת A person's disposition toward people should always be congenial. *Likkutei Geonim* cites two explanations of this statement. The first, followed by our commentary, is that a person should always speak well of others, even if they do not deserve it, just as Bet Hillel ruled in the case of the bride. The second is that a person should behave pleasantly so that others will treat him favorably, in the way Bet Hillel said brides should be treated.

Meiri explains that, just as Bet Hillel said we should

HALAKHAH

כַּלָּה נָאָה וַחֲסוּדָה A beautiful and graceful bride. "It is a commandment to entertain the bride and the bridegroom and to dance before them, singing: 'A beautiful and graceful bride,' even if the bride is not really beautiful," following Bet Hillel. (*Shulḥan Arukh, Even HaEzer* 65:1.)

TRANSLATION AND COMMENTARY

כִּי אֲתָא רַב דִּימִי [1]**When Rav Dimi came** to Babylonia from Eretz Israel, **he said:** [2]**This is how they sing before a bride in the West** (in Eretz Israel, which is to the west of Babylonia): [3]"She uses **no mascara, and no rouge, and does not dye her hair,** [4]**and yet** she is **a graceful gazelle."**

כִּי סָמְכוּ רַבָּנַן [5]Having mentioned the wedding song customarily sung in Eretz Israel, the Gemara now relates that **when the Rabbis** of Eretz Israel **ordained Rabbi Zera,** [6]the students **sang** the wedding song **to him** — as if he were a bride — **as follows:** [7]"He uses **no mascara, and no rouge, and does not dye his hair, yet** he is **a graceful gazelle."**

כִּי סָמְכוּ רַבָּנַן [8]Continuing the subject of ordination ceremonies, the Gemara relates that **when the Rabbis** of Eretz Israel **ordained Rabbi Ammi and Rabbi Assi,** [9]the students **sang** a special ordination song **to them as follows:** [10]**"Anyone like this one and like that one** (like Rabbi Ammi and Rabbi Assi) **ordain for us.** [11]**Do not ordain for us** [12]**either *sarmisin* or *sarmitin*."** These are rhyming terms for incompetent and worthless pseudo-scholars. *Sarmisin* are sophists who pervert the meaning of the law, and *sarmitin* are people who have nothing worthwhile to say. [13]The Gemara notes that **some say** the students used other rhyming epithets in their ordination song, and cites: [14]**"Neither *ḥamisin* nor *turmisin*."** *Ḥamisin* are incompetents who cannot follow an argument through to its conclusion, and *turmisin* are base, vulgar people.

[1]כִּי אֲתָא רַב דִּימִי, אֲמַר: [2]הָכֵי מְשָׁרוּ קַמֵּי כַּלָּתָא בְּמַעַרְבָא: [3]"לֹא כָּחָל, וְלֹא שָׂרָק, וְלֹא פִּירְכּוּס, [4]וְיַעֲלַת חֵן".
[5]כִּי סָמְכוּ רַבָּנַן לְרַבִּי זֵירָא, [6]שָׁרוּ לֵיהּ הָכֵי: [7]"לֹא כָּחָל, וְלֹא שָׂרָק, וְלֹא פִּירְכּוּס, וְיַעֲלַת חֵן".
[8]כִּי סָמְכוּ רַבָּנַן לְרַבִּי אַמִי וּלְרַבִּי אַסִי, [9]שָׁרוּ לְהוּ הָכֵי: [10]"כָּל מִן דֵּין וְכָל מִן דֵּין סְמוֹכוּ לָנָא. [11]לָא תִּסְמְכוּ לָנָא [12]לָא מִן סַרְמִיסִין וְלָא מִן סַרְמִיטִין". [13]וְאָמְרִי לָהּ: [14]"לָא מִן חֲמִיסִין וְלָא מִן טוּרְמִיסִין".

LITERAL TRANSLATION

[1]When Rav Dimi came, he said: [2]This is how they sing before brides in the West: [3]"No paint, and no rouge, and no dyeing [the hair], [4]and [yet] a graceful gazelle."

[5]When the Rabbis ordained Rabbi Zera, [6]they sang to him as follows: [7]"No paint, and no rouge, and no dyeing [the hair], and [yet] a graceful gazelle."

[8]When the Rabbis ordained Rabbi Ammi and Rabbi Assi, [9]they sang to them as follows: [10]"Anyone like this one and anyone like this one ordain for us. [11]Do not ordain for us, [12]not *sarmisin* and not *sarmitin*." [13]And some say: [14]"Not *ḥamisin* and not *turmisin*."

RASHI

משרו = משוררים. **לא כחל** — אינה צריכה כחל. **ולא שרק** = צבע המאדים את הפנים. **פירכוס** = קליעת שיער. זו לא כחלה ולא שרקה ולא פירכסה והרי היא יעלת חן. **כל מן דין** — כל כמות אלו הוו סומכין לנו לקרותן רבי ולמנותם דיינין. **סרמיסין** — מסרסין הלכות בהיפך טעמיהן. **סרמיטין** — לשון סמרטוטין. **חמיסין** — אומרים חמישית הטעם. **טורמיסין** — לא איתפרש. (טורמיסין — כי ההיא דאמר בבראשית רבא [פרשה מא] על טורמיסין למיקרב למסאנא דמטרוניתא — אנשים ריקנים).

BACKGROUND

כִּי סָמְכוּ רַבָּנַן **When the Rabbis ordained.** Ordination, in the precise, Halakhic meaning of the term and not in the expanded meaning given to it today, was an official ceremony in which a man was given the title of "Rabbi." This appointment entailed more than permission to issue Halakhic injunctions and to pass judgment in all aspects of Torah law (capital crimes as well as civil suits). The newly ordained Rabbi was regarded as continuing the chain of Sages beginning with Moses. The ceremony of ordination was performed only in Eretz Israel and required the agreement of the head of the Sanhedrin. Not every Sage — even those whose Torah learning rendered them worthy of ordination — received it. Therefore the granting of this title became a ceremonial matter and an occasion of great joy. From the words of the Sages' song, we may infer that occasionally men who were not fit were nevertheless ordained. However, a Sage such as Rabbi Zera, who was beloved and honored by all the Sages of Eretz Israel, was certainly worthy of the crown of ordination, like the two other Sages who were also originally from Babylonia, Rav Ammi and Rav Assi.

כָּחָל וְשָׂרָק **Paint and rouge.** "Paint," (כָּחָל) was a dark-blue (or black) dye derived from the oxide of antimony, which was applied around the eyes (to make them look larger), and was also used for medicinal purposes. "Rouge" (שָׂרָק) was a red dye used to paint the cheeks.

LANGUAGE

טוּרְמִיסִין ***Turmisin.*** Some scholars derive this word from the Latin *tremissis,* which was a Roman coin worth one-third of a dinar. By extension, the term was applied to a person with "partial" (i.e., deficient) knowledge. Others read טוּלְמִיסִין and derive the word from the Greek τόλμησις, *tolmesis,* which means "being bold," or "daring."

NOTES

not be too meticulous about the truth when praising a bride, so too should we not be too meticulous in our assessment of other people, behaving toward them more generously than they deserve, both in word and in deed.

הָכֵי מְשָׁרוּ קַמֵּי כַּלָּתָא בְּמַעַרְבָא **This is how they sing before brides in the West.** *Maharal* explains that even Bet Hillel showed a degree of reticence in praising a bride, in order to avoid a gross falsehood. For even a blind or lame bride can be beautiful and graceful in the eyes of her bridegroom, just as one may choose to buy merchandise that others consider inferior. But in Eretz Israel the custom was to go beyond the ruling of Bet Hillel, and to praise every bride as if she were a great beauty who had no need for makeup.

כִּי סָמְכוּ רַבָּנַן לְרַבִּי זֵירָא **When the Rabbis ordained Rabbi Zera.** *Yad Ramah* explains that the Rabbis sang the wedding song for Rabbi Zera by way of analogy. Just as a truly beautiful bride does not need makeup and expensive clothes, so too was Rabbi Zera's wisdom obvious to all, even though his demeanor was extremely modest.

Maharsha explains that the wedding song was intended as a play on words. The word for "makeup" in Hebrew, צֶבַע, also means "hypocrisy." Thus, in this ordination song, as in the one described below, the Rabbis were hinting that the Rabbi they were ordaining was no hypocritical pseudo-scholar.

סַרְמִיסִין ***Sarmisin.*** It is clear that all these terms are unflattering epithets, but it is not clear exactly what they mean. Our commentary follows *Rashi,* who explains that *sarmisin* comes from the root סרס, which means "to pervert"; *sarmitin* comes from סְמַרְטוּט, which means "rag," and refers to people who have nothing worthwhile to say; *ḥamisin* comes from חָמֵשׁ, meaning "five," and refers to people who know only one-fifth of the reasoning. In the parallel passage in *Sanhedrin, Rashi* explains that *ḥamisin* comes from חָמָס — "robbery" — and refers to people who reject demands for explanations. *Rashi* does not explain *turmisin,* but a medieval marginal note inserted in his commentary says it is a variant of the word *tulmisin,* which appears in the Jerusalem Talmud at the end of the seventh chapter of *Ketubot,* and refers to base, vulgar people.

Arukh cites a Geonic tradition that *sarmisin* comes from

[1] רַבִּי אַבָּהוּ כִּי הֲוָה אָתֵי מִמְּתִיבְתָּא לְבֵי קֵיסָר, [2] נָפְקָן אַמְהָתָא דְּבֵי קֵיסָר לְאַפֵּיהּ וּמְשָׁרְיָין לֵיהּ הָכִי: ״רַבָּא דְּעַמֵּיהּ וּמְדַבְּרָנָא דְּאוּמְּתֵיהּ, [3] בּוּצִינָא דִּנְהוֹרָא, בְּרִיךְ מֶתָּיָיךְ לִשְׁלָם״. [4] אָמְרוּ עָלָיו עַל רַבִּי יְהוּדָה בַּר אִילְעַאי [5] שֶׁהָיָה נוֹטֵל בַּד שֶׁל הֲדַס וּמְרַקֵּד לִפְנֵי הַכַּלָּה, [6] וְאוֹמֵר: ״כַּלָּה נָאָה וַחֲסוּדָה״. [7] רַב שְׁמוּאֵל בַּר רַב יִצְחָק [8] מְרַקֵּד אַתְּלָת. [9] אָמַר רַבִּי זֵירָא: קָא מַכְסִיף לָן סָבָא. [10] כִּי נָח נַפְשֵׁיהּ, [11] אִיפְסִיק עַמּוּדָא דְנוּרָא בֵּין דִּידֵיהּ לְכוּלֵּי עָלְמָא, [12] וּגְמִירִי דְּלָא אַפְסִיק עַמּוּדָא דְנוּרָא [13] אֶלָּא אִי לְחַד בְּדָרָא

LITERAL TRANSLATION

[1] When Rabbi Abbahu used to come from the academy to the emperor's house, [2] the maidservants of the emperor's house would come out to him and sing to him as follows: "Master of his people and leader of his nation, [3] candle of light, blessed be your coming in peace."

[4] They said of Rabbi Yehudah bar Il'ai [5] that he would take a twig of myrtle and dance before the bride, [6] and say: "A beautiful and graceful bride."

[7] Rav Shmuel bar Rav Yitzḥak [8] would dance with three. [9] Rabbi Zera said: The old man is putting us to shame. [10] When he passed away, [11] a pillar of fire separated between him and the whole world, [12] and we have a tradition that a pillar of fire [13] only makes a separation for one [person] in a generation

TRANSLATION AND COMMENTARY

רַבִּי אַבָּהוּ [1] Continuing the topic of the songs sung in honor of scholars, the Gemara relates that **whenever Rabbi Abbahu,** who acted as the representative of the Jews of Eretz Israel before the Roman authorities, **used to go from the academy to the emperor's house in Caesarea, [2] the maidservants of the emperor's house would come out to him and sing to him as follows: "Master of his people and leader of his nation, [3] candle of light, blessed be your coming in peace."**

אָמְרוּ עָלָיו [4] The Gemara now returns to the topic of songs sung in praise of the bride at wedding celebrations. **They said of Rabbi Yehudah bar Il'ai [5] that he would take a twig of myrtle and dance** with it **before the bride, [6] and say: "A beautiful and graceful bride,"** in accordance with the viewpoint of Bet Hillel mentioned above.

רַב שְׁמוּאֵל בַּר רַב יִצְחָק [7] The Gemara relates that **Rav Shmuel bar Rav Yitzḥak,** who was a very elderly and venerable scholar, took this custom a step further by [8] **dancing with three** myrtle twigs and juggling them as he danced. Some of his disciples, however, considered this behavior undignified. [9] **Rabbi Zera said: The old man is putting us to shame.** Although it is important to rejoice at a wedding, a scholar must still maintain a dignified demeanor, respecting the dignity of the Torah he represents. The Gemara relates that there was a divine indication of support for Rav Shmuel bar Rav Yitzḥak's opinion that a Rabbinic scholar is permitted to compromise his diginity at a wedding celebration: [10] **When** Rav Shmuel bar Rav Yitzḥak **passed away, [11] a pillar of fire separated him from the whole world** (i.e., his body was surrounded by fire), [12] **and we have a tradition that a separation made by a pillar of fire** does not happen to ordinary people, or even to people of great moral stature, [13] but **only to one** outstanding **person in a generation,**

RASHI

ממתיבתא = מבית המדרש. **רבא דעמיה** = נשיא בעמו. **מדברנא** = מנהיג. **בריך מתייך לשלם** = ברוך בואך לשלום. **בוצינא דנהורא** — על שהיה קלסתר פניו מבהיק, כדאמרינן בבבא בתרא (נח, א): שופריה דרבי אבהו מעין שופריה דרבי יוחנן, דנפקי זיהרורית מיניה, כדמפרש התם. **אתלת** — שלש בדין, זורק אחת ומקבל אחת. **מכסיף לן סבא** — שמזלזל בכבוד תלמידי חכמים, ונוהג קלות ראש בעצמו.

NOTES

the root סכסך, which means "to tangle"; *sarmitin* comes from סרטט, meaning "to underline" (as in lined writing paper), and refers to people who do not express themselves clearly; *ḥamisin* comes from the root חמס, meaning "to seize," and refers to people who are impatient; and *turmisin* comes from תּוּרְמוּס, a very bitter bean that required special preparation before it could be eaten.

בּוּצִינָא דִּנְהוֹרָא Candle of light. *Yad Ramah* explains that Rabbi Abbahu's wisdom was a light to the world. *Rashi* offers a literal interpretation of this description of Rabbi Abbahu: The Gemara (*Bava Batra* 58a) states that Rabbi Abbahu had an unusually radiant face.

בְּרִיךְ מֶתָּיָיךְ לִשְׁלָם Blessed be your coming in peace. *Ritva* has a slightly different reading: "Blessed be He who brings you in peace."

מְרַקֵּד אַתְּלָת Would dance with three. Our commentary follows *Rashi,* who explains that Rav Shmuel bar Rav Yitzḥak would juggle three myrtle twigs. This explanation finds support in the version of this story which appears in *Bereshit Rabbah* (59:4).

Maharsha suggests that this expression may mean that Rav Shmuel bar Rav Yitzḥak "danced for three" — i.e., danced with three times the energy of anyone else, in spite of his age. *Kikayon DeYonah* explains that Rav Shmuel bar Rav Yitzḥak could walk only with a cane, but he still danced with more energy on his "three legs" than the younger celebrants did on two.

SAGES

רַבִּי יְהוּדָה בַּר אִילְעַאי Rabbi Yehudah bar Il'ai. Known in the sources simply as Rabbi Yehudah, he was one of the most important Tannaim of the fifth generation. His father, Rabbi Il'ai, had been a student of Rabbi Eliezer ben Hyrcanus. Rabbi Yehudah himself was a leading disciple of Rabbi Akiva, and one of the Sages who continued in his path. However, Rabbi Yehudah also learned Torah from his father, from Rabbi Tarfon, and from other Sages in Yavneh. He seems to have supported himself by manual labor, and although he was extremely poor he accepted his poverty with love. He was a cordial person and saw things in a favorable light, so much so that he sought to praise the actions of the Romans, even though he lived at a time of cruel persecution after the suppression of the Bar Kokhba revolt. It is said (*Bava Kamma* 103b) that in many places where a "righteous man" is mentioned with no further qualification, the reference is to Rabbi Yehudah bar Il'ai.

When the Sanhedrin convened again after the Bar Kokhba revolt, the Sages assembled at Usha, in Galilee, which was where Rabbi Yehudah lived. He was the "chief speaker," a kind of temporary Nasi of the Sanhedrin. It seems that after Rabban Shimon ben Gamliel, of the House of Hillel, was appointed Nasi, Rabbi Yehudah continued to serve as the mentor of the House of the Nasi.

Rabbi Yehudah's son, Rabbi Yose, was an important Sage in the next generation and a colleague of Rabbi Yehudah HaNasi.

רַב שְׁמוּאֵל בַּר רַב יִצְחָק Rav Shmuel bar Rav Yitzḥak. A Babylonian Amora of the third generation. See *Ketubot,* Part I, p. 25.

BACKGROUND

לְבֵי קֵיסָר To the emperor's house. Rabbi Abbahu lived in Caesarea, and he was highly esteemed by the Roman authorities. Even though he held no official political position, he served as the representative of the Jews to the Roman

TRANSLATION AND COMMENTARY

[1]or at most **to two in a generation.** The disciples of Rav Shmuel bar Rav Yitzḥak interpreted this miracle as divine approval of his behavior at wedding celebrations. [2]Indeed, **Rabbi Zera said:** It was **the old man's twig** that **benefited him.** [3]**And some say:** It was **the old man's folly** (his undignified behavior). [4]**And some say:** It was **the old man's custom** of juggling twigs at weddings. (In Aramaic, the words for "twig," "folly," and "custom" are very similar.)

רַב אַחָא [5]The Gemara now relates another unusual wedding practice of one of the Sages: **Rav Aḥa would place the bride on his shoulders and dance** with her, in apparent violation of the laws forbidding immodest behavior. [6]**The** other **Rabbis asked** Rav Aḥa: **"May we do this** too? Are you issuing a general dispensation permitting this custom at weddings, or is there some special reason that applies only to you?" [7]Rav Aḥa **said to them** in reply: **"If you** are able to place young brides on your shoulders and feel that **they are like beams** of wood, as I am able to do, **very well,** [8]**but if not,** you are **not** permitted to act in this way." Thus, at a wedding it is permitted to behave in a manner that appears somewhat immodest, so long as the only impropriety is one of appearance.

אָמַר רַבִּי שְׁמוּאֵל בַּר נַחְמָנִי [9]The Gemara now relates another example of seemingly improper behavior which some authorities permitted at wedding celebrations: **Rabbi Shmuel bar Naḥmani said in the name of Rabbi Yonatan:** Normally it is forbidden to look at the face of a married woman, [10]but **it is permitted to look at the face of a bride during all seven days** of the wedding celebration, [11]**in order to endear** the bride **to her husband.** For if the husband notices that everyone is looking admiringly at his wife, he will become even more appreciative of her beauty. [12]Nevertheless, the Gemara rules that **the Halakhah is not in accordance with** Rabbi Shmuel bar Naḥmani, and it is forbidden to look at the face of a bride.

LITERAL TRANSLATION

[1]or for two in a generation. [2]Rabbi Zera said: His twig benefited the old man. [3]And some say: His folly [benefited] the old man. [4]And some say: His custom [benefited] the old man.

[5]Rav Aḥa would place her [the bride] on his shoulder and dance. [6]The Rabbis said to him: "May we do this?" [7]He said to them: "If they are like a beam for you, very well, [8]but if not, no."

[9]Rabbi Shmuel bar Naḥmani said in the name of Rabbi Yonatan: [10]It is permitted to look at the face of a bride all seven [days], [11]in order to endear her to her husband. [12]But the Halakhah is not in accordance with him.

[1]אִי לִתְרֵי בְּדָרָא. [2]אֲמַר רַבִּי זֵירָא: אַהַנְיָיה לֵיהּ שׁוֹטִיתֵיהּ לְסָבָא. [3]וְאָמְרִי לָהּ: שְׁטוּתֵיהּ לְסָבָא. [4]וְאָמְרִי לָהּ: שִׁיטָתֵיהּ לְסָבָא.

[5]רַב אַחָא מַרְכֵּיב לָהּ אַכַּתְפֵּיהּ וּמְרַקֵּד. [6]אָמְרִי לֵיהּ רַבָּנַן: ״אֲנַן מַהוּ לְמֶיעֱבַד הָכִי״? [7]אֲמַר לְהוּ: ״אִי דָמְיָין עֲלַיְיכוּ כְּכָשׁוֹרָא, לְחַיֵּי, [8]וְאִי לָא, לָא״.

[9]אָמַר רַבִּי שְׁמוּאֵל בַּר נַחְמָנִי אָמַר רַבִּי יוֹנָתָן: [10]מוּתָּר לְהִסְתַּכֵּל בִּפְנֵי כַּלָּה כָּל שִׁבְעָה, [11]כְּדֵי לְחַבְּבָהּ עַל בַּעֲלָהּ. [12]וְלֵית הִלְכְתָא כְּוָותֵיהּ.

RASHI

שוטיתיה — שוט של הדס שהיה מרקד בו. **שיטתיה** — שיטתו ומנהגו. **שטותיה** — שהיה מתנהג כשוטה. **מרכיב לה אכתפיה** — את הכלה. **כי כשורא** — כקורה בעלמא, שאין אתם מהרהרין עליה. **לחבבה** — כשרואה הכל מסתכלים בה — נכנס יופיה בלבו.

government. "The emperor's house" here apparently refers to the palace of the Roman governor in Caesarea, where Rabbi Abbahu lived and where his yeshivah was located.

NOTES

אַהַנְיָיה לֵיהּ שׁוֹטִיתֵיהּ לְסָבָא **His twig benefited the old man.** The commentators ask: Since Rav Shmuel bar Rav Yitzḥak was a very saintly man in every way, how did Rabbi Zera know that the miracle was the result of his behavior at wedding celebrations? *Etz Yosef* explains, on the basis of the version of this story in *Bereshit Rabbah*, that the fire took the form of a myrtle branch.

לְהִסְתַּכֵּל בִּפְנֵי כַּלָּה **To look at the face of a bride.** The Gemara (*Avodah Zarah* 20a) says: "It is forbidden to gaze at a beautiful woman, even if she is unmarried, and at a married woman, even if she is ugly." The word used there, as well as in our passage, is לְהִסְתַּכֵּל, which means "to look" (i.e., to glance at a woman for a moment in the course of some ordinary activity), as well as "to gaze" (for a period of time, to enjoy her beauty). There is some discussion among the Rishonim as to how this word should be explained in the context of our Gemara.

The Rishonim note that our Mishnah implies that people are expected to notice whether the bride wore a *hinuma* and let her hair down, and for this they obviously have to

HALAKHAH

לְהִסְתַּכֵּל בִּפְנֵי כַּלָּה **To look at the face of a bride.** "It is forbidden to gaze at a bride, just as it is forbidden to gaze at any other married woman. It is not even permitted to do so during the wedding celebration as a means of endearing her to her husband," following the Gemara's conclusion rejecting the ruling of Rabbi Shmuel bar Naḥmani. (*Shulḥan Arukh, Even HaEzer* 65:2.)

LANGUAGE

אַגְרִיפַּס Agrippa. This Hebrew word is apparently the Greek form (Ἀγρίππας, *Agrippas*) of the king's name.

PEOPLE

אַגְרִיפַּס הַמֶּלֶךְ King Agrippa. The Gemara is apparently referring to King Agrippa I (d. 44 C.E.), who was the grandson of Herod and Miriam the Hasmonean. Agrippa lived in Rome in his youth, where he associated with the emperor's court, and was presumably exposed to its intrigues and debauchery. However, after he came to Eretz Israel on being appointed king over the areas ruled by Herod, he seems to have undergone a major spiritual transformation, as a result of which he drew close to the Rabbis and began to observe the Torah's laws punctiliously. Even though the Rabbis did not officially recognize his kingship, they treated him respectfully, and his good deeds are mentioned in various places in the Talmud.

TRANSLATION AND COMMENTARY

תָּנוּ רַבָּנַן [1]Continuing the theme of the importance of wedding celebrations, the Gemara now cites a Baraita. **Our Rabbis taught** the following Baraita. [2]**"We make a funeral procession give way before a bride."** Both funerals and wedding celebrations involved large processions, as the Gemara describes below. If a funeral and a wedding happened to be scheduled for the same time, the two processions would interfere with each other if they were allowed to take the same route. Hence the Baraita rules that the wedding procession takes precedence, and the funeral must wait or take a different route. [3]The Baraita continues: **"Both** a funeral **and** a wedding procession must move aside **before the King of Israel."** The respect accorded the King of Israel is greater than that accorded a wedding or a funeral, as the Gemara explains below, and when the king travels with a large procession, he takes precedence. [4]Nevertheless, the Baraita relates that **"they said of King Agrippa,** who reigned toward the end of the Second Temple period, **that he made way for a bride,** even though he had the right to take precedence, [5]**and the Sages praised him** for going beyond the strict letter of the law in this way."

[1]תָּנוּ רַבָּנַן: [2]"מַעֲבִירִין אֶת הַמֵּת מִלִּפְנֵי כַלָּה, [3]וְזֶה וְזֶה מִלִּפְנֵי מֶלֶךְ יִשְׂרָאֵל. [4]אָמְרוּ עָלָיו עַל אַגְרִיפַּס הַמֶּלֶךְ שֶׁעָבַר מִלִּפְנֵי כַלָּה, [5]וְשִׁבְּחוּהוּ חֲכָמִים."

LITERAL TRANSLATION

[1]Our Rabbis taught: [2]"We make [the funeral procession of] a dead person give way before a bride, [3]and this and that before the King of Israel. [4]They said of King Agrippa that he made way for a bride, [5]and the Sages praised him."

RASHI

מעבירין – כשכלה יוצאה מבית אביה לבית חתונתה, ונושאי מת יוצאים, וזו וזו אוכלוסים הרבה ואין רוצין להתערב – מעבירין את המת (אפילו) דרך אחרת.

NOTES

look at her, if only for a moment. Nevertheless, *Rosh* rules that it is forbidden even to glance at a woman's face, and the Mishnah permits people to look only at the back of her head, to see whether she is wearing a *hinuma. Maharshal,* however, rules that the prohibition applies only to gazing at the woman's beauty, but it is permitted to glance at a woman briefly when necessary. Other Rishonim (*Ramban, Remah,* and others) also support this view, which has been reflected in our translation and commentary.

מַעֲבִירִין אֶת הַמֵּת מִלִּפְנֵי כַלָּה We make the funeral procession of a dead person give way before a bride. This Baraita is taken from tractate *Semakhot,* chapter 11. *Semakhot* is one of the so-called "minor tractates" — collections of Baraitot on topics which the Mishnah did not cover, and which were arranged into tractates after the completion of the Talmud. The full text of the Baraita reads as follows: "If the eulogies of a dead person and the praises of a bride conflict with each other, we make the dead person give way before the bride, because the respect due to the living takes precedence over that due to the dead." There is also another, related Baraita in chapter 12 of tractate *Semakhot:* "If one must choose between going to a mourner's house or to a wedding party, the wedding party takes precedence. If one must choose between attending the circumcision of a son and the gathering of bones for reburial in a permanent grave, the circumcision of the son takes precedence."

From these Baraitot, *Ramban* and other Rishonim infer that the respect accorded to the living always takes precedence over funerals, not only in regard to conflicting ceremonies, but also in regard to financial arrangements and the like. *Tosafot* adds that, in the synagogue as well, a bridegroom and his family take precedence over a mourner and his family in the distribution of honors.

However, the conclusion of the second Baraita appears to refute this inference: "Nevertheless, the ancient pious men used to give a mourner's house precedence over wedding parties, as the verse (Ecclesiastes 7:2) says: 'It is better to go to the house of mourning than to go to the house of feasting, for that is the end of all men, and the living will lay it to his heart.'" Indeed, *Rambam* (*Hilkhot Evel* 14:8) disagrees with the other Rishonim, and rules (citing the verse from Ecclesiastes) that "someone who has a dead person and a bride before him should leave the bride and attend to the dead." According to *Rambam,* only when a funeral procession and a wedding celebration interfere with each other do we "make the dead give way before the bride." Apparently, even though the respect due to the living takes precedence over that due to the dead (hence the precedence given to a wedding procession), when the question is not so much one of respect as one of active involvement the spiritual lesson associated with burying the dead has overriding importance (*Leḥem Mishneh*).

שֶׁעָבַר מִלִּפְנֵי כַלָּה That he made way for a bride. In the full version of this Baraita found in tractate *Semakhot,* Agrippa explains to his courtiers: "I can wear my crown on any day, whereas this lady has only this one opportunity to wear a crown."

אַגְרִיפַּס הַמֶּלֶךְ King Agrippa. Agrippa was not, Halakhically, a true King of Israel, as he was a member of the half-Jewish Herodian dynasty, and was appointed by the Roman government. Nevertheless, it is clear from many sources in the Talmud that he was scrupulous in following the practices expected of a King of Israel, and was treated like a king. Thus, in tractate *Sotah* (41a), the Mishnah relates that

HALAKHAH

מַעֲבִירִין אֶת הַמֵּת מִלִּפְנֵי כַלָּה We make the funeral procession of a dead person give way before a bride. "If a funeral procession coincides with a wedding procession and impedes its progress, the funeral procession must make way

TRANSLATION AND COMMENTARY

שִׁבְּחוּהוּ [1]The Gemara considers the last clause of this Baraita, which states that the Sages **"praised"** King Agrippa for his exemplary humility. [2]**This** surely **proves by implication that he behaved correctly.** Although the respect to which a king is entitled is greater than that accorded a wedding procession, it is the mark of a humble and pious man that he waives the respect to which he is entitled. [3]**But surely,** objects the Gemara, while it is true that waiving honors is praiseworthy for most people — indeed, even for people who have every right to expect respect, like Talmudic scholars, or even the president of the Sanhedrin during Talmudic times — this principle does not apply to kings. For **Rav Ashi said:** [4]**Even according to the** opinion of the Sage **who says** (*Kiddushin* 32b) **that if a Nasi** (president of the Sanhedrin) **waives the respect** to which he is entitled, [5]**his respect is waived** — because an eminent person normally has the right to waive the respect to which he is entitled — this does not apply to the king. [6]**If the king waives the respect** to which he is entitled, **his respect is not waived,** because the dignity of a king is not simply a matter of recognition of the importance of his office, as it is, for example, in the case of a Nasi. On the contrary, it is the king's duty, as an integral part of his office, to instill a sense of submission in the hearts of the people. [7]**For** there is an authoritative interpretation by **a certain Sage** in the Halakhic Midrash, Sifrei, of the following verse (Deuteronomy 17:15): [8]"The verse says: **'You shall surely set a king over you.'** This verse uses the emphatic double verb form (שׂוֹם תָּשִׂים — 'you shall surely set') to teach us that we must set the king high above us and behave humbly toward him, [9]so **that his fear shall be upon us."** This is the purpose of appointing a king, and the king himself is bound by this commandment no less than are his subjects.

[1]"שִׁבְּחוּהוּ". [2]מִכְּלָל דְּשַׁפִּיר עֲבַד! [3]וְהָא אֲמַר רַב אַשִׁי: [4]אֲפִילּוּ לְמַאן דְּאָמַר נָשִׂיא שֶׁמָּחַל עַל כְּבוֹדוֹ, [5]כְּבוֹדוֹ מָחוּל, [6]מֶלֶךְ שֶׁמָּחַל עַל כְּבוֹדוֹ, אֵין כְּבוֹדוֹ מָחוּל, [7]דְּאָמַר מָר: [8]"'שׂוֹם תָּשִׂים עָלֶיךָ מֶלֶךְ' [9]שֶׁתְּהֵא אֵימָתוֹ עָלֶיךָ"!

LITERAL TRANSLATION

[1]"They praised him." [2][This proves] by implication that he acted correctly! [3]But surely Rav Ashi said: [4]Even according to the one who says [that if] a Nasi waived his dignity, [5]his dignity is waived, [6][if] a king waived his dignity, his dignity is not waived, [7]for a Master said: [8]"'You shall surely set a king over you,' [9]that his fear shall be upon you"!

RASHI

אפילו למאן דאמר — פלוגתא בפרק קמא דקדושין. **שום תשים עליך מלך** — ישראל הוזהרו שישימו עליהם שימות הרבה, כלומר: שתהא אימתו עליהם. הלכך אין כבודו מחול, שלפיכך ריבה הכתוב שימות הרבה.

NOTES

Agrippa performed the ceremony that occurs once in seven years in which the King of Israel reads selections from the Book of Deuteronomy before the assembled people (Deuteronomy 31:10-13). Moreover, he is described as introducing an innovation which the Sages greeted with approval, by reading Deuteronomy standing rather than sitting. Nevertheless, the Gemara makes it clear that even though Agrippa's reign was unobjectionable in practice, this still did not give him the right to rule (*Tosafot*).

מֶלֶךְ שֶׁמָּחַל עַל כְּבוֹדוֹ If a king waived his dignity. Generally, a person is entitled to waive honors, even where they are fully deserved. Indeed, the Gemara (*Kiddushin* 32a) notes that God Himself set an example by waiving the respect to which He was entitled. Thus a father may forgo the tokens of respect that his son would normally be required to show him. But a problem arises when a person representing something higher than himself — such as a Torah scholar, who represents the Torah — wishes to waive the respect to which he is entitled. Rav Ḥisda rules that the waiver is invalid, because the scholar has no authority to waive the respect due to the Torah. But Rava concludes (based on Psalm 1:2) that the scholar is considered the owner, as it were, of the Torah that he has learned, and he thus has the right to waive the respect due to him.

Rav Ashi then states that, even if we concede that a Torah scholar may waive honors, the same does not apply to the Nasi, who was the leader of the Jewish community in Eretz Israel during Talmudic times, serving also as president of the Sanhedrin. For the Nasi does not own the community he represents, and cannot waive its honor. But the Gemara argues that the example shown by God Himself still applies, and concludes that the Nasi, too, may choose to waive the honor to which he is entitled.

The Gemara then cites a different version of Rav Ashi's statement, in which he said: Even according to those who say that the Nasi may waive the respect due to him —

HALAKHAH

for the wedding procession. Moreover, if either procession impedes the progress of the King of Israel, it must make way before him," following the Baraita. (*Rambam, Sefer Shofetim, Hilkhot Evel* 14:8; *Shulḥan Arukh, Even HaEzer* 65:4.)

נָשִׂיא שֶׁמָּחַל עַל כְּבוֹדוֹ If a Nasi waived his dignity. "A person who sees the Nasi walking by must stand until the Nasi sits, or until he can no longer see him. But a scholar, even the Nasi, may waive the respect due to him, and if he does so, the waiver is effective. Nevertheless, it is still proper to show him respect, even where this is not demanded, and to stand up at least briefly." (*Rambam, Sefer Madda, Hilkhot Talmud Torah* 6:6; *Shulḥan Arukh, Yoreh De'ah* 244:14.)

[1] פָּרָשַׁת דְּרָכִים הֲוַאי.
[2] תָּנוּ רַבָּנַן: [3] ״מְבַטְּלִין תַּלְמוּד תּוֹרָה לְהוֹצָאַת הַמֵּת וּלְהַכְנָסַת כַּלָּה. [4] אָמְרוּ עָלָיו עַל רַבִּי יְהוּדָה בְּרַבִּי אִלְעַאי [5] שֶׁהָיָה מְבַטֵּל תַּלְמוּד תּוֹרָה לְהוֹצָאַת הַמֵּת וּלְהַכְנָסַת כַּלָּה. [6] בַּמֶּה דְּבָרִים אֲמוּרִים? [7] כְּשֶׁאֵין עִמּוֹ כָּל צָרְכּוֹ. [8] אֲבָל יֵשׁ עִמּוֹ כָּל צָרְכּוֹ, [9] אֵין מְבַטְּלִין״.

LITERAL TRANSLATION

[1] It was a crossroads.

[2] Our Rabbis taught: [3] "We suspend Torah study for burying [lit., 'taking out'] a dead person and for bringing in a bride. [4] They said about Rabbi Yehudah the son of Rabbi Il'ai [5] that he would suspend Torah study for burying a dead person and for bringing in a bride. [6] In what [case] are these things said? [7] When he does not have with him all he needs. [8] But if he has with him all he needs, [9] we do not suspend."

TRANSLATION AND COMMENTARY

פָּרָשַׁת דְּרָכִים הֲוַאי [1] The Gemara answers: The incident in which King Agrippa gave way took place **at a crossroads.** The king would not have stepped aside if this would have deflected him from his route. But in fact there were two ways to go, and King Agrippa chose the route that would avoid the wedding procession, although he could have asserted his prerogative and made the wedding procession give way. Thus the king in no way diminished his authority, yet he clearly demonstrated his outstanding humility, which the Sages praised.

תָּנוּ רַבָּנַן [2] Continuing the theme of the importance of wedding celebrations, the Gemara now cites another Baraita. **Our Rabbis taught** the following Baraita: [3] **"We suspend Torah study in order to attend a funeral, and to bring in a bride** (for a wedding procession). Scholars and students engaged in the study of Torah may suspend their studies to join such processions. [4] Indeed, **they said about Rabbi Yehudah the son of Rabbi Il'ai** [5] **that he would suspend Torah study in order to attend the burial of a dead person or to bring in a bride."** The Baraita notes that this dispensation does not apply to all wedding and funeral processions: [6] **"When does this** ruling **apply?** [7] **When** the subject of the procession — the dead person or the bride — **does not have with him** or her in the procession **all** the people **he** or she **needs.** If the number of people present at the procession is small, the study of Torah may be interrupted. [8] **But if he has with him all those he needs,** in accordance with the respect to which the dead person or the bride is entitled, [9] **we do not suspend** Torah study merely to provide additional people."

RASHI

פרשת דרכים הוה — ולא ניכר שעבר מלפניה, אלא כאילו הוא צריך לפנות לאותו הדרך.

NOTES

because everyone, even the Nasi, has the right to waive the respect due to him — this does not apply to the King of Israel, because the verse (Deuteronomy 17:15) says: "You shall surely set a king over you," using a double verb form, and this verse is explained authoritatively in *Sifrei* (*Shofetim* 30) as meaning that we must set the king high above us and behave humbly towards him, so that fear of him may be upon us. (It is this statement of Rav Ashi that is cited in our Gemara.)

The Gemara does not explain exactly how this verse implies that a king may not waive the honor due him, even according to the opinion that everyone else has the right to do so. In our commentary we have followed *Tosafot* (*Sanhedrin* 19a), who explains that the respect due to a king is not simply a matter of recognition of the importance of his office, as it is in the case of a Nasi. Rather, the whole idea behind the commandment to appoint a king is to instill a sense of submission in the hearts of the people. The king is as obligated by this duty as are his subjects, and can no more avoid it than he can any other commandment. *Tosafot* adds (19b) that the positive commandment, that fear of the king be upon his subjects, implies a negative commandment prohibiting fear of his subjects from being upon the king.

מְבַטְּלִין תַּלְמוּד תּוֹרָה לְהוֹצָאַת הַמֵּת We suspend Torah study for burying a dead person. According to the plain meaning of this passage, Torah study should be suspended for the funeral of even a moderately learned Jew, as it is rare indeed for a funeral to be attended by as many as 600,000 mourners (see below). *Shittah Mekubbetzet* cites an opinion that the Baraita permits, but does not require, Torah study to be suspended. But most Rishonim reject this viewpoint. The Rishonim agree, however, that Torah study is suspended only for the funeral procession itself. The other needs of the dead may be delegated to a few people, and the rest of the community need not disturb their Torah study (*Ramban* and others).

Regarding abstention from work, the Gemara in tractate *Mo'ed Katan* (27b) rules that when someone dies, the entire

HALAKHAH

מְבַטְּלִין תַּלְמוּד תּוֹרָה לְהוֹצָאַת הַמֵּת We suspend Torah study for burying a dead person. "We suspend Torah study in order to allow students to attend a funeral procession or a wedding celebration, if the funeral or the wedding is not well attended. But if there are already enough people present, we do not suspend Torah study merely in order to provide a greater number of people." (*Rambam, Sefer Shofetim, Hilkhot Evel* 14:9; *Shulḥan Arukh, Yoreh De'ah* 361:1.)

[1]וְכַמָּה "כָּל צָרְכּוֹ"? [2]אָמַר רַב שְׁמוּאֵל בַּר אֵינִי מִשְּׁמֵיהּ דְּרַב: [3]תְּרֵיסַר אַלְפֵי גַבְרֵי וְשִׁיתָּא אַלְפֵי שִׁיפּוּרֵי. [4]וְאָמְרִי לָהּ: תְּלֵיסַר אַלְפֵי גַבְרֵי, [5]וּמִינַּיְיהוּ שִׁיתָּא אַלְפֵי שִׁיפּוּרֵי.

[6]עוּלָּא אָמַר: [7]כְּגוֹן דְּחַיְיצִי גַּבְרֵי מֵאַבּוּלָּא וְעַד סִיכְרָא.

[8]רַב שֵׁשֶׁת וְאִיתֵּימָא רַבִּי יוֹחָנָן אָמַר: [9]נְטִילָתָהּ כִּנְתִינָתָהּ. [10]מַה נְּתִינָתָהּ בְּשִׁשִּׁים רִבּוֹא, [11]אַף נְטִילָתָהּ בְּשִׁשִּׁים רִבּוֹא.

LITERAL TRANSLATION

[1]And how many are "all he needs"? [2]Rav Shmuel bar Eini said in the name of Rav: [3]Twelve thousand men and six thousand trumpets. [4]And some say: Thirteen thousand men, [5]and of them six thousand trumpets.

[6]Ulla said: [7]For example, where men form a line from the city gate to the grave.

[8]Rav Sheshet and some say Rabbi Yoḥanan said: [9]Its taking away is like its giving. [10]Just as its giving was with sixty myriads, [11]so too its taking away is with sixty myriads.

TRANSLATION AND COMMENTARY

וְכַמָּה כָּל צָרְכּוֹ [1]The Gemara asks: In the case of a funeral, **how many are "all** the people the dead person **needs,"** at which point suspending Torah study is no longer justified? [2]**Rav Shmuel bar Eini said in the name of Rav:** [3]If the funeral procession includes **twelve thousand men and six thousand trumpeters** — [4]**and some** versions of Rav's statement **say thirteen thousand men,** [5]**and of them six thousand** trumpeters — the funeral is considered well attended, and there is no further justification for suspending Torah study.

עוּלָּא אָמַר [6]**Ulla** suggested a different way of determining whether a procession is well attended, **saying:** [7]A funeral is considered well attended **when men form a line from the city gate to the grave.**

רַב שֵׁשֶׁת [8]**Rav Sheshet — and some say Rabbi Yoḥanan** — suggested a very different standard for a well-attended funeral, **saying:** When a scholar dies, the Torah he studied also leaves the world. [9]Therefore, **the departure** of Torah **should be like the giving** of the Torah on Mount Sinai. [10]**Just as it was given in the presence of sixty myriads,** for there were 600,000 adult Israelite men present at the time, [11]**so too should its departure be in the presence of sixty myriads.** Any funeral of a scholar attended by less than 600,000 men is considered poorly attended, and justifies the suspension of Torah studies.

RASHI

שיפורי — מכריזין עליו, שיבואו לכבדו. **דחייצי גברי מאבולא לסיכרא** — משער העיר ההיא, עד הקבר. **נטילתה** — של תורה ממנו כנתינתה בסיני. **נטילתה** — היינו כשמת, ותלמודו בטל.

NOTES

city must stop working until the dead person is buried. But if the community is subdivided into groups, work need only be suspended by the dead person's group, and not by the entire community. *Tosafot* suggests that this dispensation may also apply to the suspension of Torah study for the purpose of attending a funeral procession, but most Rishonim reject this view.

וְכַמָּה כָּל צָרְכּוֹ And how many are "all he needs"? The Baraita rules that Torah study may be suspended both for a funeral and for a wedding procession. But the ensuing discussion in the Gemara considers only funeral processions. *Talmidei Rabbenu Yonah* suggests that a wedding is considered well attended when the bride and the groom are satisfied; hence there is no fixed number. The Geonim explain that the stipulation in the Baraita — that Torah study is suspended only when the procession is not well attended — applies specifically to funerals, but a bridal procession warrants suspending Torah study in every case.

HALAKHAH

וְכַמָּה כָּל צָרְכּוֹ And how many are "all he needs"? "At what point is a funeral considered well attended, so that further suspension of Torah study is not justified? It depends on the status of the deceased. If the dead person was unlearned, it is sufficient if ten people attend his funeral. If he was a scholar, or at least studied Scripture or Mishnah, but was not a teacher, his funeral is not considered well attended unless 600,000 people are present. If he taught Torah to others, there is no limit to the number of people who must attend his funeral.

"Rema cites *Smag,* who rules that nowadays every Jew is assumed to have learned sufficient Scripture or Mishnah to be at least in the second category (although *Arukh HaShulḥan* notes that this assumption may no longer be warranted). Some say that an unlearned woman is considered like a scholar who did not teach, but others say that she is considered like an unlearned man, and the Halakhah follows the latter opinion, as we usually follow the lenient opinion in questions of mourning. *Arukh HaShulḥan* adds that the foregoing applies to adults, but children of school age and their teachers should not interrupt their Torah study to attend a funeral.

"Even when a person is not required to attend a funeral, if he sees a funeral procession passing before him, he must accompany it for at least a distance of four cubits, and he must stand as a sign of respect." (*Rambam, Sefer Shofetim, Hilkhot Evel* 14:11; *Shulḥan Arukh, Yoreh De'ah* 61:1,3,4.)

SAGES

רַב שְׁמוּאֵל בַּר אֵינִי Rav Shmuel bar Eini. Very little is known of this Amora, who apparently lived in Eretz Israel. Various versions of his father's name are given: Ini, Onya, Yona, and Yanai. He was probably a Palestinian Amora of the third and fourth generations, though he presents many Aggadic teachings in the name of Rav, and this has led scholars to argue that there was another Sage with a similar name who was a second-generation Babylonian Amora.

עוּלָּא Ulla. A Palestinian Amora of the second and third generations. See *Ketubot,* Part I, p. 103.

רַב שֵׁשֶׁת Rav Sheshet. A Babylonian Amora of the second and third generations. See *Ketubot,* Part I, p. 150.

BACKGROUND

תְּרֵיסַר אַלְפֵי גַבְרֵי Twelve thousand men. In Talmudic times it was customary to accompany the dead with the playing of flutes and the sounding of the shofar. The presence of a large number of mourners and the use of the shofar to sound the call of mourning is in accordance with the Sages' view that the law requires that a funeral be attended by a great multitude, because the loss of any Jew, especially one learned in Torah, is supposed to be an event known to all and felt by all.

נְטִילָתָהּ כִּנְתִינָתָהּ Its taking away is like its giving. The death of a Jew is likened to the tearing of a Torah scroll, for when a person becomes an instrument for maintaining and teaching the Torah, he himself becomes like a Torah scroll. This is why attending a funeral is compared to being present at the giving of the Torah on Mount Sinai.

LANGUAGE

מֵאַבּוּלָּא From the city gate. Most commentators interpret אַבּוּלָּא as "city gate"; thus it is derived from the Greek ἔμβολος, *embolos,* meaning "gate" or "city gate."

LITERAL TRANSLATION

[1]And these words [apply] to someone who read [Scripture] and studied [Mishnah]. [17B] [2]But for someone who taught, [3]there is no limit for him.

[4]And if there are witnesses that she went out with a *hinuma*, etc." [5]What is a *hinuma?*

[6]Surḥav bar Pappa said in the name of Ze'iri: A canopy of myrtle. [7]Rabbi Yoḥanan said: A veil (lit., "city") under which the bride can doze.

[1]וְהָנֵי מִילֵּי לְמַאן דְּקָרֵי וְתָנֵי. [17B] [2]אֲבָל לְמַאן דְּמַתְנֵי, [3]לֵית לֵיהּ שִׁיעוּרָא.

[4]"וְאִם יֵשׁ עֵדִים שֶׁיָּצְתָה בְּהִינוּמָא, וכו׳". [5]מַאי הִינוּמָא? [6]סוּרְחַב בַּר פַּפָּא מִשְּׁמֵיהּ דִּזְעִירִי אֲמַר: תַּנּוּרָא דְּאָסָא. [7]רַבִּי יוֹחָנָן אָמַר: קְרִיתָא דִּמְנַמְנָה בָּהּ כַּלְּתָא.

RASHI

למאן דקרי — מקרא. **ותני** — משנה, אבל עדיין לא שנה לתלמידים. **אבל למאן דמתני** — לאחרים. **לית ליה שיעורא** — וממילא שמעינן דלמאן דלא קרי ולא תני אין מבטלין אם יש לו מתעסקין כדי קבורה בעלמא — בשאלתות דרב אחאי מצאתי כן. **תנורא דאסא** — כמין חופה של הדס עגולה. **קריתא** — צעיף על ראשה משורבב על עיניה, כמו שעושין במקומינו. ופעמים שמנמנמת בתוכו, מתוך שאין עיניה מגולין, ולכך נקרא הינומא, על שם תנומה.

TRANSLATION AND COMMENTARY

וְהָנֵי מִילֵּי [1]Moreover, says the Gemara, **this applies to** a minor scholar **who read Scripture and studied Mishnah,** but never reached the stage of deeper study. [17B] [2]**But for** a scholar **who taught** others — [3]the proper size of **his** funeral **has no limit,** because the respect due to such a person has no bounds.

וְאִם יֵשׁ עֵדִים [4]We now return to our Mishnah, which ruled that the wife need not bring direct proof that she was a virgin when she married; it is sufficient for her to demonstrate that at her wedding she was treated in the manner customary for virgins. Thus, the Mishnah states, **"if there are witnesses that,** at her wedding ceremony, **she went out** to meet her bridegroom **with a *hinuma*** on her head, and the hair on her head was loose, she is considered to have proved her case." [5]On this clause of the Mishnah the Gemara asks: **What** exactly **is a *hinuma?***

סוּרְחַב בַּר פַּפָּא [6]**Surḥav bar Pappa said** in reply **in the name of Ze'iri:** It is **a canopy of myrtle.** [7]**Rabbi Yoḥanan** disagreed, and **said:** The word *hinuma* comes from the word *tenumah*, which means "a nap." A *hinuma* is a large **veil,** which covers **the bride's** face so well that she **can doze under it** without anyone noticing.

LANGUAGE

סוּרְחַב **Surḥav.** This is apparently the Persian word *surchav,* meaning "red" or "ruddy." Similar names (or nicknames) were used by other Rabbis as well, e.g., Yitzḥak Summaka (סוּמָּקָא — "the red").

קְרִיתָא **A veil.** Different views obtain about the meaning of this word. Some interpret it as a diminutive of קִרְיָה, meaning "city." *Rabbenu Ḥananel* (cited by *Arukh*) explains that this was a type of diadem, in the shape of a city, which was placed on the bride's head. Others explain that it was a small seat for the bride, or a carriage in which she was led out. In any case, the word's exact etymology remains unclear.

SAGES

סוּרְחַב בַּר פַּפָּא **Surḥav bar Pappa.** This Babylonian Amora is mentioned only here. According to one tradition, he was the son of Rav Pappa Saba (the elder), and thus belonged to the third generation.

NOTES

לְמַאן דְּקָרֵי וְתָנֵי **To someone who read Scripture and studied Mishnah.** The Gemara does not specify how many people are considered sufficient for the funeral of an uneducated man, but there is a Geonic tradition, cited in the *Sheiltot,* that ten men are enough. Nevertheless, the Rishonim declare that when a person sees a funeral procession pass before him — even if the deceased was totally uneducated — he should walk with it for at least a few yards.

The Rishonim discuss the case of a woman, who did not study Scripture or Mishnah. Some say that she should be treated like a man who did study Mishnah or Scripture, since a woman is not obliged to study Torah, whereas others argue that an uneducated woman should be treated no differently from an uneducated man. *Talmidei Rabbenu Yonah* concludes that an exceptionally devout woman, who took pains to see to it that her sons studied Torah, should be treated no differently from a scholarly man, as this is all that is required of her.

דְּקָרֵי וְתָנֵי **Who read Scripture and studied Mishnah.** It is not clear whether a scholar who studied Talmud in addition to Scripture and Mishnah, but did not teach others, is included in this category or in the higher one of a teacher. *Shittah Mekubbetzet* cites an opinion that such a scholar is indeed the equal of a teacher, even though he only taught himself.

Ritva translates this phrase as "someone who read Scripture *or* studied Mishnah." According to this explanation, this category should include anyone (other than a teacher) who studied at least Scripture or Mishnah. *Ritva* concludes that in practice all devout Jews, except for outstanding scholars, should be included in this category.

הִינוּמָא ***Hinuma.*** Our Gemara gives two interpretations of the word *hinuma,* both of which employ terms that are not entirely clear. Surḥav bar Pappa explains *hinuma* as תַּנּוּרָא דְּאָסָא, which literally means "an oven of myrtle." *Rashi* explains that the "oven" is actually a sort of canopy, whereas *Ri Migash* explains that it is a sort of tent. The tent, or canopy, is called an "oven" because of its shape — round and wide at the bottom and narrow at the top. The Rishonim note that the word *hinuma* was also employed by the Jerusalem Targum (Isaiah 31:9) as the Aramaic word for "oven." *Talmidei Rabbenu Yonah* suggests that the use of the word *hinuma* for "oven" is derived from the valley of the sons of Hinnom (Gehinnom), which has a connotation of fires and ovens.

Rabbi Yoḥanan explains *hinuma* as קְרִיתָא דִּמְנַמְנָה בָּהּ, which literally means "a city in which she dozes." In our commentary we have followed *Rashi,* who explains the "city" as a veil that covers the bride's face so well that she can doze under it. It is not clear how "city" came to mean veil. *Rabbenu Ḥananel* explains it as a sort of canopy in the shape of a city.

In the parallel passage in the Jerusalem Talmud, the question of the definition of the *hinuma* is presented as a dispute between the Sages of Babylonia and those of Eretz Israel. The Sages of Babylonia present the view that is mentioned here in the name of Rabbi Yoḥanan, whereas the Sages of Eretz Israel identify *hinuma* with פְּרִיוּמָא. The

[1] "רַבִּי יוֹחָנָן בֶּן בְּרוֹקָא אוֹמֵר, וכו'". [2] תָּנָא: [3] "בִּיהוּדָה, רְאָיָה". [4] בְּבָבֶל מַאי?
[5] אֲמַר רַב: דַּרְדּוּגֵי דְּמִשְׁחָא אַרֵישָׁא דְּרַבָּנַן.
[6] אֲמַר לֵיהּ רַב פַּפָּא לְאַבַּיֵי: [7] מִשְׁחָא דַּחֲפִיפוּתָא קָאֲמַר מָר? [8] אֲמַר לֵיהּ: יַתְמָא, [9] לָא עָבְדָא לָךְ אִמָּךְ דַּרְדּוּגֵי מִשְׁחָא אַרֵישָׁא דְּרַבָּנַן בִּשְׁעַת מַעֲשֶׂה? [10] כִּי הָא דְּהַהוּא מֵרַבָּנַן דְּאִיעֲסַק לֵיהּ לִבְרֵיהּ בֵּי רַבָּה בַּר עוּלָּא — [11] וְאָמְרִי לַהּ רַבָּה בַּר עוּלָּא אִיעֲסַק לֵיהּ לִבְרֵיהּ בֵּי הַהוּא מֵרַבָּנַן — [12] וְדַרְדֵּיג מִשְׁחָא אַרֵישָׁא דְּרַבָּנַן בִּשְׁעַת מַעֲשֶׂה.
[13] אַרְמַלְתָּא מַאי?

LITERAL TRANSLATION

[1] "Rabbi Yoḥanan ben Beroka says, etc." [2] It was taught: [3] "In Judea, [this is] proof." [4] What [is proof] in Babylonia?

[5] Rav said: Dripping oil on the heads of the Rabbis.

[6] Rav Pappa said to Abaye: [7] Did the Master say oil for rubbing?

[8] He said to him: Orphan, [9] did your mother not do drippings of oil for you on the heads of the Rabbis at the time of the occasion? [10] As when one of the Rabbis who made [a wedding party] for his son in the house of Rabbah bar Ulla — [11] and some say [that] Rabbah bar Ulla made [a wedding party] for his son in the house of one of the Rabbis — [12] and he dripped oil on the heads of the Rabbis at the time of the occasion.

[13] What [happens in the case of] a widow?

TRANSLATION AND COMMENTARY

רַבִּי יוֹחָנָן בֶּן בְּרוֹקָא [1] The Gemara now considers the next clause of the Mishnah: **"Rabbi Yoḥanan ben Beroka says:** The distribution of parched grain at a wedding is also proof that the bride is a virgin." Where Rabbi Yoḥanan ben Beroka lived, it was customary to distribute parched grain among the children attending the wedding of a virgin. Thus, according to Rabbi Yoḥanan ben Beroka, it is sufficient for the wife to prove that parched grain was distributed at her wedding, for her to receive the 200 zuz she is demanding. [2] Referring to this clause of the Mishnah, the Gemara notes that **it was taught in a Baraita:** [3] "The distribution of parched grain **is** a good **proof in Judea,"** where Rabbi Yoḥanan ben Beroka lived. [4] **What,** asks the Gemara, serves as **proof in Babylonia?** Is there a custom practiced here that is equivalent to the distribution of parched grain?

אֲמַר רַב [5] **Rav said** in reply: **Dripping oil on the heads of the Rabbis.** In Babylonia the women were accustomed to anoint with an aromatic oil the heads of the Rabbinic students attending a wedding celebration. Since this was done only at the weddings of virgins and not at those of widows, it could be used as proof, just like the parched grain mentioned in the Mishnah.

אֲמַר לֵיהּ [6] In a later generation, the Amoraim reviewed this passage and considered Rav's statement. In the meantime, however, the custom described by Rav had become less common, and **Rav Pappa** did not understand what Rav had meant. He **said to Abaye:** [7] **Did the Master** (i.e., Rav) **say oil** used **for rubbing?** Why would the students rub oil in their hair? Did they have sores on their heads which required oil as medication?

אֲמַר לֵיהּ [8] Abaye **said to** Rav Pappa in reply: You are like an **orphan** who goes through life without witnessing the customary rites. [9] **Did your mother not drip oil on the heads of the Rabbis for you at the time of your wedding?** [10] **As** happened **when one of the Rabbis held a wedding party for his son in Rabbah bar Ulla's house** (i.e., Rabbah bar Ulla was the bride's father) — [11] **and some say that Rabbah bar Ulla held a wedding party for his son in the house of one of the Rabbis** — [12] **and** the bridegroom's father **dripped oil on the heads of the Rabbis on that occasion,** as a sign that the bride was a virgin.

אַרְמַלְתָּא מַאי [13] The Gemara now returns to the Mishnah, which stated that parched grain was distributed only at the weddings of virgins. **What,** asks the Gemara, **happens in the case of a widow?** What custom was practiced at the wedding of a widow to show that the bride was a widow? For the Gemara declared

RASHI

ביהודה ראיה — כל הני דמתניתין, שאם היו רגילין בסימנין הללו לבתולה. **דרדוגי מישחא** — הגשים נותנים שמן בראש התלמידים, ושפות. **מישחא דחפיפותא** — [שמן של בשמים שמתוקן לחופות] קאמר מר — וכי בעלי חפיפות הן, לסוכן שמן? **יתמא** — יתום ממנהג הנוהג. **איעסק לבריה** — לישא לו אשה. **ודרדיג מישחא** — שף שמן בראש התלמידים. **ארמלתא מאי** — מה סימנין עוסים לאלמנה להודיע שאלמנה נישאת.

BACKGROUND

מִשְׁחָא דַחֲפִיפוּתָא Oil for rubbing. Oil used for anointing the head generally contained soap or aromatic herbs, which would not be fitting for a public wedding celebration. However, the pouring of oil on the heads of Sages was a ceremonial act, which was perhaps connected to the symbolic relationship between oil and wisdom.

SAGES

רַבָּה בַּר עוּלָּא Rabbah bar Ulla. A Babylonian Amora of the fourth generation. Although Rabbah bar Ulla's teachings are found in several places in the Talmud, we know very little about him. We find him debating with Abaye and Rava as their equal, and he may have been somewhat older than they were. In addition to his Halakhic teachings, we also find Aggadot in his name.

NOTES

latter term is explained in *Arukh* as meaning a thin, light cloak, whereas *Korban HaEdah* and *Pnei Moshe* derive it from the word אפיריון — "covered litter" — and again explain it as a sort of canopy.

בְּבָבֶל מַאי What is proof in Babylonia? *Shittah Mekubbetzet* points out that there was nothing preventing virgin brides from wearing a *hinuma* in Babylonia as well, but the Gemara wished to determine whether there was some custom there that was analagous to the distribution of parched grain.

SAGES

רַב יוֹסֵף Rav Yosef. A Babylonian Amora of the third generation. See *Ketubot*, Part I, p. 102.

TRANSLATION AND COMMENTARY

(above, 16b) that, in order to avoid problems, it is preferable to institute a custom for widows as well as a custom for virgins.

תָּאנֵי רַב יוֹסֵף [1]The Gemara answers that when **Rav Yosef taught** our Mishnah, [2]he explained that there is in fact no special custom practiced at **a widow's** wedding. But those present **do not** distribute **parched grain,** so as not to suggest that the bride is a virgin.

וּמוֹדֶה רַבִּי יְהוֹשֻׁעַ [3]The Gemara now considers the next clause of the Mishnah, which describes a case in which a plaintiff's claim has so much credibility that even Rabbi Yehoshua — who normally insists that the burden of proof must fall on the plaintiff — agrees that here the burden of proof falls on the defendant. **"And Rabbi Yehoshua agrees that if someone** who is in possession of a field **says to another person:** 'This field originally belonged to your father, and I bought it from him,' then the person in possession is believed without proof." Even though the person in possession of the field is considered the plaintiff — since, by his own admission, the field originally belonged to the other person's father, and no evidence exists that it was ever sold — nevertheless in this case we accept without further proof his claim that he bought the field, because his claim is supported by the argument called "the mouth that forbade is the mouth that permitted." Presumably, the Mishnah did not illustrate the law of "the mouth that forbade" with a case related to divorce and to ketubot, because no such case exists. [4]**But** it is not clear why the Mishnah illustrated its point using the complicated case of a person in possession of a field who claims that he bought the real estate from the father of the claimant of the field, because there are other, simpler illustrations of "the mouth that forbade." For example, **let the Mishnah state:** [5]**"Rabbi Yehoshua agrees that if someone** who is in possession of a field **says to another person:** [6]**'This field** originally **belonged to you** (rather than "to your father"), **and I bought it from you,'** the person in possession is believed without proof," because his claim is supported by the argument of "the mouth that forbade." Why did the Mishnah need to bring in the other person's father?

מִשּׁוּם [7]The Gemara answers: The Mishnah constructed a case in which the field was bought from the claimant's father **because it wished to teach the last clause,** which informs us that where the claimant has independent proof, the person in possession is not believed, because his claim is no longer supported by

[1]תָּאנֵי רַב יוֹסֵף: [2]אַרְמַלְתָּא לֵית לָהּ כִּיסָנֵי.

[3]"וּמוֹדֶה רַבִּי יְהוֹשֻׁעַ בְּאוֹמֵר לַחֲבֵירוֹ, כו'". [4]וְלִיתְנֵי: [5]"מוֹדֶה רַבִּי יְהוֹשֻׁעַ בְּאוֹמֵר לַחֲבֵירוֹ: [6]'שָׂדֶה זוֹ שֶׁלְּךָ הָיְתָה, וּלְקַחְתִּיהָ מִמְּךָ'"!

[7]מִשּׁוּם דְּקָא בָּעֵי לְמִיתְנֵי סֵיפָא:

LITERAL TRANSLATION

[1]Rav Yosef taught: [2]A widow does not have parched grain.

[3]"And Rabbi Yehoshua agrees that if someone says to his fellow, etc." [4]But let [the Mishnah] teach: [5]"Rabbi Yehoshua agrees that if someone says to his fellow: [6]'This field was yours, and I bought it from you'"!

[7]Because it wished to teach the last clause:

RASHI

לית לה כיסני — אין לה קליות, וזה סימנה. **וליתני מודה רבי יהושע כו' שדה זו שלך היתה** — כיון דטעמא משום דאין שור שחוט לפניו הוא, שלא היה אדם תובעו — מה לי של אביו ומה לי שלו, ומאי שנא של אביך דנקט?

NOTES

אַרְמַלְתָּא לֵית לָהּ כִּיסָנֵי A widow does not have parched grain. The Mishnah uses the Hebrew word קְלָיוֹת, meaning "parched grain," in reference to virgins, whereas the Gemara uses the Aramaic word כִּיסָנֵי in reference to widows. In our translation of this word we have followed *Rashi,* who explains that the latter word too means parched grain. Thus the answer to the Gemara's question is that parched grain is distributed only at a virgin's wedding, but not at a widow's.

But it is difficult to see how this answers the Gemara's question. The Gemara was looking for a custom that singled out a widow in a positive way, in the light of the Gemara's statement (above, 16b) that it is not sufficient for a widow not to perform the customs of a virgin, in case the celebrants fail by mistake to perform the customs of a virgin. What, then, is the Gemara's answer? *Tosafot* explains that in Rabbi Yoḥanan ben Beroka's town they were extremely careful not to distribute parched grain at the wedding of a widow. *Rabbenu Tam* explains that the Gemara's statement (above, 16b) applies only to the customs relating to virgins discussed there, which are difficult to perform. A difficult custom of this kind may sometimes be neglected by mistake; but distributing parched grain, which is very easy to do, would never be neglected in this way.

Some Rishonim have a different reading in their versions of the Gemara, in which it says that widows *have* (rather than do not have) כִּיסָנֵי. According to this explanation, כִּיסָנֵי, which are distributed at the wedding of a widow, must be different in some way from קְלָיוֹת, which are distributed for virgins. The Geonim explain that כִּיסָנֵי is a mixture of grain, beans, and raisins, whereas קְלָיוֹת are parched grains. *Rabbenu Tam* explains that the קְלָיוֹת given at the wedding of a virgin were fresh, whereas the כִּיסָנֵי distributed for widows were pre-roasted — a subtle hint that the bride had been married before.

מִשּׁוּם דְּקָא בָּעֵי לְמִיתְנֵי סֵיפָא Because it wished to teach the last clause. In our commentary we have followed

TRANSLATION AND COMMENTARY

the "mouth that forbade" argument. Under Talmudic law, if we know that a piece of real estate originally belonged to someone else, physical possession alone is not sufficient to create a presumption of ownership. Hence the person in possession is the plaintiff, and the burden of proof falls on him. However, this clause makes sense only if the person in possession bought the field from the other person's father, but not if he bought it directly from the other person. For if we were to substitute "him" for "his father" in the last clause, it would read: [1]**"If** the claimant produces **witnesses that** the field originally **belonged to him,** [2]**and** the person in possession continues to **say: 'I bought** this field **from you,'** without bringing proof, [3]the person in possession **is not believed."** The Gemara now explains why this hypothetical last clause would not make sense. While it is true that, in a dispute regarding real estate, physical possession alone is not sufficient to create a presumption of ownership, in practice the Rabbis modified this law with a regulation called "years of *ḥazakah*" (שְׁנֵי חֲזָקָה). Under this regulation, if a person holds uncontested possession of a piece of real estate for three full years (making full use of it and consuming its crops), and the original owner could have contested the possession but said nothing, and after three years the original owner tries to repossess the property, claiming that the person in possession is there illegally, his suit is rejected. If the person in possession claims that he bought the field and has lost the deed of sale, he is believed without proof, because it is unreasonable to expect a buyer to keep a deed of sale for more than three years. Given that this is the law, the hypothetical last clause we described above would not make sense. For were it to appear in the Mishnah, we would ask: [4]**How do we visualize the case?** What are the precise circumstances of the dispute between the person in possession and the claimant as described in this last clause? [5]**If** the person in possession **consumed the produce** of the field for the full three **"years of *ḥazakah*,"** [6]**why is he not believed** when he claims that he bought the field? Having held the field for three years, he no longer needs to prove his claim by producing a deed!

[1]״אִם יֵשׁ עֵדִים שֶׁהִיא שֶׁלּוֹ, [2]וְהוּא אוֹמֵר: ׳לְקַחְתִּיהָ מִמֶּנּוּ׳, [3]אֵינוֹ נֶאֱמָן״. [4]הֵיכִי דָמֵי? [5]אִי דַּאֲכָלָהּ שְׁנֵי חֲזָקָה, [6]אַמַּאי לָא

LITERAL TRANSLATION

[1]"If there are witnesses that it was his, [2]and he says: 'I bought it from him,' [3]he is not believed." [4]How do we visualize the case (lit., "how is it like")? [5]If he consumed it [the produce during] the years of *ḥazakah*, [6]why is he not

RASHI

שני חזקה – שלש שנים, שתיקנו חכמים לכל מחזיקים בקרקע. דמשאכלה שלש שנים בלא עירעור – נאמן לומר לקחתיה ואבד שטרי, דכולי האי לא מזדהר איניש בשטרא.

NOTES

Rashi, Ramban, and other Rishonim, who explain that the only way to "neutralize" the effect of the "years of *ḥazakah*" rule is to construct a case in which the owner was a minor for at least a part of the three years. This is only possible if the field was bought from the father, who then died, transferring his rights to his minor son. For if the claimant was an adult during the entire time, and produces witnesses that he originally owned the field, it is obvious that if the person in possession can prove that he has occupied the field for three years, he will be believed without proof; and if not, not. But it is unclear whether the "years of *ḥazakah*" rule applies to minors. Hence, the Mishnah needs to teach us that if the claimant was a minor, the person in possession is not believed, even if he has been in possession of the field for three years.

שְׁנֵי חֲזָקָה The years of *ḥazakah*. The term *ḥazakah* (חֲזָקָה) has several meanings, depending on the context, and there is little or no connection between them. In this passage, the Gemara is referring to a Rabbinic institution designed to protect buyers of real estate from unscrupulous sellers. The law is that physical possession alone is insufficient to create a presumption of ownership in a dispute over real estate. Hence, if a person in possession claims to have bought a field, and the original owner denies selling it, the onus is on the possessor to prove that he bought the field, e.g., by producing a deed of sale. Thus it is the buyer's duty to keep the deed. Eventually, however, if the seller makes no complaints, the buyer is likely to discard or lose the deed of sale. Thus an unscrupulous seller could wait in silence for a few years, and then come forward and deny that he ever sold the field. For this reason, the Rabbis placed a time limit of three years on the owner's right to complain. If the owner has refrained from complaining for three full years, the buyer can discard his deed, as any claim he makes henceforth will be believed without proof.

The "years of *ḥazakah*" principle is subject to many detailed regulations, which form the topic of the third chapter of tractate *Bava Batra*. Some of the most important of these are: (1) The years of *ḥazakah* serve as evidence of ownership, not as a form of legal acquisition. The

HALAKHAH

אִם יֵשׁ עֵדִים שֶׁהִיא שֶׁלּוֹ If there are witnesses that it was his. "There is a legal presumption that real estate remains in the ownership of its last known owner, even if someone else is in physical possession of it. Therefore, if someone has witnesses that a field in the possession of someone else was his, and the person in possession claims to have bought it from its rightful owner, but the owner denies selling it, then, if the person in possession has not occupied

TRANSLATION AND COMMENTARY

[1] **And if he did not consume its produce** for the full three **"years of *ḥazakah*,"** [2] **it is obvious that he is not believed,** because he does not have a deed to prove his claim, and the Mishnah would not have needed to tell us something so obvious. Thus the last clause of the Mishnah would not have been written if the Mishnah had been dealing with a case where the field was bought directly from the claimant. Hence the Mishnah constructed a case where the field was supposedly bought from the claimant's father.

אִי הָכִי [3] The Gemara asks: **If so,** if the Mishnah avoided the case of a direct purchase because of complications arising from the "years of *ḥazakah*" regulation, the same problem **also** arises **with regard to** the case that actually appears in the Mishnah, where the person in possession claims that he bought the field from the other person's **father.** [4] **If** the person in possession **consumed the produce** of the field for the full three **"years of *ḥazakah*,"** [5] **why is he not believed** when he claims that he bought the field from the claimant's father? Having held the field for three years, he does not need to prove his claim by producing a deed! [6] **And if he did not consume its produce** for the full three **"years of *ḥazakah*,"** [7] **it is obvious that he is not believed,** because he does not have a deed. Why, then, is a case where the person in possession claims he bought the field from the other person's father preferable to a case where he claims he bought it from the son?

בִּשְׁלָמָא [8] The Gemara answers: In the hypothetical case, where the person in possession claims he bought the field directly from the claimant, the "years of *ḥazakah*" regulation clearly applies, and if the person in possession occupied the field for three years, he is believed, and if not, not. But **with regard to** the case that actually appears in the Mishnah, where the person in possession claims he bought the field from the other person's **father,** [9] **you can find** the following **case** in which the person in possession held the field for three years, and yet the "years of *ḥazakah*" regulation does not apply. In such a case, the Mishnah needs to teach us that the person in possession is not believed: [10] **For example, where** the person in possession held the field and **consumed its produce for** three full years, but **two** of those **years were during the lifetime of the father,** [11] **and one was during the lifetime of the son,** after the death of the father, while the son was

מְהֵימָן? [1] וְאִי דְּלָא אֲכָלָהּ שְׁנֵי חֲזָקָה, [2] פְּשִׁיטָא דְּלָא מְהֵימָן! [3] אִי הָכִי, גַּבֵּי אָבִיו נַמִּי: [4] אִי דַּאֲכָלָהּ שְׁנֵי חֲזָקָה, [5] אַמַּאי לָא מְהֵימָן? [6] וְאִי דְּלָא אֲכָלָהּ שְׁנֵי חֲזָקָה, [7] פְּשִׁיטָא דְּלָא מְהֵימָן! [8] בִּשְׁלָמָא גַּבֵּי אָבִיו, [9] מַשְׁכְּחַתְּ לָהּ: [10] כְּגוֹן, שֶׁאֲכָלָהּ שְׁתַּיִם בְּחַיֵּי הָאָב, [11] וְאַחַת בְּחַיֵּי בְנוֹ.

LITERAL TRANSLATION

believed? [1] And if he did not consume it [the produce during] the years of *ḥazakah,* [2] it is obvious that he is not believed!

[3] If so, with regard to his father also: [4] If he consumed it [the produce during] the years of *ḥazakah,* [5] why is he not believed? [6] And if he did not consume it [the produce during] the years of *ḥazakah,* [7] it is obvious that he is not believed!

[8] Granted with regard to his father, [9] you will find [a case]: [10] For example, where he consumed it [the produce for] two [years] during the lifetime of the father, [11] and [for] one [year] during the lifetime of his son.

RASHI

בשלמא גבי אביו משכחת לה — דאיצטריך למיתנייה, כגון דאכלה שני חזקה ואפילו הכי לא מהימן. וכגון שאכלה שתי שנים ראשונות בחיי אביו, ומת. ואכלה השלישית לפני הבן הזה,

NOTES

person in possession must still assert a claim that, if true, would justify his presence in the field (e.g., purchase, inheritance, or gift). If he simply says: "I have been here for three years and you did not complain," he must surrender the field. (2) The person in possession must prove that he made full use of the property — which in the case of a field means that he consumed its crops — for the full three years. (3) The previous owner must have been in a position to protest. If the owner was a minor, or (according to some opinions) if he was out of town, the period during which he was unable to protest does not count toward the years of *ḥazakah*.

HALAKHAH

it for three full years, the onus is on him to prove that he bought the field, and if he cannot, the original owner may take back the field after taking the Rabbinic *heset* oath. If, however, the person in possession has occupied the field for three full years, the onus is on the original owner to prove that he did not sell the property and if he cannot, the person in possession may take the *heset* oath and keep the field. And if the original owner cannot produce witnesses to prove that he ever owned the field — even if the person in possession admits that the plaintiff was the original owner — the person in possession is believed if he claims to have bought the field, even if he has not occupied it for three full years," following our Gemara. (*Rambam, Sefer Mishpatim, Hilkhot To'en VeNit'an* 11:1-2; *Shulḥan Arukh, Ḥoshen Mishpat* 140:1.)

שֶׁאֲכָלָהּ שְׁתַּיִם בְּחַיֵּי הָאָב Where he consumed its produce for two years during the lifetime of the father. "If the purchaser bought the field and consumed the crops for a

TRANSLATION AND COMMENTARY

still a minor. In such a case, we might have thought that the person in possession should be believed without proof, on the basis of the "years of *ḥazakah*" law. But the Mishnah teaches us that this is not so, [1]**and this is in accordance with** the viewpoint of **Rav Huna.** [2]**For Rav Huna said:** A person who claims to have bought the property of a minor must prove his claim with a deed of sale, [3]because **people do not have presumptive ownership of a minor's estate** since a minor cannot be expected to contest the claim of someone in possession of his field. [4]Moreover, this rule applies **even if** the minor **has grown up** in the meantime, so that during part of the three-year period he was in fact an adult. The "years of *ḥazakah*" law applies only where the original owner was in a position to contest the possession during the entire three years but refrained from doing so. Hence the Mishnah needed to teach us that in a case involving a minor, the "years of *ḥazakah*" law does not apply, and the person in possession is not believed unless his claim is supported by "the mouth that forbade" argument. Therefore, the Mishnah constructed a case in which the person in possession claims he bought the field from the father of the claimant.

[1]וְכִדְרַב הוּנָא. [2]דְּאָמַר רַב הוּנָא: [3]אֵין מַחֲזִיקִין בְּנִכְסֵי קָטָן, [4]אֲפִילּוּ הִגְדִּיל.

LITERAL TRANSLATION

[1]And [this is] in accordance with Rav Huna. [2]For Rav Huna said: [3][People] do not have presumptive ownership of a minor's estate, [4]even if he has grown up.

RASHI

והוא היה קטן ולא עירער. ואיצטריך לאשמועינן, דכיון דקטן היה — אין השנה הזאת עולה מן המנין. **וכדרב הונא דאמר אין מחזיקין בנכסי קטן** — המחזיק בנכסי קטן שלש שנים אינה חזקה. דהאי דלא מיחה — משום דקטן הוא, ואפילו הגדיל לאחר מיכן והחזיק זה בפניו כמה שנים — אינה חזקה, הואיל ותחלתו כשהוא קטן ראהו מוחזק בה — לא ידע כשהגדיל שהיתה של אביו, עד ששומע מפי אחרים.

NOTES

אֲפִילּוּ הִגְדִּיל **Even if he has grown up.** It would appear, according to our Gemara, that not only does the "years of *ḥazakah*" law not apply to the property of a minor, it does not even apply to an adult heir. On the other hand, the Gemara in tractate *Bava Batra* (42a) states that if a person in possession claimed that he had bought a field from someone who later died, and he continued to hold it for three years — partly during the former owner's lifetime and partly after his death — the possessor may claim the "years of *ḥazakah*." Clearly, then, there are circumstances under which the "years of *ḥazakah*" law does apply to an adult heir. The Rishonim disagree as to how to resolve these two passages.

In our commentary we have followed *Rambam* and *Ri Migash*, who explain that the "years of *ḥazakah*" law applies to any heir who is not a minor. When our Gemara says, "even if he has grown up," it means that the time when the owner was a minor does not count toward the three years, even if the minor reached adulthood before the three years were over and had time to protest, because the owner must be allowed three full years as a competent adult in which to register his complaint. But if three years have passed since the owner reached majority, the possessor can claim the "years of *ḥazakah*," because the owner has now had ample time to register a protest.

Rashi and many other Rishonim disagree with this explanation. According to their view, even if the possessor held the field for many years after the minor grew up, he still cannot claim the "years of *ḥazakah*," so long as the father died while his heir was still a minor. For the minor might not have been aware that the field had been stolen from his father, and that he should register a protest, until many years had passed. The "years of *ḥazakah*" law applies only if the heir was an adult when his father died.

Rashbam has a third view. According to his explanation, when the Gemara says, "even if he has grown up," it means that the "years of *ḥazakah*" law does not apply to any heir, even an adult, who was a minor at the time of the original alleged purchase. For the minor might not have realized at the time that the field had been stolen from his father, and his father might not have told him about it before he died. Thus, if the possessor moved into the property while the

HALAKHAH

year, and then the seller died leaving an adult heir, and the purchaser continued to consume the crops for two more years, or if he consumed the crops for two years before the father died and one year afterwards, the "years of *ḥazakah*" law has been fulfilled, provided that the heir was an adult when the original owner died." (*Rambam, Sefer Mishpatim, Hilkhot To'en VeNit'an* 12:8; *Shulḥan Arukh, Ḥoshen Mishpat* 144:4.)

אֵין מַחֲזִיקִין בְּנִכְסֵי קָטָן, אֲפִילּוּ הִגְדִּיל **People do not have presumptive ownership of a minor's estate, even if he has grown up.** "The "years of *ḥazakah*" law does not apply to a minor's property, even if he grew up in the interval, following our Gemara. *Shulḥan Arukh* rules, in the name of *Rambam* and *Ri Migash,* that this is true only if less than three years have passed since the minor grew up (even if the field was in the occupier's possession for more than three years, if we include the period when the owner was a minor), because the owner did not have a full three years to protest as an adult. But if three years have passed since the owner grew up, the "years of *ḥazakah*" law applies. *Rema,* however, rules, in the name of *Rashi, Ra'avad, Ramban,* and *Rashba,* that the "years of *hazakah*" law does not apply even if three years have passed since the minor grew up, because the former minor may not have been aware that the field was stolen from his father. *Maggid Mishneh* notes that our Gemara is the main source for this law, but it can be explained either way." (*Rambam, Sefer Mishpatim, Hilkhot To'en VeNit'an* 14:7; *Shulḥan Arukh, Ḥoshen Mishpat* 149:19.)

BACKGROUND

דִּיּוּקָא דְּמַתְנִיתִין קָאָמַר **Stated the inference of the Mishnah.** In general, the statements of Sages contain something innovative, and if a teaching does not appear to be innovative, it is commonly challenged with the expression פְּשִׁיטָא — "it is obvious" — which implies that there was no need to say something that was self-evident. An Amora would certainly not repeat a Halakhah contained in the Mishnah unless there was something innovative about it, the determination of an alternative reading, or the like. Here, however, there is something new in the words of Rav Huna, because his teaching was not explicit in the Mishnah, but was derived from it by implication. While this implication may appear convincing, there is nevertheless something novel in the deduction of this Halakhic conclusion from the Mishnah.

TRANSLATION AND COMMENTARY

וְרַב הוּנָא ¹**But,** the Gemara asks, **did Rav Huna merely intend to inform us of the ruling of the Mishnah?** According to the explanation just given, the Mishnah makes sense only if it is teaching us Rav Huna's ruling. But if so, what was Rav Huna teaching us? Everyone is aware of the Mishnah and its implications.

אִיבָּעֵית אֵימָא ²The Gemara offers two answers to this question: (1) **If you wish,** you can **say:** ³Rav Huna **stated the implication of the Mishnah.** It is true that a careful examination of the Mishnah would have yielded the same results, and indeed this is the basis of Rav Huna's viewpoint. But the Mishnah is not clear, and Rav Huna wished to make the point explicit. (2) ⁴**And if you wish,** you can **say:** Rav Huna added something that cannot be derived from the Mishnah. ⁵**He informed us that** this law **applies even** after the minor **has grown up,** whereas the Mishnah could be referring to a case where the son was still a minor.

וְלִיתְנְיֵיהּ בְּדִידֵיהּ ⁶**But** even so, the Gemara objects, it is still not clear why the Mishnah illustrated its point by using the complicated case of a person in possession of a field who contends that he bought it from the claimant's father. **The Mishnah could teach** us about the principle of "the mouth that forbade" by using a case involving **the claimant himself,** as there is another case in which the "years of ḥazakah" law does not apply, even though the person in possession has held the field for three years, because the owner was unable to protest for part of the time. ⁷**Let the Mishnah construct a case, for example, where** the person in possession occupied the field for the full three years and **consumed its produce,** but during **two of the years** the original owner **was present,** ⁸**and** during **the one** remaining **year** he was **not present.** ⁹The Gemara explains: This could happen, **for example, where** the owner was forced **to flee** his home before the three years had elapsed. In such a case, the Mishnah needs to teach us that the person in possession is not believed, even though he has occupied the field for three years, because the "years of ḥazakah" law does not apply if the owner is not able to contest the possession for part of the time. Why, then, does the Mishnah complicate the case by introducing the claimant's father?

LITERAL TRANSLATION

¹But did Rav Huna come to inform us of the Mishnah?
²If you wish, say: ³Rav Huna stated the inference of the Mishnah. ⁴And if you wish, say: ⁵He tells us [that it applies] even if he has grown up.
⁶But let [the Mishnah] teach it about [the claimant] himself, ⁷and establish it [as referring], for example, to where he consumed it [the produce] two [years] in his presence, ⁸and one [year] not in his presence, ⁹and, for example, where he fled!

וְרַב הוּנָא מַתְנִיתִין אָתָא
לְאַשְׁמוּעִינַן? ²אִיבָּעֵית אֵימָא: ³רַב הוּנָא
דִּיּוּקָא דְּמַתְנִיתִין קָאָמַר. ⁴וְאִיבָּעֵית אֵימָא: ⁵אֲפִילוּ
הִגְדִּיל קָא מַשְׁמַע לָן.
⁶וְלִיתְנְיֵיהּ בְּדִידֵיהּ, ⁷וְלוֹקְמָהּ
כְּגוֹן שֶׁאֲכָלָהּ שְׁתַּיִם בְּפָנָיו,
⁸וְאַחַת שֶׁלֹּא בְּפָנָיו, ⁹וּכְגוֹן
שֶׁבָּרַח!

RASHI

ורב הונא מתניתין אתא לאשמועינן — בתמיה; כיון דמתניתין בהכי עסקינן, ולא מיתוקמא אלא בהכי — מאי אתא רב הונא לאשמועינן? הרי כבר שנויה ועומדת, ודבר השנוי במשנתינו שגור בפי הכל. דיוקא דמתניתין אתא לאשמועינן — משום דמתניתין לא מיפרשא בהדיא דבהכי עסקינן, ואתא רב הונא לאשמועינן בהדיא, ומדיוקא דמתניתין קא יליף לה. וליתנייה בדידיה — שדה זו שלך היתה אם יש עדים כו' אינו נאמן, ואף על גב שאכלה שני חזקה, וכגון שהיו שתים בפניו ואחת שלא בפניו. כגון שברח — ואשמעינן דהיא שמא לא סלקא ליה.

NOTES

owner's son was a minor, and a year later he reached majority, and a year after that the father died, the possessor cannot claim the "years of ḥazakah," even if he holds the property for many years thereafter. According to this view, the passage in tractate *Bava Batra* refers only to an heir who was an adult when the possessor moved into the property.

וְרַב הוּנָא מַתְנִיתִין אָתָא לְאַשְׁמוּעִינַן **But did Rav Huna come to inform us of the Mishnah?** The Rishonim note that Rav Huna never stated in so many words that the "years of ḥazakah" law does not apply to the property of a minor. He simply issued a ruling in a case in which he apparently applied this principle, and he may never have meant to claim that his ruling was in any way original.

The Gemara (*Bava Metzia* 39a) considered the problem of how to care for the property of a man who dies leaving a minor as an heir. It is necessary to appoint a guardian to take care of the property until the child grows up. Rav Huna, however, declares that a relative must not be appointed as guardian, in case he declares that the property was in fact his own, and that he inherited it from the child's father. A non-relative, however, can be appointed, since he could not make such a claim. When a later generation of Amoraim considered Rav Huna's statement, Rava declared that we can infer from it that the "years of ḥazakah" law does not apply to a minor's property, even after the minor grows up. For if this law were to apply, there would be just as much danger in appointing a non-relative as a relative, since in either case the guardian could claim to have bought the field and to have occupied it unchallenged for three years.

The Gemara's question here is actually directed at Rava

LITERAL TRANSLATION

[1]Because of what did he flee? [2]If he fled because of [danger to his] life, [3]it is obvious that he is not believed, because he cannot protest. [4]And if he fled because of money, [5]he should have protested. [6]For we maintain [that] a protest not in his presence is a [valid] protest.

[1]בָּרַח מֵחֲמַת מַאי? [2]אִי דְּבָרַח מֵחֲמַת נְפָשׁוֹת, [3]פְּשִׁיטָא דְּלָא מְהֵימַן, דְּלָא מָצֵי מָחֵי. [4]וְאִי דְּבָרַח מֵחֲמַת מָמוֹן, [5]אִיבָּעֵי לֵיהּ לְמָחוּיֵי. [6]דְּקַיְימָא לַן מְחָאָה שֶׁלֹּא בְּפָנָיו הָוְיָא מְחָאָה.

RASHI

אי ברח מחמת ממון – שאינו ירא מן המלכות, אלא מלעוקת הלועקים בעיר. **איבעי ליה למחויי** – במקום שהוא שם, וכיון דלא מיחה – חזקה מעלייתא היא.

TRANSLATION AND COMMENTARY

בָּרַח מֵחֲמַת מַאי [1]The Gemara answers: If you say that the Mishnah could have constructed a case **where** the owner **fled,** then you must specify **what** the circumstances were that forced him to leave town. [2]**If** you are referring to a case where the owner **fled because of danger to his life** (e.g., where he was the victim of government persecution), [3]**it is obvious that** the person in possession **is not believed, because** the owner **cannot protest** even at a distance as this would reveal his hiding place. [4]**And if** you are referring to a case where the owner **fled because of** some **financial** matter, and does not want to return, the "years of *ḥazakah*" law continues to apply. [5]For an owner who is unable to come to town for some reason **must** register a **protest** in front of witnesses wherever he is, and if he fails to do so for three years, the person in possession is entitled to discard his deed of sale. [6]**For** although there is a Tannaitic and Amoraic dispute about this matter, **we maintain** that the law is **that a protest not** made **in the presence** of the person in possession **is** still considered **a valid protest.** In *Bava Batra* (38a) the Gemara considers whether the owner is required to confront the possessor in person, or whether it is sufficient for him to summon witnesses (or, according to one opinion, an *ad hoc* court of three) wherever he is and to publicize the fact that he is contesting the possessor's claim, on the assumption that rumors travel and the possessor will find out if there has been any protest. According to the former opinion, the owner must be given three years to confront the possessor in person, and if he was unable to do so for part of the time — such as when he was away from town — the "years of *ḥazakah*" law does not apply. But according to the Halakhah, which follows the second opinion, the owner need not return to town to register a protest, and hence he has no excuse for failing to do so. This being the law, the last clause of the Mishnah would have made no sense if the Mishnah had

NOTES

— who should have inferred this principle from the Mishnah rather than from Rav Huna's statement — and not at Rav Huna himself, who may indeed have been applying the law of the Mishnah. For the sake of brevity, however, the Gemara did not cite the entire passage from *Bava Metzia*, and attributed Rava's remark to Rav Huna, since he was the author of the original ruling (*Tosafot, Rosh, Ramban*).

מְחָאָה שֶׁלֹּא בְּפָנָיו A protest not in his presence. The Rishonim ask: The language of the Gemara suggests that (according to the opinion that disqualifies protests which were not made in the possessor's presence) if the original owner registers his protest out of town, the protest is invalid, and the person in possession is entitled to claim the "years of *ḥazakah*," as if the protest had not been made. In fact, however, precisely the opposite is the case: According to this view, if the original owner is out of town, physical possession of the field is of no significance, and the person in possession cannot claim the "years of *ḥazakah*," even if the owner made no protest at all. Why, then, does the Gemara consistently say: "A protest not made in the occupier's presence is not a valid protest"? It should say: "'Years of *ḥazakah*' not in the owner's presence are not 'years of *ḥazakah*'"!

Tosafot and *Rosh* explain that, while it is true that possession in the owner's absence is invalid (according to this view), it is invalid not because the possession itself is defective in some way, but because the owner's protest would be unlikely to reach the ears of the person in possession. The news that the person in possession has occupied the field does travel from town to town, and the owner cannot claim not to have heard about it, as it is

HALAKHAH

בָּרַח מֵחֲמַת מַאי Because of what did he flee? "If the owner of the field was forced to flee town because of danger to his life — such as where he was being persecuted by the government — the 'years of *ḥazakah*' law does not apply to his property, because he may be afraid to protest in case his pursuers discover his hiding place. But if he fled because of a financial matter, the regular 'years of *ḥazakah*' law applies, as financial fugitives are not as fearful as fugitives whose lives are in danger. *Ba'er Hetev* rules that this is true only if the fugitive was fleeing a private debt, but a person fleeing a debt he owes the government is considered too frightened to protest, even if the government wants only his money and is not threatening his life." (*Rambam, Sefer Mishpatim, Hilkhot To'en VeNit'an* 14:10; *Shulḥan Arukh, Ḥoshen Mishpat* 143:3.)

מְחָאָה שֶׁלֹּא בְּפָנָיו A protest not in his presence. "If the owner of a field protests the presence of someone occupying the field, the 'years of *ḥazakah*' law does not apply, and the person in possession must retain his deed of sale. The protest must be registered before witnesses,

BACKGROUND

יְהוּדָה וְעֵבֶר הַיַּרְדֵּן וְהַגָּלִיל **Judea and Transjordan and Galilee.** These were the three principal regions into which Eretz Israel was divided. Transjordan was separated from the main part of Eretz Israel by the Jordan River, and between Galilee and Judea lay the "Samaritan zone," which was an independent region. Sometimes, because of the enmity between the Jews and the Samaritans, it was actually a barrier, denying free movement between Judea and Galilee.

At various times these regions were divided into separate administrative areas under Roman rule, and sometimes also under other rulers. In the generation after Herod, for example, when Judea was under direct Roman rule, Galilee was ruled by Herod's son as a kind of independent principality.

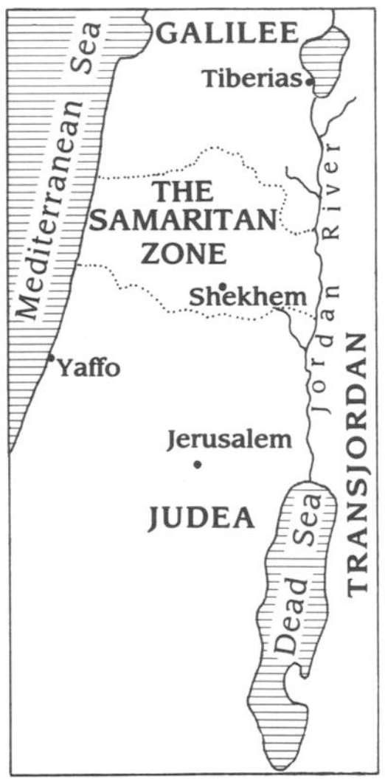

TRANSLATION AND COMMENTARY

been dealing with a case where the field was bought directly from the claimant, even if he had fled after two years. Consequently the Mishnah constructed a case where the field was bought from the claimant's father. Before considering another case which the Mishnah could have used to illustrate its ruling, the Gemara cites the entire passage in tractate *Bava Batra* in which the Gemara decided in favor of the view that a protest not made in the possessor's presence is still considered a valid protest: [1]**For we have learned** in a Mishnah (*Bava Batra* 38a): "We must distinguish between **three** different **regions** within Eretz Israel **for** the purpose of the **'years of *ḥazakah*'** law, namely, [2]**Judea and Transjordan and Galilee."** [3]The Mishnah elaborates: "**If** the owner **was in Judea, and the other person took possession** of a field belonging to **him in Galilee,** [4]**or** vice versa, if the owner was **in Galilee and the other person took possession** of a field belonging to him **in Judea,** [5]the time the possessor spent occupying the field **does not count as 'years of *ḥazakah*,'** unless the owner **is with him in the same province,** because the owner cannot register a protest in Galilee and expect the possessor to hear about it in Judea."

וְהָוֵינַן [6]Our Gemara notes that the Gemara in *Bava Batra* **analyzed this** Mishnah and asked: [7]**What does** the author of this Mishnah **maintain?** [8]**If he maintains that a protest not** made **in** the possessor's **presence is** nevertheless considered **a valid protest,** then the "years of *ḥazakah*" law **should apply,** [9]**even** if one party was **in Judea and** the other in **Galilee!** For the owner can register his protest where he is, without returning to his home. [10]**And if** the author of the Mishnah **maintains that a protest not** made **in** the possessor's **presence is not** considered **a valid protest,** then the "years of *ḥazakah*" law **should also not** apply, [11]**even** if the owner was in the same region **(e.g., in Judea)** but not in the same town!

אָמַר רַבִּי אַבָּא בַּר מֶמֶל [12]In response to this question, **Rabbi Abba bar Memel said:** [13]**In fact,** the author of the Mishnah **maintains that a protest not** made **in** the possessor's **presence is** still considered

[1]דִּתְנַן: "שָׁלֹשׁ אֲרָצוֹת לַחֲזָקָה:
[2]יְהוּדָה וְעֵבֶר הַיַּרְדֵּן וְהַגָּלִיל.
[3]הָיָה בִּיהוּדָה וְהֶחֱזִיק בַּגָּלִיל,
[4]בַּגָּלִיל וְהֶחֱזִיק בִּיהוּדָה, [5]אֵינָהּ
חֲזָקָה עַד שֶׁיְּהֵא עִמּוֹ בַּמְּדִינָה".
[6]וְהָוֵינַן בָּהּ: [7]מַאי קָסָבַר? [8]אִי
קָסָבַר מְחָאָה שֶׁלֹּא בְּפָנָיו הָוְיָא
מְחָאָה, [9]אֲפִילּוּ בִּיהוּדָה וְגָלִיל
נַמִּי. [10]וְאִי קָסָבַר מְחָאָה שֶׁלֹּא
בְּפָנָיו לָא הָוְיָא מְחָאָה,
[11]אֲפִילּוּ יְהוּדָה וִיהוּדָה נַמִּי
לָא!
[12]אָמַר רַבִּי אַבָּא בַּר מֶמֶל:
[13]לְעוֹלָם קָסָבַר מְחָאָה שֶׁלֹּא

LITERAL TRANSLATION

[1]For we have learned: "There are three lands for *ḥazakah:* [2]Judea and Transjordan and Galilee. [3]If he was in Judea and [another] took possession in Galilee, [4][or if he was] in Galilee and [another] took possession in Judea, [5]it is not *ḥazakah* unless he is with him in the [same] province."

[6]And we discussed this: [7]What does he maintain? [8]If he maintains [that] a protest not in his presence is a [valid] protest, [9][this should be so] even in Judea and Galilee as well. [10]And if he maintains [that] a protest not in his presence is not a [valid] protest, [11][it should] not [be so] even [in] Judea and Judea also!

[12]Rabbi Abba bar Memel said: [13]In fact, he maintains [that] a protest not in his presence

RASHI

שלש ארצות לחזקה – שלש ארצות של ארץ ישראל חשובות חלוקות זו מזו לענין חזקה, כאילו הן ארצות נכריות. ואם היה בזו והחזיק אחר בקרקע שיש לו בחברתה – אינה חזקה. **במדינה** – או שניהם בגליל, או שניהם ביהודה, ואפילו הן בשתי עיירות. **אפילו יהודה וגליל נמי** – הוה ליה למחויי היכא דהוי, ומדלא מחי – תיהוי חזקה. **ואי קסבר מחאה שלא בפניו לא הויא מחאה** – כגון אם היה בעיר אחת, ומיחה שלא בפניו בפני שנים בעיר אחרת. **אפילו יהודה ויהודה** – בשתי עיירות נמי לא תיהוי חזקה, דלא הוה ליה למחויי שלא בפניו.

NOTES

known to the whole town, and in any case the owner has ways of keeping informed about his field. But since news of the owner's protest would not reach the attention of the person in possession, the owner would be justified in not going to the trouble of registering it. Hence, because the "years of *ḥazakah*" rule applies only when the owner is able to protest, the *ḥazakah* is ineffective.

HALAKHAH

but need not be made in the presence of the person in possession. Indeed, the protest is valid even if the owner was in another country, provided there are regular communications between the two countries," following the Gemara's conclusion. (*Rambam, Sefer Mishpatim, Hilkhot To'en VeNit'an* 14:2; *Shulḥan Arukh, Ḥoshen Mishpat* 146:1.)

SAGES

רַבִּי אַבָּא בַּר מֶמֶל **Rabbi Abba bar Memel.** A Palestinian Amora of the second and third generations, Rabbi Abba bar Memel studied in the yeshivah of Rabbi Oshaya in Caesarea. Rabbi Elazar ben Pedat calls him his teacher. He is found in Talmudic sources in discussion with Rabbi Ammi, Rabbi Assi, Rabbi Zera, and others.

TRANSLATION AND COMMENTARY

a valid protest, [1]**and the teaching of this Mishnah was referring to a time of war,** when the roads are unsafe, and news does not travel between Judea and Galilee. Therefore the owner cannot register a protest in one region if the field is in another, and the "years of *ḥazakah*" law does not apply.

וּמַאי שְׁנָא [2]**But,** the Gemara asks, if the reason for the Mishnah's ruling is a state of war, **what is special about Judea and Galilee?** Why did the Mishnah **single them out,** since this law has nothing to do with distance? The same ruling would apply to two towns in the same district if communications between them were disrupted by war.

[18A] דִּסְתַם יְהוּדָה וְגָלִיל [3]The Gemara answers: The Mishnah used the example of Judea and Galilee **because the ordinary situation between Judea and Galilee is considered like a time of war.** These two regions suffered from frequent wars, and in addition the roads connecting them passed through hostile territory controlled by Samaritans. As a result, communications between them were frequently disrupted.

וְלִיתְנֵי [4]The Gemara asks: We have established that the only way our Mishnah could have illustrated how the law of "the mouth that forbade" applies to real estate was by constructing a complicated case of a person in possession of a field who claimed to have bought it from the claimant's father. **But** it is still not clear why the Mishnah needed to illustrate its point by using a case involving real estate, since there is another, simpler illustration of "the mouth that forbade," involving an ordinary debt. **Let the Mishnah state:** [5]**"Rabbi Yehoshua agrees that if someone says to another person:** [6]**'I borrowed a maneh from you, but I have**

בְּפָנָיו הָוְיָא מְחָאָה, [1]וּמַתְנִיתִין בִּשְׁעַת חֵירוּם שָׁנוּ.
[2]וּמַאי שְׁנָא יְהוּדָה וְגָלִיל דְּנָקַט?
[18A] [3]דִּסְתַם יְהוּדָה וְגָלִיל כִּשְׁעַת חֵירוּם דָּמוּ.
[4]וְלִיתְנֵי: [5]"מוֹדֶה רַבִּי יְהוֹשֻׁעַ בְּאוֹמֵר לַחֲבֵירוֹ: [6]'מָנֶה לָוִיתִי

LITERAL TRANSLATION

is a [valid] protest, [1]and they taught our Mishnah [as referring] to a time of war (lit., "exclusion").

[2]And what is different about Judea and Galilee that he took [them as an example]?

[18A] [3]Because ordinarily [communications between] Judea and Galilee are like a time of war.

[4]But let [the Mishnah] teach: [5]"Rabbi Yehoshua agrees that if someone says to his fellow: [6]'I borrowed a maneh

RASHI

הויא מחאה — דאמרך חברא אית ליה, דהני דמחי באנפייהו מגלו לאחריני, ובא הדבר לאזני המחזיק, והוה ליה לאזדהורי בשטריה. **ומתניתין** — דקתני יהודה וגליל לא. **בשעת חירום שנו** — דיכול לומר: לא נגלית לי מחאתו שאשמור את שטרי. **ומאי שנא יהודה וגליל דנקט** — אם יש חירום — נמי מעיר לעיר, אפילו שתי עיירות באותה מדינה, נמי לא. **וליתני מנה לויתי ממך** — מלתיה דרבי יהושע דאשמועינן דמודה היכא דאין שור שחוט לפניך, מאי שנא

NOTES

וּמַאי שְׁנָא יְהוּדָה וְגָלִיל And what is different about Judea and Galilee? If the Mishnah is referring to emergency situations, why were Judea and Galilee singled out? Our commentary follows *Rashi*, who explains that in a time of emergency even two towns in the same district may be cut off from each other, so that a protest registered in one would not be effective in the other. *Rashbam* (*Bava Batra* 38a) disagrees with *Rashi* about the issue of two towns in the same district, arguing that it is most unlikely for communications to be disrupted to that extent. According to his explanation, the Gemara is asking why Judea and Galilee were singled out instead of any other two districts. Why did the Mishnah not simply say: "If they were in different districts with no communications between them, the *ḥazakah* is ineffective"?

דִּסְתַם יְהוּדָה וְגָלִיל כִּשְׁעַת חֵירוּם דָּמוּ Because ordinarily communications between Judea and Galilee are like a time of war. *Tosafot* asks: In tractate *Gittin* (2a), the Mishnah rules that a bill of divorce sent by a husband living in a foreign country to a woman living in Eretz Israel requires a special procedure to establish its validity, but a bill of divorce brought from one town to another within Eretz Israel does not, because any questions that may arise can easily be settled later, if necessary. The Gemara (4b) considers the case of a bill of divorce brought from Judea to Galilee, and rules that, since there is a great deal of communication and travel between these two regions (regular pilgrimages to the Temple in Jerusalem, and even after its destruction frequent travel to the great Rabbinic academies of the Sanhedrin), they are treated as a single country for the purpose of bills of divorce. How, then, can our Gemara state that communications were normally disrupted between them?

Rabbenu Yonah suggests that the Mishnah in *Bava Batra* refers to a later period than does the Mishnah in *Gittin* — a time when conditions in Eretz Israel had deteriorated. The passage in *Gittin*, on the other hand, refers to the period before the destruction of the Temple and the period immediately following the destruction, when the Jews in Eretz Israel still maintained an orderly community. *Rabbenu Yonah* notes, however, that it is difficult to explain that two Mishnas refer to entirely different periods.

Tosafot and most other Rishonim explain that even though communications between the two regions were not very good, it was still possible to convey information by making an effort, and to ratify a bill of divorce this is sufficient. But for a protest against unlawful possession of a field to be valid, it is necessary that news of the protest reach the ears of the person in possession without any particular exertion on his part, and for this proper communications are essential.

וְלִיתְנֵי מוֹדֶה רַבִּי יְהוֹשֻׁעַ But let the Mishnah teach: "Rabbi Yehoshua agrees." The Gemara considers two cases of

מִמְּךָ וּפְרַעְתִּיו לְךָ׳, [1]שֶׁהוּא נֶאֱמָן״!
[2]מִשּׁוּם דְּקָא בָּעֵי לְמִיתְנֵי סֵיפָא: [3]״אִם יֵשׁ עֵדִים שֶׁהוּא לָוָה מִמֶּנּוּ, [4]וְהוּא אוֹמֵר: ׳פְּרַעְתִּיו׳, [5]אֵינוֹ נֶאֱמָן״. [6]וְהָא קַיְימָא לַן: [7]הַמַּלְוֶה אֶת חֲבֵירוֹ בְּעֵדִים אֵינוֹ צָרִיךְ לְפָרְעוֹ בְּעֵדִים.

LITERAL TRANSLATION

from you but I repaid it to you,' [1]that he is believed"!

[2]Because it wished to teach the last clause: [3]"If there are witnesses that he borrowed from him, [4]and he says: 'I repaid it,' [5]he is not believed." [6]But surely we maintain: [7]Someone who lends to his fellow before witnesses need not repay him before witnesses.

TRANSLATION AND COMMENTARY

repaid it to you,' [1]the borrower **is believed** without proof, because the mouth that forbade is the mouth that permitted." Why was it necessary for the Mishnah to construct a case involving real estate and to involve the claimant's father?

מִשּׁוּם דְּקָא בָּעֵי [2]The Gemara answers: Our Mishnah did not illustrate its point with a case involving a debt **because it wanted to inform** us of the law contained in **the last clause,** which teaches that where the claimant has independent proof, the person in possession is not believed, because his claim is no longer supported by the "mouth that forbade" argument. This clause makes sense only in a dispute involving real estate, not in a dispute involving a debt. For if we were to substitute "him" for "his father" and "borrowed" for "was his" in the last clause, it would read: [3]**If** the claimant produces **witnesses that** the borrower **did** in fact **borrow from him,** [4]**and** the borrower continues to **say: "I repaid** my debt," without bringing proof, [5]the borrower **would not be believed.** [6]**But surely** this is not true! Regarding the case of real estate actually cited in the Mishnah, since we know that the field originally belonged to the father, the possessor's physical possession is not sufficient to create a presumption of ownership; hence the possessor is the plaintiff, and the burden of proof falls on him. But with regard to monetary debts, although there is an Amoraic dispute about the matter, **we maintain** [7]that if **someone lends** money **to another person in the presence of witnesses,** and can prove that the loan was made, the borrower **need not repay him in the presence of witnesses,** because he does not need to prove that he repaid the debt. Even though the lender has proved that he lent the money, he is nevertheless considered the plaintiff, and the onus is on him to prove that the debt has not been repaid.

RASHI

דאשמעינן בקרקע, ואיצטריך למתנייה באביו משום סיפא, לנקוט מלתיה במטלטלין, ולישמעינן בדידיה גופיה! **נאמן** — מדאורייתא, בלא שבועה.

NOTES

monetary debts that do not involve real estate, which could have been used to illustrate the "mouth that forbade" argument, but which are unsuitable for other reasons. The Rishonim ask: There is one other situation involving a monetary debt which would fit the Mishnah perfectly: If one party (parallel to the person in possession of the field in the Mishnah) says to a second party (parallel to the son in the Mishnah): "I stole 100 zuz from you, but later I returned them," the thief is believed, because the mouth that forbade is the mouth that permitted; but if the second person has witnesses to prove that the first person stole the money, and the first person continues to claim, without proof, that he has returned it, he is not believed and must return the money he stole. Why, then, did the Mishnah not illustrate the "mouth that forbade" argument by using a case of theft, instead of a case of real estate involving a father and a son?

Because of this objection, *Yad Ramah* rules in favor of *Ramban*, who maintains that a thief who claims to have returned stolen property is believed, even if witnesses testify to the theft, just as a debtor who claims to have returned his debt is believed, even if the loan was originally conferred in the presence of witnesses. Many Rishonim, however, follow *Rabbi Shlomo Min HaHar,* who rules that a thief who claims to have returned a stolen object is not believed.

Rashba explains that no proof can be brought from our Gemara, because it is considering cases in which we are in doubt as to whose claim to believe, whereas a thief is in any case not believed because he is a criminal. *Meiri* adds that in general we prefer to illustrate a law by using cases involving honest people and an ordinary monetary dispute, rather than by constructing a situation relevant only to thieves and other criminals. *Ritva* agrees with *Ramban*'s ruling, but argues that no proof can be brought from our passage one way or the other, because our Gemara is seeking a case that is as similar as possible to the ketubah disputes of the first chapter of the tractate, and a case of theft is no better for that purpose than the case of real estate actually presented in the Mishnah.

הַמַּלְוֶה אֶת חֲבֵירוֹ בְּעֵדִים Someone who lends to his fellow before witnesses. The Rishonim ask: Whenever a promissory note is drawn up, the borrower accepts that he will not be able to claim that he has repaid it unless he can

HALAKHAH

הַמַּלְוֶה אֶת חֲבֵירוֹ בְּעֵדִים אֵינוֹ צָרִיךְ לְפָרְעוֹ בְּעֵדִים Someone who lends to his fellow before witnesses need not repay him before witnesses. "If someone lends money in the presence of witnesses, without a document or an act of acquisition, the money need not be returned in the presence of witnesses. Therefore, if the borrower claims

TRANSLATION AND COMMENTARY

וְלִיתְנֵי [1]**But,** the Gemara continues, there is another case involving a debt that the Mishnah could have used to illustrate its principle. **Let the Mishnah state:** [2]**"Rabbi Yehoshua agrees that if someone says to another person: 'Your father lent me a maneh, and I have** already **repaid him part** of it,' [3]the borrower **is believed** regarding the other part without proof, because the mouth that forbade is the mouth that permitted." Here, argues the Gemara, there would be no problem with the last clause of the Mishnah, because it would teach us that if the son has independent proof that the defendant did borrow the money, the borrower is not believed about the remaining part. For when a creditor demands payment of a debt, and the debtor admits owing part of the money but insists that his debt is less than the amount claimed, the debtor is not believed unless he takes "the oath of one who admits part of a claim." Thus, by describing such a case, the Mishnah would be teaching us that a person who admits part of a debt need not take an oath if his claim is supported by the "mouth that forbade" argument; but if there is independent proof of the existence of the original debt, he must take the oath.

[1]וְלִיתְנֵי: [2]"מוֹדֶה רַבִּי יְהוֹשֻׁעַ בְּאוֹמֵר לַחֲבֵירוֹ: 'מָנֶה לְאָבִיךָ בְּיָדִי, וְהֶאֱכַלְתִּיו פְּרָס', [3]שֶׁהוּא נֶאֱמָן"!

LITERAL TRANSLATION

[1]But let [the Mishnah] teach: "Rabbi Yehoshua agrees that if someone says to his fellow: [2]'A maneh of your father's was in my possession, and I repaid (lit., "fed") him part,' [3]he is believed"!

RASHI

וניתני מודה רבי יהושע כו' והאכלתיו פרס — פרעתיו חציו, שהוא נאמן בלא שבועה, הואיל ואין שור שחוט לפניו. דאשמועינן רבותא, דאף על גב דמודה במקצת — פטור, הואיל ואינו תובעו.

LANGUAGE

פְּרָס Part. This word is derived from the root פרס or פרש, whose principal meaning is "to break." Accordingly, פרס means a fraction, or a part of something. Generally, when the word appears in the context of a certain quantity or sum, it refers to half of that sum, which is the simplest fraction. However, this is not necessarily the case here in our Gemara, and the essential meaning of the word is that a certain sum was borrowed, and part of it was repaid.

NOTES

prove this. Moreover, when any act is ratified by a formal act of acquisition, the parties are considered to have given permission to write it down. Thus, if the money was lent in the presence of witnesses and a formal act of acquisition was performed, the witnesses are permitted to draw up a document attesting to the debt. Even if the witnesses did not draw up such a document, the borrower should be regarded as having agreed that he cannot claim to have repaid without proof. Why, then, did the Mishnah not select such a case to illustrate its law?

Ra'ah and *Ritva* prove from our Gemara that the borrower does not need to prove that he repaid the debt if the debt had been ratified by a formal act of acquisition, but most Rishonim (*Sefer HaTerumot, Ra'avad,* and others) reject this view, and accept a ruling of *Rav Hai Gaon* that if a debt was ratified by a formal act of acquisition, the burden of proof is on the borrower.

מָנֶה לְאָבִיךָ בְּיָדִי A maneh of your father's was in my possession. The Gemara suggests that the Mishnah could have illustrated the "mouth that forbade" argument by using as an example the case of a borrower who admitted part of a debt, but it rejects this solution because of complications arising from the Tannaitic dispute about the oath imposed by the Torah on such borrowers. The Rishonim comment: All the previous suggestions of the Gemara were rejected because they could not be reconciled with the last clause of the Mishnah. This is the only suggestion that was rejected for a different reason. But surely this case could not be reconciled with the last clause either. For it would read: "If the son of the lender had witnesses to prove that the borrower had indeed borrowed the money from his father (so that the borrower's claim is no longer supported by the 'mouth that forbade' argument), then the borrower's claim to have repaid half is not believed." But surely this is not true! The witnesses only testify that the money was originally lent, not that it remained unpaid. If the borrower claims to have repaid half while the father was still alive, he should be believed, because a debt incurred in the presence of witnesses need not be returned in the presence of witnesses.

Shittah Mekubbetzet explains that this is in fact the Gemara's question: According to Rabbi Eliezer ben Ya'akov, the first clause of the Mishnah does not make sense (because he maintains that a partial admission is never believed without an oath, even when it is supported by the "mouth that forbade" argument), whereas according to the Sages the second clause does not make sense, because the borrower does not need to prove that he has repaid half, or even to take an oath, since a debt contracted in the presence of witnesses need not be returned in the presence of witnesses (see *Tosafot*'s view in the following note).

Ritva and *Ra'ah* explain that the last clause of the Mishnah could have been explained as referring to a case where the witnesses testify not only to the original loan, but also to the fact that the borrower admitted he had not yet repaid half of it when the father died. In the first clause, where there are no witnesses, and "the mouth that forbade is the mouth that permitted," the borrower would be believed about the half he claims to have repaid. But in the last clause, since he made his admission in the presence of witnesses, he could not deny that he owed at least half the money at the time of the father's death. Hence he would not be believed about the other half without an oath, as he is not "returning a lost object."

HALAKHAH

that he has repaid the debt, he is believed without proof, although he must take the special *heset* oath imposed by the Rabbis on anyone who denies a claim without proof." (*Rambam, Sefer Mishpatim, Hilkhot Malveh VeLoveh* 11:1; *Shulḥan Arukh, Ḥoshen Mishpat* 70:1.)

מָנֶה לְאָבִיךָ בְּיָדִי A maneh of your father's was in my possession. "If one person says to another: 'My father told me that you owe him a maneh,' and the borrower replies, 'I have already repaid half of it,' then the borrower need repay only the other half. Regarding the half that the

SAGES

רַבִּי אֱלִיעֶזֶר בֶּן יַעֲקֹב Rabbi Eliezer ben Ya'akov. There were two Tannaim of this name. The first belonged to the second generation of Tannaim, and lived when the Second Temple was still standing. The second belonged to the fourth generation. He was a student of Rabbi Akiva and a colleague of Rabbi Akiva's disciples. He is found in various passages in the Talmud discussing the Halakhah with them.

LITERAL TRANSLATION

[1]According to whom? [2]If according to the Rabbis, surely they say: [3]He is [like] a returner of a lost object. [4]If according to Rabbi Eliezer ben Ya'akov, [5]surely he says [that] he needs [to take] an oath.

[1]אַלִּיבָּא דְּמַאן? [2]אִי אַלִּיבָּא דְּרַבָּנַן, הָא אָמְרִי: [3]מֵשִׁיב אֲבֵידָה הָוֵי. [4]אִי אַלִּיבָּא דְּרַבִּי אֱלִיעֶזֶר בֶּן יַעֲקֹב, [5]הָא אָמַר שְׁבוּעָה בָּעֵי.

RASHI

אליבא דמאן – תנאי פליגי בהא מילתא בשבועות (מב,א), ואי אמר רבי יהושע הכי – לא כחד מנייהו הוא. דאי כרבנן הא אמרי אפילו תובעו וזה מודה במקצת – משיב אבידה הוא, דתנן בשבועות: "מנה לאבא בידך" – "אין לך בידי אלא חמשים דינר" – פטור, משום שהוא כמשיב אבידה. ומאי אשמעינן רבי יהושע באין שור שחוט? אפילו שור שחוט לפניו נמי נאמן! ואי אליבא דרבי אליעזר בן יעקב, כי לא תבע ליה נמי – האמר שבועה בעי.

TRANSLATION AND COMMENTARY

אַלִּיבָּא דְּמַאן [1]The Gemara rejects this possibility: The Mishnah could not have used "the oath of one who admits part of a claim" to illustrate its principle, because this law is itself the subject of a Tannaitic dispute between Rabbi Eliezer ben Ya'akov and the Rabbis (explained in detail below), and according to both opinions, the "mouth that forbade" argument does not apply. For **according to which** of the Tannaim would it make sense to apply the "mouth that forbade" argument to "the oath of one who admits part of a claim"? [2]**If** we maintain that it is **according to the Rabbis** who disagree with Rabbi Eliezer ben Ya'akov, **surely they say:** [3]Even where the creditor sues the debtor and the debtor admits part of the claim, **he is** regarded **as someone returning a lost object** and need not take an oath, even when his claim is not supported by the "mouth that forbade" argument! [4]And **if** we maintain that it is **according to Rabbi Eliezer ben Ya'akov,** [5]**surely he says that** every debtor who admits part of a claim **needs to take an oath,** even where his claim is supported by the "mouth that forbade" argument! Hence the Mishnah could not have used a case of debt to illustrate the "mouth that forbade" argument, and it was forced to use a case of real estate bought by the person in possession from the claimant's father while the claimant was still a minor, in accordance with Rav Huna's ruling, as explained above (17b).

NOTES

אַלִּיבָּא דְּמַאן According to whom? At first glance, the Gemara's question is difficult to understand. Admittedly, our Mishnah could not have been written by Rabbi Eliezer ben Ya'akov, because he maintains that the borrower must take an oath even if his claim is supported by the "mouth that forbade" argument. But why could it not have been written by the Sages? Perhaps the "mouth that forbade" argument is equivalent to "returning a lost object," and the borrower is believed without an oath only when the son of the lender has no independent proof of the debt (as in the first clause), but not if he can produce witnesses (as in the second clause)?

Our commentary follows *Rashi,* who explains that the "mouth that forbade" argument is in fact a silent *miggo* (see above, 16a). Now the Mishnah in *Shevuot* (38b) cites the Sages as considering the borrower to be "returning a lost object," even if the son of the lender presses him for payment, and in such a case the borrower has at most an ordinary *miggo* but not a silent *miggo.* Hence the first clause of our Mishnah could not have been written by the Sages.

According to *Tosafot,* the "mouth that forbade" argument is in fact a regular *miggo* (see above, 16a). Hence *Tosafot* disagrees with *Rashi,* and explains that the Sages could indeed have written the first clause of our Mishnah. According to this view, however, they could not have written the second clause. For even if the son has witnesses to attest to the debt, the borrower should still be believed when he claims to have repaid half, as he still has a *miggo,* because he could have claimed to have repaid the whole debt, since, according to the Sages, the psychology underlying the oath of partial admission does not apply to an inherited debt.

מֵשִׁיב אֲבֵידָה A returner of a lost object. In his book on the laws of oaths, *Rav Hai Gaon* outlined the rules that determine when a debtor who makes a partial admission is subject to an oath, and when he is considered to be "returning a lost object." He distinguishes between a case where the debtor denies ever borrowing part of the alleged debt, and a case where he claims to have repaid part of it. In the former case, to be considered a returner of lost objects the debtor must have made his admission before the creditor approached him, and the court must be satisfied that this was done in good faith, and not as an

HALAKHAH

borrower claims to have repaid, *Rambam* rules (apparently following the view of the Sages in our Gemara) that the borrower is believed without proof, and need not take any oath — not even the Rabbinic *heset* oath — because he is considered as one who has returned a lost object. *Ra'avad* rules that the borrower is not believed unless he takes a Torah oath (following the view of Rabbi Eliezer ben Ya'akov). *Maggid Mishneh* notes that *Rambam* ruled that the borrower is believed only if the son had no personal knowledge of the debt beyond what his father told him; but if the son claims to know about the debt from personal knowledge, it is possible that even *Rambam* would agree that the borrower must take an oath." (*Rambam, Sefer Mishpatim, Hilkhot To'en VeNit'an* 4:5; *Shulḥan Arukh, Ḥoshen Mishpat* 75:3,21,22.)

LITERAL TRANSLATION

[1]For it was taught: [2]"Rabbi Eliezer ben Ya'akov says: Sometimes a person takes an oath about his own claim. [3]How so? [4]'A maneh of your father's was in my possession, and I repaid him half,' [5]he takes an oath. [6]And this is [a case of] one who takes an oath about his own claim. [7]But the Sages say: He is only like a returner of a lost object, [8]and he is exempt." [9]But does Rabbi Eliezer ben Ya'akov not maintain [that] a returner of a lost object is exempt? [10]Rav said: [11]Where a minor claims from him.

[1]דְּתַנְיָא: [2]"רַבִּי אֱלִיעֶזֶר בֶּן יַעֲקֹב אוֹמֵר: פְּעָמִים שֶׁאָדָם נִשְׁבָּע עַל טַעֲנַת עַצְמוֹ. [3]כֵּיצַד? [4]'מָנֶה לְאָבִיךָ בְּיָדִי, וְהֶאֱכַלְתִּיו פְּרָס' [5]הֲרֵי זֶה נִשְׁבָּע. [6]וְזֶהוּ שֶׁנִּשְׁבָּע עַל טַעֲנַת עַצְמוֹ. [7]וַחֲכָמִים אוֹמְרִים: אֵינוֹ אֶלָּא כְּמֵשִׁיב אֲבֵידָה, [8]וּפָטוּר". [9]וְרַבִּי אֱלִיעֶזֶר בֶּן יַעֲקֹב לֵית לֵיהּ מֵשִׁיב אֲבֵידָה פָּטוּר? [10]אָמַר רַב: [11]בְּטוֹעֲנוֹ קָטָן.

RASHI

ורבי אליעזר לית ליה משיב אבידה פטור — מן השבועה, בתמיה, הא תקנתא דרבנן היא במסכת גיטין (מח,ב): המוצא מציאה לא ישבע, מפני תיקון העולם. וכיון דכי אינו תובעו נמי מחייב ליה שבועה — הרי אין לך משיב אבידה גדולה מזה, וחייב.

TRANSLATION AND COMMENTARY

דְּתַנְיָא [1]The Gemara now explains in detail the difference of opinion between Rabbi Eliezer ben Ya'akov and the Rabbis. **It was taught in a Baraita:** [2]"Rabbi Eliezer ben Ya'akov says: Sometimes a person takes an oath about his own claim. Even though nobody has claimed anything from him, he must still take 'the oath of one who admits part of a claim' to confirm his own statement. [3]**How so?** How can such a situation occur? [4]If one person says to another: **'Your father lent me a maneh and I have** already **repaid him half** of it,' [5]he is not believed unless **he takes an oath** that he really has repaid the other half, [6]**and this is the case of** a borrower **who takes an oath about his own claim.** [7]**But the Sages** disagree, and **say:** In a case such as this, the borrower **is regarded as someone who is returning a lost object,** because he could have remained silent and avoided paying anything. Thus the money was effectively lost to the creditor, and the borrower recovered it for him by his admission. [8]And the rule is that someone who returns a lost object **is exempt** from 'the oath of one who admits part of a claim.'" The Rabbis instituted (*Gittin* 48b) that if someone finds and returns a lost object, such as a wallet full of money, and the owner insists that there was more money in the wallet than the amount returned to him, the finder need not take an oath, even though technically he is admitting part of the owner's claim. The purpose of this enactment was to see to it that honest people would not be afraid to return lost objects.

וְרַבִּי אֱלִיעֶזֶר בֶּן יַעֲקֹב [9]**But,** objects the Gemara, **does Rabbi Eliezer ben Ya'akov not maintain that someone who returns a lost object is exempt** from "the oath of one who admits part of a claim," in accordance with the Rabbinic enactment? Why, then, should this person be required to take an oath, when nobody has claimed anything from him, and he has come forward of his own volition to return a sum of money that he admits to owing?

אָמַר רַב [10]In reply to this question, **Rav said:** The case in dispute between Rabbi Eliezer ben Ya'akov and the Sages is not one where nobody at all has claimed anything from the borrower. In such a case everyone would agree that the borrower is considered like someone who is returning lost property. [11]Rather, it is a case **where** the original creditor has died, leaving a child as his heir, and this **minor** then confronts the borrower and **claims** a maneh **from him,** which he alleges the borrower was lent by his late father. The

NOTES

attempt to evade the oath. In the latter case, there are two further conditions: (1) There must be no witnesses to testify that the debtor owes the creditor anything; and (2) there must be no general rumor that he owes him anything. If any one of these conditions is not met, the debtor is not considered to be "returning a lost object," and he is subject to the regular oath for his partial admission (*Shakh, Hoshen Mishpat* 88:32).

רַבִּי אֱלִיעֶזֶר בֶּן יַעֲקֹב וְרַבָּנַן Rabbi Eliezer ben Ya'akov and the Rabbis. The Rishonim had difficulty in deciding how to rule in this Tannaitic dispute. The Gemara (*Gittin* 67a) declares that "Rabbi Eliezer ben Ya'akov's teachings are few and perfect." Based on this statement, the Rishonim generally rule in favor of Rabbi Eliezer ben Ya'akov whenever he disagrees with another Sage. On the other hand, *Ramban* (*Shevuot* 42b) argues, based on a passage in tractate *Eruvin* (46b), that all statements of this kind are generalizations that are not completely accurate, and there may be cases where the Halakhah does not follow Rabbi Eliezer ben Ya'akov. In particular, it is not clear whether Rabbi Eliezer ben Ya'akov is to be followed even against the anonymous "Sages," who are presumed to outnumber him.

Most Rishonim, including *Rabbenu Ḥananel* and *Rambam,* follow a Geonic tradition and rule in favor of the Sages. *Ra'avad,* however, rules in favor of Rabbi Eliezer ben Ya'akov. *Rif* originally ruled in favor of the Sages, but in later years changed his opinion and ruled in favor of Rabbi Eliezer ben Ya'akov (see *Rif, Shevuot* 42b, and the comment of *Ran*).

אָמַר רַב בְּטוֹעֲנוֹ קָטָן Rav said: Where a minor claims from him. According to Rav, even Rabbi Eliezer ben Ya'akov would agree that where the debtor comes forward

LITERAL TRANSLATION

[1] But surely the Master said: [2] We do not take an oath because of the claim of a deaf-mute, an imbecile, or a minor!

[3] What is a minor? An adult. [4] And why does he call him a minor? [5] Because with regard to his father's affairs he is [like] a minor.

[1]וְהָאָמַר מָר: [2]אֵין נִשְׁבָּעִין עַל טַעֲנַת חֵרֵשׁ, שׁוֹטֶה, וְקָטָן! [3]מַאי קָטָן? גָּדוֹל. [4]וְאַמַּאי קָרֵי לֵיהּ קָטָן? [5]דִּלְגַבֵּי מִילֵּי דְּאָבִיו קָטָן הוּא.

RASHI

אין נשבעין על טענת חרש שוטה וקטן – משנה היא בשבועות.

TRANSLATION AND COMMENTARY

borrower then admits that he borrowed the money, but claims that he has already repaid half of it. Normally we pay no attention to the claims of a child. Hence the Sages maintain that the child's claim is to be ignored and the borrower is to be considered as one who came forward of his own volition, without any demand on the part of the creditor. Consequently the Sages exempt the borrower from the oath, because his action is tantamount to returning lost property. But Rabbi Eliezer ben Ya'akov argues that even though the claim of the child is itself not very strong, nevertheless since the borrower did not come forward of his own volition but waited until pressed by the child, he is regarded as an ordinary person who admits part of a claim, and not as someone who is returning a lost object.

וְהָאָמַר מָר [1] **But surely,** the Gemara objects, **a certain Sage** (the anonymous author of the Mishnah in tractate *Shevuot* 38b) **said:** [2] **We do not take an oath in response to the claim of a deaf-mute, an imbecile, or a minor!** Commenting on this Mishnah, the Gemara (*Shevuot* 42a and *Bava Kamma* 106b) infers from a verse (Exodus 22:6) that a litigant can be compelled to take an oath only if his opponent was a legally competent person throughout the transaction. How, then, could Rabbi Eliezer ben Ya'akov attribute significance to the claim of a minor?

מַאי קָטָן [3] The Gemara answers: To **what** kind of **minor** was Rav referring? To **an adult** son of the original creditor, who demanded payment of the debt owed to his father, as explained above. [4] **And why does** Rav **call** this son **a minor,** if in fact he was a legally competent adult? [5] **Because with regard to his father's affairs he is** considered **like a minor.** Even an adult son is not usually familiar with his father's financial affairs. Nevertheless, Rabbi Eliezer ben Ya'akov argued that the borrower's action in responding positively to the

NOTES

completely of his own accord, without even a minor demanding money from him, he is considered a returner of a lost object and is exempt from the oath. The commentators ask: Why could the Mishnah not have illustrated the "mouth that forbade" argument according to Rabbi Eliezer ben Ya'akov by using a case where the debtor came forward completely of his own accord and admitted that he still owed half? In such a case, the debtor would be exempt as a returner of lost objects in the first clause, where the creditor's son has no independent proof of the debt, but would be required to take an oath in the second clause, where witnesses testify to the debt.

Shittah Mekubbetzet notes that this objection would not pose a problem according to *Tosafot* and other Rishonim who hold that the "mouth that forbade" argument is a regular *miggo* rather than a silent one. According to these Rishonim, the "mouth that forbade" argument applies even where the plaintiff has made a claim, so long as he has not produced witnesses, whereas according to Rabbi Eliezer ben Ya'akov, "returning a lost object" applies only where the creditor's son has made no claim at all. Therefore, if the Mishnah had selected this case to illustrate its ruling, the second clause would be misleading, because it would imply that the debtor is considered a returner of a lost object and is believed unless the creditor's son produces witnesses, whereas in fact it would be sufficient for the creditor's son to make a claim without witnesses. But this solution does not accord with the viewpoint of *Rashi,* who maintains that the "mouth that forbade" argument applies only when the creditor's son makes no claim, thus providing the debtor with a silent *miggo.* According to *Rashi,* the Mishnah could indeed have selected this case to illustrate its ruling, and the second clause would teach us that even where the plaintiff makes no claim, the defendant is not believed if witnesses testify to the original obligation. Why, then, did the Mishnah not select this case to illustrate its ruling?

This question is discussed at length by the Aḥaronim (see *Maharshal, Ḥatam Sofer,* and others). *Maharsha* explains that, according to Rabbi Eliezer ben Ya'akov, the hypothetical second clause of the Mishnah would be untrue. For if the debtor claims to have repaid part of the debt and the creditor's son makes no claim at all, the debtor is considered like a returner of lost objects and is believed, even where there are witnesses to attest to the original loan. Testimony about the original loan is irrelevant if the creditor does not claim that the debt is still outstanding, since a person who borrowed money in the presence of witnesses is not required to repay in the presence of witnesses (see also *Rosh,* who cites a similar explanation).

מַאי קָטָן? גָּדוֹל What is a minor? An adult. The Gemara explains that the adult son was called a minor because he was unfamiliar with his father's affairs. But in the parallel

HALAKHAH

אֵין נִשְׁבָּעִין עַל טַעֲנַת חֵרֵשׁ שׁוֹטֶה וְקָטָן We do not take an oath because of the claims of a deaf-mute, an imbecile, or a minor. "If a deaf-mute, an imbecile, or a minor claims that a sum of money is owed to him, and the debtor

TRANSLATION AND COMMENTARY

son's claim is not the equivalent of returning a lost object, because he did not come forward of his own volition.

אִי הָכִי [1]But the Gemara objects: **If in fact** we are referring to a case where the creditor's adult son made a claim against the debtor, then it does not fit the language used by Rabbi Eliezer ben Ya'akov. He said: "Sometimes a person takes an oath about his own claim," i.e., where the debtor comes forward of his own volition. But **is this "his own claim"?** [2]**It is the claim of someone else** — the son! For according to Rav's revised explanation, the debtor admitted nothing until he was sued by the creditor's son.

טַעֲנַת אֲחֵרִים [3]The Gemara answers: Rabbi Eliezer ben Ya'akov called it "his own claim," even though **it was** really **the claim of others,** because it was **his own admission** that obliged him to take the oath. For a person who denies owing anything is believed by Torah law without taking an oath.

כּוּלְּהִי [4]But the Gemara objects again: **All claims** that lead to the oath of partial admission **are** a combination of **the claims of others and** the defendant's **own admission!** In every case the creditor makes a claim and the debtor chooses to admit part of it. In what way is this case different? Why did Rabbi Eliezer ben Ya'akov say about this case: "*Sometimes* a person takes an oath about *his own* claim"?

[1]אִי הָכִי, "טַעֲנַת עַצְמוֹ"? [2]טַעֲנַת אֲחֵרִים הִיא! [3]טַעֲנַת אֲחֵרִים וְהוֹדָאַת עַצְמוֹ. [4]כּוּלְּהִי טַעֲנָתָא טַעֲנַת אֲחֵרִים וְהוֹדָאַת עַצְמוֹ נִינְהוּ!

LITERAL TRANSLATION

[1]If so, [is this] "his own claim"? [2]It is the claim of others!

[3]It is the claim of others and his own admission.

[4]All claims are the claim of others and his own admission!

RASHI

טענת אחרים הוא – ומאי "פעמים" דקאמר? ומאי "טענת עצמו"?

NOTES

passage in tractate *Shevuot* (42b), the Gemara concludes that Rabbi Eliezer ben Ya'akov and the Sages disagree only in a case where the son claims with certainty that the debtor owes the money. But if the son has no real knowledge of the debt at all, and merely assumes that it is still outstanding, even Rabbi Eliezer ben Ya'akov agrees that the partial admission amounts to returning a lost object.

There is a difference of opinion among the Rishonim as to how much the son really knew about his father's affairs. *Ramban* — and apparently *Rif* — explains that the dispute between Rabbi Eliezer ben Ya'akov and the Sages concerns a case where the son was present when the loan was finalized and had personal knowledge of it. *Ra'avad* explains that the dispute concerns a case where the son had no personal knowledge of the loan, but received detailed information from his father. But if the son had direct knowledge of the loan, even the Sages would agree that the debtor must take the oath.

The dispute revolves around a passage in tractate *Shevuot* (47a), in which the Gemara assumes that when a son makes a definite claim in the name of his father, the defendant must take the oath of partial admission. *Rif* explains that this passage follows the view of Rabbi Eliezer ben Ya'akov, and that the Sages would consider the defendant to be a returner of lost objects. *Ra'avad,* however, explains that this passage can follow either opinion, since it refers to a son who was directly involved. Some Rishonim (*Rabbenu Ḥananel, Rashba*) dismiss the proof from the Gemara (47a) by arguing that, according to the Gemara's conclusion, the dispute between Rabbi Eliezer ben Ya'akov and the Sages concerns only a case where the son was an actual minor who made a definite claim; but where the son was an adult (as in 47a), everyone agrees that an oath is imposed. *Rashi,* however, insists that the dispute concerns both a minor and an adult son.

טַעֲנַת אֲחֵרִים וְהוֹדָאַת עַצְמוֹ It is the claim of others and his own admission. Our commentary follows *Rashi*, who explains (in the parallel passage in *Gittin* 51b) that the Gemara is suggesting that the expression "his own claim" should be stretched to mean "his own partial admission of the plaintiff's claim." The Gemara then objects that, according to this explanation, the expression would cover every partial admission, including those that are in no way subject to dispute between Rabbi Eliezer ben Ya'akov and the Sages. The Gemara then accepts this objection, and turns to another explanation (see following note).

Meiri and *Rabbenu Ḥananel* have a very different explanation of this matter, according to which the expression "his own claim" is equivalent to "returning a lost object," and "his own admission to another's claim" is the equivalent of a regular partial admission, which is not considered the return of a lost object. The Gemara explains that the dispute between Rabbi Eliezer ben Ya'akov and the Sages refers to an adult son, which the Sages consider as an instance of "his own claim" and Rabbi Eliezer considers as a regular case of "his own admission to another's claim." The Gemara then objects that, regardless of whether the debtor or the son spoke first, any case in which the son makes a claim is manifestly "his own admission to another's claim"; why, then, do the Sages exempt the debtor as a returner of lost objects? The

HALAKHAH

admits part of the claim, the debtor need pay only the part he admits, and need not take the normal Torah oath. He must, however, take the Rabbinic *heset* oath. This is true regardless of whether the alleged debt was owed to the minor directly, or was inherited from his father," following the Gemara's conclusion. (*Rambam, Sefer Mishpatim, Hilkhot To'en VeNit'an* 5:9; *Shulḥan Arukh, Ḥoshen Mishpat* 96:1-2.)

TRANSLATION AND COMMENTARY

אֶלָּא [1] **Rather,** says the Gemara, in the light of the words chosen by Rabbi Eliezer ben Ya'akov, we must abandon this explanation. In fact, Rabbi Eliezer ben Ya'akov and the Sages are referring to a minor, after all. For the Mishnah in tractate *Shevuot* that disqualified claims made by a minor was referring to a claim made by the minor on his own behalf, regarding a property transaction in which he himself allegedly engaged. In such cases, the minor's words have no legal standing. But if the minor inherited a debt owed to his father, the verse cited in tractate *Shevuot* does not apply, and the borrower may indeed be required to take an oath. [2] The Gemara explains: **The disagreement** between Rabbi Eliezer ben Ya'akov and the Sages about a minor revolves **around** the following **explanation** given **by Rabbah.** [3] **For Rabbah said: Why did the Torah state** [4] **that someone who admits part of a claim** against him **must take an oath** regarding the rest of the claim, which he denies? Why did the Torah not consider all cases of partial admission to be the equivalent of returning a lost object? For if the borrower had simply denied the claim, he would have been believed, since the law is that a person who denies all liability is believed without an oath,

[1] אֶלָּא, [2] הָכָא בִּדְרַבָּה קָמִיפַּלְגִי. [3] דְּאָמַר רַבָּה: מִפְּנֵי מָה אָמְרָה תּוֹרָה: [4] ״מוֹדֶה מִקְצָת הַטַּעֲנָה

LITERAL TRANSLATION

[1] Rather, [2] here they disagree about Rabbah's [explanation]. [3] For Rabbah said: Why did the Torah say: [4] "He who admits part of a claim

RASHI

אלא הכא בדרבה קא מיפלגי – אלא לעולם בטוענו קטן. ודקשיא לך אין נשבעין על טענת קטן – הני מילי בשטוענו קטן "אני נתתיו לך", וקרא כתיב "כי יתן איש אל רעהו" – ולא קטן, ומהכא יליף לה בשבועות. אבל הכא שבא בטענת אביו – אית ליה לרבי אליעזר בן יעקב נשבעין. ורבנן פליגי עליה אפילו בטוענו גדול, וקרו ליה משיב אבידה, ובדרבה קא מיפלגי.

NOTES

Gemara answers that, because of Rabbah's reasoning, the claim of the son is not the same as the claim of the creditor himself; hence the Sages do indeed consider this to be a case of "his own claim." According to this explanation, the text of the Gemara must be amended to remove the word "rather," since the Gemara does not change its explanation (see following note).

אֶלָּא, הָכָא בִּדְרַבָּה קָמִיפַּלְגִי Rather, here they disagree about Rabbah's explanation. The word אֶלָּא, which we translate as "rather," is a technical term meaning that the Gemara accepts that the previous line of argument has been refuted, and is not attempting to answer the objection immediately preceding, but is retracing its steps and presenting an alternative answer to an earlier objection. There is, however, no direct way of determining how far back the Gemara is going, and this is often the subject of dispute among the commentators. Thus, in our passage, the word "rather" means that the Gemara agrees that its attempt to explain the words, "his own claim," as "the claim of others and his own admission," was unsuccessful, and it is looking for another solution to the problem of the ruling by Rabbi Eliezer ben Ya'akov about the returner of lost objects. It is not clear, however, how much of the previous discussion still remains unrefuted.

Our commentary follows *Rashi,* who explains that the Gemara still accepts Rav's explanation that the creditor's son was a minor, and is offering an alternative response to the objection that a minor's claims are legally insignificant. Previously the Gemara argued that Rav's "minor" was really an adult, but it now concedes that he was indeed a minor. For even if the claim of a minor regarding his own property is of no consequence, the claim of a minor who has inherited a debt from his father may still be significant, because of its psychological effect, as explained by Rabbah. According to *Rashi,* the dispute between Rabbi Eliezer ben Ya'akov and the Sages actually applies to any son, adult or minor, but the Baraita illustrated the dispute using the case of a minor in order to point out that Rabbi Eliezer ben Ya'akov does not consider the debtor to be a returner of lost objects, whatever claim is made against him, even where the claimant is a minor and the defendant's response is legally "a claim made of his own accord." (See also *Rashba,* who gives a similar explanation, although he differs with *Rashi* regarding the adult son.)

Tosafot explains that the Gemara still maintains that Rav was referring to an adult son, who is called a minor because he is unfamiliar with his father's affairs, but if the son really *was* a minor, Rabbi Eliezer ben Ya'akov would agree that the debtor is a returner of lost objects. According to this explanation, the Gemara has given up its attempt to explain away the words "his own claim" linguistically, and instead argues that Rabbi Eliezer calls the claim of the son "his own claim" because of Rabbah's argument. According to Rabbah, the reason a creditor's unsupported claim can force a debtor to take an oath is due to psychological considerations; but if these do not apply, the debtor need not respond at all, but if he does respond, he is in effect obligating himself to pay part by "his own claim." Thus Rabbi Eliezer ben Ya'akov argues that claims which the Sages consider to be "his own claim" can sometimes oblige the debtor to take an oath.

מִפְּנֵי מָה אָמְרָה תּוֹרָה Why did the Torah say? Rabbah's language suggests that he is asking a question about the reasoning underlying the Torah's decrees, and indeed many Rishonim understand him in precisely this way. The Rishonim note, however, that there is a Tannaitic dispute (*Bava Metzia* 115a) as to whether our understanding of the Torah's reasoning is of any significance in determining the Halakhah, and this passage, in which Rabbah analyzes the reasoning behind a law and insists that it applies only where the reasoning applies, would appear to be related to that dispute. According to Rabbi Shimon, when the reasoning behind a law is obvious and unambiguous, the law applies only when the reasoning applies. Thus, when the Torah forbade seizing a pledge from a widow (Deuteronomy 24:17), it is clear from the context that the intention was to protect a helpless, poor person. Hence Rabbi Shimon rules that this law does not apply if the widow happens to be wealthy. Rabbi Yehudah, on the other hand, rules that the laws of the Torah are completely independent of their reasoning, even where the reasoning itself is

SAGES

רַבָּה Rabbah. Rabbah bar Naḥmani the Priest, called Rabbah for short, was one of the greatest Babylonian Amoraim of the third generation. Rabbah studied under Rav Huna, Rav's disciple, and his entire method in the Halakhah followed that of Rav. He also studied Torah with Rav Yehudah and Rav Naḥman, and was a student and colleague of Rav Ḥisda. While still a young man he was considered greater than all the others of his generation in his sharpness of mind, and he was called "the uprooter of mountains" (עוֹקֵר הָרִים). After Rav Yehudah's death, Rabbah was chosen, despite his youth, to be the head of the yeshivah of Pumbedita, though he did not accept the full appointment until close to the time of his death. Rabbah was involved in Halakhic discussions with all the great Sages of his generation, and the famous controversies between him and his colleague, Rav Yosef (in which the Halakhah follows Rabbah in almost every instance), are an important element of the Babylonian Talmud.

Rabbah trained many students. In fact, all the Sages of the following generation were his students, especially his nephew, Abaye, his outstanding student. His private life was full of suffering, and his sons apparently died in his lifetime. He was also very poor, supporting himself with difficulty by agricultural labor. The people of his city also treated him badly. Although Rabbah died relatively young, he established himself as one of the pillars of the Babylonian Talmud. His son Rava (רָבָא בְּרֵיהּ דְּרַבָּה) was an important Sage in the following generation.

TRANSLATION AND COMMENTARY

because the burden of proof falls on the creditor. Hence the creditor has no way of recovering his debt unless the debtor is honest andfulfills his obligation. For that reason the debtor's partial admission amounts to returning a lost object, and he should be exempt from taking an oath. [1] Rabbah answers that the oath of partial admission is based on a psychological **presumption** regarding the behavior of the defendant. [2] We presume **that a person would not be so insolent** as to stand **before his creditor** and deny his debt. For the creditor knows the truth, and it is difficult to lie to him to his face. Hence the borrower is not someone who is returning a lost object. We must, therefore, try to explain his behavior as follows: It is possible that the borrower really owes the full sum and is lying when he denies part of it. [3] Indeed, **he would have preferred to deny it all, and** the only reason [4] **he did not totally deny it is because a person would not be so insolent** as to deny the claim completely, as we have explained. [18B] [5] Hence the debtor feels emotionally compelled to admit his debt, **and he would have admitted all of**

יִשָּׁבַע״? [1] חֲזָקָה [2] אֵין אָדָם מֵעִיז פָּנָיו בִּפְנֵי בַּעַל חוֹבוֹ. [3] וְהַאי בְּכוּלֵּהּ בָּעֵי דְּלִכְפְּרֵיהּ, [4] וְהַאי דְּלָא כָּפַר לֵיהּ מִשּׁוּם דְּאֵין אָדָם מֵעִיז פָּנָיו הוּא. [18B] [5] וּבְכוּלֵּהּ בָּעֵי דְּלוֹדֵי לֵיהּ,

LITERAL TRANSLATION

shall swear"? [1] [Because of] a presumption [that] [2] a person is not [so] insolent before his lender. [3] And this [person] wanted to deny the whole [claim], [4] and [the reason] that he did not deny it is because a person is not [so] insolent. [18B] [5] And he wanted to admit all of it to him,

BACKGROUND

אֵין אָדָם מֵעִיז פָּנָיו A person would not be so insolent. The assumption here is psychological, and it is based on normal human behavior and the motivations of normal people. Since every legal loan discussed in the Talmud is a loan without interest, the very act of lending money is an act of kindness toward the recipient, and we assume that a person feels grateful toward someone who has done him a kindness, and that he would be ashamed to lie to him and deny the whole transaction.

וְהַאי בְּכוּלֵּהּ בָּעֵי דְּלִכְפְּרֵיהּ And this person wanted to deny the whole claim. Rabbah's explanation is an effort to reconstruct what transpired in the mind of the man who denied part of the claim against him. The various stages in the man's thinking are described: his desire not to pay at all, and, by contrast, his feeling of shame (or of gratitude), which prevents him from denying the entire debt; the tendency, on the other hand, to acknowledge the entire debt; and his reluctance to undertake to pay a sum which he does not possess. Finally, he reaches a sort of inner compromise: admitting only part of the debt, yet appeasing his conscience with respect to the rest of the obligation by promising himself that he will pay it all when he can.

NOTES

not in dispute. Our passage would appear to follow Rabbi Shimon, against the Halakhah, which follows Rabbi Yehudah.

Shittah Mekubbetzet cites an opinion that Rabbah's explanation does indeed follow the opinion of Rabbi Shimon and not that of Rabbi Yehudah. According to this explanation, when the Gemara states that Rabbi Eliezer ben Ya'akov and the Sages "disagree about the statement of Rabbah," it means that the Sages accept the Halakhic significance of Rabbah's explanation of the Torah's reasoning, following Rabbi Shimon, whereas Rabbi Eliezer ben Ya'akov maintains that Rabbah's statement has no Halakhic significance, following Rabbi Yehudah. Most Rishonim, however, reject this explanation.

According to *Rashi* and other Rishonim, who insist that "returning a lost object" is in fact identical with the Rabbinic decree exempting a "finder of a found object" from taking an oath, this objection does not arise. For Rabbi Yehudah does not disagree with Rabbi Shimon that the reasoning behind the law is as he states; he merely argues that the Torah's reasoning has no Halakhic impact. Hence, even if Rabbah is explaining the reasoning behind the Torah law of the oath of partial admissions, this is not problematic, so long as the practical implications are only on the Rabbinic level. But according to those Rishonim who insist that "returning a lost object" is in fact a Torah exemption, this passage is difficult to understand.

Tosafot argues that Rabbah's explanation has nothing to do with the Tannaitic dispute about the Halakhic significance of the Torah's reasoning. According to this explanation, Rabbah is troubled by the fact that the oath of partial admissions conflicts with the idea of *miggo*. A person who admits part of a claim, where he could have successfully denied the whole claim, has an obvious *miggo* which the Torah does not accept for some reason, and this could imply that the Torah rejects the very concept of *miggo* altogether. Hence Rabbah explains that the debtor has no *miggo* because he is under psychological pressure to admit something. But where there is a valid *miggo* — as in the case of the returner of a lost object — the claimant is believed on the basis of the *miggo* without taking the oath.

Meiri points out that this explanation does not fit Rabbah's language very well. In addition, it is not at all clear that *miggo* is effective to exempt a person from taking an oath, and indeed most authorities rule against this idea. *Meiri* explains that at times it is difficult to tell whether a claim should be categorized as a partial admission or as a total denial. Hence Rabbah asks why the Torah made this distinction in the first place, in order to use the Torah's reasoning as a defining characteristic.

אֵין אָדָם מֵעִיז פָּנָיו בִּפְנֵי בַּעַל חוֹבוֹ A person is not so insolent before his creditor. There are three major explanations of this idea in the Rishonim. *Rashi* explains that a person who has borrowed money owes a debt of gratitude to the lender (particularly since the Torah forbids charging interest), and while he may be tempted to deny the debt in order to steal the money, his conscience will inhibit him from doing so while directly confronting the lender. The Rishonim note that this explanation is satisfactory only when the debt was a regular loan, but not in other instances where the oath of partial admission applies — such as if the debt arose out of a payment for damage, part of which the defendant contests (see *Shevuot* 44b), or if it concerned a deposit, part of which the recipient denies receiving (see *Shevuot* 43a).

Our commentary follows *Riva,* who explains that a person who owes money finds it hard to deny his debt when confronting a person who knows the truth. *Rabbenu Tam* explains that people find it difficult to tell a total lie, and prefer to say something that has an element of truth in it. The dispute between these three Rishonim revolves around a passage in tractate *Bava Kamma* (107a) in which the Gemara states that Rabbah's reasoning applies primarily to loans, and, according to one reading, not to deposits at all. The precise interpretation of this passage has important Halakhic implications regarding the law (Exodus 22:6-12) that a bailee who claims that a deposit held by him was stolen or destroyed must take an oath (see *Tosafot's* comments, *Bava Kamma* 107a).

וּבְכוּלֵּהּ בָּעֵי דְּלוֹדֵי לֵיהּ And he wanted to admit all of it to him. This part of the Gemara's argument is puzzling. It has already established that the Torah imposed an oath on

[1]וְהַאי דְּלָא אוֹדֵי לֵיהּ כִּי הֵיכִי דְּלִישְׁתַּמֵּיט לֵיהּ. [2]וְסָבַר: עַד דַּהֲוָה לִי זוּזֵי, [3]וּפָרַעְנָא לֵיהּ. [4]וְרַחֲמָנָא אָמַר: רְמֵי שְׁבוּעָה עֲלֵיהּ [5]כִּי הֵיכִי דְּלוֹדֵי לֵיהּ בְּכוּלֵּיהּ.

[6]רַבִּי אֱלִיעֶזֶר בֶּן יַעֲקֹב סָבַר: [7]לָא שְׁנָא בּוֹ וְלָא שְׁנָא בִּבְנוֹ — [8]אֵינוֹ מֵעִיז, [9]וְהִלְכָּךְ לָאו מֵשִׁיב אֲבֵידָה הָוֵי.

TRANSLATION AND COMMENTARY

it. [1]**The** only **reason that he did not admit** the whole claim, but only part of it, **was in order to put off** the creditor temporarily. [2]The debtor is short of money, **and he thinks:** I will pay my creditor as much as I can afford now, and regarding the rest **I will put him off until I have** enough **money,** [3]**and** then **I will repay him.** Therefore, since it is possible that the partial admission is the result of these conflicting pressures on the defendant, [4]**the Torah says: Impose an oath on him** [5]in order to induce him **to make a complete admission** of the claim against him. The difference between a person returning a lost object and a person who admits part of a claim is that the former was in no way pressed to come forward, whereas the debtor may have felt emotionally compelled by the presence of his creditor to admit at least part of the claim.

רַבִּי אֱלִיעֶזֶר בֶּן יַעֲקֹב [6]Following Rabbah's reasoning, we can explain the difference of opinion between Rabbi Eliezer ben Ya'akov and the Sages as follows: **Rabbi Eliezer ben Ya'akov maintains** that [7]**there is no difference between the** original **lender and his** minor **son** — [8]if either of them presses **the borrower,** the latter feels compelled to admit part of the claim, because he **is not so insolent** as to deny his debt to his creditor's face. [9]**Therefore** the debtor **is not** considered **like a person returning a lost object,** even though the minor's claim itself is worthless, and the debtor is taking an oath merely because of his own unsolicited claim.

LITERAL TRANSLATION

[1]and [the reason] that he did not admit to him is in order to put him off. [2]And he thinks: [I will put him off] until I have money, [3]and [then] I will repay him. [4]And the Torah (lit., "the Merciful One") says: Impose an oath on him [5]so that he will admit all of it to him.

[6]Rabbi Eliezer ben Ya'akov maintains: [7]There is no difference [between] him [the lender] and his son — [8]he [the borrower] is not [so] insolent, [9]and therefore he is not [like] a returner of a lost object.

RASHI

לא שנא בו ולא שנא בבנו — ואפילו הוא קטן. **אינו מעיז** — ולהכי קרי ליה טענת עצמו, משום דטענת קטן בעלמא לית בה מששא.

NOTES

a person who admits part of a claim because he may be acting under psychological pressure to admit at least part of the claim. What difference does it make that he admitted only part and not all of it?

In our commentary we have followed *Rosh* and most of the Rishonim, who explain that the Gemara's reasoning is as follows: If this person in fact owes the full sum but cannot bring himself to deny his debt in the face of his creditor, how does he manage to deny part of it? And if this person is capable of denying part of his debt, why does he not deny it completely? Surely the most likely explanation is that he is simply telling the truth! The Gemara answers that it is possible that he owes the full sum but cannot afford to pay all of it now, and so steels himself to deny the part he cannot afford to repay at present, rationalizing that he will pay it later.

Rashi (*Bava Metzia* 3b) explains the Gemara differently and argues that it is asking a totally different question. He points out that, generally, under Jewish law, oaths are imposed only on people who are considered honest. A known criminal is not permitted to take an oath, because he will probably swear falsely. Oaths are designed primarily to influence honest people who may be tempted to rationalize and tell a partial truth, or to impose accuracy on people whose recollection may be hazy. Following this reasoning, the Gemara (*Bava Metzia* 5b) asks whether an oath is also imposed on a person who has no previous criminal record, but who is accused of seeking to withhold money without any excuse. Do we impose an oath in the hope that this will cause the purported thief to reconsider? Or do we say that, to the degree that he is suspected of theft, he is disqualified from taking an oath? The Gemara cites an Amoraic dispute on this matter, and most Rishonim agree that we rule that a person who is merely suspected of theft is permitted to take an oath.

Rashi explains that the Gemara's question here is based on precisely this idea: How can we impose an oath on a person who admits part of a claim, since to the degree that he is suspected of lying he is suspected of theft, and hence of being prepared to swear falsely? The Gemara's answer is that the debtor could be an honest person who is justifying his action as a temporary measure until he can raise the rest of the money. The Rishonim note that *Rashi*'s explanation is not consistent with the consensus among the Rishonim — that in practice a person who is merely suspected of theft is permitted to take an oath. The Aḥaronim discuss whether *Rashi* disagrees with the other Rishonim and rules in favor of the opinion that a person suspected of theft may not take an oath, or whether there is some distinction between the Gemara here and the Gemara in *Bava Metzia*.

כִּי הֵיכִי דְּלִישְׁתַּמֵּיט לֵיהּ In order to put him off. The debtor has no intention of denying the debt permanently, but only wants to gain extra time. Nevertheless, the Torah imposes an oath on him, as one is not permitted to delay payment unilaterally in this way. The Rishonim explain that even if the debtor tells himself that he will repay the debt eventually, there is a danger that once he leaves the court

TRANSLATION AND COMMENTARY

[1]By contrast, **the Sages maintain:** A debtor **is not so insolent** as to deny a debt to the face of **his creditor himself,** [2]**but toward his** creditor's minor **son he would be** willing to display **insolence** and deny the claim completely, because the presence of the son exerts little emotional influence on him. Since the minor's claim itself is worthless, the debtor's statement is legally viewed as unsolicited. Thus the debtor could easily have denied the whole claim without feeling any remorse, and the creditor's son would have had no recourse. [3]**But since** the debtor **was not** in fact **so insolent** and did not deny the whole claim, but admitted part of it, [4]**he is** considered **like someone returning a lost object,** and is exempt from the oath, in accordance with the general law which exempts those who dutifully return lost objects from having to establish their honesty by taking an oath.

MISHNAH הָעֵדִים שֶׁאָמְרוּ [5]This Mishnah considers another case in which a claim is accepted only when "the mouth that forbade is the mouth that permitted." Under Jewish law, the strongest evidence is the testimony of two qualified witnesses, once such testimony has been thoroughly examined in court and found credible. After witnesses have testified, they may not retract their testimony unless the retraction is supported by the "mouth that forbade" argument. Under Talmudic law, a document signed by a pair of witnesses is considered the equivalent of testimony in court, provided the authenticity of the signatures has been established. However, **if** a promissory note is brought to court to be certified because the debtor claims that it is a forgery, and **the witnesses** who signed the document come forward and say: [6]**"This is our handwriting"** — thereby establishing the authenticity of the document — [7]**"but** even though the document was signed by us, and we are now qualified witnesses, the document is not valid, because when we signed it **we were** acting **under duress** and were forced to sign a false document," [8]or alternatively: **"We were minors** at the time,"

[1]וְרַבָּנַן סָבְרִי: בּוֹ הוּא דְּאֵינוֹ מֵעִיז, [2]אֲבָל בִּבְנוֹ מֵעִיז, [3]וּמִדְּלָא הֵעִיז, [4]מֵשִׁיב אֲבֵידָה הָוֵי.

מִשְׁנָה [5]הָעֵדִים שֶׁאָמְרוּ: [6]"כְּתַב יָדֵינוּ הוּא זֶה, [7]אֲבָל אֲנוּסִים הָיִינוּ, [8]קְטַנִּים הָיִינוּ,

LITERAL TRANSLATION

[1]And the Sages maintain: It is toward him [the lender] that he is not [so] insolent, [2]but toward his son he may be [so] insolent, [3]and since he was not [so] insolent, [4]he is [like] a returner of a lost object.

MISHNAH [5][If] witnesses said: [6]"This is our handwriting, [7]but we were under duress, [8]we were minors,

RASHI

אבל בבנו מעיז — ואפילו הוא גדול.

משנה העדים שאמרו כו׳ — שהיו מעידים על חתימתם לקיים את השטר.

NOTES

and no longer needs to confront the creditor, he will change his mind and decide not to pay at all (*Rosh* and others).

It should be noted that the debtor need not be desperately poor for this kind of self-justification to occur to him. Even wealthy people sometimes decide that they "cannot afford" to do their duty because of "urgent needs."

Maharam Schiff (*Gittin* 51b) brings support from this Gemara for a ruling of *Rambam* (*Hilkhot Malveh VeLoveh* 13:6), that even if the debtor and the creditor agree about the amount of a debt, and the sole matter in dispute is whether the debt has already fallen due, the debtor can still be subject to a Torah oath.

HALAKHAH

הָעֵדִים שֶׁאָמְרוּ: כְּתַב יָדֵינוּ הוּא זֶה If witnesses said: "This is our handwriting." "If witnesses have signed a promissory note, and the debtor challenges the note's authenticity, and there is no way to certify it except by summoning the witnesses themselves, and the witnesses admit that they signed the document, but immediately add that they were minors or relatives at the time (and have since grown up or ceased to be related), or that there was some mistake, or that there was some condition attached to the debt that was not mentioned in the note — even if only one witness testifies to the problem and the other denies it — in all these cases, the witnesses are believed, and the document is not certified. But if the signatures on the document can be authenticated without summoning the witnesses, and the witnesses nevertheless come forward and authenticate their signatures and testify to one of these problems, the witnesses are not believed, because the signature of witnesses on a document is considered like oral testimony that has already been examined in court, and once a witness has given such testimony, he may not return to court to retract it or alter it," following our Mishnah. (*Rambam, Sefer Shofetim, Hilkhot Edut* 3:6; *Shulḥan Arukh, Ḥoshen Mishpat* 46:37.)

אֲנוּסִים הָיִינוּ We were under duress. "If the witnesses admit signing the document, but immediately add that they did so under duress, and that the contents of the document are false, then the ruling depends on the type of threat they claim to have faced. If their lives were threatened, the law is the same as for other cases where the witnesses claim that there was a problem with the note: If their authentication is indispensable, they are believed, and the document is considered uncertified, but if it is possible to authenticate their signatures in some other way, they are not believed (see previous entry). On the other hand, if their lives were not threatened, but they claim that they signed the document because of financial threats or bribes, they are not believed in any case, since accepting a bribe or surrendering to blackmail is a crime, and a person is not

TRANSLATION AND COMMENTARY

[1] or alternatively: **"We were disqualified from giving evidence** by ties of kinship to each other or to one of the parties, and thus our testimony was worthless," [2] the Mishnah rules that in such circumstances these witnesses **are believed** and the document is invalid. Since we are relying on their present testimony to authenticate the document, we must accept this testimony in full, even though it effectively refutes the earlier testimony established by their signatures on the document, because "the mouth that forbade is the mouth that permitted." [3] **But if there are** other **witnesses** who can testify **that the handwriting** on the document **is authentic** and belongs to the first pair of witnesses, [4] **or if their handwriting is authenticated from another place** (i.e., if the court itself is able to ascertain the authenticity of the signatures by comparing them with other known examples of the witnesses' signatures), and the witnesses then come forward and claim that they were under duress, or were minors, or were disqualified when they signed, [5] then **they are not believed,** because a witness cannot refute his own testimony unless his refutation is part of the testimony itself, in accordance with the "mouth that forbade" argument.

LITERAL TRANSLATION

[1] we were disqualified [from giving] evidence," [2] they are believed. [3] But if there are witnesses that it is their handwriting, [4] or where their handwriting came out from another place, [5] they are not believed.

[1] פְּסוּלֵי עֵדוּת הָיִינוּ״, [2] הֲרֵי אֵלּוּ נֶאֱמָנִים. [3] וְאִם יֵשׁ עֵדִים שֶׁהוּא כְּתַב יָדָם, [4] אוֹ שֶׁהָיָה כְּתַב יָדָם יוֹצֵא מִמָּקוֹם אַחֵר, [5] אֵינָן נֶאֱמָנִין.

RASHI

הרי אלו נאמנים — כיון דאין כתב ידם ניכר אלא על פיהם, הפה שאסר הוא הפה שהתיר, כי היכי דמהימנת להו אהא — הימנינהו אהא. **יוצא ממקום אחר** — חתומים בשטר אחר שהוחזק בבית דין, וכתוב בו הנפק. ובא אותו שטר לפנינו עם זה, וכתב חותמן דומין של זה לשל זה — אין כאן הפה שאסר, ואין נאמנים לומר פסולים היינו.

NOTES

פְּסוּלֵי עֵדוּת הָיִינוּ We were disqualified from giving evidence. There are many people who are disqualified from giving evidence under Jewish law, including some whose credibility in itself is not in question (e.g., women, and people who are blind or deaf or mute). Among those disqualified by the Torah from giving evidence are close relatives — witnesses who are related to each other or to one of the parties. Relatives are disqualified from giving evidence even where there is no credibility problem *per se* — such as where their testimony is unfavorable to the relative concerned (see *Rambam, Hilkhot Edut* 13:15). The Torah also disqualifies criminals from giving testimony, especially those who violate monetary laws of the Torah for the sake of financial gain, as well as those who flagrantly violate other laws of the Torah when it is to their advantage (*Sanhedrin* 27a). In addition, the Sages disqualified a number of categories of people who engage in unbecoming financial practices (e.g., gambling), even if they are not technically criminals under Torah law (*Sanhedrin* 24b).

Normally, the term, "people disqualified from giving evidence," refers to people disqualified by the Torah for engaging in crimes, or by the Sages for improper behavior (the last two categories above). In our Mishnah, however, this interpretation presents a problem. The Gemara establishes (below) that the witnesses are not believed if the effect is to disqualify themselves, even if their testimony is supported by the "mouth that forbade" argument, if they are actually confessing to a crime, because under Torah law a person cannot incriminate himself. But surely, if the witnesses testify that they were criminals when they signed the document, they are doing precisely that!

Ri Migash (cited by *Ramban*) explains that our Mishnah is indeed referring to witnesses who incriminate themselves in this way. He points out that we are referring to a case in which the disqualification has lapsed, i.e., where the criminals have paid their debt to society and are considered as sincere penitents (see following note). Hence, when they admit to having been criminals, they are not incriminating themselves.

Our commentary follows *Rambam, Ramban, Rid,* and other Rishonim, who explain that the Mishnah is referring to witnesses who were related at the time of the signing (e.g., through marriage), and have since ceased to be related. It is also possible to add slaves who have subsequently been freed, and people who were blind or deaf or mute, but who have subsequently recovered (*Meiri*).

Rashi explains that the Mishnah is referring to relatives and slaves, as well as to people who were disqualified by the Sages for improper behavior, such as gamblers, but it is not referring to outright criminals. *Ramban* explains that gamblers are not exactly guilty of a crime, because the Gemara's conclusion (*Sanhedrin* 24b) is that they are disqualified, not for gambling *per se*, but rather because they do not engage in an honest profession. Hence *Rashi* could maintain that admitting to having been a gambler is not included in the rule against accepting self-incriminating testimony.

הֲרֵי אֵלּוּ נֶאֱמָנִים They are believed. The Mishnah rules that where the witnesses' retraction is part of their testimony certifying the authenticity of the document, we must accept it. The reason is that we cannot use the document without their certification, and we cannot accept part of their certification testimony without accepting all of it, because

HALAKHAH

believed if he makes himself out to be wicked. Similarly, they are not believed if they claim that they were disqualified from giving testimony at the time they signed because of crimes they had committed previously," following Rami bar Ḥama, as explained in the Gemara's conclusion. (*Rambam, Sefer Shofetim, Hilkhot Edut* 3:6; *Shulḥan Arukh, Ḥoshen Mishpat* 46:37.)

גמרא [1]אָמַר רָמִי בַּר חָמָא: [2]לֹא שָׁנוּ אֶלָּא שֶׁאָמְרוּ: ״אֲנוּסִים הָיִינוּ מֵחֲמַת מָמוֹן״. [3]אֲבָל: ״אֲנוּסִים הָיִינוּ מֵחֲמַת נְפָשׁוֹת״, [4]הֲרֵי אֵלּוּ נֶאֱמָנִין.

LITERAL TRANSLATION

GEMARA [1]Rami bar Ḥama said: They only taught [this] where [the witnesses] said: [2]"We were under duress because of money." [3]But [if they said]: "We were under duress because of [danger to] life," [4]they are believed.

TRANSLATION AND COMMENTARY

GEMARA אָמַר רָמִי בַּר חָמָא [1]The Gemara begins its analysis of the Mishnah by considering the last clause, which states that where the "mouth that forbade" argument does not apply — because the court has found another way to authenticate the document — the witnesses cannot refute their previous testimony by claiming that they signed the document under duress. Commenting on this clause, **Rami bar Ḥama said:** [2]**This ruling was given only where the witnesses said: "We were under duress because of money."** If the witnesses testify that the lender bribed them, or threatened them with financial ruin to coerce them into putting their signatures on a false document, they are not believed (unless their testimony is supported by the "mouth that forbade" argument), since testifying falsely is a crime that cannot be excused by a threat to property, and under Jewish law a person who announces that he is guilty of a crime is not believed (see below). [3]**But if** the witnesses **say: "We were under duress because of danger to life"** — where the lender threatened to kill them if they did not sign falsely — [4]in this case **they are believed,** because a person is permitted to testify falsely to save his life. Hence the witnesses are not admitting to a crime, and their testimony can be accepted, even where it is not supported by the "mouth that forbade" argument.

RASHI

גמרא לא שנו — דאם כתב ידן יוצא ממקום אחר — אין נאמנין. **אלא שאמרו אנוסים היינו מחמת ממון** — דלאו כל כמינייהו לשויי נפשייהו רשעים בעדות פיהם, ולפסול את השטר. דאדם קרוב אצל עצמו, ואינו נאמן על עצמו לא לזכות ולא לחובה בדיני נפשות, ובפסולי עדות להעשות רשע ופסול על פיו. ואלו פוסלים עצמן באומרם "חתמנו שקר בשביל אונס ממון". ורישא טעמא משום הפה שאסר הוא הפה שהתיר. **מחמת נפשות** — שאמר בעל השטר הזה להרגנו, ואדם חזק הוא.

SAGES

רָמִי בַּר חָמָא Rami bar Ḥama. Rami (Rabbi Ammi) bar Ḥama was one of the most important Babylonian Amoraim of the fourth generation. As a boy he was the outstanding student of Rav Ḥisda, whose daughter he subsequently married. Rami bar Ḥama learned Torah from Rav Naḥman and Rav Sheshet, and also discussed Halakhic issues with them. He was famous for his brilliant intellect, but some of his contemporaries observed that because of his great intelligence and creativity, he did not always submit problems to precise analysis. Rami bar Ḥama had close ties with his younger colleague, Rava, who survived him and married his widow, Rav Ḥisda's daughter. Rami bar Ḥama's daughter was the mother of the Amora Amemar.

NOTES

"the mouth that forbade is the mouth that permitted." *Tosafot* asks: The Gemara (above, 16a) established that the "mouth that forbade" argument is in fact a kind of *miggo*. But the strongest kind of evidence under Torah law is the testimony of two witnesses. And the Gemara (below, 20a) rules that the signatures of the witnesses on the document are the full equivalent of oral testimony — so much so that even if two other witnesses testify that these witnesses acted under duress, they only create a doubt. But if the testimony of other witnesses is not enough to make us believe that these witnesses acted under duress, how can a mere *miggo* add enough credibility to the second testimony of these witnesses to make us believe it outright?

Tosafot explains that the signatures on a document are not considered the equivalent of testimony until the document has been certified. Since the certification in our case is combined with a retraction, it is itself invalid, and the document remains uncertified.

Tosafot asks further: Even where the witnesses' testimony is not needed to certify the document, they should still be believed if the effect is to invalidate it. For although they do not have the support of the "mouth that forbade" argument, they still have another *miggo,* because they could have testified that the debt recorded in the document had been repaid. *Tosafot* answers that an ordinary *miggo* does not add to the credibility of testimony. However, the "mouth that forbade" argument in our Mishnah is in fact a silent *miggo,* which is more powerful than a regular *miggo.* This would seem to lend support to *Rashi*'s view that the "mouth that forbade" argument is in fact identical with the silent *miggo* (see above, 16a), a view which *Tosafot* rejected.

לֹא שָׁנוּ אֶלָּא שֶׁאָמְרוּ: אֲנוּסִין הָיִינוּ מֵחֲמַת מָמוֹן They only taught this where the witnesses said: "We were under duress because of money." The Gemara later dismisses this version of Rami bar Ḥama's statement and explains the Mishnah as referring to a case where the witnesses' lives had been threatened, because a witness cannot retract his testimony unless his retraction is supported by the "mouth that forbade" argument. According to this version, however, Rami bar Ḥama apparently maintains that witnesses can retract their testimony, provided that they do not incriminate themselves. The Rishonim ask: According to the first version of Rami bar Ḥama's statement, the witnesses are believed without the support of the "mouth that forbade" argument, provided that they do not incriminate themselves. Why, then, are the witnesses not believed, without the "mouth that forbade" argument, if they testify that they were minors or relatives when they signed, since they are not incriminating themselves?

Rashba explains that, according to the first version of Rami bar Ḥama's statement, the witnesses' testimony that they were minors or relatives is rejected when it is *not* supported by the "mouth that forbade" argument, for the same reason that the Gemara suggests below that Rabbi Meir rejects such testimony even when it *is* supported by the "mouth that forbade" argument. For it is extremely unlikely that a lender drawing up a document attesting to his loan would deliberately render it invalid by having it signed by disqualified witnesses. Hence Rami bar Ḥama could argue that such testimony is not credible unless it is supported by the "mouth that forbade" argument.

Ramban explains that when witnesses testify that they signed as minors or as relatives, they are in effect testifying that they behaved improperly when they signed the document. And although, according to the Halakhah, the rule that a person cannot incriminate himself applies only to real crimes, it is possible that in the first version of Rami

LITERAL TRANSLATION

[1] Rava said to him: Is this really in his power? [2] Since he has testified (lit., "told"), he cannot come back and testify again. [3] And if you say: These words [apply to] oral [testimony], [4] but not to a document,

[1] אֲמַר לֵיהּ רָבָא: כָּל כְּמִינֵיהּ? [2] כֵּיוָן שֶׁהִגִּיד, שׁוּב אֵינוֹ חוֹזֵר וּמַגִּיד. [3] וְכִי תֵּימָא: הָנֵי מִילֵּי עַל פֶּה, [4] אֲבָל בִּשְׁטָר לָא,

TRANSLATION AND COMMENTARY

אֲמַר לֵיהּ רָבָא [1] **Rava said to** Rami bar Ḥama: **Is this really in his power?** Can a witness simply come back to court and alter his previous testimony (provided that he is not thereby admitting to a crime) without the support of the "mouth that forbade" argument? Surely the Torah (Leviticus 5:1) states: "And if a soul...is a witness...if he does not tell he will bear his iniquity," and we have an authoritative interpretation of the word "tell" (see note), [2] which teaches us that **once he has testified, he cannot come back and testify again.** The Torah requires witnesses to tell everything the first time, holding nothing back. A witness may retract or alter his testimony only while it is being considered by the court. After the court has examined it thoroughly and accepted it, he cannot return to court and change his story. [3] Rava continues: **And if you say:** Perhaps **this applies** only **to oral testimony** formally presented to a court, [4] **but not to a** written **document.** Perhaps it is only after testifying in court that a witness is not permitted to retract, but a witness who

RASHI

כיון שהגיד שוב אינו חוזר ומגיד — דגבי עדות חדא הגדה כתיבא, "אם לא יגיד וגו׳" (ויקרא ה). והכא נמי, כיון דחתימי בשטרא — היינו הגדה דידהו, והיכי מהימני תו למיעקר, הואיל וכתב ידן יוצא ממקום אחר? בשלמא רישא, כשאין כתב ידן יוצא ממקום אחר, ועלייהו סמכינן — כולה חדא הגדה היא, דהא באותו דבור (בכדי שאילת שלום קאמרי "אבל אנוסים היינו". אבל הכא לאו אפומייהו סמכינן. **הני מילי על פה** — כגון המעיד בבית דין, ולאחר כדי דבור בא לשנות בו. **אבל בשטר לא** — דהגדה כתיב.

BACKGROUND

כֵּיוָן שֶׁהִגִּיד, שׁוּב אֵינוֹ חוֹזֵר וּמַגִּיד Since he has testified, he cannot come back and testify again. In Jewish law, the authenticated testimony of two valid witnesses is considered absolute proof that an event has taken place. Interrogation and examination of the witnesses in court is designed to determine, on the one hand, the qualifications of the witnesses to give evidence and their degree of knowledge with respect to the matters about which they are testifying, and, on the other hand, whether their testimony contains some fundamental defect (for example, if it becomes evident that the two witnesses are contradicting each other). However, after such interrogation and examination, their testimony is regarded as having firmly established the truth of the event regarding which they have given evidence. Therefore, even if other valid witnesses are produced in large numbers to refute the original testimony, this does not invalidate it, but merely leads the court to doubt its veracity. Therefore, once witnesses have testified, and their evidence has been accepted by the court, whatever they say later will not be regarded as testimony, but as words lacking juridical meaning. Moreover, if witnesses later admit that they have committed perjury, they are categorizing themselves as evildoers, and such a self-incriminatory admission is unacceptable in court.

NOTES

bar Ḥama's statement we are assuming that he extends it to confessions of improper behavior as well. Hence this testimony, too, is considered self-incriminatory, and is not believed unless it has the support of the "mouth that forbade" argument.

כֵּיוָן שֶׁהִגִּיד, שׁוּב אֵינוֹ חוֹזֵר וּמַגִּיד Since he has testified, he cannot come back and testify again. Our commentary follows *Rashi*, who explains that this law is derived from the verb "to tell," which appears in the verse commanding witnesses not to withhold testimony (Leviticus 5:1: "If he does not tell, he will bear his iniquity"). It is not clear, however, how this law is derived from this word. *Talmidei Rabbenu Yonah* explains that we derive it from the fact that the verb "to tell" appears in the future tense, whereas normally we would expect it to be in the past tense.

Ritva cites two possible explanations of *Rashi*'s interpretation: (1) The wording of this verse ("If he does not tell...") is reminiscent of Deuteronomy 25:9, which deals with levirate marriage and reads: "Who does not build his brother's house." From the latter verse, the Gemara (*Yevamot* 10b) derives the law that a brother-in-law who formally refuses to perform the levirate marriage and instead carries out the ceremony of release (חֲלִיצָה) may not subsequently change his mind and marry that sister-in-law, because the verse said: "Who does not build," from which we infer that "since he has not built, he may no longer return and build." Similarly, we may infer that "since he has not testified, he may no longer return and testify." Once a witness has declared his testimony complete, he may no longer return and add to it. (2) *Ritva*'s second explanation is that the verse in Leviticus refers to a sacrifice brought by a witness who withheld testimony and took an oath that he knew nothing more. If it were permissible for the witness to add to his testimony, he would never be subject to this sacrifice, since he could always amend his declaration and testify again. This explanation is difficult, however, because the sacrifice enjoined by the verse in Leviticus is not imposed for false testimony in itself, but only where the witness swore falsely that he knew nothing, and that oath remains false, even if the witness is allowed to testify again.

Ritva himself disagrees with *Rashi* and derives this law from a different verse. In Deuteronomy 19:15, the Torah declares: "By the mouth of two witnesses...shall the matter be established," implying that the court's decision is established on the basis of testimony. But if testimony can be altered, the court's decision is not permanently established.

HALAKHAH

כֵּיוָן שֶׁהִגִּיד שׁוּב אֵינוֹ חוֹזֵר וּמַגִּיד Since he has testified, he cannot come back and testify again. *"Rambam* rules that after a witness has been examined in court, he may not retract and say: 'I made a mistake,' or 'I spoke out of fear,' or 'I forgot,' and the like, even if he gives a very plausible reason for his retraction. *Shulḥan Arukh* omits the clause about the witness being examined in court, and *Sma* explains that this is because we do not perform a full examination of witnesses in the monetary cases that are normally considered today. *Rema* adds that the witness can retract or alter his testimony if he does so immediately, without hesitation [תּוֹךְ כְּדֵי דִּיבּוּר]." (*Rambam, Sefer Shofetim, Hilkhot Edut* 3:5; *Shulḥan Arukh, Ḥoshen Mishpat* 29:1.)

[1]וְהָא אֲמַר רֵישׁ לָקִישׁ: עֵדִים הַחֲתוּמִים עַל הַשְּׁטָר, [2]נַעֲשָׂה כְּמִי שֶׁנֶּחְקְרָה עֵדוּתָן בְּבֵית דִּין! [3]אֶלָּא, כִּי אִתְּמַר, [4]אַרֵישָׁא אִתְּמַר: [5]״הֲרֵי אֵלּוּ נֶאֱמָנִין״. [6]אָמַר רָמִי בַּר חָמָא: לֹא שָׁנוּ אֶלָּא שֶׁאָמְרוּ: [7]״אֲנוּסִין הָיִינוּ מֵחֲמַת נְפָשׁוֹת״. [8]אֲבָל אָמְרוּ:

LITERAL TRANSLATION

[1]but surely Resh Lakish said: [If] witnesses are signed on a document, [2]it is considered (lit., "made") as if their testimony has been examined in court! [3]Rather, when [this] was said, [4]it was said [in connection] with the first clause: [5]"They are believed." [6]Rami bar Ḥama said: They only taught [this] where [the witnesses] said: [7]"We were under duress because of [danger to] life." [8]But [if] they said:

TRANSLATION AND COMMENTARY

signed a document without appearing in court is permitted to retract his signature in court. [1]**Surely** this is not so, for **Resh Lakish said: If witnesses have signed a document,** [2]**it is considered as if** they have testified orally and **their testimony has been examined in court!** Thus their signatures on the document are the equivalent of oral testimony in court, and cannot be retracted.

אֶלָּא [3]**Rather,** says the Gemara, we must amend Rami bar Ḥama's statement. **When it was said,** [4]**it was said** not in connection with the last clause, as we have assumed until now, but rather **in connection with the first clause,** which states that if the court has no way of authenticating the document other than through the testimony of the witnesses themselves, they can retract their previous testimony by including in their authentication a claim that they signed the document under duress. [5]The Mishnah ruled that "in this case **they are believed,"** because we cannot use the document without their authentication, and we cannot accept part of their testimony authenticating their signatures without accepting all of it, in accordance with the argument that "the mouth that forbade is the mouth that permitted." [6]Commenting on this clause, **Rami bar Ḥama said: This ruling was meant to apply only where the witnesses said:** [7]**"We were under duress because of danger to life."** If the witnesses testify that the lender threatened to kill them if they did not sign falsely, they are believed, because a person is permitted to testify falsely to save his life. Hence the witnesses are not admitting to a crime, and their testimony can be accepted, provided that it is supported by the "mouth that forbade" argument. [8]**But if they said: "We were under duress because of money,"** i.e., if the lender threatened them with financial ruin

RASHI

לא שנו – דאמרינן הפה שאסר כו׳. אלא דאמרי מחמת **נפשות** – נאנסנו, דלא משוו נפשייהו רשעים. וכיון דעלייהו **סמכינן** – הא בתוך כדי דבור עקרוה לסהדותייהו, והפה שאסר התיר.

SAGES

רֵישׁ לָקִישׁ **Resh Lakish.** Rabbi Shimon ben Lakish, commonly known as Resh Lakish, was one of the greatest of the Palestinian Amoraim. He was a student, colleague, and brother-in-law of Rabbi Yoḥanan.

As a youth, Resh Lakish studied Torah and showed great talent. However, apparently constrained by dire poverty, he sold himself as a gladiator in the Roman arena. Many stories are told of his exceptional courage and physical strength. In time, following a meeting with Rabbi Yoḥanan, he returned to the world of Torah, beginning as Rabbi Yoḥanan's student and then becoming his colleague and marrying his sister.

Rabbi Yoḥanan and Resh Lakish had many Halakhic differences of opinion. However, in great measure Resh Lakish's intention was not to disagree with Rabbi Yoḥanan, but rather to clarify and elucidate matters by means of dialectical argument. Rabbi Yoḥanan regarded him with great respect, and used to say, "My equal disagrees with me."

Resh Lakish was famous for his piety and rigor, and it was said that one could lend money without witnesses to a person with whom Resh Lakish spoke in public, for he spoke only to people of unblemished character. When he died, he left a son who was notable for his talents and genius.

NOTES

נַעֲשָׂה כְּמִי שֶׁנֶּחְקְרָה עֵדוּתָן בְּבֵית דִּין **It is considered as if their testimony has been examined in court.** The Tosefta (2:1) declares: "Witnesses who testified to render impure or pure, to forbid or to permit, to oblige or to exempt, until the examination of their testimony has been completed, if they say: 'We were lying,' they are believed, but if they say this after the examination of their testimony has been completed, they are not believed." The Jerusalem Talmud (commenting on our Mishnah) explains that Resh Lakish issued his ruling in connection with this Tosefta. In effect, Resh Lakish is saying that the witnesses' signatures on a document are not merely the equivalent of oral testimony; they have the status of testimony that has been examined and accepted by the court — which the Tosefta declared can no longer be altered.

In tractate *Gittin* (3a), the Gemara derives another law from Resh Lakish's maxim, declaring that by Torah law it is not necessary to certify a document, even when the alleged debtor claims that the note is a forgery. Since the witnesses' signatures on the document are considered the equivalent of testimony that has been examined, no further objections can be raised against them. It is only by Rabbinic decree that the creditor must prove the authenticity of the signatures when challenged, in order to close the obvious opening for forgery that this law presents.

Rav Sa'adyah Gaon raised a question about Resh Lakish's maxim: When the court certifies the document, does it also need to ascertain that the witnesses could read and knew what they were signing, or is it sufficient for them to authenticate the witnesses' signatures, as Resh Lakish's maxim covers all doubts about the document, provided that it is not a forgery? *Rav Hai Gaon* answered that Resh Lakish's maxim does not cover a case where the witnesses could not read or did not know what they were signing. If we know this to be the case, as when the document was written in a language which the witnesses did not know, we cannot certify the document. However, if we have no reason for suspicion, we need not investigate the witnesses on this matter, as the Gemara (*Sanhedrin* 32a) says that the Rabbis exempted witnesses who testify on monetary matters from the detailed examinations to which other witnesses must submit, in order not to discourage people from lending money.

HALAKHAH

עֵדִים הַחֲתוּמִים עַל הַשְּׁטָר **If witnesses are signed on a document.** "The signatures of witnesses on a document are the equivalent of oral testimony that has been thoroughly examined in court. Hence witnesses who have signed a document may not reappear in court later and retract their testimony." (*Rambam, Sefer Shofetim, Hilkhot Edut* 3:6.)

TRANSLATION AND COMMENTARY

to force them to sign their names to a false document, [1]**they are not believed.** In spite of the argument that "the mouth that forbade is the mouth that permitted," we divide their testimony in two and believe them when they authenticate their signatures, but not when they claim to have testified falsely, as testifying falsely is a crime that cannot be excused because of a threat to property, and under Jewish law self-incriminatory testimony is not accepted. [2]**What is the reason?** How can we divide their testimony in this way? [3]Because **a person cannot make himself out to be wicked.** Under Jewish law, a person who is not trusted to testify in someone else's favor (e.g., a close relative) is also not believed when he testifies against that person. But a person is considered his own closest relative. Hence, if a person testifies against himself and confesses to a crime — even if he does so voluntarily and sincerely — his testimony has no validity. Hence, in the case of our Mishnah, in order that these witnesses should be categorized as wicked people whose testimony is disqualified, other qualified witnesses must testify against them. Their own confession is not sufficient. Therefore the part of the witnesses' testimony relating to their alleged crime must be ignored by the court, and we accept only the part authenticating their signatures.

"אֲנוּסִין הָיִינוּ מֵחֲמַת מָמוֹן", [1]אֵין נֶאֱמָנִין. [2]מַאי טַעְמָא? [3]אֵין אָדָם מֵשִׂים עַצְמוֹ רָשָׁע.

LITERAL TRANSLATION

"We were under duress because of money," [1]they are not believed. [2]What is the reason? [3]A person cannot make himself [out to be] wicked.

RASHI

אין אדם משים עצמו רשע — אינו נאמן לפסול את עצמו מחזקתו. דקרוב הוא אצל עצמו, וקרוב פסול לעדות.

CONCEPTS

אֵין אָדָם מֵשִׂים עַצְמוֹ רָשָׁע A person cannot make himself out to be wicked. The formal aspect of this Halakhic ruling is based on the principle that we do not accept the testimony of relatives. Obviously, if we do not accept any testimony, either favorable or unfavorable, from relatives, and since אָדָם קָרוֹב אֵצֶל עַצְמוֹ — "a person is his own closest relative" — a person is certainly not permitted to testify about himself.

In a deeper sense, the principle behind this ruling is that testimony must be objective, and whenever there are grounds for suspecting that it is not objective, it is not juridically valid — such as when it is clear that a witness has an interest in the matter about which he is testifying. This is why the testimony of relatives is unacceptable: because of their relationship, they lose their objectivity (and in this respect there is no difference between testimony in favor of the relative or against him). It is clear that with respect to himself, a person cannot be objective. Therefore testimony regarding oneself — even self-incriminatory testimony — cannot be accepted in court.

Consequently, although in most juridical systems in the world an admission of guilt is regarded as the strongest testimony, it is entirely disregarded in Jewish law. *Rambam* speaks of the psychological problems that might lead a person to confess to a crime he has not committed, and judicial scholars (as well as many police investigators) have been led by experience to the conclusion that confessions extorted under pressure (and, even more so, under torture) are very unreliable indications of guilt.

NOTES

אֲנוּסִין הָיִינוּ מֵחֲמַת מָמוֹן, אֵין נֶאֱמָנִין "We were under duress because of money," they are not believed. According to the explanation of *Yad Ramah,* followed by our commentary, this line of the Gemara is fully consistent with the source of this law in tractate *Sanhedrin* (see previous note). According to Rava, those aspects of the witnesses' testimony that concern their own misdeeds must be ignored by the court, because a person can no more testify concerning himself than he can concerning a relative. Hence the portion of the witnesses' testimony that concerns themselves — "We were under duress because of money" — is ignored, and we are left with a straightforward authentication of the signatures.

According to *Tosafot,* however, Rava maintains that we erase the self-incriminating words from the witnesses' testimony, and accept all the rest. Why, then, do we not simply erase the words "because of money," and consider the witnesses to have said: "The signatures are valid, but we acted under duress," without specifying the nature of the duress? We could then interpret their testimony as though they had said: "Under duress because of danger to life," just as we erase the word "voluntarily" from the testimony of a person who testifies that he engaged in homosexual relations voluntarily, and interpret his testimony as though he had said "as a result of homosexual rape"! Because of this question, *Ramban* suggests that Rami bar Ḥama may in fact disagree with Rava and maintain that we do not divide testimony up, and although it is Rava who is explaining Rami's words in our passage, he may be doing so in accordance with Rami's opinion rather than his own.

Tosafot himself gives a number of answers to this question. (1) Testimony may be divided only in order to separate two distinct points. "Danger to life" and "because of money" are explanations of the term "duress," not separate testimony, and we cannot replace one explanation with another; but "voluntarily" and "involuntarily" do not change the meaning of the act committed by the other person, and are essentially additional points. (2) Once the witnesses testify that they signed falsely, they are already confessing to a crime, unless they expressly excuse themselves by saying that it was done out of fear for their lives. Moreover, it is rare to find a case where witnesses signed a document because of threat to life. Hence we cannot interpret their testimony in this way unless they explicitly say so. (3) By Torah law, it is not necessary to certify the signatures on a document. Hence the Rabbis were not prepared to invalidate the document by dividing up the witnesses' testimony.

Tosafot in *Sanhedrin* explains this passage in the light of a parallel passage in *Bava Batra* (134b). There the Gemara considers a case where a husband claims to have divorced his wife on a certain day some time ago, and the situation is that he is not believed about the date, although he would have been believed if he had simply said that he had divorced his wife. The Gemara asks whether according to Rava we can divide his statement up, and ignore the part about the date. And the Gemara answers that dividing up a statement of a witness is possible only where the two parts concern two different people, but not where both concern the same person. But in our case, "we were under duress" and "because of money" both concern the same people — the witnesses. Hence it is not possible to divide up this portion of the testimony (see also *Ritva*).

אֵין אָדָם מֵשִׂים עַצְמוֹ רָשָׁע A person cannot make himself out to be wicked. The commentators ask: Even if the witnesses testify that they were related to one of the litigants or to each other at the time of the transaction, they are still placing themselves in the category of the wicked, because they were guilty of fraud by signing a document when they knew themselves to be disqualified.

Sma answers that since the loan about which the witnesses were testifying really did take place, they were not exactly committing a crime, even though their impropriety could cause legal problems later on. Moreover, they can claim that they thought that other, qualified, witnesses would sign alongside their signatures. *Taz* explains that the witnesses thought that no one would take the document seriously because it had been improperly drawn up. *Tosefot Rabbi Akiva Eger* notes that, according to *Sma,* the

TRANSLATION AND COMMENTARY

תָּנוּ רַבָּנַן [1] **Our Rabbis taught** the following Baraita, which explains the first clause of our Mishnah: "If witnesses testify that their signatures on a document are authentic, but that they acted under duress, or were minors, or were disqualified, **they are not believed and cannot** thus **invalidate** the document. [2] **These are the words of Rabbi Meir,** who disagrees with the ruling of our Mishnah for reasons which the Gemara will explain. [3] **But the Sages say: They are believed,** because the mouth that forbade is the mouth that permitted, as our Mishnah ruled."

[1] תָּנוּ רַבָּנַן: "אֵין נֶאֱמָנִים לְפוּסְלוֹ. [2] דִּבְרֵי רַבִּי מֵאִיר. [3] וַחֲכָמִים אוֹמְרִים: נֶאֱמָנִים".

LITERAL TRANSLATION

[1] Our Rabbis taught: "They are not believed to invalidate it. [2] [These are] the words of Rabbi Meir. [3] But the Sages say: They are believed."

RASHI

אין נאמנין לפוסלו – ארישא דמתניתין פליג; העדים שאמרו כתב ידינו הוא אבל אנוסים היינו כו'.

NOTES

Mishnah must be referring to a case where the witnesses insist that the contents of the note were true, although the note itself was invalid, but according to *Taz* it is not necessary to restrict ourselves in this way.

אֵין אָדָם מֵשִׂים עַצְמוֹ רָשָׁע A person cannot make himself out to be wicked. In most legal systems a person cannot be compelled to testify against himself. Jewish law, however, goes much further, rejecting self-incriminatory testimony, even when it is given voluntarily and sincerely. It follows that a person cannot be convicted of a crime in a Jewish court on the basis of his own confession. This is consistent with the general principle of Jewish jurisprudence, that where a witness is not believed when he testifies in favor of someone else, he is also not believed when he testifies against that person. Thus a person cannot testify concerning a close relative, regardless of whether the testimony is in the relative's favor or against him.

Although a person who confesses to a crime is not believed in court, this does not mean that his confession is entirely without consequence. To the extent that his confession concerns only his own behavior and does not directly affect anyone else, a person is obliged to behave in accordance with his own confession, and the courts may even intervene to oblige him to do so. The two most important applications of this rule are: (1) If a person admits owing money to someone else, his admission is better than the testimony of 100 witnesses. (2) If a person declares that a legal situation exists which places him at a disadvantage, the law is that he must behave in accordance with the situation he has described. Thus if a man claims to have married a certain woman, he may not marry her sister, even though we do not accept the man's testimony *per se,* and the woman in question is permitted to marry another man, or even this man's brother.

There is an important application of this rule in our Mishnah: In all the cases where the witnesses are not believed, we consider the document valid, and the debtor must pay the debt. However, where the witnesses insist that the document is false, and admit that they were guilty of a crime in signing it, *Tur* rules, in the name of *Rosh,* that the debtor can sue the witnesses and compel them to reimburse him, because by their own admission their misdeed caused him to pay a debt he did not really owe, and the Halakhah follows the opinion that a person who indirectly causes a loss to another person is liable. *Rosh* explains that even though the court does not believe the witnesses' story, their admission is binding to the extent that it affects their own financial obligations.

אֵין אָדָם מֵשִׂים עַצְמוֹ רָשָׁע A person cannot make himself out to be wicked. This passage can be better understood in the light of a passage in tractate *Sanhedrin* (9b). The Gemara there considers a case where a person "turns state's evidence" and testifies that he assisted another person in committing a crime. In the case considered by the Gemara, the witness and the defendant had engaged in homosexual intercourse — a crime by Torah law (Leviticus 18:22). Rav Yosef rules that where the witness claims to have been the victim of homosexual rape, his testimony is valid, and if a second witness can be found, the defendant is subject to the death penalty, as prescribed by the Torah (Leviticus 20:13). But if the witness admits that homosexual intercourse took place with his consent, he is in effect incriminating himself, and since a criminal is disqualified from giving testimony, his entire testimony must be rejected. Rava, however, disagrees, arguing that we accept the witness's testimony concerning the defendant, although we reject it concerning himself. Three arguments are mentioned in the Gemara in connection with Rava's ruling: (1) A person is his own relative, and therefore may not testify about himself. (2) A person cannot make himself out to be wicked. (3) We divide the witness's testimony, accepting part and rejecting part. The Rishonim disagree as to the meaning of these three arguments, and their relation to each other.

In our commentary we have followed *Yad Ramah*'s commentary on *Sanhedrin.* According to this explanation, Rava argues as follows: A person is his own closest relative, and the Torah disqualifies relatives from giving testimony, even if it is unfavorable (argument 1). Hence it follows that self-incriminating testimony is invalid and must be ignored by the court (argument 2). Therefore the court ignores those aspects of the testimony that concern the witness's own crime, and accepts the testimony only insofar as it concerns the defendant (argument 3). According to this explanation, the court ignores some of the implications of the witness's testimony, but does not tamper with the testimony itself.

Tosafot and other Rishonim understand Rava to be arguing that, where part of a witness's statement is unacceptable, the court is empowered to divide the testimony, removing the problematic words and phrases and leaving only the part that presents no problem. According to this explanation, the three arguments are logically independent, and it is possible to agree with the first two arguments while still maintaining that it is not possible to divide up speech in this way (see *Ramban*).

SAGES

רַבִּי מֵאִיר Rabbi Meir. He was one of the greatest Tannaim of the generation before the completion of the Mishnah. We do not have definite information about Rabbi Meir's parentage, though it is said that he came from a family of converts descended from the imperial family in Rome.

While he was still a very young man, his extraordinary sharpness of mind in Torah studies was noted, and he studied with two of the greatest scholars of the generation, Rabbi Yishmael and Rabbi Akiva. He was also the only student who continued to draw upon traditions taught by Elisha ben Avuyah, despite the latter's abandonment of Judaism. Rabbi Meir was one of the closest disciples of Rabbi Akiva, who ordained him at a very early age. He was ordained again later by Rabbi Yehudah ben Bava.

Rabbi Meir was officially appointed as "Ḥakham," the third in rank below the Nasi, or president, of the Sanhedrin. The discussions between him and his colleagues, Rabbi Yehudah, Rabbi Yose, Rabbi Shimon, and Rabbi Elazar, are among the most important elements of the Mishnah.

Rabbi Meir's greatest achievement was apparently a continuation of the (oral) editing and organization of the Halakhah according to the Oral Law. Rabbi Yehudah HaNasi followed Rabbi Meir in this task, and for that reason we have the principle that all anonymous Mishnayot are to be attributed to Rabbi Meir (סְתָם מִשְׁנָה רַבִּי מֵאִיר).

Because he was involved in the effort to force the resignation of Rabban Shimon ben Gamliel, the head of the Sanhedrin, Rabbi Meir was fined by him, and for a long period his teachings were not cited in his name, being instead introduced by the expression "others say" (אֲחֵרִים אוֹמְרִים).

His private life was full of suffering. His two sons died during his lifetime, though he is known to have left a daughter. His wife, Beruriah, famous for her wisdom and

[1]בִּשְׁלָמָא לְרַבָּנַן, [2]כִּי טַעֲמַיְיהוּ, [3]שֶׁהַפֶּה שֶׁאָסַר הוּא הַפֶּה שֶׁהִתִּיר. [4]אֶלָּא לְרַבִּי מֵאִיר, מַאי טַעֲמָא? [5]בִּשְׁלָמָא פְּסוּלֵי עֵדוּת, [6]מַלְוֶה גּוּפֵיהּ מֵעִיקָּרָא מֵידָק דָּיֵיק וּמַחֲתָם. [7]קְטַנִּים נַמִי, כִּדְרַבִּי שִׁמְעוֹן בֶּן לָקִישׁ. [8]דְּאָמַר רֵישׁ לָקִישׁ: [19A] [9]חֲזָקָה אֵין הָעֵדִים חוֹתְמִין עַל

LITERAL TRANSLATION

[1]Granted according to the Rabbis, [2][who go] in accordance with their reasoning, [3]that the mouth that forbade is the mouth that permitted. [4]But according to Rabbi Meir, what is the reason? [5]Granted [with regard to] people disqualified [from giving] evidence, [6]the lender himself takes great care [about the witnesses] from the outset and has [them] sign. [7]Minors too, in accordance with Rabbi Shimon ben Lakish. [8]For Resh Lakish said: [19A] [9]There is a presumption [that] witnesses do not sign a document

TRANSLATION AND COMMENTARY

בִּשְׁלָמָא לְרַבָּנַן [1]The Gemara explains: **Granted** that, **according to the Rabbis** who disagree with Rabbi Meir, their ruling is perfectly understandable. Since the witnesses were needed to authenticate the document, and as part of the same testimony they declared that their signatures had been extracted under duress (because of danger to life, as explained above), they are believed. [2]This is **in accordance with the reasoning** of the Mishnah [3]**that the mouth that forbade is the mouth that permitted.** [4]**But according to Rabbi Meir, what is the reason** why the witnesses are not believed and cannot thus invalidate the document? The Gemara now refines its question, distinguishing between the case of duress arising from a threat to life, on the one hand, and the case of witnesses who were minors or disqualified, on the other. A witness who testifies that he acted under duress is in effect testifying that the document he signed was a fabrication, and that the events described in it never took place. By contrast, a witness who testifies that he was a minor or was disqualified does not totally undermine the authenticity of the document he signed, but merely seeks to invalidate it on technical grounds. [5]The Gemara explains: **Granted with regard to** witnesses who testify that the document they signed was invalid because they were **disqualified from giving evidence** when they signed it — in such a case we understand how Rabbi Meir could reject their testimony, because their story is extremely unlikely. [6]For **the lender himself is very careful from the outset when he has the witnesses sign.** If the events described in the document really took place, why would the lender invalidate it by having it signed by disqualified witnesses? [7]Likewise, if the witnesses testify that they were **minors**, their testimony **is also** very unlikely, because of the **following** statement of **Rabbi Shimon ben Lakish.** [8]**For Resh Lakish said:** [19A] [9]**There is a presumption that witnesses do not sign a document unless** the parties to the transaction are legally

RASHI

הפה שהתיר — וכיון דמחמת נפשות קאמרי נאנסנו לא משוו נפשייהו רשעים. ופסולי עדות דקאמרי — היינו טעמא: דלאו בעדותן משוו נפשייהו רשעים, אלא דאמרי קרובים או עבדים היינו, ועכשיו אנו משוחררים. **בשלמא פסולי עדות** — או קטנים, כיון דמודים הם שהשטר כדין נכתב, שההלואה או המקח אמת, אבל אנחנו לא היינו ראוים, והויא לה כמלוה על פה, או אי מכירה היא לא נקנה הקרקע בשטר זה — אמר רבי מאיר דלא מהימני, דאם כן מלוה לא שדי זוזי בכדי, וכי מחתים עדים על שטרו — מידק דייק שיהו כשרים.

NOTES

מַלְוֶה גּוּפֵיהּ מֵעִיקָּרָא מֵידָק דָּיֵיק **The lender himself is very careful about the witnesses from the outset.** In our commentary we have noted that this entire passage is based on the assumption that the witnesses continue to confirm the content of the document but seek to invalidate it for technical reasons. For if the loan really took place, it is not reasonable to imagine that the lender would harm his own interests by having disqualified witnesses sign the document and invalidate it, instead of selecting qualified witnesses. But if the loan did not take place, and the witnesses' testimony was false from the beginning, the Gemara's reasoning would be invalid, as the lender would presumably find it easier to persuade disqualified witnesses to testify falsely than to make use of qualified witnesses (*Ra'ah, Rashba,* and others).

We are thus referring to a case where the witnesses are now qualified to testify, and are prepared to testify to the loan. It is thus immaterial to the borrower's obligation whether or not the witnesses' self-disqualification is believed. Nevertheless, the commentators explain that it is still important to determine whether or not the document is valid. For if it is valid, and the borrower has no money to pay the loan, the creditor can seize real estate that the debtor has sold to a third party, because a documented loan automatically creates a lien on the borrower's landed property. However, if the document is invalid, the loan was in effect oral, and the creditor cannot collect (see *Taz*).

Ramban asks: Why should we interpret the Mishnah in this way? Perhaps the witnesses are saying that the loan never took place, and are justifying the retraction of their previous testimony by saying they were not qualified to serve as witnesses at the time? *Ramban* explains that where they admit that they signed falsely, they are confessing to a crime, and it is obvious that neither Rabbi Meir nor the Sages would accept their testimony. Therefore the Gemara considers only the case where they confirm the fact of the loan but seek to disqualify the document on technical grounds.

חֲזָקָה אֵין הָעֵדִים חוֹתְמִין **There is a presumption that**

piety, died in tragic circumstances. Ultimately he had to go into exile in Asia Minor, where he died. In his will he requested that his body be taken to Eretz Israel, and that it be buried temporarily near the sea, whose waves reach Eretz Israel.

During his lifetime, Rabbi Meir was famous not only for his extraordinary sharpness of mind, which exceeded that of all his generation, but also for his virtuous qualities. He was peace-loving and modest. He was known as an outstanding preacher, and it is said that his death marked the end of "the tellers of parables." Some of his animal fables were retold over many generations. He was also known as a miracle-worker; charity boxes in his name, "Rabbi Meir the Miracle-Worker" (רַבִּי מֵאִיר בַּעַל הַנֵּס), were a primary source of contributions to Eretz Israel for many years.

הַשְּׁטָר אֶלָּא אִם כֵּן נַעֲשָׂה בְּגָדוֹל. [1]אֶלָּא אֲנוּסִין, [2]מַאי טַעְמָא?
[3]אָמַר רַב חִסְדָּא: קָסָבַר רַבִּי מֵאִיר: [4]עֵדִים שֶׁאָמְרוּ לָהֶם:

LITERAL TRANSLATION

unless it was done by adults. [1]But [regarding] people under duress, [2]what is the reason?

[3]Rav Ḥisda said: Rabbi Meir maintains: [4]Witnesses who were told:

RASHI

אלא אנוסים מאי טעמא לא — נימא: הפה שאסר הוא שהתיר. **אלא אם כן נעשה בגדול** — כל מעשה השטר בגדולים, הלוקח והמוכר. וגבי עדים נמי אמרינן: חזקה אין הלוקח מחתים בו קטנים.

TRANSLATION AND COMMENTARY

competent **adults,** and similarly that the parties do not accept a document unless it is signed by legally competent adults. If the events described in the document really took place, why would the lender render it invalid by having it signed by minors? Thus Rabbi Meir's ruling, that witnesses are not to be believed if they claim they were minors, is convincing. [1]**But** in the case where the witnesses testify that they acted **under duress,** and the events described in the document never took place, [2]**what is** Rabbi Meir's **reason** for not believing them? Since their lives were threatened, they are not confessing to a crime, and we should argue that the mouth that forbade is the mouth that permitted.

אָמַר רַב חִסְדָּא [3]**Rav Ḥisda said** in reply: **Rabbi Meir maintains** [4]that **if witnesses are told: "Sign a falsehood**

NOTES

witnesses do not sign. Even though the witnesses' testimony is supported by the "mouth that forbade" argument, it conflicts with a legal presumption. Rabbi Meir apparently maintains that a legal presumption overrides the "mouth that forbade" argument, whereas the Sages maintain that the "mouth that forbade" argument is stronger.

The Rishonim compare this passage with one in tractate *Bava Batra* (5b). There the Gemara states that a debtor who claims to have repaid an oral debt which has not yet come due is not believed, because there is a legal presumption that debtors do not repay their debts before they fall due. The Gemara then considers a case where a creditor tried to collect a debt some time after it had fallen due, and the debtor responded that he had repaid it early. Ordinarily we would not accept such a claim, but in this case it is supported by a *miggo*: the debtor could have claimed that he repaid the debt on time, instead of saying that he repaid it early. The Gemara notes that in this case the *miggo* conflicts with the legal presumption, and leaves open the question of which argument takes precedence.

Comparing the two passages, *Tosafot* asks: The "mouth that forbade" argument is a kind of *miggo,* and according to our Gemara the Sages are of the opinion that it takes precedence over the legal presumption, whereas Rabbi Meir favors the legal presumption. Hence it would appear that the question of the Gemara in *Bava Batra* — what happens when a *miggo* conflicts with a legal presumption? — is in fact a dispute between Rabbi Meir and the Sages. Yet in *Bava Batra* the Gemara treated this as an open question raised by the Amoraim.

To answer this question, *Rosh* notes that, according to the Gemara's conclusion, Rabbi Meir's reasoning is based on Rav Huna's ruling that once a debtor concedes the authenticity of a document, he can no longer claim a *miggo.* Although the Gemara only uses this argument to explain the claim that the witnesses acted under duress, it would apply equally well to their other claims. Therefore our Gemara in its initial explanations of Rabbi Meir's viewpoint is merely exploring a possibility, and the Gemara is aware that these answers will not be needed in the end.

According to *Rashi,* who maintains that the "mouth that forbade" argument is a silent *miggo, Tosafot*'s question is not so difficult. For all we can prove from our Mishnah is that the "mouth that forbade" argument — a particularly strong form of *miggo* — takes precedence over a legal presumption, but the question of how to proceed when an ordinary *miggo* conflicts with a legal presumption may still be open (*Shittah Mekubbetzet, Pnei Yehoshua*). This explanation would apply only to the Sages' viewpoint and not to that of Rabbi Meir, who maintains that a legal presumption takes precedence even over the "mouth that forbade" argument; but it is not unreasonable to explain the Gemara in *Bava Batra* according to the view of the Sages, since their view is followed by the Halakhah.

It is important to note, however, that there are several other passages in the Talmud in which the comparative effectiveness of *miggo* and a legal presumption are examined, and the Rishonim have difficulty in explaining them all in a consistent manner (see *Tosafot*'s comments on *Bava Batra* 5b and on *Yevamot* 115a). Accordingly, *Rashba* explains that objections cannot be raised from one case to another, since some legal presumptions are powerful enough to override a *miggo,* but others are not.

אֵין הָעֵדִים חוֹתְמִין **Witnesses do not sign.** Our commentary follows *Rashi,* who explains that Resh Lakish's legal presumption is being used to make the same point that the Gemara made previously about relatives: If the loan really did take place, why would the lender invalidate the document by employing disqualified witnesses? But it is difficult to understand why the Gemara would need to cite Resh Lakish's legal presumption to prove this point. Why

HALAKHAH

חֲזָקָה אֵין הָעֵדִים חוֹתְמִין עַל הַשְּׁטָר אֶלָּא אִם כֵּן נַעֲשָׂה בְּגָדוֹל **There is a presumption that witnesses do not sign a document unless it was drawn up by adults.** "If the witnesses who signed a document come to court and testify that the borrower was a minor when the document was drawn up, and was therefore not legally competent to borrow money, they are not believed, even where their testimony is needed to authenticate the document. *Shakh* explains that there is a legal presumption that the witnesses would not sign such a document unless they were certain that the borrower was an adult. Hence, by claiming that they neglected to follow this procedure, the

SAGES

רַב חִסְדָּא Rav Ḥisda. A Babylonian Amora of the second generation. See *Ketubot* Part I, pp. 34–5.

TRANSLATION AND COMMENTARY

and you will not be killed," [1]**they should** allow themselves to **be killed rather than sign a falsehood.** According to Rabbi Meir, it is forbidden to give false testimony, even to save one's life. Hence, by saying they acted under duress, the witnesses are in effect confessing to a crime and are not believed, even where their confession is supported by the "mouth that forbade" argument.

אָמַר לֵיהּ רָבָא [2]**Rava said to** Rav Ḥisda: Your explanation is not plausible. **If they had appeared before us** prior to signing, **to ask for advice** on whether to sign falsely or to give up their lives, [3]**we would have said to them: "Go and sign, and do not** let yourselves **be killed."** [4]**For the Master said** (*Sanhedrin* 74a): Ordinarily a person is permitted — indeed required — to violate the laws of the Torah if this is necessary to protect him when his life is in danger, whether because of illness, or dangerous circumstances, or because someone is threatening to kill him if he obeys the Torah. [5]**There is nothing that takes precedence over the saving of life except idolatry,** [6]**and adultery or incest, and murder.** A person who can save his life only by worshipping idols, or by committing adultery or incest, or by killing another person (other than the person threatening him), is required to sacrifice his life rather than commit

"חִתְמוּ שֶׁקֶר וְאַל תֵּהָרְגוּ", [1]יֵהָרְגוּ וְאַל יַחְתְּמוּ שֶׁקֶר. [2]אֲמַר לֵיהּ רָבָא: הָשְׁתָּא אִילּוּ אָתוּ לְקַמָּן לְאִמְלוּכֵי, [3]אָמְרִינַן לְהוּ: "זִילוּ חֲתוּמוּ, וְלָא תִּתְקַטְלוּן". [4]דְּאָמַר מָר: [5]אֵין לְךָ דָּבָר שֶׁעוֹמֵד בִּפְנֵי פִּיקּוּחַ נֶפֶשׁ אֶלָּא עֲבוֹדָה זָרָה, [6]וְגִלּוּי עֲרָיוֹת, וּשְׁפִיכוּת דָּמִים בִּלְבָד.

LITERAL TRANSLATION

"Sign a falsehood and you will not be killed," [1]should be killed and should not sign a falsehood. [2]Rava said to him: Now if they had come before us to ask for advice, [3]we would have said to them: "Go [and] sign, and do not be killed." [4]For the Master said: [5]You do not have anything that comes (lit., "stands") before the saving of life except idolatry, [6]and forbidden sexual relations, and bloodshed alone.

RASHI

יהרגו ואל יחתמו שקר — הלכך כי אמרי נמי "אנוסים היינו מחמת נפשות" — משוו נפשייהו רשעים.

NOTES

not simply say: "Regarding disqualified witnesses or minors, the lender himself is very careful from the outset when he arranges for the witnesses to sign"?

Shittah Mekubbetzet explains that with moderate care a lender can be certain not to employ relatives, criminals or the like as witnesses. But it is quite possible for a lender to imagine that a mature-looking boy has reached the age of majority when in fact he has not, unless he takes great care to be certain that the witness is of age. Hence the Gemara cites Resh Lakish, who states that there is a legal presumption that the witnesses take precisely such care regarding the parties, and, by implication, that the lender is just as careful regarding the witnesses.

יֵהָרְגוּ וְאַל יַחְתְּמוּ שֶׁקֶר Should be killed and should not sign a falsehood. This expression of the Gemara posed great difficulties for the Rishonim. How could anyone imagine that danger to life does not justify signing a false document? Admittedly *Ramban* cites a Baraita (not mentioned anywhere in the Talmud) which states that Rabbi Meir is of the opinion that a person must give up his life rather than steal, and it may be possible to extend this idea to cover assisting in a theft by signing a false document, but it is hard to explain the Gemara's argument this way. For if Rabbi Meir's opinion was based on this Baraita, how could the Gemara challenge it by citing the opposing opinion — that only where a threat involves the three cardinal sins is a person required to sacrifice his life (*Rashba*)?

There are two schools of thought on this matter. According to many Rishonim, a person who chooses to die a martyr's death rather than violate a law of the Torah is performing a meritorious act, even where such a sacrifice is not strictly required (see following note). Following this idea, *Ramban* explains that Rabbi Meir expected the witnesses to go beyond the law and to martyr themselves rather than sign the document. This explanation is difficult to accept because it implies that a person who behaves in accordance with the letter of the law is considered to be "making himself out to be wicked" if he admits that he did not choose to martyr himself. Although *Ramban* explains that this is precisely the Gemara's objection below ("Now if they had come before us..."), it is hard to imagine that the Gemara ever entertained such an idea, even as a hypothesis (but see *Shev Shma'ateta,* who tries to justify this idea in practice in certain cases).

Ra'ah and *Ritva* explain that the Gemara does not mean that Rabbi Meir maintains that witnesses are encouraged to die a martyr's death rather than to sign falsely, but rather that people have the mistaken impression that this is what they should do, so that it is almost unheard of for a person to agree to sign a false document to save his life. According to this explanation, the problem with the witnesses' testimony is not that it is self-incriminating, but rather that it is extremely implausible. But the Gemara responds that since in fact the witnesses did the right thing by agreeing to sign, the fact that most people would not have done so cannot be taken into consideration.

אֵין לְךָ דָּבָר שֶׁעוֹמֵד בִּפְנֵי פִּיקּוּחַ נֶפֶשׁ You do not have anything that comes before the saving of life. The source of this law is a passage in tractate *Sanhedrin* (74a).

HALAKHAH

witnesses are effectively making themselves out to be wicked," following the statement of Resh Lakish here. (*Rambam, Sefer Mishpatim, Hilkhot Malveh VeLoveh* 24:5; *Shulḥan Arukh, Ḥoshen Mishpat* 46:38.)

אֵין לְךָ דָּבָר שֶׁעוֹמֵד בִּפְנֵי פִּיקּוּחַ נֶפֶשׁ You do not have anything that comes before the saving of life. "All Jews are commanded to sanctify the name of God and not to profane it, by giving their lives, if necessary, as martyrs.

[1]הָשְׁתָּא דְּחָתְמוּ, [2]אָמְרִינַן לְהוּ: ״אַמַּאי חָתְמִיתוּ״? [3]אֶלָּא, טַעְמָא דְּרַבִּי מֵאִיר כִּדְרַב הוּנָא אָמַר רַב. [4]דְּאָמַר רַב הוּנָא אָמַר רַב: [5]מוֹדֶה

LITERAL TRANSLATION

[1]Now that they have signed, [2]can we say to them: "Why did you sign?"?

[3]Rather, Rabbi Meir's reason is in accordance with what Rav Huna said in the name of Rav. [4]For Rav Huna said in the name of Rav: [5][If a borrower] admits that

RASHI

מודה בשטר שכתבו – לוה שהודה בשטר שכתבו, ועל פיו נחתמו העדים.

TRANSLATION AND COMMENTARY

any of these transgressions. But the prohibition against giving false testimony is an ordinary commandment of the Torah, not one of the three exceptions just mentioned. Hence, if these witnesses had been in a position to ask us, we would have told them to do whatever was necessary to save their lives, even if it meant signing a false document. [1]**Now that they** have followed our advice, as it were, and **have signed** the document, [2]**can we say to them: "Why did you sign?"**? Clearly their signature under duress was not a crime. Therefore their present testimony is not tantamount to making themselves out to be wicked, and since it is supported by the "mouth that forbade" argument, it should be believed.

אֶלָּא [3]**Rather,** explains the Gemara, **Rabbi Meir's reasoning** in rejecting the "mouth that forbade" argument in this case **is in accordance with** the following statement **that Rav Huna made in the name of Rav.** [4]**For Rav Huna said in the name of Rav:** [5]**If** a borrower **admits that he wrote a promissory note, the lender does**

NOTES

Rabbi Yoḥanan reports in the name of Rabbi Shimon ben Yehotzadak that no sin comes before the saving of life, except murder, idolatry, and adultery or incest. The Gemara then cites many other Tannaim who support Rabbi Yoḥanan's ruling, which is followed by the Halakhah.

Rabbi Yoḥanan then goes on to state that even though the pressure to violate other commandments of the Torah does not justify giving up one's life, this is so only in ordinary times; but if a wicked government is trying to eradicate the practice of Judaism, Jews are required to martyr themselves rather than violate *any* law of the Torah. Moreover, even in ordinary times, Jews are permitted to violate the other laws of the Torah only when the violation is private, but if the violation is to be done in public, a Jew must sacrifice his life rather than violate the law.

The Gemara qualifies this last statement of Rabbi Yoḥanan, saying that pressure to violate publicly ordinary laws of the Torah in ordinary times justifies martydom only if the Jew plays an active role in the violation, and when the purpose of the wicked person ordering the violation is to demonstrate his contempt for the Torah. But if the Jew plays a passive role (as when a non-Jew shaves a Jew's beard with a razor and the Jew does not resist), or where the wicked person has some personal interest in mind, and the fact that this involves a transgression is incidental to him (as when the wicked man is hungry and orders the Jew to cook food for him on the Sabbath), the Jew should violate the law, even in public, if his life is at stake. *Tosafot* (above, 3b) discusses whether these exceptions apply to the three cardinal sins as well (as when a married woman is raped and does not resist).

There is a dispute among the Rishonim about when a person is permitted to violate the Torah in order to save his life. *Tosafot* (*Avodah Zarah* 27b) rules that a person who chooses a martyr's death rather than violate the Torah is performing a meritorious act. *Rambam* (*Hilkhot Yesodei HaTorah* 5:4) rules that it is forbidden to choose a martyr's death rather than violate the Torah, and a person who does so, far from performing a meritorious act, is considered to be the moral equivalent of a suicide. *Kesef Mishneh* and others note that Jewish practice throughout the ages supports *Tosafot*. *Ritva* rules that only extremely pious people may become voluntary martyrs in this way, if they see that unusual circumstances warrant it, but ordinary people are forbidden to risk their lives when this is not demanded by the Torah.

טַעְמָא דְּרַבִּי מֵאִיר כִּדְרַב הוּנָא Rabbi Meir's reason is in accordance with what Rav Huna said. *Rashi* explains that the difference of opinion between Rabbi Meir and the Sages concerns a case where the borrower admitted that the promissory note was authentic, but claimed that he had already repaid the debt, and asked to be believed on the basis of a *miggo*. The lender then produced the witnesses who signed the note. They confirmed the authenticity of their signatures, but claimed that they were disqualified or minors, or had been acting under duress. In such a case, Rabbi Meir, who is of the same opinion as Rav Huna, rules that the document is valid, because it was

HALAKHAH

Nevertheless, if someone orders a Jew to violate a law of the Torah, threatening to kill him if he disobeys, the Jew should violate the law, as the Torah says of its laws (Leviticus 18:5): "that a man shall do them and live by them," from which we learn that the Torah was given to live by, and not to die by. This law applies only to ordinary laws of the Torah, but if the Jew was ordered to commit one of the three cardinal sins — idol worship, adultery or incest, or murder — he must give his life as a martyr rather than violate the law.

"This law applies only when the person ordering the transgression had some personal reason for it (e.g., where he ordered the Jew to do work for him on the Sabbath [an ordinary sin], or to kill an enemy of his [one of the three cardinal sins]). But if his specific purpose was to show that he could force a Jew to violate the Torah, then (depending on the circumstances) the Jew may be required to give his life as a martyr, even if he was ordered to commit an ordinary sin." (*Rambam, Sefer Madda, Hilkhot Yesodei HaTorah* 5:1-3.)

בִּשְׁטָר שֶׁכְּתָבוֹ, אֵין צָרִיךְ לְקַיְּימוֹ.

[1]גּוּפָא: אָמַר רַב הוּנָא אָמַר רַב: [2]מוֹדֶה בִּשְׁטָר שֶׁכְּתָבוֹ, אֵין צָרִיךְ לְקַיְּימוֹ. [3]אֲמַר לֵיהּ רַב נַחְמָן: גְּנוּבָא גְּנוּבֵי לָמָּה לָךְ?

LITERAL TRANSLATION

he wrote a note, he [the lender] does not have to authenticate it.

[1]Concerning the previous statement (lit., "the thing itself"): Rav Huna said in the name of Rav: [2][If a borrower] admits that he wrote a note, he [the lender] does not have to authenticate it. [3]Rav Naḥman said to him: Why do you need to behave like a thief?

RASHI

אין המלוה צריך לקיימו — בעדים החתומים בו, שאין הלוה שוב נאמן לומר פרעתיו. ולא אמרינן בהאי הפה שאסר הוא שהתיר, דמכיון שאמר כשר היה — הרי הוחזק השטר. וכי אמר ״פרעתיו״ — לא מהימן, שהרי ביד המלוה הוא. ורבי מאיר נמי, דאמר אין נאמנים לפוסלו — במודה לוה שכתבו קאמר. וקסבר לא צריכינן תו לעדים, ולאו אפומייהו מיקיים שטרא. **גנבא** — מתגנב אתה לומר דבריך בלשון שלא נחלקו בו היחיד והמרובים, כדי שלא יבטלו את דבריך, דאמרת כיחידאה.

TRANSLATION AND COMMENTARY

not have to authenticate it. If a borrower claims that a promissory note was forged, everyone agrees that the lender must authenticate the document by proving that the signatures of the witnesses are genuine. But if the borrower admits that the document is genuine, and seeks to invalidate it for some other reason — by claiming, for example, that he has repaid it but forgotten to reclaim the promissory note — there is a difference of opinion among the Tannaim and the Amoraim. Some of the Sages argue that the borrower should be believed on the basis of *miggo,* because he could have claimed that the document was forged. According to this view, the lender must either disprove the borrower's actual claim, or authenticate the signatures on the document independently, in order to undermine the *miggo.* But Rav Huna is of the opinion that the lender need not authenticate the document in such a case, because a borrower is believed only if he claims that the document was forged. But if the borrower admits that the document is genuine, and claims a *miggo* on the grounds that he *could* have claimed that it was forged, he is not believed. Similarly in our case, if the witnesses testify that their signatures were forged, everyone agrees that they should be believed. But if they admit that their signatures were genuine, and wish to be believed about some other claim — that they were minors, or were disqualified, or acted under duress when they signed — the author of the Mishnah maintains that they are believed when their testimony is supported by the special *miggo* called "the mouth that forbade." Rabbi Meir, however, maintains that they are not believed, even though their testimony is supported by the "mouth that forbade" argument, because Rabbi Meir agrees with Rav Huna that a *miggo* cannot be constructed on the basis of a hypothetical claim of forgery.

גּוּפָא [1]**Returning to the previous statement,** the Gemara now gives it detailed consideration: **Rav Huna said in the name of Rav:** [2]**If a** borrower **admits that he wrote a promissory note, the lender does not have to authenticate it,** because a *miggo* cannot be constructed on the basis of a hypothetical claim of forgery, as explained above. [3]**Rav Naḥman said to** Rav Huna: **Why must you behave like a thief,** expressing

NOTES

not necessary to authenticate it in the first place, whereas the Sages rule that the document needs to be authenticated, and since the witnesses claim, as part of the authentication procedure, that the document is not valid, they are believed, because "the mouth that forbade is the mouth that permitted."

According to this explanation, the dispute between Rabbi Meir and the Sages revolves around the *miggo* argument used by the borrower. This is difficult, because the language of the Baraita suggests that the dispute concerns the credibility of the witnesses, not the credibility of the debtor, and moreover, in a parallel passage in *Bava Batra* (154b), the Gemara makes this point explicitly. Additional objections are raised by the Rishonim (see *Tosafot* and *Rashba*).

Our commentary follows *Tosafot,* who explains that Rabbi Meir is not referring to the same case as Rav Huna, but is applying the same reasoning as Rav Huna to a different case. Rav Huna said that a borrower who admits the authenticity of a promissory note but claims that it has been repaid is not believed, even though he is supported by a *miggo.* Similarly, Rabbi Meir said that witnesses who admit the authenticity of their signatures but claim that they were disqualified, or were minors, or acted under duress are not believed, even though they have the support of the special *miggo* called "the mouth that forbade."

מוֹדֶה בִּשְׁטָר שֶׁכְּתָבוֹ, אֵין צָרִיךְ לְקַיְּימוֹ **If a borrower admits that he wrote a note, the lender does not have to authenticate it.** Most Rishonim rule that the Halakhah follows Rav Naḥman against Rav Huna, and follows the Sages against Rabbi Meir. Therefore, a borrower who claims to have repaid a debt is believed with a *miggo,* since he could have claimed that the document was forged, unless the lender undermines the *miggo* by authenticating

HALAKHAH

מוֹדֶה בִּשְׁטָר שֶׁכְּתָבוֹ **If a borrower admits that he wrote a note.** "If the creditor has not authenticated the note, and the debtor says: 'It is true that I wrote this document, but I have already repaid you,' or: 'I planned to borrow the money but never did so,' or makes any similar claim, the alleged debtor is believed, because he has a

TRANSLATION AND COMMENTARY

yourself obliquely and hiding the background to your ruling? [1] **If you are of the same opinion as Rabbi Meir,** [2] **say: "The Halakhah is in accordance with Rabbi Meir."** Do not hide the fact that your ruling is the subject of a Tannaitic dispute!

אֲמַר לֵיהּ [3] Rav Huna **said to** Rav Naḥman in reply: **And you, sir, what is your opinion?** Do you rule in favor of Rabbi Meir, as I do, and reject any *miggo* constructed on the basis of a hypothetical claim of forgery? Or do you rule in favor of the Sages, and accept such a *miggo*?

[1] אִי סְבִירָא לָךְ כְּרַבִּי מֵאִיר, [2] אֵימָא: "הֲלָכָה כְּרַבִּי מֵאִיר"! [3] אֲמַר לֵיהּ: וּמָר, הֵיכִי סְבִירָא לֵיהּ?

LITERAL TRANSLATION

[1] If you maintain in accordance with Rabbi Meir, [2] say: "The Halakhah is in accordance with Rabbi Meir"!

[3] He said to him: And you, sir, how do you maintain?

RASHI

אי סבירא לך כרבי מאיר אימאהלכה כרבי מאיר — ולא תנקוט לה כמילתא בלאפי נפשה. **ומר היכי סבירא ליה** — במודה בשטר שכתבו.

NOTES

the document. But the Gemara does not explain the reasoning of Rav Huna. Why is this *miggo* unacceptable according to him?

Tosafot explains that a *miggo* is valid only when the claim that was not made was fully available to the claimant, both legally and psychologically. But the debtor may be afraid to claim that the document is forged, in case the creditor authenticates the document and proves him to be a liar. Hence the debtor prefers to claim that the debt has been repaid, and asks to be believed on the basis of a *miggo*. For this reason the *miggo* is flawed.

Several Rishonim cite *Rashbam* (*Bava Batra* 170a), who explains that by Torah law it is not necessary to authenticate a document at all. Once witnesses have signed a document, it is considered as if their testimony has been cross-examined in court. In order to avoid the obvious opportunity this presents for committing forgery, the Rabbis instituted a process of authentication if an alleged debtor claims that a note is forged. But if the debtor makes no such claim, we revert to Torah law and do not permit any other claims based on a *miggo* argument.

Rosh cites another explanation (in the name of *Rashi*) — that Rav Huna is of the opinion that the borrower is not believed on the basis of a *miggo* because his claim is so unlikely. While some documents may be forged, it is most unlikely that a document will remain intact *in the possession of the creditor* after the debt has been repaid. *Rashbam* (*Bava Batra* 154b) gives a similar explanation, adding that once we know that the document is genuine, we all become, as it were, witnesses that the debtor owes the money, and a mere *miggo* cannot refute such a degree of certainty. Most Rishonim reject this explanation (*Tosafot*, *Shittah Mekubbetzet*), but some Aḥaronim defend it (*Maharsha* and *Maharam Schiff*).

אִי סְבִירָא לָךְ כְּרַבִּי מֵאִיר If you maintain in accordance with Rabbi Meir. This line of the Gemara appears to indicate that the positions of Rabbi Meir and Rav Huna are identical, and that there is no way of distinguishing between them. In fact, however, it is theoretically possible to distinguish between them. Indeed, in tractate *Bava Batra* (154b), Rabbi Yoḥanan makes just such a distinction, arguing that even if we accept Rav Huna's argument that the borrower is not believed on the basis of a *miggo*, the witnesses can still be believed on the basis of the "mouth that forbade" argument (as the Sages ruled), because witnesses have a degree of credibility far exceeding that of the debtor. Why, then, does Rav Naḥman assume that Rav Huna is ruling in favor of Rabbi Meir?

Tosafot explains that Rav Naḥman disagreed with Rabbi Yoḥanan about the distinction between the debtor and the witnesses. *Rashba* adds that Rav Huna himself may have made the same distinction as Rabbi Yoḥanan, and this is why he chose to "behave like a thief," but Rav Naḥman considered Rabbi Yoḥanan's distinction to be forced, and felt that there was no room for Rav Huna to pretend that he was issuing an independent ruling.

וּמָר, הֵיכִי סְבִירָא לֵיהּ And you, sir, how do you maintain? From the context, it would appear that Rav Huna was asking Rav Naḥman how he ruled on the question of the dispute between Rabbi Meir and the Sages, and this is how most Rishonim, including *Rashi*, explain it. But this explanation is difficult, because Rav Naḥman has already made it perfectly clear that he does not agree with Rabbi Meir, by objecting when Rav Huna concealed the fact that his ruling was subject to a Tannaitic dispute.

Shittah Mekubbetzet offers an alternative explanation, according to which Rav Naḥman's original remark to Rav Huna was unclear. Was he objecting to Rav Huna's ruling on the grounds that it followed the discredited view of Rabbi Meir (as the other Rishonim explained), or was he encouraging Rav Huna to support his ruling by citing Rabbi Meir? According to this explanation, Rav Huna was asking Rav Naḥman to clarify his own position, and Rav Naḥman responded that he avoided all problems by having the creditor authenticate his documents in advance. *Shittah Mekubbetzet* notes, however, that this explanation does not fit the language of the Gemara very well.

HALAKHAH

miggo, since he could have denied the authenticity of the document. But if the creditor subsequently has the document authenticated independently, the debtor's claims are of no effect, as the *miggo* no longer exists," following Rav Naḥman against Rav Huna, and the Sages against Rabbi Meir. (*Rambam, Sefer Mishpatim, Hilkhot Malveh VeLoveh* 14:5; *Shulḥan Arukh, Ḥoshen Mishpat* 82:1.)

LITERAL TRANSLATION

[1]He said to him: When they come before us for judgment, [2]we say to them: "Go [and] authenticate your documents, [3]and [then] come down to judgment."

[4]Rav Yehudah said in the name of Rav: [5]Someone who says: "This is a promissory note [signed on] trust," is not believed.

[1]אֲמַר לֵיהּ: כִּי אָתוּ לְקַמָּן לְדִינָא, [2]אָמְרִינַן לְהוּ: "זִילוּ קַיְּימוּ שְׁטָרַיְיכוּ, [3]וְחוּתוּ לְדִינָא".

[4]אָמַר רַב יְהוּדָה אָמַר רַב: [5]הָאוֹמֵר: "שְׁטַר אֲמָנָה הוּא זֶה", אֵינוֹ נֶאֱמָן.

TRANSLATION AND COMMENTARY

אֲמַר לֵיהּ [1]Rav Naḥman **said to** Rav Huna in reply: **When** a lender **comes before** the court **for judgment** with a document whose authenticity the borrower concedes, [2]**we tell him** as a matter of course: "Even though the borrower concedes the authenticity of **your document, go and authenticate it,** [3]**and then come** to the court **for judgment.**" If the document is authenticated by the borrower's admission alone, the borrower can claim to have already repaid the loan, and if he does so, he will be believed on the basis of *miggo,* because he could have claimed that the document was forged. But once the document has been authenticated independently, the borrower can no longer raise other claims, because his *miggo* argument will be undermined. Thus we see that Rav Naḥman rules in favor of the Sages, against Rabbi Meir.

אָמַר רַב יְהוּדָה [4]The Gemara now considers the following statement, which effectively sums up the previous discussion. **Rav Yehudah said in the name of Rav:** [5]**If someone says: "This is a promissory note signed on trust," he is not believed.** Occasionally a person would draw up a document describing himself as a borrower, and would give it to the person named in the note as the lender, even though no loan had been granted. The note could be intended as a guarantee that the borrower would fulfill some unrelated promise, or to prepare for a later loan, or for some other personal reason. Such documents are called "promissory notes signed on trust," because the borrower effectively places himself in the hands of the lender, trusting him not to make improper use of the note. It is forbidden to draw up a promissory note signed on trust, and Rav Yehudah tells us that if someone claims that a seemingly authentic note was drawn up in this way, he is not believed without proof.

RASHI

כי אתו לקמן — מלוין מביאין שטרות. **קיימו שטרייכו** — כך אני רגיל לומר למלוים המביאים שטרותיהם לפני ואין עדיהם עמהם, אני אומר להם: לכו ובקשו עדיכם וקיימוהו. דאי לאו הכי, אף על גב דמודה לוה שכתבו — מצי למימר פרעתיו. **שטר אמנה** — לא לוה כלום, אלא כתבו ומסרו למלוה, שאם יצטרך ללות — ילוה. והאמינו שלא יתבענו אלא אם כן מלוהו.

CONCEPTS

שְׁטַר אֲמָנָה **A promissory note signed on trust.** An illegal document attesting to a loan that has not taken place. The borrower plans to borrow the money later on, and writes the promissory note in advance for reasons of convenience, trusting the lender not to produce the document for collection unless and until he actually lends the money. שְׁטַר אֲמָנָה is by nature false testimony, and hence illegal. The Sages forbade the use of such documents lest the lender's heirs or creditors discover them and present them for collection.

NOTES

אָמְרִינַן לְהוּ: זִילוּ קַיְּימוּ שְׁטָרַיְיכוּ **We say to them: "Go and authenticate your documents."** Our commentary follows *Rashi,* who explains that Rav Naḥman routinely advised creditors appearing before him to authenticate their documents in advance, in order to avoid problems later on if the borrowers were to claim that the debts had been repaid. This explanation is somewhat difficult: How does it prove that Rav Naḥman disagrees with Rav Huna? Perhaps Rav Naḥman advised creditors to authenticate their documents so that the debtors could not claim that they had been forged!

Gra disagrees with *Rashi,* arguing that it would have been improper for Rav Naḥman to give any advice to a claimant appearing before him. Accordingly, he explains that Rav Naḥman was issuing a ruling, not giving advice. According to this explanation, Rav Naḥman was referring to a case where the borrower had already claimed that he had repaid the debt. In such a case, Rav Naḥman would require the creditor to authenticate his document, even though the debtor had implicitly conceded its authenticity. Thus Rav Naḥman clearly disagreed with Rav Huna.

שְׁטַר אֲמָנָה **A promissory note signed on trust.** A document signed on trust is a document attesting to a loan that has not taken place, which the person named as the lender promises not to use improperly. The Rishonim suggest several different situations in which such a document may be drawn up. Many Rishonim, including *Rashi,* cite an explanation of the Geonim that the borrower might not yet have decided whether or not to borrow money, and asked the lender to draw up a document in advance, just in case. The Geonim explain that the scribe might have been available that day, and the parties feared that he might not be available when the money was actually lent. The Geonim add that the borrower might have had other, personal, reasons for trusting the lender with the document (e.g., he left it there for safekeeping until he had a chance to collect it); and they also describe a case in which such a document was drawn up as security for a sale that never took place in the end. These explanations have been followed by our commentary.

Rashi's explanation presents a problem. For the Mishnah (*Bava Batra* 167b, cited in *Bava Metzia* 12b) rules that it is permitted to draw up a document in advance in this way, at the request of the borrower alone, without

HALAKHAH

הָאוֹמֵר: שְׁטַר אֲמָנָה הוּא זֶה **Someone who says: "This is a promissory note signed on trust."** "If a creditor admits that a promissory note in his possession was signed on trust, and that in fact no loan took place, he is believed, because an admission by a litigant is worth the testimony of 100 witnesses. But if he owes money to other people,

[1]דְקָאָמַר מַאן? [2]אִילֵימָא דְקָאָמַר לֹוֶה, [3]פְּשִׁיטָא. [4]כָּל כְּמִינֵּיהּ? [5]וְאֶלָּא, דְקָאָמַר מַלְוֶה, [6]תָּבוֹא עָלָיו בְּרָכָה! [7]אֶלָּא, דְקָאָמְרִי עֵדִים, [8]אִי דִּכְתַב יָדָם יוֹצֵא מִמָּקוֹם אַחֵר, [9]פְּשִׁיטָא דְּלָא מְהֵימְנֵי. [10]וְאִי דְּאֵין כְּתַב יָדָם יוֹצֵא מִמָּקוֹם אַחֵר, [11]אַמַּאי לָא מְהֵימְנֵי? [12](סִימָן בא״ש)

LITERAL TRANSLATION

[1]Who said [this]? [2]If we say that the borrower said [it], [3]it is obvious. [4]Is it at all in his power? [5]But rather, [if we say] that the lender said [it], [6]may a blessing come upon him! [7]Rather, [if we say] that the witnesses said [it], [8]if their handwriting comes out from another place, [9]it is obvious that they are not believed. [10]And if their handwriting does not come out from another place, [11]why are they not believed?

[12](Mnemonic: בא״ש.)

RASHI

כל כמיניה – והלא עדים חתומים בו, פשיטא דיתקיים בחותמיו!

TRANSLATION AND COMMENTARY

דְקָאָמַר מַאן [1]The Gemara asks: **Who makes this statement,** claiming that the promissory note was signed on trust? There are three parties to a loan — the borrower, the lender, and the witnesses. Rav Yehudah did not specify which party made the statement that is not believed, and there are difficulties in explaining it as referring to any of them. [2]For **if we say that the borrower** refused to pay, and **said** that the promissory note was signed on trust, [3]**it is obvious** that his claim is not believed. [4]**Is it in any way in his power** to make such a claim? Since the authenticity of the note is not in question, the burden of proof is on the borrower to prove that no loan took place. The borrower is not even believed if he claims that he has repaid the loan, let alone that the note was signed on trust! [5]**On the other hand, if we say that** Rav Yehudah was referring to a case where **the lender** produced such a note, and then decided not to use it to collect his loan, **saying** that the note was in fact signed on trust and no loan had taken place, why would Rav Yehudah rule that he is not believed? [6]**May a blessing come upon him** for his honesty in refraining from pressing a false claim when he had the opportunity! [7]**On the other hand, if we say that** Rav Yehudah was referring to a case where **the witnesses** came forward and **said** that although their signatures on the note were authentic, no loan in fact had taken place, it is still difficult to explain why Rav Yehudah would rule that they are not believed. For this is precisely the case of our Mishnah, in which the witnesses confirm that the signatures are their own, but claim that they were disqualified or signed under duress. [8]The ruling of our Mishnah should apply to such a case, and **if** the witnesses' **handwriting is authenticated from other sources,** [9]**it is obvious that they are not believed,** because witnesses are not permitted to alter their previous testimony, as explained above (18b). [10]**And if their handwriting is not authenticated from other sources,** and the document is certified by the witnesses' testimony alone, [11]**why are they not believed?** Surely the mouth that forbade is the mouth that permitted, as the Mishnah ruled!

סִימָן בא״ש [12]The Gemara gives three possible answers to this problem, represented by a **mnemonic** — בא״ש — which refers to the names of the Amoraim who gave each answer: ב for רָבָא, who gave the first answer; א for אַבַּיֵי, who gave the second answer; and ש for רַב אַשִׁי, who gave the third answer.

BACKGROUND

תָּבוֹא עָלָיו בְּרָכָה May a blessing come upon him. This is an expression of praise for someone who does a good deed. It is used especially when the action performed is one that, by law, a person is not required to do.

סִימָן בא״ש Mnemonics of this kind were developed while the Talmud was still an oral corpus, and it was necessary to remember a series of topics, such as various approaches to a single issue, several challenges to a given teaching, etc. Since these mnemonics were intended merely to help students retain the material, they did not have to be precise. Hence in the present case we have the use of different letters from the Sages' names. When a mnemonic was created, an attempt was usually made to formulate it as a word or concept that would be easy to remember. The first initials of these Sages' names would not have formed a meaningful word, but the letters actually used mean "in the fire."

NOTES

consulting or even informing the lender, because the note imposes no obligations on the lender. *Tosafot* explains that the Mishnah permits signing a note on trust only if it remains in the custody of the borrower, but not if it passes into the lender's possession. *Rosh* adds that the witnesses are culpable only if they were involved when the document changed hands.

Tosefot Rid rejects *Tosafot's* solution, arguing that if the borrower wishes to trust the lender with the note, he is within his rights, and it is not the witnesses' concern. Accordingly, he rejects *Rashi's* explanation, and explains that a document signed on trust is a form of "document of persuasion" (שְׁטַר פַּסִּים) described below (19b), which attests to a completely fictitious loan or sale. Occasionally, a person may wish to give the impression that he is wealthy or that he is poor. In such a case, he may collaborate with a friend, and (if he wishes to appear wealthy) persuade his friend to sign a fictitious document attesting that the friend owes him a substantial sum of money ("a document of persuasion"), or (if he wishes to appear poor) entrust his friend with a fictitious document attesting that he owes the friend money ("a document signed on trust"). *Meiri* adds that such documents not only amount to false testimony, but can also be used to defraud innocent third parties. Hence, both of these documents are illegal, and witnesses must not sign them.

HALAKHAH

and cannot pay it back without collecting this debt, his admission is not believed, because it impinges on the interests of his creditors. Hence, if the document has been authenticated in court, or if the document was deposited with a third party, the debtor must pay the debt to his creditor's creditors," following Abaye's explanation of Rav Yehudah's statement. (*Rambam, Sefer Mishpatim, Hilkhot Malveh VeLoveh* 2:6; *Shulhan Arukh, Hoshen Mishpat* 47:1.)

¹אֲמַר רָבָא: לְעוֹלָם דְּקָאָמַר לֹוֶה, ²וְכִדְרַב הוּנָא. ³דְּאָמַר רַב הוּנָא אָמַר רַב: מוֹדֶה בִּשְׁטָר שֶׁכְּתָבוֹ, ⁴אֵין צָרִיךְ לְקַיְּימוֹ.
⁵אַבַּיֵי אֲמַר: לְעוֹלָם דְּאָמַר

TRANSLATION AND COMMENTARY

אֲמַר רָבָא [1](1) **Rava said: In fact,** Rav Yehudah was referring to a case where **the borrower admitted** drawing up the document, but claimed that it was signed on trust, and asked to be believed on the basis of a *miggo,* since he could have claimed that the document was forged. [2]**And** Rav Yehudah's statement **is in accordance with** the ruling of **Rav Huna.** [3]**For Rav Huna said in the name of Rav:** If a borrower **admits that he wrote a document,** [4]**the lender does not need to authenticate it,** because Rav Huna is of the opinion that it is impossible to construct a *miggo* on the basis of a hypothetical claim of forgery, as explained above. Thus Rav Yehudah is teaching us that a borrower who claims that a promissory note was "signed on trust" is not believed, even when the document cannot be authenticated in any other way, and even though his claim appears to be supported by a *miggo.*

אַבַּיֵי אֲמַר [5](2) **Abaye said: In fact,** Rav Yehudah was referring to a case where **the lender** produced the promissory note, and then decided not to collect with it, **saying** that the note had in fact been signed on trust and no loan took place. We objected above that there is surely no reason not to believe the lender

LITERAL TRANSLATION

[1]Rava said: In fact, the borrower said [it], [2]and it is in accordance with Rav Huna. [3]For Rav Huna said in the name of Rav: [If a borrower] admits that he wrote a note, [4]he [the lender] does not have to authenticate it.

[5]Abaye said: In fact, the lender

RASHI

כדרב הונא — ואשמעינן רב יהודה נמי הכי: דלוה שאמר כתבתיו ומסרתיו לו, אבל שטר אמנה הוא — אין צריך המלוה לחזור ולהביא להעיד על החתימה, דאין נאמן לוה לפוסלו, דלא עביד איניש דכתב ומסר בלא הלואה.

NOTES

לְעוֹלָם דְּאָמַר מַלְוֶה In fact, the lender said it. According to Abaye, the lender's admission is not believed, as it affects the rights of the lender's creditor. The Rishonim ask: If the lender had wished, he could simply have waived the debt, and the lender's creditor would have had no recourse. Now that he chooses to claim instead that the document was fictitious, he should have a *miggo.* Why, then, is he not believed?

Several answers are found in the Rishonim. Some argue that we learn from Rabbi Natan that a creditor cannot waive a debt due to him if it is needed to pay a debt of his own, because the debtor has a direct obligation to the creditor's creditor which the middleman cannot abrogate (*Ritva* in the name of *Ra'avad* and others). This explanation is difficult, because the Gemara (below, 85b) rules that a creditor who sells his promissory note to someone else may then waive the loan, thereby preventing the buyer from collecting. Surely the debtor in that case also has a direct obligation to the buyer, and yet the middleman can abrogate it! Some Rishonim explain that a sale of a promissory note does not in fact create a direct obligation, as only the lien on the debtor's property can be sold, but the debt itself is still owed to the original creditor. Moreover, many authorities maintain that it was the Rabbis who instituted the procedure for selling promissory notes, and the sale is not valid by Torah law. When the creditor borrows money, on the other hand, the original debtor has a direct obligation to the creditor's creditor, by virtue of Rabbi Natan's ruling (*Rashba, Ran*).

Some Rishonim explain that it is generally possible to waive a loan, even where the interests of a third party are involved, but it is not possible to do so in the circumstances of our case. *Ri Migash* notes that in our case the document has already been presented in court, and once this has happened, the third party's rights can no longer be abrogated. *Ramban* suggests that we may be referring to a case where the lender specifically mortgaged all his interests in future property to pay his debt to his creditor, and this formulation precludes him from waiving his rights by waiving the loan.

Other Rishonim explain that the lender could indeed have canceled his debt if he had waived it, even where this would harm a third party. They argue that the reason why the *miggo* argument submitted by the lender was insufficient to invalidate the document is because his *miggo* was flawed. Some Rishonim explain that the *miggo* was invalid because the lender is admitting to a crime and accusing the witnesses of a crime (*Ri Migash, Ramban* in the name of *Ra'avad*), but *Rosh* insists that the rule against self-incrimination applies only to testimony and the like, but not to a creditor who admits that he is not owed money.

Ra'ah explains that when the lender presented the document, it was considered as though he admitted to his creditor that it was valid, and no *miggo* can undermine such an admission. *Ritva* cites an opinion that *miggo* is effective only if the claimant wishes to retain an interest, on the grounds that he could have done so in some other way, but here the lender wishes to lose his interest in the loan by invalidating the document. *Tosafot* explains that the *miggo* is flawed because the lender prefers to invalidate the document rather than waive the debt. For even if he declares the document invalid, the borrower knows the truth, and his conscience may compel him to pay the debt of his own volition; but once the debt has been waived, the debtor will not feel any obligation to pay. *Ba'al HaMa'or* explains, along similar lines, that the lender will find it easier to change his story and claim the debt again — perhaps in a different court — if he invalidates the document rather than waives the debt.

מַלְוֶה, [1]וּכְגוֹן שֶׁחָב לַאֲחֵרִים, [2]וְכִדְרַבִּי נָתָן. [3]דְּתַנְיָא: "רַבִּי נָתָן אוֹמֵר: [4]מִנַּיִן לְנוֹשֶׁה בַּחֲבֵירוֹ מָנֶה, וַחֲבֵירוֹ בַּחֲבֵירוֹ, [5]מִנַּיִן שֶׁמּוֹצִיאִין מִזֶּה וְנוֹתְנִין לָזֶה? [6]תַּלְמוּד לוֹמַר: 'וְנָתַן לַאֲשֶׁר אָשַׁם לוֹ'". [7]רַב אַשִׁי אֲמַר: לְעוֹלָם דְּקָאָמְרִי עֵדִים, [8]וּדְאֵין כְּתַב יָדָם יוֹצֵא מִמָּקוֹם אַחֵר.

LITERAL TRANSLATION

said [it], and it is, [1]for example, where he harms other people, [2]and in accordance with Rabbi Natan. [3]For it was taught: "Rabbi Natan says: [4]From where [do we know] that if someone is owed a maneh by his fellow, and his fellow by his fellow, [5]from where [do we know] that we take from this one and give to that one? [6]The verse states: 'And he shall give [it] to him against whom he has trespassed.'"

[7]Rav Ashi said: In fact, the witnesses said [it], [8]and [it applies] where their handwriting does not come out from another place.

TRANSLATION AND COMMENTARY

in such a case, and indeed he is deserving of praise. [1]But in fact, says Abaye, Rav Yehudah's ruling does apply, **for example, where** the lender's admission **harms** the interests of **other people.** This could occur in a situation where the lender owes money to other people, and does not have enough money to repay his debts unless he collects this sum. In such a case, the lender is not at liberty to invalidate the document by claiming that it was signed on trust, because the rights of his own creditors are also involved. [2]The Gemara adds: Rav Yehudah's ruling on this matter is **in accordance with Rabbi Natan's** statement in the following Baraita. [3]**For it was taught** in a Baraita: **"Rabbi Natan says:** [4]**From where do we know that if someone is owed a maneh by another person, and** this **other person** is owed a similar sum **by yet another person —** [5]**from where do we know that** in such a case the court **takes** the money **from** the ultimate debtor **and gives it to** the ultimate creditor, without involving the middleman at all? [6]**The** verse **states** (Numbers 5:7): **'And he shall give it to him against whom he has trespassed.'"** The Gemara in tractate *Bava Kamma* (110a) explains that the word אָשַׁם ("he has trespassed"), which also appears in the following verse, refers there to the principal of the debt. Applying the same idea to this verse, it can be read: "He shall give it to him to whom the principal belongs." Thus we learn that a debtor can fulfill his obligation by paying his debt to the ultimate creditor, without involving the middleman. By implication, we can infer that the debtor has a direct obligation to the ultimate creditor, as well as to the person who lent him money. Therefore the lender cannot invalidate the document without proof, because his admission impinges on the interests of other people as well.

רַב אַשִׁי אָמַר [7](3) **Rav Ashi said: In fact,** Rav Yehudah was referring to a case in which **the witnesses** came forward and **said** that although their signatures on the document were authentic, no loan transaction actually took place. We objected, above, that this was simply the case of our Mishnah. If the witnesses' handwriting can be produced from other sources, it is obvious that they are not believed, and if their handwriting cannot be produced from other sources, there is no reason why they should not be believed. But in fact Rav Yehudah's ruling does [8]**apply where their handwriting cannot be produced from other sources.**

RASHI

שחב לאחרים — בהודאה זו, שהוא מודה שהוא שטר אמנה — חב ומפסיד את אחרים הנושים בו, ואין לו מה להגבותם, והיו רוצים לגבות חוב זה. **ונתן לאשר אשם לו** — ולא כתב "לאשר הלוהו" אלא לאשר האשם שלו. ואשם הוא קרן כדאמרינן ב"הגוזל" (בבא קמא קי,א) — למי שהקרן שלו.

NOTES

וּכְגוֹן שֶׁחָב לַאֲחֵרִים And it is, for example, where he harms other people. According to Abaye, the lender is not believed to the extent of invalidating the document, because this could harm a third party, namely the lender's creditor, who would thus be prevented from collecting his debt. There is a difference of opinion among the Rishonim as to the status of the document if the lender subsequently finds a way to satisfy his own creditor without collecting this debt. Does our authentication of the document still stand, or do we now believe the lender's admission, because it no longer harms other people?

Ra'avad rules that the document remains valid, and the lender can collect with it, because his admission that the document was signed on trust was rejected by the court. *Rabbenu Yonah* agrees with *Ra'avad* if the admission was made in response to a claim by the lender's creditor, because it may not have been intended seriously. But if the admission was made at the lender's own initiative, *Rabbenu Yonah* rules that it must be accepted regarding the lender himself, because his admission was rejected only insofar as it affected the rights of a third party, but not if no third pary was involved. Therefore the lender is bound by his admission, and cannot use the document to collect for himself.

HALAKHAH

רַבִּי נָתָן אוֹמֵר Rabbi Natan says. "If a debtor owes money to a creditor, and the creditor owes money in turn to his creditor, we take the money from the debtor and give it directly to his creditor's creditor, regardless of when the two loans were made. This law applies regardless of whether the debt arose as a result of a loan, a sale, unpaid

BACKGROUND

שֶׁחָב לַאֲחֵרִים Where he harms other people. The principle that "the admission of a litigant is equal to the testimony of 100 witnesses" is not based on the essential reliability of a confession. For, as we have seen above, a confession in a criminal trial has no legal validity whatsoever. Rather, the admission of a monetary obligation is regarded as the making of a gift — something a person can do in any way he wishes. An admission thus effects the transfer of money or property from one person to another. But if such an admission has direct monetary consequences for a third party, then the admission is of no legal effect, because it "harms other people."

SAGES

רַבִּי נָתָן Rabbi Natan. This is Rabbi Natan the Babylonian, who immigrated to Eretz Israel and was one of the greatest Tannaim during the generation before the completion of the Mishnah. Rabbi Natan was the son of the Exilarch in Babylonia, a member of a family descended from King David, the family with the highest lineage among the Jews. Because of his greatness as a Torah scholar and his noble lineage, he was named deputy to the president of the Sanhedrin. He was famous for his profound knowledge of civil law. Similarly, he was known for his piety, and it is said that Elijah the Prophet used to appear to him.

Rabbi Natan, together with Rabbi Meir, tried to alter the procedure for choosing the president of the Sanhedrin. This effort failed, and as a kind of punishment it was decreed that Rabbi Natan should not be mentioned by name in the Mishnah, but that his teachings be introduced anonymously with the phrase, "Some say." But this decision was not always observed in practice.

Rabbi Natan edited a number of collections of Mishnaic teachings, and the tractate *Avot DeRabbi Natan* is named after him. Many Sages of the following generation were his students, the most prominent of whom was Rabbi Yehudah HaNasi.

SAGES

רַב שֵׁשֶׁת בְּרֵיהּ דְּרַב אִידִי **Rav Sheshet the son of Rav Idi.** This Babylonian Amora of the fourth generation was also known as Rav Shisha. He and his brother, Rav Yehoshua, were sons of Rav Idi bar Avin, a disciple of Rav Ḥisda. Rav Sheshet the son of Rav Idi discussed the Halakhah with other Sages of his generation, in particular with Rav Pappa.

TRANSLATION AND COMMENTARY

[1]**And as for what you** asked before: **"Why are they not believed?"** — in accordance with the law of the Mishnah, as they would be if they had claimed to be minors, or to have acted under a threat to life — we can answer that Rav Yehudah was teaching us that his ruling is [2]**in accordance with** the viewpoint of **Rav Kahana,** who rules that a claim that a note was signed on trust is the equivalent of a claim to have acted under duress because of money, not because of a threat to life. [3]**For Rav Kahana said: It is forbidden for a person to retain in his house a promissory note signed on trust,** [4]**because the verse** (Job 11:14) **states: "Do not let wickedness dwell in your tents."** According to Rav Kahana, a note attesting to a loan that never took place is simply false testimony, and is considered wicked — even if the borrower drew it up of his own free will. Not only is it forbidden to draw up such a note, but it is also forbidden to keep it in one's home. [19B] [5]**And,** the Gemara continues, **Rav Sheshet the son of Rav Idi said:** [6]We can **conclude from this statement of Rav Kahana** [7]that if **witnesses said: "Our words were on trust,"** i.e., the document the witnesses signed was in fact signed on trust, [8]they **are not believed.** [9]**What is the reason?** [10]**Since** Rav Kahana ruled that a deed signed on trust **is** a form of **wickedness,** honest witnesses **would not sign** a **wicked** document. Thus, when the witnesses claim that they signed the document on trust, they are in effect confessing to a crime, and we have already seen (above, 18b) that such claims are not believed, even when they are supported by the argument that "the mouth that forbade is the mouth that permitted."

[1]וּדְקָאָמְרַתְּ: "אַמַּאי לָא מְהֵימְנֵי"? [2]כִּדְרַב כָּהֲנָא. [3]דְּאָמַר רַב כָּהֲנָא: אָסוּר לוֹ לְאָדָם שֶׁיַּשְׁהֶה שְׁטָר אֲמָנָה בְּתוֹךְ בֵּיתוֹ, [4]מִשּׁוּם שֶׁנֶּאֱמַר: "אַל תַּשְׁכֵּן בְּאֹהָלֶיךָ עַוְלָה". [19B] [5]וַאֲמַר רַב שֵׁשֶׁת בְּרֵיהּ דְּרַב אִידִי: [6]שְׁמַע מִינָּהּ מִדְּרַב כָּהֲנָא: [7]עֵדִים שֶׁאָמְרוּ: "אֲמָנָה הָיוּ דְּבָרֵינוּ", [8]אֵין נֶאֱמָנִין. [9]מַאי טַעְמָא? [10]כֵּיוָן דְּ"עַוְלָה" הוּא, אַעַוְלָה לָא חָתְמֵי.

LITERAL TRANSLATION

[1]And as for what you said: "Why are they not believed?" [2]it is in accordance with Rav Kahana. [3]For Rav Kahana said: It is forbidden for a person to retain inside his house a promissory note [signed on] trust, [4]because it is said: "Do not let wickedness dwell in your tents." [19B] [5]And Rav Sheshet the son of Rav Idi said: [6]Conclude from this [statement] of Rav Kahana: [7]Witnesses who said: "Our words were on trust," [8]are not believed. [9]What is the reason? [10]Since it is "wickedness," they do not sign on wickedness.

RASHI

ואמר רב ששת — גרסינן. **אעולה לא חתמי** — וכי אמרי "אמנה" — אין נאמנים להרשיע את עצמן.

NOTES

אַמַּאי לָא מְהֵימְנֵי **"Why are they not believed?"** The conclusion of our Gemara is that since it is forbidden to retain a document signed on trust, it is also forbidden to sign it. Therefore witnesses who testify that they signed it are in effect incriminating themselves, and are not to be believed. This conclusion appears to be disputed by the Jerusalem Talmud, in its comment on our Mishnah. There Rav Huna is quoted as stating, in the name of Rav, that witnesses are believed when they claim that a document was signed on trust. This ruling is then contrasted with another statement of Rav, forbidding witnesses to sign such a document. In order to resolve the contradiction, the Jerusalem Talmud amends the latter statement slightly, explaining that Rav did not forbid the witnesses to sign a document on trust, but rather forbade the lender to retain it in his possession. To support this emendation, the Jerusalem Talmud cites yet another statement of Rav, in which he declares that retaining a document signed on trust is considered iniquitous. This last statement is also cited by our Gemara (below, 19b) in the name of the Sages of the West — i.e., of Eretz Israel.

Thus the conclusion of the Jerusalem Talmud is that witnesses are permitted to sign a document on trust, although the lender is forbidden to keep it in his possession; hence witnesses who testify that they signed a document on trust are believed, if their testimony is supported by the "mouth that forbade" argument. In this conclusion, the Jerusalem Talmud appears to disagree with our Gemara. Presumably, however, the Jerusalem Talmud means that the witnesses claim that they thought that the

HALAKHAH

wages, or any other factor. It applies, however, only where the middleman has no other convenient way of paying his creditor, such as when his property is in another country. But if the middleman has property available here, we do not take away the debtor's property and give it to the creditor's creditor," following Rabbi Natan. (*Rambam, Sefer Mishpatim, Hilkhot Malveh VeLoveh* 2:6; *Shulḥan Arukh, Ḥoshen Mishpat* 86:1,2.)

אֲמָנָה הָיוּ דְּבָרֵינוּ **"Our words were on trust."** "If the witnesses confirm their signatures on a document but claim that the document was signed on trust, they are not believed, even where there is no other way to certify the document, because signing a document on trust amounts to false testimony, and confessing to it amounts to self-incrimination," following Rav Sheshet the son of Rav Idi, Rav Naḥman, and Mar bar Rav Ashi. (*Rambam, Sefer Shofetim, Hilkhot Edut* 3:7; *Shulḥan Arukh, Ḥoshen Mishpat* 46:37.)

TRANSLATION AND COMMENTARY

אָמַר רַבִּי יְהוֹשֻׁעַ בֶּן לֵוִי [1]Having mentioned Rav Kahana's interpretation of the verse from Job as referring to a document signed on trust, the Gemara now cites a slightly different application of the same verse. **Rabbi Yehoshua ben Levi said: It is forbidden for a person to retain in his house a promissory note** attesting to a loan that has already been **repaid,** [2]**because the verse states: "Do not let wickedness dwell in your tents."** Rabbi Yehoshua ben Levi also interprets the verse from Job as referring to "wicked" documents. However, while Rav Kahana explains it as referring to a promissory note signed on trust, Rabbi Yehoshua ben Levi says that it refers to a repaid promissory note. Normally, when a loan is repaid, the promissory note testifying to it is torn up. Occasionally, however, the parties may have some reason not to tear the note up (as the Gemara explains below). According to Rabbi Yehoshua ben Levi, it is forbidden to retain such a repaid note, even though the note was originally valid and the borrower trusts the lender not to make improper use of it, because it is wrong to retain an instrument that can later be used to "prove" a falsehood.

בְּמַעֲרָבָא [3]The Gemara now cites another, slightly different interpretation of the verse from Job (11:14). **In Eretz Israel they said in Rav's name:** The entire verse from Job can be interpreted as referring to improperly drawn-up documents. [4]The first part of the verse reads: **"If iniquity is in your hand, put it far away." This** refers to **a promissory note signed on trust, and** to **a document of persuasion** (a document attesting to a fictitious transfer of ownership, which one party persuades another to accept in a conspiracy to defraud a third party). These two documents are called "iniquity," which is worse than "wickedness," because they involve false testimony. [5]The second part of the verse reads: **"And do not let wickedness dwell in your tents." This** refers to **a paid promissory note,** as explained by Rabbi Yehoshua ben Levi above.

[1]אָמַר רַבִּי יְהוֹשֻׁעַ בֶּן לֵוִי: אָסוּר לוֹ לְאָדָם שֶׁיַּשְׁהֶה שְׁטָר פָּרוּעַ בְּתוֹךְ בֵּיתוֹ, [2]מִשּׁוּם שֶׁנֶּאֱמַר "אַל תַּשְׁכֵּן בְּאֹהָלֶיךָ עַוְלָה". [3]בְּמַעֲרָבָא מִשְּׁמֵיהּ דְּרַב אָמְרִי: [4]"אִם אָוֶן בְּיָדְךָ, הַרְחִיקֵהוּ" — זֶה שְׁטָר אֲמָנָה וּשְׁטָר פַּסִּים. [5]"וְאַל תַּשְׁכֵּן בְּאֹהָלֶיךָ עַוְלָה" — זֶה שְׁטָר פָּרוּעַ.

LITERAL TRANSLATION

[1]Rabbi Yehoshua ben Levi said: It is forbidden for a man to retain a paid promissory note inside his house, [2]because it is said: "Do not let wickedness dwell in your tents."

[3]In Eretz Israel (lit., "in the West") they said in Rav's name: [4]"If iniquity is in your hand, put it far away" — this is a promissory note [signed on] trust and a document of persuasion. [5]"And do not let wickedness dwell in your tents" — this is a paid promissory note.

LANGUAGE

שְׁטָר פַּסִּים A document of persuasion. Some commentators explain that the word פַּסִּים, like the word פִּיּוּס, means "persuasion," because the borrower attempts to "persuade" the lender to grant him a loan. However, the Jerusalem Talmud appears to read שְׁטָר פִּסְטִיס. According to this reading, the second word in our expression is the Greek word πίστις, *pistis,* meaning "trust." Thus a "deed of *pistis*" would be similar to a promissory note signed on trust (שְׁטָר אֲמָנָה).

NOTES

note would be left in the borrower's possession. *Rosh* explains that in such a case even our Gemara would agree that the witnesses are believed, because it is permitted to draw up a document on trust, provided that it is left with the borrower.

אִם אָוֶן בְּיָדְךָ "If iniquity is in your hand." It is clear from the context that "iniquity" is even more abhorrent than "wickedness." *Tosafot* explains that "iniquity" refers to something irredeemably evil, whereas "wickedness" refers to something good that has been perverted. Thus Rav is of the opinion that both a document signed on trust and a document of persuasion are inherently iniquitous, because they are total fabrications, whereas a paid promissory note was originally valid, and only became wicked when the lender retained it. *Maharam Schiff* adds that the verse commands us to keep "iniquity" far from us, whereas we are only forbidden to allow "wickedness" to dwell among us. This is because we should never have anything to do with documents of persuasion or trust, but a paid document may come into our possession legitimately, although it becomes wickedness if it is allowed to overstay its time and "dwell" among us.

שְׁטָר פַּסִּים A document of persuasion. Our commentary follows *Rashi* (below, 79a), who explains that the Gemara is referring to a document attesting to a fictitious transfer of property, as part of a conspiracy to defraud a third party. *Tosefot Rid* and *Meiri* explain that a document of persuasion is a form of "document signed on trust" (שְׁטָר אֲמָנָה) described above (19a). Occasionally, a person may wish to give the impression that he is wealthy or that he is poor. In such a case, he may approach a friend, and (if he wishes to appear wealthy) *persuade* his friend to sign a fictitious document attesting that the friend owes him money (a document of persuasion), or (if he wishes to appear poor) *trust* his friend with a fictitious document attesting that he owes the friend money (a document signed on trust).

HALAKHAH

אָסוּר לוֹ לְאָדָם שֶׁיַּשְׁהֶה שְׁטָר פָּרוּעַ It is forbidden for a man to retain a paid promissory note. "A lender may not retain a promissory note in his possession after the loan has been repaid, following Rabbi Yehoshua ben Levi. *Shulhan Arukh* rules, following *Ran,* that the lender must not retain the document, even if the borrower has not yet paid the scribe's fee. However, *Shakh* notes that many Rishonim — *Tosafot, Rosh,* and *Ritva* — rule that it is permitted to retain the document until the scribe's fee has been paid. Moreover, *Shakh* concludes that it is permitted to retain the note, even according to *Ran,* if the lender marks it in such a way that it is clear that the loan has already been repaid." (*Shulhan Arukh, Hoshen Mishpat* 57:1.)

BACKGROUND

סֵפֶר שֶׁאֵינוֹ מוּגָּה A scroll that is not corrected. A handwritten sacred book that has not been proofread, and for this reason probably contains scribal errors, can lead people into error on two counts. (1) A scribal error may change or distort the meaning of the text, and thus lead the reader to derive incorrect theoretical or practical conclusions. (2) Moreover, if it is a sacred scroll which is meant to be read publicly, to satisfy a religious obligation that it be read and heard, any error in it, even though it may not change the meaning, makes it impossible to regard the book as part of the Scriptures, which must be copied exactly from the original source, letter by letter and word by word. An error in such a text makes the entire scroll invalid until it has been corrected.

[1] מַאן דְּאָמַר: "שְׁטָר פָּרוּעַ" — [2] כָּל שֶׁכֵּן שְׁטַר אֲמָנָה. [3] וּמַאן דְּאָמַר: "שְׁטַר אֲמָנָה" — [4] אֲבָל שְׁטָר פָּרוּעַ לָא, [5] דִּזְמְנִין דְּמַשְׁהֵי לֵיהּ אַפְּשִׁיטֵי דְסַפְרָא.
[6] אִתְּמַר: סֵפֶר שֶׁאֵינוֹ מוּגָּה, [7] אָמַר רַבִּי אַמִי: עַד שְׁלֹשִׁים יוֹם מוּתָּר לְשְׁהוֹתוֹ; [8] מִכָּאן וְאֵילָךְ, אָסוּר לְשְׁהוֹתוֹ, [9] מִשּׁוּם שֶׁנֶּאֱמַר: "אַל תַּשְׁכֵּן בְּאֹהָלֶיךָ עַוְלָה".

LITERAL TRANSLATION

[1] The one who says: "A paid promissory note" — [2] how much more so a promissory note [signed on] trust. [3] But the one who says: "A promissory note [signed on] trust" — [4] but not a paid promissory note, [5] because he sometimes retains it because of the scribe's coins.
[6] It was stated: [Regarding] a scroll that is not corrected, [7] Rabbi Ammi said: Up to thirty days it is permitted to retain it; [8] from then (lit., "here") onward, it is forbidden to retain it, [9] because it is said: "Do not let wickedness dwell in your tents."

TRANSLATION AND COMMENTARY

מַאן דְּאָמַר [1] The Gemara observes that whereas Rav Kahana described notes signed on trust as "wickedness" but made no reference to paid notes, Rabbi Yehoshua ben Levi described paid notes as "wickedness" but made no reference to notes signed on trust. However, **the one** (Rabbi Yehoshua ben Levi) **who said** that **"a paid promissory note** is wickedness" — [2] **how much more so** would he say that **a promissory note signed on trust** is wickedness. [3] **But the one** (Rav Kahana) **who said** that **"a promissory note signed on trust** is wickedness" [4] would **not** describe the retention of **a paid promissory note** as wickedness, [5] **because** he maintains that there can **sometimes** be a legitimate reason for not tearing up a note after a loan has been repaid. By law, the borrower must pay the scribe's fee for drawing up the note. Occasionally, however, if the borrower has no money on hand, the lender may provide the money temporarily. Now, if the borrower has still not paid this fee when he repays the loan itself, the lender may **retain** the document **against the scribe's charge,** until it is paid. Rabbi Yehoshua ben Levi, however, is of the opinion that the possibility of iniquity occasioned by retaining such a note is so great that no consideration of the kind just mentioned can justify it.

אִתְּמַר [6] Having mentioned the verse from the Book of Job, the Gemara now cites another interpretation of the same verse. **The Amoraim made a statement regarding a scroll** of the Bible **that has not been corrected.** Traditionally, the Books of the Bible were handwritten on scrolls. Each copy had to be precisely correct — to the letter, and even to the shape of the letter. Copying a Book of the Bible was, therefore, an exacting task, and could only be performed by a highly trained scribe. If a scribal error was found in a Book of the Bible, or if one of the letters was erased by accident, the scroll had to be brought to a scribe to be corrected. Occasionally, the scroll's owner might delay making the correction for some reason. In such a case, [7] **Rabbi Ammi said:** For a period of **up to thirty days it is permitted to retain** the uncorrected scroll in one's house; [8] **from then onward, it is forbidden to retain it,** [9] **because the verse states: "Do not let wickedness dwell in your tents."** If someone were to read the uncorrected scroll, he might be led into error, and this is considered wickedness.

RASHI

על פשיטי דספרא — שעל הלוה ליתן שכר הסופר, ופעמים שאין לו, ונותנו המלוה, וחוזר וגובהו ממנו בשעת פרעון, ומעכב השטר עליו. **ספר שאינו מוגה** — תורה נביאים וכתובים. **מוגה** — מן טעיות שבו.

NOTES

סֵפֶר שֶׁאֵינוֹ מוּגָּה A scroll that is not corrected. Our commentary follows *Rashi*, who explains that Rabbi Ammi is referring to Books of the Bible, whose wording and lettering must be precise. *Ri Migash* explains that only a Torah scroll of the type that is read in the synagogue must be corrected immediately. But if the error appears in some other Book of the Bible, it can be left uncorrected for a longer period of time. This also appears to be the view of *Rif* and *Rambam*. Many Rishonim, however, rule that it is forbidden to leave even a non-Scriptural book uncorrected, such as a volume of the Talmud (*Ritva, Rosh, Rabbenu Yonah*, and others), and *Bet Yosef* points out (*Bedek HaBayit, Yoreh De'ah* 279) that the dangers of being misled by a faulty book of Halakhah are perhaps greatest of all.

עַד שְׁלֹשִׁים יוֹם Up to thirty days. From the language of Rabbi Ammi, it would appear that he derives the law forbidding one to retain an uncorrected scroll from the verse in Job (11:14) which forbids leaving wicked things in

HALAKHAH

סֵפֶר שֶׁאֵינוֹ מוּגָּה A scroll that is not corrected. "It is forbidden to retain in one's possession for more than thirty days a Torah scroll that needs correcting. Rather, it must be corrected or put away in a genizah, where sacred objects that are no longer usable are stored, following Rabbi Ammi. *Rema* adds, in the name of *Rashi*, that the same law applies to other Books of the Bible, and, in the name of *Rabbenu Yeruḥam*, that the same law applies to Talmud texts and the like." (*Rambam, Sefer Ahavah, Hilkhot Sefer Torah* 7:12; *Shulḥan Arukh, Yoreh De'ah* 279:1.)

LITERAL TRANSLATION

[1]Rav Naḥman said: [2]Witnesses who said: "Our words were on trust," are not believed; [3]"our words were [accompanied by] a protest," are not believed.

[1]אָמַר רַב נַחְמָן: [2]עֵדִים שֶׁאָמְרוּ: "אֲמָנָה הָיוּ דְּבָרֵינוּ", אֵין נֶאֱמָנִין; [3]"מוֹדָעָא הָיוּ דְּבָרֵינוּ", אֵין נֶאֱמָנִין.

RASHI

עדים – החתומים בשטר, ואמרו: אמנה היו דברינו. לא הלוהו כלום, אלא כתבנו לו: לכשיצטרך ילוה לו. וזה שיעבד לו נכסיו מעכשיו אם ילוה אפילו לאחר זמן, דלאו מוקדם ליהוי לטרוף שלא כדין. מודעא היו דברינו – אם שטר מכר הוא, ואמרו עדים החתומים בו: המוכר מסר מודעא בפנינו והראנו אונסו, והכרנו בו. אין נאמנין – דלא אתי על פה ומרע ליה לשטרא.

TRANSLATION AND COMMENTARY

אָמַר רַב נַחְמָן [1]The Gemara now returns to the topic of promissory notes signed on trust. Rav Yehudah ruled above (19a) that a person who claims that a note was signed on trust is not believed, and Rav Ashi explained this as referring to a statement made by witnesses who authenticated their signatures on a promissory note but claimed that the note was signed on trust. Even though their testimony is supported by the "mouth that forbade" argument, they are not believed, because signing such a note is a crime and criminals are not qualified to be witnesses. Using the same reasoning, **Rav Naḥman said:** [2]If witnesses said: "Our words were on trust" (i.e., the note signed by the witnesses was in fact signed on trust), **they are not believed,** as explained above. Rav Naḥman now goes on to apply this idea to another case: [3]If the witnesses said: **"Our words were accompanied by a protest** on the part of the seller," **they** too **are not believed.** If someone is being coerced into selling his property and being threatened with harm if he refuses, the proper procedure is for the threatened person to inform witnesses about the threat in advance, and then to sign whatever document the buyer is forcing him to sign. Later, if the buyer tries to enforce the document in court, the victim can produce the witnesses to testify that they were informed of the threat prior to the signing of the document, and that the threatened party declared that the document he was about to sign was null and void. This procedure of protest is called *moda'a* (מוֹדָעָא). Rav Naḥman is informing us by his ruling that if the witnesses who heard the threatened person deliver his formal protest were the same witnesses who later signed the document, and these people came to court and said: "The signatures are ours, but the seller made a formal protest beforehand in our presence," they are not believed, because by signing the document they became accessories to a crime, and witnesses are not believed if the effect is to incriminate them.

NOTES

one's house. Some Rishonim explain that the dispensation to keep the uncorrected scroll for thirty days is derived from the same verse. *Ritva* explains that the verse uses the verb שכן — "to dwell" — and the Gemara (*Sanhedrin* 112a) explains in connection with a verse (Deuteronomy 13:16) referring to "those who dwell in the city" that a person is not considered to be "dwelling" in a place until he has been there for thirty days. *Shittah Mekubbetzet* derives the dispensation from the word אַל — "do not" — which precedes the word "let dwell" in the verse. The word אַל has a numerical value of thirty-one in the Talmudic system of numerology called gematria. Thus the verse is saying, as it were, "do not let it dwell thirty-one days," and by implication thirty days are permitted.

מוֹדָעָא הָיוּ דְּבָרֵינוּ אֵין נֶאֱמָנִין "Our words were accompanied by a protest," they are not believed. According to Rav Naḥman, witnesses are not believed if they claim that the document they signed had been annulled earlier by a formal protest made by one of the parties that he was acting under duress. In our commentary we have followed *Ran*, who explains that Rav Naḥman is of the opinion that the witnesses were not permitted to sign the document, since they knew that it was null and void. Hence, when they now claim that the document was preceded by a formal protest, they are in effect incriminating themselves, and should not be believed, even where "the mouth that forbade is the mouth that permitted." *Ran* compares this case with that of witnesses who claim they signed falsely because of a financial threat, noting that in this case as well the pressure imposed on the party to the transaction was essentially financial. Hence Rav Naḥman maintains that the witnesses must refuse to sign, even if this means that the claimant will suffer financial loss. Mar bar Rav Ashi, by contrast, maintains that the witnesses are permitted to sign, in order to save the claimant from the person exerting pressure on him, even though they would not have been permitted to sign in order to save themselves from similar financial pressure. Hence they are believed, provided they are supported by the "mouth that forbade" argument.

Rashi, *Tosafot*, and *Rosh* agree with *Ran*'s explanation of Mar bar Rav Ashi, but not concerning Rav Naḥman, arguing that his reasoning has nothing to do with self-incrimination. Rather, he maintains that the witnesses are not believed if the effect is to invalidate the document because their "mouth that forbade" argument is flawed. In the case of the Mishnah above (18b), where the witnesses admitted signing but claimed that they were disqualified, or had acted under duress, they were in effect canceling the

HALAKHAH

מוֹדָעָא הָיוּ דְּבָרֵינוּ "Our words were accompanied by a protest." "If witnesses claim that, before they signed the document, one party to the transaction delivered a protest before them that he was acting under duress, *Rambam* and

SAGES

מָר בַּר רַב אַשִׁי Mar bar Rav Ashi. A Babylonian Amora of the seventh generation, Mar bar Rav Ashi was the son of the famous Amora, Rav Ashi. His personal name was Tavyumi. He studied under his father, inheriting his position as head of the Mata Meḥasya Yeshivah twenty-four years after his father's death. He held this position for thirteen years.

TRANSLATION AND COMMENTARY

מָר בַּר רַב אַשִׁי אָמַר [1] **Mar bar Rav Ashi said:** Regarding witnesses who said: **"Our words were on trust,"** I agree with Rav Naḥman that **they are not believed,** because they are incriminating themselves. [2] But regarding witnesses who said: **"Our words were** accompanied by **a protest** on the part of the seller," I maintain that **they are believed,** if their claim is supported by the "mouth that forbade" argument. [3] **What is the reason?** [4] A document of sale preceded by a formal protest by the seller **is allowed to be written,** unlike a note signed on trust, [5] which **is not allowed to be written.** Just as the person who is threatened is allowed to write a false document to save himself from harm, so too are the witnesses allowed to sign it. Hence the witnesses are not confessing to a crime when they testify that the note was annulled in advance by means of a formal protest.

[1] מָר בַּר רַב אַשִׁי אָמַר: ״אֲמָנָה הָיוּ דְּבָרֵינוּ״, אֵין נֶאֱמָנִין; [2] ״מוֹדָעָא הָיוּ דְּבָרֵינוּ״, נֶאֱמָנִין. [3] מַאי טַעְמָא? [4] הַאי נִיתָּן לִיכָּתֵב, [5] וְהַאי לֹא נִיתָּן לִיכָּתֵב.

LITERAL TRANSLATION

[1] Mar bar Rav Ashi said: [Witnesses who said:] "Our words were on trust," are not believed; [2] "our words were [accompanied by] a protest," are believed. [3] What is the reason? [4] This is permitted to be written, [5] but that is not permitted to be written.

RASHI

מודעא – ניתן לעדים לכתוב את השטר כדי להציל האנוס מאונסו, אמנה לא ניתן להכתב, דעולה הוא. וכי אמרו חתמנו – משוי לנפשייהו רשעים, ואין אדם נאמן לשום עצמו רשע.

NOTES

validity of the document by saying that it was procedurally flawed. Hence, since we had no other way of authenticating the document, we were forced to believe them, in accordance with the "mouth that forbade" argument. But in our present case, the witnesses admit that there was no procedural flaw in the document itself. They themselves were qualified witnesses and were under no coercive threat. Hence their authentication stands, and their subsequent oral testimony cannot refute the written testimony of the document, for once a witness has testified, he cannot return and amend his testimony. *Pnei Yehoshua* notes that this argument applies only to the witnesses who signed the note; but if other witnesses were to say that a formal protest was made, they would be believed.

הַאי נִיתָּן לִיכָּתֵב This is allowed to be written. Our commentary follows *Rashi* and most of the Rishonim, who explain that Mar bar Rav Ashi meant that the *document attesting to the loan* was permitted to be written. According to this explanation, witnesses who admit signing a document on trust are incriminating themselves, but witnesses who admit that a document they signed had previously been canceled through a protest are not incriminating themselves, because they were permitted to sign it. *Rashi* explains that the witnesses are permitted to sign the document in order to save the claimant from the person who is threatening him. *Ri Migash* explains that the witnesses are permitted to sign because a document annulled by a protest is merely canceled; it is not false testimony, like a document signed on trust.

Ba'al HaMa'or cites a different explanation of Mar bar Rav Ashi, in the name of *Rabbenu Nissim Gaon*. According to this explanation, Mar bar Rav Ashi meant that the witnesses are believed because it is permitted to write a *document of protest*. For even Rav Naḥman would agree that it is permitted to draw up a document of protest, annulling a subsequent document, and that the witnesses are permitted to sign both documents. Rav Naḥman, however, maintains that this is true only if the protest was drawn up in writing; but if the witnesses testify orally, they are not believed, because this amounts to altering previous testimony. Mar bar Rav Ashi, by contrast, maintains that since a written protest is believed, the witnesses are also believed when they testify orally.

Ran points out that there is an important practical difference between the two explanations. According to the first, Mar bar Rav Ashi considers a claim that a protest was made to be the equivalent of other nonincriminating claims (like the claims in our Mishnah). Hence he would presumably believe the witnesses only when their testimony is needed to authenticate the document, because "the mouth that forbade is the mouth that permitted." According to *Rabbenu Nissim Gaon*, by contrast, Mar bar Rav Ashi considers a verbal claim that a protest was made to be the equivalent of a formal written protest, and would believe them in all circumstances, even where the document has already been authenticated in some other way.

וְהַאי לֹא נִיתָּן לִיכָּתֵב But that is not allowed to be written. Our Gemara presents the question as to whether witnesses are believed if they claim that a document they signed was preceded by a formal protest by one of the parties as a

HALAKHAH

Shulḥan Arukh rule, following Mar bar Rav Ashi, that they are believed, even if the signatures on the document have already been authenticated in some other way. *Shakh*, however, notes that *Rosh* and many other Rishonim maintain that the witnesses are believed only when their testimony is necessary to authenticate their signatures, because the mouth that forbade is the mouth that permitted; but where their testimony is not necessary to authenticate the signatures, they are not believed. Moreover, *Rav Hai Gaon* and others rule that these witnesses are never believed, even when their testimony is needed to authenticate their signatures, following Rav Naḥman." (*Rambam, Sefer Shofetim, Hilkhot Edut* 3:8; *Shulḥan Arukh, Ḥoshen Mishpat* 46:37.)

TRANSLATION AND COMMENTARY

בְּעָא מִינֵּיהּ רָבָא מֵרַב נַחְמָן [1]**Rava asked Rav Naḥman,** who ruled that even witnesses who testify to a protest are not believed: [2]According to you, **what** is the law **concerning** witnesses who say: **"Our signatures** are authentic, but they were affixed to a document to which **a condition** was attached"? In other words, a verbal condition was attached to the document, and this was not fulfilled (for example, where the document records a sale, but the seller agreed to the sale only on condition that the buyer would do him some service, which in fact he failed to do). Are the witnesses believed when they say that a condition was attached to the document, if their testimony is supported by the "mouth that forbade" argument? [3]Rava explains the basis of his problem: **In the cases of protest and signing on trust,** in which you ruled that the witnesses are not believed, [4]**the reason** you ruled that way **is that** by giving this testimony the witnesses **annul the document,** and according to you this is not acceptable, even when they are not incriminating themselves (as in the case of protest). [5]If so, you should agree that testimony characterizing a document as conditional **also annuls the document,** and you should

[1]בְּעָא מִינֵּיהּ רָבָא מֵרַב נַחְמָן: [2]״תְּנַאי הָיוּ דְּבָרֵינוּ״ מַהוּ? [3]מוֹדָעָא וַאֲמָנָה [4]הַיְינוּ טַעְמָא — דְּקָא עָקְרֵי לֵיהּ לִשְׁטָרָא, [5]וְהַאי נַמִּי קָא עָקַר לִשְׁטָרָא.

LITERAL TRANSLATION

[1]Rava asked Rav Naḥman: [2]What about: "Our words were [accompanied by] a condition"? [3][In the case of] protest and [signing on] trust, [4]this is the reason — that they uproot the document, [5]and this too uproots the document.

RASHI

תנאי היו דברינו — על תנאי מכרה לו, שיעשה לו כך וכך, ולא ראינו שקיים לו תנאו. וזה אומר: לא קיים לי, ואינו מכר. **מודעא ואמנה** — טעמא מאי קאמר מר אין נאמנין. **דקא עקרי ליה לשטרא** — בעדותן זה, ולא אתי על פה ומרע לשטרא. הכא נמי כו׳.

NOTES

dispute between Rav Naḥman and Mar bar Rav Ashi, who lived several generations after Rav Naḥman. Many Rishonim rule in favor of Rav Naḥman, as the Halakhah is normally in accordance with Rav Naḥman on all monetary questions (*Rav Hai Gaon*, *Rid*, *Ran*, and others). Support for this view can be brought from Rava's question, later in the passage, about conditional documents. Rava assumes Rav Naḥman's position, that a claim of protest is not believed (*Ritva*). Most Rishonim, however, including *Rif*, *Rambam*, and *Rosh*, rule in favor of Mar bar Rav Ashi, as he was one of the final editors of the Talmud, and there is a Geonic tradition that the Halakhah always follows him (with only a few possible exceptions).

Among the Rishonim who rule in favor of Mar bar Rav Ashi, there is a dispute about the law in a case where the document can be authenticated in some other way. Our commentary follows *Tosafot* and others who explain that the ruling of Mar bar Rav Ashi applies only where the witnesses' testimony was needed to authenticate the document, because of the "mouth that forbade" argument. But where the document can be authenticated in some other way, and the witnesses claim to have heard a formal protest, even Mar bar Rav Ashi would agree that the witnesses are not believed, since their claim is not supported by the "mouth that forbade" argument. *Rambam*, however, rules that a claim of protest is believed, even where the witnesses' testimony is not needed to authenticate the document. *Pnei Yehoshua* notes that, even according to *Tosafot*, it is only the witnesses who signed the note who are not believed, because they cannot alter their testimony; but if other witnesses testify that a certain document was annulled by a formal protest, they are believed, even without the support of the "mouth that forbade" argument.

הַיְינוּ טַעְמָא דְּקָא עָקְרֵי לֵיהּ לִשְׁטָרָא This is the reason — that they uproot the document. From the wording of Rava's question to Rav Naḥman, it appears that Rav Naḥman's reason for not believing witnesses who claim that a formal protest was made is because witnesses are unable to annul a document which they themselves have signed. Hence Rava queries whether a condition is also an annulment, or whether it is a separate matter. *Rashba* argues that Rava's query supports the view of *Rashi* and *Tosafot* — that Rav Naḥman's reason for not believing the witnesses who claim that a protest was made is not based on self-incrimination, but rather on the principle that witnesses cannot come forward and alter their written testimony unless they point to procedural flaws.

Tosefot Rid, however, points out that Rava's question can also be explained according to *Ran*, who maintains that Rav Naḥman considered a claim of protest to be self incriminatory. For if a condition is considered to be a material part of the transaction, the witnesses should have insisted on writing it in the document itself. Hence it was wrong to sign the document on the basis of an oral condition, and the witnesses' claim is self-incriminatory. But if a condition is considered a separate matter, there is nothing technically improper about leaving it out of the document; and although the parties would have been wise to write it down anyway, the witnesses are not required to be more solicitous than the parties themselves about this matter. Hence their claim is not self-incriminatory.

HALAKHAH

תְּנַאי הָיוּ דְּבָרֵינוּ "Our words were accompanied by a condition." "If witnesses concede that their signatures are genuine, but claim that there was a verbal condition attached to the transaction that has not been fulfilled, they are believed, following Rav Naḥman. In *Ḥoshen Mishpat* 46, *Shulḥan Arukh* rules in favor of *Rambam*, who argues that this applies only where there is no other way of authenticating their signatures, because of the 'mouth that forbade' argument, but where their signatures have been authenticated in some other way, they are not believed. In

TRANSLATION AND COMMENTARY

invalidate it. [1]On the other hand, **perhaps** testimony about **a condition** attached to a document does not annul the document, but merely adds **another matter** — a condition that must be fulfilled — and it is the nonfulfillment of this condition, not the testimony, that annuls the document? If so, the witnesses to the condition should be believed, because they are permitted to add additional testimony. This is yet another application of the principle that "the mouth that forbade is the mouth that permitted." Knowledge of the condition comes to us only from the testimony of the witnesses, who seek to invalidate their prior, signed testimony.

אֲמַר לֵיהּ [2]Rav Naḥman **said to** Rava in reply: **When** litigants **come before us for judgment** bearing a document whose authenticity has been attested by the witnesses themselves, together with testimony that a verbal condition was attached, [3]**we tell them: "Go and fulfill your conditions,** [4]**and then come** to court **for judgment."** If the document is authenticated by the witnesses' testimony alone, they are believed when they testify that a verbal condition was attached, just as they are believed if they say they were minors or acted under duress.

LITERAL TRANSLATION

[1]Or perhaps a condition is another matter?
[2]He said to him: When they come before us for judgment, [3]we say to them: "Go [and] fulfill your conditions, [4]and [then] come down to judgment."

[1]אוֹ דִּלְמָא תְּנַאי מִילְּתָא אַחֲרִיתֵי הִיא?
[2]אֲמַר לֵיהּ: כִּי אָתוּ לְקַמָּן לְדִינָא, [3]אָמְרִינַן לְהוּ: "זִילוּ קַיְּימוּ תְּנָאַיְיכוּ, [4]וְחוּתוּ לְדִינָא".

RASHI

או דלמא — הא לא עקרתא — דשטרא הוא, דמודים הם שהשטר אמת, אלא שתנאי היה ביניהם. וזו עדות אחרת היא, ושטרא ממילא מיעקר לאחר זמן, ביום שלא קיים תנאו בזמנו. **כי אתו לקמן** — לקוחות שעידיהם מעידים שתנאי היו דבריהם. **אמרינן להו זילו קיימו תנאייכו** — לבעלים. **וחותו לדינא** — אם יעכב שוב הקרקע.

NOTES

תְּנַאי מִילְּתָא אַחֲרִיתֵי הִיא A condition is another matter. A straightforward reading of Rava's question suggests that the reason why the witnesses are believed is because a condition is a completely independent matter, with no bearing on the content of the document itself. It is thus in the same category as, for example, testimony that a loan has been repaid. But if a condition were considered capable of annulling the document, the witnesses would not be believed, even with the support of the "mouth that forbade" argument.

The Rishonim note that Rava's question appears to contradict the authoritative ruling of Rav Huna the son of Rav Yehoshua later on in this passage. For Rav Huna the son of Rav Yehoshua declares that the only reason why the witnesses are permitted to amend their previous testimony and to attach a condition to the document is because they are considered to be uprooting their previous testimony. Now the word used by Rava for "annulling" is עָקְרֵי, and Rav Huna the son of Rav Yehoshua uses the same word for "uprooting." Thus it would appear that according to Rava the witnesses are not believed if they "uproot" their testimony, whereas according to Rav Huna the son of Rav Yehoshua that is precisely the reason why they *are* believed. Moreover, Rav Huna the son of Rav Yehoshua rules that if even one witness testifies that there was a condition, he is believed. But if a condition is really a completely independent matter — analogous to testimony that a loan has been repaid — a single witness is not believed, just as he would not be believed if he were to testify that a loan has been repaid (*Tosafot*).

The Rishonim offer several resolutions of this apparent contradiction. *Tosafot* explains that testimony about a condition is neither a completely independent matter nor an "uprooting" of the document. Rather, the condition leaves the document theoretically intact, but leaves it open to be "uprooted" if the condition is not fulfilled. *Ran* explains that when the verb "to uproot" is used the second time, it should be translated as "to interpret." Thus Rav Huna the son of Rav Yehoshua is saying that the witnesses are believed because they are interpreting, rather than contradicting, their previous testimony.

In our commentary we have followed *Ritva*, who notes that when Rava uses the verb "to uproot," it is the document that is being uprooted, whereas when Rava Huna the son of Rav Yehoshua says it, it is the witnesses' subsequent testimony that is being uprooted. *Ritva* explains that the witnesses are not trying to uproot (i.e., annul) the document itself, as they would be if they testified that it was signed on trust, because testimony about a condition is a separate matter unrelated to the veracity of the document itself. But they are uprooting their subsequent testimony authenticating the document, by attaching a condition to it, and this is why they are believed when their testimony is needed to authenticate the document.

זִילוּ קַיְּימוּ תְּנָאַיְיכוּ "Go and fulfill your conditions." Our translation and commentary follow *Rashi*. Some Rishonim have a slightly different reading: זִילוּ קַיְּימוּ שְׁטָרַיְיכוּ — "Go and certify your document." *Talmidei Rabbenu Yonah*

HALAKHAH

Ḥoshen Mishpat 82, *Shulḥan Arukh* rules in favor of *Rav Hai Gaon* and *Ra'avad*, who argue that witnesses who claim that a condition was attached to a transaction are believed, even without the support of the 'mouth that forbade' argument (see also *Shakh*)." (*Rambam, Sefer Shofetim, Hilkhot Edut* 3:9; *Shulḥan Arukh, Ḥoshen Mishpat* 46:37 and 82:12.)

TRANSLATION AND COMMENTARY

עֵד אוֹמֵר [1]Having established that even Rav Naḥman would agree that witnesses who testify to a verbal condition are believed, provided that their testimony is supported by the "mouth that forbade" argument, the Gemara now considers a case in which only one of the witnesses testifies to the condition. **If one witness says: "There was a condition,"** [2]**and the other** witness **says: "There was no condition,"** but both witnesses confirm the authenticity of their signatures, there is a difference of opinion between Amoraim as to how such a case should be decided. [3]**Rav Pappa said: Both** witnesses **are testifying about a valid document.** Both agree that the document in question was signed by them, without any condition being included in it. [4]The document is thus certified as genuine, **and the one** witness **who said: "There was** a verbal **condition** attached to the transaction," **is** only **one** witness, [5]**and the words of one** witness **are not valid against the testimony of two** witnesses. Once the document has been authenticated, it has the same status as the testimony of two witnesses, and no single witness can impair its validity.

[1]עֵד אוֹמֵר: "תְּנַאי", [2]וְעֵד אוֹמֵר: "אֵינוֹ תְּנַאי", [3]אָמַר רַב פַּפָּא: תַּרְוַיְיהוּ בִּשְׁטָרָא מַעַלְיָא קָא מַסְהֲדִי, [4]וְהַאי דְּקָאָמַר: "תְּנַאי", הֲוָה לֵיהּ חַד, [5]וְאֵין דְּבָרָיו שֶׁל אֶחָד בִּמְקוֹם שְׁנַיִם.

LITERAL TRANSLATION

[1][If one] witness says: "[There was] a condition," [2]and [one] witness says: "There was no condition," [3]Rav Pappa said: Both of them are testifying about a valid document, [4]and the one who says: "[There was] a condition," is one, [5]and the words of one are not [valid] in place of two.

RASHI

תרוייהו בשטרא מעליא קא מסהדי — שניהם מעידים שהשטר אמת, וכמות שהוא כתוב, בלא תנאי, חתמוהו. **והאי דקאמר תנאי חד הוא** — ואינו נאמן לעקור שטר ששניים חתומים בו.

NOTES

explains that, according to this alternative version, Rav Naḥman used to advise the lender to authenticate his document independently, so that the witnesses would not be believed if they were to claim that there was an oral condition attached to the transaction, because their testimony would not then be supported by the "mouth that forbade" argument.

זִילוּ קַיִּימוּ תְּנָאַיְיכוּ, וְחוּתוּ לְדִינָא "Go and fulfill your conditions, and then come down to judgment." Rav Naḥman rules that witnesses who claim that there was an oral condition attached to the document they signed are believed, since they are not annulling the document, but rather adding another point. Our commentary follows *Rashi*, *Rambam*, and other Rishonim, who explain that Rava's question concerned a case where there was no other way to authenticate the signatures, so that the witnesses' testimony was supported by the "mouth that forbade" argument. Even in such a case, Rava thought that the witnesses should not be believed, just as they are not believed if they claim that the document was written on trust, or preceded by a formal protest. But where the signatures can be authenticated in some other way, Rav Nahman would agree that the witnesses' statement concerning an oral condition attached to the document is not accepted.

Many Rishonim disagree with this explanation, arguing that the witnesses are believed, even if their signatures were authenticated in a different way (*Rav Hai Gaon*, *Ra'avad*, and others). These Rishonim argue that since the mention of a condition is considered a separate matter, and not an alteration of the original testimony, the witnesses are not considered to be altering their previous testimony, even when that testimony is not needed to authenticate their signatures.

Ramban objects: The Gemara rules (below) in favor of the argument of Rav Huna the son of Rav Yehoshua — that it is sufficient for one of the witnesses, without the support of the other witness, to claim that there was a condition, because "the witnesses are coming to uproot their testimony." According to *Rashi* and *Rambam*, this is logical, because the testimony about the condition is an integral part of the authentication of the document, and both witnesses are needed to authenticate the document. But if a condition is considered a completely separate matter, as *Rav Hai Gaon* argued, we should accept Rav Pappa's argument that the testimony of one witness cannot alter a document signed by two witnesses. Why, then, is one witness believed about a condition?

Ran answers that Rav Huna the son of Rav Yehoshua did not mean that the witnesses were considered to be *contradicting* their previous testimony concerning the document, for in such a case they would not be believed at all, just as in the case of a document signed on trust or after a formal protest. Rather, Rav Huna the son of Rav Yehoshua meant that the witnesses were *interpreting* their previous testimony, which was unclear on the question of a possible condition. And even one witness is believed when he interprets his previous testimony, provided his fellow-witness does not contradict him.

עֵד אוֹמֵר: תְּנַאי If one witness says: "There was a condition." From the wording of the Gemara's question, it would appear that the two witnesses disagreed with each

HALAKHAH

עֵד אוֹמֵר: תְּנַאי If one witness says: "There was a condition." "If the witnesses who signed the document come forward and confirm their signatures, and one of them claims that there was an oral condition attached to the transaction, and that it was not fulfilled, the defendant need not fulfill his obligations under the contract, provided that he takes the special *heset* oath imposed on anyone who denies a claim without bringing proof. *Sma* notes that, according to some authorities, he must take a full Torah oath, since there is one witness who testifies that he owes the money." (*Rambam*, *Sefer Shofetim*, *Hilkhot Edut* 3:10; *Shulḥan Arukh*, *Ḥoshen Mishpat* 46:37 and 82:12.)

[1]מַתְקִיף לָהּ רַב הוּנָא בְּרֵיהּ דְּרַב יְהוֹשֻׁעַ: [2]אִי הָכִי, אֲפִילּוּ תַּרְוַיְיהוּ נַמִי! [3]אֶלָּא אָמְרִינַן: [4]הָנֵי לְמִיעֲקַר סַהֲדוּתַיְיהוּ קָאָתוּ. [5]הַאי נַמִי לְמִיעֲקַר סַהֲדוּתֵיהּ קָאָתֵי! [6]וְהִלְכְתָא כְּרַב הוּנָא בְּרֵיהּ דְּרַב יְהוֹשֻׁעַ.

LITERAL TRANSLATION

[1]Rav Huna the son of Rav Yehoshua objected to this: [2]If so, even both of them also! [3]Rather, we say: [4]These come to uproot their testimony. [5]This one, too, comes to uproot his testimony! [6]And the Halakhah is in accordance with Rav Huna the son of Rav Yehoshua.

TRANSLATION AND COMMENTARY

מַתְקִיף לָהּ [1]**Rav Huna the son of Rav Yehoshua objected to** Rav Pappa's reasoning: [2]**If so, even** if **both of them** testify that there was a condition attached to the transaction, they **too** should not be believed, because they are seeking to alter the validity of an authenticated document, and we have already established (above, 18b) that witnesses who deny the validity of an authenticated document which they themselves signed are not believed, because a witness cannot retract or alter his previous testimony. But surely we have established that even Rav Naḥman accepts the testimony of the witnesses when they both say that the document was conditional! [3]**Rather,** says Rav Huna the son of Rav Yehoshua, when both witnesses who signed the document testify that the transaction recorded in it was conditional, we accept their testimony, because **we say:** [4]**These** witnesses **have come to annul their testimony.** We do not view them as first authenticating the document and then testifying about a condition, but rather as canceling the effect of their original authentication. [5]And **this** individual witness, **too,** should be viewed as **coming to annul his testimony** by canceling the effect of his authentication. Hence the document must be viewed as having been authenticated by only one witness, and it is invalid. [6]**And** the Gemara concludes that **the Halakhah is in accordance with Rav Huna the son of Rav Yehoshua** in this matter, and even one witness is believed when he testifies that the transaction was conditional, provided that his testimony is needed to authenticate the signatures.

RASHI

אי הכי אפילו תרוייהו נמי אלא אמרינן כו' – אי הכי דכיון שהעיד על כתב ידו עשית לזה אחד ממקיימי השטר כמות שהוא כתוב בלא תנאי, והוי להו עדיו שנים, ועדות אחרונה דברי אחד במקום שנים. **אפילו תרוייהו נמי** – אמרי: תנאי היו דברינו – לא ליתהימנו. דכיון שהעידו על כתב ידן – קיימו השטר כמות שהוא כתוב, וכי אמרי תנאי היו דברינו – הוו להו מגידים וחוזרים ומגידים, ואמאי אמר רב נחמן קיימו תנאייכו כו'? **אלא** – על כרחך לאו חתימה מקויימת הוא, דכיון דתוך כדי דבור מסקי דבורייהו, ואמרי: אבל תנאי היה ביניהן. אמרינן: הני למיעקר סהדותייהו, שאמרו "כתב ידינו הוא" קאתו, ולומר: לא חתמנו אלא על מנת שיקיים את התנאי, וכיון דתנאי מלתא אחריתי היא, שאינה עוקרתו אלא לאחר זמן – לא דמיא למודעא ואמנה, ומהימני, דעדות בפני עצמה היא. **האי נמי** – כי קיים ואמר תנאי הוה – עקר לחתימת ידיה, לומר: לא חתמתי אלא על מנת כן, וכיון דאית לן דמלתא אחריתי היא, ושטרא ממילא מיעקר – אישתכח דאין בשטר חתום אלא עד אחד.

SAGES

רַב הוּנָא בְּרֵיהּ דְּרַב יְהוֹשֻׁעַ Rav Huna the son of Rav Yehoshua. A fifth-generation Babylonian Amora, Rav Huna the son of Rav Yehoshua was one of the outstanding disciples of Abaye and Rava. He was a close colleague of Rav Pappa from his youth, and these scholars are frequently mentioned together in the Talmud. After Rava's death, Rav Pappa became head of the yeshivah in the city of Neresh, while Rav Huna the son of Rav Yehoshua became his deputy. His teachings are found throughout the Talmud.

Little is known about the private life of Rav Huna the son of Rav Yehoshua, although he apparently owned property and was prosperous. The Talmud relates various anecdotes about his piety and his convivial nature.

NOTES

other, one claiming that there was a condition and the other insisting that there was not. However, the Rishonim explain that this is not possible. For if the two witnesses were in fact contradicting each other, one of them would have to be giving false testimony, and the law in such a case is that, while both witnesses are given the benefit of the doubt and can serve as witnesses in other cases, they are not permitted to testify together again. Hence their testimony authenticating the signatures would have to be rejected, and the document would lose its authentication. Accordingly, the Rishonim explain that the Gemara is referring to a case where one witness claimed that there was a condition and the other said that he knew nothing of the matter (*Ramban, Ritva*).

אֲפִילּוּ תַּרְוַיְיהוּ נַמִי Even both of them also. Our commentary follows *Rashi* and most of the Rishonim, who explain that if we were to accept Rav Pappa's reasoning, and consider testimony about the condition as separate from testimony authenticating the signatures, then we could not accept the testimony about the condition, even if both witnesses said it, because we have already learned (above, 18b) that the witnesses who signed the document cannot return to court and alter their testimony, unless their new testimony is an integral part of the authentication process. But we know that Rav Naḥman ruled (above) that if both witnesses testify about a condition, their testimony is accepted. Therefore, we must reject Rav Pappa's reasoning and conclude that testimony about a condition amounts to an "uprooting" of the authentication testimony, leaving us with only one witness to authenticate the document.

Ran objects to this explanation, arguing that if the evidence about the condition were really considered an "uprooting" of the authentication, we would consider that the evidence about the condition contradicts the document, and we would not believe it, just as in the case of a document signed on trust or a document preceded by a protest. Accordingly, *Ran* explains that it is clear that a condition is an entirely separate matter — not affecting the validity of the document itself — and the dispute between Rav Pappa and Rav Huna the son of Rav Yehoshua is about how the document should be viewed. Rav Pappa argues that, since the document says nothing about a condition, it should be understood as implying that there *was* no condition, and, if so, the testimony of one witness is not

[1]תָּנוּ רַבָּנַן: "שְׁנַיִם חֲתוּמִין עַל הַשְּׁטָר וּמֵתוּ, [2]וּבָאוּ שְׁנַיִם מִן הַשּׁוּק וְאָמְרוּ: 'יָדַעְנוּ שֶׁכְּתַב יָדָם הוּא, [3]אֲבָל אֲנוּסִים הָיוּ, קְטַנִּים הָיוּ, פְּסוּלֵי עֵדוּת הָיוּ', [4]הֲרֵי אֵלּוּ נֶאֱמָנִים. [5]וְאִם יֵשׁ עֵדִים שֶׁכְּתַב יָדָם הוּא זֶה, [6]אוֹ שֶׁהָיָה כְּתַב יָדָם יוֹצֵא מִמָּקוֹם

LITERAL TRANSLATION

[1]Our Rabbis taught: "[If] two [witnesses] were signed on a deed and they died, [2]and two [witnesses] came from the marketplace and said: 'We know that it is their handwriting, [3]but they were under duress, they were minors, they were disqualified [from giving] evidence,' [4]they are believed. [5]But if there are witnesses that this is their handwriting, [6]or where their handwriting came out from

TRANSLATION AND COMMENTARY

תָּנוּ רַבָּנַן [1]Until now we have been dealing with cases in which the witnesses who originally signed the document subsequently testify that the signatures were genuine, but that the document is invalid for some other reason. The Gemara now considers a case in which other witnesses give this testimony. **Our Rabbis taught** the following Baraita: **"If two witnesses signed a deed and died,** and there was a need to certify the document, [2]**and two witnesses came from the marketplace and said: 'We know that this is the handwriting** of the deceased witnesses, [3]**but** when they signed the document **they were** acting **under duress,** or **they were minors,** or **they were disqualified from** giving evidence,' [4]**they are believed,** because we need their testimony to authenticate the document, and 'the mouth that forbade is the mouth that permitted.' [5]**But if there are** other **witnesses** beside the first pair who can testify **that this is the handwriting** of the deceased original witnesses, [6]**or if their handwriting can be authenticated from other**

BACKGROUND

וּבָאוּ שְׁנַיִם מִן הַשּׁוּק And two witnesses came from the marketplace. The term "marketplace" (שׁוּק) in Hebrew essentially means a street or public square. As is still common in many countries, the city streets were used for commerce, whether carried out from stands on the street itself (the marketplace) or else from stalls adjacent to it. The term "two men from the marketplace" means simply two men who come in from the street — who are not connected with the case or with the witnesses, but who simply testify to a certain fact.

NOTES

sufficient to outweigh the document and persuade us that there was a condition. Rav Huna the son of Rav Yehoshua argues that if Rav Pappa is correct, we should not even believe *both* witnesses if they say that there was a condition, because by so doing they are contradicting their previous testimony. Rather, we must understand the document as implying nothing at all about a condition. Hence, when the witnesses testify that there was a condition, they are *interpreting* their previous testimony, and this can even be done by a single witness. (In this explanation, *Ran* translates the word לְמִיעֲקַר — which normally means "to uproot" — as "to interpret.") *Ran*'s explanation is closely related to the dispute between *Rashi* and *Rav Hai Gaon* as to whether witnesses who testify that there was a condition are believed without the support of the "mouth that forbade" argument (see above, "Go and fulfill your conditions, and then come down to judgment").

שְׁנַיִם חֲתוּמִין עַל הַשְּׁטָר וּמֵתוּ If two witnesses were signed on a deed and they died. According to the explanation attributed to *Rashi* (see next note), it was important for the Baraita to specify that the first pair of witnesses had died. For if they had still been alive, and the second pair had testified that the first pair were disqualified, the second pair would be believed without any *miggo*. It is only because the first pair are dead that the second pair are viewed as attacking the first pair's testimony and not their persons. According to the other Rishonim, however, there is no difference between a case where the first witnesses were alive and a case where they were dead. *Ritva* explains that the Baraita speaks of deceased witnesses so that we should not wonder why they were not summoned to authenticate their own signatures.

אֲבָל אֲנוּסִים הָיוּ... פְּסוּלֵי עֵדוּת הָיוּ But they were under duress... they were disqualified from giving evidence. The Baraita employs very similar language to that used in the Mishnah, but it is not clear to what extent it is referring to the same cases. The Gemara explained above (18b) that when the Mishnah says that the witnesses claimed to be acting under duress, it is referring to a case where their lives were threatened, but not to a mere financial threat. Moreover, according to most Rishonim, when the witnesses in the Mishnah claim to have been disqualified, they mean that they were related to one of the parties; but if they had claimed that they themselves were thieves, they would not have been believed. The reason for both these limitations is the rule that a witness cannot incriminate himself — a factor that clearly does not apply here, where other witnesses are disqualifying the witnesses who signed the document (*Meiri*).

Nevertheless, most Rishonim explain that the Baraita is in practice subject to the same limitations as the Mishnah, albeit for a different reason. For the Gemara rules (*Sanhedrin* 27a) that where two witnesses testify that two other witnesses have committed a crime, the accusing witnesses are believed outright, and the accused witnesses are disqualified from ever testifying again. The Gemara does not consider this to be a case of two against two, because the accusing witnesses are attacking the accused

HALAKHAH

יָדַעְנוּ שֶׁכְּתַב יָדָם הוּא, אֲבָל אֲנוּסִים הָיוּ "We know that it is their handwriting, but they were under duress." "If the witnesses who signed a document have died, and other witnesses come forward to authenticate their signatures, and the latter witnesses say that the signatures are authentic but the witnesses signed under duress or were disqualified from testifying or were minors at the time, their testimony is accepted, and the document is destroyed, provided that there is no other way of authenticating the signatures, following the Baraita. If the lender requests an extension of time in order to find some other way to authenticate the signatures on the document, the destruction of the document is delayed (but if he does not explicitly make such a request, we destroy the document immediately — *Sma*)." (*Shulḥan Arukh, Ḥoshen Mishpat* 46:37.)

אַחֵר — [1]מִשְּׁטָר שֶׁקָּרָא עָלָיו עַרְעָר וְהוּחְזַק בְּבֵית דִּין — [2]אֵין אֵלּוּ נֶאֱמָנִין״.
[3]וּמַגְבִּינַן בֵּיהּ כִּבְשְׁטָרָא מַעַלְיָא? [4]וְאַמַּאי? [5]תְּרֵי וּתְרֵי נִינְהוּ!

LITERAL TRANSLATION

another place — [1]from a document that had been contested (lit., 'on which [someone] had called a protest') and had been confirmed in court — [2]they are not believed."

[3]But do we collect with it as with a valid document? [4]But why? [5]They are two against two!

TRANSLATION AND COMMENTARY

sources, for instance if the court compares the signatures on this document with the signatures on some other [1]**document that has been contested and confirmed in court,** [2]in such a case the witnesses **are not believed** when they testify that the deceased witnesses acted under duress etc., because here the 'mouth that forbade' argument does not apply."

וּמַגְבִּינַן [3]**But,** the Gemara objects, in the last clause, when the witnesses are not supported by the "mouth that forbade" argument, **do we collect with** this note **like** we do **with a valid document?** Admittedly, when the witnesses who originally signed a document subsequently testify that it was invalid, we do not believe them without the support of the "mouth that forbade" argument, because they are not allowed to retract their original testimony. [4]**But why** should we totally reject the testimony of these other witnesses? Surely we should view them as contradicting the original witnesses — one pair of witnesses testifying that the document is valid, and the other pair that it is invalid — [5]and since **they are two against two,** we should view this as a matter that is in doubt because of conflicting testimony!

RASHI

שקרא עליו ערער — שרצה הנתבע לפוסלו. **ומגבינן ביה** — בתמיה. **תרי ותרי נינהו** — עדי השטר שנים, ואלו שנים מעידים עליהם שפסולים היו באותה שעה.

NOTES

witnesses' persons, and not their testimony. Hence, in our case as well, if the second pair of witnesses were to testify that the first pair had committed a crime, they would be believed outright, even without the support of the "mouth that forbade" argument. Therefore, our Baraita must be referring to a case where the witnesses who signed the document were not accused of committing a crime (*Tosafot, Ramban, Rashba*).

But there is an opinion (attributed by *Ramban* to *Rashi*, but not appearing in our texts of *Rashi*) which maintains that disqualifying witnesses are believed outright only if the disqualified witnesses are alive; but if the disqualified witnesses are dead (as in our Baraita), the disqualifying witnesses are not attacking the persons of the witnesses, but rather their testimony. Hence the ordinary rules governing contradictory testimony apply, and both types of witnesses are treated as equal (except where the "mouth that forbade" argument applies). This explanation is difficult, however, because it appears to contradict the conclusion of Rav Naḥman (below, 20a), that dead witnesses cannot have more credibility than they would have had if they were still alive (*Ritva*).

אֵין אֵלּוּ נֶאֱמָנִין They are not believed. If the evidence of the second pair of witnesses is needed to authenticate the document, they are believed, and they disqualify the pair of witnesses who signed it, but if their evidence is not needed, they are not believed. The Rishonim ask: Even if the signatures on the document can be authenticated in some other way, the second pair of witnesses could have disqualified the first pair by declaring that the first pair were thieves (see previous note). Instead, they declared that the first pair acted under duress, or were disqualified as relatives. The second pair thus have a *miggo*, since they could have made a better claim, but refrained from doing so because of their scrupulous honesty. Why, then, are they not believed?

Tosafot and *Rashba* explain that the *miggo* is flawed. For the principle of *miggo* is based on the assumption that if a claimant had been prepared to make a false statement, he would have made a better claim. But two witnesses cannot make any false statement without careful coordination. Thus it is possible that they chose the false claim that they found easiest to coordinate. Hence the only *miggo* that can be claimed by witnesses is a silent *miggo*, as in the Mishnah or the Baraita, since there is nothing easier to coordinate than a strategy of silence.

Ramban and *Ra'ah* explain that the testimony of witnesses is already greater than that of any other form of evidence, and no mere *miggo* can enhance it. In the case of the Baraita and the Mishnah, however, the witnesses are believed not because the *miggo* enhances their testimony, but because they have not properly authenticated the document.

תְּרֵי וּתְרֵי נִינְהוּ They are two against two. It is clear that the second pair of witnesses who testify that the first pair signed the document improperly are the first "two" here, but it is not clear who the other "two" are who contradict them. According to most Rishonim, the other "two" are the witnesses who signed the document. This, however, leads to certain difficulties, as it is not clear how the witnesses who signed the document can be considered as testifying about their qualifications, nor is it clear whether they would be believed if they were to do so. *Ri Migash* suggests that the entire discussion in the Gemara concerns only the case where the witnesses were accused of signing under duress, because this amounts to accusing them of lying, but not the cases which do not impinge on the contents of the document itself.

Rosh explains that the other "two" are not a regular pair of witnesses at all, but rather a powerful legal presumption called אֲנַן סָהֲדֵי — "we are [all] witnesses." We are so certain that the document would not have been drawn up with false witnesses, that it is as if we all testify to that effect. According to this explanation, the second pair of

TRANSLATION AND COMMENTARY

To answer this question, the Gemara considers some of the rules pertaining to contradictory testimony. Under Jewish law, the highest form of proof is the testimony of two qualified witnesses after it has been thoroughly investigated and confirmed in court. It is impossible to enhance it — even the testimony of 100 other witnesses is no better than that of two — and it is impossible to refute it, except by the testimony of two (or more) other witnesses. Indeed, as we have seen above (18b), even if the witnesses admit that their original testimony was false, they cannot alter it. When the testimony of one pair of witnesses is contradicted by the testimony of another pair, we have the situation called "contradiction." We must assume that one of the two pairs have committed perjury, but we have no way of knowing which. Therefore, we regard the case as doubtful, and treat each pair of witnesses as having possibly lied. Nonetheless, we continue to accept testimony from either pair, since each one must be presumed innocent of perjury until proved guilty. However, the Torah (Deuteronomy 19:16-21) does describe a situation in which a court is able to determine that a witness perjured himself, and decrees that the false witness should receive the punishment that he conspired to bring on the defendant. Clearly, then, it is sometimes possible to make an absolute determination as to which pair of witnesses are telling the truth and which are not. The Rabbinic interpretation of the passage from Deuteronomy is that the Torah is referring to a process called *hazamah* (הֲזָמָה — the word is derived from the root זמם, "to conspire," that appears in this verse). In a case of *hazamah*, the second pair of witnesses are not testifying about the case in question, but are testifying directly that the first pair gave false evidence. The second pair of witnesses testify that the first pair were not present where the alleged event took place at the time it was said to have taken place. They thus refute the first pair of witnesses without reference to the events themselves, which for all they know took place as described. The Gemara seeks here to answer the objection raised earlier — that the second pair of witnesses are contradicting the first pair, and should at least create a state of doubt. [1] **Rav Sheshet said: This** Baraita **tells us** that **contradiction is the beginning of *hazamah*.** In other words, contradiction is a lesser form of *hazamah,* and although we cannot impose the penalties associated with *hazamah*, because we cannot determine with certainty who is telling the truth, nevertheless the regulations applicable to *hazamah* apply to contradiction as well. [20A] [2] Therefore, **just as we make witnesses *zomemim*** (i.e., find them guilty of conspiracy by proving that they were not present at the event about which they gave evidence) **only in their presence,** as *hazamah* involves a criminal penalty, and we may try a person for a crime only in his presence, [3] **so too we contradict witnesses only in their presence.** Hence, since the original witnesses are dead, they can no longer be contradicted.

[1] אָמַר רַב שֵׁשֶׁת: זֹאת אוֹמֶרֶת הַכְחָשָׁה תְּחִלַּת הֲזָמָה הִיא, [20A] [2] וּכְשֵׁם שֶׁאֵין מְזִימִין אֶת הָעֵדִים אֶלָּא בִּפְנֵיהֶם, [3] כָּךְ אֵין מַכְחִישִׁין אֶת הָעֵדִים אֶלָּא בִּפְנֵיהֶם.

LITERAL TRANSLATION

[1] Rav Sheshet said: This says [that] contradiction is the beginning of *hazamah,* [20A] [2] and just as we do not make witnesses *zomemim* except in their presence, [3] so too we do not contradict witnesses except in their presence.

RASHI

וכשם שאין מזימין העדים אלא בפניהם — שהרי הם באין לחייבן כדי לעונשן, או נפש או ממון. והתורה אמרה "והועד בבעליו" — יבא בעל השור ויעמוד על שורו (בבא קמא קיב,ב). **כך אין מכחישין** — אפילו לבטל עדותן.

CONCEPTS

הַכְחָשָׁה Contradictions. When a pair of witnesses contradict testimony given previously by other witnesses, the testimony of both pairs is nullified, and the evidence of neither is accepted. No greater weight is attached to the evidence of several witnesses than to that of two. In contrast to a case of *hazamah*, in a case of contradiction the later witnesses contradict the earlier witnesses' description of the facts of the case, and do not focus on the presence of the first pair of witnesses at the scene.

הֲזָמָה *Hazamah.* This term refers to a situation in which witnesses are proved to have perjured themselves to make someone lose a monetary dispute or be punished by the court. There are two ways in which the testimony of witnesses can be invalidated: (1) If two other witnesses testify that something did not happen as described by the first pair of witnesses. In such a case, the testimony of neither pair is accepted, and the matter is left undecided. (2) If two witnesses testify that the first pair of witnesses, whose testimony condemned the defendant, were elsewhere (with the second pair of witnesses) when the incident transpired, and thus could not have witnessed the events about which they testified. The second pair of witnesses are not contradicting the evidence of the first pair (which may indeed be true). They are testifying that the first two were not present, and therefore were not in a position to know. In such a case, the testimony of the second pair of witnesses is accepted, and the testimony of the first pair is rejected.

NOTES

witnesses are never believed outright (except where they are supported by the "mouth that forbade" argument) — regardless of whether the witnesses they are accusing are alive or dead, or whether they are accusing them of crimes or of technical disqualifications. In several places, the "we are all witnesses" presumption has the status of testimony (see, for example, *Bava Metzia* 3a). However, the idea that the presumption that "we are all witnesses" should be considered powerful enough to contradict the testimony of regular witnesses is novel (see also *Hatam Sofer*).

הַכְחָשָׁה וַהֲזָמָה Contradiction and *hazamah*. In Jewish law, the highest form of proof is the testimony of two qualified witnesses, after this testimony has been thoroughly investigated and confirmed in court. It is impossible to enhance it — even the testimony of 100 other witnesses is no better than that of two — and no other sort of evidence can outweigh it, except the admission of the defendant in a monetary case. Indeed, as we have seen above (18b), even if the witnesses themselves now claim that their testimony was false, they cannot alter it.

When the testimony of one pair of witnesses is contradicted by the testimony of another pair, we have the situation called "contradiction." We must assume that one of the two pairs have perjured themselves in court, but we have no way of knowing which. It is immaterial how many witnesses are in each set, as the testimony of 100 witnesses is no better than that of two, and even if one pair now claim that they were lying, this has no effect, because a witness may not retract his testimony. Therefore, we treat the case in accordance with the laws for doubtful cases, and treat each set of witnesses as having possibly lied in court.

TRANSLATION AND COMMENTARY

אָמַר לֵיהּ רַב נַחְמָן [1]**Rav Naḥman said to** Rav Sheshet: Your reasoning is incorrect. For according to you, **if** the witnesses who signed the document **had been** present **before us** in court, [2]**and** the other witnesses **had contradicted them, it would have been a** valid **contradiction,** [3]**and** even if the first pair had adhered to their account, **we would have paid no attention to them.** We would not have accepted their evidence as the absolute truth, but would have left the matter in doubt, [4]**because it is testimony** that has been **contradicted.** [5]But **now that** the first pair **are not present,** you say that we cannot contradict their testimony. Why should their absence enhance their credibility? If there was some claim that they could have made but did not make because they were absent, there might be an argument for enhancing their credibility. [6]But **if they had been before us,** [7]**they might perhaps have admitted** that the second pair of witnesses were telling the truth. This is the only thing they could have added that they are not now in a position to say .But surely this would only strengthen our conviction that their original testimony was contradicted. Thus, since they are not present to affirm or deny the testimony of the second pair of witnesses, do you say that **they are believed** outright?

[1]אָמַר לֵיהּ רַב נַחְמָן: אִילּוּ הָווּ קַמָּן, [2]וּמַכְחִישִׁין לְהוּ, הֲוָה הַכְחָשָׁה, [3]וְלָא הֲוָה מַשְׁגִּיחִין בְּהוּ, [4]דְּהָוֵי לַהּ עֵדוּת מוּכְחֶשֶׁת. [5]הָשְׁתָּא דְּלֵיתְנְהוּ, [6]דְּאִילּוּ הָווּ לְקַמָּן, [7]דִּלְמָא הָווּ מוֹדוּ לְהוּ, מְהֵימְנֵי?

LITERAL TRANSLATION

[1]Rav Naḥman said to him: If they had been before us, [2]and they had contradicted them, it would have been a contradiction, [3]and we would have paid no attention to them, [4]for it is contradicted testimony. [5]Now that they are not present, [6]so that if they had been before us, [7]perhaps they might have admitted to them, are they believed?

RASHI

לא הוו משגיחין בהו — בעדי הסטר לגבות על פיהם. **השתא** — דליכא למימר אילו הוו קמן הוו מודו להני, אמרת מהימני?!

NOTES

Following this argument to its logical conclusion, we might think that it is never possible for a court to determine with certainty that a pair of witnesses have testified falsely. However, the Torah (Deuteronomy 19:16-21) describes a situation in which a court punishes a perjurer by inflicting on him the punishment that he conspired to inflict on the defendant. Clearly, then, it must occasionally be possible to make an absolute legal determination that a pair of witnesses testified falsely.

According to Rabbinic tradition, the Torah is referring here to the process called *hazamah* (the word is derived from the root זמם — "to conspire" — which appears in this verse). In a case of *hazamah*, the second pair of witnesses say nothing about the case in question, but testify instead that the first pair of witnesses were not at the place where the alleged event took place at the time it took place. They thus refute the first testimony without entering into the events themselves, which, for all they know, may have taken place as described.

There are three main differences between contradiction and *hazamah*:

(1) In a case of contradiction, the second pair of witnesses attack the first pair's testimony, whereas in a case of *hazamah*, they attack their persons (*Rambam, Hilkhot Edut* 18:2).

(2) Contradiction is based on logical argument, whereas *hazamah* is, at least to some degree, a decree of the Torah that goes beyond logic. For, in the final analysis, why should we believe the second pair more than the first? Nevertheless, *hazamah* is not entirely without precedent in the laws of testimony: If one pair of witnesses testify about a matter, and a second pair testify that the first pair are relatives or criminals, and are thus disqualified from giving testimony, the second pair are believed, because they are not attacking the first pair's testimony, but rather their persons (*Sanhedrin* 27a).

(3) In a case of contradiction, we do not know who is telling the truth. Therefore, the defendant and both pairs of witnesses must all be given the benefit of the doubt, and no one is punished. Moreover, we continue to accept testimony on other matters from both pairs of witnesses, since each one must be presumed innocent of perjury until proved guilty. On the other hand, we do not accept testimony from a pair consisting of one witness from one of these pairs and another from the other (*Bava Batra* 31b). In a case of *hazamah*, by contrast, we know for certain that the first pair of witnesses perjured themselves. Hence we release the defendant with certainty, and inflict on the first pair of witnesses the punishment they sought to inflict on the defendant.

דִּלְמָא הָווּ מוֹדוּ לְהוּ **Perhaps they might have admitted to them.** The wording of Rav Naḥman's objection suggests that if the contradicted witnesses admit that their testimony was false, we accept this as clear proof that the second pair of witnesses were telling the truth, and we invalidate the document, even where the signatures have been independently authenticated. This, however, appears to contradict the rule mentioned above (18b), that witnesses cannot retract testimony once it has been accepted by the court. Because of this statement by Rav Naḥman, *Sho'el U'Meshiv* suggests that the rule that witnesses cannot retract their testimony does not apply when there is contradictory testimony. *Sho'el U'Meshiv* admits, however, that this idea is extremely novel, and does not find support in the classic commentators (although it may find support in the words of *Rabbenu Shimshon* cited by *Tosafot*).

Maharam Schiff explains that it makes no practical difference whether or not the witnesses admit that their testimony was false; in either case we treat the testimony as contradicted, and the document as doubtful. According to *Maharam Schiff*, Rav Naḥman was making a psychological point: If the witnesses were alive, we would consider

¹אֶלָּא אֲמַר רַב נַחְמָן: ²אוֹקֵי תְּרֵי לַהֲדֵי תְּרֵי, ³וְאוֹקֵי מָמוֹנָא בְּחֶזְקַת מָרֵיהּ.

LITERAL TRANSLATION

[1] Rather, Rav Naḥman said: [2] Set two against two, [3] and leave the money in the possession of its owner.

RASHI

ואוקי ממונא בחזקת מריה — בחזקת הלוה. ואם קרקע היא — תעמוד בחזקת המוכר. ודקתני בברייתא אין נאמנים — לא דליהוי שטרא מעליא למיגבי ביה, אלא דלא קרעינן ליה. ואי תפיס מידי והדר אתי האי ותבע מיניה — לא מפקינן מיניה, דאמרינן: אוקי תרי לבהדי תרי, וממונא בחזקת היכא דקאי.

TRANSLATION AND COMMENTARY

אֶלָּא אֲמַר רַב נַחְמָן [1] **Rather, Rav Naḥman said:** We must understand the Baraita's ruling as follows: If the second pair of witnesses are needed to authenticate the document, so that their testimony is supported by the "mouth that forbade" argument, they are believed outright, and we disqualify the document. But if their testimony is not needed to authenticate the document, we do not give them total credence; [2] instead, we **set** the **two** witnesses who signed the document **against** the **two** who claim, for example, that the first two signed under duress, [3] **and** we treat the matter as being subject to the conflicting testimony of two pairs of witnesses. We must treat such a case in accordance with the law governing doubtful matters, and **leave the money in the possession of its** present **owner** (i.e., the borrower, who is the defendant), since the plaintiff has not proved his case.

NOTES

their testimony to be contradicted, even if they stood by their account and insisted that they were telling the truth. The difference here between living witnesses and dead witnesses is that dead witnesses cannot explicitly stand by their account, and while this makes little practical difference, it is surely not grounds for increasing their credibility.

אוֹקֵי תְּרֵי לַהֲדֵי תְּרֵי **Set two against two.** In this situation we follow the rules for cases in doubt, and since the onus is on the plaintiff to prove his case, the defendant does not have to pay the debt. The Rishonim ask: The Baraita that Rav Naḥman is trying to explain consists of two clauses. In the first clause, the second pair of witnesses are believed and they invalidate the document, because their testimony is necessary to authenticate the signatures. In the second clause, by contrast, the second pair of witnesses are not believed and they do not invalidate the document, because they are not needed to authenticate the signatures. The dispute between Rav Sheshet and Rav Naḥman concerns the second clause: Rav Sheshet explains it in accordance with its simple meaning, whereas Rav Naḥman rules that even though we do not believe the second pair of witnesses, we treat the document as doubtful and leave the money with the defendant. Thus, according to Rav Naḥman, we invalidate the document in the second clause as well. What, then, is the practical difference between the two clauses?

Ramah and *Ri Migash* explain that there is in fact little difference between the two clauses, except that in the first clause we destroy the document, whereas in the second we put it aside intact until the matter is clarified and the two parties agree about the facts. Most Rishonim, however, follow *Rashi*, who explains that if the creditor seizes the debtor's property to recover his debt, we do not compel him to return it, since the document is not invalid. The only reason it cannot be used is because of the principle that the burden of proof is on the plaintiff. Hence, if the creditor seizes the debtor's property and the debtor sues him for its return, the burden of proof should revert to the debtor, who is now the plaintiff.

The assumption underlying *Rashi*'s explanation is that when there is a dispute about a property right in which the defendant receives the benefit of the doubt, and the plaintiff seizes the property, the former defendant becomes the plaintiff and the burden of proof falls on him. Many Rishonim rule that seizure is effective, even if the creditor seizes the debtor's property in front of us (*Rif, Ramban, Rosh*). This question is discussed at length in a passage in tractate *Bava Metzia* (6a-b), and according to the plain reading of the Gemara there, its conclusion is that seizure is not effective. However, *Rosh* explains that the passage in *Bava Metzia* is referring to a case where the creditor himself is uncertain about the debt; but where the creditor is certain, seizure is effective.

Other Rishonim agree with *Rashi* that there are circumstances where the creditor enjoys the benefit of the doubt, but insist that seizure alone is not sufficient to change the debtor's status to that of plaintiff. *Tosafot* explains that we are referring to a case where the creditor seized the property before the validity of the document was called into question. *Rabbenu Yonah* rules that we are referring to a case where the court mistakenly issued a ruling granting the property to the creditor.

Some Rishonim explain that the case referred to is where the creditor had covertly seized the debtor's property. In such a case, the creditor has a *miggo* argument, because he could have claimed that the property was his own and had been in his possession all along. Hence he is believed when he claims that the document is valid and the seizure legitimate. But if the property was seized in front of witnesses, we return it to the debtor (*Ritva*).

There is a way of explaining this Baraita without invoking the concept of seizure at all: *Tosafot* cites *Rabbenu Shimshon*, who explains that the Baraita is referring to a receipt attesting that a debt has already been paid. In the first clause, the witnesses are believed and the receipt is invalidated, and the debtor must pay the debt, but in the second clause, we treat the matter as doubtful and leave the money in the possession of the debtor.

וְאוֹקֵי מָמוֹנָא בְּחֶזְקַת מָרֵיהּ **And leave the money in the possession of its owner.** Rav Naḥman concludes that, since the testimony of the witnesses is contradictory, we

HALAKHAH

אוֹקֵי תְּרֵי לַהֲדֵי תְּרֵי **Set two against two.** "If the witnesses who signed a document have died, and other witnesses come forward and say that the first witnesses signed under duress, or were disqualified from testifying, or were minors

[1]מִידֵי דַּהֲוָה אַנִּכְסֵי דְּבַר שָׁטְיָא. [2]דְּבַר שָׁטְיָא זַבֵּין נִכְסֵי. [3]אָתוּ בֵּי תְּרֵי אָמְרִי: ״כְּשֶׁהוּא שׁוֹטֶה זַבֵּין״, [4]וַאֲתוּ בֵּי תְּרֵי וְאָמְרִי: ״כְּשֶׁהוּא חָלִים זַבֵּין״. [5]אֲמַר רַב אַשִׁי: אוֹקֵי תְּרֵי לַהֲדֵי תְּרֵי,

LITERAL TRANSLATION

[1][It is] something that is like [the case of] the property of a [certain] madman. [2]For a [certain] madman sold property. [3]Two [witnesses] came [and] said: "When he was mad he sold [it]," [4]and two [witnesses] came and said: "When he was sane he sold [it]." [5]Rav Ashi said: Set two against two,

RASHI

זבין נכסיה = מכר קרקעותיו. **חלים** = בריא.

TRANSLATION AND COMMENTARY

מִידֵי דַּהֲוָה [1]The Gemara adds: Rav Naḥman's ruling in this case is **analogous to the** ruling given in **the case of the property of a certain madman** who suffered from intermittent fits of insanity. [2]**For this madman sold** his landed **property** in a manner that appeared less than advantageous to him. [3]**Two witnesses came and said: "When he sold** this property, **he was mad,** and therefore the sale was invalid." [4]**But two** other **witnesses came and said: "When he sold** this property, **he was sane,** and therefore the sale was valid." [5]The case came before **Rav Ashi,** who **said: Set** the first **two** witnesses **against** the second **two,** since the matter involves the conflicting testimony of

LANGUAGE

בַּר שָׁטְיָא A certain madman. Here the word בַּר does not mean "son of," as it does literally, but "someone who possesses a certain characteristic." This meaning is attested in other Hebrew and Aramaic phrases, e.g., בֶּן בְּלִיַּעַל "an evil person"; בַּר מִצְוָה "a person required to fulfill the commandments." Hence בַּר שָׁטְיָא here means "madman."

BACKGROUND

כְּשֶׁהוּא שׁוֹטֶה When he was mad. Certain mental illnesses (particularly manic-depressive conditions) occur on a periodic basis, with their victims experiencing periods of normality which alternate with periods of mental disturbance. In such cases, the illness takes effect gradually, and hence it is not always clear whether such a person was sane or not at any given time.

NOTES

must follow the procedure for cases in which we are in doubt, and give the defendant the benefit of the doubt, in accordance with the general rule that the onus is on the plaintiff to prove his case. The Rishonim ask: The rule in a case of contradictory testimony is that we give each pair of witnesses the benefit of the doubt, and treat them all as qualified witnesses for future testimony, the only exception being that we disqualify a mixed pair that includes witnesses from both original pairs, since such a pair would definitely include someone who testified falsely in the past (*Bava Batra* 31b). Thus, if the witnesses who signed this document were to sign another document, it would be valid, and the defendant in that case could not claim that the witnesses are of doubtful status, and that he should be permitted to keep the money because of the doubt. Why, then, do we not confirm the validity of this document for the same reason, and require the debtor to pay his debt?

Because of this question, *Ba'al HaMa'or* and *Rabbenu Ḥananel* rule that, in an ordinary case, where witnesses sign a document and other witnesses testify that they did so improperly, we give the witnesses who signed the document the benefit of the doubt, and the document is completely valid (unless the disqualifying witnesses were needed to authenticate the signatures). The law is thus in complete accord with the plain meaning of the Baraita. The only reason the Gemara had difficulty with the Baraita, and insisted that the validity of the document should be in doubt, was because the Baraita specified that the witnesses had died. *Ba'al HaMa'or* explains that we cannot give the benefit of the doubt to deceased people, because the benefit of the doubt is based on a legal presumption that the witnesses were originally honest people and continue to be so until proved otherwise, and this does not apply deceased people. Thus it is only where the witnesses are dead that we give the defendant the benefit of the doubt and permit him to keep the money.

Many Rishonim reject this interpretation, and follow the view of *Rif* (below, 22a), who explains that Rav Naḥman's ruling would apply even if the witnesses who signed the document were still alive. *Ran* explains that it is only regarding subsequent documents that we give the benefit of the doubt to the witnesses rather than to the defendant; but regarding this document we have two contradictory pairs of witnesses, and we must give both the benefit of the doubt. Hence we ignore this argument entirely, and rely on the general principle that the burden of proof is on the plaintiff (see also *Tosafot* and *Ramban*).

בַּר שָׁטְיָא A certain madman. *Ritva* notes that the assumption underlying this passage is that a person who has fits of insanity is treated like a completely sane person when he is well and like a completely insane person when he is sick, in accordance with a Tosefta (*Terumot* 1:2) cited by the Gemara in tractate *Rosh HaShanah* (28a).

כְּשֶׁהוּא שׁוֹטֶה זַבֵּין When he was mad he sold it. *Ran* asks: We learned above (19a) that there is a legal presumption that witnesses do not sign a document until they have ascertained that the parties are competent adults. Why, then, should there be any doubt about the madman? Surely the fact that the witnesses signed the deed of sale proves that the madman was sane at the time!

Ran answers that the madman did not draw up a document, but rather bought and sold property in some other way. *Rambam*, however, notes (*Hilkhot Mekhirah* 29:5) that there are sometimes situations in which a madman's state of mind is difficult to determine, e.g., when he is just entering or recovering from a fit of madness.

HALAKHAH

at the time, their testimony is not accepted, and we do not destroy the document, if it is possible to authenticate the signatures in some other way — through yet another pair of witnesses, or by comparing the signatures on the document with a known example of their handwriting. *Rema* adds that even in this case the validity of the document is doubtful, and we do not allow the creditor to use the document to collect his debt. But if the creditor seizes the debtor's movable property, we allow him to keep it, following the conclusion of the Gemara here. *Rema* adds further that, according to some opinions, this law applies only if the witnesses who signed the document have died; but if they are still alive, we believe the second pair and tear up the document, even if the document is authenticated independently." (*Rambam, Sefer Shofetim, Hilkhot Edut* 7:7; *Shulḥan Arukh, Ḥoshen Mishpat* 46:37.)

¹וְאוֹקֵי מָמוֹנָא בְּחֶזְקַת בַּר שָׁטְיָא. ²וְלָא אֲמָרַן אֶלָּא דְּאִית לֵיהּ חֲזָקָה דַּאֲבָהָתֵיהּ. ³אֲבָל לֵית לֵיהּ חֲזָקָה דַּאֲבָהָתֵיהּ, ⁴אָמְרִינַן: כְּשֶׁהוּא שׁוֹטֶה זָבַן, ⁵וּכְשֶׁהוּא שׁוֹטֶה זַבֵּין.

⁶אָמַר רַבִּי אַבָּהוּ: ⁷אֵין מְזִימִין אֶת הָעֵדִים אֶלָּא בִּפְנֵיהֶן, ⁸וּמַכְחִישִׁין אֶת הָעֵדִים שֶׁלֹּא

LITERAL TRANSLATION

¹and leave the money in the possession of the madman. ²And we only say [this] where he has an ancestral *ḥazakah* (lit., "the *ḥazakah* of his fathers"). ³But [if] he does not have an ancestral *ḥazakah*, ⁴we say: When he was mad he bought, ⁵and when he was mad he sold.

⁶Rabbi Abbahu said: ⁷We do not make witnesses *zomemim* except in their presence, ⁸but we contradict witnesses not in

RASHI

ולא אמרן — דאוקי נכסי בחזקת בר שטיא. **אלא דאית ליה** — בנכסים הללו חזקה דאבהתא, שהיו של אבותיו, דחזקה מעלייתא היא. **אבל לית ליה בהו חזקה דאבהתא** — אלא חזקה דנפשיה, שקנאן הוא והוחזקו בידו — כקנייתו כך מכירתו, ואין חזקתו חזקה לבטל מכירתו.

TRANSLATION AND COMMENTARY

two pairs of witnesses. ¹We must treat the case in accordance with the law governing doubtful matters, **and leave the money in the possession of the madman,** because the legal presumption in cases of real estate is that the land remains in the ownership of the last undisputed owner, until it is proved otherwise. Similarly, in a case of a loan, we leave the money in the possession of the borrower, because the legal presumption in cases of movable property is that it remains in the ownership of the person in physical possession of it. ²The Gemara now adds a stipulation to the ruling in the case of the madman: **We say** that the legal presumption of ownership supports the madman **only if he has an ancestral *ḥazakah***, that is, where the madman inherited the land from his father or from some other close relative and then sold it. In such a case, since we are in doubt as to whether the sale was valid, we restore the land to the madman as the last undisputed owner. ³**But if** the madman **does not have an ancestral *ḥazakah***, but bought the land from a third party and subsequently sold it, ⁴**we say:** It is possible that **when he bought** it, **he was mad,** ⁵**and when he sold** it, **he was** also **mad.** Hence the madman cannot be considered the last undisputed owner, and since the party from whom the madman bought the field is making no claim, we must leave the land in the ownership of the buyer, who is at present in physical possession of it.

אָמַר רַבִּי אַבָּהוּ ⁶The Gemara now returns to the dispute between Rav Sheshet and Rav Naḥman as to whether we must reject the contradiction of witnesses not in their presence, because contradiction is a lesser form of *hazamah*. **Rabbi Abbahu said:** The Halakhah is in accordance with Rav Naḥman. ⁷Therefore, even though **we make witnesses *zomemim* only** in their presence, ⁸**we** may **contradict witnesses although they are not present.** Moreover, not only do we accept contradiction although the witnesses are not present,

NOTES

כְּשֶׁהוּא שׁוֹטֶה זָבַן, וּכְשֶׁהוּא שׁוֹטֶה זַבֵּין When he was mad he bought, and when he was mad he sold. Our commentary follows *Ran* and *Ra'ah*, who explain that both the purchase and the sale are presumed invalid. According to this explanation, if the original owner who sold the madman the property were to come forward, he could claim the return of the property; but since he is apparently content, the purchaser who bought the property from the madman is permitted to keep it, since in any case it does not belong to the madman. Some Rishonim, however, explain that both the purchase and the sale are valid (*Rabbenu Yonah, Ri Migash, Meiri*). According to this explanation, an insane person may purchase property by Rabbinic decree, like a deaf-mute or a minor (see *Gittin* 59a). Moreover, he may also sell any property that he purchases in this way. He may not, however, sell property that he purchased or inherited when he was sane, as such property belongs to him by Torah law (see also *Rambam, Hilkhot Mekhirah* 29:1-4, and the accompanying comments of *Ra'avad* and *Maggid Mishneh*).

HALAKHAH

וְאוֹקֵי מָמוֹנָא בְּחֶזְקַת בַּר שָׁטְיָא And leave the money in the possession of the madman. "If a person who suffers from fits of insanity sells property while he is sane, the sale is valid; if he sells while he is insane, the sale is void. It is, therefore, the duty of the witnesses at the time of the sale to be absolutely certain of his state of mind. *Rema* adds that if he has sold property, and it is not clear what his state of mind was at the time, and two pairs of witnesses come forward, one testifying that he was sane and one that he was insane, we treat the sale as doubtful. Therefore, if he sold movable property, we leave it in the possession of the buyer, and if he sold real estate, we leave it in the possession of the madman. *Rabbi Akiva Eger* cites *Bet Yosef,* who rules that this applies only to real estate inherited by the madman from his ancestors, but not to real estate he bought, unless we are confident that he was sane at the time of the purchase." (*Rambam, Sefer Kinyan, Hilkhot Mekhirah 29:5; Shulḥan Arukh, Ḥoshen Mishpat* 235:21.)

וּמַכְחִישִׁין אֶת הָעֵדִים שֶׁלֹּא בִּפְנֵיהֶן But we contradict witnesses not in their presence. "*Hazamah* (proving that witnesses were not present at the event about which they

CONCEPTS

עַרְעָר A protest. עַרְעָר — sometimes written as עִרְעוּר — is any claim that challenges the validity of a document or the ownership of property. Such a challenge may be presented on various grounds. The claimant may argue that the document was drawn up fraudulently or under coercion, or that the document itself was written improperly or was forged. A charge commonly made against a promissory note is that it was forged by the person in possession of it. In such a case, the note is brought to court, and the signatures of the witnesses are examined. If the court concludes, relying on the testimony of the witnesses who signed the note or on that of other witnesses, or by comparing the handwriting, that the signatures are genuine, it authenticates the note by writing on it that it was examined and authenticated. The judges sign this certificate of authentication, so that another court may rely upon it.

TRANSLATION AND COMMENTARY

but we maintain that even [1]***hazamah* not in their presence, granted that it is not** considered real ***hazamah,*** [2]**is nevertheless** considered **contradiction.** Therefore, if *hazamah* is done to witnesses who have died, we consider their testimony to have been contradicted, and we treat the case as a doubtful matter, even though the second pair of witnesses did *hazamah* to the persons of the dead witnesses, and said nothing about the content of their testimony.

אָמַר מָר [3]The Gemara now considers in detail one of the clauses of the Baraita discussed in the previous passage (19b). **The Sage** who was the author of the Baraita **said:** "If the testimony of the second pair of witnesses is necessary to authenticate the document, we believe their testimony that the first pair of witnesses acted under duress, because 'the mouth that forbade is the mouth that permitted.' **But** we do not believe them if their testimony is not needed to authenticate the document." The Baraita then tells us under what circumstances their testimony is not needed to authenticate the document: [4]"Their testimony is not needed **if there are** other **witnesses** who can testify **that this is the handwriting** of the deceased original witnesses, [5]**or where their handwriting can be verified from another source**, such as when the court is able to establish the authenticity of the signatures by comparing them with known examples of the signatures of these witnesses." The Baraita then explains how the court obtains known examples of the signatures of these witnesses. [6]"It must select **a document** attesting to some other transaction which these same witnesses signed — a document **whose** authenticity **has been contested and has been confirmed in court,**" i.e., where the signatures on this second document were authenticated in response to a challenge by the defendant in that case. The signatures on such a document are known to be authentic, whereas there remains a remote possibility that the signatures on a document that has never been contested (and has thus not been investigated by a court) may themselves have been forged. The Baraita concludes that if the court can authenticate the signatures in this way, the second pair of witnesses are not needed, [7]and "**they are not believed**" when they testify that the deceased witnesses acted under duress. Rather, we treat the debt as a doubtful matter subject to the conflicting testimony, as explained above.

קָרָא עָלָיו עַרְעָר [8]On this point the Gemara observes: From the wording of the Baraita it appears that an example of the witnesses' signatures can be used to authenticate other signatures only **if** the document on which their signatures appear **was contested** and the challenge was defeated in court; [9]but **if it was not contested**, such a document may **not** be used.

בִּפְנֵיהֶן. [1]וַהֲזָמָה שֶׁלֹּא בִּפְנֵיהֶן, נְהִי דַּהֲזָמָה לָא הָוֵי, [2]הַכְחָשָׁה מִיהָא הָוְיָא.
[3]אָמַר מָר: [4]"אִם יֵשׁ עֵדִים שֶׁכְּתַב יָדָם הוּא זֶה, [5]אוֹ שֶׁהָיָה כְּתַב יָדָם יוֹצֵא מִמָּקוֹם אַחֵר — [6]מִשְּׁטָר שֶׁקָּרָא עָלָיו עַרְעָר וְהוּחְזַק בְּבֵית דִּין — [7]אֵין נֶאֱמָנִין".
[8]קָרָא עָלָיו עַרְעָר — אִין; [9]לֹא קָרָא עָלָיו עַרְעָר — לָא.

LITERAL TRANSLATION

their presence. [1]And *hazamah* not in their presence, granted that it is not *hazamah*, [2]is nevertheless a contradiction.

[3]The Master said: [4]"[But] if there are witnesses that this is their handwriting, [5]or where their handwriting came out from another place — [6]from a document that had been contested (lit., 'on which [someone] had called a protest') and had been confirmed in court — [7]they are not believed."

[8][If] it had been contested — yes; [9][if] it had not been contested — no.

RASHI

נהי דהזמה לא הויא – לעונשם לא נפש ולא ממון, הכחשה הויא לבטל עדותן.

NOTES

קָרָא עָלָיו עַרְעָר אִין; לֹא קָרָא עָלָיו עַרְעָר לָא If it had been contested — yes; if it had not been contested — no. Our translation and commentary follow the reading in *Rashi*'s text of the Talmud. *Rashi* explains that a document that has not been contested and confirmed may not be used to confirm another document, because we suspect that it too may have been forged. The language of the Gemara and of *Rashi* suggests that a document that has been confirmed in court without having been challenged may not be used for this purpose either, and a ruling to

HALAKHAH

gave testimony) can only be done in the witnesses' presence, but contradiction can be established even in their absence. Moreover, if a second pair of witnesses do *hazamah* in the first pair's absence, although it is not considered *hazamah*, it is considered contradiction. Therefore, if the first pair of witnesses died before the *hazamah*, the second pair are considered to have contradicted them, and one doubts the testimony of both sets," following Rabbi Abbahu. (*Rambam, Sefer Shofetim, Hilkhot Edut* 18:5.)

TRANSLATION AND COMMENTARY

מְסַיַּיע לֵיהּ [1] The Gemara continues: **This** Baraita **supports the** following **ruling of Rabbi Assi.** [2] **For Rabbi Assi said: We can authenticate a document only from a document that has been contested and confirmed in court.**

אָמְרִי נְהַרְדְּעֵי [3] **The Neharde'ans**, however, **said**: If a document that has been contested and confirmed in court is not available, we can authenticate the signatures on the original document by means of two examples of uncontested documents. However, there are limitations on the kind of uncontested document that can be used. [4] **We can authenticate a document only from two** uncontested

[1] מְסַיַּיע לֵיהּ לְרַבִּי אַסִי. [2] דְּאָמַר רַבִּי אַסִי: אֵין מְקַיְּימִין אֶת הַשְּׁטָר אֶלָּא מִשְּׁטָר שֶׁקָּרָא עָלָיו עַרְעָר וְהוּחֲזַק בְּבֵית דִּין. [3] אָמְרִי נְהַרְדְּעֵי: [4] אֵין מְקַיְּימִין

LITERAL TRANSLATION

[1] This supports [the ruling of] Rabbi Assi. [2] For Rabbi Assi said: We do not authenticate a document except from a document that has been contested and confirmed in court.

[3] The Neharde'ans say: [4] We do not authenticate a document

RASHI

אין מקיימין את השטר — מתוך שטר אחר. **אלא אם כן קרא ערער** — על אותו שטר האחר, והוחזק בבית דין על ידי עדיו. דאי לא קרא עליו ערער — חיישינן דלמא ההוא גופיה מזוייף הוא.

SAGES

אָמְרִי נְהַרְדְּעֵי The Neharde'ans say. Although this expression is a general one and refers to the Sages of the city of Neharde'a, nevertheless the Sages in the Talmud (*Sanhedrin* 17b) apply it to a particular Sage, Rav Ḥama, who was one of the most important Rabbis of that city. Occasionally this expression is used because the opinion expressed is not only Rav Ḥama's personal view but reflects the approach taken by all the Sages of Neharde'a.

NOTES

this effect was issued explicitly by *Ba'al HaIttur* and *Remah*, and also finds support in the language of *Rambam*.

Ritva objects, arguing that we never cast doubt on a court decision. *Shakh* explains that everyone agrees that where we recognize the signatures of the judges who signed the authentication, we do not question its validity, even if the note was confirmed without a challenge. But the Gemara is referring to a case where we do not recognize the signatures of the judges, and in such a case we suspect that the note and its authentication are both fabrications, unless we know that it passed the scrutiny of a court.

Rosh and *Ritva* rule that it is not necessary for the document to have been contested, provided that it has been confirmed. They explain that Rabbi Assi was merely describing the normal situation in which a document is not confirmed unless it is challenged, but in fact this is not a requirement. This explanation is supported by a variant reading found in *Rif*'s text of the Talmud: הוּחְזַק — אִין, לא הוּחְזַק — לא ("confirmed — yes; not confirmed — no").

אֵין מְקַיְּימִין אֶת הַשְּׁטָר אֶלָּא מִשְּׁטָר שֶׁקָּרָא עָלָיו עַרְעָר We do not authenticate a document except from a document that has been contested. There are two slightly differing versions of Rabbi Assi's statement (see *Ran*). Our translation and commentary follow the reading in *Rashi*'s text of the Talmud. *Rashi* explains that only a document that has been contested and carefully confirmed may be used to confirm another document. If any other — unconfirmed — document is used, there remains a remote possibility that it too was forged.

Many Rishonim (*Rif, Ramban, Ritva*) have a different reading in their texts: "We do not authenticate a document from a document that has been contested, unless it has been confirmed in court." According to this reading, we can use any document that has not been challenged (subject to the conditions laid down below by the Neharde'ans; see following note), but not a document that has itself been challenged, unless the challenge was carefully examined by the court and dismissed. According to this reading, Rabbi Assi's purpose is apparently to exclude a document that has been challenged but not confirmed. *Rosh* objects, arguing that it is obvious that a document whose authenticity is in doubt cannot be used to authenticate another document until it itself has been authenticated. *Ran* explains that Rabbi Assi's purpose is to exclude a case where a challenge to a document was withdrawn by the challenger before a thorough examination was made by the court.

Rif's explanation can be maintained only in accordance with the variant reading in the Gemara: "confirmed — yes; not confirmed — no," but not according to our reading: "contested — yes; not contested — no" (see previous note). But *Rashi*'s explanation can be maintained according to either reading.

Regarding a document that has not been confirmed, there is no difference in practice between the two versions; all agree that it can be used, provided that it meets the criteria set by the Neharde'ans (below). There may be a difference, however, regarding a document that has been challenged and then confirmed: According to *Rashi*, only one such document is needed, whereas according to *Rif* it may be necessary to present two such documents (see following note).

אָמְרִי נְהַרְדְּעֵי The Neharde'ans say. The Rishonim agree that the Neharde'ans do not disagree with Rabbi Assi that a document that has been contested and confirmed can

HALAKHAH

אֵין מְקַיְּימִין אֶת הַשְּׁטָר אֶלָּא מִשְּׁטָר שֶׁקָּרָא עָלָיו עַרְעָר וְהוּחֲזַק בְּבֵית דִּין We do not authenticate a document except from a document that has been contested and confirmed in court. "The court can authenticate a document by comparing the signatures on it with the signatures of the same witnesses appearing on another document, provided that the other document has itself been authenticated in a court, following Rabbi Assi and the Baraita. *Shulḥan Arukh* rules that only a document authenticated as a result of a challenge in court may be used. *Rema*, however, cites the view of *Rosh* that any authenticated document can be used, even if the authentication was not in response to a challenge. *Rema* adds that, according to *Tur*, only an authenticated document in someone else's possession can be used, but according to *Ran* even a document in the creditor's possession can be used, provided that it was authenticated in court." (*Rambam, Sefer Shofetim, Hilkhot Edut* 6:3; *Shulḥan Arukh, Ḥoshen Mishpat* 46:7.)

TRANSLATION AND COMMENTARY

ketubot, or from the uncontested **deeds of sale of two fields**, because it is extremely unlikely that such documents would not have been contested by the husbands or by the fields' original owners if they had been forged. Moreover, in the case of deeds of sale, there is one further proviso: [1]We may use a deed attesting a sale only if the new **owners** (i.e., the purchasers) **used** the fields **for the three** full **years** of undisputed possession **in peace**, without any complaint from the original owner who sold the field. The Sages instituted the rule that a landowner who claims that another person is squatting in his field illegally has three years to register a protest,

אֶת הַשְּׁטָר אֶלָּא מִשְּׁתֵּי כְּתוּבּוֹת אוֹ מִשְּׁתֵּי שָׂדוֹת, [1]וְהוּא שֶׁאֲכָלוּם בַּעֲלֵיהֶן שָׁלֹשׁ שָׁנִים וּבְשׁוּפִי.

LITERAL TRANSLATION

except from two ketubot or from [the deeds of sale of] two fields, [1]provided that their owners used (lit., "ate") them [for] three years and in peace.

RASHI

משתי שדות — מעדים האלה, אם חתומים על שני שטרות אחרים, שהן מכר שתי שדות ואכלום הלקוחות על ידי שטרות הללו שלש שנים — מקיימין שטר שלישי מהן, אם החתימות דומות. **בשופי** — בלא ערעור.

NOTES

be used to authenticate another document, since Rabbi Assi's view is supported by the Baraita (*Rosh*, *Ran*, and others). The Rishonim differ, however, as to the precise relationship between the two statements. This dispute is closely related to the two versions of Rabbi Assi's statement (see previous note).

Baḥag and *Ra'avad* follow the reading of *Rif*, according to which Rabbi Assi said that it is possible to use an unchallenged note *or* a note that has been challenged and confirmed in court. These Rishonim explain that the Neharde'ans are interpreting two points in Rabbi Assi's statement: (1) Rabbi Assi implied that any unchallenged document can be used, but the Neharde'ans insist that only a ketubah or a deed of sale can be used, because they attest to transactions that would certainly have been contested if the documents had been forged. (2) The wording of Rabbi Assi's statement seems to suggest that one confirmed document is sufficient, but the Neharde'ans insist that there must always be at least two documents, regardless of whether challenged or unchallenged documents are selected (see *Bet Yosef*).

Our commentary follows the opinion of *Rambam*, *Ritva*, and others, who interpret Rabbi Assi's ruling literally. They explain that the Neharde'ans are not interpreting Rabbi Assi's ruling that a single contested and confirmed document is sufficient, but are offering an alternative procedure in the event that a contested and confirmed document is not available. According to this explanation, one may use a single contested and confirmed document (as Rabbi Assi said), or else two unconfirmed documents, provided these documents are ketubot or deeds of sale of real estate. This explanation can follow either the reading of *Rif* or that of *Rashi*, who said that Rabbi Assi allowed only contested and confirmed documents to be used, whereas the first explanation can only follow the reading of *Rif*.

אֵין מְקַיְּימִין אֶת הַשְּׁטָר אֶלָּא מִשְּׁתֵּי כְּתוּבּוֹת We do not authenticate a document except from two ketubot. *Mordekhai* explains that two documents are needed because signatures vary slightly, and it is impossible to make a fair comparison unless two examples are used.

The Jerusalem Talmud declares that nonlegal written material may also be used, such as a book written by one of the witnesses, but the use of a letter remains questionable. *Meiri* and *Korban HaEdah* explain that a book is normally written with care, but a letter is often written quickly, and the handwriting in it may vary considerably. *Ritva* explains that we can be confident that a book was really written by its author, but we are not as certain about a letter. According to this view, a letter whose authorship has been absolutely determined can presumably be used.

According to both these explanations, it would appear from the Jerusalem Talmud that it is not necessary to choose a signature as an example of the witnesses' handwriting. Any carefully written text can be used. It is not entirely clear whether the Halakhah follows the Jerusalem Talmud in this matter. *Rosh* and *Mordekhai* note that this ruling is contradicted by a statement in our Gemara (below, 21a), from which it appears that only signatures may be used as examples: The Gemara rules that where a witness is asked to provide a handwriting sample, he should sign his name on a piece of pottery. The Gemara explains that pottery is selected rather than parchment, so that the signature cannot later be misused as part of a forged document. But if any handwriting sample can be used as an example, and it is not necessary to use a signature, why does the witness sign his name at all? According to these Rishonim, the ruling of the Jerusalem Talmud is rejected, since the Halakhah always follows the Babylonian Talmud when it conflicts with the Jerusalem Talmud. Indeed, *Bet Yosef* cites an explanation of *Ran* (not found in our texts), who says that even the Jerusalem Talmud was referring only to a case where the author of the book or the letter actually signed it.

Other Rishonim, however, rule in favor of the Jerusalem Talmud (*Rashba*, *Ritva*, *Meiri*). *Rashba* explains that there is no contradiction between our Gemara and the Jerusalem Talmud: Ordinary handwriting can be used as a handwriting sample, as the Jerusalem Talmud ruled, but witnesses who are asked to provide a handwriting sample do in fact normally sign their names; hence our Gemara advises them to do so on a piece of pottery. *Meiri* goes even further,

HALAKHAH

אֵין מְקַיְּימִין אֶת הַשְּׁטָר אֶלָּא מִשְּׁתֵּי כְּתוּבּוֹת We do not authenticate a document except from two ketubot. "If an authenticated document with these witnesses' signatures is not available, unauthenticated documents can also

אֲמַר רַב שִׁימִי בַּר אַשִׁי: [1] וּבְיוֹצֵא מִתַּחַת יַד אַחֵר, [2] אֲבָל מִיַּד עַצְמוֹ — לָא.

LITERAL TRANSLATION

[1] Rav Shimi bar Ashi said: And where it goes out from under someone else's hand, [2] but from his own hand — no.

RASHI

וביוצא מתחת ידי אחר — שהשטרות הללו שמקיימין את השלישי מהם יוצא מתחת ידי אחר, ולא מתחת ידיו של זה המוציא את השלישי.

TRANSLATION AND COMMENTARY

after which the other person's claims are believed without proof (see above, 17b). Hence, if an uncontested deed of sale is used as an example of the witnesses' signatures, it must be at least three years old, because if three years have not yet passed from the date on the deed of sale, it is still possible that the original owner plans to register a complaint. However, once three years have passed, it is clear that the original owner has no intention of protesting, and it is extremely unlikely that this would have happened if the signatures on the deed of sale had been forged. Hence two such deeds can be used to check the authenticity of witnesses' signatures.

אֲמַר רַב שִׁימִי בַּר אַשִׁי [1] **Rav Shimi bar Ashi said:** If we wish to compare the signatures on a document with those on other documents, we must select documents **in someone else's possession**, documents registering transactions to which the present creditor was not a party; [2] **but** if the documents **were in his own possession**, we do **not** use them for comparison, because we are afraid that the creditor may have forged the present document by carefully copying the authentic signatures on the other documents in his possession.

SAGES

רַב שִׁימִי בַּר אַשִׁי Rav Shimi bar Ashi. A Babylonian Amora of the fifth generation, Rav Shimi bar Ashi was a close disciple of Abaye, and also studied with Rava. After the death of his teachers he attended Rav Pappa's yeshivah, and the members of his generation regarded him as a great man and honored him. His teachings are transmitted by a number of Sages of the following generation, though he did not apparently have a yeshivah of his own. In several places in the Talmud he is shown to have been extremely sharp-witted, so that his contemporaries feared his questions. He may have been a physician by profession, but we do not know anything about his family or have detailed information about his life.

NOTES

ruling that a book can be used as an example, even if it was in the possession of the creditor (unlike a legal document), because it is harder to forge a signature by studying the handwriting in a book than it is to copy another signature.

מִשְּׁתֵּי כְתוּבּוֹת אוֹ מִשְּׁתֵּי שָׂדוֹת From two ketubot or from the deeds of sale of two fields. *Ran* explains that the Neharde'ans did not permit ordinary promissory notes to be used for this purpose because it is possible to forge such a note, and as long as it is not presented for collection, the "borrower" may know nothing about the matter. But in the case of a ketubah or a deed of sale, it is easy to ascertain whether the woman is indeed married to the man who wrote the ketubah or that the person who bought the field did indeed take possession of it. *Meiri* adds that these documents were selected because they are normally drawn up in public. According to either opinion, it is extremely unlikely that the husband or the original owner would fail to challenge such a document if it had been forged.

וּבְשׁוּפִי And in peace. The word שׁוּפִי literally means "peace" or "comfort" (*Talmidei Rabbenu Yonah*). Our translation and commentary follow *Rashi*, who explains that the word refers to the original owner of the field, who has kept his peace and issued no challenge. *Rambam* explains that it refers to the person who bought the field. He must occupy it comfortably, confident that he does not need to hide or concern himself about a potential lawsuit.

וּבְיוֹצֵא מִתַּחַת יַד אַחֵר And where it goes out from under someone else's hand. Our commentary follows *Rashi*, who explains that we suspect that the creditor may have forged this document by copying the signatures from other documents. *Rambam* explains that our concern is that the creditor may have forged all three documents (see also *Ramban* and *Ritva*). According to *Rambam*, if the documents in his possession have themselves been confirmed in court, there is no further room for concern, whereas according to *Rashi* this would make no difference (*Meiri*, *Ritva*).

The Rishonim note that, according to *Rashi*, if the creditor has samples of the witnesses' signatures in his possession, we should not allow him to confirm the document, even if he uses documents in someone else's possession as the means of authentication. So long as the creditor has samples of the witnesses' signatures in his possession, even if they are not presented as samples, he can use them to forge signatures on other documents. Indeed, *Ba'al HaIttur* rules this way in practice. *Meiri*, however, argues that this is an unnecessary stringency, and that we suspect forgery only if the documents in the creditor's possession are used to authenticate the signatures. *Rabbenu Tam* and *Rosh* rule in favor of *Ba'al HaIttur* where the document is authenticated by comparing it with other examples of the witnesses' signatures, but not if there are witnesses who recognize the handwriting, and certainly not where the witnesses themselves come forward and authenticate their own signatures. For it is relatively easy to copy a signature well enough that it appears similar on comparison, but it is much harder to deceive people who know a signature well enough to recognize it on sight.

HALAKHAH

be used to confirm the witnesses' signatures, provided that there are at least two such documents. The only documents that are permitted to be used for this purpose are ketubot and deeds of sale of real estate in which the purchaser has taken possession of the real estate and occupied it openly and confidently for three years without any complaint from the seller, following the Neharde'ans. Moreover, only documents in someone else's possession can be used for this purpose, but documents in the creditor's own possession must not be used, for we are afraid that he may have forged these documents as well, following Rav Shimi bar Ashi." (*Rambam, Sefer Shofetim, Hilkhot Edut* 6:3; *Shulḥan Arukh, Ḥoshen Mishpat* 46:7.)

TRANSLATION AND COMMENTARY

מַאי שְׁנָא [1]The Gemara asks: **What difference is there that we do not accept** documents **in his own possession?** [2]Clearly it is because we are afraid that **he may perhaps have forged them.** [3]But surely the same concern **also** applies where the documents **were in someone else's possession!** [4]**Perhaps** the present creditor **went** to the person who had the other documents, **saw** the signatures, [5]**and came** back **and forged** the signatures on his false document!

כּוּלֵּי הַאי לָא מָצֵי מְכַוֵּין [6]The Gemara answers: **He cannot be as exact as all that.** It is one thing to be concerned that a person may carefully copy signatures on a document in his possession, and quite another to imagine that he could make an exact copy based on memory alone. Such an effort would never pass the careful scrutiny of the court.

תָּנוּ רַבָּנַן [7]We mentioned above (17b) that the signatures of witnesses on a document are the equivalent of oral testimony that has been thoroughly examined and confirmed in court. This law is an exception to the general rule that witnesses must testify orally and that testimony delivered in writing is not acceptable. The Gemara now cites a Baraita from which we learn an additional exception: that witnesses are permitted to make use of written materials to refresh their memories. **Our Rabbis taught** the following Baraita: "**A person may write his testimony on a document,** [8]**and may give evidence by means of it even after several years.**" The witness must testify orally, but he can take notes for himself and use them to refresh his memory.

LITERAL TRANSLATION

[1]What difference is there under his own hand that not? [2]Perhaps he forged [it]. [3]From under someone else's hand, too, [4]perhaps he went and saw, [5][and] came and forged!

[6]He cannot be all that exact.

[7]Our Rabbis taught: "A man may write his evidence on a document, [8]and may give evidence by means of it even after several years."

[1]מַאי שְׁנָא תַּחַת יַד עַצְמוֹ דְּלָא? [2]דִּלְמָא זַיּוּפֵי מְזַיֵּיף. [3]מִתַּחַת יְדֵי אַחֵר נַמִי, [4]דִּלְמָא אֲזַל וַחֲזָא, [5]אֲתָא וְזַיֵּיף! [6]כּוּלֵּי הַאי לָא מָצֵי מְכַוֵּין. [7]תָּנוּ רַבָּנַן: "כּוֹתֵב אָדָם עֵדוּתוֹ עַל הַשְּׁטָר, [8]וּמֵעִיד עָלֶיהָ אֲפִילּוּ לְאַחַר כַּמָּה שָׁנִים".

RASHI

זיופי זייף — הסתכל בכתב של אותן שטרות, וכוון וחתם הוא עצמו את השלישי דוגמת אותה חתימה. **מכוין** — מצמצם כתב בכתב, הואיל ואינו לפניו. **כותב אדם** — אם עשאוהו עד בדבר, וירא לשוכחו — כותבו על חתיכת קלף ומצניעה. **ומעיד** — על פי אותו כתב אפילו לאחר כמה שנים.

NOTES

כּוֹתֵב אָדָם עֵדוּתוֹ A man may write his evidence. The verse (Deuteronomy 19:15) says: "At the mouth of two witnesses." The Gemara (*Yevamot* 31b) infers from this that testimony must come from the witnesses' own lips, and not from written testimony or from testimony by proxy. According to *Rashi* in his commentary on the Torah, this means that the witnesses must appear in person in court. But *Rabbenu Tam* rules that the verse only forbids a witness who was unable to testify orally from testifying in writing (e.g., if was struck dumb, or did not remember the testimony), but a witness who is physically able to testify orally is permitted to send a written deposition instead.

There is an obvious conflict between this law and the laws governing legal documents. Under Jewish law, a legal document is drawn up at the behest of the party who is assuming an obligation (e.g., the debtor), and is delivered to the person who is to benefit from the obligation (e.g., the creditor). The document must be witnessed to ensure that it was not forged by the beneficiary, and that it was delivered to him by the obligated person. There are three ways this can be done: (1) The obligated person can draw up the document in his own handwriting. (2) The document can be signed by witnesses while it is still in the possession of the obligated person (this is the normal procedure). (3) The document can be delivered in the presence of witnesses. (The relative effectiveness of the last two procedures is the subject of a Tannaitic dispute, and a dispute among the Rishonim; see *Gittin* 36a and 86a, and see *Tosafot*, *Ramban*, and others.)

The conflict with the rule that testimony must be delivered orally arises only when the second method is used. For when the document is presented in court, it appears that the witnesses who signed it (who may have died a long time ago) are testifying in writing. *Rambam* rules that the second method of attesting to the validity of a document is a Rabbinic institution. The Rishonim note, however, that this procedure is derived by the Gemara (*Gittin* 36a) from a Biblical verse (Jeremiah 32:10). *Kesef Mishneh* explains that a verse from the Prophets does not necessarily have Torah authority. *Rashi* (*Gittin* 86b) explains that Jeremiah was not issuing a legal ruling, but rather a piece of prophetic advice.

Many Rishonim maintain, however, that by Torah law a document can be authenticated in writing. *Tosafot* explains that when a document is signed by two witnesses, it is as though they have already been investigated by the court (see above, 18b), and when the document is later presented in court, it is no longer considered testimony about the events, but rather a proof that a court ruling was issued. According to this explanation, the reason why our Gemara

HALAKHAH

כּוֹתֵב אָדָם עֵדוּתוֹ עַל הַשְּׁטָר A man may write his evidence on a document. "A witness is permitted to take notes, and he may later review his notes to refresh his memory before testifying, following the Baraita. Even if he does not

LITERAL TRANSLATION

[1] Rav Huna said: And this is [provided] that he remembers it by himself.

[2] Rabbi Yoḥanan said: Even though he does not remember it by himself.

[3] Rabbah said: Conclude from Rabbi Yoḥanan's [statement that if] there are two [witnesses] who know testimony, [4] and one of them forgets [it], one may remind the other.

[5] It was asked of them: What about [the litigant] himself?

[1] אָמַר רַב הוּנָא: וְהוּא שֶׁזּוֹכְרָהּ מֵעַצְמוֹ.

[2] רַבִּי יוֹחָנָן אָמַר: אַף עַל פִּי שֶׁאֵין זוֹכְרָהּ מֵעַצְמוֹ.

[3] אֲמַר רַבָּה: שְׁמַע מִינָּהּ מִדְּרַבִּי יוֹחָנָן הָנֵי בֵּי תְּרֵי דְּיָדְעִי סַהֲדוּתָא, [4] וּמִנְשֵׁי חַד מִנַּיְיהוּ, מַדְכַּר חַד לְחַבְרֵיהּ.

[5] אִיבַּעֲיָא לְהוּ: עַצְמוֹ מַאי?

RASHI

שזוכרה מעצמו — בלא ראיית השטר נזכר קצת מעדותו מאליו. **אף על פי שאין זוכרה מעצמו** — אלא לאחר שרואה בשטר — נתן בלבו ונזכר, שלא נשתכח ממנו כל כך, שכשמזכירים לו נזכר. אבל אינו נזכר לגמרי — לא, דרחמנא אמר: מפיהם ולא מפי כתבם. **עצמו מאי** — אם בעל דין עצמו מזכירו עד שנזכר, מאי.

TRANSLATION AND COMMENTARY

אָמַר רַב הוּנָא [1] The Gemara now cites an Amoraic discussion about this Baraita. **Rav Huna said**: Notes can be used, as the Baraita ruled, **provided that** the witness also **remembers** the testimony **by himself**, without the notes, and merely uses the notes to refresh his memory on details. But if the witness has basically forgotten the testimony, he is not permitted to use notes he made at the time, because this amounts to testimony delivered in writing.

רַבִּי יוֹחָנָן אָמַר [2] **Rabbi Yoḥanan** disagreed with Rav Huna, and **said**: Notes may be used **even** if the witness **does not remember** the testimony at all **by himself,** and is wholly dependent on his notes. Even according to Rabbi Yoḥanan, however, the witness must remember the testimony after he is reminded. If he has no recollection at all, and merely testifies that he read something in his notes, his testimony is no better than the notes themselves.

אֲמַר רַבָּה [3] **Rabbah said: We can conclude from Rabbi Yoḥanan's statement** that **if there are two witnesses who know testimony,** [4] **and one of them forgets it, the one** who remembers **is permitted to remind the other** — provided, again, that the witness recalls the testimony after he has been reminded, and is not merely giving hearsay evidence about what he has been told.

אִיבַּעֲיָא לְהוּ [5] In a later generation, the following question **was asked of** the Rabbis in the academy: **What about the litigant himself?** What if the witnesses have forgotten, and they are reminded by the litigant in whose favor they are testifying? Is such testimony acceptable or not?

NOTES

rules that a witness who took notes may testify only if he remembers the events, is because his notes did not constitute a legal document. *Tosafot* explains that only a document signed by two witnesses is considered a valid document. Alternatively, only a note written at the behest of the person obligating himself is considered a valid document.

כּוֹתֵב אָדָם עֵדוּתוֹ עַל הַשְּׁטָר A man may write his evidence on a document. Our commentary follows *Rashi* and other Rishonim, who explain that the Baraita is referring to a witness who takes notes as an aid to his memory. *Ritva* notes that this explanation is somewhat difficult, because the Baraita uses the word שְׁטָר — "document" — and this normally refers to a legally binding document and not to private notes. But *Rambam* insists that this objection is not decisive, and that *Rashi*'s explanation is still to be preferred.

Many Rishonim explain that the Baraita is indeed referring to a legal document. *Rav Hai Gaon* explains that the Baraita is referring to a case where the witnesses were told to draw up a document, or where the loan was confirmed by means of a formal act of acquisition, in which case they are considered to have been told to draw up a document (*Bava Batra* 40a) but failed to do so immediately. The Baraita is telling us that the witnesses may draw up this document at any time, and need not be concerned that the loan may already have been repaid. *Ramban* rejects this explanation, arguing that the witnesses have no reason to assume that the debt has not been repaid. *Rashba*, however, defends this explanation, arguing that the debtor should have assumed that a note would be drawn up, and should not have repaid the loan without tearing up the note, or at least demanding a receipt.

HALAKHAH

remember the events without studying the notes, he may still testify, and this is not considered written testimony, following Rabbi Yoḥanan, because the Halakhah normally follows Rabbi Yoḥanan, even when he disagrees with Rav (Rav Huna's teacher), and all the more so when he disagrees with Rav Huna. However, this ruling applies only if the witness remembers the events after reading the notes; but if he remembers nothing at all, and merely testifies on the basis of what he has read, it is considered written testimony and is unacceptable. Indeed, if a witness who signed a document cannot remember anything of the transaction even after being reminded, he may not even testify that the signature on the document is his, because witnesses who authenticate their signatures are considered to be testifying about the content of the document, and not just about their signatures." (*Rambam, Sefer Shofetim, Hilkhot Edut* 8:1-2; *Shulḥan Arukh, Ḥoshen Mishpat* 28:13 and 46:10.)

[1]רַב חֲבִיבָא אֲמַר: אֲפִילּוּ עַצְמוֹ. [2]מָר בְּרֵיהּ דְּרַב אַשִׁי אֲמַר: עַצְמוֹ לֹא.
[3]וְהִלְכְתָא: עַצְמוֹ לֹא. [20B] [4]וְאִי צוּרְבָא מֵרַבָּנַן הוּא, אֲפִילּוּ עַצְמוֹ.
[5]כִּי הָא דְּרַב אַשִׁי הֲוָה יְדִיעַ לֵיהּ בְּסַהֲדוּתָא לְרַב כָּהֲנָא.

LITERAL TRANSLATION

[1]Rav Ḥaviva said: Even [the litigant] himself. [2]Mar the son of Rav Ashi said: [The litigant] himself not. [3]And the Halakhah is: [The litigant] himself not. [20B] [4]But if he is a Rabbinic scholar, even [the litigant] himself.

[5]As [happened] in that [case], where Rav Ashi knew evidence for Rav Kahana.

TRANSLATION AND COMMENTARY

רַב חֲבִיבָא אֲמַר [1]**Rav Ḥaviva said: Even the litigant himself** is permitted to remind the witnesses, provided that the witnesses recall the testimony after they have been reminded (as the Gemara states below). Since we have seen that witnesses are permitted to testify after being reminded, provided that they are then able to remember their testimony, it is immaterial who does the reminding. However, [2]**Mar the son of Rav Ashi said: The litigant himself** is **not** permitted to remind the witnesses. For if the litigant is allowed to coach the witnesses, he is liable to influence them improperly.

וְהִלְכְתָא [3]**And** the Gemara concludes that **the Halakhah is** that **the litigant himself** is **not** permitted to remind the witnesses — even if they claim that they remembered by themselves after being reminded — as every effort must be made to avoid the possibility of their being unduly influenced. [20B] [4]**But if** the witness in question **is a Rabbinic scholar,** whom no one would suspect of falsehood, **even the litigant himself** is permitted to remind him, provided that he remembers the testimony after being reminded.

כִּי הָא דְּרַב אַשִׁי [5]The Gemara illustrates this ruling by citing what **happened in the following case, where Rav Ashi was in possession of evidence supporting Rav Kahana.** In other words, Rav Kahana was the litigant

RASHI

ואי צורבא מרבנן הוא – העד. **אפילו לעצמו** – של בעל דין. דצורבא דרבנן, אי לאו דכי רמי אנפשיה מדכר שפיר – לא הוה סמיך אספיקא למיקם ואסהודי.

NOTES

וְאִי צוּרְבָא מֵרַבָּנַן הוּא **But if he is a Rabbinic scholar.** The Gemara does not make clear who has to be a Rabbinic scholar — the witness or the litigant who reminds him. Moreover, in the story cited by the Gemara in support of its ruling, both the litigant (Rav Kahana) and the witness (Rav Ashi) were scholars of the highest rank.

Our commentary follows *Rashi* and most Rishonim, who explain that it is the witness, not the litigant, who must be a Rabbinic scholar. For we have confidence that a Rabbinic scholar will be careful not to be influenced by the prompting of the litigant, and that he will testify only if he is certain that he remembers the events unaided (*Ritva*). According to this explanation, the point of the story was that Rav Ashi was a Rabbinic scholar, and the fact that Rav Kahana was also a Rabbinic scholar was a mere coincidence.

Rav Hai Gaon and *Rambam* explain that it is the litigant, not the witness, who must be a Rabbinic scholar. We have confidence that a Rabbinic scholar will not attempt to exert undue influence on a witness, and will only remind him, just as an outsider would do. According to this explanation, the point of the story was that Rav Kahana was a Rabbinic scholar, and the fact that Rav Ashi was also a Rabbinic scholar was a mere coincidence.

Rabbenu Yonah objects to this explanation, arguing that, as a litigant, even a Rabbinic scholar cannot be trusted not to say too much, because the fact that he knows that what he is saying is true is liable to cloud his judgment. Only when the witness is a Rabbinic scholar can we be confident that he will be a dispassionate observer. *Ritva* adds that even if the litigant is very careful, it is the witness who must decide if he really remembers after being reminded, and this requires the scrupulous honesty of a Rabbinic scholar. Further support for *Rashi*'s explanation can be found in the words of Rav Ashi: "Do you think that I was relying on you? It was I who took it upon myself and remembered." This remark suggests that it was Rav Ashi, and not Rav Kahana, who was making the kind of subtle judgment that can be expected from a scholar.

Sma rules that in practice both opinions are followed by the Halakhah, and if either the litigant or the witness is a Rabbinic scholar, the litigant is permitted to remind the witness.

HALAKHAH

עַצְמוֹ לֹא **The litigant himself not.** "If a witness is reminded by someone else about the events he witnessed, and after being reminded he recalls them himself, he may testify, even if the person reminding him is the other witness. But if the litigant in the case reminds him, he may not testify, even if he recalls the events himself after being reminded, following the conclusion of the Gemara which follows Rabbah and Mar the son of Rav Ashi. If, however, the witness is a Rabbinic scholar, he may testify, even if he was reminded by the litigant, following the ruling of the Gemara (below) as explained by *Rashi*. According to *Rambam*, this law applies if the litigant is a Rabbinic scholar, even if the witness is not. *Sma* rules that both opinions are correct, and if either the witness or the litigant is a Rabbinic scholar, the witness may testify, even if he was reminded by the litigant, provided that he recalls the events himself after being reminded." (*Rambam, Sefer Shofetim, Hilkhot Edut* 8:2-3; *Shulḥan Arukh, Ḥoshen Mishpat* 28:14.)

LANGUAGE

צוּרְבָא מֵרַבָּנַן **A Rabbinic scholar.** This is a common term in the Talmud for a scholar (usually a young person), though its source and precise meaning are not clear. Some suggest that it derives from the root צרב — something hot, burning with the fire of Torah. Others suggest that it is derived from the Arabic word meaning "hard" or "strong," for indeed a צוּרְבָא מֵרַבָּנַן has a sharp and powerful mind (*Rav Hai Gaon*).

SAGES

רַב חֲבִיבָא **Rav Ḥaviva.** A sixth-generation Babylonian Amora. See *Ketubot*, Part I, p. 95.

רַב אַשִׁי **Rav Ashi.** A sixth-generation Babylonian Amora. See *Ketubot*, Part I, p. 14.

רַב כָּהֲנָא **Rav Kahana.** There were many Sages of this name during different periods, and it is not always clear which one was the author of any given statement. In the present context, however, it seems clear that the Rav Kahana quoted was Rav Ashi's teacher.
This particular Rav Kahana was a Babylonian Amora of the fifth generation. He came from the city of Pum Nahara, and was head of the Pumbedita Yeshivah for twenty years.
His most important student was Rav Ashi, who speaks often in the Talmud about his studies in the home of Rav Kahana. Apparently, despite Rav Ashi's youth, Rav Kahana greatly respected him, and sometimes dignified him with the title *Mar* (מָר) — "Master."

TRANSLATION AND COMMENTARY

and Rav Ashi was one of the witnesses testifying in his favor. [1]Rav Kahana **said to** Rav Ashi: **"Do you, sir, remember this evidence?"** [2]Rav Ashi **said to him** in reply: **"No."** [3]Rav Kahana then said: **"But was it not so and so?"** [4]Rav Ashi then **said to him: "I do not know**; I am still unable to remember." [5]**Finally, Rav Ashi recalled** the evidence **and testified for** Rav Kahana. [6]**He saw that Rav Kahana was hesitant,** fearful of accepting a ruling in his favor based on hearsay evidence, since Rav Ashi had not been able to remember the facts of the case, even after being reminded. [7]Rav Ashi then **said to him: "Do you think that** when I testified **I was relying on** what **you** told me? Certainly not! [8]After we spoke, **I made an effort, and** in the end **I did remember** the facts of the case." Thus we see that where the witness is a scrupulous Rabbinic scholar like Rav Ashi, who would never give evidence about something he did not know from his own knowledge, it is permissible even for the litigant to remind the witness, provided that the witness does ultimately recall the matter.

תְּנַן הָתָם The question of a witness's memory leads the Gemara to cite a Mishnah which has no immediate relevance to the problems we have been considering. The Mishnah deals with a question of ritual impurity. By Torah law, if a person stands over a grave or walks over one, he becomes ritually impure. This law effectively divides the world into three categories: (1) Places where a human body is known to have been buried, which definitely impart ritual impurity; (2) places where we are certain that a human body has never been buried, which are definitely ritually pure; and (3) places where we have no knowledge of any burial, but we do not know for certain that no burial has taken place there. The status of a person who stands or walks over such a place is decided on the basis of certain legal presumptions applicable to ritual impurity. The Mishnah cited by our Gemara deals with this last category.

[9]**We learned** in a Mishnah **elsewhere** (*Ohalot* 16:2): "If a person stands on **a mound** of earth in which we are not certain whether or not a body has been buried, the ritual status of the person depends on the

[1]אֲמַר לֵיהּ: ״מִי דְּכִיר מָר הַאי סַהֲדוּתָא?״ [2]אֲמַר לֵיהּ: ״לָא״. [3]״וְלָאו הָכִי וְהָכִי הֲוָה?״ [4]אֲמַר לֵיהּ: ״לָא יָדַעֲנָא״. [5]לְסוֹף אִידְכַּר רַב אַשִׁי, אַסְהֵיד לֵיהּ. [6]חַזְיֵיהּ לְרַב כָּהֲנָא דַּהֲוָה מְחַסֵּם. [7]אֲמַר לֵיהּ: ״מִי סָבְרַתְּ עֲלָךְ קָא סָמֵיכְנָא? [8]אֲנָא הוּא דִּרְמַאי אַנַּפְשַׁאי וְאִדַּכְּרִי״. [9]תְּנַן הָתָם: ״הַתְּלוּלִיּוֹת

LITERAL TRANSLATION

[1]He said to him: "Do you, sir, remember this evidence?" [2]He said to him: "No." [3]"But was it not so and so?" [4]He said to him: "I do not know." [5]In the end, Rav Ashi remembered, [and] he testified for him. [6]He saw that Rav Kahana was hesitant. [7]He said to him: "Do you think [that] I was relying on you? [8]It was I who took (lit., 'cast') it upon myself and remembered."

[9]We have learned elsewhere: "Mounds that are near,

RASHI

מחסם = מגמגם, תמה על רב אשי שהעיד בדבר. **התלוליות** — תילי קרקע. ודרך בני אדם לקבור בתל, משום דאין בני אדם מטין מן הדרך לעבור עליו. ועיר ודרך לקמן מפרש להו.

LANGUAGE

מְחַסֵּם Hesitant. Various readings are attested by the manuscripts and other sources, the three main ones being מְחַסֵּם, מְהַסֵּם, and מְהַסֵּס. The third form, מְהַסֵּס, is used in modern Hebrew (where it means "hesitate"), although the other readings can also be supported on various grounds. For example, מְחַסֵּם may be derived from the root חסם, meaning "to be uncertain," or it may be related to another meaning of this root, "to overpower."

NOTES

חַזְיֵיהּ לְרַב כָּהֲנָא דַּהֲוָה מְחַסֵּם He saw that Rav Kahana was hesitant. Since Rav Ashi had declared that he did not remember, even after having been reminded, Rav Kahana thought that he was testifying only on the basis of what he, Rav Kahana, had told him. Even though Rav Kahana knew that he was telling the truth, and that Rav Ashi believed him absolutely as though he had remembered it himself, Rav Kahana was not prepared to win his case on the basis of hearsay evidence (*Sefer VeHizhir*).

The law on the question of hearsay evidence is very clear. *Rambam* writes (*Hilkhot Edut* 17:1,5): "Even if a number of great, wise, and saintly people tell someone that they witnessed a certain crime or a monetary transaction, and even though he is as certain about it as if he had witnessed it himself, he is not permitted to testify on the matter unless he himself was there. Anyone who gives hearsay evidence is a false witness, and violates the ninth commandment (Exodus 20:13): 'You shall not bear false witness against your neighbor.'" Moreover: "Even if a man's teacher says to him: 'You know that I would never tell a lie for all the money in the world. I am owed money by So-and-so, and I have only one witness. Please serve as the second witness' — even in such a case, if the student agrees to serve as the second witness, he is guilty of the crime of giving false evidence."

The Midrash (*Shemot Rabbah* 46:1, cited by *Maharsha, Yevamot* 62a) illustrates this principle in a striking way. The Torah relates that God informed Moses on Mount Sinai that the Israelites had sinned and worshipped a golden calf, and told him to go down (Exodus 32:7-8). Moses then went down, bearing the two tablets of the Ten Commandments (Exodus 32:15). The Torah goes on to relate that when Moses saw the calf he broke the tablets (Exodus 32:19). The Midrash asks: Moses did not break the tablets when God told him about the calf, so why did he break them now, when he saw it? And the Midrash answers that we see from here that even when a person hears information from an absolutely trustworthy source — in this case God Himself — he may not rely on it for legal purposes until he sees for himself that the information is correct.

הַתְּלוּלִיּוֹת Mounds. *Rashi* explains that a body is more likely to be buried in a mound than in a flat place, because

TRANSLATION AND COMMENTARY

location of the mound. If the mound is **near a city or a road**, [1]regardless of **whether** the mound **is new or old**, it must be presumed to be **ritually impure**, even though we have no knowledge of any bodies having been buried there. [2]For **distant** mounds, on the other hand, the law is different. **If** the mound is nowhere near a city or a road, and **is new** (i.e., freshly raised), we presume it **to be ritually pure,** [3]but **if** the mound **is old, it** must be presumed **to be ritually impure."**

אֵיזוֹהִי קְרוֹבָה [4]The Mishnah now defines the terms it has used, citing a Tannaitic dispute on the matter: "**What is** meant by the term **'near'**? Within **fifty cubits** [about twenty-five meters] of the city or the road. [5]**And what is** meant by the term **'old'**? Anything over **sixty years.** [6]**These are the words of Rabbi Meir.** [7]**Rabbi Yehudah says:** There is no objective definition of these terms. Rather, the term **'near'** refers to a situation **where there are no** mounds **closer** to the city or the road **than** this one." Thus, according to Rabbi Yehudah, where there are two mounds within fifty cubits of the city or the road, only the nearer one is considered near, whereas the one further away is considered distant. [8]"Likewise," continues the Mishnah, "the term **'old,'** has a relative definition; it refers to a situation **where nobody remembers** the mound first being raised." Thus, according to Rabbi Yehudah, if the mound is more than sixty years old but people remember its construction, it is considered new; conversely, if the mound is less than sixty years old but people do not remember its construction, it is considered old.

הַקְּרוֹבוֹת, [1]בֵּין לָעִיר וּבֵין לַדֶּרֶךְ, אֶחָד חֲדָשׁוֹת וְאֶחָד יְשָׁנוֹת, טְמֵאוֹת. [2]הָרְחוֹקוֹת, חֲדָשׁוֹת, טְהוֹרוֹת; [3]יְשָׁנוֹת, טְמֵאוֹת.

[4]"אֵיזוֹהִי קְרוֹבָה? חֲמִשִּׁים אַמָּה. [5]וְאֵיזוֹ הִיא יְשָׁנָה? שִׁשִּׁים שָׁנָה. [6]דִּבְרֵי רַבִּי מֵאִיר. [7]רַבִּי יְהוּדָה אוֹמֵר: קְרוֹבָה שֶׁאֵין קְרוֹבָה הֵימֶנָּה. [8]יְשָׁנָה שֶׁאֵין אָדָם זוֹכְרָהּ".

LITERAL TRANSLATION

either to the city or to the road, [1]whether (lit., 'one') new or whether old, are ritually impure. [2]Distant ones, [if they are] new, are ritually pure; [3][if they are] old, they are ritually impure.

[4]"What is near? Fifty cubits. [5]And what is old? Sixty years. [6][These are] the words of Rabbi Meir. [7]Rabbi Yehudah says: Near is where none is closer than it. [8]Old is where no person remembers it."

RASHI

אחד חדשות – שאין זמן רחוק שלא היה כאן תל, דאיכא למימר כיון דחדשה היא, אם איתא שנקבר שם מת – מדכר דכיר ליה. אפילו הכי טמאות מספק, דכיון דסמוכה לעיר, איכא למימר: אשה יחידה הלכה וקברה שם נפל שלה. **הרחוקות** – דאין אשה יחידה הולכת שם. **חדשות טהורות** – דאם איתא דנקבר ביה – הוו ידעי ליה. **ישנות טמאות** – שכבר נשתכח הדבר מן היודעים. **ואיזו היא קרובה** – לעיר, שאנו אומרים עליה שאף החדשה טמאה – חמשים אמה. **ואיזו היא ישנה** – שאנו אומרים עליה שאפילו היא רחוקה טמאה – ששים שנה. **שאין קרובה הימנה** – אבל אם יש קרובה הימנה, אפילו היא בתוך חמשים אמה – הויא כרחוקה. וחדשה טהורה, דאם איתא דהלכה אשה יחידה לקבור – לא שבקה קרובה הימנה ואזלא לגבי דהך. **שאין אדם זוכרה** – שאין אדם אומר: זכור אני שלא היה כאן תל ובימי נעשה תל זה כאן.

BACKGROUND

שִׁשִּׁים שָׁנָה **Sixty years.** One of the reasons given for a statute of limitations on the prosecution of criminal offenses lies in the problem discussed here: How much can we rely on the memory of witnesses after a great deal of time has passed? The Halakhic conclusion of the Gemara here accords with Jewish law: No statute of limitations applies to crimes, and a person may be put on trial for a transgression he committed long ago.

In the case of mounds, there is an additional element; for even when no one remembers the event itself, there is nevertheless a certain public interest that creates a tradition passed from father to son. Today, scholars maintain that oral traditions (which have not been written or fixed in a final literary form, such as a saga), can be remembered for as long as 150 years.

NOTES

people try to bury their dead in a secluded area. Preferably, they bury their dead in a graveyard, but where this is not practicable, they bury them away from the road, in a place where it is not easy to walk.

Shittah Mekubbetzet notes that we are clearly not referring to a mound raised specifically for burial purposes. For an unmarked burial mound would be unlikely to stay in place for very long — certainly not for the sixty years referred to in the Mishnah — and if the mound was marked with a gravestone, the Mishnah would not consider it a doubtful burial site. Rather, we are referring to a small natural hill, which may have been selected for burials because of its seclusion.

רַבִּי יְהוּדָה אוֹמֵר: קְרוֹבָה שֶׁאֵין קְרוֹבָה הֵימֶנָּה **Rabbi Yehudah says: Near is where none is closer than it.** Our commentary follows *Tiferet Yisrael*, who explains that Rabbi Yehudah disagrees with Rabbi Meir only about mounds that are "near." He would agree that a mound more than fifty cubits away is considered "distant," even if no other mound is nearer, but he argues that where two mounds are within fifty cubits, only the closer one is considered "near." This explanation finds support in the discussion in the Gemara, in which it is assumed that the maximum distance is fifty cubits, even though the Halakhah normally follows Rabbi Yehudah against Rabbi Meir.

HALAKHAH

הַתְּלוּלִיּוֹת הַקְּרוֹבוֹת **Mounds that are near.** "Mounds that are near a city that is itself near a graveyard or a road leading to a graveyard are presumed to impart ritual impurity, because women bury their aborted fetuses there, and those afflicted with leprosy bury their lost limbs. This law applies even where the mound is fresh. But a mound that is not near a city or a graveyard imparts ritual impurity only if it is old, since we suspect that there may once have been a city or a road nearby, but not if it is fresh (*Kesef Mishneh* notes that this follows *Rabbenu Ḥananel*'s explanation of the Mishnah rather than *Rashi*'s; see note). For the purposes of this law, a mound is considered 'old' if no one remembers when it was raised, and a mound is considered 'near' if there is no mound nearer than it, following Rabbi Yehudah against Rabbi Meir." (*Rambam, Sefer Tohorah, Hilkhot Tumat Met* 8:3.)

[1]מַאי עִיר וּמַאי דֶּרֶךְ? [2]אִילֵימָא עִיר עִיר מַמָּשׁ, דֶּרֶךְ דֶּרֶךְ מַמָּשׁ, [3]מִסְפֵּיקָא מִי מַחֲזְקִינַן טוּמְאָה? [4]וְהָאָמַר רֵישׁ לָקִישׁ: עִילָּה מָצְאוּ וְטִהֲרוּ אֶרֶץ יִשְׂרָאֵל!

[5]אָמַר רַבִּי זֵירָא: עִיר הַסְּמוּכָה לְבֵית הַקְּבָרוֹת, [6]וְדֶרֶךְ דֶּרֶךְ בֵּית הַקְּבָרוֹת.

[7]בִּשְׁלָמָא דֶּרֶךְ בֵּית הַקְּבָרוֹת, [8]דִּזְמְנִין דְּמִתְרַמֵּי בֵּין הַשְּׁמָשׁוֹת, [9]וּמִקְרוּ קָבְרוּ בְּתֵל. [10]אֶלָּא עִיר הַסְּמוּכָה לְבֵית הַקְּבָרוֹת, כּוּלְּהִי לְבֵית הַקְּבָרוֹת אָזְלֵי!

LITERAL TRANSLATION

[1]What is a city and what is a road? [2]If we say: A city is actually a city, [and] a road is actually a road, [3]do we presume ritual impurity from doubt? [4]But surely Resh Lakish said: They found a pretext and purified Eretz Israel!

[5]Rabbi Zera said: A city is a city that is next to a graveyard, [6]and a road is a road to a graveyard.

[7]Granted [regarding] a road to a graveyard, [8]for sometimes [the funeral] occurs at dusk, [9]and they happen to bury [the body] in a mound. [10]But [regarding] a city next to a graveyard, they all go to the graveyard!

RASHI

עילה מצאו — עלילה בעלמא מצאו חכמים, והחזיקו בה לתלות עליה ולטהר את ארץ ישראל, במסכת נזיר בפרק בתרא. אלמא מספיקא לא מחזקינן טומאה בקרקעה של ארץ ישראל. וטיהרו את ארץ ישראל גרסינן ולא גרסינן כל. **דמתרמי בין השמשות** — של ערב השבת, ואין שהות לילך עד בית הקברות.

TRANSLATION AND COMMENTARY

מַאי עִיר [1]The Gemara asks: **What** does the Mishnah mean by the term "**city**," **and what** does it mean by the term "**road**"? [2]**If we say** that the Mishnah is to be understood literally, and **"a city" is actually a city and "a road" is actually a road,** and whenever there is a mound near a city or near a road we assume that it contains a grave, then it follows that the Mishnah is ruling that we must suspect nearly every mound of containing a grave, even where there is no basis for our suspicion. [3]But is it true that **whenever** we have the slightest **doubt** about a piece of land **we presume it to be ritually impure?** [4]**Surely,** on the contrary, we are normally very lenient about the laws of ritual impurity, as we see from the following statement of **Resh Lakish**, who **said:** The Sages **found a pretext and purified Eretz Israel!** We are prepared to declare a piece of land in Eretz Israel ritually pure, even on the basis of a very weak argument.

אָמַר רַבִּי זֵירָא [5]**Rabbi Zera said** in reply: The Mishnah in tractate *Ohalot* is not referring to a mound near an ordinary city or an ordinary road. Rather, by **"city"** it means **a city** situated **next to a graveyard,** [6]**and by "road"** it means **a road** leading **to a graveyard.** Thus the Mishnah is ruling that a mound in the vicinity of a graveyard — even though it is not in the graveyard itself — is to be presumed ritually impure, even though the mound is not old and we have no knowledge of any graves there. The reason for the Mishnah's ruling is that in the case of a mound near a graveyard, there are grounds for suspicion that it has been used to bury the dead, as the Gemara explains below, but in the case of ordinary mounds there is no reason to suspect that they have been used in this way.

בִּשְׁלָמָא [7]The Gemara asks: **Granted** that it is reasonable to imagine that a burial may have taken place in a mound by the side of **a road** leading **to a graveyard,** [8]because **a funeral sometimes takes place at dusk** on Friday afternoon, just before the onset of Shabbat, and because of lack of time the funeral does not reach the graveyard itself, [9]**and they happen to bury the body in the mound** by the side of the road, on the way to the graveyard. [10]**But regarding** a mound in **a city** situated **next to a graveyard, they all go to the graveyard!** Why would a body be buried in a mound near the city, and not in the city graveyard itself?

BACKGROUND

עִילָּה מָצְאוּ They found a pretext. In every country where settlement dates from antiquity, it is always possible at any time, in any place, to find an ancient tomb which has been covered with a layer of earth over the generations, and so has disappeared from view and from memory. The Sages determined that where there is serious doubt (such as when a single corpse has been discovered, and it is not clear whether the place was a cemetery), the only positive way of ascertaining that there are no more corpses is to dig until one reaches virgin soil or bedrock. Since according to the Halakhah the ritual impurity of the dead "rises up to the sky," a body imparts ritual impurity even if covered with a stone or a layer of earth. Thus there was legitimate reason to be concerned about every place that was not verified. This placed an enormous burden residents of Eretz Israel, and explains what Resh Lakish meant when he said that the Sages were lenient about Eretz Israel, relying on even slender evidence so as not to consider a place to be of doubtful impurity.

CONCEPTS

בֵּין הַשְּׁמָשׁוֹת Dusk. The twilight period between the end of day and the beginning of night. Usually understood as the period between sunset and the time the stars come out. This period is treated as of doubtful status. There is a debate among the Sages concerning its duration, and when it begins and ends.

NOTES

עִילָּה מָצְאוּ They found a pretext. Resh Lakish's statement is cited in tractate *Nazir* (65b). The Mishnah rules that when the remains of one or two bodies are found near each other, we need not assume that there are any more bodies in the area; but when three or more are found near each other, we must assume that the entire field is a graveyard. The Gemara cites Resh Lakish's statement to support an interpretation of this ruling that is so lenient that it appears to defy logic.

Our translation and commentary follow *Rashi,* who explains that the word עִילָּה is a variant of the Hebrew word עֲלִילָה, meaning "pretext." According to this explanation, the Halakhic argument by which they declared the general area where they found the bodies ritually pure was little more than a legal fiction, and the real reason was the need to keep as much of Eretz Israel as possible ritually pure, so that people could walk through it on their way to the Temple. Many other Rishonim, however, follow *Rabbenu Ḥananel,* who spells the word as עִילְעָא and explains it as the Aramaic word for "rib." He explains that when investigating the fields around a city they found one rib, and on the basis of that alone they declared that all the bodies were buried nearby, and that the rest of the area was ritually pure. According to both explanations, it follows from Resh Lakish's statement that the mere existence of a mound should not cause us to assume that a body has been buried in it.

In the parallel passage in *Nazir* (65b), *Rashi* follows *Rabbenu Ḥananel*'s explanation. The contradiction between *Rashi*'s comment here and his explanation in *Nazir* is not

LITERAL TRANSLATION

[1] Rabbi Ḥanina said: Because women bury their abortions there, [2] and those afflicted with leprosy [bury] their arms. [3] Up to fifty cubits, she goes by herself; [4] more, she takes a man with her and goes to the graveyard. [5] Therefore, we do not presume ritual impurity in Eretz Israel.

[1] אָמַר רַבִּי חֲנִינָא: מִתּוֹךְ שֶׁהַנָּשִׁים קוֹבְרוֹת שָׁם נִפְלֵיהֶן, [2] וּמוּכֵּי שְׁחִין זְרוֹעוֹתֵיהֶם. [3] עַד חֲמִשִּׁים אַמָּה, אָזְלָא אִיהִי לְחוּדָהּ; [4] טְפֵי, דָּבְרָא אִינִישׁ בַּהֲדָהּ וּלְבֵית הַקְּבָרוֹת אָזְלָא. [5] הִלְכָּךְ, טוּמְאָה בְּאֶרֶץ יִשְׂרָאֵל לָא מַחֲזְקִינַן.

TRANSLATION AND COMMENTARY

אָמַר רַבִּי חֲנִינָא [1] **Rabbi Ḥanina said:** Bodies are not normally buried in such a mound, but sometimes **women bury their aborted fetuses there,** [2] **and those afflicted with leprosy** use the mound to **bury their** lost **arms**, as such burials are often done privately outside a graveyard. Why, then, are mounds ritually impure only if they are near a city? [3] It is because the women (or the lepers) **go by themselves** if the distance is **less than fifty cubits** from the city. [4] But if they must walk **more** than that, **they take a man with them** to assist them, **and** they **go** all the way **to the graveyard** itself. [5] **Therefore, we do not presume ritual impurity in Eretz Israel** except in old mounds, or in new mounds in the vicinity of a graveyard, as we have explained.

RASHI

ומוכי שחין — שאבריהן נופלין, או שחותכין אותן. ואבר מן החי מטמא כאבר מן המת, כדאמרינן ב״העור והרוטב״ (חולין קכט, ב).

BACKGROUND

קוֹבְרוֹת שָׁם נִפְלֵיהֶן Bury their abortions there. According to the Halakhah, when very small children die, they are not given a funeral, but buried privately. This applies even more so to aborted fetuses, although in general one does not erect a tombstone for them or provide any other form of memorial. Understandably, a miscarriage is a sad and unpleasant event, which people are not anxious to make public. For this reason, it was feared that a woman might bury the fetus herself somewhere, without taking the trouble to go to a cemetery.

וּמוּכֵּי שְׁחִין And those afflicted with leprosy. The word שְׁחִין, often translated as "boils," is a general term for various skin diseases. Most skin diseases are painful to the patient, but have no serious effects. However, among these diseases is צָרַעַת — leprosy (or Hansen's disease) — which in its late stages can cause certain parts of the body to fall off, and these must by law be buried. In other cases limbs are amputated — as the result of an accident or for medical reasons — and they, too, must be buried.

NOTES

unusual, because it is generally agreed that the commentary to tractate *Nazir* attributed to *Rashi* was not, in fact, written by *Rashi* (see also *Shittah Mekubbetzet*).

אָמַר רַבִּי חֲנִינָא Rabbi Ḥanina said. *Tosefot Yom Tov* notes that Rabbi Ḥanina's explanation applies only to a mound near a city; but regarding a mound near a road leading to a graveyard, our previous explanation still stands. We are concerned lest a funeral party on the way to the graveyard had to bury the body by the side of the road because of the imminent onset of Shabbat.

מִתּוֹךְ שֶׁהַנָּשִׁים קוֹבְרוֹת שָׁם נִפְלֵיהֶן Because women bury their abortions there. Normally, bodies are buried in a graveyard. But the burial of aborted fetuses and diseased limbs is embarrassing, and the people concerned may have conducted the burial secretly outside the regular graveyard. But when it is necessary to go with an escort, there is no justification not to go to the graveyard (*Shittah Mekubbetzet*).

מִתּוֹךְ שֶׁהַנָּשִׁים קוֹבְרוֹת שָׁם נִפְלֵיהֶן, וּמוּכֵּי שְׁחִין זְרוֹעוֹתֵיהֶם Because women bury their abortions there, and those afflicted with leprosy bury their arms. The law is that a miscarried fetus imparts ritual impurity (*Rambam, Hilkhot Tumat Met* 2:1). *Mishneh LeMelekh* adds that this applies only after 40 days of gestation. Any part of a dead body, even blood, imparts ritual impurity (ibid., 2:12). If, however, tissue is removed from a living body, it does not impart ritual impurity unless the tissue is a complete limb (ibid., 2:3). To be considered complete, the limb must include a complete bone together with the muscles and sinews that are normally attached to it.

By leprosy the Gemara is clearly referring to the disease that causes parts of the body to shrivel up and fall off. The Mishnah rules below (77a) that if a husband contracts such a disease, his wife is entitled to a divorce. Moreover, even if the husband told his wife about his disease before their marriage, and his wife accepted the situation, she is still entitled to a divorce, as she can argue that she did not realize how terrible it would be.

עַד חֲמִשִּׁים אַמָּה Up to fifty cubits. It is clear from the Gemara that women occasionally chose to bury their aborted fetuses in a mound rather than in a graveyard, but it is not clear why, if so, we need be concerned only about a mound near a city. What if there was no mound near a particular city, and the woman chose to bury her fetus in a distant mound?

Rashi explains that women do indeed occasionally bury their aborted fetuses in a distant mound, but when they do so they need an escort, and the escort publicizes the matter. The Rishonim object to this explanation, noting that the Gemara says that if the mound is distant, the woman "takes a man with her *and goes to the graveyard,*" implying that the escort accompanies the woman to the graveyard, and not to the distant mound. *Ramban*, however, explains the Gemara as meaning that since the man who went with her said nothing, we can assume that they went to the graveyard and not to the distant mound, and *Ritva* suggests that these words may not have appeared in *Rashi*'s text (see also *Maharsha* and *Maharam Schiff*).

Our commentary follows *Tosafot* and other Rishonim, who accept the explanation of *Rabbenu Ḥananel*. He explains that women bury their aborted fetuses in a mound only when they act on their own, but if the woman has an escort, she does not bury her abortion in a mound at all, but goes to a proper graveyard.

According to *Rashi*'s explanation, it is clear why an old mound is assumed to be ritually impure, even if it is distant. According to *Rashi*, women do occasionally bury aborted fetuses in distant mounds, although it becomes public knowledge when they do so. Therefore, if the mound is old, we suspect that a woman may have buried her aborted fetus there long ago, and the incident lapsed from memory. According to *Rabbenu Ḥananel*, however, women never bury their aborted fetuses in distant mounds, and there is no danger of a distant mound having been used in this way, even if it is old. According to this explanation, the reason we suspect an old mound of containing a grave is because it is possible that long ago there was a settlement or a road nearby, which subsequently disappeared and was forgotten. *Ritva* notes that this explanation finds support in the expanded version of this Mishnah that appears in the Tosefta (*Ohalot* 16:1).

TRANSLATION AND COMMENTARY

אָמַר רַב חִסְדָּא [1]The Gemara now makes an inference from this Mishnah that has a bearing on the question of witnesses who forget their testimony. **Rav Ḥisda said:** [2]**We can infer from Rabbi Meir's statement** — that a mound is considered old after sixty years — that a similar law applies to **evidence:** [3]**Up to sixty years,** a witness can be trusted to **remember;** [4]**more** than that, **he does not remember,** and even if he claims to remember the events clearly, he is not permitted to testify about them if sixty years or more have elapsed. Just as Rabbi Meir is of the opinion that we cannot trust our memory about mounds after sixty years, so too a witness cannot trust his memory about events that occurred sixty or more years ago, and even if he claims to remember with perfect clarity, his testimony is unacceptable as he might be mistaken.

וְלָא הִיא [5]**But,** the Gemara concludes, **this** inference **is not** well founded. In fact, a witness is permitted to testify even after sixty years, and no proof to the contrary can be brought from Rabbi Meir's ruling. [6]**There**, in tractate *Ohalot*, the Mishnah is referring to a case **where it is no** particular person's **duty** to remember whether or not a burial took place. Hence Rabbi Meir is not prepared to rely on local traditions after sixty years have elapsed, and he rules that all mounds must be assumed to be ritually impure. [7]**But here**, in the case of a witness, **it is his duty** to remember his testimony. Thus, in a case of testimony, Rabbi Meir would agree with Rabbi Yehudah's ruling that if the witness claims to remember his testimony clearly, [8]he is believed after an interval of **even more** than sixty years, until he himself admits that his memory is unreliable.

MISHNAH זֶה אוֹמֵר [9]This Mishnah continues the discussion of documents that are confirmed by summoning the witnesses themselves to authenticate their signatures. In general, testimony is acceptable in court only if every detail is attested by two witnesses. Hence, if we wish to authenticate the signatures on a document by summoning other witnesses who recognize them, each signature must be authenticated by two witnesses. But if the witnesses who signed the document come forward themselves to authenticate their own signatures, the situation is not quite so straightforward. **If one** of the witnesses **says**: **"This is my handwriting, and that is the handwriting of my fellow witness,"** [10]**and the other** witness likewise **says**: **"This is my handwriting, and that is the handwriting of my fellow witness,"** there is no problem, as there are two witnesses who can authenticate each of the signatures (the one who wrote the signature and his fellow witness). [11]Hence, **they are believed** in this case, according to all opinions.

[1]אֲמַר רַב חִסְדָּא: [2]שְׁמַע מִינָּהּ מֵרַבִּי מֵאִיר: הַאי סַהֲדוּתָא, [3]עַד שִׁיתִּין שְׁנִין, מִידְכַּר; [4]טְפֵי, לָא מִידְכַּר.

[5]וְלָא הִיא: [6]הָתָם הוּא דְּלָא רַמְיָא עֲלֵיהּ; [7]אֲבָל הָכָא, כֵּיוָן דְּרָמֵי עֲלֵיהּ, [8]אֲפִילּוּ טוּבָא נַמִי.

מִשְׁנָה [9]זֶה אוֹמֵר: ״כְּתַב יָדִי, וְזֶה כְּתַב יָדוֹ שֶׁל חֲבֵירִי״, [10]וְזֶה אוֹמֵר: ״זֶה כְּתַב יָדִי, וְזֶה כְּתַב יָדוֹ שֶׁל חֲבֵירִי״, [11]הֲרֵי אֵלּוּ נֶאֱמָנִין.

LITERAL TRANSLATION

[1]Rav Ḥisda said: [2]Conclude from Rabbi Meir's [statement]: This evidence, [3]up to sixty years, he remembers; [4]more, he does not remember.

[5]But it is not so: [6]There it is because it is not imposed (lit., "thrown") on him; [7]but here, since it is imposed on him, [8]even more also.

MISHNAH [9][If] this one says: "[This is] my handwriting, and that is the handwriting of my fellow," [10]and that one says: "This is my handwriting, and that is the handwriting of my fellow," [11]they are believed.

RASHI

שמע מינה — מדקתני לעיל אינו היא ישנה ששים שנה, וטעמא משום דלא דכירי לה הוא — האי סהדותא כו׳. **אבל הכא** — שעשאוהו עד בדבר, אפילו טובא נמי סמכינן אסהדותיה, אי מסהיד.

משנה הרי אלו נאמנין — דאיכא תרי סהדי דמסהדי אכל כתב וכתב.

NOTES

עַד שִׁיתִּין שְׁנִין **Up to sixty years.** Rav Huna's inference is based on Rabbi Meir's ruling. At first glance, it would appear that since the Halakhah follows Rabbi Yehudah, it has no relevance. But *Shittah Mekubbetzet* suggests that Rav Huna may have thought that his inference applies even according to Rabbi Yehudah. For perhaps Rabbi Yehudah disagrees with Rabbi Meir only regarding burial spots, which people are very careful to remember in order to avoid becoming ritually impure. But regarding all other matters, Rav Huna may have thought that Rabbi Yehudah would agree with Rabbi Meir that memory can be trusted only for sixty years.

HALAKHAH

כֵּיוָן דְּרָמֵי עֲלֵיהּ, אֲפִילּוּ טוּבָא נַמִי **Since it is imposed on him, even more also.** "There is no time limit on a person's ability to testify about events that he witnessed, provided that he still remembers them clearly. We do not assume that after a number of years the witness's memory is no longer reliable," following the conclusion of our Gemara. (*Shulḥan Arukh, Ḥoshen Mishpat* 28:13).

LITERAL TRANSLATION

[1] [If] this one says: "This is my handwriting," and that one says: "This is my handwriting," [2] they must add another [person] with them. [3] [These are] the words of Rabbi. [4] But the Sages say: They do not need to add another [person] with them; [5] rather, a person is believed to say: "This is my handwriting."

[1] זֶה אוֹמֵר: "זֶה כְּתַב יָדִי", וְזֶה אוֹמֵר: "זֶה כְּתַב יָדִי", [2] צְרִיכִין לְצָרֵף עִמָּהֶם אַחֵר. [3] דִּבְרֵי רַבִּי. [4] וַחֲכָמִים אוֹמְרִים: אֵינָם צְרִיכִין לְצָרֵף עִמָּהֶן אַחֵר; [5] אֶלָּא נֶאֱמָן אָדָם לוֹמַר: "זֶה כְּתַב יָדִי".

RASHI

צריכים לצרף עמהן אחר – שיכיר כתב ידי שניהם, דתרי סהדי בעינן אכל כתב וכתב, וטעמא מפרש בגמרא.

TRANSLATION AND COMMENTARY

זֶה אוֹמֵר [1] However, **if one** of the witnesses **says**: "**This is my handwriting,** but I cannot positively identify the other signature," **and the other** witness likewise **says**: "**This is my handwriting,** but I cannot positively identify the other signature," then there is only one witness for each signature (the witness who signed), and there is a Tannaitic dispute about this matter. [2] **Rabbi** Yehudah HaNasi rules that **they must bring another person with them** (i.e., they must find another witness who recognizes both signatures) so that each signature is authenticated by two witnesses — by the one who wrote the signature and by the other person. Alternatively, they could find two other people, each of whom recognizes one of the signatures. But if they cannot find another witness who recognizes the signatures, we are left with only one witness for each signature, and this testimony is unacceptable. [3] **This is the opinion of Rabbi** Yehudah HaNasi. [4] **But the Sages say: They do not need to bring another person with them;** [5] **rather, a person is believed to** be telling the truth when he **says: "This is my handwriting."** The Sages agree that only the testimony of two witnesses is acceptable. However, the issue in question here is not the authenticity of the signatures, but rather the content of the document. Hence, since the document was signed by two witnesses, and the signatures are authenticated, each by the witness who signed, the content of the document is considered to have been attested by two witnesses.

NOTES

זֶה אוֹמֵר: זֶה כְּתַב יָדִי If this one says: "This is my handwriting." The second clause of the Mishnah refers to a case where each witness recognizes his own handwriting but cannot determine anything about the handwriting of his fellow (*Meiri*). In such a case, there is a dispute between Rabbi Yehudah HaNasi and the Sages as to whether it is sufficient that a witness authenticates his own signature without corroboration. The Gemara explains that, according to Rabbi Yehudah HaNasi, there is no difference between a case where the witnesses authenticate their own signatures and a case where other witnesses authenticate them; in either case two witnesses must authenticate each signature, whereas, according to the Sages, witnesses who authenticate their own signatures are considered to be testifying about the content of the document, and do not need corroboration.

The Jerusalem Talmud (commenting on the previous Mishnah) considers a case where the witnesses who authenticate their own signatures are contradicted by two other witnesses who testify that the signatures are forged. The Jerusalem Talmud rules that this is considered contradictory testimony, and the document is of doubtful validity. This ruling is fairly straightforward according to Rabbi Yehudah HaNasi, since there are indeed two witnesses who authenticate each of the signatures, and these two are contradicted by two other witnesses who insist that they are forged. But the Rishonim explain that this ruling also fits the viewpoint of the Sages, who maintain that each witness authenticates his own signature by himself. Even though there is only one witness per signature who testifies that it is genuine (the one who signed it), and two witnesses who testify that it is forged, it is nevertheless considered two against two, because the witnesses are considered to be testifying about the content of the document (*Ra'ah, Ritva*).

The Jerusalem Talmud also considers the opposite case — where each of the witnesses who allegedly signed the document claims that his signature was forged, but other witnesses are prepared to testify that the signatures are genuine. The Jerusalem Talmud rules that in this case the other witnesses are believed outright, and the document is valid. *Ritva* and *Ra'ah* explain that this ruling applies only where each witness denies his own signature and says nothing about the signature of the other witness, because there are two authenticators and only one denier for each signature; but where the witnesses deny the authenticity of both signatures, it is considered to be contradictory testimony. *Ketzot HaḤoshen* disagrees, citing a Tosefta (*Gittin* 1:6) which rules that where the signatures have been independently authenticated, nothing the witnesses

HALAKHAH

זֶה אוֹמֵר: זֶה כְּתַב יָדִי If this one says: "This is my handwriting." "If the two witnesses who signed a document come forward to authenticate their signatures, and say: 'This is my handwriting, and that is the handwriting of my fellow witness,' they are believed. Moreover, even if they do not recognize each other's handwriting, it is sufficient if each of them authenticates his own signature (provided that they still remember the events attested in the document) because the witnesses are viewed as testifying about the contents of the document rather than about their signatures *per se*," following the view of the Sages. (*Rambam, Sefer Shofetim, Hilkhot Edut* 6:2; *Shulḥan Arukh, Ḥoshen Mishpat* 46:7.)

TRANSLATION AND COMMENTARY

GEMARA כְּשֶׁתִּימְצִי לוֹמַר [1] The Gemara proceeds to explain the basis of the dispute between Rabbi Yehudah HaNasi and the Sages. **When you analyze the matter,** says the Gemara, you will arrive at the following explanation: [2] **According to Rabbi** Yehudah HaNasi, when the witnesses who signed the document come forward to authenticate their signatures, [21A] **they are** considered to be **testifying about their handwriting.** Hence they are treated like independent witnesses summoned to identify the signatures on the document, and we require two witnesses to authenticate each signature. We cannot accept the witnesses' uncorroborated authentication of their own signatures, and it is necessary to find an additional witness who recognizes the signatures in order to corroborate their evidence. [3] **According to the Sages,** on the other hand, when the witnesses who signed the document come forward to authenticate their signatures, they are not considered to be testifying about their signatures *per se*, as if they were independent witnesses brought in to identify the signatures of the witnesses on the document. [4] Rather, **they are testifying about the maneh** (the sum of money) **in the promissory note.** They are considered to be testifying that they were present at the time, and witnessed the transaction attested in the document. Hence it is not necessary to find two witnesses to authenticate each signature, since two witnesses have effectively testified about the actual contents of the document.

פְּשִׁיטָא [5] But the Gemara objects: **This is obvious!** This is clearly how the dispute in our Mishnah is to be understood. Why, then, introduce it with the phrase "when you analyze the matter"? How else could the Mishnah have been explained?

גמרא [1] כְּשֶׁתִּימְצִי לוֹמַר, [2] לְדִבְרֵי רַבִּי [21A] עַל כְּתַב יָדָן הֵם מְעִידִים; [3] לְדִבְרֵי חֲכָמִים, [4] עַל מָנֶה שֶׁבַּשְּׁטָר הֵם מְעִידִים. [5] פְּשִׁיטָא!

LITERAL TRANSLATION

GEMARA [1] When you analyze the matter, [2] [you will find that] according to Rabbi [21A] they are testifying about their handwriting; [3] according to the Sages, [4] they are testifying about the maneh in the [promissory] note.

[5] This is obvious!

RASHI

גמרא כשתימצי לומר לדברי רבי – כשתעמוד לסוף דבריו, קסבר. **על כתב ידן** – הן באין להעיד, כשמקיימין השטר בבית דין. לפיכך צריך שנים על כל כתב וכתב. **לדברי חכמים על מנה שבשטר הם מעידים** – אנחנו ראינו המלוה וחתמנו. הלכך בתרי סגי, ולא צריך חד מינייהו לאסהודי אחבריה.

LANGUAGE

כְּשֶׁתִּימְצִי לוֹמַר **When you analyze the matter.** The root מצי literally means "to squeeze out juice or blood." Idiomatically, it means to deduce an explanation on the basis of a thorough logical analysis of the facts. Our explanation of this expression in the context of our Gemara follows *Rashi*, who explains it as follows: When you delve deeply into the views of Rabbi Yehudah HaNasi and the Sages, until you reach the basis of their statements, etc.

NOTES

say can make any difference. *Ketzot* argues that if the witnesses who signed the document deny their signatures after they have been authenticated, they are considered to be retracting their testimony.

עַל מָנֶה שֶׁבַּשְּׁטָר הֵם מְעִידִים **They are testifying about the maneh in the promissory note.** According to Rabbi Yehudah HaNasi, a witness who authenticates his own signature is just like a witness who authenticates someone else's signature; according to the Sages, a witness who authenticates his own signature is testifying about the contents of the document, unlike a witness who authenticates someone else's signature, who is testifying about the signature without reference to the contents of the document.

There is a dispute among the Rishonim as to what extent the Sages and Rabbi Yehudah HaNasi accept each other's arguments. What is the law, according to Rabbi Yehudah HaNasi, if the witnesses stipulate that they are testifying about the maneh in the document? *Rav Hai Gaon* rules that if the witnesses clearly remember the events attested in the document, even Rabbi Yehudah HaNasi would agree that they can testify about the maneh in the document and can authenticate their own signatures without corroboration. *Tosafot,* however, rules that this argument would not be accepted.

The Rishonim discuss the case where the witness recognizes his signature but has completely forgotten the events attested in the document, even after reading it. According to Rabbi Yehudah HaNasi, this would present no problem, as the witness is always considered to be testifying about his signature; but according to the Sages, it would seem that he cannot testify about the maneh in the document. Among the Rishonim, there are four views about this case.

Rav Hai Gaon explains that this is precisely the case in dispute between Rabbi Yehudah HaNasi and the Sages. Even Rabbi Yehudah HaNasi would agree that the witnesses can testify about the contents of the document if they still remember them; but according to the Sages, the witnesses are testifying about the contents of the document, even when they remember nothing. Most Rishonim, however, reject this interpretation of our Mishnah.

Tosafot and other Rishonim argue that if the witness no longer remembers the events attested in the document, he

HALAKHAH

עַל מָנֶה שֶׁבַּשְּׁטָר הֵם מְעִידִים **They are testifying about the maneh in the promissory note.** "When a witness who has signed a document comes forward to authenticate his own signature, he is considered to be testifying about the maneh in the promissory note, and not about the signature, following the view of the Sages. Therefore he may authenticate his signature only if he remembers the events attested in the document. But if the witnesses no longer

LITERAL TRANSLATION

[1] You might have said: Rabbi is uncertain whether they are testifying about their handwriting [2] or they are testifying about the maneh in the [promissory] note.

[3] And there is a practical difference (lit., "goes out from it"): Where one of them died,

[1] מַהוּ דְּתֵימָא: לְרַבִּי סַפּוּקֵי מְסַפְּקָא לֵיהּ אִי עַל כְּתַב יָדָם הֵם מְעִידִים [2] אוֹ עַל מָנֶה שֶׁבַּשְּׁטָר הֵם מְעִידִים.

[3] וְנָפְקָא מִינָּהּ: הֵיכָא דְּמִית חַד

TRANSLATION AND COMMENTARY

מַהוּ דְּתֵימָא [1] The Gemara answers: It is true that there is no other explanation of the position of the Sages. Clearly the reason why they accept the witnesses' authentication of their own signatures without corroboration is because they maintain that the witnesses are testifying about the promissory note itself, rather than about their signatures. But it is not obvious that Rabbi Yehudah HaNasi maintains that the witnesses are testifying specifically about their handwriting. **You might have said** that **Rabbi** Yehudah HaNasi **was uncertain whether** the witnesses should be considered to be **testifying about their handwriting** (in which case their testimony would require additional corroboration) [2] **or about the maneh in the promissory note** (in which case their testimony would be sufficient by itself). Hence Rabbi Yehudah HaNasi was stringent, and refused to accept the witnesses' authentication of their signatures without corroboration because he was not sure how to view their testimony.

וְנָפְקָא מִינָּהּ [3] The Gemara explains: **There is a practical difference** whether Rabbi Yehudah HaNasi was ruling with certainty that the witnesses were testifying specifically about their handwriting, or was being stringent because of doubt. For if Rabbi Yehudah HaNasi was being stringent because of doubt, then he would agree with the Sages in a case where their view is stricter, such as **where one of** the two witnesses

RASHI

מהו דתימא לרבי ספוקי מספקא ליה אי על כתב ידן — אנו נזקקין שיעידו. **או על מנה שבשטר** — ומשום שמא על כתב ידן הן מעידין — מצריך תרי לכל כתב וכתב. ומיפשט מיהא לא פשיטא ליה. **ונפקא מינה** — בין ספק לודאי, לשנים החתומים על השטר ומת אחד מהן — צריך שנים מן השוק להעיד עליו, ואין זה כשר להעיד על כתב ידו ועל של חבירו ולצרף אחד עמו שיעיד על שתיהן. דדלמא על מנה שבשטר הן מעידין, וכי אומר זה כתב ידי — נפיק פלגא דממונא אפומיה, וזה שמעיד עמו על חתימתו — לא מעלה ולא מוריד, דאינו צריך לו. וכי הדר מצטרף עם ההוא מן השוק להעיד על חתימת המת — הדר נפיק ריבעא דממונא אפומיה, אשתכח דכולא ממונא נכי ריבעא נפיק אפומיה, ואנן "על פי שנים עדים" בעינן,

NOTES

is treated like any other person who recognizes his signature. Thus, in effect, the ruling of Rabbi Yehudah HaNasi would apply, and the witness could authenticate his signature together with another witness.

Most Rishonim, including *Rif* and *Rambam,* rule that the Sages do not accept Rabbi Yehudah HaNasi's ruling under any circumstances. According to this view, the witness can authenticate his own signature only by attesting to the events in the document, and if he does not remember these events, he cannot certify the document at all. On the other hand, if the document can be certified in some other way — such as where independent witnesses recognize the signatures — the document is valid, even if the witness no longer remembers, since the entire point of documented testimony is that it should continue to be effective even after the witnesses die.

There is a fourth opinion, cited by *Bahag.* He argues that documents are certified on the assumption that the witnesses still remember; but if the witnesses declare that they have forgotten the events attested in the document, the document is invalid, even if the signatures can be authenticated in some other way. If the document has already been certified, however, a witness cannot subsequently invalidate it by declaring that he no longer remembers.

HALAKHAH

remember the events attested in the document and can testify only about their signatures, it is not sufficient if each authenticates his own signature, and the procedure to follow is subject to a dispute among the Rishonim.

"*Rosh* rules that the two witnesses must each authenticate the other's signature or find an additional witness who recognizes their signatures, in accordance with the view of Rabbi Yehudah HaNasi. *Rambam* rules that even this is not sufficient, and that two completely independent witnesses must attest to each signature, since the view of Rabbi Yehudah HaNasi is rejected by the Gemara, and the witnesses can testify only about the maneh in the document and not about their signatures. *Kesef Mishneh* questions whether *Rambam* really disagrees with *Rosh,* and suggests that *Rambam* too would permit a witness who signed the document to authenticate his own signature together with another witness, but *Shakh* argues that this suggestion is unfounded, and that even *Kesef Mishneh* eventually withdrew it. Yet another view is cited by *Shakh* in the name of *Bahag:* A document can be validated only on the assumption that the witness remembers the testimony; once the witness has declared that he does not remember the events attested in the document, the document cannot be validated, even if the signatures are subsequently authenticated by independent witnesses." (*Rambam, Sefer Shofetim, Hilkhot Edut* 8:1,4; *Shulḥan Arukh, Ḥoshen Mishpat* 46:10.)

מִינַּיְיהוּ, [1]לִבָעֵי שְׁנַיִם מִן הַשּׁוּק לְהָעִיד עָלָיו, [2]דְּאִם כֵּן, קָנָפֵיק נְכִי רִיבְעָא דְּמָמוֹנָא אַפּוּמָא דְּחַד סָהֲדָא, [3]וְהָכָא לְחוּמְרָא וְהָכָא לְחוּמְרָא. [4]קָא מַשְׁמַע לָן דְּרַבִּי מִיפְשַׁט פְּשִׁיטָא לֵיהּ, [5]בֵּין לְקוּלָּא בֵּין לְחוּמְרָא.

[6]דְּאָמַר רַב יְהוּדָה אָמַר רַב: שְׁנַיִם הַחֲתוּמִין עַל הַשְּׁטָר וּמֵת אֶחָד מֵהֶן, [7]צְרִיכִין שְׁנַיִם מִן

LITERAL TRANSLATION

[1]two [witnesses] from the marketplace would be needed to testify about it; [2]for if not (lit., "so"), three-quarters (lit., "less one-quarter") of the money goes out on the testimony (lit., "on the mouth") of one witness, [3]and here [we lean] toward stringency and here toward stringency. [4][Therefore] it tells us that Rabbi is certain, [5]whether for leniency or for stringency.

[6]For Rav Yehudah said in the name of Rav: [If] two [witnesses] are signed on a [promissory] note and one of them died, [7]two [witnesses] from the

RASHI

חצי דבר על פיו של זה וחצי דבר על פיו של זה, הלכך ניבעי תרי. דכיון דספיקא היא — ניזיל הכא לחומרא והכא לחומרא: היכא דשניהם קיימים אזלינן לחומרא, ואמרינן: על כתב ידן הן מעידין, ובעינן תרין על כל כתב וכתב. והיכא דמית חד מנייהו — בעינן תרין מן השוק, שיעיד האחד על כתב יד המת, ואחד מהן יעיד על כתב יד המת והחי. דאי הוה פשיטא לן דעל כתב ידן מעידין — הוי סגי בחד מן השוק שיעיד על שתי החתימות, והחי יעיד גם הוא על שתיהם, ולא נפיק כולא ממונא נכי ריבעא אפומא דחד — דאיהו נמי צריך לאותו מן השוק שיעיד על חתימתו. אבל השתא דמספקא לן דלמא על מנה שבשטר הן מעידין, ועל כתב ידו הוא נאמן ואין צריך לצירוף, ועוד אנו צריכים לו שיעיד על חותם המת — נפקי תלתא ריבעי אפומיה, אי ליכא תרין מן השוק שלא יהא זה צריך להעיד על המת. קמשמע לן דפשיטא ליה, וסגי בחד מן השוק, ושניהם יעידו על שתיהן. **בין לקולא** — כי הכא, דאילו לרבנן בעי שנים מן השוק שיעידו על של מת, וזה לבדו יעיד על חתימתו. **נכי ריבעא** — חסר ריבעא. **צריך שנים** — לדברי חכמים.

TRANSLATION AND COMMENTARY

who signed the document **died,** and the other witness came forward to authenticate his own signature and that of his fellow witness. If Rabbi Yehudah HaNasi is certain that the witnesses are testifying about their handwriting and about nothing else, there would be no difference between a case where one witness died and the case of the Mishnah, and it would be sufficient for the living witness together with a single independent witness to authenticate both signatures. But if Rabbi Yehudah HaNasi maintains that the witnesses are testifying about the document (where that view leads to a stringency), he would not allow the living witness to authenticate his own signature and then serve as one of the witnesses assigned to authenticate the dead man's signature. [1]Rather, **he would require two** independent **witnesses from the marketplace to testify about** the dead man's signature. [2]**For if** we allow the living witness to authenticate his own signature and then to serve as one of the authenticators of the dead man's signature as well, **three-quarters of the money would be decided on the testimony of one witness**. By Torah law, the two witnesses who are required for each item of testimony must have the same relative importance. Where for some reason one witness is believed by himself concerning one point, he cannot combine with another witness and testify about another point, because he is in effect determining three-quarters of the testimony, and the other witness merely one-quarter. Hence, according to the view that the witnesses are testifying about the maneh in the document, if the living witness authenticates his own signature, he cannot also serve as one of the authenticators of the dead man's signature. [3]Now, if Rabbi Yehudah HaNasi was uncertain about his ruling, **he would lean toward stringency** in both cases. In the case of our Mishnah, he would require an additional witness lest the witnesses who signed the document are testifying about their signatures; and in the case where one of the witnesses died, he would require two independent witnesses to authenticate the signature of the dead witness, lest the witnesses who signed the document are testifying about the maneh in the promissory note. [4]**Therefore we were informed** at the beginning of this passage that if you analyze the matter carefully, you will discover **that Rabbi Yehudah HaNasi is certain** that the witnesses are testifying about their signatures, [5]and that he maintains this position regardless of **whether** it leads to a **lenient** ruling **or to a stringency.**

דְּאָמַר רַב יְהוּדָה [6]The Gemara now demonstrates that this line of reasoning is correct. **For Rav Yehudah said in the name of Rav: If two witnesses have signed a promissory note and one of them dies,** [7]**two**

HALAKHAH

וּמֵת אֶחָד מֵהֶן **And one of them died.** "If one of the witnesses who signed a document died, the surviving witness may authenticate his own signature, and two independent witnesses must authenticate the dead man's signature. The remaining witness cannot serve as one of the two to authenticate the dead man's signature if he is also authenticating his own signature, as this would lead to three-quarters of the money being determined by one of the witnesses," following the view of the Sages as explained by the Gemara. (*Rambam, Sefer Shofetim, Hilkhot Edut* 7:5; *Shulhan Arukh, Hoshen Mishpat* 46:13.)

הַשּׁוּק לְהָעִיד עָלָיו. [1]בְּזוֹ, רַבִּי לְקוּלָּא [2]וְרַבָּנַן לְחוּמְרָא.
[3]וְאִי לֵיכָּא תְּרֵי אֶלָּא חַד, מַאי?
[4]אֲמַר אַבַּיֵי: לִכְתּוֹב חֲתִימַת יְדֵיהּ אַחַסְפָּא, וְשָׁדֵי לֵיהּ בְּבֵי דִינָא, [5]וּמַחְזְקִי לֵיהּ בֵּי דִינָא וְחָזוּ לֵיהּ, [6]וְלָא צָרִיךְ אִיהוּ לְאַסְהוּדֵי אַחֲתִימַת יְדֵיהּ, [7]וְאָזֵיל אִיהוּ וְהַאי וּמְסַהֲדֵי אַאִידָךְ.

LITERAL TRANSLATION

marketplace are needed to testify about it. [1]About this, Rabbi is for leniency [2]and the Rabbis are for stringency.

[3]And if there are not two but one, what [should be done]?

[4]Abaye said: He should write the signature of his hand on a potsherd, and place it (lit., "cast it") before the court, [5]and the court will confirm it and see it, [6]and he himself will not need to testify about the signature of his hand, [7]and he himself and that [other] one will go and testify about the other.

TRANSLATION AND COMMENTARY

witnesses from the marketplace are needed to testify about the deceased's signature, because the Halakhah is in accordance with the Sages, and the witnesses are considered to be testifying about the maneh in the promissory note.

[1]And Rav Yehudah added: **About this** case, **Rabbi** Yehudah HaNasi **is lenient**, permitting the surviving witness to serve as one of the authenticators of the dead witness's signature, together with a single independent witness, [2]whereas **the Rabbis** who disagreed with him **are strict**, requiring two independent witnesses. Thus we see that Rabbi Yehudah HaNasi maintains his position that the witnesses are authenticating the signatures, even where it causes him to issue a lenient ruling.

וְאִי לֵיכָּא תְּרֵי [3]The Gemara now asks a parenthetical question about the ruling issued by Rav Yehudah in the name of Rav. According to the Sages, if one of the witnesses dies, two independent witnesses must authenticate the dead witness's signature. However, **if two** independent witnesses **cannot be found, but** only **one** in addition to the surviving witness, **what should be done?** If the living witness authenticates his own signature (which he can do by himself, according to the Sages), can he also join with the one independent witness to authenticate the deceased's signature?

אֲמַר אַבַּיֵי [4]**Abaye said** in reply: According to the Sages, if one of the witnesses died, the living witness should not testify about his own signature at all. Rather, **he should write his signature on a potsherd and place it before the court,** [5]**and the court will see** his signature, compare it with the signature on the document, **and confirm** the document. [6]If the living witness follows this procedure, **he will not himself need to testify about his** own **signature,** [7]and this will allow **him and the one** independent witness **to go and testify about the other** signature (that of the dead man), thus leaving the testimony balanced.

RASHI

ואי ליכא שנים — שיכירו כתב המת. **אלא חד** — וזה האי נמי מכירה, מאי ניעביד? **לכתוב** — זה שנשאר בחיים. **חתימת ידיה אחספא ונשדייה בבי דינא** — ויטלוהו הדיינים, ויקיפוהו אצל חתימתו שבשטר. **ומחזקי** — ההיא דשטרא מהך דאחספא, דלא צריך לאסהודי אחתימת ידיה.

NOTES

וְאִי לֵיכָּא תְּרֵי אֶלָּא חַד מַאי **And if there are not two but one, what should be done?** Normally, the Gemara would not ask this sort of question. If there are two witnesses, we validate the document, and if there are not, we do not. But in this case, it is clear that the document is in fact genuine, as one of the witnesses has authenticated his own signature, and the other signature is confirmed by two witnesses. It is only a formal difficulty that prevents us from confirming the document — the fact that one of the witnesses who is authenticating the dead man's signature is the living witness, and we thus have an imbalance in the testimony. Therefore the Gemara seeks a way of surmounting this difficulty so that justice will be done (*Shittah Mekubbetzet*).

וְשָׁדֵי לֵיהּ בְּבֵי דִינָא **And place it before the court.** *Rambam* rules that the surviving witness should sign the potsherd in front of two independent witnesses, so that the independent witnesses can bring the potsherd to court and testify that it is an example of the living witness's signature. *Shakh* explains that, according to *Rambam,* the witness should not come to court himself and sign the potsherd in front of the judges, as this would be tantamount to

HALAKHAH

לִכְתּוֹב חֲתִימַת יְדֵיהּ אַחַסְפָּא **He should write the signature of his hand on a potsherd.** "If only one independent witness can be found, the living witness should not authenticate his own signature. Rather, he should sign his name on a potsherd in the presence of two witnesses. The two witnesses who saw him sign should then bring the potsherd to court, and testify that this is an example of the living witness's signature. Afterwards, the living witness himself and the single independent witness can authenticate the dead man's signature, following Abaye. The sample signature need not be on a potsherd, but the Rabbis recommended the use of a potsherd rather than a piece of parchment so that the signature cannot be misused later if it is found by an unscrupulous person (*Sma* and *Kesef Mishneh;* see also *Shakh*). *Sma* points out that if the witness signs his name at the top of a piece of parchment, it cannot be misused, because valid documents are signed only at the bottom." (*Rambam, Sefer Shofetim, Hilkhot Edut* 7:5; *Shulḥan Arukh, Ḥoshen Mishpat* 46:13.)

[1] וְדַוְקָא אַחַסְפָּא, אֲבָל אַמְּגִלְּתָא לָא, [2] דִּלְמָא מַשְׁכַּח לָהּ אִינִישׁ דְּלָא מַעֲלֵי, וְכָתַב עִילָּוֵיהּ מַאי דְּבָעֵי. [3] וּתְנַן: "הוֹצִיא עָלָיו כְּתַב יָדוֹ, שֶׁהוּא חַיָּיב לוֹ,

LITERAL TRANSLATION

[1] And specifically on a potsherd, but not on a parchment, [2] [because] perhaps an unscrupulous person will find it, and write on it what he wants. [3] And we have learned: "[If] he produced his [the debtor's] handwriting against him, that he owes him [money],

RASHI

וכתב עליה מאי דבעי — למעלה מן החתימה יכתוב שזה החתום לוה ממנו מנה, וכותב כך: אני פלוני החתום למטה לויתי מנה מפלוני.

TRANSLATION AND COMMENTARY

וְדַוְקָא אַחַסְפָּא [1] The Gemara notes: When Abaye said that the surviving witness is required to provide a sample of his signature, he **specifically** mentioned **a potsherd.** The witness does **not** sign his name **on a piece of parchment, because** signing one's name on a blank piece of parchment may lead to problems — after the court has finished with the parchment, it will be thrown away, and [2] **an unscrupulous person may perhaps find** it **and write** above the signature **whatever he wants.** For example, if the witness signed his name on the blank parchment, the finder can write above the signature that the person who signed below owes him a certain sum of money. He can then produce this fraudulent document and demand payment. [3] Admittedly, the fraudulent document would not have been signed by any witnesses, **but we have learned** in the following Mishnah (*Bava Batra* 175b) that: **"If** a creditor **produces** an unwitnessed document to use **against** a debtor, and it was written and signed in **the debtor's** own **handwriting,** the document is considered conclusive proof of the debt, even

NOTES

authenticating his own signature. But *Tur* appears to disagree with *Rambam*'s ruling. *Perishah* explains that, according to *Tur,* it is sufficient to sign in front of the court, because the Rabbis were lenient about the certification procedure, seeing that it is not required by Torah law.

וְדַוְקָא אַחַסְפָּא And specifically on a potsherd. The Rishonim note that there are other ways of producing a handwriting sample that cannot be misused, besides using a potsherd. *Tosafot* suggests that the witness sign his name at the very top of a piece of parchment. For the law is that only that part of a document that is written above the signatures is valid, but any text appearing below the signatures is presumed to have been added later. *Ritva* suggests, basing himself on the Jerusalem Talmud, that the witness should write the alphabet on a piece of parchment, rather than sign his name. The court can then compare the appropriate letters of the alphabet with the signature on the document. *Rosh,* however, argues that this is not acceptable according to the Babylonian Talmud. *Rashba* and *Ritva* explain that while these other methods would be perfectly acceptable, most people who are asked to provide a handwriting sample sign their names without thinking; hence the Gemara recommends using a potsherd, to avoid problems later.

אֲבָל אַמְּגִלְּתָא לָא But not on a parchment. From the simple meaning of the text, it would appear that a document written on a potsherd is invalid. *Ramban* and others explain that a potsherd may not be used because erasures cannot be detected on it. For a document may be written only on material that reveals erasures, such as a fresh piece of paper and the like, but not if it is impossible to tell if something was erased, such as on an erased piece of paper or a potsherd. This explanation is somewhat difficult, however, because the Mishnah (*Gittin* 21b) declares that the use of erased paper is subject to a Tannaitic dispute: Rabbi Meir forbids its use, and Rabbi Elazar permits it. Moreover, it is difficult to explain that our Gemara follows the view of Rabbi Meir, since the Halakhah is in accordance with Rabbi Elazar (*Shakh*).

Tosafot notes that our Gemara can be explained as following an opinion in tractate *Gittin* (22b), according to which Rabbi Elazar was referring only to bills of divorce, and not to other documents. However, there are other passages of the Gemara which permit using a potsherd to write other documents, such as a bill of marriage (*Kiddushin* 9a) or a deed of sale (*Kiddushin* 26a). *Tosafot* explains that a bill of marriage and a deed of sale are included in the category of "bills of divorce," because all these documents are primarily intended to effect a transaction, and not to serve as proof of an obligation. But regarding promissory notes and the like, the Gemara follows the opinion that they may not be written on erased parchment or on a potsherd, even according to Rabbi Elazar.

Many Rishonim reject this distinction. *Ritva* cites *Rabbenu Tam* as explaining that the Gemara permitted using a potsherd only if the text of the document was chiseled onto the potsherd; but if the text was written in the usual way, only material that revealed erasures could be used (except for bills of divorce, according to Rabbi Elazar).

Some Rishonim explain that a potsherd may in fact be used to write any document, without restriction. *Ritva* cites *Rabbenu Yeḥiel,* who explains that Talmudic pottery had a very smooth finish that would reveal erasures. According to this view, our Gemara recommends the use of a potsherd because it is unlikely that an unscrupulous person will pick up a discarded potsherd to hunt for a signature around which to construct a forged document. *Shakh* explains that writing on the potsherd is a deliberate alteration of the regular routine. Thus, if the unscrupulous person produces the potsherd with a forged statement added to it, the potsherd will serve to remind the witness, so that he will be able to explain the story to the court.

HALAKHAH

הוֹצִיא עָלָיו כְּתַב יָדוֹ If he produced his handwriting against him. "If a creditor produces a document which states that someone owes him money, and the document was written in the alleged debtor's handwriting, or was

LITERAL TRANSLATION

[1] he collects from free property."

[2] Rav Yehudah said in the name of Shmuel: The Halakhah is in accordance with the words of the Sages.

[3] This is obvious! [In a dispute between] an individual and many, [4] the Halakhah is in accordance with the many!

[1] גּוֹבֶה מִנְּכָסִים בְּנֵי חוֹרִין״. [2] אָמַר רַב יְהוּדָה אָמַר שְׁמוּאֵל: הֲלָכָה כְּדִבְרֵי חֲכָמִים. [3] פְּשִׁיטָא! יָחִיד וְרַבִּים, [4] הֲלָכָה כְּרַבִּים!

RASHI

מנכסים בני חורין – וממשעבדי לא, דלית ליה קלא לדבר שאינו עשוי בעדים.

TRANSLATION AND COMMENTARY

though it was not witnessed, [1] and the creditor can use it to **collect from** the debtor's **free property** (i.e., property owned by the debtor and in his actual possession)." A document signed by witnesses fulfills two functions: (1) It serves as proof that a debt exists, and (2) it establishes a lien that enables the creditor to seize property sold by the debtor to a third party after the debt was incurred. An unwitnessed document signed by the debtor does not establish a lien, but it is conclusive proof that the debt exists, and it can be used to collect the debt from property still in the debtor's possession. Hence, if the witness needs to give the court a sample of his signature, he should not sign a blank piece of parchment, but should instead write his name on a potsherd, which cannot be used as a document.

אָמַר רַב יְהוּדָה אָמַר שְׁמוּאֵל [2] The Gemara now returns to the dispute in our Mishnah between Rabbi Yehudah HaNasi and the Sages. **Rav Yehudah said in the name of Shmuel: The Halakhah is in accordance with the Sages.** The witnesses who authenticate their signatures are considered to be testifying about the maneh in the promissory note, and it is therefore sufficient for each witness to authenticate his own signature, without corroboration.

פְּשִׁיטָא [3] The Gemara objects: **It is obvious** that the Halakhah is in accordance with the Sages! For while there are many exceptions, the general rule is that **in a dispute between an individual** Sage **and many** Sages, [4] **the Halakhah is in accordance with the many!** Why, then, did Shmuel feel it necessary to state that this Mishnah follows the general rule?

NOTES

גּוֹבֶה מִנְּכָסִים בְּנֵי חוֹרִין **He collects from free property.** An unwitnessed document signed by the debtor does not establish a lien on property sold later by the debtor to a third party, because a lien is established only by a public document about which the third party could have been expected to know, and a document drawn up without witnesses is not considered "public." But the document does serve as convincing proof that the debt exists.

There is a dispute among the Rishonim as to whether a debt attested by such a document is considered the equivalent of an oral debt (*Rif* and *Rambam*), or a debt covered by a document, albeit a flawed document that does not establish a lien (*Tosafot*). There is an important practical difference regarding repayment. In the case of an oral debt, the Gemara ruled (above, 18a) that if the debtor claims to have repaid the debt, he is believed without proof. Regarding a documented debt, by contrast, a claim of repayment must be supported by substantial proof. Hence, if the creditor produces an unwitnessed document signed by the debtor, and the debtor claims that the debt has been repaid, *Rif* and *Rambam* maintain that he is believed without proof, whereas *Tosafot* rules that he is not believed unless he produces a receipt or witnesses to confirm the repayment.

According to the view that the debtor is believed, the Rishonim ask: What is the danger if the witness in our passage signs his name on a piece of parchment? Even if an unscrupulous person finds the parchment and writes a promissory note above the signature, the witness need only claim that the debt has been repaid! Moreover, he need not lie; he can also explain what really happened — that he had signed his name on a piece of parchment as a handwriting sample — and be believed with a *miggo,* since he could have claimed that the debt had been repaid (*Sefer HaTerumot,* cited by *Bet Yosef*).

Ritva explains that we fear that the unscrupulous finder will include in the forged document a clause in which the "debtor" waives his right to claim repayment without proof. *Ra'ah* explains that the finder may perhaps include a clause in the document stipulating a date for repayment, in which case the "debtor" will not be believed if he claims that he repaid early. Alternatively, the Rishonim explain that we fear that the witness will neither claim that the debt has been repaid nor describe what happened and

HALAKHAH

signed by the debtor, the document constitutes valid proof of the debt, and can be used to collect from the debtor's free property, even though it was not signed by witnesses. But it may not be used to collect from property sold to a third party unless it was signed by witnesses.

"If the alleged debtor claims that the document is a forgery, the creditor must authenticate the handwriting in the usual way. If the document has been authenticated, and the alleged debtor claims that the debt has already been repaid, *Rambam* and *Shulḥan Arukh* rule that he is believed, provided that he takes the *heset* oath imposed by the Rabbis on anyone who wins his case without proof; but *Rema* cites *Mordekhai,* who rules that he is not believed. Moreover, *Shulḥan Arukh* rules that, if the debtor admits the authenticity of his signature but claims that he signed a blank piece of parchment which the creditor then used to construct the document, he is believed because of a *miggo,* since he could have claimed that the debt had been repaid." (*Rambam, Sefer Mishpatim, Hilkhot Malveh VeLoveh* 11:3; *Shulḥan Arukh, Ḥoshen Mishpat* 69:1,2.)

TRANSLATION AND COMMENTARY

מַהוּ דְּתֵימָא [1] The Gemara answers: If Shmuel had not explicitly ruled here in favor of the Sages, **you might have said** that this is one of the exceptions to the general rule. For the Gemara (*Eruvin* 46b; see also *Ketubot* 51a) declares that in any dispute between Rabbi Yehudah HaNasi and an individual fellow Sage, **the Halakhah is in accordance with Rabbi Yehudah HaNasi against his fellow,** [2] **and** you might have thought that the Halakhah is in accordance with Rabbi Yehudah HaNasi **even against** several **fellow** Sages. [3] Therefore Shmuel issued his ruling to **inform us** that the Halakhah is in accordance with Rabbi Yehudah HaNasi only when he is in dispute with a single fellow Sage, but where Rabbi Yehudah HaNasi's view is an individual opinion and is opposed by many, the Halakhah is in accordance with the many.

[1] מַהוּ דְּתֵימָא: הֲלָכָה כְּרַבִּי מֵחֲבֵירוֹ, [2] וַאֲפִילּוּ מֵחֲבֵירָיו. [3] קָא מַשְׁמַע לָן.

[4] סִימָן: נח נד חד.

[5] אֲמַר לֵיהּ רַב חִנָּנָא בַּר חִיָּיא לְרַב יְהוּדָה, וְאָמְרִי לָהּ: רַב הוּנָא בַּר יְהוּדָה לְרַב יְהוּדָה, וְאָמְרִי לָהּ: רַב חִיָּיא בַּר יְהוּדָה לְרַב יְהוּדָה: [6] וּמִי אֲמַר שְׁמוּאֵל הָכִי? [7] וְהָא הַהוּא שְׁטָרָא דְּנָפֵיק מִבֵּי דִּינָא דְּמָר שְׁמוּאֵל,

LITERAL TRANSLATION

[1] You might have said: The Halakhah is in accordance with Rabbi [Yehudah HaNasi] against his fellow, [2] and even against his fellows. [3] [Therefore] it tells us [that this is not so].

[4] Mnemonic: נח נד חד

[5] Rav Ḥinnana bar Hiyya said to Rav Yehudah, and some say: Rav Huna bar Yehudah [said] to Rav Yehudah, and some say: Rav Ḥiyya bar Yehudah [said] to Rav Yehudah: [6] But did Shmuel say this? [7] But surely there was a certain [promissory] note that went out from the court of Mar Shmuel,

RASHI

מהו דתימא — כי היכי דהלכה כרבי מחבירו — הכי נמי אפילו מחביריו. **דנפיק מבי דינא דמר שמואל** — שקיימוהו בבית דינו, וכן נמצא כתוב בהנפק שכתבו הדיינים בו.

סִימָן [4] The Gemara now cites an objection raised against Rav Yehudah's report of Shmuel's ruling. It is not clear who raised the objection, and there are three versions, referred to in the following **mnemonic**. In the first version, the objection was raised by Rav Ḥinnana (חִנָּנָא) bar Ḥiyya (חִיָּיא), and the mnemonic is נח. In the second version, the objection is ascribed to Rav Huna (הוּנָא) bar Yehudah (יְהוּדָה), and the mnemonic is נד. In the third version, it is ascribed to Rav Ḥiyya (חִיָּיא) bar Yehudah (יְהוּדָה), and the mnemonic is חד.

אֲמַר לֵיהּ [5] **Rav Ḥinnana bar Ḥiyya said to Rav Yehudah, and some say Rav Huna bar Yehudah said to Rav Yehudah, and some say Rav Ḥiyya bar Yehudah said to Rav Yehudah:** [6] **Did Shmuel** really issue **this** ruling in favor of the Sages? [7] **Surely there was a certain promissory note authenticated by the court of Mar Shmuel** (i.e., Shmuel headed a court of three judges who certified this promissory note). The witnesses who

BACKGROUND

הֲלָכָה כְּרַבִּי מֵחֲבֵירוֹ The Halakhah is in accordance with Rabbi Yehudah HaNasi against his fellow. Some authorities have understood this principle to mean that whenever a ruling by Rabbi Yehudah HaNasi opposes the opinion of any other single Sage, the Halakhah follows Rabbi Yehudah HaNasi. One problem connected with this principle is whether it applies to *every* Sage who disagrees with Rabbi Yehudah HaNasi, or specifically to the members of his own generation. This problem is not merely a theoretical one, for its resolution affects the conclusions one draws whenever Rabbi Yehudah HaNasi disagrees with his father, Rabban Shimon ben Gamliel. The fact that various Sages disagree with Rabbi Yehudah HaNasi may sometimes be significant, because those Sages represent differing approaches to the Halakhah. Sometimes, however, it is merely a stylistic device. Hence doubt can arise as to whether the Halakhah is in accordance with him even against the opinion of more than one of his colleagues.

NOTES

be believed with a *miggo*. Rather, he will instantly cry out that the document is a forgery, and that no such loan ever took place. And once the forger succeeds in authenticating the signature, the "debtor" will be considered a confirmed liar, and will no longer be permitted to make other claims (*Rosh, Ran, Ritva, Meiri,* and others).

הֲלָכָה כְּרַבִּי מֵחֲבֵירוֹ The Halakhah is in accordance with Rabbi Yehudah HaNasi against his fellow. In tractate *Eruvin* (46b), the Gemara cites an authoritative statement of Rabbi Ya'akov and Rabbi Zerika that the Halakhah follows Rabbi Akiva against any single fellow Sage; that the Halakhah follows Rabbi Yose even against several fellow Sages; and that the Halakhah follows Rabbi Yehudah HaNasi against any single fellow Sage. The Gemara then cites three opinions as to whether this statement is to be taken as a ruling, as a guiding principle in issuing rulings, or merely as an indication.

Significantly, general rules such as these are not infallible, even where they are issued as rulings. Thus, the Gemara cites below (51a) a dispute between Rabbi Yehudah HaNasi and his father, Rabban Shimon ben Gamliel. The Gemara rules in favor of Rabban Shimon, declaring that notwithstanding the rule that the Halakhah always follows Rabbi Yehudah HaNasi against any single fellow Sage, this particular case is an exception. By contrast, in tractate *Bava Batra* (124b) the Gemara cites an Amoraic dispute as to whether the Halakhah follows Rabbi Yehudah HaNasi even against several fellow Sages, and the Gemara concludes that as a guiding principle the Halakhah follows the Sages, but if a court issues a ruling in accordance with Rabbi Yehudah HaNasi, the ruling stands.

It is thus easy to understand why Shmuel feared that an erring court might issue an exceptional ruling in favor of Rabbi Yehudah HaNasi. Moreover, there are special reasons for ignoring the general rule in this case, because the reasoning of the Sages appears, at first glance, to be flawed. A loan covered by a document that is signed by witnesses establishes a lien, whereas a loan attested by oral witnesses does not. Thus one might think that it is important to authenticate the signatures quite apart from confirming the events attested in the document (*Rashba, Ritva,* others). But the Sages reason that, just as these witnesses were able, by themselves, to make this document effective and to establish the lien, so too should they be able to confirm its effectiveness by themselves (*Rabbenu Shlomo Min HaHar*).

TRANSLATION AND COMMENTARY

originally signed the promissory note were Rav Anan bar Ḥiyya and Rav Ḥanan bar Rabbah, [1]**and** the confirmation of the document by the judges **was worded** as follows: [2]**"Since Rav Anan bar Ḥiyya came and testified about his own signature and that of the** witness **who** signed **with him,** [3]**who was Rav Ḥanan bar Rabbah;** [4]**and since Rav Ḥanan bar Rabbah came and testified about his own signature and that of the** witness **who** signed **with him,** [5]**who was Rav Anan bar Ḥiyya;** [6]therefore **we** [the judges] have **confirmed** this document **and certified it, as is proper."** Thus we see that Shmuel required both witnesses to testify about each signature. But according to the Sages, it is sufficient for each witness to testify only about his own signature. Evidently Shmuel follows the opinion of Rabbi Yehudah HaNasi, who requires two witnesses for each signature, and not the opinion of the Sages, as Rav Yehudah reported in his name.

אֲמַר לֵיהּ [7]In reply, Rav Yehudah **said to** the questioner: The particular document that Shmuel's court authenticated happened to be **a promissory note** in which the creditors were **orphans** (i.e., the original creditor died and his rights were inherited by his heirs), and the rule is that courts must take special care to defend the interests of orphans, who may not be able to defend themselves effectively in court. [8]Therefore, even though the Halakhah is in accordance with the Sages, **Shmuel** wrote the confirmation in accordance with the strict view of Rabbi Yehudah HaNasi, because he **was concerned about** the possibility of **an erring court** ruling in accordance with the opinion of Rabbi Yehudah HaNasi. [9]**For Shmuel thought: There may possibly be a court which is** mistakenly **of the opinion** [10]that while **the law is** normally **in accordance with Rabbi** Yehudah HaNasi **against** a single **fellow** Sage **but not against** several **fellow** Sages, [11]**in this matter** the law is in accordance with Rabbi Yehudah HaNasi **even against** several **fellow** Sages. If the note ever came before such a court, with a confirmation that was valid only according to the Sages, the court might invalidate it. In an ordinary case, Shmuel would not have concerned himself about such a possibility, since the creditor can be relied upon to guard his own interests and seek a competent court; but if the creditor is an orphan, he may be unsure as to how to look after his interests. [12]**Therefore Shmuel thought:** Since each witness in this particular case recognizes the other's signature, and there is no difficulty in confirming the document in accordance with all opinions, **I will do more than is** strictly **necessary,** [13]**in order** to avoid even the slightest possibility of **the orphans losing** what is rightfully theirs.

[1]וַהֲוָה כְּתִיב בֵּיהּ: [2]"מִדַּאֲתָא רַב עָנָן בַּר חִיָּיא וְאַסְהֵיד אַחֲתִימוֹת יְדֵיהּ וְאַדְּחַד דְּעִמֵּיהּ — [3]וּמַנּוּ? רַב חָנָן בַּר רַבָּה — [4]וּמִדַּאֲתָא רַב חָנָן בַּר רַבָּה וְאַסְהֵיד אַחֲתִימוֹת יְדֵיהּ וְאַדְּחַד דְּעִמֵּיהּ — [5]וּמַנּוּ? רַב עָנָן בַּר חִיָּיא — [6]אַשַּׁרְנוּהִי וְקִיַּימְנוּהִי, כִּדַחֲזֵי"!

[7]אֲמַר לֵיהּ: הַהוּא שְׁטָרָא דְּיָתְמֵי הֲוָה, [8]וְחָשׁ שְׁמוּאֵל לְבֵית דִּין טוֹעִין. [9]וְסָבַר שְׁמוּאֵל: דִּלְמָא אִיכָּא דִּסְבִירָא לֵיהּ: [10]הֲלָכָה כְּרַבִּי מֵחֲבֵירוֹ וְלֹא מֵחֲבֵירָיו, [11]וּבְהָא, אֲפִילּוּ מֵחֲבֵירָיו. [12]סָבַר: אַעֲבֵיד רַוְוחָא, [13]כִּי הֵיכִי דְּלָא מַפְסְדֵי יַתְמֵי.

LITERAL TRANSLATION

[1]and there was written on it: [2]"Since Rav Anan bar Ḥiyya came and testified about the signatures of his hand and of the one who was with him — [3]and who was it? Rav Ḥanan bar Rabbah — [4]and since Rav Ḥanan bar Rabbah came and testified about the signatures of his hand and of the one who was with him — [5]and who was it? Rav Anan bar Ḥiyya — [6]we confirmed it and certified it, as is proper"!

[7]He said to him: That was a [promissory] note of orphans, [8]and Shmuel was concerned about an erring court. [9]For Shmuel thought: Perhaps there is someone who maintains: [10]The law is in accordance with Rabbi against his fellow and not against his fellows, [11]but in this [matter], even against his fellows. [12][Therefore] he thought: I will do more than is necessary (lit., "I will make room"), [13]so that the orphans will not lose.

RASHI

מדאתא רב ענן כו' – אלמא כרבי סבירא ליה, שצריך לומר: זה כתב ידי וזה כתב ידו של חבירי. **שטרא דיתמי הוה** – שהוצרך לעיין בתקנתם. **וחש שמואל** – שאם לא כתב בו אלא: פלוני העיד על כתב ידו ופלוני על כתב ידו, שמא כשיגיעו היתומים שטר זה בבית דין לגבות יהא אותו בית דין טועה, לומר: שהלכה כרבי, ויאמרו שאין זה קיום. **איכא דסבירא ליה** – בעלמא ולא מחביריו, ובהא אפילו מחביריו.

NOTES

מִדַּאֲתָא רַב עָנָן בַּר חִיָּיא **Since Rav Anan bar Ḥiyya came.** Based on this Gemara, *Ba'al HaIttur* rules that when a court certifies a document, it must list the names of the witnesses authenticating the signatures. *Ritva,* however, maintains that it would have been sufficient for Shmuel to have simply written: "The signatures were authenticated by the witnesses, and the document was certified," without listing the names of the witnesses. Since this was a case

TRANSLATION AND COMMENTARY

אָמַר רַב יְהוּדָה [1]The Gemara now considers another ruling reported by Rav Yehudah in the name of Shmuel on the certification of documents. If a document produced in court carries a certification issued by another court, and the alleged debtor claims that both the document and the certification are forgeries, the creditor has two options. He can either certify the document once again, by authenticating the signatures of the witnesses who signed it, or he can authenticate the signatures of at least two of the three judges who signed the certification. However, **Rav Yehudah said in the name of Shmuel:** [2]There is a third option: One of the two **witnesses** who signed the document **and** one of the three **judges** who signed the certification can come forward and authenticate their signatures. We can then **combine** their two statements and confirm the validity of the document.

אָמַר רָמִי בַּר חָמָא [3]When a later generation of Amoraim studied this statement by Rav Yehudah in the name of Shmuel, **Rami bar Ḥama said: How good this tradition is!** This is an excellent way to confirm the validity of a disputed document.

[1]אָמַר רַב יְהוּדָה אָמַר שְׁמוּאֵל: [2]עֵד וְדַיָּין מִצְטָרְפִין. [3]אֲמַר רָמִי בַּר חָמָא: [4]כַּמָּה מַעַלְיָא הָא שְׁמַעְתָּא!

LITERAL TRANSLATION

[1]Rav Yehudah said in the name of Shmuel: [2]A witness and a judge can be combined.

[3]Rami bar Ḥama said: [4]How good this tradition is!

RASHI

עד ודיין — שטר שכתוב בו הנפק, וחתמו הדיינין על הנפק שלו. ולאחר זמן, כשהוציאו המלוה לגבות, ערער הלוה לומר מזוייף הוא, ובא אחד מעדי השטר והעיד על כתב ידו, ואחד מן הדיינים העיד על כתב ידו — מצטרפין להכשירו.

NOTES

involving orphans (as the Gemara explains below), Shmuel described the procedure in detail, so that there would be no problems later. Nevertheless, even *Ritva* agrees that there are cases where it is necessary to list the names of the witnesses in the certification, for instance where the court has not established with certainty that the witnesses authenticating the signatures are qualified to testify in this case.

Rambam and *Shulḥan Arukh* rule in favor of *Ritva*'s position in principle, but declare that in practice the custom is that courts certifying documents must describe the procedure in detail. *Shakh*, however, rules that this is no longer customary.

עֵד וְדַיָּין מִצְטָרְפִין A witness and a judge can be combined. There are several interpretations of this passage. Most Rishonim explain that we are referring to a case where a document that has already been confirmed in one court is later presented for collection before another court, and the debtor challenges the authenticity of both the document and the certification. Our commentary follows *Rashi*, who explains that in response to the debtor's challenge, one the witnesses who signed the document and one of the judges who took part in the original confirmation come forward to authenticate their respective signatures. Rav Yehudah rules that the testimony of the judge and of the witness can be combined. But Rava rules that we have, in effect, one witness to testify that the loan took place and one to testify that the document was certified, and we require two witnesses who testify to the same thing. This explanation finds support in the Jerusalem Talmud (*Sanhedrin* 3:12).

Ritva objects to this explanation, arguing that even if we ignore the fact that the judge and the witness are not testifying about the same thing, the judge is at best one witness. Thus we have, in effect, authenticated the signature of one of the original witnesses, and produced one witness (the judge) to authenticate the other, and this is obviously inadequate. To account for *Rashi*'s opinion, *Ritva* explains that Rav Yehudah's argument is that it is extremely unlikely that the creditor would have forged the signatures of the witnesses and of the judges. Since the certification of documents is in any case merely a Rabbinic requirement, it is sufficient to determine that the signatures of at least one judge and at least one witness are authentic. But Rava replies that even if this were so, the testimony of the judge and that of the witness cannot be combined, because they are not testifying about the same thing (see also *Ran*).

Rif, commenting on a parallel passage in *Bava Batra* (165b), has a totally different explanation. According to him, we are not dealing with the certification of documents at all, but rather with a case where witnesses testified before a court that the debtor owed money to the creditor. Later, the creditor sued the debtor in a different court, and one of the original witnesses and one of the original judges came forward to testify. Normally, in a monetary case, it is

HALAKHAH

עֵד וְדַיָּין מִצְטָרְפִין A witness and a judge can be combined. "If we recognize neither the signatures of the witnesses nor the signatures of the judges who confirmed the document, it is sufficient if two of the judges come forward to authenticate their own signatures (or if witnesses can be found who recognize the judges' signatures — *Shakh*), for they provide valid testimony that the document was certified. But it is not sufficient to authenticate the signatures of one witness and one judge. Even if one of the witnesses and one of the judges come forward themselves to authenticate their own signatures, we cannot combine their testimony, because the witness is testifying about the content of the document, whereas the judge is testifying about the certification of the witnesses' signatures," following the rulings of Rava and Rav Ashi. (*Rambam, Sefer Shofetim, Hilkhot Edut* 4:6; *Shulḥan Arukh, Ḥoshen Mishpat* 30:12 and 46:14,15.)

[1] אֲמַר רָבָא: מַאי מַעַלְיוּתָא? [2] מַאי דְּקָא מְסַהֵיד סָהֲדָא לָא קָא מְסַהֵיד דַּיָּינָא, [3] וּמַאי דְּקָא מְסַהֵיד דַּיָּינָא לָא קָא מְסַהֵיד סָהֲדָא!

[4] אֶלָּא, כִּי אֲתָא רָמִי בַּר יְחֶזְקֵאל, אֲמַר: [5] לָא תְּצִיתִינְהוּ לְהָנֵי כְּלָלֵי דְּכָיֵיל יְהוּדָה אָחִי מִשְּׁמֵיהּ דִּשְׁמוּאֵל.

LITERAL TRANSLATION

[1] Rava said: What is so good [about it]? [2] What the witness testifies about the judge does not testify about, [3] and what the judge testifies about the witness does not testify about!

[4] Rather, when Rami bar Yeḥezkel came, he said: [5] Do not listen to these rules that my brother Yehudah laid down in the name of Shmuel.

RASHI

מאי דקא מסהיד סהדא כו׳ — עדי השטר מעידין על מנה שבשטר כרכנן, והדיינין מעידין: בפנינו נתקיים. רב יהודה אחוה דרמי בר יחזקאל הוה.

TRANSLATION AND COMMENTARY

אֲמַר רָבָא [1] But **Rava said** to him: **What is so good about it?** [2] It is based on faulty logic: **What the witness testifies about, the judge does not testify about,** [3] **and what the judge testifies about, the witness does not testify about!** The witness is testifying about the actual transaction recorded in the document, and the judge is testifying about the certification process. Hence we have only one witness for each matter, and we cannot combine them.

אֶלָּא [4] **Rather,** says the Gemara, instead of following the tradition of Rav Yehudah in the name of Shmuel, we should follow the tradition of Rav Yehudah's brother, Rami bar Yeḥezkel. For **when Rami bar Yeḥezkel came** back to Babylonia from Eretz Israel, **he said:** [5] **Do not listen to these rules that my brother Yehudah laid down in the name of Shmuel**, as they are sometimes based on an erroneous report of Shmuel's words. Thus the Gemara concludes that we cannot use the evidence of a judge and a witness together in order to confirm the validity of a document. We must authenticate either the signatures of both witnesses who signed the document, or the signatures of at least two of the three judges who signed the certification.

SAGES

רָמִי בַּר יְחֶזְקֵאל Rami bar Yeḥezkel. Rami (an abbreviated form of "Rav Ammi") bar Yeḥezkel was a second-generation Babylonian Amora, and Rav Yehudah's younger brother. He apparently studied with Rav and Shmuel in his youth, although he later immigrated to Eretz Israel, where he learned many ancient teachings, particularly little-known Baraitot. In the Jerusalem Talmud he is referred to as Ammi (or Immi) bar Yeḥezkel. He returned later to Babylonia (and hence the Gemara's use of the term כִּי אֲתָא — "when he came"), and brought with him teachings he had learned in Eretz Israel. His versions of the ancient teachings were renowned for their accuracy and importance, and were even considered superior to the teachings of his older brother, Rav Yehudah.

NOTES

sufficient if two witnesses testify about the same obligation from two different perspectives — for example, if one witness says that he saw the loan, and the other that he heard the debtor admit the debt (*Sanhedrin* 30b). Hence Rav Yehudah thought that, in our case as well, the testimonies of the judge and the witness could be combined. But Rava argued that witnesses with different perspectives can be combined only if their testimonies are closely linked, so that it is logically impossible for one to be telling the truth and the other to be lying. But here, even if the witness is lying about the debt, the judge may still theoretically be telling the truth that the document was certified by a court; and even if the judge is lying about the court, the witness may still theoretically be telling the truth that there was a debt (*Rashba*).

וּמַאי דְּקָא מְסַהֵיד דַּיָּינָא And what the judge testifies about. From the language of the Gemara, it would appear that when a certified document is presented in a different court and the debtor challenges the authenticity of the certification, the onus of proof is on the creditor to authenticate the signatures of the judges. This position finds support in the Jerusalem Talmud, which explicitly discusses the authentication of the judges' signatures (*Sanhedrin* 3:12). It would seem, therefore, that it is futile to certify a document in advance, since the debtor can always demand that the certification be certified. Yet several sources make it clear that creditors routinely certified their documents in advance (see above, 19a). *Ran* explains that a document certified in advance is easier to certify a second time, because the creditor has the option of authenticating either the judges' signatures or the witnesses' signatures. Moreover, *Rashba* points out that where the certification is carried out before an established court, the judges' signatures are likely to be well-known to everyone (see also *Ritva*).

The Rishonim note an apparent contradiction to this ruling from a Tosefta (*Shevi'it* 8:9), which rules that a document issued by a court does not need to be certified. *Talmidei Rabbenu Yonah* explains that we must reject the Tosefta in the face of our Gemara and the Jerusalem Talmud, and assume that the Amoraim had a tradition that this particular Baraita was not reliable. *Rashba* suggests that the Tosefta may perhaps be referring to an established court, whose signatures were well-known to everyone. Most Rishonim explain that the Tosefta is referring only to a *prosbul* — a special document issued to circumvent the law canceling debts in the Sabbatical year — but not to other deeds issued by a court (*Tosafot, Ran,* and others).

The commentators discuss the procedure to be followed when the judges authenticate their signatures on a document of certification. *Talmidei Rabbenu Yonah* rules that, according to the Sages, the judges are considered to be testifying about the certification procedure itself, and not about their signatures *per se*; hence they can authenticate their signatures by themselves, just like the original witnesses who signed the document. But *Rosh* rules that a judge is considered to be testifying about his signature, even according to the Sages; hence he cannot authenticate his signature without the assistance of another witness. It is not entirely clear whether *Rosh* disagrees with *Talmidei Rabbenu Yonah,* or whether he is making a distinction between a single judge and two judges (see *Shakh*).

The Rishonim also discuss how many of the judges' signatures need to be authenticated to confirm the document of certification. Most Rishonim follow *Ba'al HaIttur,* who rules that it is sufficient to authenticate two of the signatures, because then we have in effect two witnesses who testify that the document was properly confirmed; and since the text of the confirmation was signed by three judges, we have no reason to suspect that the court was not properly constituted, even though we have no direct evidence that the third signature is authentic (*Ritva, Ran,* and others).

TRANSLATION AND COMMENTARY

אִיקְלַע [21B] [1] The Gemara now describes how other Amoraim had the same discussion and came to a similar conclusion: **Rabbenai the brother of Rabbi Ḥiyya bar Abba happened to come to buy sesame, and he said:** [2] **Shmuel said as follows: A witness and a judge can be combined.** One of the two witnesses who signed a document and one of the three judges who signed an authentication of the document can come forward and each can authenticate his own signature. We can then combine their two statements and confirm the validity of the document.

אָמַר אֲמֵימָר [3] In a later generation, **Amemar said: How good this tradition is!** This is an excellent way of confirming the validity of a disputed document.

אֲמַר לֵיהּ רַב אַשִׁי [4] **Rav Ashi said to Amemar: Because your mother's father,** Rami bar Ḥama, **praised it, you also praise it!** [5] **Rava has already refuted** Rami bar Ḥama's statement (above, 21a), arguing that the witness is testifying about the maneh in the document and the judge is testifying about the certification process. Hence we have only one witness for each matter, and we cannot combine them.

אָמַר רַב סָפְרָא [6] The Gemara continues the subject of how judges certify a document. **The following statement was made by Rav Safra in the name of Rabbi Abba,** who said it **in the name of Rav Yitzḥak bar Shmuel bar Marta,** who said it **in the name of Rav Huna,** [7] **and some say** that **Rav Huna** was not himself the author of this statement, but **said it in the name of Rav:** [8] **If three judges convene to certify a document, and two** of them **recognize the signatures of the witnesses** without need for testimony, **and one** of them **does not recognize** the signatures, and requires testimony, can the two judges who recognize the

LITERAL TRANSLATION

[21B] [1] Rabbenai the brother of Rabbi Ḥiyya bar Abba happened to come to buy sesame, and he said: [2] Shmuel said as follows: A witness and a judge can be combined.

[3] Amemar said: How good this tradition is!

[4] Rav Ashi said to Amemar: Because your mother's father praised it, you also praise it! [5] Rava has already refuted it.

[6] Rav Safra said in the name of Rabbi Abba, in the name of Rav Yitzḥak bar Shmuel bar Marta, in the name of Rav Huna, [7] and some say: Rav Huna said in the name of Rav: [8] [If] three sat down to certify a document, [and] two recognize the signatures of the witnesses and one does not recognize [them],

---

[21B] ¹ אִיקְלַע רַבְּנַאי אֲחוּהּ דְּרַבִּי חִיָּיא בַּר אַבָּא לְמִזְבַּן שׁוּמְשְׁמֵי, וַאֲמַר: ² הָכִי אֲמַר שְׁמוּאֵל: עֵד וְדַיָּין מִצְטָרְפִין. ³ אֲמַר אֲמֵימָר: כַּמָּה מַעַלְיָא הָא שְׁמַעְתָּא! ⁴ אֲמַר לֵיהּ רַב אַשִׁי לַאֲמֵימָר: מִשּׁוּם דְּקַלְסָהּ אֲבוּהּ דְּאִמָּךְ, אַתְּ נַמֵי מְקַלְּסַת לַהּ! ⁵ כְּבָר פִּרְכַהּ רָבָא. ⁶ אֲמַר רַב סָפְרָא אָמַר רַבִּי אַבָּא אָמַר רַב יִצְחָק בַּר שְׁמוּאֵל בַּר מָרְתָּא אָמַר רַב הוּנָא, ⁷ וְאָמְרִי לֵיהּ: אָמַר רַב הוּנָא אָמַר רַב: ⁸ שְׁלֹשָׁה שֶׁיָּשְׁבוּ לְקַיֵּים אֶת הַשְּׁטָר, שְׁנַיִם מַכִּירִין חֲתִימוֹת יְדֵי עֵדִים וְאֶחָד אֵינוֹ מַכִּיר,

RASHI

אִיקְלַע רבנאי למיזבן שומשמי גרסינן, ולא גרסינן דאיקלע, ולא גרסינן לגגן. ולאו רמי אמרה, דאי אפשר לומר כן שאמר רמי עדות זו על אמימר ורב אשי, שהרי רב אשי כמה דורות היה אחריו, דאמרינן בקדושין (עב,ג): יום שמת רב יהודה נולד רבא, יום שמת רבא נולד רב אשי. אבוה דאמך — רמי בר חמא. שלשה שישבו — בבית דין. לקיים השטר — ונלא העדאת עדים שיעידו על כתב ידן, לפי שהדיינין עצמן מכירין אותה. השנים מכירין אותה ואחד אינו מכיר.

BACKGROUND

מִשּׁוּם דְּקַלְסָהּ אֲבוּהּ דְּאִמָּךְ **Because your mother's father praised it.** It is not clear whether Amemar truly made his remark because he relied upon the teaching of his grandfather, Rami bar Ḥama, or whether Rav Ashi was noting that the family connection influenced Amemar to relate to the matter in the same fashion.

LANGUAGE

מְקַלְּסָת **Praise.** Here the root קלס means "to praise," although in Biblical Hebrew it has the opposite meaning — "to scorn," or "to deride." The root קלס in the sense attested here is derived from the Greek καλός, *kalos*, meaning "beautiful" or "good."

SAGES

רַבְּנַאי אֲחוּהּ דְּרַבִּי חִיָּיא בַּר אַבָּא **Rabbenai the brother of Rabbi Ḥiyya bar Abba.** This Sage, whose full name was apparently Rav Bannai, was a Babylonian Amora of the second and third generations. His brother, Rabbi Ḥiyya bar Abba, moved to Eretz Israel where he became a disciple of Rabbi Yoḥanan, and one of the greatest Sages of his generation. His teachings are cited frequently in both the Babylonian and Jerusalem Talmuds. By contrast, Rabbenai seems to have remained in Babylonia, or to have lived most of his life there, and he is less well-known. To distinguish him from other Sages of the same name, he is associated with his brother.

Rabbenai seems to have been a close disciple of Shmuel, he consulted Shmuel frequently, and most of his teachings are delivered in Shmuel's name. Some scholars are of the opinion that when the name Rabbenai appears in the Talmud with no other appellation, it refers to the brother of Rabbi Ḥiyya bar Abba.

אֲמֵימָר **Amemar.** One of the greatest Babylonian Amoraim of the fifth and sixth generations, Amemar was born in Neharde'a, and was one of its chief Sages. He studied under Rav Zevid and Rav Dimi of Neharde'a, and also with the

---

NOTES

אִיקְלַע רַבְּנַאי אֲחוּהּ דְּרַבִּי חִיָּיא בַּר אַבָּא **Rabbenai the brother of Rabbi Ḥiyya bar Abba happened to come.** Our translation and commentary are in accordance with the standard Vilna Talmud, which follows *Rashi's* version of the text. According to this version, the story of Rabbenai, Amemar, and Rav Ashi is a repetition of the story of Rav Yehudah, Rami bar Ḥama, and Rava. The Talmud frequently notes that a later generation of Amoraim raised the same question, had the same discussion, and arrived at the same conclusion as an earlier generation.

Tosefot Rid had a slightly different reading in his version of the Talmud: "For Rabbenai happened to come *before us* to buy sesame seeds, etc." According to this version, the story of Rabbenai is a continuation of the previous story. The Gemara has just cited Rami bar Yeḥezkel as dismissing his brother's reports of Shmuel's rulings as unreliable. Rami bar Yeḥezkel then supports this contention by relating that Rabbenai once came before them to buy sesame seeds, and made a statement similar to that of Rav Yehudah; and although it was praised by Amemar, it was

HALAKHAH

שְׁלֹשָׁה שֶׁיָּשְׁבוּ לְקַיֵּים אֶת הַשְּׁטָר **If three sat down to certify a document.** "If three judges convene to certify a document, and two of them recognize the signatures but the third does not, the two who recognize the signatures testify before the third who does not, and then all three may sign the certification. The two judges must testify before the

elders of Pumbedita. He cites the teachings of Rava, Rav Pappa, and others. He was the head of the yeshivah in his city. On several occasions he is found in the company of Mar Zutra and Rav Ashi. Rav Aḥa bar Rava and Rav Gamda were among his most prominent students. He also had a son who was a Sage known as Mar.

SAGES

רַב סַפְרָא Rav Safra. A Babylonian Amora of the third and fourth generations. He is found in Halakhic discussions as a student and a colleague of the greatest Sages of the third generation, such as Rabbah and Rav Yosef. He remained active during the generation of their students, Abaye and Rava. Rav Safra was apparently a merchant, and frequently visited Eretz Israel, where he held discussions with Sages such as Rabbi Abba and Rabbi Abbahu. He was an expert in Halakhah, and is not quoted so frequently in Aggadic passages. Rav Safra was famous for his personal qualities, in particular his punctiliousness in avoiding the slightest deviation from the truth. Since Rav Safra traveled widely, he did not have his own yeshivah, and was not often found in the House of Study.

רַבִּי אַבָּא Rabbi Abba. An Amora of the third generation, Rabbi Abba was born in Babylonia. He was a disciple of Rav Huna and Rav Yehudah. He immigrated to Eretz Israel like his colleague Rabbi Zera, and probably settled in Tiberias.

רַב יִצְחָק בַּר שְׁמוּאֵל בַּר מָרְתָא Rav Yitzḥak bar Shmuel bar Marta. Rav Yitzḥak was an Amora of the second generation in Babylonia. His father, Rav Shmuel bar Marta, was a cousin of Rav. Rav Yitzḥak bar Shmuel bar Marta was a close disciple of Rav, and transmits teachings in his name. Rav Yitzḥak seems to have been young at the time of Rav's death, and also studied with Rav Huna. Rav Yitzḥak was friendly with many of Rav's younger students. Important Sages of the following generation studied Torah from him, and he also seems to have been a judge in his hometown.

TRANSLATION AND COMMENTARY

signatures serve as witnesses and testify before the third judge? [1] The rule is that **as long as** the first two judges **have not yet signed** the certification, **they are permitted to testify before** the third judge, **and he can sign** with them; [2] but **once they have signed** the certification, **they are not permitted to testify before him, and he is not permitted to sign** together with them. The first two judges had no right to sign the certification in the first place, because at the time they did so the third

[1] עַד שֶׁלֹּא חָתְמוּ, מְעִידִין בְּפָנָיו וְחוֹתֵם; [2] מִשֶּׁחָתְמוּ, אֵין מְעִידִין בְּפָנָיו וְחוֹתֵם.

LITERAL TRANSLATION

[1] as long as they have not [yet] signed, they may testify before him and he signs; [2] once they have signed, they may not testify before him and he may [not] sign.

RASHI

עד שלא חתמו – השנים על ההנפק. **מעידין** – לפני השלישי שזהו כתב ידן של חתומים. **וחותם** – עמהם על מה שכותבין "אשרנוהי וקיימנוהי לשטרא דנן במותב תלתא דאשתמודענא דחתימת ידא דסהדי היא". **משחתמו אין מעידין** – דחתימה קמייתא בשקרא הוה, דלאו תלתא הוו דידעי.

NOTES

dismissed by Rav Ashi. However, *Rashi* rejects this explanation as anachronistic, since Amemar and Rav Ashi lived several generations after Rav Yehudah and Rami bar Yeḥezkel.

מְעִידִין בְּפָנָיו וְחוֹתֵם They may testify before him and he signs. From the plain meaning of the text, it would appear that when the two judges who recognize the signatures testify, the third judge is seated alone. The Rishonim ask: There is a discussion in the Gemara below (22a) of the precise language used in the certification procedure, and the Gemara refers to three judges seated together as a court. How, then, can the third judge hear the testimony by himself? When the other two judges are testifying, the court consists of only one member! *Ramban* says that we must explain that in our Gemara two other people were seated next to the third judge when he heard the testimony. But *Ritva* dismisses this explanation as inconsistent with the language of the Gemara.

Alternatively, *Ramban* suggests that the Gemara may be referring to a case where the third judge was of outstanding caliber and was universally accepted as a judge. The Gemara (*Sanhedrin* 5a) rules that such a judge may adjudicate a monetary case by himself, although this procedure is not recommended (see *Pirkei Avot* 4:8 and *Shulḥan Arukh, Ḥoshen Mishpat* 3:3). But *Ritva* rejects this explanation as well, because the Gemara insists that all three judges must sign the certification, and because there is no indication in the Gemara that we are dealing with an outstanding judge. Moreover, many Rishonim are of the opinion (based on a passage in tractate *Bava Batra* 40a) that there is a special Rabbinic decree that documents must never be certified before fewer than three judges (*Rashbam, Tosafot*). This position finds support below (22a), where the Gemara specifically bars the Rabbis of Rav Ashi's household from certifying a document with fewer than three judges, even though Rav Ashi's household included judges of outstanding ability (*Ritva*).

Accordingly, Ritva explains that even when they are acting as witnesses, the two standing judges are still considered to be judges; hence the court still has a full complement. *Rosh* explains that there is no need for the witnesses to testify before all the judges at the same time, provided that all the judges eventually hear the testimony. These explanations find support in tractate *Gittin* (5b), where the Gemara also discusses the idea of having one of the judges serve as a witness, and it is clearly not referring to adding another judge, or to a judge with unusual qualifications. *Ran* adds, in the name of *Rashba*, that even though for the sanctification of the New Moon, the Mishnah does require two other people to be seated next to the third judge, we are lenient regarding the certification of documents, because certification is merely a Rabbinic requirement.

מִשֶּׁחָתְמוּ, אֵין מְעִידִין Once they have signed, they may not testify. Our commentary follows *Rashi* and *Rabbenu Ḥananel*, who explain that the signatures of the first two judges are invalid because it is a blatant falsehood for them to sign as part of a court of three before the third judge can sign. According to this explanation, the three judges must sign a new certification document after the testimony has been given (*Talmidei Rabbenu Yonah*). *Talmidei Rabbenu Yonah* and *Meiri* note that, according to this explanation, the certification would be invalid even if independent witnesses were to testify before the third judge, so long as the two judges signed before the third judge heard the evidence.

Tosafot and *Tosefot Rid* have a different explanation, according to which it is the *testimony* that is invalid, not the signatures. They explain that the first two judges are disqualified from testifying before the third judge once they have signed the document, since they now have an interest in persuading the third judge to sign with them. Having signed the certification, the two judges are committed in writing, and it would be embarrassing for them to discover that their colleague disagrees with them. According to this explanation, there would be no problem if independent witnesses were to testify before the third judge (*Talmidei Rabbenu Yonah*). On the other hand, it would not be sufficient for the two judges to draw up a new document of certification after the third judge has heard their testimony.

HALAKHAH

certification is signed, following Rav Huna and the other Amoraim. *Rosh* and *Tur* rule that it is not sufficient for the testimony to be delivered before the certification is signed; it must be delivered before the certification is drawn up, following the conclusion of our Gemara, which follows Rav Pappi. But *Rif* and *Rambam* are of the opinion that the view of Rav Pappi is rejected, and that it is sufficient for the testimony to be delivered before the certification is signed. *Shakh* notes that this is also the view of *Rashba, Smag,* and most other authorities." (*Rambam, Sefer Shofetim, Hilkhot Edut* 7:6; *Shulḥan Arukh, Ḥoshen Mishpat* 46:24.)

TRANSLATION AND COMMENTARY

judge had not yet heard their testimony. Hence the certification is invalid.

וּמִי כָּתְבִינַן [1]**But**, the Gemara objects, **can we write this?** May a document of certification be written before testimony has been heard? From the wording of the earlier statement, it would appear that the judges are permitted to draft the certification at the beginning of the procedure, provided that they do not sign it. [2]**But surely Rav Pappi said in the name of Rava:** If **the judges write the certification before the witnesses have given evidence about their signatures** — even if they have not yet signed it — the certification **is invalid,** [3]**because it looks like a falsehood.** The standard language of the judges' document of certification implies that the testimony has already been heard: "We were three judges sitting together, and this document came before us, and So-and-so and So-and-so, the witnesses, testified before us, and we certified the document." But at the time the certification was written, the witnesses had not yet testified. And even though the witnesses did testify before the certification was signed, it is not acceptable for a court to write something that is less than absolutely true at the time. Hence the certification is invalid. [4]In the same way, **here too** the certification **looks like a falsehood.** For even though the certification had not been signed when the first two judges testified before the third judge, it had nevertheless been written before the three judges could confirm the authenticity of the signatures.

[1]וּמִי כָּתְבִינַן? [2]וְהָאָמַר רַב פַּפִּי מִשְּׁמֵיהּ דְּרָבָא: הַאי אַשַׁרְתָּא דְּדַיָּינֵי דְּנִיכְתַּב מִקַּמֵּיהּ דְּנִיחֲווּ סָהֲדֵי אַחֲתִימַת יְדַיְיהוּ פְּסוּלָה, [3]דְּמִתְחֲזֵי כְּשִׁקְרָא. [4]הָכָא נַמִי מִתְחֲזֵי כְּשִׁקְרָא!

LITERAL TRANSLATION

[1]But do we write [this]? [2]But surely Rav Pappi said in the name of Rava: A certification of the judges which was written before the witnesses gave evidence about the signature of their hands is invalid, [3]because it looks like a falsehood. [4]Here too it looks like a falsehood!

RASHI

ומי כתבינן – לאשרתא דידיה? בתמיה. וכי קודם שנתקיים לפני שלשתן יכתבו "במותב תלתא הוינא ואשתמודענא כו'"? **אשרתא** – לשון חוזק, שמחזקים [את השטר] וכותבין אשרנוהי. **דנכתבא מקמי דניחוו סהדי כו'** – עד שלא העידו העדים על כתב ידם כתבו הדיינין "במותב תלתא הוינא ונפיק שטרא דנן קדמנא ואסהידו פלוני ופלוני אחתימת ידייהו ואשרנוהי וקיימנוהי".

NOTES

וּמִי כָּתְבִינַן? וְהָאָמַר רַב פַּפִּי But do we write this? But surely Rav Pappi said. Rav Pappi's ruling, disqualifying documents that are true but appear false, is cited in several places in the Talmud. The Gemara concludes below (85a) that his view is rejected, and that such documents are in fact valid. Accordingly, most Rishonim, including *Rif, Rambam, Rashba,* and others, rule that the Gemara's question and answer have no Halakhic relevance, and that it is in fact permitted to write the certification before the testimony, provided that it is not signed. It is difficult to understand why the Gemara cites this view here as an objection to Rav's ruling, particularly since the Gemara specifically notes (*Gittin* 26b) that Rav — the author of the statement in our Gemara — disagrees with Rav Pappi. However, *Rabbenu Tam* notes that the Talmud does sometimes raise an objection from an opinion that is not accepted as the Halakhah.

Some Rishonim, however, insist that the Gemara's question and answer are Halakhically significant. *Tosafot* cites an opinion that Rav Pappi's view was rejected only insofar as he declared improper-looking court documents to be invalid, but that everyone agrees that it is improper for a court to draw up such a document in the first place. Hence our Gemara objects to Rav permitting the court to follow this procedure.

Rosh notes that Rav Pappi's ruling was issued in connection with the certification of documents, whereas the passages below (85a) and in tractate *Gittin* were attempting to extrapolate from his ruling to other legal documents not drawn up by a court. Hence *Rosh* suggests that it was the extrapolation that was rejected by the Gemara, not the ruling itself. According to this explanation, legal documents drawn up outside a court may be used, even if they do not appear to be genuine (provided that they are in fact true), but court actions (such as the certification of documents) must not even appear to be false.

וְהָאָמַר רַב פַּפִּי מִשְּׁמֵיהּ דְּרָבָא But surely Rav Pappi said in the name of Rava. *Ritva* asks: Rava was a late Amora, whereas Rav belonged to the first generation of Amoraim, and in some respects is considered one of the Tannaim. It is almost unheard of for a later Amora to dispute his words. How, then, can the Gemara raise an objection against Rav from the words of Rav Pappi in the name of Rava? *Ritva* explains that the Gemara is in effect raising an objection against Rava and Rav Pappi, not against Rav. The Gemara is saying, as it were, that Rav Pappi's view is refuted by Rav's statement.

Ra'ah explains that Rav's statement was itself based on the argument later used by Rav Pappi. The only reason for Rav to forbid the two judges to sign before the third judge had heard the testimony was because the certification would appear false. Hence the Gemara objected that, following this principle, Rav should have forbidden the judges to draw up the document, even if they did not sign it. *Tosafot* rejects this explanation, however, because the Gemara explicitly states (*Gittin* 26b) that Rav disagrees with Rav Pappi's ruling.

Tosafot maintains that Rav disagreed only with Rav Pappi's ruling invalidating improper-looking court documents, but would have agreed that a court should not draw up such a document in the first place. Hence our Gemara objects to Rav permitting the court to draw up the certification before the third judge has heard the testimony.

דְּמִתְחֲזֵי כְּשִׁקְרָא Because it looks like a falsehood. According to most Rishonim, Rav Pappi's view is rejected

SAGES

רַב פַּפִּי Rav Pappi. A Babylonian Amora of the fifth generation. See *Ketubot*, Part I, p. 73.

BACKGROUND

מִתְחֲזֵי כְּשִׁקְרָא It looks like a falsehood. This expression does not refer to outright lies, but to statements which merely appear to be false. For example, it could refer to a promissory note or a certificate of some kind which, for the sake of convenience, has been written although the transaction to which it attests has not yet been properly witnessed. The words of the Torah (Exodus 23:7), "Keep far from a false matter," emphasize that one must not only avoid absolute falsehood, but also keep a distance from it. Hence making a statement which merely appears to be a lie is severely deprecated. Since this verse refers explicitly to the actions of a court, Rava infers from it that one must be particularly scrupulous in a court to avoid anything that looks like a lie.

[1]אֶלָּא אֵימָא: עַד שֶׁלֹּא כָּתְבוּ, [2]מְעִידִין בְּפָנָיו וְחוֹתֵם; [3]מִשֶּׁכָּתְבוּ, אֵין מְעִידִין בְּפָנָיו וְחוֹתֵם. [4]שְׁמַע מִינָּהּ תְּלַת. [5]שְׁמַע מִינָּהּ: עֵד נַעֲשֶׂה דַּיָּין. [6]וּשְׁמַע מִינָּהּ: דַּיָּינִין הַמַּכִּירִין חֲתִימוֹת יְדֵי עֵדִים, אֵינָן צְרִיכִין לְהָעִיד

LITERAL TRANSLATION

[1]Rather, say: As long as they have not [yet] written [it], [2]they may testify before him and he signs; [3]once they have written [it], they may not testify before him and he may [not] sign.

[4]Conclude from this three [things]. [5]Conclude from this: A witness can be made a judge. [6]And conclude from this: [If] the judges recognize the signatures of the hands of the witnesses, it is not necessary to testify

RASHI

עד נעשה דיין — שהרי השנים העידו על החתימות.

TRANSLATION AND COMMENTARY

אֶלָּא אֵימָא [1]**Rather,** we must amend the statement slightly and **say:** The rule is that **as long as** the judges **have not yet written** the certification, [2]the first two judges **are permitted to testify before** the third judge, **and he is permitted to sign** with them, [3]but **once they have written** the certification, **they are not permitted to testify before him, and he is not permitted to sign** together with them.

שְׁמַע מִינָּהּ תְּלַת [4]The Gemara now considers the implications of this statement. We can **infer three things from this** statement. (1) [5]We can **infer** that **a witness can be made a judge.** For we see that two of the judges testified before the third, and then sat down and served as judges together with him. [6]**And** (2), we can **infer** that **if the judges recognize the signatures of the witnesses, it is not necessary to testify before them.** For we see that the two judges who recognized the signatures of the witnesses were able to sign on that basis without further testimony, and

TERMINOLOGY

שְׁמַע מִינָּהּ תְּלַת **Conclude from this three things.** This expression and others similar to it are efforts to exhaust all the inferences that can be drawn from a single Halakhic ruling. In the case at hand, although we are dealing with a single Halakhah, upon analysis it can be seen to be based on a number of Halakhic principles not stated explicitly in the Halakhic ruling.

NOTES

by the Halakhah. Nevertheless, the Rishonim note that in several places (*Bava Kamma* 70a, *Bava Batra* 172a) the Gemara does disqualify court actions because of appearances, even though the Halakhah does not follow Rav Pappi (*Ritva, Shittah Mekubbetzet*). *Ritva* explains that these cases refer to documents that have already been signed. According to this view, Rav Pappi's opinion was rejected only in relation to documents in which the problem of appearance is slight; but if the document has already been signed, there is a severe problem of appearance, and the document is invalid, even according to the Halakhah, which does not follow Rav Pappi. A pupil of *Rashba*, quoted in *Shittah Mekubbetzet*, explains that when the Gemara disqualifies documents because they appear false, the document retains the false appearance permanently; but in a case such as ours — in which the problem disappears after the third judge has heard the testimony — the document is valid, according to the Halakhah, which does not follow Rav Pappi.

Some Rishonim distinguish between cases where the action of the court actually involves a falsehood and cases where it merely appears to do so. The rejected ruling of Rav Pappi refers to a court action that merely appears objectionable, but where there is a genuine falsehood all would agree that the court action is invalid. *Rosh* explains that this is the difference between *drawing up* the certification before the third judge has heard the testimony, and *signing* it. If the certification has already been signed before the two judges testify in front of the third judge, even Rav agrees that it is a blatant falsehood. But a document is devoid of legal significance until it is signed; hence there is no problem of actual falsehood with a certification document drawn up in advance, provided that it was not signed until after the testimony was heard. The only problem with such a document is its improper appearance, and this is of no concern according to the Halakhah, which does not follow Rav Pappi (see also *Ra'ah* and *Ritva*).

עֵד נַעֲשֶׂה דַּיָּין **A witness can be made a judge.** *Rashash* asks: How can the same person serve as a witness and as a judge? For the Gemara rules (*Shevuot* 30b) that when the testimony is heard, the judges must sit and the witnesses must stand. *Rashash* answers that the Gemara also rules that if the witnesses are eminent Torah scholars, they are permitted to sit; and the judges presumably belong in this category.

HALAKHAH

עֵד נַעֲשֶׂה דַּיָּין **A witness can be made a judge.** "The same man cannot serve as both witness and judge in the same case, even if it is a monetary matter. Hence, if a judge witnessed an event and testified about it, he may not adjudicate it. If the judge witnessed the event but did not actually testify about it, *Rambam* rules that he may serve as a judge for all cases, monetary or capital. *Shulḥan Arukh* adds that if three judges witnessed an event together, and the event took place during the daytime, when it was possible for them to sit as a court, the judges may rule on the basis of their observation, without formally hearing testimony. *Rema* adds that if the testimony is required only by Rabbinic decree, as is the case regarding the certification of documents, a judge may testify," following our Gemara. (*Rambam, Sefer Shofetim, Hilkhot Edut* 5:8; *Shulḥan Arukh, Ḥoshen Mishpat* 7:5.)

דַּיָּינִין הַמַּכִּירִין חֲתִימוֹת יְדֵי עֵדִים **If the judges recognize the signatures of the hands of the witnesses.** "If the judges themselves recognize the signatures of the witnesses, they may certify the document without a formal process of hearing testimony, following the Gemara's second inference from Rav Huna's statement." (*Rambam, Sefer Shofetim, Hilkhot Edut* 6:2; *Shulḥan Arukh, Ḥoshen Mishpat* 46:7.)

בִּפְנֵיהֶם. [1]וּשְׁמַע מִינָּהּ: דַּיָּינִין שֶׁאֵין מַכִּירִין חֲתִימוֹת יְדֵי עֵדִים, צְרִיכִין לְהָעִיד בִּפְנֵי כָּל אֶחָד וְאֶחָד.

[2]מַתְקִיף לָהּ רַב אַשִׁי: בִּשְׁלָמָא עֵד נַעֲשֶׂה דַּיָּין שָׁמְעִינַן מִינָּהּ. [3]אֶלָּא דַּיָּינִין הַמַּכִּירִין חֲתִימוֹת יְדֵי עֵדִים, [4]אֵין צְרִיכִין לְהָעִיד בִּפְנֵיהֶם? [5]דִּלְמָא, לְעוֹלָם אֵימָא לָךְ: צְרִיכִין, [6]וְשָׁאנֵי הָכָא, דְּקָא מְקַיְּימָא הַגָּדָה בְּחַד! [7]וְדַיָּינִין שֶׁאֵין מַכִּירִין חֲתִימוֹת יְדֵי עֵדִים, [8]צְרִיכִין לְהָעִיד בִּפְנֵי כָּל אֶחָד וְאֶחָד?

LITERAL TRANSLATION

before them. [1]And conclude from this: [If] the judges do not recognize the signatures of the hands of the witnesses, it is necessary to testify before each and every one.

[2]Rav Ashi objected to this: Granted [that] we may conclude from this [that] a witness can be made a judge. [3]But [if] the judges recognize the signatures of the hands of the witnesses, [4]do they not need to testify before them? [5]Perhaps, in fact, I can say to you: They do need to, [6]but it is different here, because testifying (lit., "telling") is fulfilled with one! [7]And [if] the judges do not recognize the signatures of the hands of the witnesses, [8]do they need to testify before each and every one?

TRANSLATION AND COMMENTARY

it was only the third judge who needed to hear testimony. [1]**And** (3), we can **infer from this** that **if the judges do not recognize the signatures of the witnesses, it is necessary to testify before each** of the three judges, and it is not sufficient for one or two of them to hear the testimony. For we see that the third judge was not able to sign on the basis of the knowledge of the first two judges, and needed to wait until he had heard the testimony himself.

מַתְקִיף לָהּ רַב אַשִׁי [2]**Rav Ashi objected to these** inferences: **Granted that** the first inference is correct, and **we can infer from this** statement that **a witness can be made a judge.** [3]But how can we deduce that **if the judges recognize the signatures of the witnesses,** [4]**it is not necessary to testify before them?** [5]**Perhaps, in fact, I can say to you** that, in general, where all the judges recognize the signatures, **it is** still **necessary** to testify before them. Perhaps the judges must actually be told about the signatures, since the verse from which we learn the laws of testimony (Leviticus 5:1) uses the expression, "to tell." [6]**But here,** in this case, **it is different, because** the act of **testifying can be fulfilled with one!** Provided that one of the judges is told the evidence, the other two can sign on the basis of their own knowledge. [7]**And** how can we deduce that, **if the judges do not recognize the signatures of the witnesses,** [8]**it is necessary to testify**

RASHI

צריכין להעיד בפני כל אחד ואחד – שאם העידו בפני השנים – אין השלישי יכול לחתום, דהא הכא הוצרכו השנים להעיד בפני השלישי. דלמא לעולם צריכין – להעיד, שאין עדות אלא על ידי הגדת עדות. ושאני הכא דקא מקיימא הגדה – בפני

NOTES

דַּיָּינִין שֶׁאֵין מַכִּירִין חֲתִימוֹת יְדֵי עֵדִים **If the judges do not recognize the signatures of the hands of the witnesses.** The Rishonim ask: Surely this is obvious! The court that certifies the document must consist of three judges. Obviously, all three must be satisfied that the signatures are authentic! *Ran* answers that since the certification of documents is a Rabbinic requirement, we might have thought that the third judge could rely on his colleagues.

Ritva explains that three judges are needed to form a court so as to have an odd number. This allows the court to reach a decision if the judges disagree. But regarding the certification of documents, this consideration does not apply, as it is not at all likely that the judges will disagree with each other, and in similar cases the Gemara does indeed permit a court of two judges. Three judges are required for certification so that the difference between the signatures of the judges and those of the original witnesses should be obvious. Hence we might have thought that it was sufficient for the third judge to be simply present, even if he did not hear the testimony.

מַתְקִיף לָהּ רַב אַשִׁי **Rav Ashi objected to this.** Normally the Halakhah is in accordance with Rav Ashi, who was the chief editor of the Talmud. But in this case the Rishonim agree that all three inferences of the Gemara are accepted, in spite of Rav Ashi's objections (*Tur, Ḥoshen Mishpat* 46:12,20). *Bet Yosef* explains that Rav Ashi did not refute the Gemara's inferences, but merely raised doubts about them, and we do not reject an unqualified statement of the Gemara because of doubts.

דְּקָא מְקַיְּימָא הַגָּדָה בְּחַד **Because testifying is fulfilled with one.** The Rishonim ask: Regarding the sanctification of the New Moon, the Gemara (*Rosh HaShanah* 25b) declares that seeing a fact is better than hearing testimony about it, and if an event took place in the presence of a court, it is not necessary for the judges to hear formal testimony (see following note). Why, then, does the Gemara need Rav's statement to infer that, if judges recognize the signatures, there is no need for formal testimony? And how can Rav Ashi disagree with this rule?

Tosafot answers that the Rabbis required that a court certifying a document should be instantly recognizable as a court, so that observers would notice the difference between the signatures of the judges on the certification and the original signatures of the witnesses on the

LITERAL TRANSLATION

[1]Perhaps, in fact, I can say to you: They do not need to, [2]but it is different here, because testifying is not being fulfilled at all!

[3]Rabbi Abba sat and recited this tradition [4]that a witness can be made a judge.

[5]Rav Safra raised an objection to Rabbi Abba: [6]"[If] three saw it, and they are a court, [7]two must stand and seat [two] of their fellows next to the one, and they must testify before them, [8]and they [then] say: 'The [new] month is sanctified, sanctified,' [9]because a single [person] is not believed by himself." [10]But if it should enter your mind that a witness can be made a judge,

[1]דִּלְמָא, לְעוֹלָם אֵימָא לָךְ: אֵין צְרִיכִין, [2]וְשָׁאנֵי הָכָא, דְּלָא קָא מִקַּיְּימָא הַגָּדָה כְּלָל!

[3]יְתֵיב רַבִּי אַבָּא וְקָאָמַר לָהּ לְהָא שְׁמַעְתָּא [4]דְּעֵד נַעֲשֶׂה דַּיָּין. [5]אֵיתִיבֵיהּ רַב סָפְרָא לְרַבִּי אַבָּא: [6]"רָאוּהוּ שְׁלֹשָׁה, וְהֵן בֵּית דִּין, [7]יַעַמְדוּ שְׁנַיִם וְיוֹשִׁיבוּ מֵחַבְרֵיהֶם אֵצֶל הַיָּחִיד, וְיָעִידוּ בִּפְנֵיהֶם, [8]וְיֹאמְרוּ: 'מְקוּדָּשׁ הַחֹדֶשׁ, מְקוּדָּשׁ', [9]שֶׁאֵין הַיָּחִיד נֶאֱמָן עַל יְדֵי עַצְמוֹ." [10]וְאִי סָלְקָא דַּעְתָּךְ דְּעֵד נַעֲשֶׂה דַּיָּין,

TRANSLATION AND COMMENTARY

before each one? [1]**Perhaps, in fact, I can say to you** that if none of the judges recognizes the signatures, it is sufficient to testify before one judge, and **it is not necessary** for all of them to hear the testimony. [2]**But here** in this case **it is different, because** the requirement of **testifying is not fulfilled at all** if the two judges do not testify before the third! Thus we see that the second and third inferences, while not unreasonable, are less than compelling.

יְתֵיב רַבִּי אַבָּא [3]The statement we have just been discussing was taught to Rav Safra by Rabbi Abba, who had heard it from the other Sages previously mentioned. The Gemara relates that when **Rabbi Abba sat and recited this tradition** — [4]the statement from which we inferred **that a witness can be made a judge** — [5]**Rav Safra raised an objection to Rabbi Abba** from the following Mishnah (*Rosh HaShanah* 25b). This Mishnah deals with the procedure to be followed when sanctifying the New Moon. Under Jewish law, the months of the year are lunar, and begin on the first day after conjunction on which the New Moon is visible. Astronomically, this occurs on the thirtieth or the thirty-first day of the previous month. The declaration of the New Moon is made by a court composed of three members of the Sanhedrin, and is based on the testimony of two qualified witnesses. All the usual laws of testimony apply to these witnesses. If witnesses come on the thirtieth day, the court sanctifies the new month with the proclamation described below. If no witnesses come on the thirtieth day, the new month, automatically begins on the thirty-first day, with no need for sanctification. The Mishnah tells us that "if no witnesses come on the thirtieth day to testify that they have seen the New Moon, [6]but **three** judges **saw it, and they** themselves **are** authorized to serve as **a court** for this purpose, [7]**two** of the judges **must stand and seat two of their fellow** judges **next to the one** who saw the New Moon, **and** the two standing judges become regular witnesses and **testify before** the three seated judges that they saw the New Moon. [8]The three seated judges **then** issue the sanctification proclamation, **saying: 'The new month is sanctified, sanctified.'** [9]This procedure must involve the introduction of two other judges **because a single person is not believed by himself** to sanctify the new month; rather, three judges are required." [10]**But**, objects Rav Safra, **if it should enter your mind that a witness can be made a**

CONCEPTS

מְקוּדָּשׁ הַחֹדֶשׁ, מְקוּדָּשׁ "The new month is sanctified, sanctified." This is the formula of the sanctification proclamation issued by the authorized Rabbinic court announcing the beginning of a new month. In ancient times, when the new month was announced on the basis of the testimony of witnesses, people who had seen the New Moon appeared before a central court (in Temple times, in Jerusalem) to testify that they had seen it. Their testimony was examined, and if found correct by the court, the new month would be announced and sanctified.

RASHI

היחיד שאינו מכיר. **דלא מקיימא הגדה כלל** — אי לא הוו מסהדי באפיה.

ראוהו שלשה — בעדות החדש קאי. **והן בית דין** — מסנהדרין המקדשין את החדש. **יעמדו השנים** — להיות עדים. והתם פרכינן: לא תהא שמיעה גדולה מראיה! ומוקמינן לה כשראוהו בלילה. לפיכך אם לא יעידו לבקר — על מה יאמרו מקודש? **שאין היחיד נאמן** — לקדש החדש ביחידי.

NOTES

of documents should be done before a court of three, and not before a single outstanding judge or a pair of judges. For the same reason, Rav Ashi suggested that the judges should also be required to go through the formality of hearing testimony.

Our commentary follows *Ritva* and *Ramban*, who explain that the laws governing most forms of testimony are derived from Leviticus 5:1, in which the word "telling" appears. Testimony about the New Moon, however, is derived by the Gemara (*Rosh HaShanah* 20a) from a different verse (Exodus 12:2), in which the word "telling" does not appear. Hence, we might have thought that the rule that seeing is even better than hearing applies only to the sanctification of the New Moon, but regarding other forms of testimony we would require the "telling" to be fulfilled literally (see *Ran*).

Ra'avad explains that justice must not only be done; it must be seen to be done. Hence Rav Ashi thought that the rule that seeing is even better than hearing applies only to the sanctification of the New Moon, as everyone can see that the New Moon has indeed appeared. But regarding other testimony, where only a select few know the facts, Rav Ashi thought that formal testimony was necessary, so that people would understand the basis of the court's decision.

רָאוּהוּ שְׁלֹשָׁה, וְהֵן בֵּית דִּין If three saw it, and they are a court. The Mishnah rules that two of the judges must stand up, and must seat two other judges next to the

TRANSLATION AND COMMENTARY

judge, as we inferred above, [1]**why do we need all of this,** i.e., the other two judges? [2]**Let** two of the judges who saw the New Moon stand up and testify before the remaining judge, and then let all three judges **sit in their places and sanctify** the new month! Clearly, this Mishnah is based on the principle that once a person has become a witness, he cannot serve as a judge in the same case.

אָמַר לֵיהּ [3]Rabbi Abba **said to** Rav Safra in reply: When I was taught this law by Rav Yitzḥak bar Shmuel bar Marta, **this** objection that you raised from the Mishnah in tractate *Rosh HaShanah* **was difficult for me, too,** [4]**and I raised** the question **with Rav Yitzḥak bar Shmuel bar Marta,** who had taught me this law, [5]**and Rav Yitzḥak** told me that he had asked the same question **of Rav Huna**, when Rav Huna had taught him the law, **and Rav Huna** replied that he had asked the same question **of Ḥiyya bar Rav, and Ḥiyya bar Rav** had asked it **of Rav,** the original author of the statement, [6]**and** Rav **had said to** his son in reply: **Leave testimony about the New Month alone.** No proof can be brought from this case, because such testimony **is required by Torah law** and is subject to the highest standards, [7]**whereas the certification of documents is of Rabbinic** origin, since by Torah law a document signed by witnesses is considered the equivalent of

[1]לָמָּה לִי כּוּלֵּי הַאי? [2]לֵיתְבוּ בְּדוּכְתַּיְיהוּ וְלִיקַדְּשׁוּ!
[3]אָמַר לֵיהּ: אַף לְדִידִי קַשְׁיָא לִי, [4]וּשְׁאֵילְתֵּיהּ לְרַב יִצְחָק בַּר שְׁמוּאֵל בַּר מָרְתָא, [5]וְרַב יִצְחָק לְרַב הוּנָא, וְרַב הוּנָא לְחִיָּיא בַּר רַב, וְחִיָּיא בַּר רַב לְרַב, [6]וַאֲמַר לְהוּ: הַנַּח לְעֵדוּת הַחֹדֶשׁ, דְּאוֹרָיְיתָא, [7]וְקִיּוּם שְׁטָרוֹת דְּרַבָּנַן.

LITERAL TRANSLATION

[1]why do I need all of this? [2]Let them sit in their places and sanctify!

[3]He said to him: This was difficult for me too, [4]and I asked it of Rav Yitzḥak bar Shmuel bar Marta, [5]and Rav Yitzḥak of Rav Huna, and Rav Huna of Ḥiyya bar Rav, and Ḥiyya bar Rav of Rav, [6]and he said to them: Leave testimony about the [new] month alone, [because it is required] by Torah law, [7]but the certification of documents is Rabbinic.

RASHI

ליתבו בדוכתייהו – אחר שהעידו בפניו.

NOTES

remaining judge, and the two standing judges must then testify before the three seated judges. Commenting on this Mishnah, the Gemara (*Rosh HaShanah* 25b) objects: We have a rule that if an event took place in the presence of a court, it is not necessary for the judges to hear formal testimony, as seeing is even better than hearing. Why, then, does the Mishnah require the judges to engage in this strange procedure? The Gemara answers that the Mishnah is referring to a case in which the court saw the New Moon after nightfall, on the night between the twenty-ninth and the thirtieth day of the month (under Jewish law, this is considered the thirtieth day, as a day begins at nightfall). Now, under Jewish law, courts decide cases only during the daytime. Hence, when the court saw the New Moon, it was unable to accept testimony. Therefore the observation could not serve as a substitute for formal testimony. But if the court saw the New Moon during the daytime (this is possible shortly before sunset on the afternoon of the twenty-ninth), it is permitted to sanctify the new month immediately, without any formal testimony (see *Rambam, Sefer Zemanim, Hilkhot Kiddush HaḤodesh* 2:9).

לֵיתְבוּ בְּדוּכְתַּיְיהוּ **Let them sit in their places.** Our commentary follows *Rashi*, who explains the Gemara's question as follows: Why is it necessary to seat two other judges next to the third judge? Let one judge sit while the other two testify before him, and then all three can sit together and sanctify the New Moon. *Tosefot Rosh* rejects this explanation, arguing that the two additional judges are needed to give the court three members when it is hearing testimony. He explains the Gemara's question as follows: Why is it necessary to select *judges* to sit next to the third judge? Why not seat two ordinary people next to the third judge during the testimony, and then have the two original judges take their places for the sanctification ceremony? Yet another explanation of the Gemara's question is offered by *Ritva*: Why do the two judges stand up and testify at all? Why do the three judges who saw the New Moon not sanctify it on the basis of their observation alone, without any formal testimony?

הַנַּח לְעֵדוּת הַחֹדֶשׁ, דְּאוֹרָיְיתָא **Leave testimony about the new month alone, because it is required by Torah law.** The Gemara's conclusion is that by Torah law a witness cannot serve as a judge, but if the court decision is required only by Rabbinic decree, a witness is permitted to serve as a judge. The Gemara reaches a similar conclusion in tractate *Gittin* (5b). There is an opinion of the *Geonim* that a witness can serve as a judge in all monetary matters, and that he is forbidden to do so only in the case of the sanctification of the new month, which has important ramifications regarding ritual questions of the utmost severity, such as Yom Kippur and Passover. But most Rishonim follow the plain meaning of our Gemara, and agree that a witness can serve as a judge only for Rabbinic matters.

The Rishonim differ as to the reason why a witness cannot serve as a judge by Torah law. *Tosafot* cites an

HALAKHAH

וְקִיּוּם שְׁטָרוֹת דְּרַבָּנַן **But the certification of documents is Rabbinic.** "The entire certification procedure is a Rabbinic institution. *Sma* cites *Haggahot Mordekhai*, who rules that this applies only to certification effected in anticipation

TRANSLATION AND COMMENTARY

oral testimony that has already been investigated by the court (see above, 18b). Thus, while it is true that by Torah law a witness cannot be made a judge, the witnesses who authenticate the signatures on a document may serve as judges, because the Rabbis were lenient regarding the certification of documents, since it is only a Rabbinic requirement.

אָמַר רַבִּי אַבָּא [1] The Gemara now relates another statement of Rabbi Abba on the subject of the certification of documents: **Rabbi Abba said in the name of Rav Huna in the name of Rav:** [2] **If three judges convene to certify a document, and an objection was raised against one of them** (i.e., two witnesses came and testified that one of the judges was unfit to serve as a judge), the question arises as to whether the two judges who recognize the signatures can serve as witnesses to remove the doubts about the third judge. [3] The rule is that **as long as** the first two judges **have not yet signed** the certification, **they may testify about** the third judge, **and he may sign** with

[1] אָמַר רַבִּי אַבָּא אָמַר רַב הוּנָא אָמַר רַב: [2] שְׁלֹשָׁה שֶׁיָּשְׁבוּ לְקַיֵּים אֶת הַשְּׁטָר, וְקָרָא עַרְעָר עַל אֶחָד מֵהֶן, [3] עַד שֶׁלֹּא חָתְמוּ מְעִידִין עָלָיו וְחוֹתֵם;

LITERAL TRANSLATION

[1] Rabbi Abba said in the name of Rav Huna in the name of Rav: [2] [If] three sat down to certify a document, and [someone] made (lit., "called") an objection against one of them, [3] as long as they have not [yet] signed, they may testify about him and he signs;

RASHI

וקרא ערער על האחד – שהוא פסול. **עד שלא חתמו** – השני דיינים על האשרתא. **מעידין** – על זה שהוא כשר.

NOTES

opinion that testimony is acceptable only if it is theoretically possible to refute it through *hazamah* (see above, 20a). But when the witness also serves as a judge, it is impossible for *hazamah* to take place, because a judge cannot judge himself. *Tosafot* rejects this opinion, however, and rules that it is sufficient for testimony to be vulnerable to *hazamah* in theory, even if the court hearing the case is unable to carry it out in practice.

Tosafot also cites *Rashbam*, who derives this law from the verse (Deuteronomy 19:17): "And the two men shall stand," from which we learn (*Shevuot* 30b) that the proper court procedure is for the judge to sit and the witnesses to stand. From here it follows that the judge and the witness cannot exchange roles. This opinion is followed by many Rishonim, and also finds support among the Geonim.

וְקִיּוּם שְׁטָרוֹת דְּרַבָּנָן **But the certification of documents is Rabbinic.** In several places the Gemara notes that the Rabbis were lenient about certain procedural regulations governing the certification of documents, since certification is in any case required only by Rabbinic decree. In tractate *Gittin* (3a), the Gemara connects this idea with Resh Lakish's maxim (see above, 18b) that witnesses who have signed a document have the status of oral witnesses who have already been examined in court. Accordingly, most Rishonim explain that by Torah law the creditor can use the document as proof of the debt, without proving that the witnesses' signatures are authentic. Following this opinion, *Rav Hai Gaon* rules that if one of the judges who signed a certification is subsequently found to be unfit, the certification remains valid, as we rely on the Torah law, by which the entire procedure is unnecessary. However, most authorities follow *Rosh*, who rejects this idea (*Shulḥan Arukh, Ḥoshen Mishpat* 26:28).

According to most authorities, even if the debtor insists that the document was forged, the onus is on him to prove his claim, and it was only by Rabbinic decree that the burden of proof was reversed. *Rabbenu Avigdor HaKohen*, however, rules that certification is Rabbinic only where the debtor does not challenge the authenticity of the document; but where the debtor expressly claims that the document is a forgery, the burden of proof is on the creditor by Torah law (*Haggahot Mordekhai, Kiddushin* 569).

Rambam has a different opinion, according to which Torah law requires that a loan must be attested orally by the witnesses who saw it effected. It is effected only by Rabbinic decree that the witnesses can testify in writing by signing a document. According to this explanation, Resh Lakish's maxim — comparing witnesses who have signed a document to oral witnesses who have been examined in court — is also Rabbinic, and refers to the rule that witnesses who have been examined in court cannot subsequently retract their testimony.

The commentators have difficulty in reconciling *Rambam*'s opinion with our Gemara and the passage in tractate *Gittin*, which appear to indicate that it is the certification, rather than the document, that is Rabbinic. *Bayit Ḥadash* explains that, according to *Rambam*, the certification of documents has no effect by Torah law. Hence, since the entire process has significance only at the Rabbinic level, the Rabbis were lenient regarding certain of the procedural regulations (see also *Shittah Mekubbetzet*).

HALAKHAH

of a claim of forgery; but where the debtor denies the authenticity of the note, certification is required by Torah law. *Shakh* disagrees, arguing that, according to most Rishonim, the debtor is not believed by Torah law if he claims that a document is forged, unless he can prove his claim. *Rema* notes that the custom is to permit an established judge to certify documents by himself, even though the law equating one outstanding judge to three ordinary judges is not in effect today, because the certification of documents is only a Rabbinic procedure, and on such matters a single outstanding judge can decide a case by himself even today." (*Rambam, Sefer Shofetim, Hilkhot Edut* 6:1; *Shulḥan Arukh, Ḥoshen Mishpat* 46:4.)

וְקָרָא עַרְעָר עַל אֶחָד מֵהֶן **And someone made an objection against one of them.** "If three judges convene to certify a document, and two witnesses come forward to testify that

[1] מִשֶּׁחָתְמוּ, אֵין מְעִידִין עָלָיו וְחוֹתֵם.
[2] עַרְעָר דְּמַאי? [3] אִי עַרְעָר דְּגַזְלָנוּתָא, [22A] תְּרֵי וּתְרֵי

TRANSLATION AND COMMENTARY

them, [1] but **once they have signed** the certification, **they may not testify about him, and he** may **not sign** with them. The two judges are permitted to testify before they sign the certification; but if they testify after they have signed the certification, the testimony is invalid, because they are then regarded as having an interest in establishing their colleague's fitness, since it is an embarrassment to sit as a court and have one of the members of the court disqualified.

עַרְעָר דְּמַאי [2] The Gemara asks: **What sort of** objection? What did the first two witnesses claim against the judge? There are two possibilities: Either that the judge had been guilty of some crime, or that there was a problem with his status or his lineage — that he was in fact a slave or a non-Jew. [3] But, argues the Gemara, **if it was an objection about robbery**, if they claimed that the judge had been guilty of a crime, [22A] **they are** evenly balanced, **two against two!** To be effective, the original protest must have

LITERAL TRANSLATION

[1] once they have signed, they may not testify about him and he may [not] sign.

[2] What sort of objection? [3] If [it was] an objection about robbery, [22A] they are two and two.

RASHI

משחתמו — הוו להו נוגעין בעדות, שגנאי להם שישבו עם פסול בדין. **תרי ותרי נינהו** — כי אמרי לא גזל — הוו להו תרי ותרי, ולא מתכשר בהכי. דקיימא לן לקמן בפרקין (כתובות כו,א): אין ערער פחות משנים.

NOTES

מִשֶּׁחָתְמוּ Once they have signed. Our commentary follows *Rashi*, who explains that once the judges have signed the certification they cannot testify about their colleague, because they now have an interest in protecting the third judge who signed with them. Having signed the certification, the two judges are committed in writing, and it would be embarrassing for them to discover that the court was not qualified. According to this view, there is no problem *per se* with establishing the status of the judge after he has signed, provided that independent witnesses can be found.

Many Rishonim, however, including *Rambam*, follow the explanation of *Rabbenu Ḥananel*, who argues that even though the judge is now qualified — because witnesses have testified that he repented of his crimes — at the time the certification was signed he was disqualified, and it is not possible to correct this problem retroactively. According to this view, the same problem would apply even if independent witnesses were to come forward with favorable testimony, if they did not come forward until after the judge had signed the document (see also following note).

עַרְעָר דְּמַאי What sort of objection? The Gemara's conclusion is that Rav was referring to a case where the judge was accused of a crime, and his fellow judges testified that he had since repented. But if the judge's lineage is called into question, his fellow judges are permitted even after signing to testify that it is unblemished, since this is merely revealing a matter of record. This distinction is easier to understand according to the explanation of *Rabbenu Ḥananel* (see previous note), for it is obvious that if a person's lineage is challenged, and the challenge is found to be baseless, the person is reinstated retroactively. Regarding repentance, however, the Gemara rules that a person who is disqualified because of a crime is retroactively disqualified from the time he committed the crime (*Sanhedrin* 27a); and it is conceivable that even when the person repents, he is not considered qualified again until witnesses have testified about his repentance (*Ramban*, *Ritva*). *Ran*, however, rejects this suggestion as illogical, because there is no reason for the disqualified person's repentance to be more dependent upon the witnesses' testimony than the crimes themselves.

According to *Rashi*'s explanation, it is more difficult to understand the difference between testimony about lineage and testimony about repentance. If the two judges are regarded as having an interest in their testimony after they have signed, what difference does it make if evidence of lineage is merely revealing a matter of record? The judges still have an interest in testifying that their fellow judge was qualified to sign with them. *Ramban* explains that testimony about lineage is less direct than testimony about repentance, because the judges are testifying about their fellow judge's family, and not directly about him. Moreover, the status of the judge's family is a matter of public record, and since we have had no knowledge of any problems, we expect the challenge to be found baseless. Therefore, we consider the favorable testimony to be a mere formality, and are even prepared to accept it from his fellow judges.

תְּרֵי וּתְרֵי נִינְהוּ They are two and two. Our commentary

HALAKHAH

one of the judges has been guilty of a crime (such as theft) and is therefore disqualified from serving as a judge, and two other witnesses come forward to testify that the judge has since repented and now lives a blameless life, if the favorable testimony is heard before any of the judges has signed the certification, it is accepted, and the three judges may all sign. If, however, the judges signed the certification before the two pairs of witnesses came forward, *Shulḥan Arukh* rules, following *Rif* and *Rambam*, that the third judge is disqualified, since he had not yet been cleared when he signed; whereas *Shakh* rules, following *Rashi*, that he is qualified, provided that the witnesses in his favor were outsiders. But if the witnesses in his favor were the other two judges in the court, even *Rashi* agrees that the favorable testimony may not be heard after the certification has been signed," following our Gemara. (*Rambam, Sefer Shofetim, Hilkhot Edut* 6:7; *Shulḥan Arukh, Ḥoshen Mishpat* 46:26.)

תְּרֵי וּתְרֵי נִינְהוּ They are two and two. "If two witnesses

TRANSLATION AND COMMENTARY

been made by at least two witnesses, and the two fellow judges who contradict it are also two witnesses. How, then, can their testimony remove the doubt about the third judge? [1]On the other hand, **if the objection was that the** judge's **family was blemished** (i.e., if the witnesses claimed that the judge was in fact a slave or a non-Jew), why should the two other judges not be permitted to testify, even after they signed the certification? [2]The information they provide **is merely revealing a matter** that will ultimately come to light in any case, and there is no danger that they will testify falsely because of embarrassment.

נִינְהוּ. [1]אִי עַרְעָר דִּפְגַם מִשְׁפָּחָה, [2]גִּלּוּי מִלְּתָא בְּעָלְמָא הוּא.

LITERAL TRANSLATION

[1]If [it was] an objection about a family blemish, [2]it is merely revealing a matter.

RASHI

דפגם משפחה — שהעידו עליו שהוא עבד, ועבד פסול לדין ולעדות קל וחומר מאשה, כדאמר בפרק ״החובל״ (בבא קמא פח,א). **גלוי מילתא בעלמא הוא** — משחתמו אמאי אין מעידין עליו? מאי חשד נוגע בעדות איכא הכא? דבר זה צריכין הן לברר, ודבר העשוי לגלות הוא, שיבדקו אחריו עד שיבורר הדבר. ואין עדותן של אלו תלוי בהגדתן, ואינן אלא מגלי דבר בעלמא.

BACKGROUND

גִּלּוּי מִלְּתָא בְּעָלְמָא הוּא It is merely revealing a matter. The strict meaning of the term "testimony" (עֵדוּת) is the transmission of information about events and matters which only the witnesses are capable of reporting. However, there are procedures in which people appear in court to clarify a certain situation, about which knowledge is not limited strictly to the witnesses, but can be discovered in various ways. In such cases we have "the mere revelation of a matter," and do not insist on all the regulations regarding judicial testimony. One of the reasons given for this leniency is that the matter is one whose existence will ultimately be made known in any event. Consequently, we believe the witnesses, since they would not lie about something that could easily be refuted. Any statement in court which is not dependent on testimony in the precise sense of the word comes under this category, and we do not insist on all the rules of evidence when we receive such information.

NOTES

follows *Rashi*, who explains that if two witnesses claim that the judge committed a crime, and two other witnesses contradict them and insist that he was not guilty, the status of the judge is doubtful, and any decisions he makes are void. According to this explanation, the Gemara is objecting to the clause in Rav Huna's statement permitting the two other judges to testify in their colleague's favor before they sign the document.

The Rishonim object: In tractate *Bava Batra* (31b) there is a dispute between Rav Huna and Rav Ḥisda concerning contradicting pairs of witnesses. According to Rav Huna there, we apply to both pairs of witnesses the legal presumption that every Jew is qualified to be a witness, and we treat all of them as qualified witnesses for future testimony, disqualifying only a mixed pair, which definitely includes someone who testified falsely in the past. The Halakhah is in accordance with Rav Huna; moreover, Rav Huna is himself the author of the statement that is the topic of our Gemara. Hence we should follow Rav Huna here, give the judge the benefit of the doubt, and consider him qualified to judge all cases.

Because of this objection, several Rishonim, including *Tosafot* and *Ba'al HaMa'or*, prefer the explanation of *Rabbenu Ḥananel*, who rules that the judge is indeed given the benefit of the doubt, in accordance with Rav Huna's ruling in *Bava Batra*. According to this explanation, the Gemara is objecting to the clause in Rav Huna's statement *forbidding* the other two judges to testify in their colleague's favor *after* the certification is signed. Since the judge is given the benefit of the doubt, and the unfavorable testimony is rejected, the judge is regarded as never having been disqualified, and the other two judges should be allowed to testify in his favor even after the certification has been signed. But the Gemara answers that the two judges do not contradict the unfavorable witnesses, but rather testify that the third judge repented of his crimes; hence the unfavorable testimony is superseded rather than rejected, and the judge does not become qualified again until the favorable testimony is heard.

Many Rishonim, including *Rif*, follow *Rashi*'s explanation. In response to *Tosafot*'s objection, they explain that in *Bava Batra* Rav Huna applied the legal presumption — that both pairs of witnesses are qualified — only to future testimony where the pairs do not contradict each other, but the legal presumption does not apply to the disputed question itself (*Ran* and others). Moreover, even if there is a legal presumption that the judge remains qualified, it is overridden by the standard legal presumption favoring the defendant in any doubtful monetary case (*Shittah Mekubbetzet*). *Rif* notes that *Rashi*'s explanation is also supported by the Gemara's statement, above (20a), that when two witnesses claim that the witnesses who signed a document were disqualified, and two other witnesses claim that they were not, the document may not be used, and we decide the case on the basis of the legal presumption favoring the defendant in any doubtful monetary case. But *Ba'al HaMa'or*, who follows *Rabbenu Ḥananel*, explains that the Gemara's ruling there applies only because the witnesses who signed that particular document had died.

Rabbenu Ḥananel's explanation can be maintained only if we accept his interpretation of Rav Huna's statement itself, according to which Rav Huna's ruling is based on the idea that the third judge cannot be reinstated retroactively. Those Rishonim who accept *Rashi*'s explanation (above, 21b) — according to which the ruling is based on the idea that the two judges have an interest in protecting their colleague — also follow *Rashi* here. The converse is not true, however, and several Rishonim, including *Rif*, follow *Rabbenu Ḥananel* there and *Rashi* here.

עַרְעָר דִּפְגַם מִשְׁפָּחָה An objection about a family blemish. Under Torah law, a major court (one that is authorized to judge capital cases) must be composed only of Jews of impeccable lineage. But witnesses, or judges in an ordinary court of three, may even be *mamzerim* (*Sanhedrin* 36b).

HALAKHAH

come forward to testify that another person has committed a crime and is therefore disqualified from serving as a witness or as a judge, and two other witnesses come forward and testify that the person has repented, he is fit to serve as a witness or as a judge. But if the second pair of witnesses contradict the first pair, and deny that the person has ever committed a crime, his status is doubtful, and he may not serve either as a witness or as a judge until it is clear that he has repented of whatever crimes he may have committed," following *Rashi*'s explanation of the Gemara. (*Rambam, Sefer Shofetim, Hilkhot Edut* 12:3; *Shulḥan Arukh, Ḥoshen Mishpat* 34:28.)

עַרְעָר דִּפְגַם מִשְׁפָּחָה An objection about a family blemish. "If two witnesses testify that a judge is disqualified because

TRANSLATION AND COMMENTARY

לְעוֹלָם אֵימָא לָךְ [1]The Gemara answers: **In fact, I can say to you that** Rabbi Abba was referring to **an objection about robbery,** where the witnesses accused the judge of having committed a crime. And as for your objection — why should we believe the two judges and not treat it as a case of two conflicting pairs of witnesses? — we are referring to a case where the two judges confirmed the allegations about the third judge's past, [2]**but they said: We know that he has repented**, and has returned the stolen object to its rightful owner. Even if a person has been disqualified from being a witness and a judge because of some criminal act, the law is that if he repents in a thorough manner, he becomes qualified to testify and to serve as a judge once again. Hence the evidence of the two judges does not contradict that of the accusing witnesses, and there is no reason not to believe the judges.

[1]לְעוֹלָם אֵימָא לָךְ: עַרְעָר דְּגַזְלָנוּתָא, [2]וְקָאָמְרִי הָנֵי: יָדְעִינַן בֵּיהּ דַּעֲבַד תְּשׁוּבָה.

LITERAL TRANSLATION

[1]In fact, I can say to you: [It was] an objection about robbery, [2]and these [two] say: We know of him that he has repented.

RASHI

דעבד תשובה — והשיב את הגזלה.

NOTES

Only non-Jews and slaves (who are not considered fully Jewish) are not qualified to testify. According to *Tosafot* and *Rambam*, this disqualification applies even after the non-Jew has been converted or the slave freed, although *Rashi* disagrees.

In the event of an intermarriage between a Jew and a non-Jew or a Jew and a slave, the status of the offspring follows the principle of matrilineal descent (*Kiddushin* 66b). Hence it could happen that a judge who was thought to be fully Jewish discovers that his maternal grandmother was in fact a non-Jewess or a slave. In such a case, the judge technically becomes a non-Jew or a slave until he undergoes a formal conversion, and any testimony he may have given or decisions he may have rendered in the meantime (and even afterwards, according to *Rambam* and *Tosafot*) are void.

דִּפְגַם מִשְׁפָּחָה **About a family blemish.** *Rashi* explains that two witnesses testified that the judge was a non-Jew or a slave, and two witnesses testified that he was fully Jewish. *Tosafot* objects: According to *Rashi*'s own explanation, when there is contradictory testimony about the qualifications of a judge, he must be considered disqualified because of doubt. How, then, could the favorable witnesses refute the testimony that the judge was disqualified because of blemished lineage? *Tosafot* cites this argument as an additional reason for rejecting *Rashi*'s explanation of Rav Huna's statement, and for following *Rabbenu Ḥananel*, who ruled that when there is a doubt the judge is considered qualified.

In response to this objection, *Ramban* explains that contradictory testimony about lineage is not like other contradictory testimony. Every Jewish family enjoys a strong legal presumption supporting its lineage, and where there is contradictory testimony, we give the family the benefit of the doubt (see also *Ritva*). Another explanation was offered by *Rid*. He explains that the unfavorable witnesses did not testify that this judge's grandmother was definitely a slave; rather, they testified that someone in the judge's family married a slave. The favorable witnesses then testified that the judge's grandmother was not that slave.

The problem posed by this passage is further complicated by an apparent contradiction between two other passages that explicitly deal with this question. Later in our chapter (26b), the Gemara rules that when one pair of witnesses challenges a person's lineage and the other defends it, we give the person the benefit of the doubt and consider his lineage to be unblemished. On the other hand, in tractate *Kiddushin* (66a), the Gemara states that when one pair of witnesses challenges a person's lineage and the other defends it, we consider the person's status doubtful, and disqualify him. The Rishonim offer several resolutions of this problem (see *Rashi*, *Tosafot*, *Ran*, and others).

דַּעֲבַד תְּשׁוּבָה **That he has repented.** A person can be disqualified from giving testimony if he has committed a serious crime subject to the penalty of lashes, or if he has committed any crime for the sake of monetary gain, even if there is no fixed punishment for his crime. In the former case, the person is restored to his former qualification as soon as he has been punished or repents. In the latter case, punishment or ordinary repentance are not enough. Rather, the person must make it clear that he has totally changed his ways and will in the future avoid anything remotely connected with his crime, even though it may technically be permitted. The Gemara (*Sanhedrin* 25a-b) explains that a gambler must smash his dice and refrain from playing any game that involves gambling, even one in which money is not at stake; a person who lends at interest must tear up his promissory notes and refrain from charging interest, even if his clients are non-Jews, and so on.

HALAKHAH

of his lineage (e.g., if they testify that he is a slave or a non-Jew), and it later transpires that the charge was baseless, the judge is completely qualified, and even documents that he signed in the meantime are valid, because the favorable testimony merely reveals matters that were previously unclear to us, and does not effect a change in status," following our Gemara. (*Rambam, Sefer Shofetim, Hilkhot Edut* 6:7; *Shulḥan Arukh, Ḥoshen Mishpat* 46:27.)

[1]אֲמַר רַבִּי זֵירָא: הָא מִלְּתָא מֵרַבִּי אַבָּא שְׁמִיעַ לִי, [2]וְאִי לָאו רַבִּי אַבָּא דְּמִן עַכּוֹ, שְׁכַחְתָּהּ: [3]שְׁלֹשָׁה שֶׁיָּשְׁבוּ לְקַיֵּים אֶת הַשְּׁטָר וּמֵת אֶחָד מֵהֶם, צְרִיכִין לְמִיכְתַּב: [4]״בְּמוֹתַב תְּלָתָא הֲוֵינָא, וְחַד לֵיתוֹהִי״.

[5]אֲמַר רַב נַחְמָן בַּר יִצְחָק: [6]וְאִי כָּתַב בֵּיהּ: ״שְׁטָרָא דְּנַן נְפַק לְקָדָמָנָא בֵּי דִינָא״, [7]תּוּ לָא צְרִיךְ.

[8]וְדִלְמָא בֵּית דִּין חָצוּף הוּא, [9]וּכְדִשְׁמוּאֵל? [10]דְּאָמַר שְׁמוּאֵל: שְׁנַיִם שֶׁדָּנוּ, דִּינֵיהֶם דִּין, [11]אֶלָּא שֶׁנִּקְרָא בֵּית דִּין חָצוּף.

LITERAL TRANSLATION

[1]Rabbi Zera said: I heard this matter from Rabbi Abba, [2]and if not [for] Rabbi Abba from Acco, I would have forgotten it: [3][If] three sat down to certify a document and one of them died, they must write: [4]"We were in a session of three, and one is no more." [5]Rav Naḥman bar Yitzḥak said: [6]And if he wrote in it: "This document came before us, the court," [7]more is not necessary. [8]But perhaps it was an arrogant court, [9]and in accordance with Shmuel? [10]For Shmuel said: [If] two judged, their judgment is a [valid] judgment, [11]but it is called an arrogant court.

TRANSLATION AND COMMENTARY

אֲמַר רַבִּי זֵירָא [1]The Gemara now relates another statement of Rabbi Abba on the subject of the certification of documents. **Rabbi Zera said: I heard the following statement from Rabbi Abba, [2]and if it had not been for Rabbi Abba from Acco, I would have forgotten it**, because he reminded me of this law: [3]**If three** judges **convene to certify a document and one of them dies** after they have heard the testimony but before they have written the certification, the two remaining judges **must write** in the certification: [4]**"We were officiating as a court of three judges, and one** of us **is** with us **no more."** Since the certification will be signed by only two of the judges, people seeing it will think that only two judges were present throughout the hearing; hence it is important to write in the certification that the third judge died before he could sign, to avoid any appearance of falsehood.

אֲמַר רַב נַחְמָן [5]However, **Rav Naḥman bar Yitzḥak said** that there is another possibility: [6]**If they wrote in** the certification: **"This document came before us, the court,"** [7]**it is not necessary** to write any **more**, since everyone knows that the word "court" implies that three judges were present.

וְדִלְמָא [8]**But**, the Gemara objects, **perhaps** people will think that there were only two judges, and **it was an arrogant court.** [9]This would be **in accordance with** the viewpoint of **Shmuel,** [10]**for Shmuel said: If two** judges **judged** a case, **their judgment is valid,** [11]**but it is called an arrogant court.** According to Shmuel, if two judges decide a case, their action is improper but valid. Hence it is possible to refer to two judges as "a court," and if people see that only two judges signed, they will not be convinced that there was a third judge merely because the word "court" was used in the wording of the certification.

RASHI

ואי לאו רבי אבא דמן עכו – שהזכירה לי לאחר זמן. **שכחתה** = שכחתיה. **ומת אחד מהן** – עד שלא חתמו. **צריכין למיכתב כו׳** – דקיום השטר בשלשה, והרואה שנים חתומין בו – יאמר ששנים קיימוהו. **ואי כתב ביה שטרא דנן נפק קדמנא בי דינא תו לא צריך** – דלא מקרי בי דינא בציר מתלתא.

BACKGROUND

בֵּית דִּין חָצוּף An arrogant court. The Hebrew word חָצוּף means "arrogant" or "impudent." Even though a certain judge may be an expert and be worthy of presiding over a court alone, the ancient Sages, in the *Ethics of the Fathers,* said: "Do not judge alone, for there is none who judges alone except One." Therefore, even when an outstanding Sage judged a case, and the judgment was in fact determined by his opinion, two other judges were placed beside him for the sake of courtesy, so that the court would be complete. Therefore, even in the opinion of Shmuel, who maintains that according to the Torah there is no obligation to seat three judges on a panel, it is "arrogant" for judges not to include a third justice in their deliberations.

NOTES

שְׁנַיִם שֶׁדָּנוּ, דִּינֵיהֶם דִּין If two judged, their judgment is a valid judgment. The source of this law is found in tractate *Sanhedrin* (5b). Shmuel rules there that when two judges decide a case, the judgment is valid; whereas Rabbi Abbahu rules that such a court is invalid, since the Torah requires three judges to constitute a court. But even Shmuel agrees that the judges who sit on such a court are called arrogant. *Rashi* explains that this is because the judges are violating the wishes of the Sages. *Shittah Mekubbetzet* cites an opinion that this is because in the event of disagreement they will be forced to seek outside assistance, and will thus publicize discussions that should have remained private. *Rabbenu Tam* follows *Bahag*, who rules in favor of Shmuel. However, most Rishonim follow *Rav Aḥai Gaon*, who rules that the Halakhah follows Rabbi Abbahu in this matter (*Rif*, *Rambam*, *Ramban*, *Ritva*, and others).

According to most Rishonim, there is no difference between two judges and one judge, and the only reason Shmuel mentioned two judges was to emphasize that any court consisting of less than three judges is considered arrogant. *Rabbenu Ḥananel* (*Sanhedrin* 3a) explains that

HALAKHAH

שְׁלֹשָׁה שֶׁיָּשְׁבוּ לְקַיֵּים אֶת הַשְּׁטָר וּמֵת אֶחָד מֵהֶם If three sat down to certify a document and one of them died. "If three judges convene to certify a document, and before they can sign the certification one of them dies, the two remaining judges must write in the certification: 'We were in a session of three, and one is no longer alive.' This clause is included so that people will understand why only two judges signed, and will not suspect that only two judges constituted the court from the outset. If the certification includes other language from which it is clear that there were three judges, this is also sufficient. But if the certification merely includes the word "court," this is

¹דִּכְתִיב בֵּיהּ: ²״בֵּי דִינָא דְּרַבָּנָא אַשִׁי״.
³וְדִלְמָא רַבָּנַן דְּבֵי רַב אַשִׁי כְּדִשְׁמוּאֵל סְבִירָא לְהוּ?
⁴דִּכְתִיב בֵּיהּ: ⁵״וַאֲמַר לָנָא רַבָּנָא אַשִׁי״.

משנה ⁶הָאִשָּׁה שֶׁאָמְרָה: ⁷״אֵשֶׁת אִישׁ הָיִיתִי, וּגְרוּשָׁה

LITERAL TRANSLATION

[1] Where it is written in it: [2] "The court of our Master Ashi."

[3] But perhaps the Rabbis of the School of Rav Ashi maintain in accordance with Shmuel?

[4] Where it was written in it: [5] "And our Master Ashi said to us."

MISHNAH [6] [If] a woman said: [7] "I was a married woman, but I am divorced,"

TRANSLATION AND COMMENTARY

דִּכְתִיב בֵּיהּ [1] The Gemara answers: Rav Naḥman bar Yitzḥak was referring to a case **where** the court **wrote in** the certification: [2] "This document came before us, **the court of our Master,** Rav **Ashi,"** or of some other famous Rabbi. For everyone would know that at the court of Rav Ashi there must have been three judges.

וְדִלְמָא רַבָּנַן [3] **But,** the Gemara objects, **perhaps the Rabbis of the School of Rav Ashi are of the same opinion as Shmuel,** and consider a court consisting of two judges to be properly constituted?

דִּכְתִיב בֵּיהּ [4] The Gemara answers: Rav Naḥman bar Yitzḥak was referring to a case **where** the court **wrote in** the certification: [5] "This document came before us, the court of our Master, Rav Ashi, **and our Master,** Rav **Ashi, told us** to certify it." In such a case there can be no doubt that the court consisted of three judges.

MISHNAH הָאִשָּׁה שֶׁאָמְרָה [6] This Mishnah returns to the subject of "the mouth that forbade is the mouth that permitted," discussed earlier in the chapter (16a, 18b). **If an** apparently unmarried **woman says:** [7] **"I was a married woman, but I am** now **divorced," she is believed** without proof, and is permitted to marry another

RASHI

בי דינא דרבנא אשי — אורחא דמילתא נקט, שהוא היה ראש ישיבה במתא מחסיא בימי רב נחמן בר יצחק דהוא מרא דשמעתא, דודאי בי דינא דרב אשי לא עבדין בתרין. **ואמר לנא רבנא אשי** — לאזדקוקי ליה ולקיומי. דכיון דרב אשי גופיה הזקיקן — איהו ודאי לתלתא אמר. ויש מפרשין: ואמר לנא רבנא אשי — תלתא נינהו. ולא נהירא לי, דאי רב אשי חד מנהון — מאי ואמר לנא דכתבי ביה?

NOTES

Shmuel is referring to the law mentioned in several other places, that where a judge is of outstanding ability and is universally accepted, his decisions are considered the equivalent of those of three ordinary judges. *Rashi* also appears to support this view. *Tosafot* and *Rambam*, however, explain that Shmuel was referring to a single judge who was not outstanding. According to this explanation, if a single, ordinary judge tries a case, he is considered arrogant but his decision is binding (according to Shmuel), whereas an outstanding judge who judges by himself is not considered arrogant. Nevertheless, *Rambam* declares that even an outstanding judge should not judge by himself, because the Sages warned that no human being should be so confident in his own abilities (*Avot* 4:8).

כְּדִשְׁמוּאֵל סְבִירָא לְהוּ **Maintain in accordance with Shmuel.** According to most Rishonim, the Halakhah does not follow Shmuel here (see previous note). Moreover, *Tosafot* explains that even Shmuel would agree that an arrogant court of two could not certify a document, because the Sages decreed that a court certifying a document must be instantly recognizable as a court, so that observers will appreciate the difference between the signatures of the judges and the original signatures of the witnesses. Nevertheless, *Tosafot* explains that we are concerned here that the Rabbis associated with Rav Ashi may mistakenly have permitted a court of two to certify a document, basing themselves on Shmuel's ruling. Indeed, it is possible that they did so even if they agree with the viewpoint of Rabbi Abbahu regarding other laws, since certification is a Rabbinic requirement, and we have seen that this results in leniencies in other matters of procedure.

וַאֲמַר לָנָא רַבָּנָא אַשִׁי **And our Master Ashi said to us.** Our commentary follows *Rashi*, who explains that the wording of the certification never indicated explicitly that there were three judges, but simply stated that the court was composed of Rav Ashi's students acting under his supervision. In such a case, we would not suspect the court of having two members, even where this is not explicit in the language of the certification, because Rav Ashi's reputation was so great that we can be confident that his students would never commit an impropriety such as convening a court with two members.

Several Rishonim explain that Rav Ashi himself was a member of the court, and the certification mentioned something that Rav Ashi told "us" — the other two judges (*Rambam, Meiri*). According to this explanation, it was clear from the language of the certification that there were three members, since Rav Ashi was one judge, and "us" implies that there were two more judges. *Rashi* rejects this explanation, because if Rav Ashi had been one of the judges he would have been one of "us," and he would not have been described as "telling us" what to do. However, *Meiri* suggests that Rav Ashi may have been described as asking the other members of the court if they recognized the signatures, and whether they were prepared to testify before him (as explained by the Gemara above, 21b).

אֵשֶׁת אִישׁ הָיִיתִי **I was a married woman.** According to

HALAKHAH

not sufficient, because sometimes courts are convened with only two judges. *Rema* adds that where all three judges did sign the document, it is not necessary to include such detailed language." (*Rambam, Sefer Shofetim, Hilkhot Edut* 6:6; *Shulḥan Arukh, Ḥoshen Mishpat* 46:29.)

הָאִשָּׁה שֶׁאָמְרָה: אֵשֶׁת אִישׁ הָיִיתִי **If a woman said: "I was**

אֲנִי״, נֶאֱמֶנֶת, [1]שֶׁהַפֶּה שֶׁאָסַר הוּא הַפֶּה שֶׁהִתִּיר. [2]וְאִם יֵשׁ עֵדִים שֶׁהָיְתָה אֵשֶׁת אִישׁ, [3]וְהִיא אוֹמֶרֶת: ״גְּרוּשָׁה אֲנִי״, אֵינָהּ נֶאֱמֶנֶת.
[4]אָמְרָה: ״נִשְׁבֵּיתִי וּטְהוֹרָה אֲנִי״, נֶאֱמֶנֶת, [5]שֶׁהַפֶּה שֶׁאָסַר

LITERAL TRANSLATION

she is believed, [1]because the mouth that forbade is the mouth that permitted. [2]But if there are witnesses that she was a married woman, [3]and she says: "I am divorced," she is not believed.

[4][If] she said: "I was taken captive but I am pure," she is believed, [5]because the mouth that forbade is the mouth

RASHI

משנה נשביתי – לבין הנכרים. **וטהורה אני** – שלא נבעלתי לנכרי. **נאמנת** – ומותרת לכהן.

TRANSLATION AND COMMENTARY

man, [1]**because the mouth that forbade is the mouth that permitted.** Had it not been for her statement that she had been married, we would have assumed that she had never been married, and we have no right to accept part of her claim and reject the rest. [2]**But if there are witnesses that she was a married woman,** [3]**and she says: "I am now divorced," she is not believed** without proof, because a woman who is known to have been married must prove that she has been divorced before she is allowed to remarry.

אָמְרָה [4]The Mishnah now considers a related case: The law is that a woman who was raped by a non-Jew is disqualified from marrying into the priesthood. The Rabbis decreed that a woman who was taken captive by bandits or by enemy soldiers is assumed to have been raped by them, unless she can prove otherwise. Hence a woman who was taken captive by non-Jews is disqualified by Rabbinic decree from marrying into the priesthood, even if she claims that she was not violated, unless she can prove her claim. **If,** however, a woman comes forward and **says: "I was taken captive but I am pure** (i.e., they did not rape me)," **she is believed** without proof and is permitted to marry a priest, [5]**because the mouth that forbade**

NOTES

some Rishonim, the woman must immediately add the fact that she was divorced. *Rabbenu Yonah* argues that she must say it within the time it takes to utter a greeting (תּוֹךְ כְּדֵי דִּיבּוּר), i.e., within a few seconds. *Yad Ramah* says that she may take a little longer, provided that she says it while she is still discussing the matter in court. *Tur*, however, rules that she may even come back later and say that she is divorced, because she is considered to be explaining her previous words rather than contradicting them.

Bet Yosef cites *Rabbenu Yehiel*, who explains that the Mishnah deliberately employed the past tense. For when the woman says that she *was* a married woman, her language suggests that she is no longer so; hence she is believed when she says that she is now divorced. If she had used the present tense, however, and then claimed to be divorced, she would have been regarded as contradicting herself, and she would not be believed, even if her claim was supported by the "mouth that forbade" argument (unless she gave a plausible explanation, as the Gemara states below).

Bet Shmuel explains that *Rabbenu Yehiel*'s explanation has relevance only according to *Tur*, who said that the woman is believed even if she said that she was divorced some time after she said that she was married. But if she said this immediately, she would be believed regardless of the tense she used, since a person who corrects himself immediately is even entitled to contradict himself momentarily.

Ritva adds that *Rabbenu Yehiel*'s distinction between past and present applies only to the woman herself. But where witnesses testify that the woman was married, and the woman responds that she is now divorced, she is not believed, even if the witnesses used the past tense. *Ritva* explains that witnesses generally use the past tense because they have no way of knowing whether the situation has changed since they last observed it. Hence their use of tense cannot be taken as any indication that the woman was divorced later.

נִשְׁבֵּיתִי וּטְהוֹרָה אֲנִי **I was taken captive but I am pure.** A Jewish woman who has sexual relations with a man

HALAKHAH

a married woman." "If an apparently unmarried woman comes forward and says: 'I was a married woman, but my husband divorced me,' she is believed without proof and without further explanation, following our Mishnah. If, however, she simply says: 'I was married' (in the past tense — *Bet Shmuel*), and some time later she says: 'My husband divorced me,' some authorities accept her second statement, because she is simply explaining her words, whereas other authorities rule that she is not believed unless she can give a plausible explanation for the delay. But if she uses the present tense, *Bet Shmuel* rules that she is considered to be contradicting herself, and she is not believed unless she corrects herself immediately, or is able to give a plausible explanation for the delay." (*Rambam, Sefer Nashim, Hilkhot Gerushin* 12:1; *Shulhan Arukh, Even HaEzer* 152:6.)

וְאִם יֵשׁ עֵדִים שֶׁהָיְתָה אֵשֶׁת אִישׁ **But if there are witnesses that she was a married woman.** "If there are witnesses who testify that the woman was married, and she claims that she was divorced, she is not believed without proof, following our Mishnah. But if she can produce witnesses to attest to her divorce, it is not necessary that the bill of divorce itself be produced. Nevertheless, even if the woman is not believed to the extent of being allowed to remarry, we take her words into account where this leads to a stringency. For example, she is not permitted to marry a priest if her alleged husband dies. And if he dies without children, she must not marry her brother-in-law in a levirate marriage, but must be released through the *halitzah* ceremony." (*Rambam, Sefer Nashim, Hilkhot Gerushin* 12:1,2; *Shulhan Arukh, Even HaEzer* 152:7.)

נִשְׁבֵּיתִי וּטְהוֹרָה אֲנִי **I was taken captive but I am pure.**

TRANSLATION AND COMMENTARY

is the mouth that permitted. Had it not been for her statement, we would have assumed that she had never been taken captive, and we have no right to accept part of her claim and reject the rest. [1]**But if there are witnesses that she was taken captive, [2]and she says: "I am pure," she is not believed** without proof, because a woman who is known to have been taken captive is assumed to have been raped, if there is no proof to the contrary.

וְאִם מִשֶּׁנִּשֵּׂאת [3]The Mishnah ruled that where there are witnesses that the woman was taken captive, she is not permitted to marry a priest unless she can prove that she was not violated. **But if** there were no witnesses that she was taken captive, and the woman made her claim, and the court permitted her to marry a priest on the grounds that "the mouth that forbade is the mouth that permitted," and later, **after she** had **married, witnesses came** forward to refute her claim, the Mishnah rules that in such a case she is permitted to rely on the court decision given before the witnesses came, [4]and **she is not** required to **leave** her new husband.

GEMARA אָמַר רַב אַסִי [5]The central theme of the Mishnayot of this chapter has been the concept called "the mouth that forbade is the mouth that permitted." When we would have no reason to imagine that a problem exists, were it not for a certain statement, and if the statement also contains a solution to the problem, we must take the statement as a single unit and view the problem as solved. We do not divide the statement in two, accepting the problem while ignoring the solution. Until now, the validity of this concept has simply been assumed. The Gemara now seeks to prove it. **Rav Assi said: From where in the Torah do we know that "the mouth that forbade is the mouth that permitted"?** [6]Our source is **the verse** (Deuteronomy 22:16) that **says: "I gave my daughter to this man as a wife."** The verse refers to the punishment to be meted out to a husband who slanders his wife, claiming that she was not a virgin when they married. The verse tells us that the woman's father must make a statement in court, charging the man with slandering his daughter. In the course of making his statement, the father briefly reviews the

הוּא הַפֶּה שֶׁהִתִּיר. [1]וְאִם יֵשׁ עֵדִים שֶׁנִּשְׁבֵּית, [2]וְהִיא אוֹמֶרֶת: "טְהוֹרָה אֲנִי", אֵינָהּ נֶאֱמֶנֶת. [3]וְאִם מִשֶּׁנִּשֵּׂאת בָּאוּ עֵדִים, [4]הֲרֵי זוֹ לֹא תֵּצֵא.

גמרא [5]אָמַר רַב אַסִי: מִנַּיִן לְ"הַפֶּה שֶׁאָסַר הוּא הַפֶּה שֶׁהִתִּיר" מִן הַתּוֹרָה? [6]שֶׁנֶּאֱמַר: "אֶת בִּתִּי נָתַתִּי לָאִישׁ הַזֶּה

LITERAL TRANSLATION

that permitted. [1]But if there are witnesses that she was taken captive, [2]and she says: "I am pure," she is not believed.

[3]But if witnesses came after she was married, [4]she does not go out.

GEMARA [5]Rav Assi said: From where [do we know] "the mouth that forbade is the mouth that permitted" from the Torah? [6]As it is said: "I gave my daughter to this man

RASHI

ואם משניסת באו עדים — נגמרא מפרש להיא קאי.

NOTES

whom she is forbidden to marry (such as a non-Jew) is disqualified from marrying into the priesthood, even if she was raped. This has four consequences: (1) The woman may never marry a priest, even if she was never married before, or was married and widowed. (2) If she was already married to a priest, she must be divorced (even if she was raped). (3) If she was herself the daughter of a priest, or was married to a priest and was not yet divorced (consequence 2), she must never again eat terumah and other sacred food that only priests and the members of their households are permitted to eat. (4) If in the future she has any children by a priest, they also become disqualified from the priesthood.

If a woman is taken captive, there is a serious possibility that she will be violated, and hence disqualified from the priesthood. It is clear from the Gemara, however, that by Torah law we need not concern ourselves with this possibility unless we are certain that the woman was raped. The Sages, however, ruled that every captive woman is presumed to have been raped — even if she claims that this did not happen — unless she can prove otherwise. Despite this presumption, the Sages were fairly lenient about the standards of proof in such cases, since by Torah law she is believed without proof.

HALAKHAH

"If a woman comes forward and declares that she was taken captive, but insists that she was not violated, she is believed, because 'the mouth that forbade is the mouth that permitted,' following our Mishnah. This law applies even if there is one witness who testifies that she was taken captive." (*Rambam, Sefer Kedushah, Hilkhot Issurei Bi'ah* 18:21; *Shulhan Arukh, Even HaEzer* 7:4.)

וְאִם יֵשׁ עֵדִים שֶׁנִּשְׁבֵּית But if there are witnesses that she was taken captive. "If there are two witnesses who testify that she was taken captive, even though they do not know for certain that she was violated, her claim that she was not violated is not believed. On the other hand, if even one witness testifies with certainty that she was not violated — even if the witness is a maidservant — she is believed, even if the witness in her favor is contradicted by another individual witness." (*Rambam, Sefer Kedushah, Hilkhot Issurei Bi'ah* 18:21; *Shulhan Arukh, Even HaEzer* 7:4.)

TRANSLATION AND COMMENTARY

history of the marriage. The review itself teaches us nothing we do not already know. Hence the Gemara understands that it was inserted in the Torah to teach us some additional law. Therefore, the Gemara interprets this verse as though it were teaching us the general principle that if a father declares that he gave his daughter in marriage to a certain man, he is believed. [1]Now, if the father had left out the word "this," and had simply said: "I gave my daughter **to a man,"** he would in effect have been declaring that his daughter was a married woman, and **she would be forbidden** to all men. [2]However, since the father included in the same sentence the word **"this,"** indicating that his daughter's husband was *this* particular man, he is believed on both counts, and his daughter is forbidden to all other men but **is permitted** to this particular man. In Hebrew, the demonstrative adjective "this" is written after the noun it modifies. Hence, in the Hebrew word-order, the father's statement reads literally: "My daughter I gave to a man, this, as a wife." Thus the father's first words effectively forbade his daughter to the entire world, and only afterwards did he utter the word that permitted her to her husband. Yet the father is believed on both counts, since the same "mouth" uttered both parts of the statement. Thus we see that where "the mouth that forbade is the mouth that permitted," we take the entire statement as a single unit. We do not divide it in two, accepting the problem while ignoring the solution.

לָמָּה לִי קְרָא [3]Rav Assi's inference from the verse is sound, but the Gemara decides that it is not necessary to cite a verse to prove that "the mouth that forbade is the mouth that permitted." **Why**, asks the Gemara, **do I need a verse?** [4]This concept can be proved by an argument **based on reason.** Although it is true that this verse implies the concept of "the mouth that forbade," this is not the reason why the Torah included it, because the principle of "the mouth that forbade" is logically inescapable. Where the only source for a problem is the statement containing the solution, it would be illogical to divide the statement in two. [5]Thus, in the case of the father, **he forbade her** by the first part of his statement **and he permitted her** by the second part!

אֶלָּא [6]**Rather,** says the Gemara, this **verse** — which teaches us that a father who claims to have given his daughter in marriage to a certain man is believed — **is needed** to teach us **the ruling issued by Rav Huna**

לְאִשָּׁה״. [1]״לָאִישׁ״ אֲסָרָהּ;
[2]״הַזֶּה״ הִתִּירָהּ.
[3]לָמָּה לִי קְרָא? [4]סְבָרָא הִיא:
[5]הוּא אֲסָרָהּ, וְהוּא שָׁרֵי לָהּ!
[6]אֶלָּא, כִּי אִיצְטְרִיךְ קְרָא לְכִדְרַב הוּנָא אָמַר רַב.

LITERAL TRANSLATION

as a wife." [1]"To [a] man" made her forbidden; [2]"this" made her permitted.

[3]Why do I need a verse? [4]It is [based on] reason: [5]He forbade her, and he permits her!

[6]Rather, where the verse needed is for [the ruling] by Rav Huna in the name of Rav.

RASHI

גמרא נתתי לאיש אסרה — לכל העולם, דלא ידעינן למאן. וכי אמר ״הזה״ התירה לו.

NOTES

סְבָרָא הִיא **It is based on reason.** In general, when a rule can be derived by logical reasoning, it has the status of a Torah law, even if it was not explicitly mentioned in the Torah. Thus our Gemara is stating that since the argument that "the mouth that forbade is the mouth that permitted" is so logical, it is not necessary to find Scriptural support for it. *Bahag* explains that if we believe the first part of the father's statement and rely on it to consider the daughter married, and therefore subject to the death penalty if she commits adultery, we must accept the second part of his statement as well, and consider her permitted to the man the father indicated as her husband.

Early in this chapter (16a), the Gemara connects the "mouth that forbade" argument, which usually appears in the context of ritual law, with *miggo*, a relatively weak argument that usually refers to monetary law. According to *Tosafot*, the terms are in fact equivalent, but according to *Rashi*, the "mouth that forbade" argument is much more powerful than *miggo*, and in fact corresponds to the silent *miggo* of monetary law.

According to those Rishonim who identify the "mouth that forbade" argument with *miggo*, our Mishnah presents a problem. For *miggo* is normally valid only if the entire claim is made immediately. A person cannot make a claim in court and ask to be believed on the basis of a *miggo*, maintaining that if he had not said something last year he would be in a better legal position today. But if our Mishnah is referring to a case where the woman said, "I was married," and then *immediately* added: "I am now divorced," it is obvious that she is believed, because in judicial proceedings a person is even believed if he retracts a statement outright, provided that he does so within the time it takes to utter a greeting. *Tosafot* explains that the *miggo* of our Mishnah is accepted even if the woman's second statement was not made immediately, because her claim to be divorced is an explanation of her previous statement, rather than a retraction of it.

Rashba explains that the Mishnah is indeed referring to a case where the woman made both statements one after the other. *Rashba* explains that the rule that a person can retract a statement within the time it takes to utter a greeting applies only to retraction, but not to additional claims. Hence the woman in our Mishnah is believed only because she has a *miggo*. According to this explanation, if the woman said, "I was married," and only later returned and said, "I am now divorced," she would not be believed.

[1]דְּאָמַר רַב הוּנָא אָמַר רַב: מִנַּיִן לָאָב שֶׁנֶּאֱמָן לֶאֱסוֹר אֶת בִּתּוֹ מִן הַתּוֹרָה? [2]שֶׁנֶּאֱמַר: "אֶת בִּתִּי נָתַתִּי לָאִישׁ".
[3]"הַזֶּה" לָמָּה לִי?
[4]מִיבָּעֵי לֵיהּ לְכִדְתָנֵי רַבִּי יוֹנָה.
[5]דְּתָנֵי רַבִּי יוֹנָה: "'אֶת בִּתִּי נָתַתִּי לָאִישׁ הַזֶּה'. 'הַזֶּה', [6]וְלֹא לְיָבָם".

LITERAL TRANSLATION

[1]For Rav Huna said in the name of Rav: From where [do we know] that a father is believed to make his daughter forbidden from the Torah? [2]As it is said: "I gave my daughter to a man."

[3]Why do I need "this"?

[4]It is needed for what Rabbi Yonah taught. [5]For Rabbi Yonah taught: "'I gave my daughter to this man.' [To] '*this*' [man], [6]and not to a *yavam*."

TRANSLATION AND COMMENTARY

in the name of Rav. [1]**For Rav Huna said in the name of Rav: From where in the Torah do we know that a father is believed with regard to making his daughter forbidden?** [2]Our source is **the verse which says: "I gave my daughter to a man."** (Rav Huna does not infer anything from the adjective "this.") By Torah law, a father is permitted to give his daughter in marriage while she is still a minor. According to Rav Huna, the verse teaches us that if the father claims to have given his daughter in marriage in this way, he is believed, and his daughter has the status of a married woman.

הַזֶּה לָמָּה לִי [3]The Gemara asks: If the purpose of the verse is to teach us that the father is believed, and his daughter has the status of a married woman, **why do we need** the word **"this"?** Once we know that the father is believed when he says that he gave his daughter in marriage, it follows automatically that he is believed with regard to permitting her to her husband, as we explained above. What specific teaching do we learn from the word "this"?

מִיבָּעֵי לֵיהּ [4]The Gemara answers that the word "this" does not teach us anything about Rav Huna's ruling. Rather, it refers to the case of the husband who slanders his wife, and **it is needed for** the law we learned in the Baraita **that Rabbi Yonah taught.** [5]**For Rabbi Yonah taught** the following Baraita: "Since the verse states that the father says: **'I gave my daughter to this man,'** we infer that the law of the husband who slanders his wife applies only when the father can say that he personally gave his daughter to **'this** man.' Hence, if the original husband died childless, and his brother performed a levirate marriage with the widow, [6]**and** the former brother-in-law (**the *yavam***) then falsely accused his wife of not being a virgin,

RASHI

שנאמן לאסור את בתו – כשהיא קטנה או נערה, שבידו לקדשה. כדאמרינן בפרק "נערה שנתפתתה": מנין שאם אמר קדשתיה לפלוני שהוא נאמן לאוסרה על הכל. **את בתי נתתי** – אלמא בדידיה תליא נתינה, והימניה קרא למימר הכי. **הזה למה לי** – כיון דלאו להפה שאסר מיבעי ליה. **ולא ליבם** – אם הוציא שם רע על נישואי אחיו, שאין היבם נידון כמוציא שם רע ליענש במאה כסף. והכי מוכח לקמן בפרק "נערה".

SAGES

רַבִּי יוֹנָה **Rabbi Yonah.** One of the leading Amoraim in Eretz Israel during the fourth generation, Rabbi Yonah was an outstanding disciple of two of Rabbi Yoḥanan's younger students, Rabbi Il'ai and Rabbi Zera, and a student-colleague of Rabbi Yirmeyah.

Many of Rabbi Yonah's teachings appear in the Jerusalem Talmud, and he was apparently one of the leading scholars of his time. Many Amoraim of the following generation were his students. Rabbi Yonah was one of the last Amoraim from Eretz Israel to be cited in the Babylonian Talmud.

Rabbi Yonah was renowned for his piety, and the Talmud mentions various miracles performed for him. He was also highly respected by the non-Jewish leaders of his time.

Rabbi Yonah's son, Rabbi Mana, was his outstanding disciple, and was considered one of the leading Amoraim in Eretz Israel during the next generation.

NOTES

מִנַּיִן לָאָב שֶׁנֶּאֱמָן לֶאֱסוֹר אֶת בִּתּוֹ מִן הַתּוֹרָה **From where do we know that a father is believed to make his daughter forbidden from the Torah?** The Rishonim explain that Rav Huna is referring to the law (*Kiddushin* 41a) that a daughter can be married off by her father as long as she is not yet an adult (i.e., while she is still a minor, or during the period called *na'arut*, the first six months after puberty). The prospective husband performs the regular betrothal ritual with the father, saying, "Behold *your daughter* is betrothed to me by the law of Moses and of Israel," instead of "behold *you* etc." The marriage is valid by Torah law, and can only be dissolved by a bill of divorce. Likewise, if the girl is divorced before she reaches adulthood, the bill of divorce must be delivered to the father. By Torah law, only the father has this power; no other relative can marry off the girl, nor may the girl marry herself off while she is a minor. Moreover, the father cannot marry off a son in this way, nor can he marry off his daughter once she reaches the age of full adulthood (בַּגְרוּת).

הַזֶּה, וְלֹא לְיָבָם **To "this" man, and not to a *yavam*.** The

HALAKHAH

מִנַּיִן לָאָב שֶׁנֶּאֱמָן לֶאֱסוֹר אֶת בִּתּוֹ **From where do we know that a father is believed to make his daughter forbidden?** "If a father declares that he married off his minor daughter and then received a bill of divorce for her, and she is still a minor, he is believed, and her status is that of a divorcee, who is forbidden to marry a priest. But if his daughter was already an adult when he made his declaration, his claim that he married her off and received a bill of divorce for her while she was still a minor is not believed. *Ḥelkat Meḥokek* adds that the same rule applies if the father claims that he married off his daughter and did not receive a bill of divorce on her behalf, so that she is still married. Here, too, the father is believed only if his daughter was still a minor when he made his declaration. The father is believed about these matters while his daughter is still a minor because the Torah believes the father concerning his daughter's marital status, following Rav Huna. If, on the other hand, the father claims that his daughter — regardless of her age — was taken captive and that he redeemed her, he is not believed, because the Torah believed the father only with regard to his daughter's marital status, but not with regard to anything else." (*Rambam, Sefer Kedushah, Hilkhot Issurei Bi'ah* 18:24; *Shulḥan Arukh, Even HaEzer* 37:25,26, and 7:8.)

הַזֶּה, וְלֹא לְיָבָם **"To this man," and not to a *yavam*.** "If a man betrothed a woman and then divorced her and

TRANSLATION AND COMMENTARY

the law does **not** apply, and the former brother-in-law is not subject to the penalty for slander."

תָּנוּ רַבָּנַן [1]**Our Rabbis taught** the following Baraita: **"If a woman says: 'I am a married woman,'** [2]**and** subsequently **she retracts and says: 'I am unmarried,' she is believed."** In this case the woman's claim is not supported by the "mouth that forbade" argument, because her two statements contradict each other and cannot be taken as an undivided whole. Nevertheless, the Baraita teaches us that if the only basis for giving her the status of a married woman is her own claim, she is believed if she withdraws her statement and claims to be unmarried.

[1]תָּנוּ רַבָּנַן: ״הָאִשָּׁה שֶׁאָמְרָה: ׳אֵשֶׁת אִישׁ אֲנִי׳, [2]וְחָזְרָה וְאָמְרָה: ׳פְּנוּיָה אֲנִי׳, נֶאֱמֶנֶת.״

LITERAL TRANSLATION

[1]Our Rabbis taught: "[If] a woman said: 'I am a married woman,' [2]and she retracted (lit., 'returned') and said: 'I am unmarried,' she is believed."

NOTES

law of the husband who slanders his wife appears in Deuteronomy 22:13-19. The Torah tells us that if a husband falsely accuses his wife of not having been a virgin when they married, he is punished by lashes (verse 18), as well as by a fine of 100 shekels, and he loses his right to divorce her, unless she herself demands a divorce (v. 19). The tradition of the Sages is that this law applies only if the husband claims that he discovered that his wife was not a virgin when the marriage was consummated, and he then brings support for his claim by producing witnesses who testify that his wife committed adultery after betrothal. The case then depends upon the witnesses. If they are found to be telling the truth, the wife is executed as an adulteress; but if they are refuted through the *hazamah* process (see above, 19b-20a), the husband is considered to have slandered his wife and he is subject to the penalties prescribed by the Torah. If the wife was not expected to show signs of virginity at the time of consummation (e.g., where she was known not to be a virgin), or if the husband does not produce witnesses to substantiate his claim, he is not subject to any penalty, even if he is found to have slandered his wife.

The law of levirate marriage appears in Deuteronomy 25:5-10. The Torah decrees that if a man dies without offspring, his wife must marry his brother or perform a ceremony called *ḥalitzah* that releases her from this obligation. Even if the wife had only been betrothed to her late husband, she must not remarry until her brother-in-law releases her or marries her himself.

Rabbi Yonah's Baraita appears below (46a), as part of a discussion of the laws governing a man who slanders his wife about her virginity. The Gemara asks whether a brother-in-law who marries the widow of his dead brother is subject to the law of the husband who slanders his wife, and replies that he is not subject to this law, citing Rabbi Yonah's Baraita.

Rambam explains that the Gemara below (46a) is referring to a case where the dead brother's marriage was not consummated. According to this explanation, the man betrothed his wife but died before the marriage was consummated, and then the brother performed a levirate marriage, and this marriage was consummated. The second husband then falsely accused his wife of not being a virgin, producing witnesses who testified that she had committed adultery while betrothed to his late brother, and the witnesses were refuted, etc. According to this explanation, Rabbi Yonah is teaching us that the brother-in-law is not subject to the penalty for slander, even though his wife's first marriage was not consummated and he had every right to expect her to be a virgin.

Rashi, however, explains that Rabbi Yonah is referring to a case where the first marriage was consummated. According to this explanation, Rabbi Yonah is teaching us that the brother-in-law is not subject to the penalty for slander, because he could not have expected his wife to have been a virgin when he consummated his marriage. If the first marriage was not consummated, however, the brother-in-law would be subject to the regular penalty, according to this explanation.

וְחָזְרָה וְאָמְרָה: פְּנוּיָה אֲנִי And she retracted and said: "I am unmarried." We have already learned in the Mishnah that a woman who declares that she was married, and then declares that she was divorced, is believed. In that case, however, the woman did not contradict herself, as it is possible that she was indeed married, and is now divorced. Therefore the Gemara asks whether the woman is believed if she contradicts herself and says that she was not married (*Ra'ah*).

The Rishonim note that it is always possible to alter or retract a statement immediately, within the time it takes to utter a greeting (תּוֹךְ כְּדֵי דִּיבּוּר). Thus it is clear that the entire discussion of our Gemara concerns a case where the retraction or alteration was not made immediately, but some time later. Support for this explanation can be found in the account (mentioned in a Baraita, below) of the important and beautiful woman who maintained her original story for some time, and retracted only when she found a suitable husband (*Shittah Mekubbetzet*).

HALAKHAH

later remarried her, and then slandered his wife, claiming that she had committed adultery during the period of their first betrothal, or if a man betrothed a woman and died, and his brother performed the levirate marriage with her and then slandered her, claiming that she committed adultery while betrothed to his brother, in both cases the husband guilty of slander is exempt from the normal penalty of lashes and a fine, and does not lose his right to divorce his wife, even if it is conclusively proved that his claims were baseless," following the Baraita of Rabbi Yonah. (*Rambam, Sefer Nashim, Hilkhot Na'arah Betulah* 3:9.)

TRANSLATION AND COMMENTARY

וְהָא [1]**But**, the Gemara objects, by her first statement **she made herself** the equivalent of **a piece of forbidden food!** The law is that when a person declares that he is certain something is forbidden, even though he may not be believed for some technical reason, he is required to follow his own strict declaration, and must treat the object as forbidden. This is called "making something a piece of forbidden food for oneself." In the case we are considering, the woman's first statement has effectively "made her a piece of forbidden food" with regard to her status, because she has declared that she is already married and forbidden to marry other men. Hence, although we have no reason apart from the woman's first statement to suppose that she is married, and she has already retracted what she said, nevertheless the retraction should not be accepted, because she is required to follow her own strict declaration and to treat herself as forbidden to marry.

אָמַר רָבָא בַּר רַב הוּנָא [2]**Rava bar Rav Huna said** in reply: The ruling in the Baraita applies, **for example, where she gave a plausible reason for her** previous **statement**. When a person declares something to be a piece of forbidden food, he is believed when he retracts his declaration, provided he gives a reasonable explanation for having declared it to be forbidden in the first place. Thus, in our case, if the woman can give a plausible reason as to why she initially declared herself to be married and then retracted, her retraction is believed.

[1]וְהָא שָׁוְיָה לְנַפְשָׁה חֲתִיכָה דְּאִיסּוּרָא!

[2]אָמַר רָבָא בַּר רַב הוּנָא: כְּגוֹן שֶׁנָּתְנָה אֲמַתְלָא לִדְבָרֶיהָ.

LITERAL TRANSLATION

[1]But she made herself a piece of prohibition!

[2]Rava bar Rav Huna said: For example, where she gave a plausible reason for her words.

LANGUAGE

אֲמַתְלָא **A plausible reason.** This word is apparently derived from the Aramaic מַתְלָא, which means "proverb," and by extension "story," or "report." Thus אֲמַתְלָא denotes an "explanation" that someone gives to account for his actions.

NOTES

שָׁוְיָה לְנַפְשָׁה חֲתִיכָה דְּאִיסּוּרָא **She made herself a piece of prohibition.** The Rishonim connect this idea with a passage above (9a), and a passage in tractate *Kiddushin* (65a). There, the Gemara states that if a person makes a declaration that limits his freedom in some way, such as where he declares that he knows a piece of food to be non-kosher, he is required to behave in accordance with his statement even if for some technical reason he is not believed. In the case in *Kiddushin*, a man declares that he is married to a certain woman, and the woman denies this. Since there are no witnesses to attest to the marriage, the man is not believed, and the woman is free to marry another man. But the man may not marry the woman's sister because he must behave in accordance with his own statement, and it is forbidden to marry two sisters.

There are two basic schools of thought about a person who renders himself "a piece of forbidden food." Both are explained at length in *Shittah Mekubbetzet* above (9a). According to one opinion, the man who declares himself married to a particular woman is believed insofar as it affects his own behavior, even though he is not believed regarding other people. According to the other opinion, "rendering oneself a piece of forbidden food" is a type of vow whereby a person obligates himself to refrain from some physical benefit. According to the latter view, the man who says that he married a certain woman is not believed at all, but is rather deemed to have said: "I hereby vow to refrain from any physical benefits that I would be forbidden to enjoy were I married to this woman." Our commentary has been written in the light of the former opinion, which is accepted by most authorities.

שֶׁנָּתְנָה אֲמַתְלָא לִדְבָרֶיהָ **Where she gave a plausible reason for her words.** The Rishonim note that not every plausible explanation is sufficient. If, for example, the woman said that she had been joking, she would not be believed (*Rambam*). *Ra'ah* explains that, although the explanation need not be proved absolutely, we must be satisfied in our own minds that it is so. *Hatam Sofer* adds that this is why, in the story of the great woman related below, Rabbi Aḥa Sar HaBirah felt the need to bring the ruling before the Great Sanhedrin at Usha, so that it should determine whether the explanation was plausible. This is also why the Baraita goes out of its way to describe the woman as unusually distinguished and beautiful, because an ordinary woman would not be believed if she were to claim that she had said she was already married merely to put off suitors.

HALAKHAH

כְּגוֹן שֶׁנָּתְנָה אֲמַתְלָא לִדְבָרֶיהָ **For example, where she gave a plausible reason for her words.** "If a woman declares that she was married, and later retracts and claims that she was not married, if she retracts her statement immediately (within the time it takes to utter a greeting), she is believed; but if not, she is not believed, unless she gives a plausible explanation for her earlier declaration, following our Gemara. Likewise, if she declared that she was married, and later betrothed herself to another man, if she gives a plausible explanation for her earlier declaration, her marriage to the other man is valid, but if not, it is doubtful, and he must give her a bill of divorce.

Rema cites *Ran* and *Ra'ah*, who rule that this law applies only if she simply said that she was already married, without mentioning the name of her husband. But if she said that she was married to a particular man, she is not believed when she retracts her statement, even if she gives a plausible explanation. *Ḥelkat Meḥokek* explains that *Ran* gave this ruling, even in a case where she retracted her statement immediately, but *Bet Shmuel* explains that this ruling applies only if she retracted after the time it takes to utter a greeting." (*Rambam, Sefer Nashim, Hilkhot Ishut* 9:31; *Shulḥan Arukh, Even HaEzer* 47:4.)

LANGUAGE

מְהוּגָּנִים **Worthy.** The general meaning of מְהוּגָּן and related terms such as הָגוּן is "worthy" or "fit." Here the expression "men who were not worthy" may have an even more negative meaning — men who are not honest, whose conduct is unworthy. Some authorities believe that the root הגן is related to the Greek εὐγενής, *eugenes*, meaning "wellborn." In this context such an interpretation seems quite apt: at first, men who were not of good family wished to marry the woman, and for that reason she rejected them.

SAGES

רַבִּי אַחָא שַׂר הַבִּירָה **Rabbi Aha Sar HaBirah.** There were apparently two scholars by this name, one of whom was a Tanna (the one mentioned here), while the other (who might have been a descendant of the first) was an Amora (cited in *Yevamot* 45a).

In both cases, it seems that the title "Sar HaBirah" ("Prince of the Castle") was passed from father to son, and was given to the head of the family in charge of the Temple Mount, which is called בִּירָה — "castle" — in Rabbinic sources.

[1]תַּנְיָא נַמִּי הָכִי: [2]״אָמְרָה: ׳אֵשֶׁת אִישׁ אֲנִי׳, וְחָזְרָה וְאָמְרָה: ׳פְּנוּיָה אֲנִי׳, [3]אֵינָהּ נֶאֱמֶנֶת. [4]וְאִם נָתְנָה אֲמַתְלָא לִדְבָרֶיהָ, נֶאֱמֶנֶת. [5]וּמַעֲשֶׂה נַמִּי בְּאִשָּׁה אַחַת גְּדוֹלָה שֶׁהָיְתָה גְּדוֹלָה בְּנוֹי, [6]וְקָפְצוּ עָלֶיהָ בְּנֵי אָדָם לְקַדְּשָׁהּ, [7]וְאָמְרָה לָהֶם: ׳מְקוּדֶּשֶׁת אֲנִי׳. [8]לְיָמִים עָמְדָה וְקִידְּשָׁה אֶת עַצְמָהּ. [9]אָמְרוּ לָהּ חֲכָמִים: ׳מָה רָאִית לַעֲשׂוֹת כֵּן?׳ [10]אָמְרָה לָהֶם: ׳בַּתְּחִלָּה, שֶׁבָּאוּ עָלַי אֲנָשִׁים שֶׁאֵינָם מְהוּגָּנִים, [11]אָמַרְתִּי: ״מְקוּדֶּשֶׁת אֲנִי״. [12]עַכְשָׁיו שֶׁבָּאוּ עָלַי אֲנָשִׁים מְהוּגָּנִים, עָמַדְתִּי וְקִדַּשְׁתִּי אֶת עַצְמִי.׳״ [13]וְזוֹ הֲלָכָה הֶעֱלָה רַבִּי אַחָא שַׂר הַבִּירָה לִפְנֵי חֲכָמִים בְּאוּשָׁא, [14]וְאָמְרוּ: ״אִם נָתְנָה אֲמַתְלָא לִדְבָרֶיהָ, נֶאֱמֶנֶת.

[15]בְּעָא מִינֵּיהּ שְׁמוּאֵל מֵרַב: [16]אָמְרָה: ״טְמֵאָה אֲנִי״, וְחָזְרָה וְאָמְרָה: ״טְהוֹרָה אֲנִי״, [17]מַהוּ?

LITERAL TRANSLATION

[1]It was also taught thus: [2]"[If] she said: 'I am a married woman,' and she retracted and said: 'I am unmarried,' [3]she is not believed. [4]But if she gave a plausible reason for her words, she is believed. [5]And it also happened with a certain great woman who was [also] great in beauty, [6]and people were eager (lit., 'jumped on her') to betroth her, [7]and she said to them: 'I am betrothed.' [8]Later (lit., 'to days'), she rose and betrothed herself. [9]The Sages said to her: 'Why did you see [fit] to do this?' [10]She said to them: 'In the beginning, when men came to me who were not worthy, [11]I said: "I am betrothed." [12]Now that worthy men have come to me, I have risen and betrothed myself.'" [13]And Rabbi Aha Sar HaBirah raised this ruling before the Sages in Usha, [14]and they said: "If she gave a plausible reason for her words, she is believed."

[15]Shmuel asked Rav: [16][If a woman] said: "I am ritually impure," and she retracted and said: "I am ritually pure," [17]what is [the law]?

TRANSLATION AND COMMENTARY

תַּנְיָא נַמִּי הָכִי [1]The Gemara now notes that the ruling of Rava bar Rav Huna — that a woman who declares herself married can withdraw her statement if she has a plausible explanation — finds support in a Baraita. **This ruling was also taught** in the following Baraita. [2]**"If a woman says: 'I am a married woman,' and** subsequently **she retracts and says: 'I am unmarried,'** [3]**she is not believed**, because she has 'made herself the equivalent of a piece of forbidden food,' as the Gemara explained above. [4]**But if she gives a plausible reason for her** previous **statement, she is believed,"** as Rava bar Rav Huna explained above. [5]The Baraita adds: **"There was also an incident** that supports this ruling. **It concerned a certain important woman who was also a great beauty,** [6]**and people were eager to betroth her.** [7]In order to rid herself of unwanted suitors, **she said to them: 'I am** already **betrothed.'** [8]Later, when a man came forward whom she was willing to marry, **she rose and betrothed herself.** The court then questioned her right to do this, since she had previously rendered herself forbidden by declaring that she was already betrothed. She replied that her previous declarations had been false. [9]But **the Sages** would not accept her repudiation of her previous declarations, and they **said to her: 'Why did you see fit to do this?** If you were not betrothed, why did you say you were?' [10]**She said to them: 'In the beginning, when men who were not worthy came to me** to propose marriage, [11]**I said: "I am** already **betrothed,"** to put them off. [12]**Now that a worthy man has come** and proposed **to me, I have risen and betrothed myself.'"** [13]The Gemara concludes that **Rabbi Aha Sar HaBirah presented this ruling before the Sages in Usha,** the seat of the Sanhedrin for part of the Mishnaic period, [14]**and they said: "If she gave a plausible reason for her words, she is believed."**

בְּעָא מִינֵּיהּ [15]The Gemara has just ruled that a person who has rendered himself forbidden by his own statement is permitted to retract his statement, provided that he gives a plausible explanation. In this connection, **Shmuel asked Rav:** [16]**If a woman said: "I am ritually impure," and she retracted and said: "I am ritually pure,"** [17]**what is the law?** According to Jewish law, when a woman menstruates, she becomes ritually impure, and until she purifies herself by immersion in a mikveh — a ritual bath — she may not have any

NOTES

אָמְרָה: טְמֵאָה אֲנִי **If a woman said: "I am ritually impure."** The Rishonim object: We have just established that if a woman claims that she was married and then changes her story, she is believed if she has a plausible explanation. But

HALAKHAH

אָמְרָה: טְמֵאָה אֲנִי **If a woman said: "I am ritually impure."** "If a wife tells her husband that she is ritually impure, and does not correct herself immediately within the time it takes to utter a greeting, but later retracts her statement,

TRANSLATION AND COMMENTARY

physical contact with her husband (Leviticus 18:19). In this situation, the woman is completely trusted to declare herself ritually pure or impure, and no proof of any kind is required. Shmuel's question is this: What if the woman declared herself ritually impure and then retracted her declaration? Is her retraction believed, or is she required to act in conformity with her original declaration, since she has "rendered herself forbidden"?

אָמַר לֵיהּ [1]Rav **said to** Shmuel in reply: **In this case too, if she gave** [22B] **a plausible explanation for her words, she is believed.**

תָּנָא מִינֵּיהּ אַרְבָּעִים זִימְנִין [2]The Gemara relates that Shmuel **reviewed** Rav's ruling **forty times** after he heard it **from him,** in order to memorize it and because he found it difficult to decide whether he could accept Rav's argument; [3]**but even** though **Shmuel** did ultimately accept it in theory, **he did not** adopt it for his personal practice. The woman who declared herself ritually impure and then retracted her declaration with a plausible explanation was Shmuel's wife. And although Shmuel did finally accept Rav's ruling that he was permitted to have sexual relations with her, he decided to wait until she had purified herself by immersion in a ritual bath.

LITERAL TRANSLATION

[1]He said to him: In this [case] too, if she gave [22B] a plausible reason for her words, she is believed. [2]He learned it from him forty times, [3]but even so Shmuel did not do a deed for himself.

[1]אֲמַר לֵיהּ: אַף בְּזוֹ, אִם נָתְנָה [22B] אֲמַתְלָא לִדְבָרֶיהָ, נֶאֱמֶנֶת. [2]תָּנָא מִינֵּיהּ אַרְבָּעִים זִימְנִין, [3]וַאֲפִילּוּ הָכִי לָא עֲבַד שְׁמוּאֵל עוּבְדָא בְּנַפְשֵׁיהּ.

RASHI

אמתלא — משל וטעם למה אמרה תחלה מקודשת אני. **אם נתנה אמתלא לדבריה נאמנת** — הואיל ונתנה אמתלא — נאמנת. **אמרה טמאה אני** — אמרה לבעלה: נדה אני. **טהורה אני** — לא הייתי נדה. **לא עבד שמואל עובדא בנפשיה** — פעם אחת אמרה לו אשתו כן, ונתנה אמתלא לדבריה — ופירש הימנה עד שטבלה.

BACKGROUND

תָּנָא מִינֵּיהּ אַרְבָּעִים זִימְנִין He learned it from him forty times. This expression, which appears several times in the Talmud, describes a situation in which a Sage hears a Halakhic teaching which is new to him, and repeats it to himself many times in order to remember it. In Shmuel's time, Rabbinic teachings were not recorded in writing but were transmitted and memorized orally, so that new material required repetition in order to fix it in the memory.

NOTES

surely adultery is a far more serious offense than intercourse with a menstruating woman! If a plausible explanation is sufficient to permit a woman to marry another man without a bill of divorce, surely it is also sufficient to allow a wife to have sexual relations with her husband!

Ritva explains that, in the case of a menstruating woman, it is possible to solve the problem without relying on the woman's explanation, simply by refraining from contact for a few days until the purification ritual is complete. But in the case of a woman who claims to be married, she is liable to be penalized for the rest of her life if we do not accept her explanation.

Rashba explains that it is hard to imagine a truly plausible explanation regarding menstruation. For if a woman has some reason other than menstruation for avoiding intercourse, she should tell her husband the truth, particularly if the husband is a righteous and understanding man like Shmuel. Therefore Shmuel felt that his wife's plausible explanation should not be accepted, but Rav ruled that even in this case the explanation is accepted.

לָא עֲבַד שְׁמוּאֵל עוּבְדָא בְּנַפְשֵׁיהּ Shmuel did not do so for himself. There are two versions of this story. One (cited by *Tosafot* and *Ritva*) is found in the Jerusalem Talmud, commenting on our Mishnah. In that version, Shmuel's wife declared one day that she had become ritually impure. The next day she came to him and said: "Now I am ritually pure." Shmuel said to her: "How could you be impure yesterday and pure today? The purification period lasts at least seven days!" She replied: "Yesterday, I was not feeling well, so I made an excuse." Shmuel then asked Rav whether a plausible explanation such as this is sufficient. Rav responded that it was, but Shmuel refused to rely on it for himself.

Shittah Mekubbetzet rejects that version of the story. He finds it hard to understand why Shmuel's wife would not simply tell her husband that she was not feeling well. He prefers another version of this story, found in the responsa of the Geonim. According to that version, Shmuel had an arrangement with his wife that he would hand her the cup of wine traditionally drunk at the end of Grace after Meals, and if she refused to drink from it, it meant that she was ritually impure (it is forbidden for a ritually impure woman to drink from the cup used by her husband). One day, Shmuel's sister paid them a visit. At the end of the blessing after the meal, Shmuel handed his wife the cup of wine, but gave nothing to his sister. Not wishing to embarrass her sister-in-law, Shmuel's wife chose not to drink from the cup, and Shmuel interpreted this as meaning that she had become ritually impure. Later, after his sister had gone

HALAKHAH

she is not believed, and she may not have physical contact with her husband. But if she gives a plausible explanation for her original statement, she is believed, and is permitted to have relations with her husband, following Rav. But if she not only declared herself impure, but began the rituals normally associated with ritual impurity — such as wearing special clothes — her explanations are not accepted and she is considered ritually impure.

Rema adds that if the husband understands the reason for the original declaration of ritual impurity, it is unnecessary for the wife to retract her statement formally. *Rema* also adds that even though the wife is believed if she gives a plausible explanation, it is permissible — and indeed virtuous — to refrain from physical contact until she purifies herself, in emulation of Shmuel." (*Rambam, Sefer Kedushah, Hilkot Issurei Bi'ah* 4:10; *Shulḥan Arukh, Yoreh De'ah* 185:3.)

[1]תָּנוּ רַבָּנַן: ״שְׁנַיִם אוֹמְרִים: ׳מֵת׳, [2]וּשְׁנַיִם אוֹמְרִים: ׳לֹא מֵת׳; שְׁנַיִם אוֹמְרִים: ׳נִתְגָּרְשָׁה׳, [3]וּשְׁנַיִם אוֹמְרִים: ׳לֹא נִתְגָּרְשָׁה׳, [4]הֲרֵי זוֹ לֹא תִּנָּשֵׂא, [5]וְאִם נִשֵּׂאת, לֹא תֵּצֵא. [6]רַבִּי מְנַחֵם בַּר יוֹסֵי אוֹמֵר: תֵּצֵא. [7]אָמַר רַבִּי מְנַחֵם בַּר יוֹסֵי: אֵימָתַי אֲנִי אוֹמֵר תֵּצֵא? [8]בִּזְמַן שֶׁבָּאוּ עֵדִים וְאַחַר כָּךְ נִשֵּׂאת. [9]אֲבָל נִשֵּׂאת וְאַחַר כָּךְ בָּאוּ עֵדִים, לֹא תֵּצֵא.״ [10]מִכְּדִי תְּרֵי וּתְרֵי נִינְהוּ,

LITERAL TRANSLATION

[1]Our Rabbis taught: "[If] two [witnesses] say: 'He died,' [2]and two say: 'He did not die'; [3][if] two say: 'She was divorced,' and two say: 'She was not divorced,' [4]she may not be married, [5]but if she is married, she need not go out. [6]Rabbi Menaḥem bar Yose says: She must go out. [7]Rabbi Menaḥem bar Yose said: When do I say she must go out? [8]When witnesses came and afterwards she was married. [9]But [if] she was married and afterwards witnesses came, she need not go out." [10]Now, since they are two and two,

RASHI

לא תצא – ולקמיה פריך: תרי ותרי נינהו! שבאו עדים – שאמרו לא מת.

TRANSLATION AND COMMENTARY

תָּנוּ רַבָּנַן [1]**Our Rabbis taught** the following Baraita: "If a man disappears, and **two witnesses** come forward and **say:** 'We have seen the husband, and **he is dead,**' [2]**and two** other witnesses come forward and contradict the first pair, **saying: 'He is not** dead'; [3]or **if** the first **two say: 'She is divorced,' and** the other **two say: 'She is not divorced,'** [4]in such a case **she is not permitted to remarry,** because her marital status is doubtful, [5]**but if she does remarry, she need not leave** her second husband. [6]However, **Rabbi Menaḥem bar Yose** disagrees with this ruling and **says:** Even if she has already remarried, **she must leave** her second husband. [7]**Rabbi Menaḥem bar Yose** explained his ruling, **saying: When do I say** that if she has remarried **she must leave** her second husband? [8]Only in a case **where** the unfavorable **witnesses came** forward before she remarried, **and she** ignored them and **remarried afterwards**, relying on the testimony of the first pair of witnesses. [9]**But if she remarried** before the second pair of witnesses came forward, when the only testimony before the court was favorable, **and only afterwards** did the second pair of **witnesses come** forward, Rabbi Menaḥem bar Yose agrees that **she need not leave** her second husband, since she had a right to rely on the first pair of witnesses at the time she remarried."

מִכְּדִי תְּרֵי וּתְרֵי נִינְהוּ [10]We see that, according to both opinions expressed in the Baraita, where the wife had a right to rely on the favorable witnesses, we do not make her leave her second husband because of doubt. The only point in dispute is whether we make her leave her second husband if she knew at the time she remarried that her status was in doubt. But the Gemara objects to this idea. **Now,** says the Gemara, how can the Baraita allow her to remain with her second husband? Surely there **are two** favorable witnesses **and two** unfavorable witnesses. We have no way of knowing whether or not she is permitted to remarry,

SAGES

רַבִּי מְנַחֵם בַּר יוֹסֵי Rabbi Menaḥem bar Yose. A Tanna of the fifth generation, Rabbi Menaḥem was the son of the famous Tanna, Rabbi Yose (the son of Ḥalafta). The teachings of Rabbi Menaḥem are found in only a few places in the Talmud and the Midrash; and it is likely that he is the Rabbi Menaḥem who is cited without any patronym in the Mishnah. From the words of the Gemara, it seems that several anonymous Mishnayot reflected his approach, and this is what earned him the appellation סְתִימְתָּאָה, meaning "the one quoted anonymously."

According to one source (*Shabbat* 118b), he also had another name, Vardimos, but other authorities believe that Vardimos was another of Rabbi Yose's sons.

NOTES

home, Shmuel's wife told him she was ritually pure, and had refused the wine in order not to embarrass her sister-in-law. Shmuel then asked Rav, etc.

In practice, the excuses cited in both versions of the story are accepted by the Halakhah as plausible explanations, in accordance with Rav's ruling. If, however, a couple prefer to emulate Shmuel, they may do so.

מִכְּדִי תְּרֵי וּתְרֵי נִינְהוּ Now, since they are two and two. The Baraita deals with a case of conflicting testimony. According to one pair of witnesses, if the woman were to remarry, she would be guilty of adultery. Nevertheless, the first Tanna rules that if the woman remarries, she need not get divorced, and even Rabbi Menaḥem bar Yose agrees with this ruling if the second pair of witnesses come forward after she has remarried. Hence the Gemara objects that we have no reason to believe one pair of witnesses more than the other. Granted that we are not certain that the second marriage is forbidden, but we must take the strict approach, because the Torah rules that people who are prepared to risk committing a transgression must offer up a special sacrifice in cases of uncertainty. The Gemara answers that we are dealing with a case where the woman and her second husband insist that they know for certain that there is no problem. Hence, since we ourselves do not know for certain, we cannot compel them to disregard what they know to be the case.

The Rishonim ask: Why is this a case of uncertainty? The Baraita appears to be dealing with a case where the

HALAKHAH

שְׁנַיִם אוֹמְרִים: מֵת If two witnesses say: "He died." "If two witnesses say that the husband is dead, and two say that he is not, the wife may not remarry; and if she does remarry, she must be divorced, since there is a real possibility that her second marriage is adulterous. If, however, she marries one of the witnesses who testified that her first husband was dead, and she herself declares that she is certain that her husband is dead, then she need not be divorced," following the Baraita and Rav Sheshet's explanation. (*Rambam, Sefer Nashim, Hilkhot Gerushin* 12:23; *Shulḥan Arukh, Even HaEzer* 17:42.)

שְׁנַיִם אוֹמְרִים: נִתְגָּרְשָׁה If two say: "She was divorced." "If two witnesses testify that a woman was divorced some time ago, and two other witnesses contradict them and

TRANSLATION AND COMMENTARY

[1] and if **someone has intercourse with her, he is subject to** the law that he must bring **a doubtful guilt-offering** as sacrifice! The law is that if a person suspects that he may unwittingly have committed a sin (in this case, unwitting adultery), which would normally require him to bring a sin-offering, he must bring a special sacrifice called "a doubtful guilt-offering" (אָשָׁם תָּלוּי). Thus we see that it is not permitted to commit an act which may be sinful, merely because there is a chance that it is permitted. Why, then, in these circumstances, where her status with regard to remarriage is unclear, is she permitted to remarry at all?

[1] הַבָּא עָלֶיהָ בְּאָשָׁם תָּלוּי קָאֵי!

LITERAL TRANSLATION

[1] he who has intercourse with her is subject to (lit., "stands in") a doubtful guilt-offering!

RASHI

באשם תלוי – כא על ספק כרת.

NOTES

woman was known to be married before the two pairs of witnesses came forward. But if so, there is a legal presumption that she has remained married, until it has been proved otherwise. Since the witnesses contradict each other, she should be considered a married woman, and her second marriage should be considered adulterous, regardless of the claims of the woman and her second husband. Indeed, such a marriage should not be subject to the doubtful guilt-offering at all, but to the penalty for adultery — death.

Tosafot answers that there is a powerful legal presumption that a woman would not remarry without making a thorough investigation. Indeed, for this reason we permit a woman who declares that her husband is dead to remarry without any proof at all. Hence the legal presumption that she is a married woman is weakened, and we are left with a balanced doubt.

Ra'ah explains that we are dealing with a case where the woman was not known to be married until the two pairs of witnesses came forward. In such a case, the legal presumption is that the woman is permitted to marry, and since the witnesses contradict each other, she should be permitted to remarry without hesitation. Nevertheless, the Rabbis forbade her to do so, in case the husband returned and the marriage was rendered adulterous; but if she had remarried already, they did not order her to be divorced. The difficulty with this explanation is that the Gemara declares that the marriage is subject to a doubtful guilt-offering, whereas according to this explanation there is only a Rabbinic prohibition. *Ra'ah* explains that the Gemara used the term "doubtful guilt-offering" to refer to the doubts that led to the Rabbinic prohibition, even though the requirement of the guilt offering was not meant literally.

Ritva notes that our Gemara would make sense according to one opinion in tractate *Yevamot* (31a), which states that when two pairs of witnesses contradict each other, legal presumptions are not applied at all, and we must treat the case as a balanced doubt. The difficulty with this explanation is that the Gemara in *Yevamot* concludes that it is only as a Rabbinic stringency that conflicting testimony is considered doubtful, whereas by Torah law legal presumptions are indeed applied. *Ritva* explains that our Gemara was not being precise when it said that the marriage would be subject to a doubtful guilt-offering. The Gemara meant that the marriage was forbidden; the term "doubtful guilt-offering" was used because this would be the law according to the first opinion in tractate *Yevamot*.

בְּאָשָׁם תָּלוּי קָאֵי Is subject to a doubtful guilt-offering. The laws governing the doubtful guilt-offering are found in Leviticus 5:17-19, and are described in detail in tractate *Keritot*. If a person unwittingly commits a sin for which the normal penalty is excision (כָּרֵת, destruction at the hands of Heaven, second only to capital punishment in severity), he must bring a female lamb or kid as a sin-offering (see Leviticus 4:27-35 and *Keritot* 2a). A sacrifice is brought only if the sin was committed unwittingly, and the sinner recognizes what he has done and is prepared to seek atonement. But if the sinner admits that he committed the sin deliberately, or if he denies his action — though witnesses testify that he did it — he does not bring a sin-offering (*Keritot* 11b). If the sinner is in doubt as to whether he unwittingly committed a sin requiring him to bring a sin-offering, he must bring a doubtful guilt-offering as a sacrifice — in this case a male ram.

For example, the Torah forbids eating certain types of fat, on penalty of excision (Leviticus 7:22-25). It follows that a person who unwittingly ate a piece of forbidden fat must bring a sin-offering. If there were two pieces of fat in front of him, one of the forbidden type and the other permitted, and he unwittingly ate one of them and threw away the other, so that he does not know whether or not he ate the

HALAKHAH

testify that she was not, she may not remarry. and if she does remarry, she must be divorced, and any children from the second marriage are doubtful *mamzerim*, because there is a real possibility that her second marriage is adulterous. If, however, she remarried one of the witnesses who said that she was divorced, and she herself insists that she was divorced, then she need not be divorced from her second husband. Even if she cannot produce a bill of divorce, this makes no difference, as it is quite normal for women to lose or discard their bills of divorce after a period of time.

"The above ruling applies only if the witnesses testify that the woman was divorced some time ago. But if they testify that she was divorced very recently, and other witnesses contradict them, the woman must produce her bill of divorce. If she cannot do so, she is presumed to be a married woman, and if she does remarry, she must be divorced, and any children from the second marriage are *mamzerim*, because we do not believe that the woman could have lost her bill of divorce so quickly. Even if she insists that she was divorced, and even if she looks her husband in the eye and says: 'You divorced me,' she is not believed, because the support she receives from the two witnesses enables her to lie brazenly to her husband's face, following Rav Assi's explanation of Rabbi Yoḥanan's statement." (*Rambam, Sefer Nashim, Hilkhot Gerushin* 12:6,7; *Shulḥan Arukh, Even HaEzer* 152:3.)

TRANSLATION AND COMMENTARY

אָמַר רַב שֵׁשֶׁת [1]**Rav Sheshet said** in reply: The Baraita is referring to a case **where, for example, she married one of the witnesses** who said that her first husband was dead. This witness claims to know for certain that she is permitted to remarry, and that the other witnesses are lying. From his point of view, there is no sin involved, and since we are lenient regarding women seeking permission to remarry, he is permitted to rely on his own testimony and to marry her.

הִיא גּוּפָהּ [2]But, the Gemara objects again, even if her new husband is certain, **she herself** has no way of knowing which pair of witnesses are telling the truth. Hence, if she remarries, she herself is **subject to** the obligation to bring **a doubtful guilt-offering.** Why, then, is she permitted to remarry?

בְּאוֹמֶרֶת [3]The Gemara replies that the Baraita is referring to a case **where she says: "I am certain** that my husband is dead." Knowing her husband, she is convinced that the only explanation for his long absence is that he is dead. Hence she is prepared to rely on the testimony that he is dead, and has no qualms about remarrying.

[1]אֲמַר רַב שֵׁשֶׁת: כְּגוֹן שֶׁנִּשֵּׂאת לְאֶחָד מֵעֵדֶיהָ.
[2]הִיא גּוּפָהּ בְּאָשָׁם תָּלוּי קַיְימָא!
[3]בְּאוֹמֶרֶת: ״בָּרִי לִי״.

LITERAL TRANSLATION

[1]Rav Sheshet said: For example, where she was married to one of her witnesses.

[2]She herself is subject to a doubtful guilt-offering!

[3]Where she says: "I am certain."

RASHI

לאחד מעדיה – שאמרו מת, דאין אשם תלוי אלא למי שלבו נוקפו, וזה אומר ברי לי. **באומרת ברי לי** – אין לבי נוקפי, שברי לי אילו היה קיים – היה בא.

NOTES

forbidden fat, he must bring a doubtful guilt-offering. There is an Amoraic dispute (*Keritot* 17b) as to whether the doubtful guilt-offering must also be brought if there was only one piece of fat and it is uncertain whether or not it was forbidden, or whether this sacrifice is brought only when we know for certain that a *possibility* existed to commit a sin.

According to the Halakhah, which follows the Sages, the doubtful guilt-offering may be brought only when it is obligatory. Rabbi Eliezer, however, maintains that it is also possible to bring such a sacrifice whenever a person suspects that he may have committed a sin, even if he has no particular reason for his suspicion. Rabbi Eliezer called this voluntary doubtful guilt-offering "the guilt-offering of the pious." Rabbi Eliezer relates that a particularly pious Sage named Bava bar Buta would bring such an offering every weekday except on the day after Yom Kippur, when he was confident that he had no sins for which to atone (*Keritot* 25a).

הַבָּא עָלֶיהָ בְּאָשָׁם תָּלוּי קָאֵי He who has intercourse with her is subject to a doubtful guilt-offering. The Rishonim ask: Why is he subject to a doubtful guilt-offering? The doubtful guilt-offering is brought only by a person who suspects that he has committed a sin unwittingly, whereas this man is deliberately doing something which may be a sin. Moreover, according to the Halakhah, the doubtful guilt-offering is brought only if there were two courses of action available — one forbidden and one permitted — and the sinner selected one of them, so that we know for certain that a possibility of committing a sin existed, even though we are not certain if a sin was actually committed. But if we do not know whether there was any opportunity at all to sin, a doubtful guilt-offering is not brought.

Talmidei Rabbenu Yonah explains that if a doubt arises because of two conflicting pairs of witnesses, these rules do not apply, and the sin is always subject to a doubtful guilt-offering. *Rosh* explains that the Gemara means that a doubtful guilt-offering is called for in principle, even if for technical reasons it is not brought.

כְּגוֹן שֶׁנִּשֵּׂאת לְאֶחָד מֵעֵדֶיהָ For example, where she was married to one of her witnesses. Other men are not permitted to marry her, because they cannot know for certain that she is permitted to remarry, and they would be subject to a doubtful guilt-offering. The witness, however, does not have to bring such an offering because he is certain that the husband is dead (*Ritva*).

The Rishonim ask: The Mishnah (*Yevamot* 25a) rules that a witness who testifies that a man is dead may not marry the man's widow, in case people suspect that he testified falsely in order to marry her. Why, then, does our Gemara permit the witness to marry this woman?

Rabbenu Ḥananel explains that our Gemara is referring to a case where there were three witnesses who testified that the husband was dead, so that there were two witnesses in addition to the one who married the widow. *Rosh* explains that there is no difference between two witnesses and three witnesses. But the Mishnah in *Yevamot* is referring to a case where the woman was given permission to remarry on the testimony of a single witness. In such a case, we do not permit the witness to marry the woman because of the suspicion this would arouse. But where two witnesses attest to the death, as in our Gemara, they are not suspected of conspiring to testify falsely, and therefore one of them is permitted to marry the widow.

בְּאוֹמֶרֶת: בָּרִי לִי Where she says: "I am certain." Our commentary follows *Rashi*, who notes that sacrifices are brought only when the sinner himself feels guilt. In particular, the doubtful guilt-offering is brought only when the person suspects that he may have committed a sin. But if a person's conscience is not troubling him, no sacrifice is brought. According to this explanation, the woman herself has no legally acceptable evidence that her husband is dead, but since she is certain — perhaps because she is confident that her husband would somehow have communicated with her if he were alive — she is not subject to the sacrifice.

Some Rishonim object to this explanation. Since two witnesses testify that the husband is not dead, the wife's

TRANSLATION AND COMMENTARY

אָמַר רַבִּי יוֹחָנָן [1]The Baraita we have just been considering made no distinction between a case where the witnesses said that the husband was dead and a case where they said that the wife was divorced. In both cases, the Sages are of the opinion that the wife may not remarry, but if she does so, she need not leave her second husband, whereas Rabbi Menaḥem bar Yose maintains that she must leave her second husband if she remarried after the second pair of witnesses came forward. The Gemara now cites an opinion that distinguishes between death and divorce: **Rabbi Yoḥanan said:** If a man has disappeared, and **two witnesses** come forward and **say:** "We saw the husband, and **he was dead,"** [2]**and two** other witnesses come forward and contradict the first pair, **saying: "He did not die,"** [3]in such a case the woman **is not permitted to remarry,** because her marital status is doubtful; [4]**but if she does remarry, she need not leave** her second husband. Rabbi Yoḥanan's statement is consistent up to this point with the view of the Sages in the Baraita we have just been considering. [5]Rabbi Yoḥanan continues: **If,** however, **two** witnesses **say: "She is divorced," and two** others **say: "She is not divorced,"** [6]**she is not permitted to remarry; and if she does remarry, she must leave** her second husband. Rabbi Yoḥanan is of the opinion that the dispensation allowing the woman to remarry in the event of conflicting testimony (where she herself and her second husband are certain that there is no impediment to her doing so) applies only to widowhood, but not to divorce. This ruling is not consistent with the view of the Sages in the Baraita we have been considering, although it can be reconciled with the viewpoint of Rabbi Menaḥem bar Yose if we assume that the second pair of witnesses came forward before she remarried.

מַאי שְׁנָא רֵישָׁא [7]The Gemara asks: **What is the difference** between **the first clause of Rabbi Yoḥanan's statement** (where he agrees with the Sages) **and the second clause** (where he agrees with Rabbi Menaḥem bar Yose)? If the woman need not leave her second husband when there is conflicting testimony about whether her first husband is dead, why should she be required to do so if there is conflicting testimony about whether her first husband has divorced her? If Rabbi Yoḥanan follows the view of the Sages in the Baraita, he should permit the woman to remain with her second husband, even in the case of divorce, and if he follows the view of Rabbi Menaḥem bar Yose, he should forbid her to remain with her second husband, even in the case of widowhood!

אָמַר אַבַּיֵי [8]**Abaye said** in reply: Rabbi Yoḥanan's statement should be **explained as referring to one**

[1]אָמַר רַבִּי יוֹחָנָן: שְׁנַיִם אוֹמְרִים: ״מֵת״, [2]וּשְׁנַיִם אוֹמְרִים: ״לֹא מֵת״, [3]הֲרֵי זוֹ לֹא תִּנָּשֵׂא, [4]וְאִם נִשֵּׂאת, לֹא תֵּצֵא. [5]שְׁנַיִם אוֹמְרִים: ״נִתְגָּרְשָׁה״, וּשְׁנַיִם אוֹמְרִים: ״לֹא נִתְגָּרְשָׁה״, [6]הֲרֵי זוֹ לֹא תִּנָּשֵׂא, וְאִם נִשֵּׂאת, תֵּצֵא. [7]מַאי שְׁנָא רֵישָׁא וּמַאי שְׁנָא סֵיפָא? [8]אָמַר אַבַּיֵי: תַּרְגְּמָהּ בְּעֵד אֶחָד.

LITERAL TRANSLATION

[1]Rabbi Yoḥanan said: [If] two [witnesses] say: "He died," [2]and two say: "He did not die," [3]she may not be married, [4]but if she was married, she need not go out. [5][If] two say: "She was divorced," and two say: "She was not divorced," [6]she may not be married, and if she was married, she must go out.

[7]What is the difference in the first clause and what is the difference in the last clause?

[8]Abaye said: Explain it [as referring] to one witness.

RASHI

תרגמה — להא דרבי יוחנן. בעד אחד — ולאו שנים איתמר, אלא עד אומר כו׳ ועד אומר כו׳.

NOTES

own feelings are irrelevant. We have a clear-cut case of two against two, and the woman must be presumed to be married until it is proved otherwise. These Rishonim explain that the woman is certain for the same reason as the first pair of witnesses are certain — because she herself saw her husband's dead body (*Ra'ah*, *Ran*, *Ritva*). But this explanation is difficult to accept. The law is that a wife who declares that she has seen her husband's dead body is believed without further testimony, and is permitted to remarry. Why, then, are we concerned with the witnesses' testimony at all? And why does the Baraita permit the woman to remain with her second husband only if she has already remarried? She should be permitted to remarry without any restriction!

Ra'ah explains that the law that we believe a woman who testifies that her husband is dead applies only where two witnesses do not testify against her. But if two witnesses testify against her — even if two other witnesses testify in her favor — her own evidence is of no value, and she may not remarry. *Ritva* explains that the presumption that a woman would never lie about her husband's death applies only if two witnesses do not testify in her favor. But if she has the support of two witnesses, we fear that she may not have investigated the matter thoroughly, relying instead on the witnesses. Therefore her own evidence is of no value, and her right to remarry depends entirely on the credibility of the witnesses.

HALAKHAH

בְּעֵד אֶחָד **As referring to one witness.** "If a single witness testifies that a woman's husband is dead, she may remarry.

TRANSLATION AND COMMENTARY

witness rather than two. Instead of reading: "If two witnesses said...and two witnesses said...," it should read: "If one witness said the husband was dead and one witness said he was alive, she may not remarry but she need not leave her second husband; but if one witness said she was divorced and one witness said she was not, she must leave her second husband." According to Abaye, Rabbi Yoḥanan would agree that if two witnesses come forward on each side, no distinction is made between death and divorce, and according to the Sages the woman may remain with her second husband, whereas according to Rabbi Menaḥem bar Yose she may not. But if only one witness comes forward on each side, the woman may remain with her second husband in the case of death, but not in the case of divorce. Abaye now explains why there is a difference between death and divorce if there is only one witness on either side. Normally, at least two witnesses are needed to give effective testimony; the evidence of a single witness is not accepted as proof. [1]However, **if** a woman claims that her husband is dead, and asks for permission to remarry, and **one witness** comes forward and **says**: "Her husband is indeed **dead,"** [2]**the Rabbis believed him as** if he were **two** witnesses, and permitted the woman to remarry without further proof. The woman's own strong conviction, coupled with her awareness of the terrible consequences she is likely to face if her husband returns alive, give the single witness's testimony added weight.

וְכִדְעוּלָּא [3]Abaye continues: My explanation **is in accordance with** the following statement of **Ulla.** [4]**For Ulla said:** In those exceptional cases **where the Torah believed one witness,** [5]we treat the matter **as if there were two** witnesses who testified about it. Hence, if another single witness subsequently comes forward and contradicts the first witness, he is considered a single witness contradicting two witnesses, and his evidence is rejected.

[1]עֵד אֶחָד אוֹמֵר: ״מֵת״, [2]הֵימְנוּהוּ רַבָּנַן כְּבֵי תְרֵי. [3]וְכִדְעוּלָּא. [4]דְּאָמַר עוּלָּא: כָּל מָקוֹם שֶׁהֶאֱמִינָה תּוֹרָה עֵד אֶחָד, [5]הֲרֵי כָּאן שְׁנַיִם.

LITERAL TRANSLATION

[1][If] one witness says: "He died," [2]the Rabbis believed him as two.

[3]And [this is] in accordance with Ulla. [4]For Ulla said: Wherever the Torah believed one witness, [5][it is as if] there are two here.

RASHI

הימנוהו רבנן כבתרי – לומר מת, כדאמרינן ביבמות ב״האשה״: מתוך חומר שהחמרת עליה בסופה – הקלתה עליה בתחלתה.

NOTES

כָּל מָקוֹם שֶׁהֶאֱמִינָה תּוֹרָה עֵד אֶחָד **Wherever the Torah believed one witness.** The Mishnah (*Yevamot* 122a) rules that if a husband disappears, his wife may remarry if one witness comes forward to testify that he is dead. Moreover, for this purpose we accept testimony even from women, slaves, and maidservants, and even hearsay testimony. The wife herself is also believed, if she testifies that she knows that her husband is dead (114b).

The Gemara explains (ibid., 87b-88a) that the Rabbis feared that if they insisted on the normal rules of evidence, many women would be permanently unable to remarry. (According to Jewish law, it is impossible to dissolve a marriage unless the husband personally orders a bill of divorce to be delivered, or we are certain that he is dead.) Therefore they imposed extremely severe penalties on any woman who remarried improperly — even as the result of an honest mistake — and they also relaxed the rules of evidence, arguing that the wife herself will be so afraid of the consequences if her first husband returns alive that she will not remarry unless she has investigated the matter thoroughly and is certain that her husband is dead.

From the language of the Gemara in *Yevamot*, it would appear that the relaxation of the regular rules of evidence is a Rabbinic institution, and that by Torah law a wife cannot remarry unless two qualified witnesses testify that they personally saw the husband's dead body. Many Rishonim, including *Rashi*, explain the Gemara this way.

Some Rishonim explain that the rule that a single witness is believed is in fact a Torah law (*Ra'ah*, *Ritva* in *Yevamot*). They explain that we are absolutely confident that the husband is dead, because the Rabbis arranged matters so that the woman would get married only after

HALAKHAH

If, before the court permits her to remarry, another witness comes forward to contradict the first witness and claims that her husband is still alive, she may not remarry; and if she does so, she must leave her second husband. If, however, the second witness comes forward only after the court has permitted her to remarry on the basis of the first witness's testimony, she does not lose her right to remarry, because the first witness who testified that the husband was dead is believed as if he were two witnesses, and hence cannot be contradicted by another single witness, following Abaye's explanation of Rabbi Yoḥanan's statement.

"Nevertheless, *Rema* rules, following *Rosh*, that if she has not yet remarried before the second witness comes forward, she should not do so, because, following Rav Assi's maxim, it appears scandalous. *Ḥelkat Meḥokek*, however, rules that Rav Assi's maxim is only a suggestion, not an obligatory ruling, and *Kesef Mishneh* explains that *Rambam* disagrees with *Rosh*, and rules that according to the Halakhah, which rejects Abaye's explanation, Rav Assi's maxim does not apply at all." (*Rambam, Sefer Nashim, Hilkhot Gerushin* 12:18; *Shulḥan Arukh, Even HaEzer* 17:37.)

TRANSLATION AND COMMENTARY

וְהַאי דְּקָאָמַר [1]Abaye now explains how Ulla's principle can be applied to Rabbi Yoḥanan's statement: In the first clause, one witness testified that the husband was dead, and we accepted his testimony because the Rabbis accept the testimony of a single witness for this purpose. Therefore, his testimony must be treated as though it had been given by two witnesses, in accordance with Ulla's principle. Hence, when **the other** witness comes forward and **says**: "Her husband **did not die,"** we must reject his testimony, because he **is only one** witness, [2]**and the words of one** witness **have no significance in a situation where there are two**, as Ulla ruled. This is why Rabbi Yoḥanan ruled that the woman is considered a widow, and if she has already married a second time, she need not leave her second husband.

אִי הָכִי [3]But, the Gemara interjects, **if so,** why did Rabbi Yoḥanan permit the woman to remain married only if she went ahead and remarried without receiving explicit permission to do so from the court? Rabbi Yoḥanan should **even** have allowed the woman to remarry ***ab initio***! According to Abaye, the testimony of the second witness is to be rejected completely, in accordance with Ulla's principle. Why, then, did Rabbi Yoḥanan rule that the woman should not remarry?

מִשּׁוּם דְּרַב אַסִּי [4]The Gemara answers: Even though the woman was indeed technically permitted to remarry, in accordance with Ulla's principle, Rabbi Yoḥanan said that she should not do so **because of** the following **statement of Rav Assi.** [5]**For Rav Assi said:** Whenever an action appears scandalous, even if it is technically permitted, it is better to refrain from doing it, in accordance with the verse (Proverbs 4:24): **"Remove from yourself a twisted mouth, and perverse lips put far from yourself."** Scandalous behavior should be avoided, even if it is not forbidden by the letter of the law. This woman should not remarry, for ordinary people may not be familiar with Ulla's principle, and may speculate that the marriage is an adulterous union.

סֵיפָא [6]Abaye has so far explained the first clause of Rabbi Yoḥanan's statement in accordance with Ulla's principle. **In the last clause,** by contrast, if we are to explain it as referring to single witnesses, we must assume that **one witness said: "She was divorced," and** the other **witness said: "She was not divorced."**

[1]וְהַאי דְּקָאָמַר: ״לֹא מֵת״, הָוֵה לֵיהּ חַד, [2]וְאֵין דְּבָרָיו שֶׁל אֶחָד בִּמְקוֹם שְׁנַיִם.
[3]אִי הָכִי, אֲפִילּוּ לְכַתְּחִלָּה נַמִּי!
[4]מִשּׁוּם דְּרַב אַסִּי. [5]דְּאָמַר רַב אַסִּי: ״הָסֵר מִמְּךָ עִקְּשׁוּת פֶּה, וּלְזוּת שְׂפָתַיִם הַרְחֵק מִמֶּךָּ״.
[6]סֵיפָא, עֵד אֶחָד אוֹמֵר: ״נִתְגָּרְשָׁה״, וְעֵד אֶחָד אוֹמֵר:

LITERAL TRANSLATION

[1]And the one who said: "He did not die," is one, [2]and the words of one are not in place of two.

[3]If so, even *ab initio* too!

[4]Because of [the saying of] Rav Assi. [5]For Rav Assi said: "Remove from yourself a twisted mouth, and perverse lips put far from yourself."

[6][In] the last clause, one witness says: "She was divorced," and one witness says:

RASHI

אפילו לכתחלה נמי – תינסח. **דרב אסי** – ביבמות, בפרק שני.

NOTES

a thorough investigation, and because we are dealing with a matter in which the single witness is afraid to testify falsely in case the husband returns and exposes his falsehood. Hence the woman is permitted to remarry by Torah law.

Rashi's interpretation is supported by the language of the Gemara in *Yevamot*, which describes this law as a Rabbinic institution. But *Ritva* explains that the Gemara may perhaps be referring to the principle that the Rabbis have the authority to interpret the Torah. *Ritva*'s interpretation is supported by the language of the Gemara here, which describes our case as one where *the Torah* believed one witness. But *Ritva* explains that proponents of the other viewpoint could argue that our Gemara is employing a phrase borrowed from other places where the Torah did believe one witness (e.g., regarding the kashrut of food). Indeed, the source of Ulla's statement (*Sotah* 31b) refers specifically to such a case.

הֲרֵי כָּאן שְׁנַיִם There are two here. According to Ulla, in those rare instances where a single witness is sufficient, if two single witnesses contradict each other, we accept the testimony of the first one to appear before us. Ulla's rule applies only if we have issued a ruling in accordance with the first witness's testimony before the second witness comes forward, but if the second witness comes forward with conflicting testimony while we are still considering the testimony of the first witness, we do not favor one over the other (*Sotah* 31b). Likewise, the first witness is only considered to be *like* two witnesses, but if two witnesses come forward to contradict him, we accept the two and reject the words of the one, even though he came forward first and we originally accepted him as two (*Yevamot* 117b).

HALAKHAH

עֵד אֶחָד אוֹמֵר: נִתְגָּרְשָׁה One witness says: "She was divorced." "If a woman is known to be married, and two witnesses come forward, one testifying that she has been divorced and the other that she has not, she may not remarry; and if she does remarry, she must be divorced, since the woman is presumed to be married until proved otherwise.

"If the woman is thought to be single, and two witnesses come forward, one testifying that she has been married and divorced and the other that she has been married and not

TRANSLATION AND COMMENTARY

Now, although the Rabbis were lenient regarding testimony about a husband's death, and accepted the evidence of one witness, they were not lenient regarding testimony about divorce. To prove that a woman known to be married has been divorced, two witnesses must testify. Now, if two single witnesses agree about one point and disagree about another, we accept the point in agreement as having been attested by two witnesses. [1] In this case, **both** witnesses **testified that the woman was married.** Hence we already know, on the evidence of two witnesses, that the woman was originally married, and we therefore need two witnesses to attest that she was later divorced. [2] **But the one witness who said: "She is divorced," is** only **one.** [3] Hence we must reject his testimony, because **the words of one** witness **have no significance if** the woman's status has been determined on the basis of the evidence of **two** witnesses.

"לֹא נִתְגָּרְשָׁה". [1] תַּרְוַיְיהוּ בְּאֵשֶׁת אִישׁ קָמְסָהֲדֵי, [2] וְהַאי דְּקָאָמַר: "נִתְגָּרְשָׁה", הֲוָה לֵיהּ חַד, [3] וְאֵין דְּבָרָיו שֶׁל אֶחָד בִּמְקוֹם שְׁנַיִם.

LITERAL TRANSLATION

"She was not divorced." [1] Both are testifying about a married woman, [2] and the one who said: "She was divorced," is one, [3] and the words of one are not in place of two.

RASHI

תרוייהו באשת איש קא מסהדי – שניהן מעידין שאשת איש היתה.

NOTES

וְעֵד אֶחָד אוֹמֵר: לֹא נִתְגָּרְשָׁה And one witness says: "She was not divorced." In this passage, it is important to bear in mind the Halakhic principle that all changes in marital status must be attested by two qualified witnesses (אֵין דָּבָר שֶׁבְּעֶרְוָה פָּחוֹת מִשְּׁנַיִם) — except in those few cases (such as the death of the husband, considered above) where the Rabbis were lenient (*Yevamot* 88a). Hence, if a woman is presumed unmarried and a single witness testifies that she is married — or if a woman is presumed to be married and a single witness testifies that she is divorced — the witness is not believed.

Accordingly, the Rishonim explain that our Gemara cannot be referring to a woman who is known to be married, because in such a case the single witness who testifies that she has been divorced would not be believed under any circumstances — even if he were not contradicted — and there would be no point in introducing the other witness. Rather, we must be referring to a woman of unknown status, who was presumed unmarried until the two witnesses both testified that she was married, after which she was presumed married. Thus the one witness who testified that she was divorced would have been believed if he had come on his own, but since we now presume that the woman is married, he is not believed, because two witnesses are needed to prove that a married woman has been divorced (*Tosafot*, *Ramban*, and others).

תַּרְוַיְיהוּ בְּאֵשֶׁת אִישׁ קָמְסָהֲדֵי Both are testifying about a married woman. The assumption underlying Abaye's explanation is that when two witnesses contradict each other, we consider the points on which they are in agreement as having been attested by two witnesses. The Rishonim ask: In tractate *Shevuot* (47b) there is a dispute between Rav Huna and Rav Ḥisda concerning two pairs of witnesses who contradict each other. Rav Ḥisda rules that we presume both pairs to be false witnesses, and disqualify all four witnesses from giving testimony in the future; whereas Rav Huna rules that we presume both pairs to be qualified until proved otherwise, and allow both pairs to testify in the future. The Halakhah follows Rav Huna, but even Rav Huna agrees that a mixed pair, made up of one witness from each pair, is disqualified, because one of its members definitely gave false testimony in the past. How, then, can we form a pair from the two conflicting witnesses in our Gemara regarding the points on which they agree? At least one of them definitely gave false testimony, and is disqualified from testifying again!

Tosafot explains that we are referring to a case where it is possible that the "false" witness made an honest mistake, such as where both witnesses agreed that a bill of divorce was delivered, but one testified that there was a flaw in the divorce procedure. *Ra'ah* rejects this explanation, arguing that it is farfetched; but *Ritva* notes that experience shows that this is the type of conflicting testimony that normally arises in cases of divorce.

Ramban explains that technically the witnesses are indeed rejected, but in practice we believe their testimony that the woman is married, not merely because of their testimony, but because we are referring to a case where the woman herself also claimed that she was married and divorced. *Ramban* argues that the "mouth that forbade" argument does not apply where there are witnesses — even where they are disqualified because of contradictions between them. Hence the woman is believed if she claims that she is married, because she is "rendering herself forbidden," but she is not believed if she claims that she is divorced, because her claim does not have the support of the "mouth that forbade" argument. *Ritva* objects to this explanation, arguing that from the wording of the Gemara

HALAKHAH

divorced, there is a dispute among the authorities. *Rambam* rules that we accept the combined testimony of the two witnesses that she has been married, and since only one witness testifies that she has been divorced, he is not believed, because one witness has no standing against the testimony of two witnesses, following Abaye. Hence *Rambam* rules that this woman, too, must not remarry, and if she does remarry, she must be divorced. *Shulḥan Arukh*, however, rules that the testimony of the conflicting witnesses can be combined only if they contradict each other on a point that is subject to human error. But if the two witnesses contradict each other outright, their testimony cannot be combined, and if the woman was thought to be single until the witnesses came forward, she may even remarry *ab initio*." (*Rambam*, *Sefer Nashim*, *Hilkhot Gerushin* 12:9; *Shulḥan Arukh, Even HaEzer* 152:5.)

LITERAL TRANSLATION

[1] Rava said: [2] In fact, they are two and two, [3] and Rabbi Yoḥanan accepted (lit., "saw") the words of Rabbi Menaḥem bar Yose about divorce, but did not accept [them] about death. [4] What is the reason? [5] [In the case of] death, she cannot contradict him; [6] [in the case of] divorce, she can contradict him.

[7] But would she be so impudent?

[1] רָבָא אֲמַר: [2] לְעוֹלָם תְּרֵי וּתְרֵי נִינְהוּ, [3] וְרָאָה רַבִּי יוֹחָנָן דְּבָרָיו שֶׁל רַבִּי מְנַחֵם בַּר יוֹסֵי בְּגֵרוּשִׁין, וְלֹא רָאָה בְּמִיתָה. [4] מַאי טַעְמָא? [5] מִיתָה, אֵינָהּ יְכוֹלָה מַכְחַשְׁתּוֹ; [6] גֵּרוּשִׁין, יְכוֹלָה מַכְחַשְׁתּוֹ.

[7] וּמִי חֲצִיפָה כּוּלֵּי הַאי?

RASHI

מיתה אינה יכולה מכחשתו — אם יבא בעלה אינה יכולה לומר "מת אתה", הלכך אי לאו דברי לה שמת — מירתתא ולא מינסבא. **גירושין יכולה מכחשתו** — אם יבא ויאמר "לא גירשתיך" היא תאמר "גירשתני". הלכך, אי שריא לה — סמכה אהכחשה, ומינסבא על פי עדים הללו מספק, ולא מירתתא למידק שפיר.

TRANSLATION AND COMMENTARY

רָבָא אֲמַר [1] **Rava** disagreed with Abaye's interpretation of Rabbi Yoḥanan's ruling and **said:** It is not necessary to amend Rabbi Yoḥanan's statement in this way. [2] **In fact,** Rabbi Yoḥanan was referring to a case where **there were two** witnesses who testified that the woman's husband was dead or that the couple were divorced, **and two** who testified that the woman was still married, in accordance with the straightforward meaning of his statement. As for the question we asked at the beginning of this passage — why Rabbi Yoḥanan distinguished between death and divorce, issuing a ruling consistent with the view of the Sages in the former and a ruling consistent with the view of Rabbi Menaḥem bar Yose in the latter — [3] the reason is simply that **Rabbi Yoḥanan accepted the viewpoint of Rabbi Menaḥem bar Yose about divorce, but not about death.** Rabbi Menaḥem bar Yose disagreed with the Sages about both cases, but Rabbi Yoḥanan ruled in favor of Rabbi Menaḥem bar Yose in the case of divorce and in favor of the Sages in the case of death. [4] Rava asks rhetorically: **What is the reason?** Why would Rabbi Yoḥanan rule in one way regarding death and in another regarding divorce? Rava answers: We have already seen that the Baraita is referring to a case where the woman claims that she is certain that her husband is indeed dead, or that she is divorced; otherwise, she would not have the right to rely on the testimony of the one pair of witnesses, because she would be subject to a doubtful guilt-offering. The reason why we are so lenient regarding the woman is because her strong convictions carry weight, since she is aware of the terrible consequences she is likely to face if her husband returns. Hence, she would not lie or take precipitate action were she not absolutely certain. [5] But in this matter there is a difference between death and divorce: **In the case of death,** the woman is very frightened indeed of the consequences of error, for if her husband returns **she cannot contradict him** and claim that he is dead, and any lie she may have told will inevitably be exposed. [6] By contrast, **in the case of divorce,** the woman is less frightened of having her lies exposed, for if her husband returns and denies divorcing her, **she can** always **contradict him** and continue to maintain that she was divorced. Hence, she may not be fully aware of the consequences she is liable to face, and her strong conviction does not carry the same weight as it did in the case of death. Nevertheless, the Sages ruled that even in a case of divorce the woman need not leave her second husband, since her strong convictions still carry some weight, but Rabbi Yoḥanan felt that the Halakhah should follow Rabbi Menaḥem bar Yose in this matter.

וּמִי חֲצִיפָה כּוּלֵּי הַאי [7] The assumption underlying Rava's explanation is that the woman may be lying about being divorced, and intends to adhere to her story should her husband return. **But,** the Gemara

NOTES

it is clear that the reason we consider the woman to be married is because we believe the witnesses, not the woman.

Rashba explains the Gemara literally, and rejects the objection from tractate *Shevuot.* A pupil of *Rashba* elaborates on his explanation, arguing that conflicting witnesses are disqualified only from testifying in the future, but the validity of their past testimony is not affected. The two conflicting witnesses in our passage both said that the woman was married, and then disagreed as to whether she was divorced. Hence they are believed regarding this point.

מִיתָה אֵינָהּ יְכוֹלָה מַכְחַשְׁתּוֹ In the case of death, she cannot contradict him. According to Rava, the difference between death and divorce is that if a woman claims that her husband is dead and he returns alive, her claim can no longer be sustained, but if she claims that she was divorced and the husband denies it, it is a case of her word against his. The Jerusalem Talmud also cites Rabbi Yoḥanan's statement, and explains the distinction between death and divorce along the same lines as Rava does. The Rishonim explain that the reasoning behind Rava's distinction is that if the woman knows that if she makes a mistake there will be no way for her to justify herself, she will make a thorough investigation and will not remarry if there is even the slightest room for doubt; but where the consequences of error are not quite so obvious, she may be a little less careful, and may rely on the favorable witnesses, even where she is slightly doubtful (*Rashi, Talmidei Rabbenu Yonah*).

SAGES

רַב הַמְנוּנָא Rav Hamnuna. A Babylonian Amora of the second generation, Rav Hamnuna was a student of Rav. Another Amora of the same name lived in the next generation and was a student of Rav Ḥisda.
The Rav Hamnuna referred to here was one of the students of Rav who remained in his House of Study and continued the tradition of "the School of Rav," so that it is said that the expression "the School of Rav" (בֵּי רַב) refers to Rav Hamnuna.

TRANSLATION AND COMMENTARY

objects, **would** the woman **dare** to lie about such matters to her husband's face? [1]**Surely Rav Hamnuna said:** If a **woman said to her husband's** face: **"You divorced me," she is believed,** [2]**because there is a presumption that a woman would not dare to say this to her husband's face** if it were not true! How, then, could this woman be planning to adhere to her story when her husband returns?

הָנֵי מִילֵּי [3]The Gemara answers: Rav Hamnuna's ruling **applies** only **where there are no witnesses who support** the woman's account. In such a case, she would not be able to look her husband in the eye and say: "You divorced me," if it were not true. [4]**But where there are witnesses who support her** account, [5]**she would certainly dare** to lie to her husband's face. Hence, when two sets of witnesses disagree about whether the husband is dead, Rabbi Yoḥanan rules in favor of the Sages. He argues that we rely on the woman's own strong convictions, since she knows that lying is useless. But in a case of divorce, Rabbi Yoḥanan rules in favor of Rabbi Menaḥem bar Yose because we are concerned that the woman may be brazenly lying.

רַב אַסִי אָמַר [6]**Rav Assi** agreed with Rava that Rabbi Yoḥanan's statement should not be amended, but he did not accept Rava's explanation that Rabbi Yoḥanan was ruling in favor of the first Tanna in the case of death and in favor of Rabbi Menaḥem bar Yose in the case of divorce. Rather, he **said,** Rabbi Yoḥanan rules in favor of the first Tanna in both cases, and ordinarily he would permit the woman to remain with her second husband, provided she insists that she knows that her first husband is dead or that she was divorced. But Rabbi Yoḥanan was referring to a special case, [7]**where, for example, the** first pair of **witnesses said:** "The husband **died** just **now,"** or: **"He divorced her** just **now,"** and the second pair of witnesses contradicted them. For where the witnesses said: "Just now," the first Tanna would also distinguish between death and divorce, and would agree with the viewpoint of Rabbi Menaḥem bar Yose in the case of divorce.

[1]וְהָאָמַר רַב הַמְנוּנָא: הָאִשָּׁה שֶׁאָמְרָה לְבַעְלָהּ: ״גֵּרַשְׁתַּנִי״, נֶאֱמֶנֶת, [2]חֲזָקָה אֵין אִשָּׁה מְעִיזָּה פָּנֶיהָ בִּפְנֵי בַּעְלָהּ! [3]הָנֵי מִילֵּי הֵיכָא דְּלֵיכָּא עֵדִים דְּקָא מְסַיְּיעֵי לַהּ; [4]אֲבָל הֵיכָא דְּאִיכָּא עֵדִים דְּקָא מְסַיְּיעֵי לַהּ, [5]מְעִיזָּה וּמְעִיזָּה.
[6]רַב אַסִי אָמַר: [7]כְּגוֹן דְּאָמְרִי עֵדִים: ״עַכְשָׁיו מֵת״, ״עַכְשָׁיו גֵּירְשָׁהּ״.

LITERAL TRANSLATION

[1]But surely Rav Hamnuna said: The woman who said to her husband: "You divorced me," is believed, [2][because there is] a presumption that a woman is not [so] impudent to her husband's face!

[3]These words [apply] where there are no witnesses who support her; [4]but where there are witnesses who support her, [5]she would certainly be [so] impudent (lit., "she is brazen and is brazen").

[6]Rav Assi said: [7]For example, where the witnesses say: "He died now," "he divorced her now."

RASHI

עכשיו מת – היום.

HALAKHAH

הָאִשָּׁה שֶׁאָמְרָה לְבַעְלָהּ: גֵּרַשְׁתַּנִי The woman who said to her husband: "You divorced me." "If a woman says to her husband's face that he has divorced her, she is believed, since a woman would not dare to make such a statement to her husband's face if it were not true. Similarly, if a woman who was presumed to be married betrothed herself to another man in her first husband's presence, it is considered the equivalent of a divorce declaration, because a woman would not dare to marry someone else in the presence of her previous husband, if she were not already divorced. *Rambam* rules that the betrothal is completely valid. *Rema*, however, cites *Ran* (who rules that she is not fully believed and therefore not allowed to remain with her second husband) and *Haggahot Maimoniyot* (who rules that she is not entitled to collect her ketubah from her first husband). She is believed only to the extent that she must receive a bill of divorce from her second husband. *Rema* also cites *Yad Ramah*, who rules that even *Rambam* would agree that in our time the woman is not fully believed, since people are now much more brazen than they used to be." (*Rambam, Sefer Nashim, Hilkhot Ishut* 4:13 and *Hilkhot Gerushin* 12:4; *Shulḥan Arukh, Even HaEzer* 17:2.)

הֵיכָא דְּאִיכָּא עֵדִים דְּקָא מְסַיְּיעֵי לַהּ Where there are witnesses who support her. "A woman is believed if she says to her husband's face that he has divorced her, because she would not dare to say this if it were not true (see previous entry). However, this law applies only if there are no witnesses who support her claim. But if two witnesses testify that the woman has been divorced and two other witnesses contradict them, the woman's claim has no weight, even if it is made to her husband's face, because the support of the witnesses gives her added courage, following Rava. *Bet Shmuel* notes that *Tur* rules this way even if only one witness testifies that she is divorced and one testifies that she is not; however, *Rosh* rules that this law applies only where two witnesses testify for each side, but where there is only one witness for each side, her claim is believed." (*Rambam, Sefer Nashim, Hilkhot Gerushin* 12:6; *Shulḥan Arukh, Even HaEzer* 17:2.)

TRANSLATION AND COMMENTARY

מִיתָה 1Rav Assi explains: In the case of **death,** it makes no difference whether the witnesses say that the husband died just now or that he died some time ago, since in any case **there is no way to clarify** the matter one way or the other. Hence the first Tanna does not require the woman to leave her second husband, even if she married him after the second pair of witnesses came forward, because we assume that the woman would not remarry without investigating the matter most carefully (as we explained above). 2In the case of **divorce,** by contrast, it makes a difference if the witnesses say that the divorce took place very recently or it took place some time ago, because **there is a way to clarify** the matter if they testify that she was divorced recently. 3**For we** can **say to her: "If it is true that it happened in this way,** and you were divorced recently, 4**show us your bill of divorce."** Although a woman is not required to keep her bill of divorce indefinitely, nevertheless if she claims to have been divorced recently and cannot show us her bill of divorce, her claim is very suspicious. Hence we cannot rely on the woman in this case, even if she says she is certain, and since there is conflicting testimony she is not permitted to remarry.

תָּנוּ רַבָּנַן 5The Gemara now cites another Baraita on a related topic: **Our Rabbis taught** the following Baraita: **"If two witnesses** come forward and **say:** 'This woman **has** already **been betrothed** to another man,' 6**and two** other witnesses come forward and contradict the first pair, **saying: 'She has not been betrothed,'** in such a **case she may not marry,** since her marital status is doubtful; 7**but if she does marry, she need not leave** her husband, because one of the pairs of witnesses testified that she was permitted to marry, and we do not make a woman leave her husband because of doubt, if she herself is certain, as we explained above. 8**If,** however, **two** witnesses agree that she was married to another man, but they **say: 'She has been divorced,'** and **two** other witnesses **say: 'She has not been divorced,'** 9**she is not permitted to remarry; and if she does remarry, she must leave** her second husband, as the dispensation mentioned in the first clause does not apply to divorce."

1מִיתָה, לֵיכָּא לְבֵרוּרָה; 2גֵּירוּשִׁין, אִיכָּא לְבֵרוּרָה. 3דְּאָמְרִינַן לָהּ: "אִם אִיתָא דְּהָכִי הֲוָה, 4אַחֲזֵי לָן גִּיטֵּיךְ". 5תָּנוּ רַבָּנַן: "שְׁנַיִם אוֹמְרִים: 'נִתְקַדְּשָׁה', 6וּשְׁנַיִם אוֹמְרִים: 'לֹא נִתְקַדְּשָׁה', הֲרֵי זוֹ לֹא תִּנָּשֵׂא, 7וְאִם נִשֵּׂאת, לֹא תֵּצֵא. 8שְׁנַיִם אוֹמְרִים: 'נִתְגָּרְשָׁה', וּשְׁנַיִם אוֹמְרִים: 'לֹא נִתְגָּרְשָׁה', 9הֲרֵי זוֹ לֹא תִּנָּשֵׂא, וְאִם נִשֵּׂאת, תֵּצֵא".

LITERAL TRANSLATION

1Death, there is no way to clarify; 2divorce, there is a way to clarify. 3For we say to her: "If it is [true] that it happened thus, 4show us your bill of divorce."

5Our Rabbis taught: "[If] two [witnesses] say: 'She was betrothed,' 6and two say: 'She was not betrothed,' she may not be married, 7but if she is married, she need not go out. 8[If] two say: 'She was divorced,' and two say: 'She was not divorced,' 9she may not be married, and if she was married, she must go out."

RASHI

ליכא לברורה — אם אמרו טבע במים, או אכלו ארי — אין אנו יכולין לברר הדברים. הלכך, לכתחלה לא תינשא, ואם ניסת — לא תצא, כרבנן, וכשניסת לאחד מעדיה. אחזי גיטיך — דכשעתא פורתא לא מהימנא למימר אירכס לי. הרי זו לא תנשא — לאחר.

NOTES

מִיתָה, לֵיכָּא לְבֵרוּרָה **Death, there is no way to clarify.** If the witnesses say that the woman was divorced very recently, we can ask her to produce her bill of divorce, but if the witnesses say that her husband died very recently, there is nothing we can do to clarify the matter. *Rashi* asks. Why do we not ask them to show us the body? *Rashi* answers that we are referring to a case where they testify that the husband drowned at sea or was eaten by a lion. *Talmidei Rabbenu Yonah* explains that it is possible that the body was taken away and can no longer be located.

Rashba notes that the argument that the woman must produce her bill of divorce, if she claims to have been divorced very recently, applies only when there are two sets of witnesses who contradict each other, so that we must rely on the woman's own investigation to clarify the doubt. But if the woman produces witnesses who testify that she was divorced and no other witnesses contradict them, they are believed — even if she is unable to produce her bill of divorce.

שְׁנַיִם אוֹמְרִים: נִתְקַדְּשָׁה **If two witnesses say: "She was betrothed."** Throughout this passage it is important to bear in mind that in Jewish law marriage is a two-stage process, and after the first stage, called *kiddushin* or *erusin*, the woman is already legally married. *Kiddushin* can be dissolved only by a bill of divorce; until such a bill is delivered, any extramarital relations are considered adulterous and are punishable by death. Following long-standing convention, we have translated *kiddushin* as "betrothal," but in reality it has nothing to do with the modern concept of betrothal.

TERMINOLOGY

תַּרְגְּמָה Explain it. The root תרגם can mean "to translate from one language to another" or "to explain something." The Talmud uses this expression when an Amora explains something, particularly a Tannaitic teaching, not according to its simple meaning but as an exceptional case, or with a change in the original language.

TRANSLATION AND COMMENTARY

מַאי שְׁנָא רֵישָׁא [23A] [1]Concerning this Baraita too, the Gemara asks: **What is the difference** between **the first clause and the last clause?** In both cases two witnesses testify that the woman is married and two testify that she is not. If the woman is not required to leave her second husband when there is contradictory testimony about her betrothal to her first husband, why should she be required to leave her second husband if there is contradictory testimony about her divorce from her first husband? If this Baraita is in accordance with the viewpoint of the Sages in the previous Baraita, it should permit the woman to remain with her second husband even in the case of divorce; and if it is in accordance with the viewpoint of Rabbi Menaḥem bar Yose, it should forbid her to remain with her second husband, even in the case of betrothal.

[23A] [1]מַאי שְׁנָא רֵישָׁא וּמַאי שְׁנָא סֵיפָא?

[2]אָמַר אַבַּיֵי: תַּרְגְּמָה בְּעֵד אֶחָד. [3]עֵד אֶחָד אוֹמֵר: "נִתְקַדְּשָׁה",

LITERAL TRANSLATION

[23A] [1]What is the difference in the first clause and what is the difference in the last clause?

[2]Abaye said: Explain it [as referring] to one witness. [3][If] one witness says: "She was betrothed,"

אָמַר אַבַּיֵי [2]**Abaye said** in reply: The Baraita should be **explained as referring to one witness**, rather than two. Instead of reading: "If two witnesses said... and two witnesses said...," it should read: "If one witness says that she has already been betrothed, and one witness says that she has not, she is not permitted to remarry, but she need not leave her second husband if she has already remarried; but if one witness says that she has been divorced and one witness says that she has not, she must leave her second husband." According to Abaye, the Baraita would agree that if two witnesses come forward on each side, no distinction is made between betrothal and divorce, and according to the Sages the woman is permitted to remain with her second husband, whereas according to Rabbi Menaḥem bar Yose she is not. But if only one witness comes forward on each side, the woman is permitted to remain with her second husband in the case of betrothal but not in the case of divorce. Abaye now explains why there is a difference between betrothal and divorce if there is only one witness on either side: In most questions involving a change in marital status, two witnesses are required. Accordingly, in order to prove that a woman known to be unmarried is in fact betrothed or that a woman known to be married is in fact divorced, two witnesses must testify. Now, when two individual witnesses agree about one point and disagree about another, we accept that the point they agree about has been attested by two witnesses. In this case, [3]**if one witness** says: **"She was**

NOTES

מַאי שְׁנָא רֵישָׁא What is the difference in the first clause? The Baraita considers two cases. In the first case, two witnesses say that an apparently unmarried woman was in fact married, and two other witnesses contradict them, and the Baraita rules that the woman is considered unmarried. In the second case, two witnesses say that an apparently married woman was in fact divorced and two other witnesses contradict them, and the Baraita rules that the woman is considered married. The Rishonim ask: Why does the Gemara object to the Baraita's distinction? There is an obvious difference between the two cases. In the first clause, we are dealing with an unmarried woman, and the contradictory testimony concerns her marriage. In the second clause we are dealing with a woman who is presumed to be married, and the contradictory testimony concerns her divorce. In both cases, since we cannot resolve the dispute between the witnesses, we presume that the woman retains her previous status until it is proved otherwise. Hence, in the first clause we presume that the woman has not been married, and in the second that she has not been divorced. Why does the Gemara have to resort to a textual emendation to explain this Baraita?

The Rishonim note that the approach of our Gemara conforms to an opinion cited in tractate *Yevamot* (31a) that when two pairs of witnesses disagree, we treat the matter as doubtful by Torah law, and do not attempt to resolve it by applying a legal presumption (*Tosefot Rid*). The difficulty with this explanation is that at the end of the passage in *Yevamot* the Gemara concludes that we treat conflicting testimony as doubtful only by Rabbinic decree, whereas by Torah law we do apply legal presumptions. *Rashba* explains that our Gemara is asking whether this Baraita can be explained according to both opinions in *Yevamot*. *Tosafot* explains that, even according to the Gemara's conclusion in *Yevamot*, we do not apply presumptions in doubtful cases by Rabbinic decree; hence our Gemara may in fact be asking why the first clause of the Baraita did not rule that by Rabbinic decree the woman must be divorced.

Ritva and *Shittah Mekubbetzet* explain that the Gemara objects to the Baraita's distinction because it assumes that both clauses of the Baraita are referring to the same case — a woman of unknown status who came from out of town. But if this is correct, the woman should be presumed

HALAKHAH

עֵד אֶחָד אוֹמֵר: נִתְקַדְּשָׁה If one witness says: "She was betrothed." "If one witness comes forward and testifies that an apparently unmarried woman was in fact betrothed, and the woman herself denies the allegation, she is

TRANSLATION AND COMMENTARY

betrothed," [1]**and the other witness says: "She was not betrothed,"** [2]**both** witnesses **are** in fact **testifying that the woman was** previously **unmarried**. Hence in this case we already know, on the testimony of two witnesses, that the woman was originally single. We therefore need two witnesses to give evidence that she was later betrothed. [3]**But the one witness who said: "She was bethrothed,"** is only one. [4]Hence we reject his testimony, because **the words of one** witness **are not significant in a situation where** the woman's status has been determined on the basis of the evidence of **two** witnesses.

[1]וְעֵד אֶחָד אוֹמֵר: ״לֹא נִתְקַדְּשָׁה״, [2]תַּרְוַיְיהוּ בִּפְנוּיָה קָמַסְהֲדֵי, [3]וְהַאי דְּקָאָמַר: ״נִתְקַדְּשָׁה״, הֲוָה לֵיהּ חַד, [4]וְאֵין דְּבָרָיו שֶׁל אֶחָד בִּמְקוֹם שְׁנַיִם.

LITERAL TRANSLATION

[1]and one witness says: "She was not betrothed," [2]both of them are testifying about an unmarried woman, [3]and the one who said: "She was betrothed," is one, [4]and the words of one are not in place of two.

RASHI

תרווייהו בפנויה קמסהדי — לדברי שניהם עד עכשיו בחזקת פנויה היתה, [קודם שנתקדשה].

NOTES

unmarried in both clauses until proved otherwise. Hence the Gemara asks why the Baraita distinguishes between a case where witnesses disagree about whether she was betrothed, and a case where they agree that she was married but disagree whether she was divorced.

Tosafot suggests yet another solution: The Gemara is not objecting to the Baraita's distinction in itself, but rather to its deviation from the previous Baraita. The Sages in the previous Baraita permitted the woman to remain with her present husband, even in the case of divorce, and Rabbi Menaḥem bar Yose distinguished between a case where she married with the court's permission before the unfavorable witnesses came, and a case where she defied the court and married later. Neither, however, distinguishes between betrothal and divorce.

עֵד אֶחָד אוֹמֵר: נִתְקַדְּשָׁה If one witness says: "She was betrothed." According to Abaye, the Baraita is referring to a case where one witness testifies that the woman was betrothed and another testifies that she was not. Hence the Baraita rules that the woman may not remarry, but if she does so, she need not leave her new husband. The Rishonim ask: In tractate *Kiddushin* (65b), the Gemara rules that if only one witness testifies to a betrothal and the woman denies his account, his testimony is rejected absolutely and the woman may marry without qualms. Why, then, does our Baraita forbid the woman to marry? Even if the favorable witness does not come forward, she should be permitted to marry without qualms!

Rambam (*Hilkhot Ishut* 9:31) accepts both passages literally, ruling that the woman may marry without qualms if there is only one witness who testifies that she was betrothed and she denies this (following the Gemara in *Kiddushin*). But if two witnesses come forward and dispute the matter, she may not marry, although she need not get divorced if she does marry (following Abaye). *Maggid Mishneh* explains that, according to *Rambam*, the credibility of the woman's denial is actually reduced when her claim is supported by a witness, because she feels less isolated and is more prepared to abide by her account even if it is not true.

Most Rishonim explain that a woman may ordinarily marry without qualms if there is only one unfavorable witness and she denies his allegation (following *Kiddushin*), regardless of whether a favorable witness supports her account, and that our Baraita is dealing with a special case. *Ra'avad* explains that Abaye's ruling applies only when the woman herself does not know for certain whether she was betrothed — for example, if one witness testifies that her father married her off as a minor and the other witness testifies that he did not. *Tosafot* explains that Abaye's ruling applies only where we have other grounds for suspecting that the woman was married — for example, if we know that a wedding ceremony was performed between this woman and this man, and the dispute between the witnesses is over legal technicalities. This position is also taken by *Shulḥan Arukh*.

תַּרְוַיְיהוּ בִּפְנוּיָה קָמַסְהֲדֵי Both of them are testifying about an unmarried woman. *Tosafot* asks: According to Abaye, why does the Baraita need to construct a case in which two individual witnesses disagree as to whether the woman was betrothed? Even if the only witness is unfavorable, and the woman alone denies the story, the witness is still not believed, because this woman was initially presumed unmarried and this presumption remains valid until two witnesses testify that her status has changed! In the second clause, dealing with divorce, we can explain that the woman's marital status is unknown, and it is the combined testimony of the two witnesses that leads us to presume that she is married. *Rosh* explains that it was not in fact necessary to introduce the second

HALAKHAH

believed, and may marry, in accordance with a passage in tractate *Kiddushin* (65a). If, on the other hand, her version of the matter is supported by one witness, she is not believed absolutely; she is not permitted to marry, but if she does so she need not get divorced, following Abaye's explanation of the Baraita. *Rambam* maintains that Abaye's ruling applies whenever the woman's account is subject to the conflicting testimony of two individual witnesses. *Ra'avad* maintains that Abaye's ruling applies only when the woman herself does not know if she was betrothed. *Shulḥan Arukh* rules that Abaye's ruling applies only where there is an independent factor leading us to believe that she was betrothed, such as where everyone admits that a wedding ceremony took place, but the witnesses disagree as to whether the betrothal was performed properly. But if the woman insists that there is no basis at all for the claim that she was betrothed, she is believed absolutely, just as she would be if there were no testimony in her favor." (*Rambam, Sefer Nashim, Hilkhot Ishut* 9:31; *Shulḥan Arukh, Even HaEzer* 47:3.)

[1]סֵיפָא, עֵד אֶחָד אוֹמֵר: ״נִתְגָּרְשָׁה״, וְעֵד אֶחָד אוֹמֵר: ״לֹא נִתְגָּרְשָׁה״. [2]תַּרְוַיְיהוּ בְּאֵשֶׁת אִישׁ קָמְסָהֲדֵי, [3]וְהַאי דְּקָאָמַר: ״נִתְגָּרְשָׁה״, הֲוָה לֵיהּ חַד, [4]וְאֵין דְּבָרָיו שֶׁל אֶחָד בִּמְקוֹם שְׁנַיִם.

[5]רַב אַשִׁי אֲמַר: [6]לְעוֹלָם תְּרֵי וּתְרֵי, [7]וְאֵיפּוּךְ: [8]שְׁנַיִם אוֹמְרִים: ״רְאִינוּהָ שֶׁנִּתְקַדְּשָׁה״,

LITERAL TRANSLATION

[1][In] the last clause, one witness says: "She was divorced," and one witness says: "She was not divorced." [2]Both are testifying about a married woman, [3]and the one who said: "She was divorced," is one, [4]and the words of one are not in place of two.

[5]Rav Ashi said: [6]In fact, they are two and two, [7]and reverse it: [8][If] two [witnesses] say: "We saw her become betrothed,"

RASHI

איפוך — ברישא תני: אם ניסת — תצא, וסיפא: אם ניסת — לא תצא.

TRANSLATION AND COMMENTARY

סֵיפָא [1]**In the last clause,** by contrast, **one witness says: "She was divorced," and** the other **witness says: "She was not divorced."** In this case we cannot believe the single witness who says that she has been divorced, [2]because **both** witnesses **have testified that the woman was** previously **married**, and we must accept this point, on which the witnesses are in agreement. Consequently, we need two witnesses to give evidence that she was later divorced. [3]**But the one** witness **who said: "She is divorced,"** has the credibility of only **one.** Hence we reject his testimony, [4]because **the words of one** witness **are not** significant **in a situation where** the woman's status has been determined on the basis of the evidence of **two** witnesses.

רַב אַשִׁי אֲמַר [5]**Rav Ashi said:** It is not necessary to amend the Baraita in this way. [6]**In fact,** the Baraita is referring to a situation where **there are two** witnesses testifying that the woman is unmarried or that she is divorced, **and two** witnesses testifying that she is still married. Rather, says Rav Ashi, the Baraita should be amended in a different way. Instead of reading: "Two witnesses said that she was married," it should read: "Two witnesses said: 'We saw her get married.' " [7]**And** in addition, the rulings of the two clauses of the Baraita must **be reversed.** The first clause of the amended Baraita should read as follows: [8]**If** a woman wishes to marry, and **two** witnesses come forward and say: **"We saw** this woman **become betrothed** to

NOTES

witness in the first clause, but since the Baraita needed to do so in the second clause, it did so in the first clause as well, for stylistic reasons.

Many Rishonim have a version of this passage in which it is Rav Pappa rather than Abaye who explains the Baraita as referring to individual witnesses. Following this reading, *Ramban* explains that this entire discussion reflects a position expressed by Rav Pappa in tractate *Kiddushin*, in which he argues that the testimony of a single witness is sufficient to alter a woman's marital status. But this explanation is rejected by most Rishonim. *Ra'ah* notes that, even according to Rav Pappa's view, one witness is believed only when the parties themselves admit the allegation. Moreover, *Ritva* notes that some versions of the passage in *Kiddushin* attribute this view to Rav Pappi rather than to Rav Pappa (see also previous note).

Ritva and *Ra'ah* explain that the first clause of the Baraita does not in fact refer to a woman who was presumed unmarried. In both clauses of our Baraita we are dealing with a woman who claims to have been married and divorced. In the second clause, one witness supports her claim and one witness refutes it. In the first clause, both witnesses support her claim that she was divorced, but one testifies that she subsequently remarried and the other denies this. Thus, in both cases, it is the combined testimony that determines her status, and not any prior presumption.

רַב אַשִׁי אֲמַר Rav Ashi said. It is not clear on what grounds Rav Ashi rejects Abaye's explanation of the Baraita. Our commentary follows *Maharam Schiff*, who explains that Rav Ashi did not agree with Abaye's emendation of the Baraita. This explanation is a little difficult, but Rav Ashi's own explanation also involves a no less radical emendation. According to those Rishonim who read "Rav Pappa" here instead of "Abaye," and explain that his explanation is valid only according to Rav Pappa's position in tractate *Kiddushin* (see the two last notes), Rav Ashi presumably disagrees because the Halakhah is not in accordance with Rav Pappa.

תְּרֵי וּתְרֵי, וְאֵיפּוּךְ They are two and two, and reverse it. The Baraita discussed in this passage is very similar to the statement of Rabbi Yoḥanan above (22b). In the earlier passage, however, three explanations are presented: Abaye's, Rava's, and a third explanation which in the Vilna edition of the Talmud is attributed to Rav Assi, but which most Rishonim attribute to Rav Ashi. In this passage, by contrast, there are only two explanations: Abaye's and Rav Ashi's.

There is no parallel in our passage to the explanation given by Rava in the previous passage — that the difference between death and divorce is that the woman can maintain her story in the case of divorce, but not if she claims that her husband is dead and he subsequently returns. Presumably, Rava did not make a similar distinction here between betrothal and divorce, because in both cases the woman's claim does not lose its force even if the husband comes forward and challenges it.

In both passages, Abaye gives essentially the same explanation — that Rabbi Yoḥanan and the Baraita are

HALAKHAH

שְׁנַיִם אוֹמְרִים: רְאִינוּהָ שֶׁנִּתְקַדְּשָׁה If two witnesses say: "We saw her become betrothed." "If two witnesses say that they saw an apparently single woman get married, and two other witnesses say that they and the woman were

וּשְׁנַיִם אוֹמְרִים: ״לֹא רְאִינוּהָ שֶׁנִּתְקַדְּשָׁה״, [1]הֲרֵי זוֹ לֹא תִּנָּשֵׂא, וְאִם נִשֵּׂאת, תֵּצֵא.
[2]פְּשִׁיטָא! [3]״לֹא רְאִינוּהָ״ אֵינָהּ רְאָיָה!
[4]לָא, צְרִיכָא דְּדָיְירֵי בְּחָצֵר אֶחָד. [5]מַהוּ דְּתֵימָא: אִם אִיתָא דְּנִתְקַדְּשָׁה, [6]קָלָא אִית לָהּ לְמִילְּתָא. [7]קָא מַשְׁמַע לָן דְּעָבְדֵי אֱינָשֵׁי דִּמְקַדְּשֵׁי בְּצִנְעָא.

LITERAL TRANSLATION

and two say: "We did not see her become betrothed," [1]she may not be married, and if she is married, she must go out.

[2]This is obvious! [3]"We did not see her" is no proof!

[4]No, it is necessary where they live in one courtyard. [5]You might have said: If it were [true] that she was betrothed, [6]the matter would have publicity (lit., "a voice"). [7][Therefore] it tells us that people do sometimes betroth in private.

TRANSLATION AND COMMENTARY

another man," **and two** other witnesses come forward and contradict the first pair, **saying: "We did not see her become betrothed,"** we believe the first pair outright, because the second pair do not really contradict them, since she may have become betrothed without their knowing it. [1]Hence **she may not remarry, and if she has remarried, she must leave** her second husband, since we are certain that she is already married.

פְּשִׁיטָא [2]The Gemara objects: Surely **this is obvious!** It is clear that we must believe the first pair, since the second pair do not contradict them, but merely say: [3]**"We did not see her** become betrothed," and this **is no proof** that she did not become betrothed at some other time, when they were unaware of the fact.

לָא [4]The Gemara answers: **No,** the Baraita's ruling **is needed** to teach us the law in a case **where** the woman and the witnesses who testify that they are unaware that she has become betrothed **live in one courtyard.** [5]**You might have said** that **if it were true that she was betrothed,** [6]**the matter would have attracted notice,** and these close neighbors would know about it. Hence, if they testify that they have no knowledge of her betrothal, this should be considered a contradiction of the evidence of the other pair of witnesses, and we should follow the law of the first Baraita, which permitted her to remain with her present husband. [7]**Therefore** the Baraita **informs us that** this is not so, because **people do sometimes become betrothed in private.**

BACKGROUND

דְּעָבְדֵי אֱינָשֵׁי דִּמְקַדְּשֵׁי בְּצִנְעָא That people do sometimes betroth in private. The betrothal ceremony, which today is performed together with the marriage ceremony, is Halakhically distinct. In Talmudic times and for many generations afterward, the betrothal ceremony was often performed months, or even years, before the wedding. Unlike marriage, betrothal requires only two witnesses, and the ceremony itself was not always regarded as a particularly festive occasion. Therefore, if the two parties were not interested in publicizing the matter, a betrothal ceremony could well have taken place in private, without even the neighbors knowing.

NOTES

dealing with a dispute between two individual witnesses, and in such a case we accept the points in agreement between the witnesses, and reject the points of contention. Rav Ashi, however, does not explain the Baraita in the same way as he explained Rabbi Yoḥanan's position (assuming the reading of the Rishonim is correct). Had he done so, he would have explained that our Baraita is referring to a case where two pairs of witnesses come forward. One pair testify that the woman was betrothed or divorced very recently, while the other pair insist that there was no betrothal or divorce. In such a situation we believe the unfavorable witnesses in the case of divorce because the woman does not produce her bill of divorce, but not in the case of betrothal because it is impossible to clarify the matter.

The commentators attempt to explain why Rav Ashi does not apply his previous explanation here. *Rashba* explains that by comparing divorce with betrothal, the Baraita is in effect comparing a case where we presume the woman to be married with a case where we presume her to be unmarried, and there is no reason to introduce an additional complicating factor. If the Baraita were speaking about "very recently" and making a distinction between testimony that can be clarified and testimony that cannot, it would have simplified matters by comparing divorce with death, rather than with betrothal. Since betrothal was selected, it is clear that the Baraita is referring to a case where the betrothal or divorce did not take place very recently, and the sole issue is the difference in our initial presumption.

This question continues to be debated by the commentators (see *Rosh*, *Maharshal*, *Maharsha*, *Maharam Schiff*).

לֹא רְאִינוּהָ אֵינָהּ רְאָיָה "We did not see her" is no proof! There are two ways of explaining this statement. (1) In general, when a witness testifies that he did not see something, his testimony has no weight, as it is possible that he was not paying attention and did not notice what happened. Only positive testimony is of value. (2) In our case, the witnesses who testify that they did not see are not believed when their statement contradicts that of the witnesses who testify that they *did* see, because the betrothal or divorce took place before the witnesses who did see, and the other witnesses played no role in it (*Likkutei Geonim*).

Meiri notes that the rule that "'we did not see' is not a proof" applies only when the witnesses testify in a general way that they did not see anything. But if the witnesses testify that they were with the other witnesses at the very

HALAKHAH

neighbors in the same courtyard and they did not see her get married, she is considered definitely married — even if she herself insists that she is not — and if she marries someone else, she must be divorced. The second pair of witnesses are not believed, because 'we did not see' is not legally significant testimony, and it is possible that she married privately, in accordance with Rav Ashi's interpretation of the Baraita. Nevertheless, *Bet Shmuel* rules that if the second pair of witnesses claim to have been present at the precise place and time that the marriage was supposed to have taken place, the testimony of the two pairs of witnesses is considered contradictory, and if she herself insists that she was not married and marries one of the favorable witnesses, she need not get divorced." (*Rambam, Sefer Nashim, Hilkhot Ishut* 9:30; *Shulḥan Arukh, Even HaEzer* 47:1.)

TRANSLATION AND COMMENTARY

סֵיפָא [1]The Gemara now returns to Rav Ashi's explanation. We have seen that in the first clause two witnesses say that they saw the woman become betrothed, and two say that they did not. Similarly, **in the last clause, two say: "We saw her get divorced,"** [2]**and two say: "We did not see her get divorced,"** [3]and the Baraita rules (following the reversal of rulings proposed by Rav Ashi) that in this case **she is not permitted to remarry, but if she does remarry, she need not leave** her second husband. Here, too, we believe the first pair outright, because the second pair do not really contradict them.

מַאי קָא מַשְׁמַע לָן [4]But, the Gemara objects, **what is** the second clause **telling us** according to this explanation? It is obvious that we believe the first pair, because the second pair do not contradict them! [5]And if you say that it is needed to teach us **that** this law **applies even** if the woman and the witnesses who testify that they are unaware that she is divorced **live in one courtyard,** and that we do not say that if she had been divorced they would have known about it, [6]then **this** case **is the same as that** case! Why do we need a second clause to teach us about neighbors in a case of divorce? We have already learned from the first clause that the fact that neighbors have heard nothing has no bearing on a woman's marital status. Why should we think that there is a difference between neighbors in a case of betrothal and neighbors in a case of divorce?

מַהוּ דְּתֵימָא [7]The Gemara answers: If we had been taught only the first clause of the Baraita, **you might have said** that **it is** only **with respect to betrothal that** we disregard the testimony of close neighbors who declare that they have seen and heard nothing about it, because **people do sometimes become betrothed in private,** [8]**but divorce** always arouses interest. Hence, we should argue that **if it were true that she was divorced,** [9]**the matter would have attracted notice,** and her neighbors would know about it. Since they testify that they know nothing about the matter, we should consider that this testimony contradicts the testimony of the other pair of witnesses, and we should not permit her to remarry. [10]**Therefore** the Baraita

[1]סֵיפָא, שְׁנַיִם אוֹמְרִים: "רְאִינוּהָ שֶׁנִּתְגָּרְשָׁה", [2]וּשְׁנַיִם אוֹמְרִים: "לֹא רְאִינוּהָ שֶׁנִּתְגָּרְשָׁה", [3]הֲרֵי זוֹ לֹא תִּנָּשֵׂא, וְאִם נִשֵּׂאת, לֹא תֵּצֵא. [4]מַאי קָא מַשְׁמַע לָן? [5]אַף עַל גַּב דְּדָיְירֵי בְּחָצֵר אֶחָד? [6]הַיְינוּ הַךְ!

[7]מַהוּ דְּתֵימָא: גַּבֵּי קִדּוּשִׁין הוּא דַּעֲבִידֵי אֱינָשֵׁי דִּמְקַדְּשֵׁי בְּצִנְעָא, [8]אֲבָל גַּבֵּי גֵּירוּשִׁין, אִם אִיתָא דְּאִיגַּרְשָׁא, [9]קָלָא אִית לַהּ לְמִילְּתָא. [10]קָא מַשְׁמַע לָן

LITERAL TRANSLATION

[1][In] the last clause, [if] two [witnesses] say: "We saw her get divorced," [2]and two say: "We did not see her get divorced," [3]she may not be married, but if she is married, she need not go out.

[4]What is it telling us? [5][That it applies] even though they live in one courtyard? [6]This is the same as that!

[7]You might have said: It is with regard to betrothal that people sometimes betroth in private, [8]but with regard to divorce, if it were [true] that she was divorced, [9]the matter would have publicity. [10][Therefore] it tells us that people do

NOTES

place and at the very time when the alleged events were said to have taken place, and the events described by the other witnesses did not take place, this is the classic case of contradictory testimony. This distinction was accepted by the Halakhic authorities (see Halakhah section).

לֹא רְאִינוּהָ שֶׁנִּתְגָּרְשָׁה "We did not see her get divorced." According to Rav Ashi, the first witnesses are believed absolutely, because the claim of "we did not see" does not eonstitute proof. The Rishonim ask: Following this reasoning, the woman should have been permitted to remarry *ab initio.* Why, then, does the Baraita permit her to remain with her husband only if she has actually remarried? *Rashi* explains that when the neighbors insist that there was no divorce — even though their testimony is legally without effect — it would nevertheless be scandalous for the woman to remarry. Hence we apply Rav Assi's maxim (above, 22b), and instruct her to refrain from remarriage until the matter has been clarified.

Ramban asks: According to Rav Ashi, the second clause of the Baraita teaches us that even if the neighbors say: "We did not see her get divorced," their testimony is rejected, and if the woman does remarry, she need not be divorced. But even if their testimony were valid, it would still be two against two, and we have already seen (above, 22b), that in such a case the law is the same — the woman may not remarry, but if she does so, she need not be divorced! What, then, is the Baraita teaching us? *Ramban* notes that the Baraita is teaching us that although "we did not see" does not constitute proof, the woman is not permitted to remarry, because the neighbors' testimony is sufficient to create a scandal. But this is clearly not the way the Gemara understands the Baraita, since the Gemara asks what the second clause teaches us that we did not learn from the first clause, and does not answer that it

HALAKHAH

שְׁנַיִם אוֹמְרִים: רְאִינוּהָ שֶׁנִּתְגָּרְשָׁה If two witnesses say: "We saw her get divorced." "If two witnesses say that they saw a woman get divorced, and two other witnesses say that they were living in the same courtyard and did not see her get divorced, and she herself insists that she is divorced, she may not remarry, in order to avoid the appearance of

דַּעֲבִידֵי אֱינָשֵׁי דִּמְקַדְּשֵׁי וּדְמְגָרְשֵׁי בִּצְנְעָא.
[1]״וְאִם מִשֶּׁנִּשֵּׂאת בָּאוּ עֵדִים, לֹא תֵּצֵא, כו׳״. [2]רַבִּי אוֹשַׁעְיָא מַתְנֵי לָהּ אַרֵישָׁא. [3]רַבָּה בַּר אָבִין מַתְנֵי לָהּ אַסֵּיפָא.

LITERAL TRANSLATION

sometimes betroth and divorce in private.

[1]"But if witnesses came after she was married, she does not leave, etc." [2]Rabbi Oshaya taught this [as applying] to the first clause. [3]Rabbah bar Avin taught it [as applying] to the last clause.

RASHI

דמגרשי בצנעא — ואפילו הכי, לכתחלה לא תנשא, משום לזות שפתים. **ארישא** — אם משניסת באו עדים שהיתה אשת איש, והיא ניסת על פי עצמה, שאמרה ״גרושה אני״. **אסיפא** — א״נשביתי וטהורה אני״ והתירוה לינשא, ואחר כך באו עדים שנשבית.

TRANSLATION AND COMMENTARY

informs us that this assumption is not correct, because **people do sometimes betroth and divorce in private.**

וְאִם מִשֶּׁנִּשֵּׂאת בָּאוּ עֵדִים [1]The Gemara now considers the last clause of the Mishnah: **"But if** the woman makes her claim and is neither supported nor contradicted by witnesses, and the court permits her to marry a priest, because the mouth that forbade is the mouth that permitted, but **witnesses come** foward later, **after she** has already **married, she is not** required to **leave** her husband," since she is permitted to rely on the court decision rendered before the witnesses came. [2]**Rabbi Oshaya taught this** clause of the Mishnah **with reference to the first clause** of the Mishnah, which deals with divorce. In other words, Rabbi Oshaya explained that the Mishnah is teaching us in this last clause that if an apparently unmarried woman comes forward of her own accord and says that she has been married and divorced, and the court permits her to remarry, because the mouth that forbade is the mouth that permitted, and afterwards witnesses come forward and testify that she has been married, she need not leave her second husband. [3]**Rabbah bar Avin taught this** clause **with reference to the second clause** of the Mishnah, which deals with the captive woman. According to Rabbah bar Avin, the Mishnah teaches us that if a captive woman is permitted to marry a priest, because of the "mouth that

SAGES

רַבָּה בַּר אָבִין **Rabbah bar Avin.** Rabbah (or, in some versions, Rava; both names are short forms of the same name, Rav Abba) bar Avin was a Babylonian Amora of the second and third generations. Few of his teachings have been preserved, and we possess no information about his private life. Some manuscripts have a different reading: Rabbah bar Avuha.

NOTES

teaches us that "we did not see" is believed to the extent of creating a scandal.

Ramban answers that, according to Rav Ashi, the Baraita is referring to a case where the witnesses say she was divorced very recently, and the neighbors insist they did not see the divorce. We have already seen (above, 22b) that in such a case the unfavorable testimony is believed outright, because the woman should have been able to produce her bill of divorce. Thus the Baraita is teaching us that "we did not see" is no proof, and the neighbors are not believed at all, although the woman may still not remarry because of the scandal.

Ra'ah explains that there is a difference between the ruling of the Baraita — that the woman may not remarry but need not be divorced — and the similar ruling of the previous Baraita in the case of two against two. In the previous case, the matter remains doubtful, and the woman is allowed to remain with her husband only if she has married one of the favorable witnesses, because of the problem of the doubtful guilt-offering. In this case, however, the unfavorable witnesses are rejected absolutely, because "we did not see" is not proof. Hence the woman is in principle permitted to marry, but must refrain from doing so because of the scandal it would cause. This distinction was accepted by the Halakhic authorities (see Halakhah section).

רַבִּי אוֹשַׁעְיָא מַתְנֵי לָהּ אַרֵישָׁא **Rabbi Oshaya taught this as applying to the first clause.** Most authorities, including *Rambam* and *Shulḥan Arukh*, rule in accordance with Rabbah bar Avin, who maintains that the Rabbis were lenient only regarding a captive woman. But an apparently unmarried woman who said: "I was married and divorced," and was permitted to remarry on the basis of the "mouth that forbade" argument, is not permitted to remain with her second husband if witnesses subsequently come forward and testify that she was married, since a woman who is known to have been married is presumed married unless she can prove that she has been divorced.

Some authorities, however, rule in favor of Rabbi Oshaya and Rav Huna (*Meiri, Hashlamah*). Support for this position can be found in the version of this passage found in the Jerusalem Talmud. There the Gemara explicitly states that the Mishnah is referring to the first clause, dealing with the woman who claims to have been divorced, and even applies to it the two rulings that appear in our Gemara at the end of the passage, in connection with the captive

HALAKHAH

wrong-doing; but if she does remarry, she need not get divorced, regardless of whom she married, because 'we did not see' is not legally significant testimony, and it is possible that she got divorced privately, in accordance with Rav Ashi's interpretation of the Baraita. *Rema* adds that if the second pair of witnesses claim to have been at the designated place at the time the alleged divorce took place, the testimony of the two pairs of witnesses is considered contradictory, and she must get divorced unless she married one of the favorable witnesses. *Bet Shmuel* cites *Ramban*, who rules that this law applies only if the second pair of witnesses claim to have been living in the courtyard at the time of the alleged divorce. But if the witnesses do not make this claim, the fact that they did not see the divorce is of no significance, and the woman is permitted to remarry." (*Rambam, Sefer Nashim, Hilkhot Gerushin* 12:8; *Shulḥan Arukh, Even HaEzer* 152:4.)

וְאִם מִשֶּׁנִּשֵּׂאת בָּאוּ עֵדִים **But if witnesses came after she was married.** "If there are witnesses who testify that a woman was married, and she claims that she was

TRANSLATION AND COMMENTARY

forbade" argument, and witnesses come forward later and testify that she was indeed taken captive, she need not leave her husband. [1]The Gemara explains: Rabbi Oshaya, **who teaches** this clause **with reference to the first clause** of the Mishnah, does not mean to imply that the same ruling does not also apply to a captive woman, the topic of the second clause. [2]On the contrary, **it applies with even greater force** to **the second clause,** [3]**because** the Rabbis **were** more **lenient in the case of a captive woman** marrying a priest than they were in the case of a possibly married woman marrying another man. [4]**But** Rabbah bar Avin, **who teaches** this clause **with reference to the second clause** of the Mishnah, did indeed mean to imply that this ruling applies only to captive women, [5]but he **does not apply it** to married women who remarry without a divorce, which is the subject of **the first clause,** because the Rabbis were lenient only with regard to a captive woman, but not with regard to a possibly married woman who married another man.

[1]מַאן דְּמַתְנֵי לַהּ אַרֵישָׁא, [2]כָּל שֶׁכֵּן אַסֵּיפָא, [3]דְּבִשְׁבוּיָה הֵקִילוּ. [4]וּמַאן דְּמַתְנֵי לַהּ אַסֵּיפָא, [5]אֲבָל אַרֵישָׁא לָא.

LITERAL TRANSLATION

[1]The one who teaches it [as applying] to the first clause [applies it] [2]all the more so to the second clause, [3]because they were lenient in [the case of] a captive woman. [4]But the one who teaches it [as applying] to the last clause [5]does not [apply it] to the first clause.

RASHI

בשבויה הקילו – דספקא בעלמא הוא דאיכא, שמא נבעלה לנכרי ונפסלה לכהונה.

NOTES

woman: (1) That the woman may still remarry, even if witnesses come forward before she has had a chance to do so, provided that they come forward after the court has given her permission. (2) That the court may give the woman permission to remarry, on the basis of the "mouth that forbade" argument, even if we believe that there are witnesses on their way to testify about her marital status, so long as they have not yet come forward (this ruling is in direct conflict with the Babylonian Talmud; see following note). Clearly, then, the Jerusalem Talmud rules in favor of Rabbi Oshaya.

Meiri notes that when there is an Amoraic dispute in the Babylonian Talmud which is not explicitly resolved, and the Jerusalem Talmud takes one side in the question, we normally follow the ruling of the Jerusalem Talmud, even though we might have decided the Amoraic dispute differently on its own merits. It is not clear why the other Rishonim did not take the Jerusalem Talmud into consideration.

דְּבִשְׁבוּיָה הֵקִילוּ Because they were lenient in the case of a captive woman. It is clear from several passages in the Talmud that the Rabbis were lenient in the standards of proof they applied regarding captive women, but the reason for this is not entirely clear. *Rashi* explains that even though it often happened that captive women were raped, it was far from inevitable, and since we do not know with certainty what happened to this particular woman, the prohibition is considered Rabbinic, and the Rabbis were lenient about it. *Rambam* (*Hilkhot Issurei Bi'ah* 18:17) explains that the laws of captive women, as well as all other laws regarding doubtful lineage, are of Rabbinic origin, whereas by Torah law only people who are definitely known to be of blemished lineage are subject to marriage restrictions.

In tractate *Kiddushin* (12b), the Gemara cites the ruling of Rabbi Ḥanina (below) that a court may permit a captive woman to marry a priest on the basis of the "mouth that forbade" argument, even when we know that there are witnesses on their way to testify that she was taken captive, so long as they have not yet come forward. The Gemara states that this law applies only to captive women, regarding whom the Rabbis were lenient, but not to matters which could entail adultery. The Rishonim cite *Rashi's* comment there (not in our editions of *Rashi*) that this is because even if the captive woman was definitely raped, a priest who marries a woman who was raped by a non-Jew is not guilty of a major sexual crime like adultery, but of (at most) only a relatively minor infraction — albeit an infraction of Torah law. *Ritva*, however, rejects this explanation, arguing that there is no room to distinguish between the regulations applying to major sexual crimes and those applying to other relationships that are forbidden by the Torah (see also *Tosafot*).

Some Rishonim have a reading in the passage in *Kiddushin* in which the Gemara says: "Rabbi Ḥanina's ruling applies only to captive women, regarding whom the Rabbis were lenient, because a captive woman tries her best to spoil her appearance to avoid being raped." According to this view, the Rabbis were lenient because the presumption that captive women are usually raped must be weighed against the presumption that a woman would do everything in her power to avoid this fate (*Ritva* and others).

HALAKHAH

divorced, she is not believed without proof. Even if there are no witnesses initially, and the court permits her to marry on the basis of the 'mouth that forbade' argument, and subsequently witnesses come forward and testify that she was married, after she has already married someone else, her second husband must divorce her, and any children by the second husband have the status of *mamzerim*, unless she can prove that she was divorced before she remarried," following Rabbah bar Avin, who explains that the Mishnah was lenient only regarding a captive woman." (*Rambam, Sefer Nashim, Hilkhot Gerushin* 12:1; *Shulḥan Arukh, Even HaEzer* 152:7.)

[1]לֵימָא בִּדְרַב הַמְנוּנָא קָמִיפַּלְגִי — [2]דְּמַאן דְּמַתְנֵי לָהּ אַרֵישָׁא [3]אִית לֵיהּ דְּרַב הַמְנוּנָא, [4]וּמַאן דְּמַתְנֵי לָהּ אַסֵּיפָא [5]לֵית לֵיהּ דְּרַב הַמְנוּנָא?

LITERAL TRANSLATION

[1]Shall we say that they disagree about [the ruling] of Rav Hamnuna — [2]that the one who teaches it [as applying] to the first clause [3]accepts (lit., "has") Rav Hamnuna, [4]and the one who teaches it [as applying] to the last clause [5]does not accept Rav Hamnuna?

RASHI

דרב המנונא — דאמר: האשה שאמרה לבעלה "גירשתני" — נאמנת. הלכך, הא דאמרה "גרושה אני" — מהימנא.

TRANSLATION AND COMMENTARY

We see, therefore, that Rabbi Oshaya and Rabbah bar Avin disagree as to whether a woman whom we have permitted to remarry on the basis of her own statement that she is divorced (because the mouth that forbade is the mouth that permitted), must leave her new husband if witnesses subsequently come forward and testify that she was married, and she still has no proof that she was divorced. The Gemara now seeks to understand the theoretical basis of their dispute. How can Rabbi Oshaya believe without proof the woman's uncorroborated claim that she is divorced, when it is no longer supported by the "mouth that forbade" argument after the witnesses have come forward? Clearly, Rabbi Oshaya must maintain that we have reason to believe a married woman's unsubstantiated claim that she is divorced, even when the "mouth that forbade" argument does not apply. Such a position was taken above (22b) by Rav Hamnuna, who declared that there is a presumption that a wife would not dare to look her husband in the eye and say: "You divorced me," if it were not true. Thus, even if the woman's claim that she has been divorced is no longer supported by the "mouth that forbade" argument, because witnesses have since come forward, the fact that she abides by her account is itself a persuasive argument, in accordance with Rav Hamnuna's maxim, and this should be sufficient for us to permit her to remain with her second husband, if she married him before the witnesses came.

לֵימָא בִּדְרַב הַמְנוּנָא קָמִיפַּלְגִי [1]It is clear, then, that Rabbi Oshaya bases his ruling on Rav Hamnuna's maxim. But why does Rabbah bar Avin disagree with him? The Gemara asks: **Shall we say that** Rabbi Oshaya and Rabbah bar Avin **disagree about Rav Hamnuna's statement** itself? [2]Perhaps Rabbi Oshaya, **who teaches that** this clause **applies to the first clause** of the Mishnah (maintaining that a woman who marries on the basis of her own statement that she has been divorced may remain with her second husband, even if witnesses subsequently come forward), [3]**accepts Rav Hamnuna's** maxim, as we explained above, [4]whereas Rabbah bar Avin, **who teaches that it applies to the second clause** (maintaining that a woman who marries on the basis of her own statement that she has been divorced must leave her second husband if witnesses subsequently came forward), [5]**does not accept Rav Hamnuna's** maxim at all, and maintains that a woman who looks her husband in the eye and says: "You divorced me," is not believed. For if Rabbah bar Avin were to accept Rav Hamnuna's maxim, he would have to give considerable weight to the woman's claim, because there is a legal presumption that she is telling the truth, and this would surely be sufficient to permit her to remain with her second husband.

NOTES

לֵימָא בִּדְרַב הַמְנוּנָא קָמִיפַּלְגִי **Shall we say that they disagree about the statement of Rav Hamnuna?** The Gemara concludes that the dispute between Rabbi Oshaya and Rabbah bar Avin revolves around Rav Hamnuna's maxim: Rabbi Oshaya is of the opinion that a wife would not dare to lie about such matters, even when her husband is absent, whereas Rabbah bar Avin maintains that this is only true when he is present. The Rishonim ask: Rav Hamnuna specifically says: "A woman would not dare to look her husband in the face and say, etc." How can Rabbi Oshaya explain that the same law applies even when the husband is absent? Moreover, how can Rabbi Oshaya apply Rav Hamnuna's ruling? Rav Hamnuna ruled that a woman who says (to her husband's face): "You divorced me," is believed without reservation and may remarry *ab initio*, even if she has no other proof. But Rabbi Oshaya permits the woman to remarry only if she was first permitted to remarry on the basis of the "mouth that forbade" argument, because the witnesses had not yet come forward!

Because of these objections, *Ramban* explains that Rabbi Oshaya does not dispute that Rav Hamnuna was referring to a case where the woman addressed her husband directly. The dispute between Rabbi Oshaya and Rabbah bar Avin is whether we may extrapolate from Rav Hamnuna's reasoning, and argue that it is extremely unlikely that a woman would lie about such matters even in the husband's absence. For the husband will eventually return, and the woman knows that if she does not tell the truth she will then be in a most difficult situation. Accordingly, Rabbi Oshaya maintains that while this argument alone is not enough to permit the woman to remarry, it is enough to permit her to remain with her second husband, since she was already permitted to remarry on the basis of the "mouth that forbade" argument (see also *Tosafot*)

In tractate *Gittin* (89b), the Gemara cites a dispute between Shmuel, who maintains that Rav Hamnuna's maxim applies only in the husband's presence, and Rav Huna, who maintains that it applies even in his absence. *Rashi* explains that Rav Huna is also inferring from, rather

[1]לָא. [2]דְּכוּלֵּי עָלְמָא אִית לְהוּ דְּרַב הַמְנוּנָא, [3]וְהָכָא בְּהָא קָמִיפַּלְגִי: [4]דְּמָר סָבַר: כִּי אִיתְּמַר דְּרַב הַמְנוּנָא, בְּפָנָיו. [5]אֲבָל שֶׁלֹּא בְּפָנָיו, מְעִיזָּה. [6]וּמָר סָבַר: שֶׁלֹּא בְּפָנָיו נַמִי אֵינָהּ מְעִיזָּה.

[7]״וְאִם מִשֶּׁנִּשֵּׂאת בָּאוּ עֵדִים, וכו׳״. [8]אֲמַר אֲבוּהּ דִּשְׁמוּאֵל: לֹא ״נִשֵּׂאת״ נִשֵּׂאת מַמָּשׁ. [9]אֶלָּא, כֵּיוָן שֶׁהִתִּירוּהָ לִינָּשֵׂא, [10]אַף עַל פִּי שֶׁלֹּא נִשֵּׂאת.

LITERAL TRANSLATION

[1]No. [2]Everyone accepts Rav Hamnuna, [3]but here they disagree about this: [4][One] Master maintains: When [the ruling] of Rav Hamnuna was said, [it meant] to his face. [5]But not to his face, she is impudent. [6]And [the other] Master maintains: Not to his face also she is not impudent.

[7]"But if witnesses came after she was married, etc." [8]Shmuel's father said: "She was married" does not [mean that] she was actually married. [9]Rather, [it means] since they permitted her to be married, [10]even though she was not married.

TRANSLATION AND COMMENTARY

לָא [1]The Gemara answers: **No.** [2]**Everyone,** including Rabbah bar Avin, **accepts Rav Hamnuna's** maxim in principle, [3]**but here,** in the particular case discussed by our Mishnah, **they disagree about** how it should be applied. [4]**One scholar,** Rabbah bar Avin, **maintains** that **Rav Hamnuna's statement** applies only when the wife says: "You divorced me," **to** her husband's **face,** because there is a strong presumption that she could not look him in the eye if her statement were not true. [5]**But** in the case described in the Mishnah, she declares to the court that she is divorced, but does **not** do so **to** her husband's **face,** so it is possible that **she would dare** to make such a declaration, even if it were not true. [6]On the other hand, **the other scholar,** Rabbi Oshaya, **maintains** that even if she makes the declaration in court, and **not to** her husband's **face,** Rav Hamnuna's maxim applies, because **she would also not dare** to make such a statement in court if it were not true. Hence we can rely on her declaration that she has been divorced, and she need not leave her second husband.

וְאִם מִשֶּׁנִּשֵּׂאת בָּאוּ עֵדִים [7]The Gemara now considers another aspect of the last clause of the Mishnah: **"But if** the woman who has been redeemed from captivity makes a claim that she has not been raped — and is neither supported nor contradicted by witnesses — and the court permits her to marry a priest, because the mouth that forbade is the mouth that permitted, but **witnesses come** forward later, **after she has** already **married,** she is not required to leave her husband," since she is permitted to rely on the court decision rendered before the witnesses came. [8]**Shmuel's father said:** The expression **"she married" should not** be taken literally, as though it **meant that she actually married** before the witnesses came. [9]**Rather, it means** that **since** the court **has permitted her to marry,** she is entitled to marry even after witnesses come, [10]**even though she did not marry** before they came.

SAGES

אֲבוּהּ דִּשְׁמוּאֵל Shmuel's father. This refers to Abba bar Abba, the father of the great Amora Shmuel and usually called "Shmuel's father" in his honor. Abba bar Abba, who was a silk merchant by profession, used to travel to distant lands on business. He also visited Eretz Israel and maintained strong ties of friendship with Rabbi Yehudah HaNasi and his sons after him.

Abba bar Abba was one of the greatest Sages of his generation, and, although he never served in public office, he was the leading authority in his city, Neharde'a. There he administered the city's affairs and was occupied extensively with charity and the redemption of prisoners. The Sage Levi (ben Sisi), upon his arrival in Babylonia, became a close friend of Shmuel's father, and Rav, too, when he returned to Babylonia, accorded him great honor. The Torah teachings of Shmuel's father are quoted frequently in both the Babylonian and the Jerusalem Talmud. He was closely affiliated with the Jewish community in Eretz Israel, which would send him various questions; and there, too, he was greatly honored.

NOTES

than applying, Rav Hamnuna's maxim. Rav Huna does not claim that we believe the woman fully in the husband's absence, but merely that we must believe her when this leads to a stringency. *Tosafot* notes that Rav Huna's position there is not necessarily the same as Rabbi Oshaya's here. Rabbi Oshaya may even agree with Shmuel that Rav Hamnuna's maxim ordinarily has no practical application when the husband is absent. But in our case, the woman also has the support of her original "mouth that forbade" argument; hence Rabbi Oshaya maintains that we may draw inferences from Rav Hamnuna's maxim, even according to Shmuel.

HALAKHAH

כִּי אִיתְּמַר דְּרַב הַמְנוּנָא, בְּפָנָיו When the ruling of Rav Hamnuna was said, it meant to his face. "If a woman says to her husband's face that he divorced her, she is believed, because a woman would not dare to make such a statement to her husband's face if it were not true. But if her husband was not present, she is not believed without proof, following Rabbah bar Avin's explanation of Rav Hamnuna's maxim. The declaration must be made before the woman remarries; but if she marries (in her husband's absence) and only then declares herself divorced, she is not believed, even if the declaration is made in her husband's presence.

"Similarly, if an apparently married woman becomes betrothed to another man in the presence of her first husband, it is considered the equivalent of a divorce declaration. With regard to a case in which her husband was not present, *Shulḥan Arukh* cites *Rambam,* who rules that the betrothal is completely void; but *Bet Shmuel* cites *Ramban,* who rules that the woman must receive a bill of divorce from her second husband.

Shulḥan Arukh cites *Rosh,* who rules that the husband is considered present if he is in town; but *Rema* cites *Maharik,* who rules that the husband must be in her immediate presence when she makes the declaration or becomes betrothed." (*Rambam, Sefer Nashim, Hilkhot Ishut* 4:13 and *Hilkhot Gerushin* 12:4; *Shulḥan Arukh, Even HaEzer* 17:2.)

TRANSLATION AND COMMENTARY

וְהָא לֹא תֵּצֵא קָתָנֵי [1]But, the Gemara objects, the Mishnah **uses the expression: "She need not leave** her second husband," and from these words it is clear that the Mishnah is referring to a case where she has already married, because the expression "to leave" always refers to getting a divorce from her husband!

לֹא תֵּצֵא מֵהֶתֵּירָה הָרִאשׁוֹן [2]The Gemara answers: In this case, the expression "she need not leave" does not mean that she need not get divorced, but rather that **she need not leave her original permitted status** and forfeit the right to remarry granted by the court before the witnesses came forward.

תָּנוּ רַבָּנַן [3]The Gemara now cites a Baraita in support of the ruling given by Shmuel's father. **Our Rabbis taught** the following Baraita: "If an apparently free woman comes to court and **says: 'I was taken captive but I am pure'** (the case of the Mishnah, in which she is believed because the mouth that forbade is the mouth that permitted), and the woman goes on to say, unnecessarily, [4]**'and I have witnesses that I am pure,** who are not in town today, but who were with me all the time I was in captivity,' [5]**we do not say** that since there are witnesses who know the truth **we will wait until the witnesses come** and clarify the matter definitively. [6]**But we immediately permit her** to marry a priest, on the basis of the 'mouth that forbade' argument." [7]The Baraita continues: **"If the court permits her to marry, and later** her **witnesses come and say:** 'It is true that we were with this woman in captivity, but **we do not know** whether she was raped,' [8]in such a case **she need not leave** her husband, even though there are now witnesses who testify that she was taken captive, and she is no longer supported by the 'mouth that forbade' argument." This ruling is in accordance with the Mishnah, as interpreted by Shmuel's father, which permits her to marry a priest on the basis of her own declaration, provided that she receives the court's permission to do so before the witnesses come forward. Even though the witnesses do not confirm her account of her captivity, as she promised they would, she is not penalized for this, because it was unnecessary for her to bring witnesses at all. "However," the Baraita concludes, "this is the case only where witnesses testify that she was taken captive, but they know nothing about whether she was raped. [9]**But if** the witnesses **who come forward are witnesses of impurity**, who testify positively that she was raped by her captors, she is not permitted to marry a priest; and if she has done so already, [10]**she must leave** her husband, **even if she has several children.** The reason for this is that the Mishnah's dispensation applies only to a captive woman about whom there is a strong likelihood but no

[1]וְהָא "לֹא תֵּצֵא" קָתָנֵי! [2]לֹא תֵּצֵא מֵהֶתֵּירָה הָרִאשׁוֹן. [3]תָּנוּ רַבָּנַן: "אָמְרָה: 'נִשְׁבֵּיתִי וּטְהוֹרָה אֲנִי, [4]וְיֵשׁ לִי עֵדִים שֶׁטְּהוֹרָה אֲנִי' [5]אֵין אוֹמְרִים: נַמְתִּין עַד שֶׁיָּבֹאוּ עֵדִים. [6]אֶלָּא מַתִּירִין אוֹתָהּ מִיָּד. [7]הִתִּירוּהָ לִינָּשֵׂא, וְאַחַר כָּךְ בָּאוּ עֵדִים וְאָמְרוּ: 'לֹא יָדַעְנוּ', [8]הֲרֵי זוֹ לֹא תֵּצֵא. [9]וְאִם בָּאוּ עֵדֵי טוּמְאָה, [10]אֲפִילּוּ יֵשׁ לָהּ כַּמָּה בָּנִים, תֵּצֵא."

LITERAL TRANSLATION

[1]But it teaches: "She does not go out"!

[2]She does not go out from her first permitted status.

[3]Our Rabbis taught: "If she said: 'I was taken captive but I am pure, [4]and I have witnesses that I am pure,' [5]we do not say: We will wait until witnesses come. [6]But we permit her immediately. [7][If the court] permitted her to be married, and afterwards witnesses came and said: 'We do not know,' [8]she does not go out. [9]But if witnesses of impurity came, [10]even if she has several children, she must go out."

RASHI

ויש לי עדים — שהיו עמי תמיד, שלא נתייחדתי עם נכרי. **ואחר כך באו עדים** — שנשבית. דהשתא לאו הפה שאסר הוא — אפילו הכי לא תלא. **אפילו יש לה כמה בנים** — מן הכהן הזה שנשאת.

NOTES

וְאָמְרוּ: לֹא יָדַעְנוּ **And said: "We do not know."** The witnesses testify that the woman was indeed taken captive, but that they have no further information as to what happened to her. Hence we would have presumed that the woman had been raped, in accordance with the general law concerning captive women, had it not been for the fact

HALAKHAH

לֹא תֵּצֵא מֵהֶתֵּירָה הָרִאשׁוֹן **She does not go out from her first permitted status.** "If a captive woman is permitted to marry a priest on the basis of her own declaration, since there is no independent evidence that she was ever taken captive, and the mouth that forbade is the mouth that permitted, the woman does not forfeit her right to marry a priest, even if witnesses come forward later and testify that she was indeed taken captive. Moreover, we appoint guardians to protect the captive woman from molestation, until she has been redeemed, following Shmuel's father. Indeed, even if her captors follow her into court immediately after the permission has been granted to her, she is permitted to marry a priest," following the ruling of Rabbi Hanina regarding Shmuel's daughters. (*Rambam, Sefer Kedushah, Hilkhot Issurei Bi'ah* 18:22; *Shulhan Arukh, Even HaEzer* 7:6.)

וְאִם בָּאוּ עֵדֵי טוּמְאָה **But if witnesses of impurity came.** "If a captive woman has been permitted to marry a priest

[1] הָנֵי שְׁבוּיָיתָא דְּאָתְיָין לִנְהַרְדְּעָא. [2] אוֹתֵיב אֲבוּהּ דִּשְׁמוּאֵל נָטוֹרֵי בַּהֲדַיְיהוּ. [3] אֲמַר לֵיהּ שְׁמוּאֵל: "וְעַד הָאִידָּנָא מַאן נָטְרִינְהוּ?" [4] אֲמַר לֵיהּ: "אִילּוּ בְּנָתָךְ הָווּיָן, [5] מִי הֲוֵית מְזַלְזֵל בְּהוּ כּוּלֵּי הַאי?" [6] הֲוַאי "כִּשְׁגָגָה שֶׁיֹּצָא מִלִּפְנֵי הַשַּׁלִּיט", [7] וְאִישְׁתַּבְיָין בְּנָתֵיהּ דְּמָר שְׁמוּאֵל, [8] וְאַסְּקִינְהוּ לְאַרְעָא דְּיִשְׂרָאֵל.

LITERAL TRANSLATION

[1] There were certain captive women who came to Neharde'a. [2] Shmuel's father appointed (lit., "seated") guards over them.

[3] Shmuel said to him: "And until now who guarded them?"

[4] He said to him: "If they had been your daughters, [5] would you have treated them so lightly?"

[6] It was "as an error which proceeds from the ruler," [7] and the daughters of Mar Shmuel were taken captive, [8] and they brought them to Eretz Israel.

RASHI

דאתיין לנהרדעא – להפדותן.

TRANSLATION AND COMMENTARY

certainty that she was raped, but if there is positive testimony that she was raped, she is definitely disqualified from the priesthood by Torah law, and her statement is of no value."

הָנֵי שְׁבוּיָיתָא [1] The Gemara illustrates the previous rulings with a story: It once happened that **there were certain captive women who came to Neharde'a** to be redeemed. [2] After **Shmuel's father,** who was the leading Halakhic authority in Neharde'a, redeemed the women, he **appointed guardians** to watch over **them** on their return home.

אֲמַר לֵיהּ שְׁמוּאֵל [3] At this point, **Shmuel said to his** father: **"Until now who guarded them?** It is strange to appoint guardians to protect these women against molestation. If you are worried that they may be taken captive and become disqualified from the priesthood, they are already disqualified. Their captors have been molesting them at will ever since they kidnapped them. Why take such precautions at this stage?"

אֲמַר לֵיהּ [4] Shmuel's father **said to him** in reply: "You should be ashamed of yourself! **If they were your daughters,** [5] **would you treat them so lightly?** These are decent women who had the misfortune of being kidnapped. Now that they are free, they must be treated with all possible dignity."

הֲוַאי [6] The Gemara relates that the rebuke delivered by Shmuel's father, in which he mentioned the possibility of something similar happening to Shmuel's own daughters, **was "as an error which proceeds from the ruler"** (Ecclesiastes 10:5), [7] **and** shortly afterwards **the daughters of Mar Shmuel were** indeed **taken captive,** in fulfillment of his father's words, [8] **and** the captors **brought them** from Neharde'a in Babylonia **to Eretz Israel**, where the local Jewish community redeemed them.

NOTES

that she was already permitted before the witnesses came, on the basis of the "mouth that forbade" argument. Thus the Baraita supports the ruling of Shmuel's father — that if witnesses come forward only after we have permitted the captive woman to remarry, she does not lose her right to remarry (*Ra'ah*).

Moreover, the Baraita goes even further than Shmuel's father, since it refers to a case where the woman claimed that these witnesses would testify in her favor, whereas in fact they did not. Hence, we might have thought that since this woman did not tell the truth about the witnesses, we should consider her a confirmed liar, and should no longer believe her original claim. But the Baraita informs us that in fact the woman is treated in the same way as if she had said nothing about witnesses supporting her claim (*Tosefot Rid*).

אִילּוּ בְּנָתָךְ הָווּיָן, מִי הֲוֵית מְזַלְזֵל בְּהוּ כּוּלֵּי הַאי If they had been your daughters, would you have treated them so lightly? *Ritva* asks: Shmuel's point, however insensitively phrased, was essentially correct. These women were indeed already disqualified from the priesthood. Why was Shmuel's father treating them as though they were still of unblemished status? *Ritva* answers that this story is closely related to the Gemara's previous statement, in which Shmuel's father ruled that once a captive woman has been permitted, on the basis of the "mouth that forbade" argument, she may marry a priest, even if witnesses subsequently come forward before she has the opportunity to do so. *Ritva* explains that these women came to court of their own volition, and Shmuel's father declared them to be pure on the basis of the "mouth that forbade" argument. Then witnesses came forward, but Shmuel's father ruled that the women should still be considered pure. According to this explanation, Shmuel, in addition to showing a disregard for the feelings of the captive women, was also criticizing his father's ruling. This perhaps sheds light on why Shmuel was punished so severely.

כִּשְׁגָגָה שֶׁיֹּצָא מִלִּפְנֵי הַשַּׁלִּיט "As an error which proceeds from the ruler." In several places, the Gemara mentions that a great scholar "caused" a tragic misfortune by a slip

HALAKHAH

on the basis of her own declaration, and two witnesses come forward later and testify that she had in fact been raped by her captors, she may not marry a priest. Moreover, if she has already married a priest, she must be divorced, and her children by the priest are disqualified from the priesthood. The evidence of one witness, however, is of no legal significance." (*Rambam, Sefer Kedushah, Hilkhot Issurei Bi'ah* 18:23; *Shulḥan Arukh, Even HaEzer* 7:6.)

BACKGROUND

נָטוֹרֵי Guards. Shmuel's father treated these captive women in the way that women who are alone at any time should be treated: He protected them to prevent them from being left alone with men. Although Shmuel thought his father's action unwarranted, since the women had already been in captivity, where they had been subject to molestation at any time, his father nevertheless wished to emphasize that he honored them. In the opinion of Shmuel's father, the absence of an escort would be an expression of contempt, showing that they were no longer regarded as worth protecting.

בְּנָתֵיהּ דְּמָר שְׁמוּאֵל The daughters of Mar Shmuel. Neharde'a, where Shmuel's family lived, was near the boundary between Persia and the Roman Empire, and so it was frequently attacked and despoiled. Some authorities maintain that Shmuel's daughters were taken captive when Pappa bar Netzer (see below, 51b) destroyed the city in 259 C.E. It would seem that Shmuel had at least three daughters, two of whom were taken captive and brought to Eretz Israel. Later, these daughters married Rav Shemen (Shimon) bar Abba, one after the death of the other, while the third, Raḥel, married Issur, a non-Jew who later converted to Judaism. Raḥel was the mother of Rav Mari bar Raḥel.

SAGES

מָר שְׁמוּאֵל Mar Shmuel. The word מָר — "Master" — is used as a form of respect in addressing an elder scholar. As a title it is used to denote scholars of the family of the Exilarch. The case of Shmuel is exceptional, because even though he did not receive formal ordination and was not called Rabbi, he was one of the greatest scholars of his time. Hence the honorific title מָר is often added to his name.

TRANSLATION AND COMMENTARY

אוקְמָן לְשָׁבוֹיָינְהוּ מֵאַבְּרַאי [1]The Gemara now relates that when Shmuel's daughters were taken to be redeemed, **they persuaded their captors to stand outside,** while **they went into Rabbi Ḥanina's House of Study.** [2]Each **one** of them then **said** in turn: **"I was taken captive, but I am pure."** [3]The Rabbis in Rabbi Ḥanina's House of Study then **permitted them** to marry priests, in accordance with the law of the Mishnah, since there was no evidence that they were in fact captives except for their own admissions, and the mouth that forbade is the mouth that permitted. [4]**In the end their captors entered** the House of Study, **and came** forward to demand their ransom money. [5]**Rabbi Ḥanina** then **said: "These women must be the daughters of a scholar."** Only women familiar with the interpretation of the Mishnah given by Shmuel's father would realize that by making their declaration in court before the court had seen the objective evidence, they would be permitted to marry priests, and even though the evidence would be produced moments later — long before they would have a chance to marry — the permission they received would not be canceled. [6]It then **became known that** these captive women **were,** in fact, none other than **the daughters of Mar Shmuel.**

אֲמַר לֵיהּ [7]**Rabbi Ḥanina** then **said to Rav Shemen bar Abba,** a priest who was related to Shmuel: [8]**"Go out and attend to your relatives** (i.e., marry one of them)."

אֲמַר לֵיהּ [9]Rav Shemen bar Abba was hesitant about relying on this ruling to marry a captive. **He said to Rabbi Ḥanina:** "The Mishnah permitted a priest to marry a captive in this way only if there were no witnesses. [10]**But surely there are witnesses abroad,** in Neharde'a, who know that Shmuel's daughters were kidnapped! How, then, can I marry one of them?"

[1]אוּקְמָן לְשָׁבוֹיָינְהוּ מֵאַבְּרַאי, וְעַיְילֵי לְבֵי מִדְרְשָׁא דְּרַבִּי חֲנִינָא. [2]הָא אָמְרָה: "נִשְׁבֵּיתִי וּטְהוֹרָה אֲנִי". וְהָא אָמְרָה: "נִשְׁבֵּיתִי וּטְהוֹרָה אֲנִי". [3]שָׁרֵינְהוּ. [4]סוֹף עוּל אָתוּ שָׁבוֹיָינְהוּ. [5]אֲמַר רַבִּי חֲנִינָא: "בְּנָן דְּמוֹרְיָין אִינּוּן". [6]אִיגְלַאי מִילְּתָא דִּבְנָתֵיהּ דְּמָר שְׁמוּאֵל הֲוֵיָין.

[7]אֲמַר לֵיהּ רַבִּי חֲנִינָא לְרַב שֶׁמֶן בַּר אַבָּא: [8]"פּוּק אִיטַּפַּל בִּקְרוֹבוֹתֶיךָ".

[9]אֲמַר לֵיהּ לְרַבִּי חֲנִינָא: [10]"וְהָאִיכָּא עֵדִים בִּמְדִינַת הַיָּם!"

LITERAL TRANSLATION

[1]They left their captors standing outside, and they went into Rabbi Ḥanina's House of Study. [2]This one said: "I was taken captive but I am pure," and that one said: "I was taken captive but I am pure." [3]They permitted them. [4]In the end their captors entered [and] came. [5]Rabbi Ḥanina said: "They are daughters of scholars (lit., 'teachers')." [6]The matter was revealed that they were the daughters of Mar Shmuel.

[7]Rabbi Ḥanina said to Rav Shemen bar Abba: [8]"Go out [and] attend to your relatives." [9]He said to Rabbi Ḥanina: [10]"But surely there are witnesses abroad (lit., 'in a country over the sea')!"

RASHI

אוקמינהו לשבויינהו אבראי — שלא יבואו לפני בית דין, ולא ידעו בית דין שהן שבויות, אלא על פי עצמן, ויתירום. **בנן דמוריין אינון** — בנות אדם גדול ובעל הוראה הוא, שידעו לעשות כן. **לרב שמן** — כהן היה. **איטפל בקרובותיך** — שא אחת מהן, שהן קרובותיך. **והא איכא סהדי במדינת הים** — שראו שנשבו, ודלמא אתו לקמן למחר וליומא אוחרן לאחר שתנשא.

NOTES

of the tongue (see, for example, *Bava Metzia* 68a and *Bava Batra* 22a). The scholar said something perfectly innocent that could also have been interpreted as a curse, and the curse promptly took effect. The Biblical verse cited by the Gemara is taken from the Book of Ecclesiastes (10:5). There, Ecclesiastes compares the injustices of the world to a careless error on the part of a king. Such errors are almost impossible to correct once committed, and lead invariably to disaster (*Rashi*). Rabbinic scholars are compared to kings, in that heavenly forces obey them. Hence, a slip of the tongue on their part can have tragic and irrevocable consequences.

The words of ordinary people, of course, are not as potent as those of scholars. However, in several places (e.g., *Berakhot* 19a) the Gemara forbids everyone (and not merely Rabbinic scholars) from making statements that can be misinterpreted as implying a curse. In the words of the Gemara: "A person must never open his mouth [i.e., offer suggestions] to Satan."

אוקְמָן לְשָׁבוֹיָינְהוּ מֵאַבְּרַאי They left their captors standing outside. Shmuel's daughters wished to be the first to tell Rabbi Ḥanina that they had been taken captive, so that they could get a favorable ruling based on the "mouth that forbade" argument, while the court still presumed them to

HALAKHAH

וְהָאִיכָּא עֵדִים But surely there are witnesses. "If an apparently free woman declares that she was taken captive but not raped, and she adds that she has witnesses to support her declaration, we permit her to marry a priest

BACKGROUND

בְּנָן דְּמוֹרְיָין Daughters of scholars. The way in which Shmuel's daughters behaved showed that they knew not only general Halakhot, but also subtleties of the Halakhah that were not widely known. Consequently, Rabbi Ḥanina concluded that they were the daughters of a great Torah scholar who was not only a learned man, but also a major Halakhic authority.

SAGES

רַבִּי חֲנִינָא Rabbi Ḥanina. When the name of the Amora Rabbi Ḥanina is used without a patronymic in the Talmud, the reference is to Rabbi Ḥanina bar Ḥama, a first-generation Amora from Eretz Israel. Rabbi Ḥanina originally came from Babylonia, although he immigrated to Eretz Israel at a relatively early age, and studied there with Rabbi Yehudah HaNasi, who was very fond of him (and indeed remarked that Rabbi Ḥanina was "not a human being, but an angel"). Rabbi Ḥanina also studied with Rabbi Yehudah HaNasi's most distinguished students, in particular with Rabbi Ḥiyya. On his deathbed, Rabbi Yehudah HaNasi designated Rabbi Ḥanina as the new head of his yeshivah, although the latter, in his great modesty, refused to accept the position as long as his older colleague, Rabbi Efes, was still alive.

Rabbi Ḥanina lived in Sepphoris, where he earned a living as a honey dealer, from which he became wealthy and established a large academy. He was renowned for his acuity, as well as for his uprightness and piety.

Numerous Halakhic and Aggadic teachings of Rabbi Ḥanina appear in the Babylonian and the Jerusalem Talmud. He lived to a great age, and had many students over an extended period, among them Rabbi Yehoshua ben Levi, who was a student-colleague of his, and Rabbi Yoḥanan, who studied with him for many years.

His son was the Amora Rabbi Ḥama the son of Rabbi Ḥanina.

רַב שֶׁמֶן בַּר אַבָּא Rav Shemen bar Abba. This is Rav Shimon bar Abba the Priest

[1]״הָשְׁתָּא, מִיהַת, [2]לֵיתְנְהוּ קַמָּן. [3]עֵדִים בְּצַד אִסְתָּן, וְתֵאָסֵר?!״

[4]טַעְמָא דְּלָא אָתוּ עֵדִים, [5]הָא אָתוּ עֵדִים, [6]מִיתַּסְרָא? [7]וְהָאֲמַר אֲבוּהּ דִּשְׁמוּאֵל: ״כֵּיוָן שֶׁהִתִּירוּהָ לִינָּשֵׂא, אַף עַל פִּי שֶׁלֹּא נִשֵּׂאת״!

[8]אֲמַר רַב אַשִׁי: ״עֵדֵי טוּמְאָה״ אִיתְּמַר.

LITERAL TRANSLATION

[1]"Now, at all events, [2]they are not before us. [3]Witnesses are in the north side, and she should be forbidden?!"

[4]The reason is that witnesses did not come, [5]but if witnesses came, [6]she would be forbidden? [7]But surely Shmuel's father said: "Since they permitted her to be married, even though she was not married"!

[8]Rav Ashi said: It was stated: "Witnesses of impurity."

RASHI

השתא מיהא לא איתנהו — קודם נישואין, ומשום דלמא אתו לא אסרינן לה השתא. **עדים בצד אסתן** — בצד צפון. [״מצפון זהב יאתה״ (איוב לז) מתרגם: מלאיסתנא]. **ותאסר** — בתמיה, הא [לא] אתו קודס נשואין.

TRANSLATION AND COMMENTARY

הָשְׁתָּא [1]Rabbi Ḥanina answered: **"Now, at all events, [2]they are not before us.** The court must rule on the basis of witnesses who come before it, not on the basis of witnesses who have not come forward. [3]Is there any reason why **she should be forbidden** just because someone says that there **are witnesses in the north** (i.e., far away in Babylonia)?" Satisfied with Rabbi Ḥanina's explanation, Rav Shemen bar Abba married one of Shmuel's captive daughters.

טַעְמָא דְּלָא אָתוּ עֵדִים [4]In a later generation, the Amoraim studied the story of Shmuel's daughters, and objected: **The reason** Rabbi Ḥanina gave **is that** the **witnesses** from Babylonia **had not** yet **come.** [5]Thus it follows that **if witnesses had come** after Rav Shemen's bride had been permitted to marry him, and had testified that she and her sister had been taken captive, [6]**she would have been forbidden** to marry a priest. [7]**But surely Shmuel's father said: "Since they permitted her to marry,** she could have relied on that dispensation, **even though she did not marry** before the witnesses came forward"! Why, then, was Rav Shemen bar Abba concerned?

אֲמַר רַב אַשִׁי [8]**Rav Ashi said** in reply: The witnesses **mentioned in the statement** of Rav Shemen bar Abba in his conversation with Rabbi Ḥanina **were "witnesses of impurity."** Rav Shemen bar Abba suspected that witnesses from Babylonia would come forward and testify positively that the daughters of Shmuel had been raped. And as we have seen in the Baraita cited above, if such witnesses were to testify, the dispensation of the Mishnah would not apply. But Rabbi Ḥanina responded that we need not concern ourselves with witnesses who have not yet come forward, and we may rely on the evidence that we have before us to issue a definitive ruling.

NOTES

be free. For their grandfather had ruled that if a favorable ruling is issued before witnesses come forward, it remains in force even afterwards. Once the captors entered the House of Study and asked for a ransom, however, the women would be presumed captive, and they could not be permitted to marry into the priesthood without proof. *Rosh* notes that for an apparently free woman to be presumed a captive, it is normally necessary for two qualified witnesses to testify against her, and the captors were certainly not qualified to give testimony.

However, Shmuel's daughters feared that their captors would seize them and behave toward them in the manner of captors, in which case everyone present would become witnesses that these women were indeed captives.

עֵדֵי טוּמְאָה אִיתְּמַר **It was stated: "Witnesses of impurity."** The Gemara suggests that Rav Shemen bar Abba suspected that witnesses from Babylonia would come forward and testify positively that the daughters of Shmuel had been raped. But Rabbi Ḥanina responded that we need not concern ourselves with witnesses who have not yet come forward, and we may rely on the evidence that we have before us to issue a definitive ruling based on the sisters' own declaration.

It is not clear from the story whether the witnessses of impurity ever did come forward. *Rabbi Ya'akov Emden* suggests that in fact they did come forward and testified that one of Shmuel's daughters had lied and had indeed been raped. Support for this ideacan be found in the fact that one of Shmuel's daughters, named Raḥel, had a son named Mari, who was himself a Sage of note (*Berakhot* 16a), and in tractate *Bava Batra* (149a) we are told that Rav Mari bar Raḥel's father was a non-Jew named Issur (who subsequently converted to Judaism). *Rashi* and *Rashbam* explain that Issur was a non-Jew who had captured Raḥel and raped her and Mari was their son.

Tosafot notes that *Rashi*'s explanation is not consistent

HALAKHAH

immediately, on the basis of her own declaration, and do not wait for the witnesses to come forward, following the Baraita. Moreover, even if there are rumors that there are witnesses elsewhere who will contradict her account and testify that she was raped, we pay no attention to them and permit her to marry a priest, until such time as the witnesses come forward, because we are lenient regarding captive women," following Rav Ashi. (*Rambam, Sefer Kedushah, Hilkhot Issurei Bi'ah* 18:23; *Shulḥan Arukh, Even HaEzer* 7:7.)

(Shemen is an abbreviation of Shimon), who belonged to the second generation of Palestinian Amoraim. Rav Shimon bar Abba was born in Babylonia, and was a relative of Shmuel. He immigrated to Eretz Israel as a young man, and studied with Rabbi Ḥanina. However, his main teacher was Rabbi Yoḥanan, whom he served with exceptional affection. Much has been said in praise of his great piety, and his wisdom was also highly praised. Not only was he poor, but circumstances prevented Rabbi Yoḥanan from granting him ordination, though he was undoubtedly one of the great Sages of his generation.

Rav Shemen bar Abba married — one after the other — the daughters of Shmuel, after they had been captured and redeemed in Eretz Israel. All the students of Rabbi Yoḥanan were his colleagues, and members of the following generation transmit teachings in his name. He had a son, Rav Amram, who was a Sage and who also transmitted teachings in his father's name.

LANGUAGE

אִסְתָּן **The north.** This word means "north wind" in Aramaic, and is apparently derived from the Assyrian term for "north." The expression "witnesses are in the north" came to be used in the sense of "there are witnesses somewhere far away."

TRANSLATION AND COMMENTARY

MISHNAH [23B] שְׁתֵּי נָשִׁים שֶׁנִּשְׁבּוּ [1]This Mishnah considers a case **where** witnesses testify that **two women were taken captive, and** each **one says: "I was taken captive but I am pure."** [2]The Mishnah rules that, since they have no proof that their claims are true, **they are not believed,** in accordance with the law of the previous Mishnah (22a), that a woman who is known to have been taken captive is assumed to have been raped in captivity, unless she can prove otherwise. [3]**But** the Mishnah rules that **when** the two captive women do not merely claim that they themselves are pure, but rather **testify about each other, they are believed.** The reason they are believed about each other is because the Rabbis were lenient regarding captive women, and where there is one witness — even another captive woman — who testifies that a captive woman was not violated, the witness is believed and the captive woman is permitted to marry a priest.

GEMARA תָּנוּ רַבָּנָן [4]The Mishnah ruled that if each of two captive women claims not to have been raped in captivity, neither one is believed, but if they testify about each other, they are both believed. The Gemara now cites a Baraita which illustrates this law by considering a series of cases where one of the women testified about herself and her fellow captive, while the other was silent. **Our Rabbis** taught the following Baraita: **"If** one of the women **says: 'I am impure** [i.e., I was raped] **but my fellow** captive **is pure,'**

LITERAL TRANSLATION

MISHNAH [23B] [1][If] two women were taken captive, [and] one says: "I was taken captive but I am pure," and one says: "I was taken captive but I am pure," [2]they are not believed. [3]But when they testify about each other, they are believed.

GEMARA [4]Our Rabbis taught: "[If she says:] 'I am impure but my fellow is pure,'

מִשְׁנָה [23B] [1]שְׁתֵּי נָשִׁים שֶׁנִּשְׁבּוּ, זֹאת אוֹמֶרֶת: "נִשְׁבֵּיתִי וּטְהוֹרָה אֲנִי", וְזֹאת אוֹמֶרֶת: "נִשְׁבֵּיתִי וּטְהוֹרָה אֲנִי", [2]אֵינָן נֶאֱמָנוֹת. [3]וּבִזְמַן שֶׁהֵן מְעִידוֹת זוֹ אֶת זוֹ, הֲרֵי אֵלּוּ נֶאֱמָנוֹת.
גְּמָרָא [4]תָּנוּ רַבָּנָן: "אֲנִי טְמֵאָה וַחֲבֶרְתִּי טְהוֹרָה'

RASHI

מִשְׁנָה קַשְׁתֵּי נָשִׁים שֶׁנִּשְׁבּוּ — שִׁיֵשׁ עֵדִים שֶׁנִּשְׁבּוּ. שְׁמְעִידוֹת זוֹ אֶת זוֹ". — כָּל אַחַת אוֹמֶרֶת "סְבַרְתִּי טְהוֹרָה". הֲרֵי אֵלּוּ נֶאֱמָנוֹת — דְּנַסְבַּיְהוּ הֵקֵילוּ לְהַאֲמִין עֵד אֶחָד, וַאֲפִילוּ אִשָּׁה.

BACKGROUND

BACKGROUND

זֹאת אוֹמֶרֶת: נִשְׁבֵּיתִי **And one says: "I was taken captive."** This Mishnah and the next one are presented in this form so as to emphasize the extent to which we follow the formal laws of testimony. The Halakhah that we do not believe a woman who testifies about herself is not based on lack of confidence in her testimony as such (for, as this Mishnah states, she is entirely believed regarding her companion). Rather, it reflects a formal principle — that a person's testimony about himself is not accepted, even when the court believes that the person is entirely trustworthy. An extreme example of this is found in another Mishnah in this chapter (below, 27b), where we reject a husband's testimony regarding his wife (who is considered Halakhically to be part of her husband's person, so that he is precluded from testifying about her), even though the husband was one of the great Sages of his generation, and no one doubted the objectivity and truth of his statement.

NOTES

with the version of this story found in the Jerusalem Talmud (commenting on our Mishnah). There, the Gemara concludes the story by relating that Rav Shemen bar Abba married one of the captive sisters, and she died. He then married the other sister, and she died as well. Observers saw this as a sign of divine displeasure, and suggested that the sisters had lied when they claimed to have been pure. But they had not lied. Rather, their early death was the result of the sin of a certain ancestor called Rabbi Ḥananyah, and there may have been a curse on the family.

Following the Jerusalem Talmud, *Tosafot* insists that Shmuel's daughters were not raped. *Tosafot* suggests that there may have been two Sages named Mari bar Raḥel, and the mother of the one who was the son of Issur was not the daughter of Shmuel. Alternatively, *Tosafot* suggests that three of Shmuel's daughters may have been taken captive, and one of them may have admitted to being raped, while the other two claimed to have remained pure. Some Aḥaronim, however, attempt to reconcile *Rashi*'s explanation with the Jerusalem Talmud by connecting the sin of Rabbi Ḥananyah with the status of Shmuel's daughters (see *Gilyon Efraim*).

וּבִזְמַן שֶׁהֵן מְעִידוֹת זוֹ אֶת זוֹ **But when they testify about each other.** *Rashi* explains that the Mishnah is teaching us that although a captive woman is presumed to have been raped unless it is proved otherwise, it is not necessary to produce two qualified witnesses or even one qualified witness to prove that she was not raped; the testimony of anyone — even of another captive woman — is believed that this captive woman was not raped. *Tosafot* notes that the law that anyone — even a slave or a maidservant — is believed to the extent of clearing a captive woman of suspicion, is stated explicitly in a later Mishnah (below, 27a). Thus our Mishnah does not need to tell us this. However, the Gemara below (24a) states that we learn something else from our Mishnah — that even where two captive women testify in each other's favor, we believe them, and do not suspect them of conspiring to testify falsely.

תָּנוּ רַבָּנָן **Our Rabbis taught.** Throughout this Baraita, only one of the women speaks. *Rosh* explains that the fellow captive insisted that she herself was pure. *Ritva* explains that the fellow captive was silent, or was not present, or was perhaps insane and hence incompetent to testify.

HALAKHAH

וּבִזְמַן שֶׁהֵן מְעִידוֹת זוֹ אֶת זוֹ **But when they testify about each other.** "The Rabbis were very lenient in cases involving captive women. Therefore, although they presumed that a woman known to have been a captive had been raped, and did not permit her to marry a priest on the basis of her own statement alone, they did permit her if a single witness testified that she had not been raped.

Even if the witness is not qualified to give formal evidence — such as a slave or maidservant — is related to the captive woman, the witness's evidence is sufficient. Moreover, two captive women may testify in each other's favor, and we do not suspect them of conspiring to give false testimony." (*Rambam, Sefer Kedushah, Hilkhot Issurei Bi'ah* 18:17; *Shulḥan Arukh, Even HaEzer* 7:1.)

נֶאֱמֶנֶת; [1]'אֲנִי טְהוֹרָה וַחֲבֶרְתִּי טְמֵאָה', אֵינָהּ נֶאֱמֶנֶת; [2]'אֲנִי וַחֲבֶרְתִּי טְמֵאָה', נֶאֱמֶנֶת עַל עַצְמָהּ, וְאֵינָהּ נֶאֱמֶנֶת עַל חֲבֶרְתָּהּ; [3]'אֲנִי וַחֲבֶרְתִּי טְהוֹרָה', נֶאֱמֶנֶת עַל חֲבֶרְתָּהּ, וְאֵינָהּ נֶאֱמֶנֶת עַל עַצְמָהּ".

[4]אָמַר מָר: "'אֲנִי טְהוֹרָה וַחֲבֶרְתִּי טְמֵאָה', אֵינָהּ נֶאֱמֶנֶת". [5]הֵיכִי דָּמֵי? [6]אִי דְּלֵיכָּא עֵדִים, עַל עַצְמָהּ אַמַּאי לָא מְהֵימְנָא?

LITERAL TRANSLATION

she is believed; [1]'I am pure but my fellow is impure,' she is not believed; [2]'I and my fellow are impure,' she is believed about herself, but she is not believed about her fellow; [3]'I and my fellow are pure,' she is believed about her fellow, but she is not believed about herself."

[4]The Master said: "'I am pure but my fellow is impure,' she is not believed." [5]How do we visualize the case (lit., "how is it like")? [6]If there are no witnesses, about herself why is

RASHI

גמרא נאמנת — על הכל. **אינה נאמנת** — על כלום. ולקמיה מפרש לה לכולה. **אי דליכא עדים** — שנשבו.

TRANSLATION AND COMMENTARY

she is believed on both counts." Regarding herself, she is believed when she says that she was raped, because the Mishnah ruled that a captive woman is presumed to have been raped even if she insists that she was not, and clearly this is all the more true if she admits that she was raped. Regarding her fellow captive, she is believed when she says that the other woman was not raped in captivity, because the Mishnah ruled that a single witness is sufficient to prove that a captive was not raped, even if the witness had herself been a captive. [1]The Baraita considers a second case: "If one of the women says: **'I am pure but my fellow** captive **is impure** [i.e., she was raped],' **she is not believed** on either count." Regarding herself, she is not believed when she says that she was not raped, because the Mishnah ruled that a captive woman is presumed to have been raped, even if she insists that she was not, unless she can prove otherwise. Regarding her fellow captive, her testimony that the other woman was raped in captivity is ignored, and if the fellow captive has proof that she was not raped, she is permitted to marry a priest; and if she has no proof, we presume that she was raped, as we did before. [2]The Baraita considers a third case: "If one of the women says: **'My fellow** captive **and I are impure** [i.e., we were both raped],' **she is believed about herself, but she is not believed about her fellow** captive." Regarding herself, she is believed when she says that she was raped, because the Mishnah ruled that a captive woman is presumed to have been raped even if she insists that she was not, and all the more so if she admits that she was raped. Regarding her fellow captive, her testimony that the other woman was raped is ignored, and if the fellow captive has proof that she was not raped, she is permitted to marry a priest; and if she has no proof, we presume that she was raped, as we did before. [3]The Baraita considers a fourth case: "If one of the women says: **'My fellow** captive **and I are** both pure [i.e., neither of us was raped],' **she is believed about her fellow** captive, **but she is not believed about herself."** Regarding her fellow captive, she is believed when she says that the other woman was not raped, because the Mishnah ruled that a single witness is sufficient to prove that a captive was not raped, even if the witness was herself a captive. Regarding herself, she is not believed when she says that she was not raped, because the Mishnah ruled that a captive woman is presumed to have been raped, even if she insists that she was not, unless she can prove her claim.

אָמַר מָר [4]The Gemara now considers the Baraita in detail. **The author** of the Baraita **said** in the second clause: "If the woman says: **'I am pure but my fellow** captive **is impure,' she is not believed** on either count." We have explained our Mishnah as referring to a case where there were witnesses who testified that the women were taken captive. [5]But, asks the Gemara, **how do we visualize the case** to which the Baraita is referring? Is it a case where there are witnesses who testify that the women were taken captive? Or is it a case where the women were presumed free when they came before us, and the sole evidence that they were ever taken captive comes from their own statements? The Gemara will now show that it is difficult to explain the entire Baraita in a consistent way. The second clause is clearly referring to a case where there are witnesses, like the case discussed in our Mishnah. [6]For **if there are no witnesses** who testify that

NOTES

הֵיכִי דָּמֵי **How do we visualize the case?** Mishnayot and Baraitot like this one illustrate the effect on complex laws of altering one variable per clause. If more than one variable is altered at a time, the effect is somewhat spoiled. Accordingly, whenever the Gemara encounters a Baraita like this one, it expects all the clauses to be consistent, regarding both the facts of the case and the schools of thought represented. Here, by asking: "How do we visualize the case?" the Gemara is seeking to discover the assumptions that must underlie this Baraita if it is to be interpreted in a consistent manner.

At times the Gemara will go to great lengths to find a

TRANSLATION AND COMMENTARY

the women were taken captive, **why is** this woman **not believed about herself?** [1]For we learned in the previous Mishnah (22a), that if an apparently free woman comes forward and **says: "I was taken captive but I am pure,"** she is believed, because the mouth that forbade is the mouth that permitted, and if the only evidence that a woman was taken captive is her own statement, we must believe it in its entirety! [2]**Rather,** says the Gemara, **it is obvious that** the second clause of the Baraita, like our Mishnah, is referring to a case where **there are witnesses** who testify that the women were taken captive, and this woman insists, without proof, that she was not raped. Hence she is not believed about herself. But if we explain the rest of the Baraita as referring to a case where there were witnesses that the women were taken captive, [3]**consider the middle** (i.e., the third) **clause:** "If one of the women says: **'My fellow** captive **and I are** both **impure,'** [4]**she is believed about herself, but she is not believed about her fellow** captive," i.e., we believe that the fellow captive was not raped. [5]**But**, argues the Gemara, **if** the Baraita is referring to a case **where there are witnesses** who testify that the women were taken captive, **why is she not believed** about her fellow captive? Her fellow captive must surely be presumed to have been raped, unless she can prove otherwise! [6]**Rather**, says the Gemara, **it is obvious that** the third clause of the Baraita, unlike our Mishnah, is referring to a case where **there are no witnesses** who testify that the women were taken captive, and this woman's testimony alone is not sufficient to establish that the other woman was taken captive and raped. But if we explain the rest of the Baraita as referring to a case where there were no witnesses that the women were taken captive, [7]**consider the last** (i.e., the fourth) **clause:** "If the woman says: **'My**

[1]״נִשְׁבֵּיתִי וּטְהוֹרָה אֲנִי״ קָאָמְרָה! [2]אֶלָּא פְּשִׁיטָא דְּאִיכָּא עֵדִים. [3]אֵימָא מְצִיעֲתָא: ״׳אֲנִי וַחֲבֶרְתִּי טְמֵאָה׳, [4]נֶאֱמֶנֶת עַל עַצְמָהּ, וְאֵינָהּ נֶאֱמֶנֶת עַל חֲבֶרְתָּהּ״. [5]וְאִי דְּאִיכָּא עֵדִים, אַמַּאי לָא מְהֵימְנָא? [6]אֶלָּא פְּשִׁיטָא דְּלֵיכָּא עֵדִים. [7]אֵימָא סֵיפָא: ״׳אֲנִי וַחֲבֶרְתִּי טְהוֹרָה׳,

LITERAL TRANSLATION

she not believed? [1]She is saying: "I was taken captive but I am pure"! [2]Rather, it is obvious that there are witnesses. [3]Read (lit., "say") the middle [clause]: "'I and my fellow are impure,' [4]she is believed about herself, but she is not believed about her fellow." [5]But if there are witnesses, why is she not believed? [6]Rather, it is obvious that there are no witnesses. [7]Read the last [clause]: "'I and my fellow are pure,'

RASHI

אלא פשיטא דאיכא עדים – הלכך, אעצמה אינה נאמנת לטהרה, וחברתה נמי, אף על גב דאנן אמרינן בחזקת טמאה קיימא – ההוא לאו משום הימנותא דהך הוא, דבלאו סהדותא דידה נמי בחזקת טומאה היא. **ואינה נאמנת על חברתה** – על כרחך משמע דחברתה בחזקת טהורה קיימא. דבשלמא אינה נאמנת דרישא, אף על גב דאכולה מילתא משמע – שייך למיתנייה משום דידה. אלא הכא, דבהדיא תנא אינה נאמנת על חברתה – קשה. **אלא פשיטא דליכא עדים** – ואדידה מהימנא, דשויתה לנפשה חתיכה דאיסורא.

NOTES

way of explaining a Mishnah or a Baraita in a consistent manner, even if it has to adopt a construction that appears forced, or amend the wording slightly. Occasionally, however, the Gemara cannot find such a solution, and is forced to accept that a Mishnah or a Baraita was not constructed in a logically sound way (see, for example, *Bava Metzia* 41a).

אֵימָא מְצִיעֲתָא Read the middle clause. Throughout the Talmud, the terms "first clause" and "last clause" are used in a relative sense, and should not be understood as necessarily referring to the very first or the very last clause of the statement under consideration. In our Gemara, in particular, "the first clause" actually refers to the second of the four clauses of the Baraita; "the middle clause" to the third; and "the last clause" to the fourth. The very first clause is not discussed by the Gemara until Rav Pappa's explanation later in the passage, where it is described as "the first part of the first clause" [רֵישָׁא דְּרֵישָׁא]. *Ritva* notes that the Gemara did not need to explain the very first clause of the Baraita because it presents no difficulty, and makes sense regardless of whether there are witnesses who testify that the women were taken captive.

The second and fourth clauses, in which the woman is not believed when she claims not to have been raped, clearly refer to cases where there were witnesses that the women were taken captive, so that the "mouth that forbade" argument does not apply. The third clause, however, cannot be explained in this way, because it states that the woman is not believed when she testifies that her fellow captive was raped. This implies that we presume that the fellow captive has not been raped, and if there were witnesses that the women had been taken captive, we would presume that the fellow captive had been raped.

Rashi asks: The same objection could have been raised within the second clause itself. There, too, the woman claims that her fellow captive was raped, and the Baraita rules that she is not believed. But there we interpret the Baraita's ruling that the woman is not believed as meaning that we ignore her statement and apply the general presumption to the fellow captive. Why do we not explain the third clause in the same way? *Rashi* answers that testimony that is ignored is not normally described as "not believed," although such a description is technically correct. Therefore, since the second clause simply says, "she is not believed," without specifying the woman and the fellow captive by name, and since this language is

[1]נֶאֱמֶנֶת עַל חֲבֶרְתָּהּ, וְאֵינָהּ נֶאֱמֶנֶת עַל עַצְמָהּ״. [2]וְאִי דְּלֵיכָּא עֵדִים, אַעַצְמָהּ אַמַּאי לָא מְהֵימְנָא? [3]אֶלָּא פְּשִׁיטָא דְּאִיכָּא עֵדִים. [4]רֵישָׁא וְסֵיפָא דְּאִיכָּא עֵדִים, [5]מְצִיעָתָא דְּלֵיכָּא עֵדִים?

[6]אֲמַר אַבַּיֵי: אִין. רֵישָׁא וְסֵיפָא, דְּאִיכָּא עֵדִים, [7]מְצִיעָתָא דְּלֵיכָּא עֵדִים.

[8]רַב פַּפָּא אֲמַר: כּוּלָּהּ דְּאִיכָּא עֵדִים, [9]וְאִיכָּא עֵד אֶחָד דְּקָא אַפֵּיךְ.

LITERAL TRANSLATION

[1]she is believed about her fellow, but she is not believed about herself." [2]But if there are no witnesses, why is she not believed about herself? [3]Rather, it is obvious that there are witnesses. [4]Are the first [clause] and the last [clause] where there are witnesses, [5][and] the middle [clause] where there are no witnesses?

[6]Abaye said: Yes. The first [clause] and the last [clause] are where there are witnesses, [7][and] the middle [clause] is where there are no witnesses.

[8]Rav Pappa said: All of it is where there are witnesses, [9]but there is one witness who says the opposite (lit., "reverses").

RASHI

דאפיך — מיפך את כל דבריה.

TRANSLATION AND COMMENTARY

fellow captive **and I are** both **pure,'** [1]**she is believed about her fellow** captive **but she is not believed about herself."** [2]**But**, argues the Gemara, **if** the Baraita is referring to a case **where there are no witnesses** who testify that the women were taken captive, **why is** this woman **not believed about herself?** [3]**Rather,** says the Gemara, **it is obvious that** the fourth clause of the Baraita, like our Mishnah, is referring to a case where **there are witnesses** who testify that the women were taken captive. Hence this woman is believed about her fellow captive, because her testimony is sufficient proof, but not about herself, because a woman known to have been a captive is not believed about herself without proof. These difficulties in explaining the Baraita in a consistent manner lead the Gemara to ask: [4]Is it possible that **the first** (i.e., the second) **clause and the last clause** of this Baraita **are** referring to cases **where there are witnesses,** [5]**and the middle** (third) **clause is** referring to a case **where there are no witnesses?** How could the Baraita have been formulated in such a seemingly inconsistent way?

אֲמַר אַבַּיֵי [6]**Abaye said** in reply: **Yes.** The Gemara's analysis is correct. **The first** (i.e., the second) **clause and the last clause of the Baraita are** indeed referring to cases **where there are witnesses,** [7]**and the middle** (third) **clause is** referring to a case **where there are no witnesses.** Although the Baraita was formulated in this unusual way, we have no choice but to accept the Gemara's interpretation of it.

רַב פַּפָּא אֲמַר [8]**Rav Pappa said:** It is possible to explain the Baraita in a consistent manner. **The entire** Baraita, like our Mishnah, **is** referring to a situation **where there are witnesses** who testify that the women were taken captive, [9]but in addition **there is one** further **witness who** testifies either that the women were raped or that they were not raped, and he **says the opposite** of the woman whose statement is recorded in the Baraita.

NOTES

literally true about the woman and technically true about the fellow captive, the Gemara does not find this clause objectionable. But the third clause specifically says that the woman is not believed about her fellow captive, and this can only mean that she is literally not believed, not that she is merely ignored. The Aḥaronim offer other solutions (see *Ḥatam Sofer*).

וְאִיכָּא עֵד אֶחָד דְּקָא אַפֵּיךְ But there is one witness who says the opposite. To understand Rav Pappa's explanation of the Baraita, three rules must be kept in mind. (1) The Rabbis were lenient regarding captive women, and accepted the testimony of a single witness with regard to declaring a captive woman pure. Moreover, the Gemara (*Sotah* 31b) rules that whenever a single witness is believed, we accept testimony even from people who are not normally qualified to testify. (2) When there are two single witnesses, one who says that the captive was raped and the other who denies this, we accept the favorable testimony outright (see following note). (3) Even when there is adequate testimony that a captive woman was not

HALAKHAH

וְאִיכָּא עֵד אֶחָד דְּקָא אַפֵּיךְ But there is one witness who says the opposite. "If there are two witnesses who testify that a woman was taken captive, and one witness testifies that she was definitely raped, and another witness testifies that she was not, she is permitted to marry a priest, even if the unfavorable witness is qualified to testify and the favorable witness is a slave or a maidservant, following Rav Pappa. *Bet Shmuel* adds that this law applies even if the unfavorable testimony was heard first and the favorable testimony was heard only afterwards, although in general in those cases where we accept the testimony of a single witness, we treat the first witness who testifies as though he were two and we do not allow another single witness to come forward later and contradict his testimony." (*Rambam, Sefer Kedushah, Hilkhot Issurei Bi'ah* 18:21; *Shulḥan Arukh, Even HaEzer* 7:5.)

TRANSLATION AND COMMENTARY

אָמְרָה [1]Rav Pappa elaborates: In the first clause of the Baraita, **where** the woman **says: "I am impure but my fellow** captive **is pure,"** [2]we must understand that there is **one witness who says to her: "You are pure but your fellow** captive **is impure."** [3]In this case the woman is believed **regarding herself,** even though the witness testifies that she has not been raped, because by her own statement **she is rendering herself** the equivalent of **a piece of forbidden food.** We have seen above (22a) that when a person declares something to be forbidden, he or she must behave in accordance with that declaration, even when other people are permitted to disregard it. Similarly here, even though we would be prepared to believe the witness and declare this woman to be permitted to marry a priest, she must act in accordance with her own declaration and treat herself as forbidden. [4]**Regarding her fellow** captive, she is also believed, [5]for the fellow captive **is permitted** to marry a priest **by her** testimony. Even though the witness contradicts her, she is believed when she claims that her fellow captive was not raped.

אֲנִי טְהוֹרָה וַחֲבֶרְתִּי טְמֵאָה [6]In the second clause of the Baraita, where the woman says: **"I am pure but my fellow** captive **is impure,"** [7]we must understand that there is **one witness who says to her: "You are impure but your fellow** captive **is pure."** [8]In this case the woman is not believed **regarding herself, because it is not in her power** to declare that she was not raped if **there are witnesses** who testify that she was taken captive, and all the more so where there is a witness who testifies that she was indeed raped. [9]**Regarding her fellow** captive, she is also not believed. [10]For the fellow captive **is permitted** to marry a priest **by the testimony of the witness** who gave evidence in her favor. Even though this woman contradicts the witness, the latter is believed when he testifies that her fellow captive was not raped.

[1]אָמְרָה: ״אֲנִי טְמֵאָה וַחֲבֶרְתִּי טְהוֹרָה״, [2]וַאֲמַר לָהּ עֵד אֶחָד: ״אַתְּ טְהוֹרָה וַחֲבֶרְתֵּיךְ טְמֵאָה״, [3]אִיהִי שָׁוִיתָא לְנַפְשָׁהּ חֲתִיכָה דְּאִיסּוּרָא, [4]חֲבֶרְתָּהּ מִשְׁתַּרְיָא [5]אַפּוּמָא דִּידָהּ.

[6]״אֲנִי טְהוֹרָה וַחֲבֶרְתִּי טְמֵאָה״, [7]וַאֲמַר לָהּ עֵד אֶחָד: ״אַתְּ טְמֵאָה וַחֲבֶרְתֵּיךְ טְהוֹרָה״, [8]אִיהִי, כֵּיוָן דְּאִיכָּא עֵדִים, לָאו כָּל כְּמִינָּהּ, [9]חֲבֶרְתָּהּ מִשְׁתַּרְיָא [10]אַפּוּמָא דְּעֵד.

LITERAL TRANSLATION

[1][If] she says: "I am impure but my fellow is pure," [2]and one witness says to her: "You are pure but your fellow is impure," [3]she has rendered herself a piece of prohibition, [4][but] her fellow is permitted [5]by her testimony (lit., "mouth").

[6]"I am pure but my fellow is impure," [7]and one witness says to her: "You are impure but your fellow is pure," [8][regarding] herself, since there are witnesses, it is not in her power, [9][but] her fellow is permitted [10]by the testimony of the witness.

RASHI

חברתה משתריא אפומא דידה – דבשבויה האמינו חכמים עד אחד להקל, ואפילו עבד או שפחה, כדקתני מתניתין (כתובות כז,א): אם יש להן עדים אפילו עבד כו׳. וכל מקום שנאמן בו עד אחד – הרי הוא כשנים, ואין דברי אחד שכנגדו לטמא עומד במקום שנים. הכי גרסינן: **איהי כיון דאיכא עדים לאו כל כמינה** – ואעדי שבויה קאי, דעד אחד בטומאה אינו כלום אלא בסוטה בלבד, שרגלים לדבר, שהרי קינא לה ונסתרה. **שויתה לנפשה חתיכה דאיסורא** – לפיכך אין העד נאמן לטהרה.

NOTES

raped, if she herself insists that she was raped she is believed and renders herself forbidden, in accordance with the rule that a person is believed when the effect is to render himself forbidden (above, 22a).

חֲבֶרְתָּהּ מִשְׁתַּרְיָא אַפּוּמָא דִּידָהּ Her fellow is permitted by her testimony. According to Rav Pappa's explanation of the Baraita, it is clear that when there are two single witnesses — one who says that the captive was raped and the other who denies this — we accept the favorable testimony outright (see previous note). There are two possible reasons for this. *Rosh* explains that we are referring to a case where the fellow captive herself insists that she was not raped. Therefore, since the Rabbis were lenient about captive women, they believed the woman herself in the event of conflicting testimony.

Ritva argues that the fellow captive is permitted, even when she herself says nothing. He explains that the Baraita is referring to a situation where the favorable testimony was given first, and the unfavorable testimony only later. For we have already learned (above, 22b) that in those rare cases where the testimony of a single witness is accepted, the testimony is treated almost like that of two witnesses. Hence, it can be contradicted only by another witness appearing at the same time, but not by one witness who comes forward later, because the second single witness is considered as one witness contradicting two (see *Sotah* 31b). This explanation is somewhat difficult, because Rav Pappa's language seems to indicate that in each case the witness spoke in response to the woman. But according to this explanation, the favorable testimony was always given first. Hence, in the second and third clauses, in which the woman's testimony was unfavorable, we have to explain that the witness spoke first, and the captive woman came forward only later, after the fellow captive had been permitted (see also *Ramban*).

Rambam makes no distinction between a case where the favorable testimony was heard first and a case where it was heard at the same time as, or even after, the unfavorable testimony. *Maggid Mishneh* explains that, according to *Rambam*, the Rabbis were lenient regarding

TRANSLATION AND COMMENTARY

אֲנִי וַחֲבֶרְתִּי טְמֵאָה [1]In the third clause of the Baraita, where the woman says: **"My fellow** captive **and I are** both **impure,"** [2]we must understand that there is **one witness who says to her: "You and your fellow** captive **are** both **pure."** [3]In this case the woman is believed **regarding herself,** even though the witness testifies that she has not been raped, because **she is rendering herself the equivalent of a piece of forbidden food.** Even though we would be prepared to believe the witness and declare this woman to be permitted to marry a priest, she must act in accordance with her own declaration and treat herself as forbidden. [4]**Regarding her fellow** captive, however, she is not believed. [5]For the fellow captive **is permitted by the testimony of the witness** who gave evidence in her favor. Even though this woman contradicts the witness, the latter is believed when he testifies that her fellow captive was not raped.

הָא תּוּ לָמָה לִי [6]The Gemara now interjects: But according to this explanation, **why do we need this** third clause of the Baraita **as well?** [7]Surely **it is the same as the first** two **clauses!** We have already learned in the first clause that the woman is believed and renders herself forbidden, and we have already learned in the second clause that if one witness testifies that her fellow captive is permitted, he is believed, even if she contradicts him. What, then, do we learn from the third clause that we did not already know?

LITERAL TRANSLATION

[1]"I and my fellow are impure," [2]and one witness says to her: "You and your fellow are pure," [3]she has rendered herself a piece of prohibition, [4][but] her fellow is permitted [5]by the testimony of the witness.

[6]Why do I need this as well? [7]It is the same as the first [clause]!

[1]"אֲנִי וַחֲבֶרְתִּי טְמֵאָה", [2]וַאֲמַר לָהּ עֵד אֶחָד: "אַתְּ וַחֲבֶרְתֵּךְ טְהוֹרָה", [3]אִיהִי שָׁוְיתָא לְנַפְשָׁהּ חֲתִיכָה דְּאִיסּוּרָא, [4]חֲבֶרְתָּא מִשְׁתַּרְיָא [5]אַפּוּמָא דְּעֵד. [6]הָא תּוּ לָמָה לִי? [7]הַיְינוּ רֵישָׁא!

RASHI

הַיְינוּ רֵישָׁא — הֲנֵי מִילֵּי תַּרְוַויְיהוּ אֶשְׁמְעִינַן בְּרֵישָׁא: חֲתִיכָה דְּאִיסּוּרָא — מֵרֵישָׁא שַׁמְעִינַן, שַׁוְיוֹתָא דְּחַבְרְתָּהּ אַפּוּמָא דְעֵד — מִסֵּיפָא דְּרֵישָׁא שַׁמְעִינַן. תַּרְתֵּי בְּנֵי קַמַּיְיתָא רֵישָׁא קָרֵי לְהוּ, דִּדְמֵיין לַהֲדָדֵי. וְתַרְתֵּי בְּנֵי בַתְרַיְיתָא חֲדָא מִילְּתָא הִיא, דְּבַכֹּל חֲדָא חֲדָא תְּנַן מִילְּתָא וְחִילּוּפָהּ, בֵּין בְּרֵישָׁא בֵּין בְּסֵיפָא.

NOTES

captive women, and accepted any favorable testimony, even when it was contradicted by other testimony (see also *Ran*). Presumably *Rambam* explains the Baraita, as did *Rosh*, as referring to a case where the fellow captive also insists that she was not raped.

אִיהִי שָׁוְיתָא לְנַפְשָׁהּ חֲתִיכָה דְּאִיסּוּרָא **She has rendered herself a piece of prohibition.** The Mishnah in tractate *Nedarim* (90b) rules that if the wife of a priest declares, without proof, that she has been raped, she is not believed, because we assume that she made up the story in order to compel her husband to grant her a divorce. From here *Meiri* infers that the captive woman in our Gemara can "render herself a piece of prohibition" and disqualify herself from the priesthood only if she has not yet been married to a priest. But if she is already married to a priest, we believe the witness who testifies that she was pure, and treat her claim just like that of any other priest's wife who declares that she has been raped.

Shiltei HaGibborim argues that this is true only if the married captive woman is contradicted by two witnesses; but if there is only one witness who testifies that the woman was not raped, and she insists that she was raped, we believe her and she renders herself forbidden. *Ḥelkat Meḥokek* objects to *Shiltei HaGibborim*'s distinction, arguing that since one witness is sufficient to establish that the captive woman was not raped, there is no reason to distinguish between a captive woman and any other priest's wife; the law of *Nedarim* should apply, and the woman should not be believed if the effect is to render herself forbidden. *Bet Shmuel* answers that, since the

woman was taken captive, her claim that she was raped is much more credible than that of an ordinary priest's wife who claims, without evidence, that she was raped. *Gra* argues that a captive woman is presumed to have been raped, unless proved otherwise, and although the Rabbis were lenient in accepting the evidence of one witness that she was not raped, so long as two witnesses have not come forward there remains an element of doubt; hence the woman is believed and renders herself forbidden, if only one witness contradicts her declaration.

חֲבֶרְתָּהּ מִשְׁתַּרְיָא אַפּוּמָא דְּעֵד **Her fellow is permitted by the testimony of the witness.** The Rishonim ask: We have already learned from the first clause of the Baraita that if there is conflicting testimony, the fellow captive is permitted to marry a priest. Indeed, in the first clause we were taught that this is the case even if the favorable testimony was given by the captive woman and the unfavorable testimony by a properly qualified witness. Why, then, does the second clause need to teach us that we permit the fellow captive, if the favorable testimony was given by the properly qualified witness and the unfavorable testimony by the woman? *Rosh* and *Ritva* answer that we might have thought that the captive woman is a better witness than the regular witness because she was personally involved, and thus in a better position to know the facts. Hence we might have thought that we always believe her rather than the regular witness. Therefore, the Baraita informs us that we always believe the favorable testimony, even if the testimony of the captive woman is unfavorable.

TRANSLATION AND COMMENTARY

מַהוּ דְּתֵימָא [1]The Gemara answers: If the Baraita had not included the third clause, **you might have said** that in such a case we would believe the witness outright, and not consider the woman to have rendered herself forbidden. For we have seen (above, 22a) that if there is a plausible explanation as to why a person rendered himself forbidden, he is not required to behave in accordance with his declaration. [2]Hence we could argue in the third clause of the Baraita that **these two** women **are** in fact **both pure,** [3]**and the reason why she said** that she was impure **was because** she was trying to incriminate her fellow captive by having her declared impure, out of spite, because of some quarrel. You might have argued that **what she was doing was** sacrificing her own status in order to lend credibility to her attempt to disqualify her fellow captive, in the spirit of Samson (Judges 16:30), who pulled a building down on himself, killing himself and his Philistine enemies, with the cry: **"Let my soul die with the Philistines."** Hence, since we do not believe her regarding her fellow captive, we should not consider her to have rendered herself forbidden either. [4]**Therefore** the Baraita **informs us that** we do **not** assume that the woman would go to such lengths to hurt her fellow captive.

אֲנִי וַחֲבֶרְתִּי טְהוֹרָה [5]Rav Pappa returns to his explanation. In the fourth clause of the Baraita, where the woman says: **"My fellow** captive **and I are** both **pure,"** [6]we must understand that there is **one witness who says to her: "You and your fellow** captive **are** both **impure."** [7]In this case the woman is not believed **regarding herself, because it is not in her power** to establish that she was not raped if **there are witnesses** who testify that she was taken captive, and all the more so if there is a witness who testifies that she was indeed raped. [8]**Regarding her fellow** captive, however, she is believed, for the fellow captive **is permitted by her testimony.** Even though the witness contradicts her, she is believed when she claims that her fellow captive was not raped.

הָא תּוּ לָמָּה לִי [9]Here too the Gemara interjects: But according to Rav Pappa's explanation, **why do we need this** fourth clause of the Baraita **as well?** The fact that the woman is not believed regarding herself is obvious, and has already been mentioned in the second clause. [10]And the fact that she is believed to the extent of contradicting the witness and rendering her fellow captive permitted **is stated in the first part of the first clause!** We have already learned in the first clause that if the woman declares that her fellow captive is permitted to a priest, she is believed, even if she is contradicted by one witness. What, then, do we learn from the fourth clause that we did not already know?

[1]מַהוּ דְּתֵימָא: [2]הָנֵי תַּרְוַיְיהוּ טְהוֹרוֹת נִינְהוּ, [3]וְהַאי דְּקָאָמְרָה הָכִי ״תָּמוֹת נַפְשִׁי עִם פְּלִשְׁתִּים״ הִיא דְּקָא עָבְדָה. [4]קָא מַשְׁמַע לָן.

[5]״אֲנִי וַחֲבֶרְתִּי טְהוֹרָה״, [6]וַאֲמַר לָהּ עֵד אֶחָד: ״אַתְּ וַחֲבֶרְתֵּךְ טְמֵאָה״, אִיהִי, כֵּיוָן דְּאִיכָּא עֵדִים, לָאו כָּל כְּמִינָּהּ, [7]חֲבֶרְתָּהּ מִשְׁתַּרְיָא [8]אַפּוּמָּא דִּידָהּ.

[9]הָא תּוּ לָמָּה לִי? [10]הַיְינוּ רֵישָׁא דְּרֵישָׁא!

LITERAL TRANSLATION

[1]You might have said: [2]These two are both pure, [3]and the reason why she said this is because she is acting [in the way of]: "Let my soul die with the Philistines." [4][Therefore] it tells us [otherwise].

[5]"I and my fellow are pure," [6]and one witness says to her: "You and your fellow are impure," [7][regarding] herself, since there are witnesses, it is not in her power, [8][but] her fellow is permitted by her testimony.

[9]Why do I need this as well? [10]It is the same as the first [part] of the first [clause]!

RASHI

מהו דתימא כו׳ — ומשום נאמנת על עצמה תנא ליה. **איהי, כיון דאיכא עדים** גרסינן. **היינו רישא דרישא** — דהא ודאי משום דאינה נאמנת על עצמה לא אצטריך למיתנייה, דהא טובא אשמועינן דבמקום עדי שביה לא מהימנא למימר טהורה אני, ומשום נאמנת על חברתה הוא דאצטריך, דאף על גב דעד קא מכחיש לה — מהימנא, והא ברישא דרישא אשמועינן.

NOTES

תָּמוֹת נַפְשִׁי עִם פְּלִשְׁתִּים "Let my soul die with the Philistines." Samson's exclamation is used throughout the Talmud as a symbol of the urge some people have to take revenge, regardless of the personal loss involved. In our case, the Gemara concludes that we need not suspect the captive woman of behaving in this way toward her fellow captive. But in many cases the Rabbis rejected testimony for precisely this reason.

The Gemara assumes that there is a potential for hostility between a wife and certain relatives by marriage who are frequently rivals for the husband's affection (the mother-in-law, the stepdaughter, the sister-in-law, and the other wife in a polygamous marriage; *Yevamot* 117a). Thus, if a woman's mother-in-law testifies that her son (the woman's husband) is dead, the woman may not remarry, because we fear that the mother-in-law may be lying in order to trick the woman into an adulterous second marriage, so that when her son returns he will be forced to divorce her. Even though the fear that a mother would deliberately put her son (and the second husband) through

LITERAL TRANSLATION

[1]You might have said: [2]When she is believed, it is where she renders herself unfit, [3]but where she renders herself fit, [4]I might say: She is not believed. [5][Therefore] it tells us [otherwise].

MISHNAH [6]And similarly [regarding] two men, [7][if] one says: "I am a priest," and one says: "I am a priest," they are not believed. [8]But when they testify about each other, [9]they are believed.

[1]מַהוּ דְּתֵימָא: [2]כִּי מְהֵימְנָא, בְּמָקוֹם דְּפָסְלָה נַפְשָׁהּ, [3]אֲבָל בְּמָקוֹם דְּמַכְשְׁרָא נַפְשָׁהּ, [4]אֵימָא: לָא מְהֵימְנָא. [5]קָא מַשְׁמַע לָן.

משנה [6]וְכֵן שְׁנֵי אֲנָשִׁים, [7]זֶה אוֹמֵר: ״כֹּהֵן אֲנִי״, וְזֶה אוֹמֵר: ״כֹּהֵן אֲנִי״, אֵינָן נֶאֱמָנִין. [8]וּבִזְמַן שֶׁהֵן מְעִידִין זֶה אֶת זֶה, [9]הֲרֵי אֵלּוּ נֶאֱמָנִין.

TRANSLATION AND COMMENTARY

מַהוּ דְּתֵימָא [1]The Gemara replies: If the Baraita had not included the fourth clause, **you might have said** that in such a case we would not believe her contradiction of the witness. [2]For we could argue that **she is believed** and contradicts the witness only in a situation **where she is rendering herself unfit,** as in the first clause. In such a case, her declaration has great credibility because it is in no way self-serving. [3]**But in a situation where she is** trying to **render herself fit,** as in the fourth clause, where she claims that both she and her fellow captive were not raped, [4]**we might say:** She claimed that her fellow captive had not been raped only in order to lend credibility to her own claim that she had not been raped either. Hence, since her claim has no special credibility, **she should not be believed** if the effect is to contradict the witness and permit her fellow captive to marry a priest. [5]**Therefore** the fourth clause **informs us that** this is **not** so, and we believe her favorable testimony against the unfavorable testimony of the witness, even if her testimony appears somewhat self-serving.

MISHNAH וְכֵן שְׁנֵי אֲנָשִׁים [6]The previous Mishnah ruled that a captive woman who claims that she was not raped is not believed, but two captive women who testify in each other's favor are believed. The Mishnah now informs us that there is a **similar** law **regarding two men** of unknown lineage who claim to be priests: [7]If each **one says** about himself: **"I am a priest," they are not believed**, because a man who claims to be a priest is not believed without proof. [8]**But when** each of the two men does not merely claim that he is a priest but **each testifies about the other**, there is a Tannaitic dispute about the matter. [9]The anonymous first Tanna of our Mishnah rules that **they are believed**, even though we might suspect that

RASHI

במקום דפסלה לנפשה — התם הוא דמהימנא אחברתה, משום דקאמרה "טמאה אני". **אבל היכא דמכשרא נמי לנפשה** — אימא משום דידה הוא דקאמרה, ולא אחברתה. קמשמע לן גרסינן. לישנא אחרינא גרסינן: מהו דתימא כי מהימנא במקום עד פסול. כגון דעד דקא מפיך הוי אשה, אבל במקום עד כשר — לא, תנא משנה יתירה דאפילו במקום עד כשר.

משנה וכן שני אנשים — לא גרסינן שנשבו. **אין נאמנים** — ליתן להן תרומה. **ובזמן שמעידין זה את זה** — שכל אחד אומר "אני וחברי כהן".

NOTES

such suffering merely for the sake of revenge appears exaggerated, experience shows that the urge for revenge should not be underestimated.

The Gemara concludes that the two women in our passage are not suspected of plotting revenge in this way. It is not clear, however, what the law would be if the two captives were in fact sisters-in-law or wives of the same husband. *Shiltei HaGibborim* rules that the testimony of even one of her traditional enemies that a captive woman was not raped is believed, since the Rabbis were lenient regarding captive women. But some commentators suggest that *Rosh* would disagree with this ruling (see *Ḥelkat Meḥokek* and *Bet Shmuel*).

HALAKHAH

זֶה אוֹמֵר: ״כֹּהֵן אֲנִי״ **If one says: "I am a priest."** "We do not elevate a person to the priesthood without proof. Hence, if a stranger comes forward and says: 'I am a priest,' he is not permitted to eat terumah — even terumah of Rabbinic status — nor may he read first from the Torah, nor may he give the Priestly Benediction in the synagogue, following the Mishnah.

"*Remakh* rules that a man who claims to be a priest is believed, without proof, and is permitted to read first from the Torah and to give the Priestly Benediction, although he may not be given terumah. *Remakh* explains that we are not concerned that allowing this man to read first from the Torah will lead to his being given terumah, as in any case terumah today is of Rabbinic status. *Maggid Mishneh*, however, rejects this ruling. *Rema* rules in favor of *Remakh* in practice, because the majority of the Jewish people live far from Eretz Israel, and the issue of terumah is not a practical one for them. But in Eretz Israel, where the laws of terumah apply, *Bet Shmuel* rules that we do not permit a man who claims to be a priest to act as a priest in the synagogue, unless he can substantiate his claim, lest he be given terumah." (*Rambam, Sefer Kedushah, Hilkhot Issurei Bi'ah* 20:13; *Shulḥan Arukh, Even HaEzer* 3:1.)

וּבִזְמַן שֶׁהֵן מְעִידִין זֶה אֶת זֶה **But when they testify about each other.** "A person claiming to be a priest is not believed unless he produces at least one witness to support

TRANSLATION AND COMMENTARY

they have conspired to fabricate their claims, because in principle people are believed on ritual questions, even when they have a material interest in the matter.

רַבִּי יְהוּדָה אוֹמֵר [1] **Rabbi Yehudah** disagrees with the first Tanna, and **says:** Each man claiming to be a priest must prove his claim by producing two qualified witnesses to testify on his behalf. The testimony of the other claimant is not sufficient, because **we do not elevate** a man **to the priesthood on the evidence of one witness,** even where the witness is qualified and disinterested. And we would certainly not do so if the evidence is provided by another claimant who has a material interest in the matter.

אָמַר רַבִּי אֶלְעָזָר [2] **Rabbi Elazar says:** Rabbi Yehudah's ruling — that the testimony of a single witness is insufficient to prove that a man is a priest — applies only when real proof is required. And **when** is real proof required? [3] **In a situation where there are objectors** — other witnesses who testify that the man is not a priest. In such a case, the evidence of one witness testifying in the man's favor — even if the witness is qualified and disinterested — is inadequate. [4] **But in a situation where there are no objectors, we** do **elevate** a man **to the priesthood on the evidence of one** qualified, disinterested **witness.**

רַבָּן שִׁמְעוֹן בֶּן גַּמְלִיאֵל [5] **Rabban Shimon ben Gamliel** takes a slightly different position, and **says in the name of Rabbi Shimon the son of the Deputy High Priest:** [6] Even in a situation where there are objectors, **we** sometimes **elevate** a man **to the priesthood on the evidence of one witness.**

[1] רַבִּי יְהוּדָה אוֹמֵר: אֵין מַעֲלִין לִכְהוּנָּה עַל פִּי עֵד אֶחָד. [2] אָמַר רַבִּי אֶלְעָזָר: אֵימָתַי? [3] בְּמָקוֹם שֶׁיֵּשׁ עוֹרְרִין. [4] אֲבָל בְּמָקוֹם שֶׁאֵין עוֹרְרִין, מַעֲלִין לִכְהוּנָּה עַל פִּי עֵד אֶחָד. [5] רַבָּן שִׁמְעוֹן בֶּן גַּמְלִיאֵל אוֹמֵר מִשּׁוּם רַבִּי שִׁמְעוֹן בֶּן הַסְּגָן: [6] מַעֲלִין לִכְהוּנָּה עַל פִּי עֵד אֶחָד.

LITERAL TRANSLATION

[1] Rabbi Yehudah says: We do not elevate to the priesthood on the evidence of one witness.

[2] Rabbi Elazar said: When? [3] In a situation (lit., "place") where there are objectors. [4] But in a situation where there are no objectors, we elevate to the priesthood on the evidence of one witness.

[5] Rabban Shimon ben Gamliel said in the name of Rabbi Shimon the son of the Deputy High Priest: [6] We elevate to the priesthood on the evidence of one witness.

RASHI

רבי יהודה אומר אין מעלין לכהונה על פי עד אחד — ואפילו היכא דליכא גומלין, וכל שכן הכא דאיכא למיחש לגומלין: העד אתה עלי ואני עליך. **עוררין** — שקורין עליו שם פסול. **מעלין** — היכא דליכא גומלין. והיינו דאיכא בין רבי אלעזר לתנא קמא דרבי יהודה. **רבן שמעון כו׳** — בגמרא מפרש מאי בינייהו.

NOTES

רַבִּי יְהוּדָה אוֹמֵר **Rabbi Yehudah says.** The Gemara gives two different explanations of Rabbi Yehudah's position. Our commentary follows *Rashi*, who explains Rabbi Yehudah's viewpoint in accordance with the Gemara's second explanation (below, 24b). According to this explanation, Rabbi Yehudah does not accept the testimony of only one witness regarding terumah, even if the witness is disinterested and qualified, and there is no contrary evidence. But according to Abaye's explanation (ibid.), Rabbi Yehudah does accept the testimony of one witness regarding terumah, provided that he is disinterested. According to Abaye, Rabbi Yehudah rejects the witness in our Mishnah because he is also claiming to be a priest, and has an interest in the matter, so we suspect a conspiracy (*Maharsha*).

According to the Gemara's second explanation, there are two unrelated issues in our Mishnah: (1) Whether the testimony of one witness is sufficient to elevate a man to the priesthood, and (2) whether we accept the testimony of one witness who has an interest in his testimony being accepted. According to this explanation, *Rashi* argues that each of the Tannaim in our Mishnah has a distinct point of view: The first Tanna accepts the testimony of one witness, even if the witness has an interest in his testimony being accepted; Rabbi Yehudah rejects the testimony of one witness, even if the witness has no interest in his testimony being accepted; and Rabbi Elazar and Rabban Shimon ben Gamliel accept the testimony of one disinterested witness, but not one who has an interest in his testimony being accepted (see previous note). According to Abaye's explanation, however, the only issue in our Mishnah is the question of a possible conspiracy, and at most there can be two views on this matter.

מַעֲלִין לִכְהוּנָּה **We elevate to the priesthood.** The question in our Mishnah is whether a presumed priest who has only one witness to support his claim is permitted to eat terumah. *Rosh* (*Gittin* 54b) explains that, in general, one witness is believed regarding ritual questions such as terumah, and even the person himself is believed. Thus, if a person claims that his food is kosher, he is believed, and we may eat from it without further proof. Our Mishnah, however, rules that a man who claims to be a priest is not believed unless he brings at least one witness to support his claim. But a single witness is sufficient, even if he is not disinterested, and even if two men who claim to be priests testify in each other's favor," following the first Tanna in our Mishnah. (*Rambam, Sefer Kedushah, Hilkhot Issurei Bi'ah* 20:11; *Shulḥan Arukh, Even HaEzer* 3:4.)

HALAKHAH

CONCEPTS

מַעֲלִין לִכְהוּנָּה **We elevate to the priesthood.** Throughout the generations the priests have enjoyed a special status within the Jewish people. This status of membership in a special, noble group was particularly prominent in Temple times and for many generations afterwards, when matters of lineage still occupied an important place in Jewish communal life.

While the Temple stood, not only did the priests alone perform the Temple service, but they also had certain economic privileges. Moreover, their social status gave them priority on religious and social occasions. At the same time, some commandments which are not binding on other Jews are incumbent upon priests — notably the prohibition against contracting ritual impurity from the dead (except close relatives), and the prohibition against marrying a divorced woman or a woman with certain flaws in her Jewish lineage.

After the destruction of the Temple, many of the priests' privileges lapsed, but they continued to receive their part of harvests from Eretz Israel — terumah and first tithe.

As the period of exile continued and there was no longer any possibility of observing the laws of ritual purity, the priests were forbidden to consume terumah and *ḥallah*. The status of the courts also declined, so that the details of family lineage were no longer preserved. Today the priesthood hardly confers any economically significant privilege, although the special prohibitions applicable to priests have not been abolished, and their privileges in synagogue ritual have been preserved.

The laws and the discussions in the Mishnah and the Gemara here relate to the situation that obtained during the generations immediately after the destruction of the Second Temple.

SAGES

רַבִּי שִׁמְעוֹן בֶּן הַסְּגָן **Rabbi Shimon the son of the Deputy High Priest.** This scholar is mentioned in a few passages in the Mishnah. The

LITERAL TRANSLATION

GEMARA [1] Why do I need all of these? [2] They are necessary. [3] For if [the Mishnah] had taught "Rabbi Yehoshua admits," [I might have thought] it was because there is money at stake (lit., "a pull of money"), [4] but [in the case of] witnesses, where there is no money at stake, [5] I would say no.

גמרא [1] כָּל הָנֵי לָמָּה לִי? [2] צְרִיכִי. [3] דְּאִי תָּנָא "מוֹדֶה רַבִּי יְהוֹשֻׁעַ" מִשּׁוּם דְּאִיכָּא דְּרָרָא דְּמָמוֹנָא, [4] אֲבָל עֵדִים, דְּלֵיכָּא דְּרָרָא דְּמָמוֹנָא, [5] אֵימָא לָא.

RASHI

גמרא כל הני — דתנא מתניתין לאשמועינן הפה שאסר הוא הפה שהתיר למה לי? **משום דאיכא דררא דממונא** — הלכך, אי לאו דפשיטא מלתא שלקחה מאביו — לא היה אומר של אביך היתה וגורס לעצמו הפסד ממון. וכשאומר תחלת דבריו — על שם סופו אמרו, לגמור בהן "ולקחתיה הימנו". **אבל עדים** — שאמרו "כתב ידינו הוא". **דליכא דררא דממונא** — לגבייהו, דלימטינהו פסידא בהאי עדות. **אימא לא** — ליתהמנו למימר "אנוסין היינו". דמעיקרא כי אמרו "כתב ידינו הוא" — אדעתא דסהדותא אמרו, ולאו למיגמר בה "אנוסים היינו", והדר אימליכו למיגמר בה הכי — קמשמע לן.

TRANSLATION AND COMMENTARY

GEMARA כָּל הָנֵי לָמָּה לִי [1] Before considering our Mishnah in detail, the Gemara explains the sequence of Mishnayot from the beginning of the chapter up to this point. Most of these Mishnayot are based on the same idea — that a person who is presumed to be in a disadvantageous situation cannot refute that presumption without proof, but a person who creates a disadvantageous situation for himself by a statement he volunteered, and then resolves the difficulty almost in the same breath, *is* believed, because the mouth that forbade is the mouth that permitted. **Why,** then, asks the Gemara, **do we need all these** Mishnayot to teach us a single principle?

צְרִיכִי [2] The Gemara answers: These Mishnayot **are** all **necessary.** Although the principle is the same in all of them, it is applied to cases with important differences between them, so that if we had been taught only one Mishnah, we would not have been certain that we could apply the principle to all cases. [3] The Gemara now elaborates, showing the special features of each case: **If the Mishnah had taught** only the first case (above, 15b) — **"Rabbi Yehoshua agrees** that if someone who is in possession of a field says to another person: 'This field originally belonged to your father and I bought it from him,' then the person in possession is believed, because the mouth that forbade is the mouth that permitted" — we might have thought that the "mouth that forbade" argument applies only to cases where a person puts himself in a situation where **there is money at stake,** and he is liable to suffer a financial loss. In other words, the *miggo* argument is very strong because we can be certain that he would never have risked his money if he had not been telling the truth. [4] **But in the case of witnesses** who authenticate their signatures on a document yet insist that their testimony was invalid (above, 18b), **there is no money at stake,** because the witnesses themselves are risking nothing even if the document is declared valid. [5] Therefore, **I might have said that** the "mouth that forbade" argument does **not** apply in such a case, because there is no *miggo* involved.

title הַסְּגָן was apparently not a personal name but an honorary title — "Deputy High Priest." Indeed, according to *Rambam*, this Rabbi Shimon was the son of Rabbi Ḥanina the Deputy High Priest, who lived at the time when the Second Temple was destroyed, and is frequently mentioned in Talmudic sources.

Some authorities are of the opinion that this Rabbi Shimon is identical to the Sage referred to in the Tosefta and other sources as Rabbi Shimon ben Kahana. In any case, as the son of the Deputy High Priest, Rabbi Shimon's testimony carries special weight as far as the genealogical status of that priests is concerned.

TERMINOLOGY

כָּל הָנֵי לָמָּה לִי Why do I need all of these? When a Mishnah presents a series of apparently similar examples, the Gemara often asks: "Why are they all necessary? They all seem to be based on a single principle, and there seems to be no need to state them all." The Gemara then answers that the cases are indeed necessary (צְרִיכָא or צְרִיכִי), and explains the special circumstances justifying their inclusion.

NOTES

his claim — even according to the lenient view of the Sages. *Rosh* explains that the prestige associated with the priesthood, and the economic advantages of receiving terumah — both for the claimant and for his descendants — are so great that we are not willing to take his word without some corroboration.

דְּרָרָא דְּמָמוֹנָא Money at stake. This concept appears in several places in the Talmud in different contexts. Its precise meaning is unclear, and various explanations have been given by the commentators. In our commentary we have followed *Rashi*, who explains that "money at stake" means "a loss of money." *Rashi* explains that the silent *miggo* of the person occupying the field is very strong because he is placing his property at risk by saying something, and he would not have done so if it were not true. By contrast, the witnesses who authenticate the document, although they are supported by a silent *miggo*, are not causing themselves any loss by testifying.

Tosafot cites *Rabbenu Ḥananel*, who explains that דְּרָרָא דְּמָמוֹנָא means that the claim is based on an undisputed connection to the property. Thus in this case the person occupying the field has indisputably been in de facto possession for some time, and his *miggo* argument merely buttresses his claim. The witnesses, by contrast, have no connection with the money attested in the document. In tractate *Bava Metzia* (2b), *Ramban* argues that *Rabbenu Ḥananel*'s explanation fits other passages better than *Rashi*'s does. *Rashba* suggests that both interpretations are correct, and each is used by the Gemara, depending on the context.

In *Bava Metzia*, *Tosafot* cites another explanation: that דְּרָרָא דְּמָמוֹנָא (lit., "a pull of money") means that the money is being pulled in different directions, i.e., it is obvious that the ownership of the property in question is problematic, even before the parties present their arguments in court. This explanation fits very well in several places (such as *Bava Kamma* 46a and *Bava Batra* 35b), but there does not appear to be a simple way of applying it to our Gemara.

[1]וְאִי תָּנָא "עֵדִים", [2]מִשּׁוּם דִּלְעָלְמָא, [3]אֲבָל אִיהוּ דִּלְנַפְשֵׁיהּ, [24A] [4]אֵימָא לָא. [5]וְאִי אַשְׁמַעִינַן הָנֵי תַּרְתֵּי, מִשּׁוּם דְּמָמוֹנָא, [6]אֲבָל אֵשֶׁת אִישׁ, דְּאִיסּוּרָא, [7]אֵימָא לָא. [8]"נִשְׁבֵּיתִי וּטְהוֹרָה אֲנִי" לָמָּה לִי? [9]מִשּׁוּם דְּקָא בָּעֵי לְמִיתְנֵי: [10]"וְאִם מִשֶּׁנִּשֵּׂאת בָּאוּ עֵדִים, [11]הֲרֵי זוֹ לֹא תֵּצֵא".

LITERAL TRANSLATION

[1]And if [the Mishnah] had taught "witnesses," [2][I might have thought] it was because it concerns others (lit., "the world"), [3]but [where] he himself [testifies] for himself, [24A] [4]I would say no. [5]And if [the Mishnah] had informed us of these two, [I might have thought] it was because [they involve] money, [6]but [in the case of] a married woman, which [involves] a prohibition, [7]I would say no.

[8]Why do I need "I was taken captive but I am pure"?

[9]Because [the Mishnah] needed to teach: [10]"But if witnesses came after she was married, [11]she does not leave."

TRANSLATION AND COMMENTARY

[1]**And** conversely, **if the Mishnah had taught** only the case of **"witnesses"** (above, 18b) and had left out the first case (above, 15b), we might have thought that the "mouth that forbade" argument applies only to cases of witnesses, [2]**because** the witnesses are "permitting the forbidden" **for others**. In other words, the *miggo* argument is very strong because the witnesses have no interest in lying about this matter. [3]**But** in the first case, **where** the person making the statement was "permitting the forbidden" **for himself,** [24A] [4]**I might have said that** the "mouth that forbade" argument does **not** apply. It is possible that the field actually belongs to the plaintiff, and that the person in possession stole it and, in a fleeting moment of repentance, was prepared to return it, but later changed his story. Hence, this Mishnah was needed to teach us that the "mouth that forbade" argument applies even to such a case. [5]**And** even **if the Mishnah had informed us of these two** cases, I would still not have been able to infer the other cases from them, **because** I might have said that the "mouth that forbade" argument applies only to cases **involving money,** [6]**but in the case of a married woman** (a woman who was presumed to be unmarried but who said: "I was married and divorced"; see above, 22a), **which involves a** religious **prohibition,** [7]**I might have said that** the "mouth that forbade" argument does **not** apply, because financial laws cannot be used as the basis for ritual laws. Therefore, the Mishnah was needed to teach us that the "mouth that forbade" argument applies even to questions of adultery.

נִשְׁבֵּיתִי וּטְהוֹרָה אֲנִי [8]But, the Gemara continues, the Mishnah did not stop there. It went on (above, 22a) to cite the case of a woman who says: **"I was taken captive but I am pure." Why do we need** this case as well? Surely it is obvious that if the "mouth that forbade" argument applies even to questions of adultery, it applies all the more so to captive women!

מִשּׁוּם דְּקָא בָּעֵי לְמִיתְנֵי [9]The Gemara replies: This law of the captive woman was mentioned by way of introduction, **because the Mishnah needed to teach** us the last clause: [10]**"But if witnesses come after** the captive woman has been permitted to marry on the basis of her own deposition, and **she has married** a priest, [11]**she need not leave** her new husband." This law applies specifically to captive women, and not to any other case where the "mouth that forbade" argument applies. If, for example, in the first Mishnah, witnesses were to come forward and testify that the field originally belonged to the plaintiff's father, the "mouth that forbade" argument would not apply, regardless of whether the witnesses came immediately or later. Hence the Mishnah must teach us about the specific case of a captive woman, who is permitted to marry on the basis of the "mouth that forbade" argument.

RASHI

דלעלמא — אין הדבור האחרון מהני לעצמו אלא לאחרים, ומשום אחרים לא הוו הדרי במלתייהו. אבל איהו גופיה דלנפשיה — מהני כי הדר ואמר "לקחתיה".

NOTES

מִשּׁוּם דְּמָמוֹנָא Because they involve money. In general, monetary matters and ritual matters are dealt with separately under Jewish law, and when a law applies to one area we cannot assume automatically that it applies to the other as well. Thus, in some places (e.g., *Bava Metzia* 20b, *Berakhot* 19b) the Gemara declares that we cannot derive a ritual law from a monetary law, whereas in others (e.g., *Kiddushin* 3b) the Gemara declares that we cannot derive a monetary law from a ritual law.

Rashi explains that the reason we are sometimes more lenient regarding monetary matters when a slight doubt remains is that a court has the power to that confiscate a person's property and deliver it to someone else, whereas in ritual cases this power does not exist. *Ritva* explains that we are sometimes more lenient regarding ritual matters because certain legal presumptions which apply to monetary questions have no parallel in ritual matters, such as the presumption that property belongs to the person in possession of it.

"נִשְׁבֵּיתִי וּטְהוֹרָה אֲנִי" לָמָּה לִי Why do I need "I was taken captive but I am pure"? *Tosafot* asks: What is the Gemara asking? Granted that we do not need to be told that the

LITERAL TRANSLATION

[1]This is well according to the one who teaches it [as applying] to the last clause, [2]but according to the one who teaches it [as applying] to the first clause, [3]what is there to say?

[4]Because [the Mishnah] needed to teach: "[If] two women were taken captive." [5]And why do I need [the case of] "two women who were taken captive"? [6]You might have said: Let us suspect [them of] mutual assistance. [7][Therefore] it tells us [otherwise]. [8]Why do I need [the case of] "and similarly two men"?

[1]הָנִיחָא לְמַאן דְּמַתְנֵי לַהּ אַסֵּיפָא, [2]אֶלָּא לְמַאן דְּמַתְנֵי לַהּ אַרֵישָׁא, [3]מַאי אִיכָּא לְמֵימַר?

[4]מִשּׁוּם דְּקָא בָּעֵי לְמִיתְנֵי: "שְׁתֵּי נָשִׁים שֶׁנִּשְׁבּוּ". [5]וּ"שְׁתֵּי נָשִׁים שֶׁנִּשְׁבּוּ" לָמָּה לִי? [6]מַהוּ דְּתֵימָא: נֵיחוּשׁ לְגוּמְלִין. [7]קָמַשְׁמַע לַן. [8]"וְכֵן שְׁנֵי אֲנָשִׁים" לָמָּה לִי?

RASHI

משום דבעי למיתני שתי נשים שנשבו — לאשמועינן דבזמן שמעידות זו את זו נאמנות.

TRANSLATION AND COMMENTARY

הָנִיחָא [1]But, the Gemara objects, **this** line of argument **is satisfactory according to** Rabbah bar Avin (above, 23a), **who teaches** that the law that if witnesses subsequently come forward, a woman who was permitted by the court to marry need not leave her new husband **applies to the last clause** of the Mishnah, and concerns only captive women. [2]**But according to** Rabbi Oshaya, **who teaches** that this law also **applies to the first clause**, which deals with adultery, [3]**what is there to say?** Rabbi Oshaya ruled that an apparently unmarried woman who says that she was married and divorced, and is permitted by the court to remarry on the basis of the "mouth that forbade" argument, need not leave her new husband, even if witnesses subsequently come forward and testify that she was previously married. Why, then, does the Mishnah need to teach us that the "mouth that forbade" argument applies to a captive woman as well? It is sufficient for it to teach us that the argument applies to a woman who claims to be divorced, and then immediately to insert the final clause, teaching us that witnesses who come forward later have no effect. For it is obvious that if the "mouth that forbade" argument applies in a case of possible adultery, it also applies to a captive woman.

מִשּׁוּם דְּקָא בָּעֵי לְמִיתְנֵי [4]The Gemara answers: The "mouth that forbade" argument was mentioned in connection with the law of the captive woman by way of introduction, **because the Mishnah needed to teach** us the next Mishnah (above, 23b): **"If two women were taken captive,** etc.," from which we learn that if there is even one witness — even another captive woman — who testifies that the captive woman was not raped in captivity, the witness is believed. This law applies specifically to captive women.

וּשְׁתֵּי נָשִׁים שֶׁנִּשְׁבּוּ [5]But, the Gemara continues, **why do we need** the case of **"two women who were taken captive"?** The ruling that even people who are not qualified to testify are believed regarding captive women is taught explicitly in another Mishnah (below, 27a). What does the Mishnah teach us here that is not mentioned there?

מַהוּ דְּתֵימָא [6]The Gemara answers: If the Mishnah had not specifically told us that the testimony of a fellow captive is accepted, **you might have said** that, even though people who are not qualified to testify are believed regarding a captive woman, another captive woman should not be believed, because **we suspect** the two women **of giving** false **evidence in each other's favor.** We suspect the two captive women of conspiring to invent a story to clear each other of suspicion. [7]**Therefore** the Mishnah **informs us that this is not so,** and that even a fellow captive is believed. In order to introduce this law, the Mishnah also mentioned that the "mouth that forbade" argument applies to captive women, even though that point is itself unnecessary.

וְכֵן שְׁנֵי אֲנָשִׁים [8]But, the Gemara continues, if the Mishnah has already taught us that there is no reason to suspect the two women of giving false evidence in each other's favor, and that a fellow captive is believed, **why do we need** the clause in our Mishnah: **"And similarly two men"?** We have already learned from the

NOTES

"mouth that forbade" argument is effective in the case of a captive woman. But we need this Mishnah for another reason: Were it not for the Mishnah, we would not have known that the law of the captive woman existed at all! Perhaps the law is that a woman who was kidnapped but claims not to have been raped is believed, even if she is not supported by the "mouth that forbade" argument?

Tosafot answers that we learn the basic law of the captive woman from a later Mishnah in our chapter (27a), which teaches us that captive women are disqualified from marrying, or remaining married to, priests unless they can prove that they were not raped in captivity. This law was taught here as well merely to inform us that the "mouth that forbade" argument is a valid proof in the case of a captive woman — a point that is obvious, as the Gemara notes.

TRANSLATION AND COMMENTARY

case of the two captive women that people are not believed when they testify about themselves, but are believed when they testify about each other. Why does the Mishnah need to cite the similar case of the two men who claim to be priests?

מִשּׁוּם דְּקָא בָּעֵי לְמִיתְנֵי [1]The Gemara answers: **The Mishnah needed to teach us** specifically that two men who claim to be priests are believed when they testify about each other, **because** there is a **dispute between Rabbi Yehudah and the Rabbis** on this matter. The first Tanna is of the opinion that the case of the two men who claim to be priests is similar to that of the two captive women. In both cases we accept the testimony of the fellow priest or fellow captive by itself, and do not worry about a possible conspiracy between them. But Rabbi Yehudah requires a man who claims to be a priest to produce two qualified witnesses to support his claim, although he agrees that two captive women are believed when they testify about each other. Hence the Mishnah needed to teach us both laws.

תָּנוּ רַבָּנַן [2]The Gemara now considers the difference of opinion between Rabbi Yehudah and the other Sages in our Mishnah, and cites a Baraita which throws light on this dispute. **Our Rabbis taught** the following Baraita: "If two men of unknown family come to town and claim to be priests, they are not believed. [3]But if each says: **'I am a priest and the man with me is** also **a priest,'** [4]the Sages maintain that **they are believed,** and each is allowed **to eat terumah** on the strength of the other's testimony. The Sages are of the opinion that a man claiming to be a priest is believed if one witness — even a companion of his, also claiming to be a priest — supports his claim. [5]**But** even according to this view, the two claimants **are not believed to** the extent of permitting each to **marry a woman** of unblemished lineage, **unless there are three** men involved who are claiming to be priests, and they all testify in each other's favor, [6]so that there are **two witnesses testifying about** each claimant." In Talmudic times, certain families would intermarry only with priests, or with other Jews of unblemished lineage. Ordinary Jews who could not prove their lineage were not accepted by such families, even though there was no known stain on their lineage and

[1]מִשּׁוּם דְּקָא בָּעֵי לְמִיתְנֵי פְּלוּגְתָּא דְּרַבִּי יְהוּדָה וְרַבָּנַן.
[2]תָּנוּ רַבָּנַן: [3]״אֲנִי כֹּהֵן וַחֲבֵרִי כֹּהֵן׳ [4]נֶאֱמָן לְהַאֲכִילוֹ בִּתְרוּמָה, [5]וְאֵינוֹ נֶאֱמָן לְהַשִּׂיאוֹ אִשָּׁה עַד שֶׁיְּהוּ שְׁלֹשָׁה, [6]שְׁנַיִם מְעִידִין עַל זֶה וּשְׁנַיִם מְעִידִין עַל זֶה.

LITERAL TRANSLATION

[1]Because [the Mishnah] needs to teach the dispute of Rabbi Yehudah and the Rabbis.

[2]Our Rabbis taught: [3]"[If a man says:] 'I am a priest and my fellow is a priest,' [4]he is believed to feed him with terumah, [5]but he is not believed to allow him to marry a woman unless there are three, [6]two testifying about one and two testifying about

RASHI

נאמן להאכילו בתרומה ואינו נאמן להשיאו אשה — מיוחסת, מעלה היא ביוחסין.

NOTES

נֶאֱמָן לְהַאֲכִילוֹ בִּתְרוּמָה He is believed to feed him with terumah. The Torah lays down that various gifts and tithes must be taken from crops grown in Eretz Israel. Two of these donations are called terumah and are given to a priest: (1) An initial amount separated by the farmer from his crops (Numbers 18:12); and (2) an additional donation separated by the Levite from the tithe he receives from the farmer (Numbers 18:26-28). The first is called terumah (תְּרוּמָה, or תְּרוּמָה גְּדוֹלָה), and is one-fiftieth of the farmer's crop. The second is called terumah of tithe (תְּרוּמַת מַעֲשֵׂר or מַעֲשֵׂר מִן הַמַּעֲשֵׂר), and is one-tenth of the tithe received by the Levite. By law, only a priest or a member of his household may eat terumah, and it may be eaten only in a state of ritual purity (Leviticus 22:10-13). Any unauthorized person who eats terumah is liable to death at the hands of Heaven (Leviticus 22:9). The Torah also lays down that whenever dough is kneaded to make bread, a certain amount must be given to the priest (Numbers 15:17-21). This additional offering, called *ḥallah*, has the same status as terumah (*Rambam, Hilkhot Bikkurim* 5:13-14).

וְאֵינוֹ נֶאֱמָן לְהַשִּׂיאוֹ אִשָּׁה But he is not believed to allow him to marry a woman. Our commentary follows *Rashi* and *Rabbenu Ḥananel*, who, on the basis of a passage in tractate *Kiddushin* (76a), explain that the Baraita is referring to the custom of certain families of unblemished lineage not to intermarry with ordinary Jews unless these could prove their lineage. Although the Torah does not require a person to prove his lineage in this way, certain families who intermarried with priests were especially strict, and the Rabbis forbade the women of these families to marry men who could not prove their lineage.

Most Rishonim reject this explanation. They argue, on the basis of a passage in tractate *Yevamot* (45a), that an unknown man who claims to be a Jew is believed without proof, and need not prove that he is not a *mamzer*. Questions of lineage are important only when a priest wishes to marry a woman whose lineage is unknown. In such a case, the woman must prove her lineage, because it is possible that she is of a family that is disqualified from marrying into the priesthood. But if a man of unknown lineage marries a woman of unblemished lineage, no harm is done, even if he is lying about his lineage, because the Torah permits a woman of priestly family to marry a man who is disqualified from the priesthood. *Rid* also notes that if *Rabbenu Ḥananel* was correct, and the Rabbis forbade a man of unknown lineage to marry a woman of unblemished lineage, this man would be forbidden to marry anyone. For on his own admission he is a priest and therefore forbidden to marry anyone but a woman of unblemished lineage!

[1] רַבִּי יְהוּדָה אוֹמֵר: אַף אֵינוֹ נֶאֱמָן לְהַאֲכִילוֹ בִּתְרוּמָה עַד שֶׁיְּהוּ שְׁלֹשָׁה, [2] שְׁנַיִם מְעִידִין עַל זֶה וּשְׁנַיִם מְעִידִין עַל זֶה". [3] לְמֵימְרָא דְּרַבִּי יְהוּדָה חָיֵישׁ לְגוֹמְלִין, [4] וְרַבָּנַן לָא חָיְישֵׁי לְגוֹמְלִין? [5] וְהָא אִיפְּכָא שָׁמְעִינַן לְהוּ, [6] דִּתְנַן: [7] "הַחַמָּרִין שֶׁנִּכְנְסוּ לָעִיר, וְאָמַר אֶחָד מֵהֶן:

LITERAL TRANSLATION

the other. [1] Rabbi Yehudah says: He is not believed even to feed him with terumah unless there are three, [2] two testifying about one and two testifying about the other."

[3] [Do you mean] to say that Rabbi Yehudah suspects [them of] mutual assistance, [4] but the Rabbis do not suspect [them of] mutual assistance? [5] But surely we have heard them [say] the opposite, [6] for we have learned: [7] "[If] ass drivers entered a city, and one of them said:

RASHI

למימרא כו' — קא סלקא דעתך דטעמא דרבי יהודה משום גומלין.
החמרים — סוחרי תבואה, ומוליכין ממקום הזול לכרכין.

TRANSLATION AND COMMENTARY

they were legally permitted to marry anyone. Thus the Baraita informs us that, even according to the view of the Sages, the evidence of a single witness is not sufficient for us to allow such a claimant to the priesthood to marry into a family of unblemished lineage, although it is sufficient to give him the right to eat terumah. [1] The Baraita continues: **"Rabbi Yehudah says:** The two claimants **are not even believed as far as the eating of terumah is concerned, unless there are three** men involved, [2] so that there are **two** witnesses **testifying about** each claimant." Rabbi Yehudah is of the opinion that someone claiming to be a priest must produce two witnesses, as we learned in our Mishnah, and the testimony of one other man claiming to be a priest is not sufficient to permit the first claimant to eat terumah.

לְמֵימְרָא [3] The Gemara now goes on to explain: The dispute between Rabbi Yehudah and the Sages in the Mishnah and in the Baraita is about a case where two men claiming to be priests testify in each other's favor. In such a case, the only support each claimant has is one witness who has an obvious interest in giving evidence in the other's favor. Rabbi Yehudah rejects such testimony, but the Sages accept it. At first glance, it appears that Rabbi Yehudah would have no objection to a single disinterested witness testifying about a man who claims to be a priest, since he rejects only the testimony of another claimant. But if this is so, we are forced **to say that** when two individual witnesses testify in each other's favor, **Rabbi Yehudah suspects them of giving** false **testimony in each other's favor,** [4] **whereas the Rabbis do not suspect them of giving** false **testimony in each other's favor.** Rabbi Yehudah suspects the two single witnesses of conspiring to invent a story to further each other's interests, whereas the Rabbis are not concerned about this possibility. [5] **But surely,** the Gemara objects, this explanation of their views is untenable. For **we have heard them say the opposite** on this question in other places, [6] **as we have learned** in the following Mishnah (*Demai* 4:7), dealing with the laws of tithing.

This Mishnah is part of a series of Mishnayot at the end of tractate *Demai* dealing with cases where a single uneducated person (called an *am ha'aretz*) is believed concerning other people's tithes. By Torah law, the testimony of one witness is sufficient to establish that produce has been tithed, and even the owner of the produce is believed. But the Rabbis decreed that an *am ha'aretz* is not believed about his own produce. The reason for this decree was that the Rabbis found that a significant minority of *ammei ha'aretz* were failing to separate all the tithes required by law. Nevertheless, when an *am ha'aretz* declared that he had tithed his produce, the Rabbis did not treat the produce as completely untithed, because they recognized that most *ammei ha'aretz* did in fact tithe their produce. Instead, they gave the produce a special status called *demai* — "doubtfully tithed produce."

The Mishnah deals with two *ammei ha'aretz* ass drivers who testify about each other's produce: [7] **"If** two **ass drivers enter a city**, each carrying grain for sale, **and one of them** says: 'Buy my companion's grain,

NOTES

Rid, Rabbenu Tam, and most other Rishonim explain that the Baraita does not mean that the man claiming to be a priest is *forbidden* to marry a woman of unblemished lineage, but rather that he must not benefit from the consequences of marrying such a woman. That is to say, we do not consider him a priest of established lineage who may serve in the Temple. And even if he marries a woman of unblemished lineage, his daughter may not marry a priest of established lineage. *Rosh* and *Ramban* note that this explanation does not fit the language of the Baraita very well. For, according to this explanation, the Baraita's main point is that this man is not considered a priest of established lineage and cannot serve in the Temple. Why, then, does the Baraita introduce the woman of unblemished lineage at all?

עַד שֶׁיְּהוּ שְׁלֹשָׁה Unless there are three. From the language

HALAKHAH

הַחַמָּרִין שֶׁנִּכְנְסוּ לָעִיר If ass drivers entered a city. "If two ass drivers come to town carrying grain, and one of them

TRANSLATION AND COMMENTARY

for it is better than mine. [1]**My** grain **is new and my companion's is old** (grain improves with age), [2]and moreover **my** grain **has not** yet **been tithed and my companion's has been tithed** and is ready to eat,' [3]**he is not believed,** and his companion's grain is still considered *demai*. Although we would ordinarily accept the ass driver's testimony about someone else's produce, in this case we suspect that the two ass drivers conspired to further each other's interests, and in the next city, in return for the first ass driver's declaration, his companion will declare that the first driver's grain is old and tithed, etc. [4]But **Rabbi Yehudah** disagrees with the first Tanna and **says: He is believed,** because Rabbi Yehudah is not concerned about the possibility of each ass driver giving false evidence in favor of his companion." Thus we see that Rabbi Yehudah and the Sages take positions regarding *demai* that are the opposite of those they took regarding priestly lineage. Regarding priestly lineage, Rabbi Yehudah was concerned about the possibility of such false testimony, and the Sages were not; whereas regarding *demai*, the Sages were concerned about the possibility of such false testimony, and Rabbi Yehudah was not. How is this contradiction to be resolved?

אָמַר רַב אַדָּא בַּר אַהֲבָה [5]**Rav Adda bar Ahavah said in the name of Rav:** We have to amend the Mishnah in tractate *Demai*. [6]**The opinions** expressed there **must be reversed,** with Rabbi Yehudah ruling that the ass driver is not believed, and with the Sages accepting that his testimony is valid.

אַבַּיֵּי אֲמַר [7]**Abaye said: In fact, we do not** need **to reverse** the opinions in tractate *Demai*. Normally, Rabbi Yehudah would not accept the testimony of one witness where there is a possibility of a conspiracy

LITERAL TRANSLATION

[1]'Mine is new and my fellow's is old; [2]mine is not tithed (lit., "prepared") and my fellow's is tithed,' [3]he is not believed. [4]Rabbi Yehudah says: He is believed"!

[5]Rav Adda bar Ahavah said in the name of Rav: [6]The opinion must be reversed.

[7]Abaye said: In fact, do not reverse.

[1]"שֶׁלִּי חָדָשׁ וְשֶׁל חֲבֵרִי יָשָׁן; [2]שֶׁלִּי אֵינוֹ מְתוּקָּן וְשֶׁל חֲבֵרִי מְתוּקָּן', [3]אֵינוֹ נֶאֱמָן. [4]רַבִּי יְהוּדָה אוֹמֵר: נֶאֱמָן"! [5]אָמַר רַב אַדָּא בַּר אַהֲבָה אָמַר רַב: [6]מוּחְלֶפֶת הַשִּׁיטָּה. [7]אַבַּיֵּי אֲמַר: לְעוֹלָם לָא תֵּיפּוּךְ.

RASHI

שלי חדש ושל חברי ישן שלי אינו מתוקן ושל חבירי מתוקן — משבח את של חבירו ומזלזל את שלו. שלי אינו מעושר, של חבירי מעושר. שלי חדש ואינו יבש עדיין כל צורכו, [ושל חבירי ישן ויבש כל צורכו]. דסתם ישן טוב מן החדש בעת הגורן, כדאמרינן ב"איזהו נשך" (בבא מציעא עב,ב): היו חדשות מארבע וישנות משלש. **אינו נאמן** — הואיל ועם הארץ הוא, ואינו נאמן על המעשר. אף על פי שמעיד על שלו שאינו מתוקן, ועוד שמוסיף עם זו דברים אחרים לשבח את של חבירו — אינו נאמן להחזיק את של חבירו בחזקת מתוקן, שאינן אלא מערימין: אמור אתה כאן, ואני במקום אחר.

TERMINOLOGY

מוּחְלֶפֶת הַשִּׁיטָּה The opinion must be reversed. Sometimes a contradiction is found in two scholars' opposed opinions as recorded in one source and their opinions as recorded elsewhere. In such cases the Talmud may propose that the names in one of the sources be reversed. This suggestion is normally introduced by the expression: "The views of the scholars cited should be reversed."

לְעוֹלָם לָא תֵּיפּוּךְ In fact, do not reverse. Sometimes the Gemara quotes another Tannaitic source when discussing a difference of opinion recorded in a Mishnah or a Baraita. It does so because there is a contradiction between that source and the Mishnah under discussion. The Gemara often resolves the contradiction by saying מוּחְלֶפֶת הַשִּׁיטָּה, reversing the names of the Rabbis in one of the conflicting sources. But occasionally it rejects this solution, saying לָא תֵּיפּוּךְ — "Do not reverse the names in one of the sources," for there is another way of reconciling the contradictory views.

NOTES

of the Baraita it is not entirely clear whether the third witness must be disinterested, so that each claimant has the support of one other claimant and one disinterested witness, or whether the third witness also claims to be a priest. If so, it would follow that although the Baraita does not accept the testimony of one other claimant, because of the danger of their conspiring to give evidence in each other's favor, it does accept the testimony of two such witnesses. Our commentary follows *Ritva*, who takes the latter position. Taking the same position, *Rashash* notes that the Baraita is actually referring to three claimants who all testify about each other, so that there are two witnesses testifying in favor of each of the three purported priests.

שֶׁלִּי חָדָשׁ וְשֶׁל חֲבֵרִי יָשָׁן Mine is new and my fellow's is old. Our commentary follows *Rashi*, who explains (based on a Mishnah, *Bava Metzia* 72b) that old grain is of better quality than new grain. According to this explanation, the only Halakhically significant statement of the ass driver was his declaration that his companion's produce was tithed, whereas his own was not. The Mishnah inserted the other clause — in which the ass driver praised the quality of his companion's grain — in order to sharpen the Mishnah's ruling: Even though the ass driver sincerely admits that his grain is of poorer quality than his companion's and is not tithed, he is still not believed when he testifies that his companion's grain is tithed, because we suspect a conspiracy between them.

מוּחְלֶפֶת הַשִּׁיטָּה The opinion must be reversed. According to Rav Adda bar Ahavah, there is no way of resolving the conflict between our Mishnah and the Mishnah in tractate *Demai*, and we are forced to concede that there was an error in transmission, so that the opinions in one of the Mishnayot must be reversed. Rav Adda bar Ahavah does not say which of the Mishnayot he thinks should be amended. Our commentary follows *Melekhet Shlomo*, who explains that it is the Mishnah in tractate *Demai* that should be changed.

HALAKHAH

says: 'My grain is untithed, but my companion's grain is tithed,' he is not believed, because we suspect that in the next town the two ass drivers will conspire and reverse their roles," following the anonymous first Tanna in the Mishnah in *Demai*. (*Rambam, Sefer Zera'im, Hilkhot Ma'aserot* 12:10.)

[1]בִּדְמַאי הֵקִילוּ, [2]רוֹב עַמֵּי הָאָרֶץ מְעַשְּׂרִין הֵן. [3]אָמַר רָבָא: [4]דְּרַבִּי יְהוּדָה אַדְּרַבִּי יְהוּדָה קַשְׁיָא, [5]דְּרַבָּנַן אַדְּרַבָּנַן לָא קַשְׁיָא?

LITERAL TRANSLATION

[1]In [the case of] *demai* they were lenient, [2][because] most *ammei ha'aretz* do tithe.

[3]Rava said: [4]There is a contradiction between Rabbi Yehudah and Rabbi Yehudah. [5]Is there no contradiction between the Rabbis and the Rabbis?

TRANSLATION AND COMMENTARY

between the two witnesses, as we see from our Mishnah in *Ketubot*. [1]But **he was lenient in the case of *demai*,** [2]**because most *ammei ha'aretz* do tithe** their produce. Hence Rabbi Yehudah accepted the testimony of the ass driver, in spite of the possibility that he was giving false testimony in his companion's favor.

אָמַר רָבָא [3]**Rava said:** Abaye's answer is incomplete. Abaye has indeed explained why Rabbi Yehudah may have been more lenient in a case involving *demai*, and has resolved [4]**the contradiction between Rabbi Yehudah's view** in *Ketubot* **and Rabbi Yehudah's view** in *Demai*. [5]But **is there not** also **a contradiction between the view of the Rabbis** in *Ketubot* **and the view of the Rabbis** in *Demai*? The Rabbis who disagreed with Rabbi Yehudah were more lenient regarding priestly lineage than regarding *demai*, and no solution of the problem is complete if it does not resolve this contradiction as well.

NOTES

דְּמַאי ***Demai.*** Produce from which tithes have not yet been separated (called *tevel*) may not be eaten by anyone, on pain of death at the hands of Heaven (*Sanhedrin* 83a). By Torah law, the testimony a single witness that produce has been tithed is sufficient, and even the owner of the produce is believed (*Yevamot* 88a). However, during the Second Temple period the Rabbis found that a significant minority of people were failing to separate all the tithes required by law (*Sotah* 48a). Accordingly, the Rabbis decreed that the owner of the produce should not be believed, unless he was known to be a very learned and scrupulous person called a *ḥaver* (*Rambam, Hilkhot Ma'aser* 10:1-2).

Other people, called *ammei ha'aretz*, are not believed about their own produce. Regarding the produce of other people, where the *am ha'aretz* has no financial interest, there is a dispute among the Rishonim: *Rambam* rules that the *am ha'aretz* is believed, whereas *Ra'avad* rules that he is not (ibid., 12:17). Nevertheless, even though an *am ha'aretz* is not believed about his own produce, the Rabbis did not treat that produce as completely untithed, because they recognized that most *ammei ha'aretz* do tithe their produce properly (as the Gemara states, below). Rather, they gave the produce a special status called *demai* — doubtfully tithed produce.

Ordinarily, *demai* produce may not be eaten until tithes are separated once more by a trustworthy person (ibid., 11:1), but under certain, unusual circumstances it may be eaten without being tithed again. Thus, when there is no other produce available on Shabbat, a *ḥaver* may rely on the tithing of an *am ha'aretz* (ibid., 12:1). Likewise, *demai* may be given as charity to a poor person, when there is nothing else available (ibid., 10:11). Many of the regulations surrounding tithing procedures are relaxed for *demai* (ibid., 9:2,6 and *Hilkhot Ma'aser Sheni* 4:8). An entire tractate of the Mishnah, called *Demai*, deals with this subject.

בִּדְמַאי הֵקִילוּ **In the case of *demai* they were lenient.** Abaye explains that the standards of proof for *demai* were relaxed, according to Rabbi Yehudah, because most *ammei ha'aretz* do tithe their produce, and the entire law of *demai* is a stringency. This argument is attributed to Rava later in this tractate (below, 56b), in connection with an opinion of Rabbi Yehudah that the regulations governing Rabbinic laws are more strict than those governing Torah laws. As a counter-example, the Gemara cites this Mishnah, in which Rabbi Yehudah accepts the ass driver's uncorroborated testimony, although there is good reason to suspect a conspiracy, even though *demai* is a Rabbinic law. In response, Rava explains that most Rabbinic laws are treated strictly, but the standards of proof for *demai* were relaxed because most *ammei ha'aretz* do tithe their produce.

דְּרַבָּנַן אַדְּרַבָּנַן לָא קַשְׁיָא **Is there no contradiction between the Rabbis and the Rabbis?** There is a dispute between *Rambam* and *Ra'avad* as to whether an *am ha'aretz* is believed about other people's produce when he has no material interest. *Rambam* (*Hilkhot Ma'aser* 12:17) rules that an *am ha'aretz* — and even someone known to be lax in his observance of tithing — is believed when he testifies about someone else (provided that there is no suspicion of conspiracy), because there is a legal presumption that a person will not sin if he has nothing to gain by it. *Ra'avad*, however, rules that such people are not believed. The dispute revolves around a Tannaitic disagreement in tractate *Bekhorot* (35a). *Rambam* rules in accordance with one Tanna, and *Ra'avad* with another. In our commentary we have followed *Rambam*'s view.

According to *Rambam*, Rava's question can be explained as follows: There is no essential difference between the case concerning priesthood and that concerning *demai*. In both cases one witness is believed, even if he is unknown to us, but a person is not believed about himself. Regarding priesthood, however, the Rabbis went further, believing one witness even if he had an obvious interest in his own testimony. But regarding *demai*, they did not accept the testimony of an *am ha'aretz* when there was a suspicion of a conspiracy. Accordingly, Rava asks: "What is the difference between priesthood and *demai*?" And he answers that in the case of priesthood, the conspiracy is only a suspicion, whereas in the case of *demai*, we are referring to a case where the conspiracy is virtually explicit.

According to *Ra'avad*, however, Rava's question can be answered quite simply, without resorting to a forced construction, because priesthood and *demai* are fundamentally different. Regarding priesthood, one witness is believed, even if he is unknown to us. The only reason Rabbi Yehudah does not believe the other man who claims to be a priest is because he suspects a conspiracy. But the

CONCEPTS

עַמֵּי הָאָרֶץ ***Ammei ha'aretz.*** The appellation *am ha'aretz*, "common person" (עַם הָאָרֶץ, lit., "nation of the earth"), is one of contempt. The expression was originally used in reference to non-Jews. In time it also came to refer to Jews who were considered similar to non-Jews because they lacked Torah knowledge, neglected the commandments, or behaved improperly. The Sages of the Mishnah disagreed about the precise definition of this term. Some used it to refer to a person who was not only ignorant ("he knows neither Bible nor Mishnah") but slighted the commandments and was suspected of transgression and theft, whereas someone who had not studied at all was known as an ignoramus (בּוּר). Other Sages stated that even people who have studied a great deal may be called *ammei ha'aretz* if they are not associated with the Sages. Generally, in matters of Halakhah, *ammei ha'aretz* are suspected of not keeping the commandment of separating tithes properly; nor are they scrupulous about ritual purity (whereas those who have taken it upon themselves to observe these commandments are known as "companions" — חֲבֵרִים).

[1]אֶלָּא, דְּרַבִּי יְהוּדָה אַדְּרַבִּי יְהוּדָה לָא קַשְׁיָא, כִּדְשָׁנֵינַן. [2]דְּרַבָּנַן אַדְּרַבָּנַן לָא קַשְׁיָא, [3]כְּדַאֲמַר רַבִּי חָמָא בַּר עוּקְבָא: [4]בְּשֶׁכְּלֵי אוּמָּנוּתוֹ בְּיָדוֹ. [24B] [5]הָכָא נַמִי, בְּשֶׁכְּלֵי אוּמָּנוּתוֹ בְּיָדוֹ.

LITERAL TRANSLATION

[1]Rather, there is no contradiction between Rabbi Yehudah and Rabbi Yehudah, as we explained. [2][And] there is no contradiction between the Rabbis and the Rabbis, [3]as Rabbi Ḥama bar Ukva said: [4]Where the tools of his trade are in his hand. [24B] [5]Here too, it is where the tools of his trade are in his hand.

TRANSLATION AND COMMENTARY

אֶלָּא [1]**Rather,** said Rava, Abaye's solution must be expanded to explain both these problems. In fact, **there is no contradiction between Rabbi Yehudah's view** in *Ketubot* **and Rabbi Yehudah's view** in *Demai*, **as** Abaye **explained.** [2]**Nor is there any contradiction between the Rabbis' view** in *Ketubot* **and the Rabbis' view** in *Demai*, [3]because the Mishnah in *Demai* can be explained **according to what Rabbi Ḥama bar Ukva said** in reference to another case, which will be discussed below. [4]There he said: We are referring to a case **where** the tradesman has **the tools of his trade in his hand**, so that it is obvious that he plans to do business. [24B] [5]**Here too** in *Demai*, Rava concludes, we are referring to a case **where** the first ass driver brought **the tools of his trade** (i.e., his scales and measures) **with him**, and it is obvious that he plans to sell his grain. Thus it is reasonable to assume that in the next city the ass drivers plan to reverse roles, and there the second driver will praise the first driver's produce. For this reason, even though the Rabbis normally accept the evidence of one witness even if there is a possibility of conspiracy, they were strict regarding *demai*, because in this case the conspiracy is a virtual certainty.

RASHI

בשכלי אומנותו בידו — חמר המביא תבואה למכור היה נושא בידו כלי היכר של מכירה, כגון מחק שמוחקין בה המדה. והמביאה להצניע אינו נושא בידו כלי אומנות מכר. והכא כגון שכלי אומנותו בידו של זה המזלזל את שלו, דאנן סהדי שלמוכרה הביאה. הלכך אין זה אלא גומל, וזה יעיד עליו בכרך שלפניהם.

SAGES

רַבִּי חָמָא בַּר עוּקְבָא **Rabbi Ḥama bar Ukva.** A Palestinian Amora of the third generation, Rabbi Ḥama bar Ukva was a disciple of Rabbi Yose bar Ḥanina. Among Amoraim of the fourth generation, the following transmitted teachings in his name: Rabbi Yonah, Rabbi Yirmeyah, and Abaye.

NOTES

Rabbis ignored this concern, and applied the general law that one witness is believed. Regarding *demai*, however, a single witness is not believed unless we know that he is scrupulous about tithing. The only reason why we might have believed this ass driver is because of his apparent sincerity in deprecating his own produce. But in view of the danger of a conspiracy, the Rabbis attached little significance to the ass driver's apparent sincerity, and applied the general law that an *am ha'aretz* is not believed. Why, then, according to *Ra'avad*, does Rava not explain the Rabbis' viewpoint in this way?

The Aḥaronim answer that, according to *Ra'avad*, Rava had no objection to the Rabbis' position in itself; he simply noted that, regarding priesthood, Rabbi Yehudah was more concerned about the possibility of a conspiracy than the Rabbis were; whereas regarding *demai*, the opposite was the case. Rava's objection was that it was most unusual for Tannaim to change sides in this way. According to this explanation, the Gemara's conclusion — that there is no contradiction in Rabbi Yehudah's words, because his reasoning in the case of priesthood had nothing to do with concern about conspiracy — resolves the question about the Rabbis as well, because their reasoning is no longer the opposite of that of Rabbi Yehudah. Hence it is no longer necessary to explain the Mishnah in *Demai* as referring to a case of explicit conspiracy (*Pnei Yehoshua, Rabbi Akiva Eger*).

אֶלָּא, דְּרַבִּי יְהוּדָה אַדְּרַבִּי יְהוּדָה לָא קַשְׁיָא, כִּדְשָׁנֵינַן **Rather, there is no contradiction between Rabbi Yehudah and Rabbi Yehudah, as we explained.** In our commentary we have followed the plain meaning of the Gemara, according to which Rava resolves the contradiction in Rabbi Yehudah's view in the same way as Abaye does. *Rashbatz* suggests that when Rava said, "as we explained," he may not have been referring to the answer of Abaye that he had just attacked, but rather to an answer given by the Gemara earlier (above, 23b). The Gemara said there that if an explicit Baraita did not exist, we might have thought that a captive woman who testifies in favor of another is believed only when she testifies against herself at the same time, but not when she testifies in her own favor as well. Applying the same reasoning to our case, we can say that Rabbi Yehudah does not believe the two men who claim to be priests, since they are also testifying in their own favor, but he does believe the ass driver, because he is testifying against himself.

הָכָא נַמִי, בְּשֶׁכְּלֵי אוּמָּנוּתוֹ בְּיָדוֹ **Here too, it is where the tools of his trade are in his hand.** Our commentary follows *Rashi, Rambam* and most Rishonim, who explain that it is the ass driver in tractate *Demai* who has the tools of his trade with him, and that the "tools" are the weights and measures he needs for selling his grain. Thus we know that he plans to sell his grain, and it is virtually certain that the ass drivers are planning to exchange roles in the next town. Hence it is obvious that the ass driver's insistence that everyone buy from his companion is anything but sincere, and we do not attach any credibility to it. In our Mishnah, however, there is no special reason to suspect that the two men claiming to be priests have conspired to testify in each other's favor, and the Rabbis were lenient and accepted their testimony at face value.

Tosafot cites another explanation in the name of *Rabbenu Ḥananel*. According to this explanation, it is the men claiming to be priests in our Mishnah who have the tools of their trade with them. The "tools" are specially designed vessels made of materials (e.g., stone vessels) that can never become ritually impure, and are used only by people who are careful about ritual impurity, such as priests. In such a case, we believe the two men who claim to be priests when they testify in each other's

TRANSLATION AND COMMENTARY

וְהֵיכָא אִתְּמַר [1]The Gemara asks: **And where was the ruling of Rabbi Ḥama bar Ukva stated?** In connection with what Halakhah did he refer to a tradesman's tools? [2]The Gemara answers: **Rabbi Ḥama bar Ukva made his statement about the following Mishnah** (*Teharot* 7:1), **in which we learn: "If a potter** who is scrupulously careful about the laws of ritual purity **leaves his pots and goes down to drink water from the river,** he must assume that an *am ha'aretz* touched his pots in his absence and rendered them ritually impure. [3]Nevertheless, **the inner ones are ritually pure,** because they were out of reach, [4]**but the outer ones are ritually impure**, because the potter must assume that they were touched by an *am ha'aretz*.

וְהָתַנְיָא [5]When that Mishnah was being discussed, an objection was raised: **But surely it was taught** in a Baraita that "if a potter leaves his pots unattended, he must assume that an *am ha'aretz* touched all his pots, [6]and **all of them are ritually impure"!** How is the contradiction between the Mishnah in tractate *Teharot* and this Baraita to be resolved?

LITERAL TRANSLATION

[1]And where was [the ruling] of Rabbi Ḥama bar Ukva stated? [2]About this that we have learned: "[If] a potter left his pots and went down to drink water from the river, [3]the inner ones are ritually pure, [4]and the outer ones are ritually impure."

[5]But surely it was taught: [6]"These and those are ritually impure"!

[1]וְהֵיכָא אִתְּמַר דְּרַבִּי חָמָא בַּר עוּקְבָא? [2]אַהָא דִּתְנַן: "הַקַּדָּר שֶׁהִנִּיחַ קְדֵירוֹתָיו וְיָרַד לִשְׁתּוֹת מַיִם מִן הַיְּאוֹר, [3]הַפְּנִימִיּוֹת טְהוֹרוֹת, [4]וְהַחִיצוֹנוֹת טְמֵאוֹת". [5]וְהָתַנְיָא: [6]"אֵלּוּ וְאֵלּוּ טְמֵאוֹת"!

RASHI

הקדר — שהוא חבר. **הפנימיות טהורות** — כולה מתרצא ואזלא לקמיה.

NOTES

favor, in spite of the danger that they are conspiring together, because there is circumstantial evidence supporting their testimony. In the Mishnah in *Demai*, however, there is no circumstantial evidence supporting the ass driver's testimony, and in view of the danger of a conspiracy, the Rabbis were strict.

This dispute has important Halakhic implications. According to the school of *Rashi*, it is the Mishnah in *Demai* that is referring to a case where "the tools of his trade are in his hand," whereas our Mishnah is referring to any case in which one man claiming to be a priest testifies in favor of another. Accordingly, *Rambam* and *Shulḥan Arukh* rule that the testimony of one witness is sufficient in matters of terumah, even when there is a danger of conspiracy (following the first Tanna, as explained by *Rashi*). According to *Tosafot*, by contrast, our Mishnah is referring to a special case, in which the men claiming to be priests have "the tools of their trade" in their hands, but in all other cases the first Tanna would agree that we cannot accept the testimony of the other man claiming to be a priest, because of the danger of conspiracy. Hence *Rosh* (*Gittin* 54b) rules that the testimony of one witness is sufficient only if he is disinterested (following the first Tanna, as explained by *Tosafot*).

הַקַּדָּר The potter. In order to understand this Mishnah, it is important to be aware of some of the laws of ritual impurity. It is possible to become ritually impure in many different ways — for example, by contact with a human corpse or with the carcasses of certain animals, or through certain diseases such as leprosy (צָרַעַת) or gonorrhea (זָב), and in several other ways. The Rabbis were aware that *ammei ha'aretz* — even though they were quite scrupulous about keeping most of the other laws of the Torah — were not keeping the laws of ritual impurity. In fact, the Torah does not require Jews to remain in a constant state of ritual purity, except when they visit the Temple in Jerusalem. Maintaining ritual purity in other situations is an optional act of piety.

Accordingly, the Rabbis decreed that *ammei ha'aretz* are assumed to be ritually impure except during the Pilgrim Festivals, when they visit the Temple in Jerusalem and purify themselves. Only scrupulous individuals, called *ḥaverim*, who make a formal commitment to follow a prescribed regimen of ritual purity, are trusted in matters of ritual purity. An *am ha'aretz* is treated as being ritually impure in the highest degree, so that even the clothes of the *am ha'aretz* impart ritual impurity to other clothes and to utensils with which they come in contact.

The potter in the Mishnah cited by our Gemara is a *ḥaver*, who is scrupulous about ritual purity, but his customers include *ammei ha'aretz*, and they are liable to render his pots ritually impure by touching them or even by brushing against them with their clothes. Even though the potter is not sure that an *am ha'aretz* passed by while he was away, the strict regimen of being a *ḥaver* requires him to assume that this did happen.

HALAKHAH

הַקַּדָּר שֶׁהִנִּיחַ קְדֵירוֹתָיו If a potter left his pots. "If a potter who is scrupulous about ritual purity leaves his pots close to the street and walks away for a moment, he must assume on his return that the outer ones were touched by passing *ammei ha'aretz* and are ritually impure, but he may assume that the inner ones are ritually pure. If it is obvious that the pots are for sale, he must assume that they were all handled and are all ritually impure, even if he left them far from the street; but if the vessels are clearly private, he may assume that none of them were touched, provided that they were left far from the street," following the Mishnah and the Baraitot as explained by our Gemara. (*Rambam, Sefer Tohorah, Hilkhot Mishkav U'Moshav* 12:23.)

BACKGROUND

הַקַּדָּר שֶׁהִנִּיחַ קְדֵירוֹתָיו If a potter left his pots. As explained in the Torah (Leviticus 11:33 and elsewhere), pottery vessels (the jars in question here are clay jars) which have become ritually impure cannot be purified, so they remain impure forever. Since any food or drink placed in a ritually impure vessel also becomes ritually impure, those who wished to be scrupulous in matters of ritual purity had to make certain that their dishes and pots were ritually pure. Generally, a potter would manufacture vessels and then sell them to customers himself. At times a potter who was himself a *ḥaver* (someone who took it upon himself to remain ritually pure, and could be relied upon to ensure that his products were ritually pure) would make vessels to order for a certain person, and he would sometimes bring them to the market and sell them to the general public. Since *ḥaverim* were scrupulous in their use of ritually pure vessels, the potter would make an effort to keep his wares ritually pure, so that they could be sold to anyone.

הַפְּנִימִיּוֹת טְהוֹרוֹת The inner ones are ritually pure. The Sages decreed that *ammei ha'aretz* were to be considered ritually impure to a severe degree, and that they conferred ritual impurity on a clay vesssel not only by touching the inside of it but also by touching it on the outside. The row of jars fronting on the public domain may well be in the way of pedestrians, who may move the pottery to make way for themselves, thus rendering the vessels ritually impure.

TRANSLATION AND COMMENTARY

אָמַר רַבִּי חָמָא בַּר עוּקְבָא [1]It was in answer to this objection that **Rabbi Ḥama bar Ukva said:** The Baraita is referring to a case **where** the potter had **the tools of his trade with him**, so that the pots were obviously for sale. In such a case, all the pots must be considered ritually impure, [2]**because everyone's hand examines them.** While the potter was away, people may well have come and examined his pots, and since it was clear that the pots were for sale, we must assume that the inner ones were touched as well.

וְהָתַנְיָא [3]Another objection was raised: **But surely it was taught** in another Baraita that "if a potter leaves his pots unattended, he is entitled to assume that they were not touched by anyone, [4]and **all of them**, both the inner and the outer pots, **are** considered **ritually pure**"! How is this Baraita to be explained in the light of the other Baraita and the Mishnah?

אָמַר רַבִּי חָמָא בַּר עוּקְבָא [5]In answer to this objection, **Rabbi Ḥama bar Ukva said:** This Baraita is referring to a case **where** the potter did **not** have **the tools of his trade with him**, so that the pots were obviously private property and not for sale. In such a case, all the pots are considered ritually pure, because we assume that people respected the potter's property rights, and did not handle his pots without permission.

וְאֶלָּא הָא דִּתְנַן [6]The Gemara asks: We have seen that if the pots are for sale, they must all be presumed ritually impure, and if they are not for sale, they are presumed to be ritually pure. Thus the two Baraitot can be reconciled without difficulty. **But what about** the ruling **that we learned** in the Mishnah — that "where the potter left his pots unattended, [7]he is entitled to assume that **the inner ones are ritually pure, but** he must assume that **the outer ones are ritually impure**"? [8]**What** are the circumstances in which the ruling of the Mishnah **applies?** If the Mishnah is referring to a case where the pots are for sale, why does it rule that the inner ones are ritually pure? And if the pots are not for sale, why does it rule that the outer ones are ritually impure?

דִּסְמִיכָא לִרְשׁוּת הָרַבִּים [9]The Gemara answers: The Mishnah **is** referring to a case where the pots were not for sale, but the potter left them **close to the public domain,** [10]**and** the reason why the outer ones are ritually impure is **because** he left them next to **the border stones of the public domain**, where people sometimes walk. Hence the potter must assume that an *am ha'aretz* may have accidentally brushed against the pots nearest the road, but not against the inner ones.

The Gemara now returns to the contradiction between our Mishnah in *Ketubot* and the Mishnah in *Demai*. Up to this point the Gemara has assumed that the issue in dispute between Rabbi Yehudah and the Sages in *Ketubot* is whether the testimony of one witness is sufficient when we have reason to suspect a conspiracy. The assumption has been that Rabbi Yehudah, who in *Ketubot* does not accept the testimony of one claimant to the priesthood about another such claimant, is concerned about a possible conspiracy between the two, and that the Sages, who accept such testimony, do not share his concern. The Gemara then objected that, in tractate *Demai*, Rabbi Yehudah and the Sages switched their positions on the question of a possible conspiracy. And the Gemara answered that Rabbi Yehudah was lenient on questions of *demai* because most *ammei ha'aretz* do tithe, whereas the Sages were stricter in the case of *demai* because it was virtually certain that the ass drivers were involved in a conspiracy.

[1]אָמַר רַבִּי חָמָא בַּר עוּקְבָא: בְּשֶׁכְּלֵי אוּמָּנוּתוֹ בְּיָדוֹ, [2]מִפְּנֵי שֶׁיַּד הַכֹּל מְמַשְׁמֶשֶׁת בָּהֶן.
[3]וְהָתַנְיָא: [4]"אֵלּוּ וְאֵלּוּ טְהוֹרוֹת"!
[5]אָמַר רַבִּי חָמָא בַּר עוּקְבָא: בְּשֶׁאֵין כְּלֵי אוּמָּנוּתוֹ בְּיָדוֹ.
[6]וְאֶלָּא הָא דִּתְנַן: [7]"הַפְּנִימִיּוֹת טְהוֹרוֹת, וְהַחִיצוֹנוֹת טְמֵאוֹת", [8]הֵיכִי מַשְׁכַּחַת לָהּ?
[9]דִּסְמִיכָא לִרְשׁוּת הָרַבִּים, [10]וּמִשּׁוּם חִיפּוּפֵי רְשׁוּת הָרַבִּים.

LITERAL TRANSLATION

[1]Rabbi Ḥama bar Ukva said: Where the tools of his trade are in his hand, [2]because the hand of everyone examines them.

[3]But surely it was taught: [4]"These and those are ritually pure"!

[5]Rabbi Ḥama bar Ukva said: Where the tools of his trade are not in his hand.

[6]But about that which we have learned: [7]"The inner ones are ritually pure, and the outer ones are ritually impure," [8]how can you find it?

[9]Where it is close to the public domain, [10]and because of the border stones of the public domain.

RASHI

בשכלי אומנותו בידו – להיכר שהוא נושאן למוכרן. **ממשמשת בהן** – לבדוק וליקח. **ומשום חיפופי רשות הרבים** – שנותנים בני אדם אבנים גדולות או יתדות לצידי רשות הרבים, להרחיק העגלות מלהזיק את הכתלים, ומתוך שהן דוחקות את רשות הרבים וזה הניח קדירותיו אצלם – דחק גם הוא את הדרך. והעוברין שם מתחככין בהן, ובגדיהן עוברין על פני אוירן. ובגדי עם הארץ טמאים הם, ומטמאים את החיצוניות.

BACKGROUND

חִיפּוּפֵי רְשׁוּת הָרַבִּים The border stones of the public domain. The word חִיפּוּפִים — "border stones" — is apparently derived from the root חפף — "to rub," or "to scrape." People who had houses or courtyards near the public domain tried to prevent bypassers from damaging their walls and fences. Thus they might leave a few stones jutting out from their walls, or line up an entire row of stones or wooden stakes at a distance from their property. The space between these stakes and people's houses was thus officially part of the public domain, although as a practical matter few people were to be found there. Therefore, this area had a special Halakhic status, something between the public domain and private property.

TRANSLATION AND COMMENTARY

וְאִיבָּעֵית אֵימָא [1] **But**, says the Gemara, **if you wish,** you can give a completely different explanation, which is consistent with the plain meaning of the Mishnah in *Demai*, according to which Rabbi Yehudah is not concerned about possible conspiracies, while the Sages are. Rabbi Yehudah might reject the testimony of the second claimant to the priesthood in our Mishnah, not because he suspects a conspiracy, but because the second claimant is only one witness, and Rabbi Yehudah requires two witnesses to testify about terumah. According to this explanation, Rabbi Yehudah would not accept the testimony of one witness regarding terumah even if there was no question of a conspiracy. But regarding *demai*, where one witness is sufficient, Rabbi Yehudah would believe the ass driver, even though there are grounds to suspect a conspiracy. [2] **Rabbi Yehudah** does not accept the testimony of one witness to enable someone to eat terumah, because he **disagrees with the Rabbis about elevating from terumah to lineage.** There is a dispute between Rabbi Yehudah and Rabbi Yose in a Tosefta (*Yevamot* 12:4, cited in *Ketubot* 28b), as to whether a farmer may give a priest's slave a share of terumah in his master's absence (a priest's slave is considered part of his household, and is permitted to eat terumah). Rabbi Yehudah is of the opinion that if a man is given a share of terumah, we may assume that his priestly lineage has been definitely established, and that he is permitted to marry any woman. Hence Rabbi Yehudah does not allow a slave to be given a share of terumah unless his owner is present with him, lest it be thought that the slave is himself a priest. Rabbi Yose, however, is of the opinion that eating terumah is not a sign of lineage. Hence he allows a slave to be given a share of terumah, and is not worried about him being regarded as a priest.

Now, in the Baraita quoted earlier by the Gemara, which elaborated on the dispute between Rabbi Yehudah and the Sages in our Mishnah, the Sages ruled that if two men of unknown family come to town, and each testifies that the other is a priest, the testimony of each is sufficient to enable the other to eat terumah, but not to permit him to marry a woman of unblemished lineage. But Rabbi Yehudah ruled that they are not even believed to the extent of enabling each other to eat terumah. All agree, however, that we do not accept the testimony of one witness to permit an unknown man to marry a woman of unblemished lineage. But Rabbi Yehudah maintains that eating terumah is in itself a sign of priestly lineage. Hence he requires two witnesses for terumah, just as he does for lineage, for if we were to accept one witness for terumah, we would in effect be indirectly accepting one witness for lineage as well. The Sages, however, follow Rabbi Yose, who maintains that eating terumah is not in itself a sign of priestly lineage. Hence they do not require two witnesses, but rather treat this as a normal case where we question the permissibility of a piece of food, and in such cases one witness is sufficient.

[1] וְאִיבָּעֵית אֵימָא: [2] רַבִּי יְהוּדָה וְרַבָּנַן בְּמַעֲלִין מִתְּרוּמָה לְיוֹחֲסִין קָמִיפַּלְגִי.

LITERAL TRANSLATION

[1] And if you wish, say: [2] Rabbi Yehudah and the Rabbis disagree about elevating from terumah to lineage.

RASHI

במעלין מתרומה ליוחסין – רבי יהודה סבר: הרואה שמאכילין תרומה לאדם בחזקת כהן – מעיד עליו בכל מקום שהוא כהן, ומעלין אותו ליוחסין. הלכך, אם תאכילהו תרומה – הרי אתה מביאו להשיאו אשה. וטעמיה לאו משום גומלין הוא. ורבנן סברי: אין מעלין מתרומה ליוחסין.

BACKGROUND

מִתְּרוּמָה לְיוֹחֲסִין **From terumah to lineage.** "Elevating to lineage" means that we consider a certain man to be a priest in every respect. When the Temple was in existence, the Sanhedrin used to clarify matters of priestly lineage, disqualifying those who proved to be of blemished lineage and those who could not provide sufficient proof of their status. After the destruction of the Temple, when there was no longer a central tribunal and priestly lineage had no monetary value beyond the right to eat terumah, there was no longer any central authority to deal with the matter. The question was whether the eating of terumah should be regarded as sufficient proof for a man to be treated as a priest in every respect — in particular, with regard to his right to marry a woman of unblemished lineage and his ability to confer priestly status on his sons.

NOTES

בְּמַעֲלִין מִתְּרוּמָה לְיוֹחֲסִין קָמִיפַּלְגִי **Disagree about elevating from terumah to lineage.** Here the Gemara abandons its first explanation, according to which Rabbi Yehudah and the Sages differ about the problem of conspiracy, and it explains instead that they disagree as to whether eating terumah is proof of priestly lineage. Rabbi Yehudah maintains that eating terumah is proof of priestly lineage, and for this reason we give terumah only to priests who can prove their lineage. According to the Rabbis, eating terumah is not proof of priestly lineage, and therefore we can accept a lower standard of proof for eating terumah than for lineage. The Rishonim agree that this latter explanation is authoritative.

Tosafot raises the following problem: Our original difficulty with the first explanation was a double contradiction between *Ketubot* and *Demai* regarding conspiracy. Rabbi Yehudah was strict in *Ketubot* and lenient in *Demai*, whereas the Rabbis were lenient in *Ketubot* and strict in *Demai*. There is no longer any contradiction in Rabbi Yehudah's view, according to the new explanation, because we are now explaining that Rabbi Yehudah was strict in *Ketubot* for reasons that have nothing to do with conspiracy. But we still have not accounted for the contradiction implicit in the view of the Rabbis. Why do they not suspect a conspiracy in the case of the man who claims to be a priest (in *Ketubot*), as they did in the case of the ass driver (in *Demai*)?

This problem is solved differently by the various Rishonim. According to *Rashi*, there are four distinct points of view in our Mishnah, and while the first Tanna is of the opinion that one witness is believed even when we suspect a conspiracy, Rabbi Elazar and Rabban Shimon ben Gamliel argue that one witness is believed only when there is no danger of a conspiracy. Thus the first opinion in the Mishnah in *Demai* can be explained as reflecting the view of Rabbi Elazar or Rabban Shimon ben Gamliel, rather than

TRANSLATION AND COMMENTARY

אִיבַּעְיָא לְהוּ [1]Having explored the Tannaitic dispute as to whether the privilege of eating terumah is proof of one's full priestly status, the Gemara turns to a related problem: The Rabbis **were asked: What is the law about elevating from documents to lineage?** If a man produces a properly witnessed promissory note in which his name appears as "So-and-so, the priest," do we consider this conclusive proof of his priestly status and permit him to marry a woman of unblemished lineage?

הֵיכִי דָּמֵי [2]The Gemara considers the problem. **How do we visualize the case** to which you refer in your question? How does the man's name appear in the document? [3]**If we say** that the purported priest was the witness in the document, and **he wrote in it: "I, So-and-so, the priest, signed as a witness,"** [4]this cannot be the case in question, for **who testifies about him?** If the purported priest is the witness in the document, he is in effect testifying about himself, and that is not testimony at all. Surely it is obvious that in such a case we do not attach any significance to the fact that he styled himself "the priest"!

[1]אִיבַּעְיָא לְהוּ: מַהוּ לְהַעֲלוֹת מִשְּׁטָרוֹת לְיוּחֲסִין? [2]הֵיכִי דָּמֵי? [3]אִילֵימָא, דִּכְתִיב בֵּיהּ: "אֲנִי, פְּלוֹנִי, כֹּהֵן, חָתַמְתִּי עֵד", [4]מַאן קָא מַסְהִיד עִילָּוֵיהּ?

LITERAL TRANSLATION

[1]It was asked of them: What is [the law] about elevating from documents to lineage? [2]How do we visualize the case? [3]If we say, where it is written in it: "I, So-and-so, a priest, signed as a witness," [4]who is testifying about him?

NOTES

that of the first Tanna of our Mishnah, and there is thus no contradiction.

Tosafot and *Rosh* answer that, even according to the new explanation, the Rabbis' view must still be understood in the way Rava did in the first explanation — that in one of the Mishnayot we are referring to a case where "the tools of his trade are in his hand." Because of this, *Rosh* rules that a single witness is believed regarding terumah only if he is disinterested, or if the man claiming to be a priest has the tools of his trade with him.

Pnei Yehoshua and *Rabbi Akiva Eger* offer a suggestion that accords with the viewpoint of *Ra'avad*, who maintains that an *am ha'aretz* is not believed about another person's tithing, even if he is disinterested.

None of these explanations can be reconciled with the viewpoint of *Rambam*, who cites the Mishnayot in *Ketubot* and *Demai* without mentioning any stipulation that one of them is referring to a case where "the tools of his trade are in his hand" (unlike *Tosafot*). *Kesef Mishneh* explains that *Rambam* disagrees with *Tosafot*, and that according to the new explanation the Rabbis are no longer referring to a case where "his tools are in his hand." It is not clear, however, how *Rambam* would have answered *Tosafot*'s question, because he disagrees with *Ra'avad* about a disinterested *am ha'aretz*, and rules in favor of the first Tanna in both Mishnayot (unlike *Rashi*). This problem continued to exercise the Aḥaronim (see *Tosefot Yomtov*, *Rashash*, and others).

מַהוּ לְהַעֲלוֹת מִשְּׁטָרוֹת לְיוּחֲסִין **What is the law about elevating from documents to lineage?** The Gemara specifically asks whether documentary evidence is sufficient to establish a priest's lineage, but it does not ask whether such evidence is sufficient for us to presume the man to be a priest to the extent of permitting him to eat terumah. *Ritva* explains that the question applies equally to both matters. He notes that the issue underlying the Gemara's question is whether the witnesses who sign a document are testifying about the entire document or only about the loan. According to the opinion that they are testifying only about the loan, their testimony is of no effect regarding other matters mentioned in the document. Hence, *Ritva* argues, the "testimony" provided by the document cannot even be used to give the claimant the presumptive status of being a priest. The reason the Gemara mentioned lineage was to teach us that the witnesses' testimony is sufficient, even for lineage, according to the opinion that the witnesses are testifying about the entire document.

Most Rishonim disagree with *Ritva* on this point. *Rambam*, *Ra'ah*, *Ramban*, and *Ran* explain that the Gemara's question concerns only lineage. Regarding terumah, however, not only do we accept the document as proof (even according to the opinion that the witnesses are testifying only about the loan), but we even believe the man claiming to be a priest if he served as a witness and signed his name "So-and-so, the priest." The Rishonim explain that if a person signs his name on a document — as a borrower, a lender, or a witness — and mentions the fact that he is a priest, it is considered a case of someone who has made an incidental, unconsidered remark (a case discussed below, 26a, in which a person mentions in the course of a story that he is a priest), and the Halakhah is that a person who incidentally mentions that he is a priest is believed without proof.

HALAKHAH

מַהוּ לְהַעֲלוֹת מִשְּׁטָרוֹת לְיוּחֲסִין **What is the law about elevating from documents to lineage?** "We do not elevate to lineage on the basis of documents. If witnesses signed a document in which it was written, 'I, So-and-so, the priest, borrowed [or lent] money to So-and-so,' we do not treat this as though two witnesses have testified that this man is definitely a priest, because the witnesses may have been interested only in the loan, and not in matters incidental to the loan. *Maggid Mishneh* explains that *Rambam* followed the stricter opinion in the dispute between Rav Huna and Rav Ḥisda because we are strict in matters of lineage.

"The above ruling applies only to questions of lineage. But regarding things that are permitted to presumed priests today, such as eating Rabbinic terumah and Rabbinic *ḥallah*, we do elevate to lineage on the evidence of

TRANSLATION AND COMMENTARY

לָא [1]The Gemara explains: **No, it is necessary** to consider the problem of a document **in which** the purported priest was the borrower or the lender, and **wrote in it:** [2]**"I, So-and-so, the priest, borrowed** [or lent] **a maneh from So-and-so,"** [3]**and** independent **witnesses signed.** In such a case the witnesses are in effect testifying to the contents of the document, including the man's assertion that he is a priest. [4]**What is the law** in such a case? [5]**Are** the witnesses merely **testifying about the maneh** which is the subject of **the document,** and not about incidental matters mentioned in the document? [6]**Or are they perhaps testifying about the entire matter**, about every detail mentioned in the document, including the borrower's assertion that he is a priest?

רַב הוּנָא וְרַב חִסְדָּא [7]The Gemara reports that when this question was asked, **Rav Huna and Rav Ḥisda disagreed** about the matter. [8](It is not clear from the Gemara which Amora held which view.) **One** Rabbi **said: We may elevate** such a man to full priestly status, and permit him to marry a woman of unblemished lineage, because the witnesses are considered to be testifying about the entire matter. [9]**But** the other Rabbi **said: We may not elevate** such a man to full priestly status, because the witnesses are testifying only about the maneh, which is the main subject of the document.

אִיבַּעְיָא לְהוּ [10]The Gemara, continuing to examine the circumstances in which a claimant to the priesthood is elevated to full priestly status, considers another problem. The Rabbis were **asked: What is the law about elevating from** the giving of **the Priestly Benediction to lineage?** The Torah commands the priests to bless the congregation of Israel by raising their hands and reciting three verses (Numbers 6:22-27; Leviticus 9:22). Only a priest is permitted to pronounce this blessing, the Priestly Benediction, which was

[1]לָא, צְרִיכָא דִּכְתִיב בֵּיהּ: [2]"אֲנִי, פְּלוֹנִי, כֹּהֵן, לָוִיתִי מָנֶה מִפְּלוֹנִי", [3]וַחֲתִימוּ סָהֲדֵי. [4]מַאי? [5]אַמָּנֶה שֶׁבִּשְׁטָר קָא מַסְהֲדֵי, [6]אוֹ דִּלְמָא אַכּוּלָּהּ מִילְּתָא קָא מַסְהֲדֵי?

[7]רַב הוּנָא וְרַב חִסְדָּא: [8]חַד אָמַר: מַעֲלִין, [9]וְחַד אָמַר: אֵין מַעֲלִין.

[10]אִיבַּעְיָא לְהוּ: מַהוּ לְהַעֲלוֹת מִנְּשִׂיאוּת כַּפַּיִם לְיוֹחֲסִין?

LITERAL TRANSLATION

[1]No, it is necessary where it is written in it: [2]"I, So-and-so, a priest, borrowed a maneh from So-and-so," [3]and witnesses signed. [4]What is [the law]? [5]Are they testifying about the maneh in the document, [6]or are they perhaps testifying about the entire matter?

[7]Rav Huna and Rav Ḥisda [disagreed]: [8]One said: We elevate, [9]and one said: We do not elevate.

[10]It was asked of them: What is [the law] about elevating from the Priestly Benediction (lit., "lifting the hands") to lineage?

CONCEPTS

נְשִׂיאוּת כַּפַּיִם **The Priestly Benediction.** The three verses of blessing (Numbers 6:24-26) recited by the priests when blessing the congregation in the synagogue. The Priestly Benediction is recited between the blessings of מוֹדִים and שִׂים שָׁלוֹם in the repetition of the Amidah prayer. As the priests turn to face the congregation to recite the Priestly Benediction, they first recite a blessing acknowledging the holiness of the priestly line and their responsibility to bless the people in a spirit of love. While reciting the Priestly Benediction, the priests lift their hands according to a traditional rite. In Eretz Israel the Priestly Benediction is recited by the priests at every Shaharit and Musaf service. In the Diaspora, however, there is a long-established Ashkenazi practice of reciting it only during the Musaf service on Festivals.

NOTES

דִּכְתִיב בֵּיהּ: אֲנִי, פְּלוֹנִי, כֹּהֵן, לָוִיתִי **Where it is written in it: "I, So-and-so, a priest, borrowed."** *Rid, Ra'ah,* and *Ritva* maintain that the Gemara's wording here is significant. The question concerns a case where the borrower wrote in the first person singular, "I, So-and-so, the priest, borrowed," but not a case where the witnesses wrote, referring to the borrower in the third person, "We saw So-and-so, the priest, borrow." *Ra'ah* explains that the witnesses would not sign the document without checking all questions of substance, however phrased, but they would sign irrelevant matters without checking, if they were written in the first person singular, because they could always argue that they had testified merely that the borrower *said* such and such, and he did indeed say it. Thus the Gemara's question is whether the borrower's self-proclaimed status as a priest is substantial or irrelevant. But if the witnesses wrote, referring to the borrower in the third person singular, that he was a priest, everyone agrees that they would not have signed such a document without checking, and their testimony is sufficient even to establish priestly lineage.

Rambam, however, phrases this Halakhah as referring to the borrower in the third person. *Ran* explains that, according to *Rambam*, the witnesses may have written that the borrower was a priest without checking, because they considered his priestly status as incidental to the loan that was the subject of the document.

Tosafot adds that where the borrower's title is significant to the loan — for example, in a town where there are two people with the same name, one a priest and the other not, and the title "priest" is included in the document to distinguish between them — the witnesses would definitely not have signed without checking, and their testimony is believed.

מַהוּ לְהַעֲלוֹת מִנְּשִׂיאוּת כַּפַּיִם לְיוֹחֲסִין **What is the law about elevating from the Priestly Benediction to lineage?** Our commentary follows *Rashi*, who explains that the Gemara is referring to a man who claims to be a priest, and who

HALAKHAH

documents. *Rema* adds, in the name of *Ran*, that regarding such matters we elevate even from a document in which the would-be priest was the witness, and signed his name, 'I, So-and-so, the priest, attest this loan.'" (*Rambam, Sefer Kedushah, Hilkhot Issurei Bi'ah* 20:9; *Shulhan Arukh, Even HaEzer* 3:2.)

מַהוּ לְהַעֲלוֹת מִנְּשִׂיאוּת כַּפַּיִם לְיוֹחֲסִין **What is the law about elevating from the Priestly Benediction to lineage?** "We

TRANSLATION AND COMMENTARY

recited regularly in the Temple and is still recited today in the synagogue service. If a man proves that he regularly recites the Priestly Benediction in the synagogue, do we permit him to marry a woman of unblemished lineage? Or is pronouncing the Priestly Benediction at best a proof of presumptive priesthood — like eating terumah is in the view of the Sages — and thus not sufficient for elevating a claimant to full priestly status?

תִּיבָּעֵי לְמַאן דְּאָמַר [1]The Gemara explains: At first glance it would seem that giving the Priestly Benediction is the same kind of proof of priestly status as eating terumah, and this question should be subject to the dispute between Rabbi Yehudah and the other Sages in our Mishnah. But in fact this question **may be asked** even **according to** Rabbi Yehudah, **who said** (above) **that we elevate from terumah to lineage,** because eating terumah may be a better proof of priestly lineage than giving the Priestly Benediction. According to Rabbi Yehudah, it would seem obvious that we should elevate from the Priestly Benediction to lineage just as we do for terumah; but the Gemara will explain that this is not necessarily the case, because there is reason to distinguish between the two. [2]Moreover, this question **may** also **be asked according to the** Sages, **who** disagreed with Rabbi Yehudah and **said that we do not elevate** from terumah to lineage, because giving

LITERAL TRANSLATION

[1]It may be asked according to the one who said [that] we elevate from terumah to lineage, [2]and it may be asked according to the one who said [that] we do not elevate.

[1]תִּיבָּעֵי לְמַאן דְּאָמַר מַעֲלִין מִתְּרוּמָה לְיוּחֲסִין, [2]וְתִיבָּעֵי לְמַאן דְּאָמַר אֵין מַעֲלִין.

NOTES

regularly gives the Priestly Benediction in the synagogue. The Gemara is asking: May we rely on the fact that this man is manifestly confident that he is a priest to permit him to marry a woman of unblemished lineage, since nobody would dare to give the Priestly Benediction if he had the slightest doubt about his status? Or is it possible that the man may have doubts about his status — or even be brazenly lying — and behave as a priest without legal justification? Accordingly, the Gemara compares a non-priest who gives the Priestly Benediction with a non-priest who eats terumah, and notes that while eating terumah is a much more serious sin, giving the Priestly Benediction is more public, and thus requires more audacity.

Rabbenu Tam explains that the Gemara's question about elevating from the Priestly Benediction to lineage is similar to the question about elevating from terumah to lineage (above, 24a). There, *Rabbenu Tam* explained that when the Gemara uses the term "lineage," it is referring to the accreditation of a man to serve as a priest in the Temple. Thus the Gemara's question here is whether an ordinary priest by presumption — who has only one witness — is permitted to give the Priestly Benediction, or whether this privilege is reserved for a priest who can produce two qualified witnesses in support of his claim. The Gemara then distinguishes between terumah and the Priestly Benediction, arguing that even if we maintain that serious matters like eating terumah are reserved for priests whose lineage has been established by two witnesses, we might be willing to rely on one witness to allow the claimant to recite the Priestly Benediction, the recital of which by a non-priest is at most a relatively minor sin. And even if we maintain that in principle one witness is sufficient for both terumah and the Priestly Benediction, and that we do not elevate from terumah to lineage, nevertheless regarding a public matter like the Priestly Benediction we might believe one witness, since a witness would never lie about a public matter, and we might then elevate the claimant to the status of full priestly lineage. Hence we should require two witnesses from the outset to avoid this problem (see *Ritva*).

Ramban and *Ra'ah* explain that the Gemara is referring to a person who claims to be a priest and wishes to give the Priestly Benediction. In principle, no more than one witness should be needed, since this is a ritual matter with no material ramifications, and one witness is believed in ritual matters. Nevertheless, the Gemara suggests that two witnesses may be needed, because we are concerned that a later generation may accept as a proof of priestly lineage the fact that this man gave the Priestly Benediction. On the other hand, we might not be concerned about this, and we could rely on one witness in accordance with the letter of the law. The Gemara then distinguishes between terumah and the Priestly Benediction, arguing that even if we are concerned that a later generation may accept a serious matter such as eating terumah as proof of a person's priestly lineage, the same does not apply to the Priestly Benediction, the recital of which by a non-priest is at most a minor sin. And even if we dismiss our concerns about a later generation mistaking the status of someone seen eating terumah, the Priestly Benediction — which is recited in public — is bound to make an impression on people, and could lead a later generation to elevate this man's son or grandson to the status of full priestly lineage.

HALAKHAH

do not elevate from the Priestly Benediction to lineage. If witnesses testify that they saw someone reciting the Priestly Benediction in the synagogue without any protest from the congregation, we do not treat this as if two witnesses were testifying that this man is definitely a priest. *Maggid Mishneh* explains that *Rambam* followed the stricter opinion in the dispute (below) between Rabbi Avina and Rav Ḥisda, because we are strict in matters of lineage.

"The above ruling applies only to questions of lineage. But regarding things that are permitted to presumed priests today, such as eating Rabbinic terumah and Rabbinic *ḥallah*, we do elevate from the Priestly Benediction to lineage." (*Rambam, Sefer Kedushah, Hilkhot Issurei Bi'ah* 20:4,9; *Shulḥan Arukh, Even HaEzer* 3:2.)

[1] תִּיבָּעֵי לְמַאן דְּאָמַר מַעֲלִין: [2] הָנֵי מִילֵּי תְּרוּמָה, דַּעֲוֹן מִיתָה הִיא, [3] אֲבָל נְשִׂיאוּת כַּפַּיִם, [4] דְּאִיסּוּר עֲשֵׂה, לָא. [5] אוֹ דִּלְמָא לָא שְׁנָא?

LITERAL TRANSLATION

[1] It may be asked according to the one who said [that] we elevate from terumah to lineage: [2] These words [apply to] terumah, which is a transgression [punishable by] death, [3] but the Priestly Benediction, which [4] is a prohibition [inferred from] a positive commandment, no. [5] Or perhaps there is no difference?

TRANSLATION AND COMMENTARY

the Priestly Benediction may be a better proof of lineage than eating terumah. According to the Sages, it would seem obvious that we should not elevate from the Priestly Benediction to lineage, because giving the Priestly Benediction is no better proof of lineage than eating terumah; but the Gemara will explain that this is not necessarily the case, because there is reason to distinguish between the two.

תִּיבָּעֵי לְמַאן דְּאָמַר [1] The Gemara elaborates: This question **may be asked according to** Rabbi Yehudah, **who said that we elevate from terumah to lineage,** because we can distinguish between terumah and the Priestly Benediction and we can argue that eating terumah is a good proof of priestly lineage, whereas giving the Priestly Benediction is not. [2] For Rabbi Yehudah's **words** may **apply** only **to terumah,** the eating of **which** by an unauthorized person **is a transgression punishable by death** at the hands of Heaven. The Torah (Leviticus 22:9) declares that an unauthorized person who eats terumah will die, although the court does not impose any penalty. Hence a purported priest who had the slightest doubt about his lineage would not eat terumah, out of fear for his life. Thus, if anyone does eat terumah, Rabbi Yehudah is of the opinion that we can be certain that he is a priest, and we can elevate him to full priestly status. [3] **But** if a non-priest **gives the Priestly Benediction,** [4] he **is** merely transgressing **a prohibition inferred from a positive commandment.** The Torah nowhere explicitly forbids non-priests from giving the Priestly Benediction. However, since the Torah commanded priests to do so, we infer that non-priests are forbidden to do so. This kind of prohibition is called "a prohibition inferred from a positive commandment," and is considered the least severe kind of sin. Hence the purported priest may be willing to take a chance, even if he has doubts about his lineage, so that even if he does give the Priestly Benediction we **cannot** be certain that he is a priest, and we do not allow him to marry a woman of unblemished lineage. [5] On the other hand, continues the Gemara, **perhaps there is no difference,** and Rabbi Yehudah would maintain that the law regarding the Priestly Benediction is the same as that regarding terumah? In either case, the purported priest is forbidden both to eat the terumah and to give the Priestly Benediction if he has doubts about his lineage. Since Rabbi Yehudah is of the opinion that a priest who eats terumah may be elevated to full priestly status, the same should apply to a priest who gives the Priestly Benediction.

RASHI

דאיסור מיתה – אם זר הוא – לא היה אוכל תרומה, שהוא עון מיתה.

דאיסור עשה – "כה תברכו" (במדבר ו) – אתם ולא זרים, ולאו הבא מכלל עשה – עשה.

NOTES

דְּאִיסּוּר עֲשֵׂה **Which is a prohibition inferred from a positive commandment.** The law barring a non-priest from giving the Priestly Benediction is "a prohibition inferred from a positive commandment." The Torah does not explicitly forbid non-priests from giving the Priestly Benediction, but we may infer from the fact that the Torah specifically imposed this commandment on the priests that non-priests are forbidden to do so (*Rashi*).

In tractate *Shabbat* (118b), the Gemara lists a series of statements of Rabbi Yose that illustrate his extraordinary piety. In one of them he says: "All my life I have never disobeyed my colleagues. I know that I am not a priest, but if my colleagues told me to go up to the platform in the synagogue where the Priestly Benediction is recited, I would do so." *Tosafot* comments on this statement that he does not know of any prohibition against a non-priest going up to the platform, except possibly the prohibition against reciting an unnecessary blessing — a Rabbinic prohibition associated with the Torah prohibition against taking the name of God in vain (Exodus 20:7). According to the usual meaning of the expression "reciting an unnecessary blessing," *Tosafot* seems to be referring to the Rabbinic blessing recited by the priests before they utter the Priestly Benediction. *Tosafot* appears to be saying that a non-priest is permitted to recite the Priestly Benediction in the synagogue, provided that he does not recite the Rabbinic blessing first. The commentators note, however, that this is in complete contradiction to our Gemara here, which clearly states that a non-priest who recites the Priestly Benediction violates a prohibition inferred from a positive commandment of the Torah, and not merely the Rabbinic prohibition against reciting an inappropriate blessing.

The commentators have proposed many different solutions to this problem. *Magen Avraham* suggests that *Tosafot* may have been referring to the Priestly Benediction itself, rather than the Rabbinic blessing preceding it, and that he was explaining the nature of "the prohibition inferred from a positive commandment" mentioned in our Gemara. *Maharsha* explains that Rabbi Yose was prepared to go up to the platform with the priests, but was not prepared to recite the Priestly Benediction; hence *Tosafot* could not find any prohibition against him doing so. *Rema* explains that the inferred prohibition applies only if the non-priest goes up by himself to give the Priestly Benediction, but if he goes up together with priests, as Rabbi Yose

TRANSLATION AND COMMENTARY

תִּיבָּעֵי לְמַאן דְּאָמַר [1]Moreover, says the Gemara, this question **may** also **be asked according to the** Sages, **who** disagreed with Rabbi Yehudah and **said that we do not elevate** from terumah to lineage, because it is possible to distinguish between terumah and the Priestly Benediction and to argue that giving the Priestly Benediction is a good proof of priestly lineage whereas eating terumah is not. [2]For the Sages' **words** may **apply** only **to terumah, which is eaten in private.** The purported priest may be willing to take a chance and eat terumah in private, even if he has doubts about his lineage. Hence the eating of terumah cannot serve as proof of lineage. [3]**But with regard to the Priestly Benediction, which is** given **in public** in the synagogue, [4]**if** the man claiming to be a priest **were not** certain that he was **a priest,** [5]**he would not be so brazen** as to bless the congregation in public. Hence the fact that he gives the Priestly Benediction in the synagogue can be taken as proof of his lineage. [6]On the other hand, continues the Gemara, **perhaps there is no difference,** and the Sages would maintain that the law regarding the Priestly Benediction is the same as that regarding terumah. In either case, the purported priest is forbidden to eat the terumah or to give the Priestly Benediction if he has doubts about his lineage, and there is no reason to imagine that he will be prepared to sin just because the sin is not committed in public. Hence, since the Sages are of the opinion that a priest who eats terumah may not be elevated to full priestly status, the same should apply to a priest who gives the Priestly Benediction.

רַב חִסְדָּא וְרַבִּי אָבִינָא [7]The Gemara reports that when this question was asked, **Rav Ḥisda and Rabbi Avina disagreed** about the matter. (It is not clear from the Gemara which Amora held which view.) [8]**One said: We elevate** such a man to full priestly status, because giving the Priestly Benediction is conclusive proof of priesthood. [9]**But** the other **one said: We do not elevate** such a man to full priestly status, because giving the Priestly Benediction is not conclusive proof of priesthood.

אֲמַר לֵיהּ [10]In a later generation, **Rav Naḥman bar Yitzḥak said to Rava: What is the law about elevating from the Priestly Benediction to lineage?**

אֲמַר לֵיהּ [11]Rava **said to him** in reply: **It is a dispute between Rav Ḥisda and Rabbi Avina.**

הִלְכְתָא מַאי [12]Rav Naḥman bar Yitzḥak then asked: **What is the Halakhah?** How do we rule in this dispute?

אֲמַר לֵיהּ [13]Rava **said to him** in reply: I did not hear any explicit ruling on the matter, but **I know a Baraita** which clearly indicates that we do not elevate from the Priestly Benediction to lineage. [14]**For it was taught** in a Baraita: "If a person wishes to do something that is permitted only to certain people (such as eating terumah, which is permitted only to a priest and members of his household), and he cannot prove

[1]תִּיבָּעֵי לְמַאן דְּאָמַר אֵין מַעֲלִין: [2]הָנֵי מִילֵּי תְּרוּמָה, דְּמִיתְאַכְלָא בְּצִנְעָא, [3]אֲבָל נְשִׂיאוּת כַּפַּיִם, דִּבְפַרְהֶסְיָא, [4]אִי לָאו כֹּהֵן הוּא, [5]כּוּלֵּי הַאי לָא מַחֲצִיף אִינָשׁ נַפְשֵׁיהּ. [6]אוֹ דִּלְמָא לָא שְׁנָא?

[7]רַב חִסְדָּא וְרַבִּי אָבִינָא: [8]חַד אָמַר: מַעֲלִין, [9]וְחַד אָמַר: אֵין מַעֲלִין.

[10]אֲמַר לֵיהּ רַב נַחְמָן בַּר יִצְחָק לְרָבָא: מַהוּ לְהַעֲלוֹת מִנְּשִׂיאוּת כַּפַּיִם לְיוּחֲסִין?

[11]אֲמַר לֵיהּ: פְּלוּגְתָּא דְּרַב חִסְדָּא וְרַבִּי אָבִינָא.

[12]הִלְכְתָא מַאי?

[13]אֲמַר לֵיהּ: אֲנָא מַתְנִיתָא יָדַעְנָא. [14]דְּתַנְיָא:

LITERAL TRANSLATION

[1]It may be asked according to the one who said [that] we do not elevate: [2]These words [apply to] terumah, which is eaten in private, [3]but [with regard to] the Priestly Benediction, which is in public, [4]if he were not a priest, [5]a person would not be so brazen. [6]Or perhaps there is no difference?

[7]Rav Ḥisda and Rabbi Avina [disagreed]. [8]One said: We elevate, [9]and one said: We do not elevate.

[10]Rav Naḥman bar Yitzḥak said to Rava: What is [the law] about elevating from the Priestly Benediction to lineage?

[11]He said to him: It is a dispute between Rav Ḥisda and Rabbi Avina.

[12]What is the Halakhah?

[13]He said to him: I know a Baraita (lit., "a teaching"). [14]For it was taught:

LANGUAGE

דִּבְפַרְהֶסְיָא Which is in public. The word פַּרְהֶסְיָא — "public" — is derived from the Greek παρρησία, *parresia*, meaning "openness," "frankness," or "free speech," and hence, by extension in Rabbinic literature, "public."

BACKGROUND

כּוּלֵּי הַאי לָא מַחֲצִיף אִינָשׁ נַפְשֵׁיהּ A person would not be so brazen. Here, as elsewhere in the Talmud, it is assumed that even a person who is not entirely honest and upright has a certain feeling of shame, and this would prevent him from transgressing openly. Whereas taking terumah and eating it is a private act, so that a person may be tempted to rely on no more than imperfect evidence or rumor and regard himself as a priest, the recital of the Priestly Benediction takes place in front of a large congregation. Hence there are two reasons why a person would be reluctant to recite the Priestly Benediction if he were not positive that he was a priest: (1) The act is an extremely public one, and (2) there may be someone in the congregation who knows the truth of the matter.

SAGES

רַבִּי אָבִינָא Rabbi Avina. A Babylonian Amora of the third generation, Rabbi Avina was a disciple of Rav Huna, but also studied with other Sages, such as Rav Yirmeyah bar Abba, Rav's disciple. He seems to have been a younger contemporary of Rav Ḥisda, in whose name he transmits teachings (though he also disagrees with him), and of Rav Sheshet.

Rabbi Avina is the only Sage who transmits the teachings of a Sage named Geniva, who left him a significant legacy.

Rabbi Avina later immigrated to Eretz Israel, and became the colleague of several of the major Sages there. His Halakhic and Aggadic teachings are found in both the Babylonian and the Jerusalem Talmud.

NOTES

proposed, there is no prohibition.

Bet Ya'akov suggests that *Tosafot* may be explaining our Gemara differently from *Rashi*. According to this explanation, there is no prohibition against non-priests reciting the Priestly Benediction. What the Gemara means is that there is a prohibition inferred from a positive commandment if a *priest* refuses to obey the Torah commandment and give the Priestly Benediction. Thus we can prove nothing from the fact that the priest gives the Priestly Benediction, because he may be doing so — in spite of doubts about his lineage — out of fear of transgressing the positive commandment.

״רַבִּי יוֹסֵי אוֹמֵר: גְּדוֹלָה חֲזָקָה, [1]שֶׁנֶּאֱמַר: ׳וּמִבְּנֵי הַכֹּהֲנִים, בְּנֵי חֲבַיָּה, בְּנֵי הַקּוֹץ, בְּנֵי בַרְזִלַּי, [2]אֲשֶׁר לָקַח מִבְּנוֹת בַּרְזִלַּי הַגִּלְעָדִי אִשָּׁה וַיִּקָּרֵא עַל שְׁמָם, [3]אֵלֶּה בִּקְשׁוּ כְתָבָם, הַמִּתְיַחְשִׂים, וְלֹא נִמְצָאוּ, וַיְגֹאֲלוּ מִן הַכְּהֻנָּה. [4]וַיֹּאמֶר הַתִּרְשָׁתָא לָהֶם אֲשֶׁר לֹא יֹאכְלוּ מִקֹּדֶשׁ הַקֳּדָשִׁים, עַד עֲמֹד כֹּהֵן לְאוּרִים וּלְתֻמִּים׳. [5]אָמַר לָהֶם: ׳הֲרֵי אַתֶּם בְּחֶזְקַתְכֶם. [6]בַּמֶּה הֱיִיתֶם אוֹכְלִים בַּגּוֹלָה? בְּקָדְשֵׁי הַגְּבוּל.

LITERAL TRANSLATION

"Rabbi Yose said: Great is legal presumption, [1]as it is said: 'And of the sons of the priests, the sons of Ḥovayah, the sons of Hakkotz, the sons of Barzillai, [2]who took a wife from the daughters of Barzillai the Gileadite and was called after their name, [3]these [people] sought their register, of those who were reckoned by lineage, but they were not found, and they were disqualified from the priesthood. [4]And the Tirshata said to them that they should not eat from the most holy things, until a priest stood with Urim and Tummim.' [5]He said to them: 'You remain in your legal presumption. [6]Of what did you eat in the exile? Of the holy things of the country (lit., "border").

TRANSLATION AND COMMENTARY

that he is in the permitted category, but he can prove that he has performed this activity in the past without hindrance, we presume that he was justified in doing it, and we allow him to continue to do what he did previously, on the basis of legal presumption. Moreover, **Rabbi Yose said:** The power of **legal presumption is great,** and we rely on it to permit activities that would otherwise be forbidden, even where there are other considerations militating against granting a dispensation. To prove his contention that legal presumptions override other considerations, Rabbi Yose cites Biblical verses (Ezra 2:61-63) which list the names of families that returned to Eretz Israel at the beginning of the Second Commonwealth. Toward the end of the list, people of doubtful lineage are mentioned, among them several purported priests who could not prove their lineage. [1]**The verse says: 'And of the sons of the priests, the sons of Ḥovayah, the sons of Hakkotz, the sons of Barzillai'** — and here the verse notes that the father of this family was not called Barzillai, but [2]**'took a wife from the daughters of Barzillai the Gileadite, and** the entire family **was called after their name** — [3]**these people sought their register, of those who were reckoned by lineage, but they were not found, and they were disqualified from the priesthood.'** The problem of these priests was brought before the religious authorities of the time, [4]**'and the Tirshata** [the ruler] **said to them that they should not eat from the most holy things, until a priest stood with Urim and Tummim.'"** The Urim and Tummim comprised part of the garments worn by the High Priest (Exodus 28:30), and they served as an oracle to resolve matters in doubt (Numbers 27:21). The Urim and Tummim were lost at the time of the destruction of the First Temple; thus the Tirshata was in effect saying that the would-be priests should not eat from the most holy things until the coming of the Messiah, when all doubts would be resolved. [5]The Baraita continues: "Rabbi Yose notes that the Tirshata **said to** the would-be priests: 'You may not eat of the *most holy* things,' implying that they could eat of ordinary holy things, even though they could not prove their lineage. According to Rabbi Yose, the Tirshata explained his ruling as follows: 'I ruled in this way because these priests **remain in their** previous **legal presumption,** [6]and continue to be permitted to eat those things **that they ate during their exile**, namely **the holy things of the country** (i.e., terumah, so called because, unlike the sacrifices, it does not have to be eaten in, or close to,

RASHI

גדולה חזקה – שאין בית דין יכולין להוציא דבר מחזקתו. **בקשו כתבם המתיחשים** – שיהו כהנים כשרים, לפי שהתחתנו כהנים בגולה בגויי הארץ וילדו להם בנים, כדכתיב בספר עזרא, והם חללים – הוצרכו הנולדים בגולה להתייחס, כשעלו מן הגולה לשרת בבנין שני. **ויגאלו** – נפסלו, מלשון ״לחם מגואל״ (מלאכי א). **התרשתא** – הוא נחמיה בן חכליה, וכן כתוב בספר עזרא (נחמיה ח). **עד עמוד כהן לאורים וגו׳** – כאדם שאומר לחבירו ״עד שיבא המשיח״. דאורים ותומים לא הוו במקדש שני, שנחסרו חמשה דברים, כדאמרינן בסדר יומא (כא,ב). **מקדשי הקדשים** – דוקא מקדשי המקדש פסלינהו, אבל תרומה שהיו רגילין בה בגולה – לא אסר עלייהו, משום דהוחזקו בה. **קדשי הגבול** – תרומה, שהיא נוהגת בגבולין, חוץ למקדש ולירושלים.

NOTES

בְּקָדְשֵׁי הַגְּבוּל Of the holy things of the country. The Tirshata specifically referred to "the most holy things" (קֹדֶשׁ הַקֳּדָשִׁים). Normally this term refers to certain kinds of sacrifices that may be eaten only by male priests in the Temple Courtyard itself, as opposed to the "holy" sacrifices (קָדָשִׁים), a portion of which is given to the priests and their households, and which may be eaten anywhere in Jerusalem. (Indeed, *Rashi* explains the verse this way in his commentary on the Book of Ezra.) In our commentary, however, we have followed *Rashi*'s comment here, which explains that the Tirshata was referring to the priestly portions of all sacrifices when he forbade "the most holy things," and that he permitted the priests of doubtful status to eat only terumah. *Rashba* explains that terumah is called

BACKGROUND

גְּדוֹלָה חֲזָקָה Great is legal presumption. A presumption is something accepted as fact, though we have no proof of it, because of an assumption (judicial, social, or psychological) that it is true. In various matters we treat presumptions as absolute proofs, and Rabbi Yose shows here that Scripture, too, provides evidence of the extent to which we depend on presumption. Even when the truth of a presumption has become doubtful, we continue to rely on it so long as it has not been refuted. Therefore, the family of "the sons of Ḥovayah," who were unable to produce full proof of priestly lineage, were not entirely demoted from the priesthood. Their status was left in doubt until the matter could be clarified.

הַתִּרְשָׁתָא The Tirshata. This title appears in four places in the Books of Ezra and Nehemiah. It is clear from the context here that the Tirshata was the highest religious authority in Eretz Israel. Etymologically, the word *tirshata* appears to be a Persian title, possibly equivalent to "governor," but also having the meaning "worthy of respect." Presumably, in the early Second Commonwealth, this title was bestowed on the highest religious authority (*Ibn Ezra*). Traditionally, when ever this title is mentioned, the reference is to Nehemiah, who was known to have borne it (Nehemiah 8:9 and 10:2). The Jerusalem Talmud (*Kiddushin* 4:1) suggests that this title is a contraction of הֶתֵּיר שְׁתִיָּה — meaning "dispensation to drink" — and refers to the special dispensation that Nehemiah was given, as the Persian king's cup-bearer, to taste the king's wine, even though it is ordinarily forbidden to drink the wine of a non-Jew.

עַד עֲמֹד כֹּהֵן לְאוּרִים וּלְתֻמִּים Until a priest stood with Urim and Tummim. When a family possesses no evidence of its lineage, there is no way of proving or disproving its claims. The issue is particularly complex in the case of priests, for a man may be descended from a priestly family without himself being a

¹אַף כָּאן בְּקָדְשֵׁי הַגְּבוּל׳״.
²וְאִי סָלְקָא דַּעְתָּךְ מַעֲלִין מִנְּשִׂיאוּת כַּפַּיִם לְיוֹחֲסִין, ³הָנֵי, כֵּיוָן דְּפָרְסֵי יְדַיְיהוּ, ⁴אָתֵי לְאַסּוּקִינְהוּ!
⁵שָׁאנֵי הָכָא, דְּרִיעַ חֶזְקַיְיהוּ.

LITERAL TRANSLATION

[1]Here too [you may eat] of the holy things of the country.'"

[2]And if it should enter your mind [that] we elevate from the Priestly Benediction to lineage, [3][then with regard to] these, since they spread out their hands, [4]we might come to elevate them!

[5]It is different here, because their legal presumption has been weakened.

RASHI

אף כאן בקדשי הגבול — ומדאמר רבי יוסי גדולה חזקה — שמע מינה נשיאות כפים נמי לא אסר עלייהו, שהרי הוחזקו בה בגבולין. **ואי סלקא דעתך כו׳ אתו לאסוקינהו** — ומה הועילו בתקנתם. **שאני הכא** — דליכא למיחש דליסוקינהו, דהא ריע חזקייהו, שהרי הכל רואין שאר כהנים אוכלין קדשי המקדש, והם אינן אוכלין — יש כאן היכר גדול שיש בהן צד פסול. אבל שאר בני אדם, כגון בזמן הזה — לעולם מעלין מנשיאות כפים ליוחסין.

TRANSLATION AND COMMENTARY

the Temple).' In Babylonia, there were no sacrifices, but terumah was separated and given to the priests, because the Rabbis decreed that produce grown in Babylonia should be tithed. Hence priests in Babylonia ate terumah even before the destruction of the First Temple, and there is a legal presumption that they were permitted to do so. [1]Therefore the Tirshata said: "'**Here, too,** in Eretz Israel, **they can** continue to **eat of the holy things of the country,** but not of the sacrifices, which are holier than terumah.' Regarding terumah, there is a legal presumption supporting their claim, since they ate terumah even in Babylonia. But regarding the sacrifices, there is no such presumption. Thus we see, says Rabbi Yose, that priests who could not prove their lineage were permitted to continue eating terumah on the basis of a legal presumption alone, and this shows that a legal presumption has the power to override other considerations."

וְאִי סָלְקָא דַּעְתָּךְ [2]**But,** concludes Rava, we can infer from this Baraita that we do not elevate from the Priestly Benediction to lineage. These purported priests were permitted to continue doing everything that they had done in exile in Babylonia, and this included giving the Priestly Benediction in the synagogue. But **if it should enter your mind that we elevate from the Priestly Benediction to lineage, [3]then with regard to these** purported priests, **since they** were permitted to continue to **spread out their hands** in blessing, [4]there was an obvious danger that **we might come to elevate them** to full priestly status! Yet the Tirshata was not concerned about this problem. Clearly, then, giving the Priestly Benediction, like the eating of terumah itself, is not sufficient proof of priestly lineage. Hence the Tirshata was able to permit these priests to continue doing so.

שָׁאנֵי הָכָא [5]But Rav Naḥman bar Yitzḥak dismisses Rava's argument: **It is different** in the case described in the Book of Ezra, **because the legal presumption** of those would-be priests **was flawed.** In the days of Ezra, all the priests ate of the sacrifices, except for the priests mentioned in this verse. Hence it was clear that they were in an inferior position, and there was no danger that someone might decide to elevate them

NOTES

"the holy things of the country" because it may be eaten anywhere in Eretz Israel, whereas the "most holy" sacrifices may not be eaten outside the Temple Courtyard, and even the "holy" sacrifices must not be removed from the city of Jerusalem.

Rashash asks: Why did the Tirshata permit the eating of terumah and forbid the eating of sacrifices? A non-priest who eats terumah is liable to death at the hands of Heaven (*Sanhedrin* 83b), whereas a non-priest who eats the "most holy" sacrifices is merely subject to lashes (*Makkot* 18b), and a non-priest who eats the priestly portion of the "holy" sacrifices is not subject to any penalty at all! Surely, if these priests were permitted to eat terumah, they should also have been permitted to eat sacrifices! *Rashash* answers that, because of the reverence associated with the sacrificial service, the priestly portions of the sacrifices were treated with great severity. In addition, it should be noted that the Torah permits some people to eat terumah but not the priestly sacrificial portions. Members of the priest's household, for example, are not permitted to eat the "most holy" sacrifices.

דְּרִיעַ חֶזְקַיְיהוּ Because their legal presumption has been weakened. Our commentary follows *Rashi*, who explains that Rav Naḥman is describing the method used by the Tirshata to distinguish the priests of doubtful status from other priests who ate terumah and recited the Priestly Benediction. In the days of Ezra, all the priests ate of the sacrifices, except for the priests mentioned in this verse. Hence it was clear that they were in an inferior position, and there was no danger that someone might decide to elevate them to full priestly status, even according to the opinion that we do elevate from terumah or the Priestly Benediction to lineage. But today, since the sacrificial service no longer exists, a priest who gives the Priestly Benediction may well be elevated to full priestly status on this basis.

Tosafot asks: According to the opinion that we elevate from terumah to lineage, why did the Tirshata find it necessary to disqualify these priests? Why did he not accept the fact that since the priests of doubtful status regularly ate terumah, this was proof of their lineage? *Rosh* answers that the fact that terumah was eaten by someone in Babylonia was not relevant, since the situation during the exile was too chaotic for terumah to serve as proof of priestly lineage. Hence the Tirshata had no difficulty in ruling that the would-be priests should eat terumah

priest, because one of the women among his ancestors may not have been permitted to marry into the priesthood, thus disqualifying her descendants from the priesthood. This issue could be resolved only by a Prophet or by the Urim and Tummim worn by the High Priest, which had prophetic power and authority.

BACKGROUND

בְּקָדְשֵׁי הַגְּבוּל Of the holy things of the country. The Hebrew word גְּבוּל — lit., "border" — was used as early as the Biblical period to indicate the entire territory within the borders of Eretz Israel. In Mishnaic Hebrew the Sages speak of גְּבוּלִין (rather than the usual plural, גְּבוּלוֹת) to refer to every place outside Jerusalem. Since all sacrifices must be eaten in Jerusalem (often within the Temple Courtyard), "the holy things of the country" refer to terumah and *ḥallah*, which, though holy, need not be eaten specifically in Jerusalem. Such "holy things" can also be eaten in the rest of the country.

TRANSLATION AND COMMENTARY

to full priestly status. But today, generations after the cessation of the sacrificial service in the Temple, a priest who gives the Priestly Benediction may well be elevated to full priestly status. Rav Naḥman explains: My reason for dismissing your argument is as follows: [1]**If you do not accept my position,** but rather reason as you did that the Tirshata permitted the would-be priests to give the Priestly Benediction and eat terumah because these actions by themselves are not sufficient proof to elevate to lineage, [2]how **then** do you explain this verse **according to** Rabbi Yehudah, **who says that we do elevate from terumah to lineage?** It is clear from the verse that the Tirshata permitted the would-be priests to continue eating terumah, [3]and **since they ate terumah,** there was a danger that people **might come to elevate them** to full priestly status, according to Rabbi Yehudah! [4]**Rather, is it not** the case that even Rabbi Yehudah would agree about the incident mentioned in the Book of Ezra, **because the presumption** of these would-be priests **was flawed,** as we explained? And if so, we can say the same thing about giving the Priestly Benediction, even according to the Sages.

וְאֶלָּא מַאי גְּדוֹלָה חֲזָקָה [25A] [5]But the Gemara now objects to this reasoning. According to Rava's explanation above, the Tirshata permitted the priests of doubtful status to continue eating terumah — even though there was a possibility that they might be elevated to full priestly status — because a legal presumption is very powerful, and we do not set it aside lightly. **But** if the legal presumption was defective, as Rav Naḥman bar Yitzḥak explained, **what is the meaning of** Rabbi Yose's remark, **"great is legal presumption"?** According to the explanation of Rav Naḥman bar Yitzḥak, the Tirshata merely ruled that the priests of doubtful status should continue eating terumah as they had before, provided that there was no danger that this would lead to complications in other areas. This does indeed show that a legal presumption is a valid proof, but it does not show that a legal presumption is so powerful that it overrides other considerations, as Rabbi Yose claimed.

[1]דְּאִי לָא תֵּימָא הָכִי, [2]לְמַאן דְּאָמַר מַעֲלִין מִתְּרוּמָה לְיוֹחֲסִין, [3]כֵּיוָן דְּאָכְלִי בִּתְרוּמָה, אָתֵי לְאַסּוּקִינְהוּ! [4]אֶלָּא לָאו מִשּׁוּם דְּרִיעַ חֶזְקַיְיהוּ?

[25A] [5]וְאֶלָּא מַאי "גְּדוֹלָה חֲזָקָה"?

LITERAL TRANSLATION

[1]For if you do not say this, [2][then] according to the one who says [that] we elevate from terumah to lineage, [3]since they eat terumah, we might come to elevate them! [4]Rather, is it not because their legal presumption has been weakened?

[25A] [5]But what is [the meaning of] "great is legal presumption"?

RASHI

[דאי לא תימא הכי – דעל זה סמיך, שיש בהן היכר תרומה, נמי תקשי למאן דאמר מעלין מתרומה ליוחסין].

ואלא מאי גדולה חזקה – דקאמר רבי יוסי, למה לנו [לחוש] להשבית חזקתם, כי מה יש לחוש לבטלה?

NOTES

and give the Priestly Benediction but not eat sacrifices. The only question was whether such a ruling would lead a later generation to elevate them to the priesthood (see also *Ritva*).

According to *Tosafot*, Rav Naḥman is explaining why the Tirshata distinguished between the priests of doubtful status and other priests, and did not accept the fact that the former had eaten terumah as proof of their lineage. According to this explanation, Rav Naḥman was arguing that the would-be priests' legal presumption was flawed because they could not find their documents of lineage, and because they were not named after a priest, but rather after Barzillai the Gileadite, whose daughter had married the father of this family. Therefore, the Tirshata did not rely on their legal presumption to elevate them to the priesthood; and for the same reason he was confident that the flaw in their legal presumption would prevent them from being elevated from eating terumah to full priestly status in the future.

וְאֶלָּא מַאי גְּדוֹלָה חֲזָקָה But what is the meaning of "great is legal presumption"? Our commentary follows *Rashi*, who explains that the Gemara's problem is that Rabbi Yose selected the verses from the Book of Ezra to illustrate the power of legal presumptions. But if the Tirshata merely applied the legal presumption, without overriding any other considerations, there is nothing novel about these verses. For why should legal presumptions not be applied where there are no conflicting considerations? In the parallel passage in tractate *Kiddushin* (69b), *Rashi* phrases his commentary a little differently, explaining that the Gemara is objecting to Rabbi Yose's choice of words: If Rabbi Yose had merely wished to prove from this verse that legal presumptions apply where they do not conflict with other considerations, he should have said: "From where do we learn about legal presumptions?" rather than: "Great is legal presumption."

Ramban explains the Gemara's question as follows: If the Tirshata had given the priests of doubtful status a privilege they did not have before, this verse would indeed be a demonstration of the power of legal presumption, as Rabbi Yose claimed. But since the Tirshata merely allowed the would-be priests to do precisely what they had done before, he was in effect reducing their status, because until now they had been considered full priests, whereas now they were in an inferior position to that of their colleagues. Why, then, did Rabbi Yose say that this verse shows the greatness of the power of legal presumption?

It is also not entirely clear against whom the Gemara's objection is directed. Our commentary follows *Tosafot* and *Ritva*, who explain that the Gemara is objecting to the explanation given by Rav Naḥman bar Yitzḥak, who disagrees with Rava. According to Rava, Rabbi Yose can

TRANSLATION AND COMMENTARY

מֵעִיקָּרָא [1]The Gemara answers: This particular legal presumption was special in that it gave these priests greater rights than those they had enjoyed previously. **Initially,** in Babylonia, **they ate Rabbinic terumah,** since by Torah law tithes need be separated only in Eretz Israel, whereas in Babylonia the separation of terumah is obligatory only by Rabbinic decree. [2]**Now,** however, **they** were permitted to **eat from Torah terumah** grown in Eretz Israel. Therefore, Rabbi Yose remarked that the power of this legal presumption was far greater than one might at first have imagined. The consequence of this answer by the Gemara is that the explanation of the Baraita given by Rav Naḥman bar Yitzḥak is satisfactory, and the Baraita has no apparent bearing on the question of whether we elevate from giving the Priestly Benediction to full priestly status.

וְאִי בָּעֵית אֵימָא [3]Having mentioned the objection of Rav Naḥman bar Yitzḥak — that according to Rabbi Yehudah, the Tirshata should not have permitted the purported priests to eat terumah, lest they be elevated to full priestly status by mistake — the Gemara cites another solution to this problem. Alternatively, **if you wish,** you can **say: Now, too, they** were permitted to **eat** only **Rabbinic terumah**, as before; [4]but **they were not** permitted to **eat Torah terumah.** By Torah law, terumah must be separated only from wheat, olives, and grapes, whereas terumah from other crops is Rabbinic, even if these crops are grown in Eretz Israel. Hence both Rabbinic and Torah terumah were available in Eretz Israel, and since the terumah eaten by these purported priests in Babylonia was Rabbinic, they were permitted to continue to eat Rabbinic terumah in Eretz Israel, but not Torah terumah. The reason the Tirshata was not concerned about the would-be priests being elevated to full priestly status, according to Rabbi Yehudah, [5]was because Rabbi Yehudah is of the opinion that **we elevate from Torah terumah to lineage,** [6]**but we do not elevate from Rabbinic terumah,** even according to Rabbi Yehudah. Hence there is no difficulty in explaining the verse according to Rabbi Yehudah, because the Tirshata was careful not to permit the would-be priests to eat Torah terumah.

[1]מֵעִיקָּרָא, אֲכוּל בִּתְרוּמָה דְּרַבָּנַן. [2]הָשְׁתָּא אֲכוּל בִּתְרוּמָה דְּאוֹרַיְיתָא.

[3]וְאִי בָּעֵית אֵימָא: הָשְׁתָּא נַמִי בִּתְרוּמָה דְּרַבָּנַן אֲכוּל, [4]בִּתְרוּמָה דְּאוֹרַיְיתָא לָא אֲכוּל. [5]וְכִי מַסְּקִינַן מִתְּרוּמָה לְיוֹחֲסִין, בִּתְרוּמָה דְּאוֹרַיְיתָא; [6]בִּתְרוּמָה דְּרַבָּנַן, לָא מַסְּקִינַן.

LITERAL TRANSLATION

[1]Initially, they ate Rabbinic terumah. [2]Now they eat Torah terumah.

[3]And if you wish, say: Now, too, they eat Rabbinic terumah, [4][and] do not eat Torah terumah. [5]And when we elevate from terumah to lineage, it is from Torah terumah; [6]but from Rabbinic terumah, we do not elevate.

RASHI

בתרומה דרבנן — שהרי בגולה היו, שאין שם תרומה מן התורה. דכל מצוה שהיא תלויה בארץ אינה נוהגת אלא בארץ, כדאמרינן בקידושין (לו,ב). **ואיבעית אימא השתא נמי בתרומה דרבנן אכול** — תרומת פירות האילן וירק. **דאורייתא** — דגן תירוש ויצהר לא אכול. ומשום הכי לא קשיא למאן דאמר מעלין מתרומה ליוחסין, **דכי מסקינן ליוחסין** — מתרומה דאורייתא כו׳.

NOTES

be understood as saying that, because of the power of legal presumption, the Tirshata permitted the would-be priests to eat terumah and give the Priestly Benediction, even though there was a possibility that this would cause confusion and lead a later generation to elevate them to full priestly status. But according to Rav Naḥman bar Yitzḥak, the Tirshata took adequate precautions to prevent this, and thus there was nothing special about this legal presumption.

Ra'ah explains that the Gemara's objection is directed both at Rava and at Rav Naḥman bar Yitzḥak. If we maintain that we elevate from the Priestly Benediction or from terumah to lineage, and that the Tirshata took no special precautions, Rabbi Yose can be understood as saying that it was because of the power of legal presumption that the Tirshata permitted the priests of doubtful status to eat terumah and give the Priestly Benediction, even though they might be elevated to full priestly status in a later generation. But according to Rava, this Baraita maintains that we do not elevate from terumah or from the Priestly Benediction to lineage; and according to Rav Naḥman, the Tirshata took adequate precautions to prevent these priests of doubtful status from being elevated. Hence, according to both views, there was nothing special about this legal presumption.

תְּרוּמָה דְּאוֹרַיְיתָא וּתְרוּמָה דְּרַבָּנַן **Torah terumah and Rabbinic terumah.** When the Torah commands that terumah be given to the priests, it refers to "your grain, your wine,

HALAKHAH

הָשְׁתָּא נַמִי בִּתְרוּמָה דְּרַבָּנַן אֲכוּל **Now, too, they eat Rabbinic terumah.** "Today all priests are merely presumed to be priests. No priest is able to prove his lineage to the point where he would theoretically be permitted to serve in the Temple. Hence priests in our time may eat only Rabbinic terumah," following the Gemara's second explanation of this Baraita. (*Rambam, Sefer Zeraim, Hilkhot Terumot* 6:2, and *Sefer Kedushah, Hilkhot Issurei Bi'ah* 2:1.)

וְכִי מַסְּקִינַן מִתְּרוּמָה לְיוֹחֲסִין, בִּתְרוּמָה דְּאוֹרַיְיתָא **And when we elevate from terumah to lineage, it is from Torah

TRANSLATION AND COMMENTARY

וְאֶלָּא מַאי גְּדוֹלָה חֲזָקָה [1] **But**, objects the Gemara, if this latter explanation is correct, and the legal presumption did not give the would-be priests greater rights than they had enjoyed previously, and it did not override any other consideration, **what is the meaning of** Rabbi Yose's remark, **"great is legal presumption"?** According to the explanation just given by the Gemara, the Tirshata merely ruled that the would-be priests should continue eating Rabbinic terumah as before. This does indeed show that a legal presumption is a valid proof, but it does not show that a legal presumption is so powerful that it overrides other considerations, as Rabbi Yose claimed.

דְּאַף עַל גַּב [2] The Gemara answers: This particular legal presumption was special in **that** the Tirshata permitted these priests to continue eating Rabbinic terumah, **even though there was** a good **reason to prohibit** them from doing so **because** they might come to eat **Torah terumah** as well. In Babylonia they had eaten any kind of terumah, but now they were permitted to eat only the terumah of certain crops, and this could easily lead to confusion. Accordingly, Rabbi Yose remarked on the fact that the purported priests were allowed to rely on their legal presumption, [3] and **we did not prohibit** them from continuing to eat Rabbinic terumah, in spite of the danger of confusion, because a legal presumption cannot be set aside lightly.

וּבִתְרוּמָה דְּאוֹרָיְיתָא לָא אֲכוּל [4] The assumption underlying this solution to the problem was that the Tirshata permitted the priests of doubtful status to eat only Rabbinic terumah. The Gemara now challenges this assumption. **But** is it true that the would-be priests were **not** permitted to **eat Torah terumah?** [5] **Surely the Biblical verse states** that the Tirshata said to them **"that they should not eat of the most holy things,"**

[1] וְאֶלָּא מַאי ״גְּדוֹלָה חֲזָקָה״? [2] דְּאַף עַל גַּב דְּאִיכָּא לְמִיגְזַר מִשּׁוּם תְּרוּמָה דְּאוֹרָיְיתָא, [3] לָא גָּזְרִנַן.

[4] וּבִתְרוּמָה דְּאוֹרָיְיתָא לָא אֲכוּל? [5] וְהָא כְּתִיב: ״אֲשֶׁר לֹא יֹאכְלוּ מִקֹּדֶשׁ הַקֳּדָשִׁים״?

LITERAL TRANSLATION

[1] But [if so], what is [the meaning of] "great is legal presumption"?

[2] That even though there is [reason] to prohibit [Rabbinic terumah] because of Torah terumah, [3] we do not prohibit [it].

[4] But did they not eat Torah terumah? [5] But surely it is written: "That they should not eat from the most holy things"?

RASHI

דאיכא למיגזר משום תרומה דאורייתא — שהרי לארץ באו, ומצויה שם תרומה גמורה דאורייתא, מה שלא היה מצוי להם בגולה, ויש לחוש פן יאכילום בה.

NOTES

and your oil" (Deuteronomy 18:4), and when it commands that tithes be given, it refers to "the increase of your seed" (Deuteronomy 14:22). From here we learn that terumah and tithes apply by Torah law to all fruit-like produce that grows from the ground, is fit for human consumption, and is cultivated. Wild produce, however, or produce that is not usually eaten, is exempt from terumah. Vegetables, which are cultivated for their leaves and stems rather than for their fruit, are not subject to terumah by Torah law, but terumah must nevertheless be separated from them by Rabbinic decree (*Rambam, Hilkhot Terumot* 2:1-6). According to many Rishonim, the same applies to all produce other than grain, grapes, and olives (*Rashi, Tosafot, Ra'avad*).

By Torah law, terumah and tithes — like most agricultural laws — apply only in Eretz Israel. For this purpose, Eretz Israel includes only those parts of the country that were actually under Israelite control (certain parts were never conquered). Moreover, the original conquest of Eretz Israel under Joshua is considered to have been terminated with the destruction of the First Temple. Thus, by Torah law, only territory in Eretz Israel that has been settled by Jews since the time of Ezra is subject to terumah and tithes. The Rabbis, however, decreed that produce grown in Transjordan, Syria, Babylonia, and Egypt should be tithed (*Rambam*, ibid., 1:1-9). Vegetables, however, which by Torah law are not subject to terumah, even in Eretz Israel, need not be tithed at all in Babylonia or Egypt (ibid., 2:7).

There is a Tannaitic dispute as to whether terumah and tithes apply today by Torah law (in the areas of Eretz Israel settled during the Second Temple period), or whether they have only Rabbinic status (*Yevamot* 81a). There is likewise a dispute on this matter among the Rishonim. According to the opinion that terumah and tithes today are only Rabbinic, a presumed priest may eat terumah, even according to the Gemara's conclusion that the Tirshata permitted the priests of doubtful status to eat only Rabbinic terumah (*Rambam, Hilkhot Issurei Bi'ah* 20:3).

HALAKHAH

terumah. "If two witnesses testify that a man claiming to be a priest eats Torah terumah, this is proof of lineage. *Gra* notes that *Rambam* is ruling in favor of Rabbi Yehudah against the Sages (but see *Maggid Mishneh*)." (*Rambam, Sefer Kedushah, Hilkhot Issurei Bi'ah* 20:4.)

¹מִקֹּדֶשׁ הַקֳּדָשִׁים הוּא דְּלָא אֲכוּל, ²הָא בִּתְרוּמָה דְּאוֹרַיְיתָא אֲכוּל!

³הָכִי קָאָמַר: ⁴לָא בְּמִידֵי דְּאִיקְּרִי ״קֹדֶשׁ״, ⁵דִּכְתִיב: ״וְכָל זָר לֹא יֹאכַל קֹדֶשׁ״; ⁶וְלָא בְּמִידֵי דְּאִיקְּרִי ״קֳדָשִׁים״, ⁷דִּכְתִיב: ״וּבַת כֹּהֵן כִּי תִהְיֶה לְאִישׁ זָר, הִיא בִּתְרוּמַת הַקֳּדָשִׁים לֹא תֹאכֵל״. ⁸וְאָמַר מָר: ⁹בַּמּוּרָם מִן הַקֳּדָשִׁים לֹא תֹאכַל.

¹⁰תָּא שְׁמַע: ״חֲזָקָה לִכְהוּנָּה נְשִׂיאוּת כַּפַּיִם בְּבָבֶל,

LITERAL TRANSLATION

[1] It was from the most holy things that they did not eat, [2] [implying that] from Torah terumah they did eat!

[3] This is what it says: [4] Not of anything that is called "holy," [5] as it is written: "And no stranger shall eat [that which is] holy"; [6] nor of anything that is called "holy things," [7] as it is written: "And if the daughter of a priest is married to a stranger, she shall not eat of an offering of the holy things." [8] And the Master said: [9] She shall not eat of what is lifted up from the holy things.

[10] Come [and] hear: "Presumption for the priesthood [is created by] giving the Priestly Benediction (lit., 'lifting the hands') in Babylonia,

TRANSLATION AND COMMENTARY

[1] from which we can infer that **it was** only **the most holy things that they were not permitted to eat** — i.e., the sacrifices — [2] **whereas** ordinary holy things, like **Torah terumah, they were permitted to eat!** How, then, can we explain that the Tirshata permitted them to eat Rabbinic terumah only?

הָכִי קָאָמַר [3] The Gemara answers: Each word in the expression "the most holy things" (קֹדֶשׁ הַקֳּדָשִׁים) must be considered separately, as though the Tirshata forbade them to eat both "holy" (קֹדֶשׁ) and "the holy things" (הַקֳּדָשִׁים). And **this is what** the Tirshata **said**: [4] The would-be priests were **not** permitted to eat terumah, **which is called "holy,"** [5] **as the verse** (Leviticus 22:10) **states: "And no stranger** [i.e., non-priest] **shall eat that which is holy."** This verse, and this entire passage in the Torah, are traditionally understood to be referring to terumah. [6] **Nor** could they eat the priestly portions of sacrifices, **which are called "holy things,"** [7] **as the verse** (Leviticus 22:12) **states: "And if the daughter of a priest is married to a stranger, she shall not eat of an offering of the holy things."** This verse, although it immediately follows the previous verse and is also referring to terumah, is traditionally understood to be teaching us about the priestly portion of the sacrifices as well. Thus we see that the Tirshata's words in the Book of Ezra can be understood as forbidding the would-be priests to eat terumah as well as sacrifices. The Gemara now explains how the latter verse can be understood as referring to the priestly portion of the peace-offering eaten by ordinary Israelites. A portion of this sacrifice is given to the priest (Leviticus 7:28-34) to be eaten by any member of his household (Leviticus 10:14). In tractate *Yevamot* (87a), the Gemara cites a Baraita which rules that if the daughter of a priest marries a non-priest, she may never again eat the priestly sacrificial portion, even if she is subsequently widowed or divorced and is permitted once again to eat terumah (Leviticus 22:13). [8] **And the Master** (Rav Ḥisda in the name of Ravina bar Shila) **said** that this law is derived from an extra word in this verse: The verse uses repetitive language — "an offering of the holy things" — rather than just saying "an offering" or "holy things," to teach us another law, [9] that a priest's daughter who marries a non-priest **shall not eat of what is lifted up from the holy things**, i.e., the priestly portions that are removed from the peace-offering and given to the priest.

תָּא שְׁמַע [10] The Gemara now returns to the question of whether giving the Priestly Benediction is sufficient proof to elevate someone to full priestly status. **Come and hear** a Baraita which suggests that it is sufficient proof: "A man **is presumed to be a priest** if he does one of three things: (1) If he **gives the Priestly Benediction**, even **in Babylonia** (which is outside Eretz Israel), and certainly in Syria or Eretz Israel.

RASHI

לא במידי דאקרי קדש — והיינו תרומה. **וכל זר לא יאכל קדש** — בתרומה משתעי, דכתיב בפרשה לעיל מיניה ״ובא השמש וטהר ואחר יאכל מן הקדשים״ ואוקמינן בתרומה, ביבמות ב״הערל״ (עד,ב). **ולא במידי דאקרי קדשים** — אפילו חזה ושוק של שלמים הנאכלים לנשי כהנים ולעבדיהם. **ואמר מר** — ביבמות, בפרק ״יש מותרות״, בבת כהן שניסת לישראל ונעשית אלמנה וגרושה וזרע אין לה, שחוזרת לתרומת אביה ואינה חוזרת לחזה ושוק. ויליף לה מהאי קרא ״כי תהיה לאיש זר היא בתרומת הקדשים לא תאכל״ עוד. **חזקה לכהונה** — להעיד עליו שהוא כהן. **נשיאות כפים בבבל** — הרואהו נושא כפיו בבבל מעיד עליו בכל מקום שהוא כהן, ומקבלין הימנו. לפי שיש שם ישיבה, ובית דין קבוע בודקין אחר נושאי כפים. אבל אכילת חלה ותרומה אינה חזקה, דחוצה לארץ לאו דאורייתא תרומה דיליה, ולא קפדי כולי האי.

CONCEPTS

סוּרְיָא Syria. The land to the north and northeast of Eretz Israel, extending to the Euphrates River. King David conquered much of Syria. Since this conquest was carried out before the full conquest of Eretz Israel proper, Syria was not incorporated into Eretz Israel. Nevertheless, the Sages decreed that in certain respects (for example, with regard to firstfruits) Syria was to be considered a part of Eretz Israel, and in other specific matters it was to be given an intermediate status between that of Eretz Israel and that of the Diaspora.

TERMINOLOGY

קָתָנֵי מִיהַת At all events it teaches.... When, as part of an objection, a lengthy Mishnah or Baraita is cited by the Talmud, and only one part is actually relevant to the objection being raised, the Talmud may first cite this Mishnah or Baraita in its entirety, and then repeat the relevant section, introducing it with this expression.

TRANSLATION AND COMMENTARY

[1]**Or** (2) if he **eats *hallah* in Syria** [a territory to the north and northeast of Eretz Israel, which is treated like Eretz Israel for some purposes and like a foreign country for others; see note]. The Torah (Numbers 15:17-21) commands that whenever dough is kneaded, a piece must be given to the priest. This piece of dough is called *hallah*, and has the same status as terumah. Thus, if a man eats *hallah* — even in Syria, where the Torah status of *hallah* is problematic — he is definitely a priest, because a non-priest who eats *hallah* is subject to death at the hands of Heaven. By implication, however, if a man eats *hallah* in Babylonia, this cannot serve as proof that he is a priest, since *hallah* outside Eretz Israel is of Rabbinic status. [2]**Or** (3) if he benefits from **the distribution of the priestly gifts in large cities** [in Eretz Israel, Syria, or even Babylonia]." The Torah (Deuteronomy 18:3) commands anyone who slaughters an ox, a sheep, or a goat to give the priest the animal's front leg, two cheeks, and maw. These so-called "priestly gifts" have no special holiness, and may be eaten by anyone, but they are the property of the priest. The owner of the animal has the right to select any priest as the recipient of these gifts. In a small town, a non-priest might lie about his status and persuade someone to give him these portions; but in a big city with good communications, a non-priest would not dare to claim priestly status for fear of being caught. Hence no priest would be given a share if his status were not absolutely certain.

קָתָנֵי מִיהַת [3]The Gemara now analyzes this Baraita. **At all events, it teaches** that a man is presumed to be a priest if he **gives the Priestly Benediction.** Thus we see that giving the Priestly Benediction is sufficient proof of priestly status. [4]Now, argues the Gemara, **is** the Baraita **not teaching** us this law **in reference to lineage?** Does the Baraita not mean that a man who gives the Priestly Benediction has full priestly status? Surely this implies that we do elevate from the Priestly Benediction to full priestly status!

לָא [5]The Gemara answers: **No,** the Baraita is referring **to terumah.** The Baraita means that a man who gives the Priestly Benediction is treated like a man who claims to be a priest, but who has only one witness. We have seen that, according to the Sages, such a man is permitted to eat terumah but is not permitted to marry a woman of unblemished lineage, and the Baraita is teaching us that the same law applies to a man who gives the Priestly Benediction.

[1]וַאֲכִילַת חַלָּה בְּסוּרְיָא, [2]וְחִלּוּק מַתָּנוֹת בִּכְרַכִּין".
[3]קָתָנֵי מִיהַת נְשִׂיאוּת כַּפַּיִם.
[4]מַאי לָאו לְיוּחֲסִין?
[5]לָא, לִתְרוּמָה.

LITERAL TRANSLATION

[1]and the eating of *hallah* in Syria, [2]and the distribution of [priestly] gifts in large cities."

[3]At all events it teaches lifting the hands. [4]Is it not [referring] to lineage?

[5]No, to terumah.

RASHI

ואכילת חלה בסוריא – היא ארם צובה שכיבשה דוד וחיברה לארץ ישראל. וקסבר האי תנא: כיבוש יחיד שמיה כיבוש, וחלתה ותרומתה דאורייתא. וקסלקא דעתך תנא: חלה, והוא הדין לתרומה. **וחילוק מתנות** – דהזרוע והלחיים. **בכרכין** – ואף על גב דאיסורן אין איסור לזרים, הואיל וכרכים מקום שווקין הן, ומצויין בו עוברים ושבים המכירין בו, אי לאו דכהן הוה – לא מחליף נפשיה. **לא לתרומה** – הרואהו נושא כפיו בבבל, או אוכל חלה דווקא בסוריא, והעיד עליו בארץ ישראל מקבלין עדותו להאכילו תרומה, אבל לא ליוחסין.

NOTES

בְּסוּרְיָא In Syria. When the Gemara discusses Syria, it is referring to certain areas outside Eretz Israel (most of which are in present-day Syria) which were conquered by King David in what is described as a "private war," undertaken without divine sanction (*Rashi*). These territories were annexed to Eretz Israel at the time, but their status remained problematic. According to some authorities, a "private war" is Halakhically effective, and these territories have the status of Eretz Israel by Torah law. Other authorities, however, maintain that a private war is not effective, and these territories have the status of foreign countries. In practice, Syria is placed in an intermediate category. It is treated like Eretz Israel in some respects, and like a foreign country in others.

Rambam (*Hilkhot Terumot* 1:2-4) has a slightly different explanation. According to him, a private war has no Halakhic effect at all, but King David's war did have divine sanction, and so was not considered "private." According to *Rambam*, the conquest of Syria was considered problematic because King David was supposed to have completed the conquest of Eretz Israel before embarking on this war.

Rashi and other Rishonim explain that this Baraita is teaching that a private war is effective, since we see that the Baraita treats Syrian *hallah* like *hallah* from Eretz Israel, and not like Babylonian *hallah*. Hence, *hallah* taken from grain grown in Eretz Israel or in Syria is a good proof of priesthood, since it is of Torah status, whereas Babylonian *hallah* is not acceptable, as it is Rabbinic. Giving the Priestly Benediction, by contrast, is convincing proof even in Babylonia, and certainly in Syria or in Eretz Israel. But it is clear from the next Baraita (below) that even giving the Priestly Benediction is sufficient proof only in a country like Babylonia, with a highly organized Jewish community, but not in a foreign country with a small Jewish community.

לָא לִתְרוּמָה No, to terumah. The Gemara explains that the Baraita may not be referring to lineage at all, and may merely be saying that giving the Priestly Benediction is

TRANSLATION AND COMMENTARY

וְהָא דוּמְיָא דַּאֲכִילַת חַלָּה קָתָנֵי [1]**But,** the Gemara objects, **surely** the Baraita **teaches** us the case of a would-be priest who gives the Priestly Benediction **as** being **analogous to eating *ḥallah*.** The Baraita listed three ways by which a person could prove that he was a priest: by giving the Priestly Benediction, by eating *ḥallah*, and by receiving a share of the priestly gifts. It can be argued that giving the Priestly Benediction and receiving the priestly gifts constitute proof that the purported priest is permitted to eat terumah, but eating *ḥallah* is definitely proof of full priestly status. For the Baraita made a clear distinction between *ḥallah* taken from grain grown in Eretz Israel or Syria, and *ḥallah* taken from Babylonian grain, implying that this law applies specifically to Torah *ḥallah*. And we do not need to be told that a person who eats Torah *ḥallah* is permitted to eat terumah, since the two are completely equivalent. [2]Therefore, **just as** the Baraita could only have been teaching us the case of **eating *ḥallah* in reference to lineage,** [3]**so too** the analogous case of **giving the Priestly Benediction** must have been **taught in reference to lineage!**

לָא [4]The Gemara answers: **No, it is the eating of *ḥallah* that is taught in reference to terumah,** and the entire Baraita is referring to terumah rather than to lineage. And if you object that the Baraita specifically referred to *ḥallah* taken from grain grown in Eretz Israel or Syria, which is a Torah obligation, and we do not need to be told that a person who eats Torah *ḥallah* may eat terumah, as the two are completely equivalent, [5]the answer is that the author of this Baraita **maintains** that ***ḥallah* today is** of **Rabbinic** status, even in Eretz Israel, [6]whereas **terumah** taken from produce grown in Eretz Israel **is a Torah obligation,** even today. [7]Thus the Baraita is teaching us that **we elevate from Rabbinic *ḥallah* to Torah terumah.** A priest of doubtful status who eats *ḥallah* taken from grain grown in Eretz Israel or even in Syria is permitted to eat terumah taken from produce grown in Eretz Israel, even though the *ḥallah* is Rabbinic and the terumah is a Torah obligation. The Gemara explains: There is, in fact, an opinion that today terumah taken from produce

[1]וְהָא דוּמְיָא דַּאֲכִילַת חַלָּה קָתָנֵי. [2]מָה אֲכִילַת חַלָּה לְיוּחֲסִין, [3]אַף נְשִׂיאוּת כַּפַּיִם לְיוּחֲסִין!

[4]לָא, אֲכִילַת חַלָּה גּוּפָהּ לִתְרוּמָה. [5]קָסָבַר: חַלָּה בַּזְּמַן הַזֶּה דְּרַבָּנַן, [6]וּתְרוּמָה דְּאוֹרַיְיתָא, [7]וּמַסְּקִינַן מֵחַלָּה דְּרַבָּנַן לִתְרוּמָה דְּאוֹרַיְיתָא.

LITERAL TRANSLATION

[1]But surely it teaches it as analogous to eating *ḥallah*. [2]Just as eating *ḥallah* [refers] to lineage, [3]so too giving the Priestly Benediction [refers] to lineage!

[4]No, the eating of *ḥallah* itself [refers] to terumah. [5]He maintains: *Ḥallah* in our (lit., "this") time is Rabbinic, [6]and terumah is from the Torah, [7]and we elevate from Rabbinic *ḥallah* to Torah terumah.

RASHI

מה אכילת חלה – עדות מוקמה. **ליוחסין** – דאי לתרומה – פשיטא, היא גופה תרומה היא, וכבר הוחזק בה. **ומסקינן מחלה דרבנן כו׳** – דאי לאו כהן הוא לא הוו ספו ליה חלה, גזירה משום תרומה.

NOTES

sufficient proof to allow the would-be priest to eat terumah. *Ramban* raises the following problem: When the Gemara first posed the question about giving the Priestly Benediction, it explained that the question was directed both at Rabbi Yehudah and at the Sages. Admittedly, according to the Sages it is possible that the Baraita is referring to terumah and not to lineage. But Rabbi Yehudah is of the opinion that we elevate from terumah to lineage. Thus, even if the Baraita were saying only that a priest who gives the Priestly Benediction may eat terumah, he would automatically be elevated to lineage as well.

Ramban answers that the Gemara is primarily interested in the viewpoint of the Sages, which is followed by the Halakhah, and the dispute between Rabbi Avina and Rav Ḥisda about giving the Priestly Benediction, which began this discussion, likewise concerns the viewpoint of the Sages alone. Thus, even if this Baraita were a proof according to Rabbi Yehudah, it would be a relatively unimportant discovery. Moreover, even according to Rabbi Yehudah, it is possible that this Baraita provides no proof. For the dispute between Rabbi Yehudah and the Sages is a Tannaitic dispute, and Baraitot are not required to cite both sides in such disputes. Thus Rabbi Yehudah could argue that the Baraita reflects the view of the Sages, who certainly maintain that giving the Priestly Benediction is sufficient for terumah, and they may indeed be of the opinion that it is a good proof of lineage as well, whereas according to Rabbi Yehudah, giving the Priestly Benediction may be no proof of anything at all.

וּמַסְּקִינַן מֵחַלָּה דְּרַבָּנַן לִתְרוּמָה דְּאוֹרַיְיתָא **And we elevate from Rabbinic *ḥallah* to Torah terumah.** The Rishonim ask: According to the Gemara's conclusion, this Baraita rules that all *ḥallah* is of Rabbinic status today, even if the grain was grown in Eretz Israel proper. Why, then, does it distinguish between *ḥallah* prepared from grain grown in Eretz Israel or Syria on the one hand and Babylonian

HALAKHAH

חַלָּה וּתְרוּמָה בַּזְּמַן הַזֶּה ***Ḥallah* and terumah today.** "Today, all terumah and all *ḥallah* — even that taken from crops grown in Eretz Israel — is Rabbinic. For the Torah requires terumah to be given only when the entire Jewish people is

BACKGROUND

בַּזְּמַן הַזֶּה **In our time.** This expression is used here to refer to the period after the destruction of the Second Temple. However, since the status of certain laws changed because of historical developments, it is important to summarize the issues and define the various stages. For every purpose, according to all opinions, the sanctity of Eretz Israel began once the Israelites had settled there after the exodus from Egypt (that is to say, following "the seven years of conquest and the seven years of settlement"). At that time, all the laws written in the Torah concerning the land came into force: the Sabbatical cycle, the Jubilee, terumah and tithing, *ḥallah* and contributions to the poor.

In the opinion of many Sages, "our time" begins with the fall of the Kingdom of Israel and the exile of the ten tribes in the eighth century B.C.E. For when the exile of the ten tribes took place, the laws of the Jubilee were annulled, and with them the laws of the Sabbatical cycle, as well as other laws sanctifying the land.

The destruction of the First Temple and the Babylonian exile brought to an end, according to all opinions, the period of "first sanctity" (קְדוּשָּׁה רִאשׁוֹנָה), and Eretz Israel and Jerusalem no longer had any particular Halakhic sanctity.

The construction of the Second Temple and the return of the Jews from Babylonia at the time of Ezra brought about the period of "second sanctity" (קְדוּשָּׁה שְׁנִיָּה). In various respects, this degree of sanctity can never be removed from the land. The Halakhic problem is whether the covenant in the Book of Nehemiah (chapter 8) — in which all the Jews agreed to bring terumah and tithes — was a social contract to accept Torah law or merely an ordinance. If it was an ordinance, then in this respect the situation remained as it was after the destruction of the Kingdom of Israel. The implication of this is that there is no longer any Torah obligation to observe these Halakhot, but the Sages of

Ezra's generation agreed to observe them, and they are therefore all Rabbinic ordinances.
The destruction of the Second Temple brought about a basic change in priestly status. Some of the obligatory laws were suspended, and they were observed as Rabbinic ordinances, as a reminder of a Torah obligation.

TRANSLATION AND COMMENTARY

grown in Eretz Israel is from the Torah, whereas *ḥallah* is Rabbinic. [1]This opinion is maintained by **Rav Huna the son of Rav Yehoshua,** who **reversed a statement of the Rabbis,** as we will see below. The Gemara explains below that certain Rabbis took the position that, in their time, *ḥallah* taken from grain grown in Eretz Israel was a Torah obligation while terumah was Rabbinic, but Rav Huna the son of Rav Yehoshua told them that the opposite was the case.

[1]וְכִדְאַפֵּיךְ לְהוּ רַב הוּנָא בְּרֵיהּ דְּרַב יְהוֹשֻׁעַ לְרַבָּנַן.

LITERAL TRANSLATION

[1]And it is as Rav Huna the son of Rav Yehoshua reversed [the statement of] the Rabbis.

RASHI

וכדאפיך – לקמן מפרש.

NOTES

ḥallah on the other, since they are all of Rabbinic status? The Rishonim explain that people are more careful in a place where *ḥallah* is, at least in principle, a Torah law, than in a place where it is inherently Rabbinic (*Tosafot*, *Ra'ah*, *Ramban*).

According to this explanation, it is difficult to reconcile this Baraita with the viewpoint of Rav Naḥman bar Yitzḥak, who explained Rabbi Yose's statement earlier — "great is legal presumption" — as meaning that where a would-be priest is able to show that he has been permitted to eat Rabbinic terumah, he may continue to eat terumah, even if it is terumah by Torah law. For Rav Naḥman bar Yitzḥak was willing to accept any Rabbinic terumah as proof, even from Babylonia, whereas this Baraita is prepared to accept only Rabbinic *ḥallah* from Eretz Israel or Syria. On the other hand, it is also difficult to reconcile this Baraita with the Gemara's second explanation above — that the Tirshata permitted the doubtful priests to eat only Rabbinic terumah but not Torah terumah — since that explanation is based specifically on the viewpoint that we do not elevate from Rabbinic terumah grown in Eretz Israel to Torah terumah, whereas this Baraita does elevate from Rabbinic *ḥallah* to Torah terumah, provided that they are both from Eretz Israel. Neither explanation distinguishes between Rabbinic terumah from Eretz Israel and Rabbinic terumah from Babylonia, whereas this Baraita does. The Rishonim had great difficulty in resolving this problem (see *Ramban*, and *Tosafot* below, 25b).

חַלָּה וּתְרוּמָה בַּזְּמַן הַזֶּה ***Ḥallah* and terumah today.** To understand why certain agricultural laws mentioned in the Torah are of Rabbinic status today, it is important to recognize that Torah laws fall into two categories: Obligations incumbent on the person himself (e.g., keeping the Sabbath or returning a lost object), and obligations that are intrinsically connected to a specific location (e.g., the agricultural laws, which can be fulfilled only in Eretz Israel, or the sacrificial laws that can be fulfilled only in the Temple). Nearly all Torah commandments directed to the person himself began to apply the moment they were given to Moses, and continue to apply in all places at all times. But most obligations connected to a specific location apply only when the location in question has been sanctified. Sanctity is not permanent: Eretz Israel itself was sanctified once, then lost its sanctity, and was then sanctified again. Shiloh was sanctified for the sacrificial service, and later lost its sanctity. Jerusalem was sanctified, and, according to one opinion, lost its sanctity (*Megillah* 10a).

When the Israelites entered Canaan for the first time, under Joshua, the parts of the country that they conquered became sanctified for the purposes of the agricultural laws. With a few exceptions (notably *ḥallah*, mentioned below), the sanctification took effect only after the first fourteen years, when the main campaign to conquer Canaan was complete. The fifteenth year became the first year of the first Jubilee cycle, the twenty-first year was the first Sabbatical Year, etc.

When the First Temple was destroyed and the population exiled, the sanctity of the land as it applied to the agricultural laws lapsed (*Ḥagigah* 3b). According to some opinions, the Jubilee Year — and perhaps even the other agricultural laws — lapsed when the ten tribes were exiled, a century-and-a-half before the First Temple was destroyed (*Arakhin* 32b). The Book of Nehemiah relates (12:27-34) that those who returned from exile in Babylonia performed a dedication ceremony to resanctify the city of Jerusalem for sacrifices. According to one opinion, this was a true sanctification, but according to another opinion, the original sanctity of Jerusalem had never lapsed, and the rededication was a mere ceremony reminiscent of a true sanctification (*Shevuot* 16a). According to all opinions, however, Eretz Israel was sanctified again for the purposes of the agricultural laws with the beginning of a new Sabbatical and Jubilee cycle (*Arakhin* 12b). As a result, the borders of Eretz Israel today, for most Halakhic purposes, are those established by Ezra and Nehemiah, rather than the wider ones in effect during the period of the First Temple (*Ḥagigah* 3b).

תְּרוּמָה בַּזְּמַן הַזֶּה **Terumah today.** There is a Tannaitic and Amoraic dispute (*Yevamot* 81a and 82b) as to whether terumah applies today by Torah law or only by Rabbinic decree. According to *Rashi* and *Tosafot* (followed by our commentary), the question is whether Ezra's resanctification of Eretz Israel for the purposes of the agricultural laws (see previous note) lapsed with the destruction of the Second Temple.

A somewhat similar question is raised in tractate *Arakhin* (32b) regarding the Jubilee Year (Leviticus 25:8-13). The Gemara adduces from a Biblical verse that the laws of the Jubilee Year apply only when the entire Jewish people is in Eretz Israel, arranged according to tribes. According to one opinion, this arrangement ceased with the exile of the ten tribes, a century-and-a-half before

HALAKHAH

living in Eretz Israel, and this has not been the situation since the destruction of the First Temple, since only a minority returned to Eretz Israel under Ezra. *Ra'avad* agrees that this is true of *ḥallah*, but rules that terumah is a Torah commandment even today, following Rav Huna the son of Rav Yehoshua. *Rema* cites *Ra'avad*'s view, but notes that in practice the custom is to be lenient and treat even terumah as Rabbinic." (*Rambam, Sefer Zeraim, Hilkhot Terumot* 1:26, and *Sefer Kedushah, Hilkhot Issurei Bi'ah* 20:3; *Shulḥan Arukh, Yoreh De'ah* 322:2 and 331:2.)

TRANSLATION AND COMMENTARY

תָּא שְׁמַע [1]The Gemara returns to the question of whether giving the Priestly Benediction is sufficient proof to elevate someone to full priestly status. **Come and hear** a Baraita which suggests that it is sufficient proof: "A man **is presumed to be a priest** if he does one of two things: (1) If he **gives the Priestly Benediction,** [2]or (2) if he benefits from **the distribution** of terumah **at the threshing floors.** Since terumah must not be eaten by non-priests, on pain of death at the hands of Heaven, the man would not be given a share if his status were not absolutely certain. These two forms of proof only apply **in Eretz Israel.** [3]**But in Syria, and anywhere** else outside Eretz Israel **where messengers travel about** to provide information about the date **of the new month,** [4]**giving the Priestly Benediction is proof, but** benefiting from **the distribution** of terumah **at the threshing floors is not proof."** At the beginning of every month, the Sanhedrin in Eretz Israel would announce, on the basis of testimony, whether the previous month had contained twenty-nine days or thirty days. Messengers would then be sent to inform Jewish communities in Eretz Israel, as well as important Jewish communities in nearby countries. The Baraita is teaching us that a community that was close enough to Eretz Israel and sufficiently well-organized to receive such messengers could be trusted not to allow non-priests to give the Priestly

[1]תָּא שְׁמַע: ״חֲזָקָה לִכְהוּנָּה נְשִׂיאוּת כַּפַּיִם [2]וְחִילּוּק גְּרָנוֹת בְּאֶרֶץ יִשְׂרָאֵל. [3]וּבְסוּרְיָא וּבְכָל מָקוֹם שֶׁשְּׁלוּחֵי רֹאשׁ חוֹדֶשׁ מַגִּיעִין, [4]נְשִׂיאוּת כַּפַּיִם רְאָיָה, אֲבָל לֹא חִילּוּק גְּרָנוֹת.

LITERAL TRANSLATION

[1]Come [and] hear: "Presumption for the priesthood [is created by] giving the Priestly Benediction [2]and the distribution at the threshing floors in Eretz Israel. [3]But in Syria and in every place to which messengers of the New Moon come, [4]giving the Priestly Benediction is proof, but the distribution at the threshing floors is not [proof].

RASHI

נשיאות כפים וחילוק גרנות — דתרומה. **בארץ ישראל** — נושאי כפים, דאיכא בית דין קבועין ובדקי. וחילוק גרנות קאי סלקא דעתך השתא דתרומה בזמן הזה דאורייתא, וכיון דעון מיתה איכא — מסקינן מינה ליוחסין. **בסוריא וכל מקום ששלוחי ארץ ישראל מגיעין** — להודיע לגולה יום שקידשו בית דין את החדש לעשות פסח בזמנו, דהיינו היושבים בתוך מהלך חמשה עשר יום. **נשיאות כפים ראיה** — לפי שבית דין קבוע שם, שמקבל שליחות החדש של בית דין הגדול. **אבל לא חילוק גרנות** — דתרומה דידהו לאו דאורייתא — ובסוריא נמי, האי תנא סבר: כיבוש יחיד לא שמיה כיבוש. ופלוגתא דתנאי היא בהך מילתא (עבודה זרה כא,א).

BACKGROUND

שְׁלוּחֵי רֹאשׁ חוֹדֶשׁ Messengers of the New Moon. In ancient times the determination of the New Moon by the Bet Din, which was of particular importance for the observance of Festivals during that month, used to be announced by lighting torches on mountaintops. When interference by the Samaritans and other factors made it impossible to continue using this method, the Temple officials began to send out messengers to announce the date of the New Moon.

The places to which the messengers were sent were regarded as part of Eretz Israel for the purpose of determining the dates of Festivals, and the Festivals were celebrated there for one day, not for two days as is done outside Eretz Israel. Moreover, the very fact that messengers were sent to a certain place was proof that there was a reliable court there. Hence it could be presumed that the priests who gave the Priestly Benediction there had been examined by an authorized court.

NOTES

the destruction of the First Temple, and was not restored during the Second Temple period. The Gemara makes it clear, however, that even according to the view that the laws of the Jubilee Year did not apply during the Second Temple period, the Jubilee cycle was counted. Hence, the laws of the Sabbatical Year applied by Torah law, although the Jubilee Year itself was not observed. In tractate *Gittin* (36a), however, the Torah obligation of the Sabbatical Year itself is questioned. *Rashi* and *Tosafot* disagree as to whether this is a variant of the Jubilee Year question raised in tractate *Arakhin*, or whether it is a separate question.

According to *Rashi* and *Tosafot*, the question in tractate *Yevamot* about terumah and the question about the Jubilee Year in tractate *Arakhin* are quite distinct. Even according to the opinion that the laws of the Jubilee Year did not apply during the Second Temple period, the years of the Jubilee and the Sabbatical cycles were counted, and the laws of terumah and tithes — which are connected to the cycle — were fulfilled in accordance with Torah law. The question in tractate *Yevamot* was not whether terumah was required by Torah law during the Second Temple period, but rather whether it was still required by Torah law after the destruction of the Second Temple.

Rambam has a very different interpretation of this entire matter. According to *Rambam*, the sanctity established by Joshua lapsed, but the sanctity established by Ezra is permanent (*Hilkhot Terumot* 1:5). Thus the destruction of the Second Temple changed nothing in this regard. Rather, the issue in *Yevamot* is the same as that in *Arakhin*: Did terumah, and the Sabbatical and Jubilee Years, apply during the Second Temple period? Or was Ezra's sanctification merely Rabbinic, since most of the Jewish people did not return to Eretz Israel? According to *Rambam*, the opinion that maintains that terumah is Rabbinic today must also maintain that terumah was Rabbinic in Ezra's day and, indeed, ever since the tribal arrangement ceased, a century-and-a-half before the destruction of the First Temple.

In practice, *Rambam* rules that the sanctity of Eretz Israel is Rabbinic, so long as a majority of the Jewish people is not living there. This is true with regard to terumah (*Hilkhot Terumot* 1:26), with regard to the Sabbatical Year, and with regard to all other agricultural laws (*Hilkhot Shemittah VeYovel* 10:8-9). This status will remain until the coming of the Messiah, when a true resanctification will take place (*Hilkhot Shemittah VeYovel* 12:15). But the special sanctity of Jerusalem as God's holy city never lapsed, since God's presence never left Jerusalem (*Hilkhot Bet HaBehirah* 6:14-16).

It is not entirely clear how *Rambam* would explain the many passages in the Gemara which suggest that the destruction of the Second Temple did effect a change, nor is it clear how he would explain passages (such as ours) which imply that some agricultural laws did not apply during the Second Temple period whereas others did. For the sake of simplicity, in our commentary we have followed *Rashi* and *Tosafot*.

אֲבָל לֹא חִילּוּק גְּרָנוֹת But the distribution at the threshing floors is not. *Rashi* and other Rishonim explain that this Baraita teaches that the conquests achieved in a private war to extend the borders of Eretz Israel do not create the

[1] וּבָבֶל כְּסוּרְיָא. [2] רַבָּן שִׁמְעוֹן בֶּן גַּמְלִיאֵל אוֹמֵר: אַף אַלֶכְּסַנְדְּרִיָּא שֶׁל מִצְרַיִם בָּרִאשׁוֹנָה, [3] מִפְּנֵי שֶׁבֵּית דִּין קְבוּעִין שָׁם״.
[4] קָתָנֵי מִיהַת נְשִׂיאוּת כַּפַּיִם.
[5] מַאי לָאו לְיוֹחֲסִין?
[6] לָא, לְחַלָּה.
[7] הָא דּוּמְיָא דְּחִילּוּק גְּרָנוֹת קָתָנֵי. [8] מַה חִילּוּק גְּרָנוֹת לְיוֹחֲסִין, [9] אַף נְשִׂיאוּת כַּפַּיִם לְיוֹחֲסִין!

LITERAL TRANSLATION

[1] And Babylonia is like Syria. [2] Rabban Shimon ben Gamliel says: Also Alexandria in Egypt in the past, [3] because a court was fixed there."

[4] At all events it teaches giving the Priestly Benediction. [5] Is it not [referring] to lineage?

[6] No, to *ḥallah*.

[7] But surely it teaches it as analogous to the distribution at the threshing floors. [8] Just as the distribution at the threshing floors [refers] to lineage, [9] so too giving the Priestly Benediction [refers] to lineage!

TRANSLATION AND COMMENTARY

Benediction; but the fact that someone was given terumah in such places is not a good proof, since terumah outside Eretz Israel is of Rabbinic status, and this Baraita teaches that even Syria is considered to be a foreign country for the purposes of terumah. [1] The Baraita continues: **"Babylonia is like Syria."** Babylonia had a highly organized Jewish community, and even in its remoter parts, which the messengers of the new month could not reach, the community could be trusted not to allow non-priests to give the Priestly Benediction. But in other, more remote, countries even the Priestly Benediction was not a proof of priestly status. [2] The Baraita continues: **"Rabban Shimon ben Gamliel says: Alexandria in Egypt, too, originally** had the same status as Babylonia, [3] **because there were permanent courts** in Alexandria, and they could be trusted not to allow non-priests to give the Priestly Benediction." In later generations, however, the Alexandrian community declined in importance, and could no longer be trusted on this matter.

קָתָנֵי מִיהַת [4] The Gemara now analyzes this Baraita. **At all events,** it **teaches** that a man is presumed to be a priest if he **gives the Priestly Benediction.** Thus we see that giving the Priestly Benediction is sufficient proof of priesthood. [5] Now, argues the Gemara, **is** the Baraita **not teaching** us this law **in reference to lineage?** Does the Baraita not mean that a man who gives the Priestly Benediction has full priestly status, and is permitted to marry a woman of unblemished lineage? Surely this implies that we do elevate from the Priestly Benediction to full priestly status!

לָא [6] The Gemara answers: **No,** the Baraita is referring **to *ḥallah*,** which has the same status as terumah. The Baraita means that a man who gives the Priestly Benediction is treated like a man who claims to be a priest but has only one witness. We have seen that, according to the Sages, such a man is permitted to eat terumah (or *ḥallah*), but is not permitted to marry a woman of unblemished lineage, and the Baraita is teaching us that the same law applies to a man who gives the Priestly Benediction.

הָא דּוּמְיָא [7] **But,** the Gemara objects, **surely the Baraita teaches** us the case of a purported priest who gives the Priestly Benediction **as** being **analogous to the distribution** of terumah **at the threshing floors.** The Baraita listed two ways in which a man could prove that he was a priest — by giving the Priestly Benediction, and by receiving a share of terumah at the threshing floors. It can be argued that giving the Priestly Benediction is proof that a purported priest is permitted to eat *ḥallah*, but eating terumah is definitely proof of full priestly status. For the Baraita specifically referred to terumah in Eretz Israel, where it is separated and given to the priests by Torah law, and we do not need to be told that a person who eats Torah terumah is permitted to eat *ḥallah*, since the two are completely equivalent. [8] Therefore, **just as** the Baraita could only have been teaching us the case of **the distribution** of terumah **at the threshing floors in reference to lineage,** [9] **so too** the analogous case of **giving the Priestly Benediction** must have been **taught in reference to lineage!**

BACKGROUND

אַלֶכְּסַנְדְּרִיָּא שֶׁל מִצְרַיִם **Alexandria in Egypt.** There were many cities in Asia and Africa named Alexandria after Alexander the Great. The one in Egypt was called "Alexandria in Egypt" to distinguish it from the others. A large and important Jewish community flourished in Alexandria for many generations, and the main synagogue there was famous for its immense size. When Jewish revolts in Judea against the Romans were cruelly suppressed (in 66 and 115 C.E.), the main Jewish communal institutions in Alexandria, including its central Rabbinic Court, were severely damaged.

NOTES

same sanctity as that enjoyed by Eretz Israel proper, since we see that the Baraita treats Syrian terumah like Babylonian terumah rather than like terumah from Eretz Israel. Thus, consuming terumah from Eretz Israel is good proof of priesthood, since it is of Torah status, whereas Syrian or Babylonian terumah is not acceptable, because it is Rabbinic. By contrast, giving the Priestly Benediction is acceptable proof in any well-ordered Jewish community, even in Babylonia and Alexandria, and certainly in Syria or Eretz Israel.

Here too the Rishonim ask: According to the Gemara's conclusion, this Baraita maintains that all terumah is of Rabbinic status today, even if the produce was grown in Eretz Israel proper. Why, then, does the Baraita distinguish between terumah from Eretz Israel on the one hand, and Babylonian and Syrian terumah on the other, since they are all of Rabbinic status? As before, the Rishonim answer that people are more careful in a place where terumah is at least in principle a Torah law than in a place where it is inherently Rabbinic.

אַף אַלֶכְּסַנְדְּרִיָּה שֶׁל מִצְרַיִם בָּרִאשׁוֹנָה **Also Alexandria in Egypt in the past.** The Rishonim ask: In later generations,

[1]לָא, חִילּוּק גְּרָנוֹת גּוּפָהּ לְחַלָּה. [2]קָסָבַר: תְּרוּמָה בַּזְּמַן הַזֶּה דְּרַבָּנַן, [3]וְחַלָּה דְּאוֹרַיְיתָא, [4]וּמַסְּקִינַן מִתְּרוּמָה דְּרַבָּנַן לְחַלָּה דְּאוֹרַיְיתָא.

[5]וְכִדְאַשְׁכַּחִינְהוּ רַב הוּנָא בְּרֵיהּ דְּרַב יְהוֹשֻׁעַ לְרַבָּנַן. [6]דְּאָמַר רַב הוּנָא בְּרֵיהּ דְּרַב יְהוֹשֻׁעַ: אַשְׁכַּחְתִּינְהוּ לְרַבָּנַן בְּבֵי רַב, [7]דְּיָתְבֵי וְקָאָמְרִי: אֲפִילּוּ לְמַאן דְּאָמַר תְּרוּמָה בַּזְּמַן הַזֶּה דְּרַבָּנַן, [8]חַלָּה דְּאוֹרַיְיתָא. [9]שֶׁהֲרֵי שֶׁבַע שֶׁכִּיבְּשׁוּ וְשֶׁבַע

LITERAL TRANSLATION

[1]No, the distribution at the threshing floors itself [refers] to *ḥallah*. [2]He maintains: Terumah today is Rabbinic, [3]and *ḥallah* is from the Torah, [4]and we elevate from Rabbinic terumah to Torah *ḥallah*.

[5]And [it is] as Rav Huna the son of Rav Yehoshua found the Rabbis [saying]. [6]For Rav Huna the son of Rav Yehoshua said: I found the Rabbis in the House of Study, [7]who were sitting and saying: Even according to the one who says [that] terumah today is Rabbinic, [8]*ḥallah* is from the Torah. [9]For [during] the seven [years] when [the Israelites] conquered and the seven

RASHI

בבי רב – בית המדרש קרי בי רב.

TRANSLATION AND COMMENTARY

לָא [1]The Gemara rejects this argument: **No,** it is **the distribution** of terumah **at the threshing floors** that **is taught in reference to *ḥallah*,** and the entire Baraita is referring to *ḥallah* rather than to lineage. And if you object that the Baraita specifically referred to Torah terumah, and we do not need to be told that a person who receives a share of Torah terumah may eat *ḥallah*, as the two are completely equivalent, [2]the answer is that the author of this Baraita **maintains** that **terumah today is of Rabbinic status,** even in Eretz Israel, [3]whereas ***ḥallah*** taken from grain grown in Eretz Israel **is from the Torah,** even today. [4]Thus the Baraita is teaching us that **we elevate from Rabbinic terumah to Torah *ḥallah*.** A man who claims to be a priest and eats terumah taken from grain grown in Eretz Israel is permitted to eat *ḥallah* separated from produce grown in Eretz Israel, even though the terumah is Rabbinic and the *ḥallah* is from the Torah.

וְכִדְאַשְׁכַּחִינְהוּ [5]The Gemara explains: There is, in fact, an opinion that today *ḥallah* taken from grain grown in Eretz Israel is from the Torah, and terumah is Rabbinic. This opinion is maintained by **the Rabbis whose views were overheard by Rav Huna the son of Rav Yehoshua,** and related in the story below. The Gemara explains there that certain Rabbis took the position that today *ḥallah* taken from grain grown in Eretz Israel is from the Torah and terumah is Rabbinic, but Rav Huna the son of Rav Yehoshua told them that the opposite was the case. [6]**For Rav Huna the son of Rav Yehoshua said:** Once **I found the Rabbis in the House of Study,** [7]**and they were saying: Even according to the** authority **who says that terumah today is of Rabbinic status** everywhere, including Eretz Israel, [8]nevertheless ***ḥallah* is from the Torah,** even today. There is a Tannaitic and Amoraic dispute (*Yevamot* 81a) as to whether terumah remains a Torah obligation today, after the destruction of the Second Temple. All agree that the Torah obligation to separate terumah ceased after the destruction of the First Temple and was renewed by Ezra with the construction of the Second Temple; but Resh Lakish rules in favor of Rabbi Yose, who maintains that the obligation ceased once more when the Second Temple was destroyed, whereas Rabbi Yoḥanan and the Sages are of the opinion that Ezra's renewal of the Torah obligation to separate terumah was permanent. The Rabbis in the House of Study were arguing that it is possible to make a distinction between terumah and *ḥallah*, and to argue that the obligation to give *ḥallah* may be from the Torah, even according to the opinion that terumah is of Rabbinic status. [9]**For during the seven years when the Israelites** under Joshua **conquered** Canaan,

NOTES

the situation in Alexandria deteriorated, and this law no longer applied. Why, then, mention it at all? *Ra'ah* answers that if a person produces witnesses that his ancestors gave the Priestly Benediction in Alexandria, this serves as proof. *Ramban* answers that Alexandria set a precedent, and the same law would apply in any other place in which a highly organized Jewish community was set up.

שֶׁהֲרֵי שֶׁבַע שֶׁכִּיבְּשׁוּ For during the seven years when the Israelites conquered. The Rabbis' argument is that, just as during the fourteen years of conquest all the agricultural laws (including terumah) were not operative, whereas *ḥallah* was in force, similarly today even the opinion that maintains that the laws of terumah lapsed after the destruction of the Second Temple would maintain that the laws of *ḥallah* remain in force. Although there is technical justification for it, it is a little difficult to understand how Eretz Israel could remain sanctified for some agricultural purposes and not for others. This problem was considered by the Aḥaronim (see *Bet HaLevi*). It is also not entirely clear why the fact that *ḥallah* applied during the fourteen years of conquest implies that it should apply by Torah law today as well.

It should be noted, however, that the laws of *ḥallah* are less closely connected to land than are most other agricultural laws. They apply to dough, which is a processed product, rather than to produce that is still growing. Indeed, it was for this reason that the Rabbis decreed that *ḥallah* should apply even outside of Eretz Israel, unlike the other agricultural laws (see *Tosafot, Bekhorot* 27b). It is also interesting to note that the *Sifra* (*Behar* 2), which is

שֶׁחִילְּקוּ, [1]נִתְחַיְּיבוּ בְּחַלָּה וְלֹא נִתְחַיְּיבוּ בִּתְרוּמָה. [2]וְאָמִינָא לְהוּ אֲנָא: [3]אַדְּרַבָּה, אֲפִילּוּ לְמַאן דְּאָמַר תְּרוּמָה בַּזְּמַן הַזֶּה דְּאוֹרַיְיתָא, [4]חַלָּה דְּרַבָּנַן.

LITERAL TRANSLATION

[years] when they divided, [1]they were obliged to [separate] *ḥallah* but they were not obliged to [separate] terumah. [2]But I said to them: [3]On the contrary, even according to the one who says [that] terumah today is from the Torah, [4]*ḥallah* is Rabbinic.

TRANSLATION AND COMMENTARY

and during **the** following **seven years, when they divided** the land among the tribes, [1]the Israelites **were under the obligation to give** the priests ***ḥallah*** whenever they kneaded dough, **but they were not obliged** to give the priests **terumah.** In general, the agricultural laws laid down in the Torah came into effect only after the war of conquest was concluded — fourteen years after the Israelites first entered Canaan. But we have a tradition that *ḥallah* was an exception to this rule, and that the Israelites were obliged to give it immediately on their arrival (see note). The Rabbis of the House of Study house argued that the same applies today. Even according to the opinion that terumah is not a Torah obligation today, *ḥallah* is an exception, because the obligation to separate it is still in force. [2]**But** Rav Huna the son of Rav Yehoshua **said to** the Rabbis of the House of Study: [3]**On the contrary,** if there is room to distinguish between these laws at all, the distinction is in the opposite direction: **Even according to** Rabbi Yoḥanan, **who says that** the obligation to give **terumah is** still **from the Torah today** (because Ezra's renewal of the agricultural laws remains in effect, even after the destruction of the Second Temple), [4]***ḥallah* is Rabbinic**, even in Eretz Israel,

RASHI

נתחייבו בחלה — דכתיב "בבואכם אל הארץ", ותניא בספרי: רבי ישמעאל אומר: שינה הכתוב ביאה זו מכל ביאות שבתורה, שבכולן נאמר "כי תבאו" "כי יביאך" וכאן "בבואכם" — ללמדך שכיון שנכנסו לה נתחייבו. **ולא נתחייבו בתרומות ומעשרות** — דכתיב "דגנך... תבואת זרעך" — המיוחדת לך. ועוד, שהרי תלה הכתוב המעשר במנין שנות השמטה, דכתיב "בשנה השלישית שנת המעשר" ושמטות לא מנו אלא משכבשו וחילקו, כדאמרינן בסדר עולם, ובמסכת ערכין (יב,ב).

NOTES

the source of the ruling that the other agricultural laws applied only after the first fourteen years (see next note), rules that all three agricultural laws that apply outside Eretz Israel (*ḥallah, orlah,* and new grain), applied from the moment of entry into Canaan, even before the conquest.

שֶׁבַע שֶׁכִּיבְּשׁוּ וְשֶׁבַע שֶׁחִילְּקוּ The seven years when the Israelites conquered and the seven years when they divided. It is clear from our Gemara that tithing was not required during the first fourteen years. It is likewise clear from tractate *Arakhin* (12b) that the reckoning of the Sabattical Year and the Jubilee Year did not begin until after the first fourteen-years. Nowhere in the Talmud is a reason given for the fourteen year delay. But the Rishonim cite comments of the *Sifra* and *Sifrei* (authoritative Tannaitic Midrashim on Leviticus and Numbers, respectively) as the sources of these laws.

Sifrei (Shelaḥ 1) explains that the fourteen-year exemption applies to all laws introduced in the Torah by the phrase "when you come into the land" (which includes the laws of the Sabbatical Year and the Jubilee Year, and most other agricultural laws). *Sifrei* explains that we learn this from another verse (Deuteronomy 26:1): "And it shall be, when you come into the land which the Lord is giving you as an inheritance, and you shall conquer it and settle it." This teaches us that "coming into the land" always means conquering and settling, so that the Israelites were not regarded as having "come" until the conquest was complete after the fourteen years.

Rambam (*Shemittah VeYovel* 10:2) and other Rishonim cite *Sifra* (*Behar* 2), which notes that the words "your field" and "your vineyard" appear in connection with the Sabbatical Year (Leviticus 25:4), from which we learn that the Sabbatical and Jubilee Years apply only when the land is "yours," i.e., after the conquest is complete. It is not clear, however, from where we know that this applies to the laws of tithes. *Rashi* gives two explanations: (1) The Torah commands that terumah be given from "your grain," and that tithes be given from "the seed of your produce." Hence these laws too applied only after the conquest, when the grain and produce were "yours." (2) The Torah (Deuteronomy 26:12) connects the laws of tithing with the Sabbatical cycle, thus creating a Halakhic connection between them.

In a parallel passage in tractate *Bava Metzia* (89a), *Rashi* gives a third explanation for tithes, unrelated to the Sabbatical cycle: The Torah connects the second tithe with the choice of a site for the Temple (Deuteronomy 14:22-23), and the temporary tabernacle in Shiloh was erected only at the end of the war (Joshua 18:1).

Ritva cites another explanation: The Torah (Deuteronomy 12:10-11) commands that various gifts and sacrifices, including terumah and tithes, be brought to the place chosen by God (i.e., Shiloh) after the Israelites "cross the Jordan and dwell in the land." From here we learn that although it is possible to separate tithes even when there is no organized Temple, the tithes should ideally be brought to the Temple. But it is unreasonable to imagine that the Torah issued commandents that could be fulfilled initially only in an incomplete way. Hence the Torah could not have expected these commandents to be fulfilled at all until after the war and the selection of Shiloh.

אֲפִילּוּ לְמַאן דְּאָמַר תְּרוּמָה בַּזְּמַן הַזֶּה דְּאוֹרַיְיתָא, חַלָּה דְּרַבָּנַן Even according to the one who says that terumah today is from the Torah, *ḥallah* is Rabbinic. The question as to whether terumah applies by Torah law today is discussed in tractate *Yevamot* (82a). Resh Lakish cites a Baraita which implies that terumah has Rabbinic status today, following the destruction of the Second Temple. But Rabbi Yoḥanan counters by citing another Baraita, which declares that Eretz Israel will be inherited only twice, not three times, from which it follows that Ezra's sanctification

[1]דְּתַנְיָא: ״׳בְּבֹאֲכֶם אֶל הָאָרֶץ׳״. [2]אִי ׳בְּבֹאֲכֶם׳, [3]יָכוֹל מִשֶּׁנִּכְנְסוּ לָהּ שְׁנַיִם וּשְׁלֹשָׁה מְרַגְּלִים. [4]תַּלְמוּד לוֹמַר: ׳בְּבֹאֲכֶם׳. [5]בְּבִיאַת כּוּלְּכֶם אָמַרְתִּי, וְלֹא בְּבִיאַת מִקְצָתְכֶם״.

LITERAL TRANSLATION

[1]For it was taught: "'When you come into the land.' [2]If it is 'when you come,' [3]I might have thought [that it means] once two or three spies have entered it. [4]Therefore the Torah states: 'When you come.' [5]I said [this referring] to the coming of all of you, and not to the coming of some

TRANSLATION AND COMMENTARY

because Ezra did not renew this law to the level of a Torah obligation. [1]Rav Huna the son of Rav Yehoshua proves his contention from the following statement that **was taught** in a Baraita. The Baraita is commenting on the Torah verse (Numbers 15:18) which contains the commandment to separate *ḥallah* from dough. "The verse begins: **'When you come into the land,'** implying that this commandment will take effect only when the Israelites have entered the land of Canaan. [2]**If** the verse had stipulated that *ḥallah* takes effect only **'when you come,'** [3]**I might have thought that it means once two or three spies have entered it** — at the very earliest stage of the conquest of the land. [4]**Therefore the Torah states: 'When you come,'** with special emphasis on the word 'you.'" The Baraita notes that the verse uses the expression בְּבֹאֲכֶם (lit., "in your coming"), rather than the usual כִּי תָבֹאוּ "when you come." [5]The Baraita concludes: "From this we learn that the Torah **is saying** that this law should apply only **when all of you come, and not when some of you come."** Hence, Rav Huna the son of Rav Yehoshua argues, the obligation to separate *ḥallah* is not dependent on the other agricultural laws, but depends on the presence of the entire Jewish people in Eretz Israel. Thus, during the time of Joshua,

RASHI

הכי גרסינן: אי בבואכם יכול משנכנסו לה שנים ושלשה מרגלים תלמוד לומר בבואכם בביאת כולכם כו׳ — והכי פירושו: כיון דשינה הכתוב ביאה זו לכתוב בה ״בבואכם״ ולא כתב ״כי תבאו״ — יכול משנכנסו לה מרגלים, תלמוד לומר כו׳.

NOTES

survived the destruction of the Second Temple and is permanent.

Our commentary follows *Rashi* and *Tosafot*, who explain that during the Second Temple period the obligation to tithe produce was of Torah authority according to everyone. The debate between Rabbi Yoḥanan and Resh Lakish about the Torah status of terumah today refers to the period following the destruction of the Second Temple. According to this view, it is easy to understand the distinction made by Rav Huna the son of Rav Yehoshua between *ḥallah* and terumah. For *ḥallah* applies only when the entire Jewish people are in Eretz Israel, and hence did not apply during the Second Temple period, whereas terumah did apply then according to all opinions. Hence it follows that the dispute between Rabbi Yoḥanan and Resh Lakish about the effect of the destruction of the Second Temple does not apply to *ḥallah*, and even Rabbi Yoḥanan — who is of the opinion that the Torah obligation to give terumah survived the destruction of the Second Temple — would agree that *ḥallah* is Rabbinic.

According to *Rambam*, the debate between Rabbi Yoḥanan and Resh Lakish about terumah today is relevant to the period when the Jewish people ceased to live entirely in Eretz Israel, a century and a half before the destruction of the First Temple. According to Resh Lakish, terumah was of purely Rabbinic status throughout the Second Temple period, whereas according to Rabbi Yoḥanan terumah is of Torah status even though the majority of the Jewish people does not live in Eretz Israel. According to *Rambam*, it is a little difficult to understand the distinction made by Rav Huna the son of Rav Yehoshua between *ḥallah* and terumah, since the issue in both cases is the same. In fact, *Rambam* rules that both terumah and *ḥallah* are of Rabbinic status today (following Resh Lakish against Rabbi Yoḥanan). *Ra'avad*, on the other hand, rules that terumah is of Torah status today (following Rabbi Yoḥanan), and that *ḥallah* is Rabbinic (following Rav Huna the son of Rav Yehoshua).

The normal practice in disputes between Rabbi Yoḥanan and Resh Lakish is to rule in favor of Rabbi Yoḥanan. *Rambam*'s ruling in favor of Resh Lakish and against Rabbi Yoḥanan is thus highly unusual. *Maggid Mishneh* explains that since this question is both a Tannaitic and an Amoraic dispute, *Rambam* followed the rules for deciding Tannaitic disputes. These tend tend to favor the position that terumah is Rabbinic, while the rules for deciding Amoraic disputes tend to favor the opposing position held by Rabbi Yoḥanan. *Gra* adds that support for *Rambam*'s ruling can be found in the Jerusalem Talmud. Moreover, *Gra* adds, it is possible that Rabbi Yoḥanan would agree with Resh Lakish in practice, and that he was merely explaining the view of one of the Tannaim.

בְּבֹאֲכֶם אֶל הָאָרֶץ "When you come into the land." Our Gemara cites two Baraitot, which derive two laws from this verse: (1) That *ḥallah* applied even during the fourteen years of conquest; (2) that *ḥallah* does not apply unless all Israelites are in Eretz Israel.

The Gemara (*Kiddushin* 38b) explains that the source of the law of the first Baraita is the following comment of the *Sifrei* (*Shelaḥ* 21). "Rabbi Yishmael says: The language of this verse is different from all other 'comings' in the Torah. All the other 'comings' are phrased, 'when you come' (כִּי תָבוֹאוּ) or 'when God brings you' (כִּי יְבִיאֲךָ), whereas this 'coming' is phrased 'in your coming' (בְּבֹאֲכֶם). From here we learn that the Israelites were obliged to give *ḥallah* immediately on their entry into the land." The Gemara explains that this Midrash in *Sifrei* can be understood only in the light of another passage in *Sifrei* (*Shelaḥ* 1), in which Rabbi Yishmael comments as follows: "Whenever the Torah declares that a law applies 'when you come into the land,' it applies only after the land has been conquered and settled (i.e., after the first fourteen years)." Thus we see that

LITERAL TRANSLATION

of you." [1]And when Ezra brought them up, [25B] not all of them went up.

[2]Come [and] hear: "Presumption for the priesthood [is created by] giving the Priestly Benediction, [3]and the distribution at the threshing floors, and testimony."

[4]Is testimony presumption? [5]Rather, is it not saying thus: Giving the Priestly Benediction is like testimony. [6]Just as testimony [is effective] for lineage, [7]so too is giving the Priestly Benediction [effective] for lineage!

[1]וְכִי אַסְּקִינְהוּ עֶזְרָא, [25B] לָאו כּוּלְּהוּ סְלוּק.

[2]תָּא שְׁמַע: "חֲזָקָה לִכְהוּנָּה נְשִׂיאוּת כַּפַּיִם, [3]וְחִילּוּק גְּרָנוֹת, וְעֵדוּת".

[4]עֵדוּת חֲזָקָה הִיא? [5]אֶלָּא לָאו הָכִי קָאָמַר: נְשִׂיאוּת כַּפַּיִם כִּי עֵדוּת. [6]מָה עֵדוּת לְיוּחֲסִין, [7]אַף נְשִׂיאוּת כַּפַּיִם לְיוּחֲסִין!

RASHI

לאו כולהו סלוק — רובן נשארו בבבל, דכתיב "כל הקהל כאחד ארבע רבוא" (עזרא ב). **ועדות** — אם באו עדים שהוא כהן שמכירין את אביו ואת אמו. **ועדות חזקה היא** — בתמיה, וכי עדות חזקה קרי ליה?

TRANSLATION AND COMMENTARY

they were obliged to give *ḥallah*, [1]**but when Ezra brought** the Jews back from Babylonia to Eretz Israel after the exile, [25B] **not all of them went up** with him. Most of the exiled Jews remained in Babylonia. Hence, although Ezra renewed the practice of separating terumah and the observance of other agricultural laws, *ḥallah* was renewed only by Rabbinic decree, even during the Second Temple period. Thus, concludes the Gemara, *ḥallah* is today in force only by Rabbinic decree, even in Eretz Israel, even according to the opinion that the Torah obligation to give terumah, reinstituted by Ezra, continued after the destruction of the Second Temple.

תָּא שְׁמַע [2]The Gemara now returns to the question of the man who claims to be a priest on the basis of the fact that he gives the Priestly Benediction, and it continues its attempt to determine whether this is sufficient proof to elevate him to full priestly status. **Come** and **hear** a Baraita which suggests that it is sufficient proof: **"A man is presumed to be a priest** if he does one of three things: (1) **If he gives the Priestly Benediction,** [3]**or** (2) **if he receives** a share of terumah **at the threshing floors, or** (3) **if there is testimony** that he is a priest."

עֵדוּת חֲזָקָה הִיא [4]The Gemara notes immediately that the wording of this Baraita presents a problem. The Baraita mentions "testimony" as one of the ways of creating a legal presumption. But **can testimony be described as a presumption?** "Presumption" is something that is applied in the *absence* of testimony! A man who can produce witnesses to testify that he is a priest has no need of any legal presumptions! [5]**Rather,** suggests the Gemara, should we **not** understand the Baraita **to be saying as follows:** "There are two ways of confirming priestly status — if a man gives the Priestly Benediction, he is *presumed* to be a priest, and if he produces witnesses, he is *known* to be a priest"? The Baraita puts these two together to tell us that **giving the Priestly Benediction is like testimony.** In other words, both are equally effective. [6]Thus it follows that **just as testimony is effective in establishing** a man's **full priestly status,** [7]**so too is** the act of **giving the Priestly Benediction effective in establishing** a man's **full priestly status.** A would-be priest who produces witnesses to support his claim is certainly permitted to marry a woman of unblemished lineage, and the same applies to a person who gives the Priestly Benediction. We can thus prove from this Baraita that we elevate from giving the Priestly Benediction to full priestly status.

NOTES

the Torah changed its wording in the case of *ḥallah* to teach us that it does not fall under this category, but rather applies immediately.

It is not clear from where we learn the law of the second Baraita — that *ḥallah* does not apply unless all Israelites are in Eretz Israel. Our commentary follows *Rashi*, who explains that this rule too is based on the idea that the Torah changed its wording from "when you come" to "in your coming," to teach us that *ḥallah* applies only when all of you have come. *Tosafot* (*Niddah* 47a) rejects this explanation, arguing that it would imply a dispute between the two Baraitot. For the first Baraita considers the expression "in your coming" (which applies immediately) to be weaker than "when you come" (which applies only after the conquest is completed), whereas the second Baraita, according to *Rashi*, considers that the expression "in your coming" (which applies only when all of you have come) is stronger than "when you come" (which applies even if only some of you have come).

Accordingly, *Tosafot* explains that the second Baraita is actually a continuation of the first Baraita, which inferred from the unusual wording of the verse that *ḥallah* applies as soon as you "come," even before you conquer. The second part of the Baraita then argues that, if so, you might have thought that it applies from the moment the first Israelites "came." Hence the verse says "when *you* come," which implies that although it is not necessary to complete the conquest, all of "you" must come across the Jordan River for this law to apply.

TRANSLATION AND COMMENTARY

לָא [1] The Gemara answers: **No.** It is possible to explain that the Baraita is simply teaching us that testimony creates a legal presumption. And as for your argument, that a man who can produce witnesses to testify that he is a priest does not need any legal presumptions, the Baraita is not referring to direct testimony that the man is a priest, but rather to testimony that he engaged in an activity that creates a legal presumption that he is a priest. [2] And the Baraita is teaching us that **testimony that comes on the strength of** a legal **presumption is the equivalent of** that legal **presumption.** Although the court did not actually see this man engage in this activity, if he can produce witnesses to testify that he did so, we accept their evidence. Accordingly, we consider this man to be a presumed priest, who is permitted to eat terumah (according to the Sages), but does not have the priestly status necessary to marry a woman of unblemished lineage.

כִּי הַהוּא [3] The Gemara now gives an example of testimony about a would-be priest that creates a legal presumption as to his status. Such a situation occurred **in the case of a certain man who came before Rabbi Ammi** to give testimony. [4] The man **said to** Rabbi Ammi: **"I am sure that this** other **man is a priest."** [5] Rabbi Ammi **said to** the witness: **"What did you see** that led you to this conclusion?" [6] The witness **said to him:** I saw **that** this man **read first** from the Torah **in the synagogue."** Portions of the Torah are read aloud on certain occasions as part of the synagogue service. Each of these portions is divided into at least three sections, and different members of the congregation are honored by being called up to take part in the reading of a section. The first congregant to be called is a priest, the second a Levite, and the third a Jew who is neither a priest nor a Levite. Thus, if the man about whom the witness is speaking was called to

[1] לָא. [2] עֵדוּת הַבָּאָה מִכֹּחַ חֲזָקָה כַּחֲזָקָה.

[3] כִּי הַהוּא דַּאֲתָא לְקַמֵּיהּ דְּרַבִּי אַמִי. [4] אֲמַר לֵיהּ: "מוּחְזְקַנִי בְּזֶה שֶׁהוּא כֹּהֵן". [5] אֲמַר לֵיהּ: "מָה רָאִיתָ"? [6] אֲמַר לֵיהּ: "שֶׁקָּרָא רִאשׁוֹן בְּבֵית הַכְּנֶסֶת".

LITERAL TRANSLATION

[1] No. [2] Testimony which comes on the strength of a presumption is like a presumption.

[3] It is like [the case of] a certain man (lit., "one") who came before Rabbi Ammi. [4] He said to him: "I am sure about this [man] that he is a priest." [5] He said to him: "What did you see?" [6] He said to him: "That he read first in the synagogue."

RASHI

עדות הבאה מכח חזקה כחזקה – העדות נקבל, ונאכילו בתרומה כאילו ראינוהו אנן לאותה חזקה שזה העיד.

SAGES

רַבִּי אַמִי **Rabbi Ammi.** A Palestinian Amora of the third generation, Rabbi Ammi (bar Natan) was a priest and a close friend of Rabbi Assi. They studied with the greatest Sages of Eretz Israel, and were especially close disciples of Rabbi Yoḥanan. Rabbi Ammi also studied with Rabbi Yoḥanan's greatest students. In the Jerusalem Talmud he is commonly known as Rabbi Immi.

After Rabbi Yoḥanan's death, Rabbi Ammi was appointed head of the Tiberias Yeshivah in his place. The Sages of Babylonia also consulted him about Halakhic problems. He is widely quoted in both the Babylonian and the Jerusalem Talmud, not only in transmitting statements from his teachers, but also in debate with Rabbi Assi and with other Sages of the generation. Most of the Palestinian Amoraim of the following generation received and transmitted his teachings. He and Rabbi Assi were known as "the distinguished priests of Eretz Israel," and stories are told of their righteousness and piety. Rabbi Ammi seems to have lived to a great age, and even the Sages of the fourth generation in Babylonia used to send him their questions.

NOTES

עֵדוּת הַבָּאָה מִכֹּחַ חֲזָקָה **Testimony which comes on the strength of a presumption.** Our commentary follows *Rashi*, who explains that testimony can sometimes create a presumption — for example, if witnesses testify that they saw a man behave as a priest. In such a case, if the court itself had seen the man's behavior, it would have given him the presumptive status of a priest. The Baraita is telling us that the same is true if witnesses testify to the man's behavior, even if the court did not see it. *Rosh* objects to this explanation, arguing that it is obvious that once a court accepts testimony, it is as though it saw the events itself. Hence, a case where witnesses attest to presumptive behavior is simply a case of presumptive behavior, and should not be described as "testimony on the strength of presumptive behavior." *Maharsha* adds that, according to *Rashi*, the wording of the Gemara is difficult. For according to *Rashi*, the testimony is normal testimony, and is accepted in the usual way, and the presumption is established by witnesses rather than by the court. Hence, the testimony is not based on the strength of the presumption; rather, the presumption is based on the strength of the testimony.

Tosafot explains that "testimony on the strength of a presumption" is a case where the testimony alone would not be sufficient to create a presumption, but the combination of the testimony and another presumption is sufficient. For example, in the case used by the Gemara, if witnesses testify that a man was called up first to the Torah, this is not sufficient to prove that he is a priest; but if they testify that the man who was called up second was a presumed Levite, the combination of the Levite's presumption and the first man's attested behavior is sufficient for us to presume him to be a priest.

שֶׁקָּרָא רִאשׁוֹן בְּבֵית הַכְּנֶסֶת **That he read first in the synagogue.** On certain days, during the morning service in the synagogue, a portion of the Torah is read from the Torah scroll. The precise portion to be read is fixed by the Halakhah, and depends on the occasion. On Sabbaths, the Torah portion is divided into seven sections, on Yom Kippur into six, on Festivals into five, on the New Moon and the intermediate days of Pesaḥ and Sukkot into four, and on all other days into three. A different congregant is called up to read each section, and he recites a blessing before and after the reading.

When a priest and a Levite are present in the congregation, they must be called up to the first and second

HALAKHAH

עֵדוּת הַבָּאָה מִכֹּחַ חֲזָקָה **Testimony which comes on the strength of a presumption.** "If one witness testifies that he saw a person being called up first to the Torah, and that a known Levite was called up after him, this evidence is sufficient to create a presumption that this person is a priest." (*Rambam, Sefer Kedushah, Hilkhot Issurei Bi'ah* 20:11.)

TRANSLATION AND COMMENTARY

read the first section, he must have been a priest. [1] But Rabbi Ammi queried further: "Was this man called to the first section **under the presumption that he was a priest,** as you claim, [2] **or** was it perhaps **under the presumption that he was a great man?"** The custom in Talmudic times was to call an outstanding Torah scholar to read first from the Torah, even if he was not a priest. Thus it is possible that the man in question was not a priest at all, but was called to the Torah as a sign of respect for his scholarship. [3] The witness replied: "I saw that **a Levite read after him."** A Levite is called to read second only when a priest has read first. When a non-priest is called first to the Torah, the rule is that non-priests are called for the second and for all subsequent sections. Thus, if a known Levite read second, and the man in question read first, he could only have been a priest. [4] The Gemara concludes by relating that **Rabbi Ammi** accepted the witness's testimony, and **elevated** the man in question **to the priesthood on the basis of** the witness's **evidence,** permitting him to do all those things that a presumed priest may do (such as eat terumah, according to the Sages). But Rabbi Ammi certainly did not elevate him to full priestly status. Thus we see that the Baraita can be interpreted as stating simply that testimony does sometimes create a presumption, but no proof can be brought from this Baraita regarding the question of whether or not we elevate from the Priestly Benediction to lineage. In fact, this question is left unresolved. It is a dispute between Rav Ḥisda and Rabbi Avina, and the Gemara is unable to reach a conclusion one way or the other.

[1] ״בְּחֶזְקַת שֶׁהוּא כֹּהֵן, [2] אוֹ בְּחֶזְקַת שֶׁהוּא גָּדוֹל״? [3] ״שֶׁקָּרָא אַחֲרָיו לֵוִי״. [4] וְהֶעֱלָהוּ רַבִּי אַמִי לִכְהוּנָּה עַל פִּיו.

LITERAL TRANSLATION

[1] "Under the presumption that he was a priest, [2] or under the presumption that he was a great man?" [3] "Where a Levite read after him." [4] And Rabbi Ammi elevated him to the priesthood on [the basis of] his evidence (lit., "his mouth").

RASHI

או בחזקת שהוא גדול — כדאמרינן בעלמא (גיטין נט,ב): רב קרי בכהני, ואף על גב דלאו כהן הוה. **שקרא אחריו לוי** — ואי לאו כהן הוא אין לוי קורא אחריו. דאמרינן במסכת גיטין (שם): אם אין שם כהן — נתפרדה חבילה. ומפרשינן: דאין לוי קורא במקום שאין כהן. ויש מפרשים: נתפרדה החבילה, שבמקום שאין כהן, אם רוצה ישראל לקרות לפני לוי — קורא. ודוקא דאין שם כהן, אבל היכא דאיכא כהן — לא נתפרדה החבילה, ולא יקרא ישראל גדול לפני לוי. והכא כהן אחר הוה התם, הלכך אי לאו דהאי כהן הוה — לא הוה לוי קרי אבתריה.

NOTES

sections respectively. When there is a priest but no Levite, the priest who was called up first (and not another priest) reads both sections. When there is a Levite but no priest, anyone may be called up for the first section, and only non-Levites for the second section onward. It is thus impossible for a Levite to read second unless the person who read first was a priest, and it is impossible for anyone but a Levite to read second if the first person who read was a priest. Hence, if a Levite reads second, the first person who read must have been a priest, and if a priest reads first, the second person to read must be a Levite, if a Levite is present. The purpose of these rules, as we see from our Gemara, is to ensure that the lineage of priests and Levites is not confused.

בְּחֶזְקַת שֶׁהוּא גָּדוֹל Under the presumption that he was a great man. In Talmudic times, it was customary to honor great scholars by calling them up to read the first section of the Torah portion, even if they were not priests and there were priests present in the congregation (*Megillah* 22a). For the Mishnah states (*Horayot* 13a): "A *mamzer* who is a Torah scholar takes precedence over a High Priest who is an ignoramus." In such a case, the reading was carried out in the same way as when there was no priest in the congregation. Nowadays, this custom has fallen into disuse, as it tended to cause quarrels (*Shulḥan Arukh, Oraḥ Ḥayyim* 135:4).

Nowadays, the practice in Ashkenazi congregations is that when a congregant is called up to the Torah, his name is announced together with the name of his father and his status, if he is a priest or a Levite. When a priest is not present, and an ordinary congregant is called up, his name is announced as "So-and-so the son of So-and-so — *in the absence of a priest,*" and when a Levite is not present, and the priest who read first is called up again, it is announced that he is reading second *"in the absence of a Levite."* The status of the congregant is thus clear from the outset, with no need for indirect proofs. From the fact that the Talmud sought indirect proofs that a congregant was a priest or a Levite, and did not rely on his name, *Rabbi Ya'akov Emden* deduces that the practice of calling up by name was not followed in Talmudic times. *Ritva* goes still further, ruling that, according to our custom, it is not essential to follow the Talmudic procedure rigidly, and it is permissible to call a priest or a Levite for one of the later sections, provided that he is announced as "So-and-so the son of So-and-so, *despite the fact* that he is a priest (or a Levite)." *Ritva*'s view was not accepted in practice by most congregations.

שֶׁקָּרָא אַחֲרָיו לֵוִי Where a Levite read after him. In our commentary we have followed *Rashi* and most Rishonim, who explain that a Levite can read the second section only if a priest has read the first section. A Levite can read the first section if no priest is available, but if anyone but a priest reads the first section for any reason, the Levite may not read the second section.

This rule is derived from a passage in tractate *Gittin* (59b). The Mishnah there rules that a priest is to be called up first, a Levite second, and a Jew who is neither a priest nor a Levite third. The Gemara then states that if there are no Levites in the congregation, the same priest who read first — but not a different priest — reads second as well. If, on the other hand, there are no priests in the congregation, "the bundle has come apart."

TRANSLATION AND COMMENTARY

הַהוּא דַּאֲתָא [1]Having mentioned the story of Rabbi Ammi and the man who read first from the Torah, the Gemara relates a similar story. **There was** once **a certain man who came before Rabbi Yehoshua ben Levi** to give testimony. [2]The man **said to** Rabbi Yehoshua ben Levi: **"I am sure that this** other **man is a Levite."** [3]Rabbi Yehoshua ben Levi **said to** the witness: **"What did you see?"** [4]The witness **said to him:** "I saw **that** this man **read second from the Torah in the synagogue."** We have already seen that the second person called to the Torah is usually a Levite. [5]But Rabbi Yehoshua ben Levi queried further: "Was this man called to the second section **under the presumption that he was a Levite,** as you claim, [6]**or** was it perhaps **under the presumption that he was a great man?"** It is possible that the man in question was not a Levite at all, but was called to the second section of the Torah reading as a sign of respect for his scholarship. [7]The witness replied: "I saw that **a priest read before him."** When a priest is called first to the Torah, only a Levite may be called after him. If there are no Levites present in the congregation, the second section is read by the priest who was called first. Only when a non-priest is called to the Torah first can an ordinary Jew be called to read the second section. Thus, if a known priest read first, and this man read second, he could only have been a Levite. [8]The Gemara concludes by relating that **Rabbi Yehoshua ben Levi** accepted the witness's testimony, and **elevated** the man in question **to the status of Levite on the basis of** the witness's **evidence,** permitting him to do all those things that a presumed Levite may do, such as receive a share of the first tithe.

[1]הַהוּא דַּאֲתָא לְקַמֵּיהּ דְּרַבִּי יְהוֹשֻׁעַ בֶּן לֵוִי. [2]אֲמַר לֵיהּ: ״מוּחְזָקְנִי בְּזֶה שֶׁהוּא לֵוִי״. [3]אֲמַר לֵיהּ: ״מָה רָאִיתָ״? [4]אֲמַר לֵיהּ: ״שֶׁקָּרָא שֵׁנִי בְּבֵית הַכְּנֶסֶת״. [5]״בְּחֶזְקַת שֶׁהוּא לֵוִי, [6]אוֹ בְּחֶזְקַת שֶׁהוּא גָּדוֹל״? [7]״שֶׁקָּרָא לְפָנָיו כֹּהֵן״. [8]וְהֶעֱלָהוּ רַבִּי יְהוֹשֻׁעַ בֶּן לֵוִי לִלְוִיָּה עַל פִּיו.

LITERAL TRANSLATION

[1]There was a certain man who came before Rabbi Yehoshua ben Levi. [2]He said to him: "I am sure about this [man] that he is a Levite." [3]He said to him: "What did you see?" [4]He said to him: "That he read second in the synagogue." [5]"Under the presumption that he was a Levite, [6]or under the presumption that he was a great man?" [7]"Where a priest read before him." [8]And Rabbi Yehoshua ben Levi elevated him to the status of Levite on [the basis of] his evidence.

RASHI

שקרא לפניו כהן – ואי לאו דהאי לוי הוא – לא היה קורא שני אלא שלישי, שנים כהנים היו קורין לפניו והוא שלישי. דהכי אמרינן במסכת גיטין: אם אין שם לוי – קורא כהן במקומו. **ללויה** – לתת לו מעשר ראשון.

SAGES

רַבִּי יְהוֹשֻׁעַ בֶּן לֵוִי **Rabbi Yehoshua ben Levi.** One of the greatest Amoraim of the first generation in Eretz Israel. Rabbi Yehoshua ben Levi was, according to some opinions, the son of Levi ben Sisi, one of the outstanding students of Rabbi Yehudah HaNasi, and it seems that Rabbi Yehoshua ben Levi was himself one of Rabbi Yehudah HaNasi's younger students. Many Halakhic disputes are recorded between him and Rabbi Yoḥanan, who was apparently younger than he and a student and colleague of his. In general, the Halakhah follows Rabbi Yehoshua ben Levi, even against Rabbi Yoḥanan, whose authority was very great.

Rabbi Yehoshua ben Levi was also a renowned teacher of Aggadah. Because of the great respect in which he was held, Aggadic statements in his name are presented at the end of the six orders of the Mishnah.

A great deal is told of his piety and sanctity, and he is regarded as one of the most righteous men who ever lived. Among other things, it is told that he would sit with the most dangerously infected lepers and study Torah. He was famous as a worker of miracles, to whom Elijah the Prophet appeared, and his prayers were always answered. According to tradition he is one of those over whom the Angel of Death had no dominion, and he entered the Garden of Eden alive.

He taught many students. All the Sages of the succeeding generation were his students to some degree, and quote Torah teachings in his name. His son, Rabbi Yosef, was also a Sage, and married into the Nasi's family.

NOTES

The Rishonim differ as to the meaning of the expression "the bundle has come apart." *Rashi* cites two explanations: (1) If there is no priest in the congregation, the Levite does not read at all, and only Jews who are not Levites are called up. (2) If there is no priest, we pay no attention to the Levite's lineage, and call him up for any section in the reading, in accordance with his importance. The Halakhah follows the first explanation. Most authorities agree, however, that even according to this view a Levite is permitted to be called up for the first section (but not for the later sections), although there is no requirement to do so, and this is the custom followed today (*Shulḥan Arukh, Oraḥ Ḥayyim* 135:6).

It is difficult to reconcile *Rashi*'s second explanation of the expression in *Gittin* with our passage. How could Rabbi Ammi establish that the first reader was a priest from the fact that the second reader was a Levite? Perhaps there were no priests in the congregation, and the first reader was a very distinguished person, and the Levite read second because he was the second most important man in the congregation? *Tosafot* explains that Rabbi Ammi knew that the Levite called up second was in fact an unimportant person. Hence it was clear that he was called up second because of his lineage, and not because of his importance.

מוּחְזָקְנִי בְּזֶה שֶׁהוּא לֵוִי **I am sure about this man that he is a Levite.** It is not entirely clear why the Amoraim were so concerned about establishing whether or not this man was a presumed Levite. The only real significance of having the status of a Levite is that Levites take part in the Temple service, but following the destruction of the Temple that is of little practical relevance. Moreover, the fact that the Levite was called up to the Torah second was not sufficient to prove his lineage. There is nothing special that a presumed Levite is forbidden to do (unlike presumed priests, who are forbidden to marry divorcees or to have contact with the dead), and there is nothing that they are exclusively permitted to do (unlike presumed priests, who are allowed to eat terumah). *Ran* explains that the Amoraim were careful to give first tithe only to definite

HALAKHAH

וְהֶעֱלָהוּ...לִלְוִיָּה **And he raised him to the status of Levite.** "If one witness testifies that he saw a person being called up second to the Torah, and that a known priest was called up before him, this evidence is sufficient to create a presumption that this person is a Levite. *Maggid Mishneh* explains that we are permitted to give such a person a share of first tithe." (*Rambam, Sefer Kedushah, Hilkhot Issurei Bi'ah* 20:11.)

[1]הַהוּא דַּאֲתָא לְקַמֵּיהּ דְּרֵישׁ לָקִישׁ. [2]אֲמַר לֵיהּ: "מוּחְזְקַנִי בְּזֶה שֶׁהוּא כֹּהֵן". [3]אֲמַר לֵיהּ: "מָה רָאִיתָ"? [4]אֲמַר לֵיהּ: "שֶׁקָּרָא רִאשׁוֹן בְּבֵית הַכְּנֶסֶת". [5]אֲמַר לֵיהּ: "רְאִיתִיו שֶׁחִילֵּק עַל הַגְּרָנוֹת"? [6]אָמַר לוֹ רַבִּי אֶלְעָזָר: [7]"וְאִם אֵין שָׁם גּוֹרֶן, בָּטְלָה כְּהוּנָּה"? [8]זִימְנִין הֲווּ יָתְבִי קַמֵּיהּ דְּרַבִּי יוֹחָנָן. [9]אֲתָא כִּי הָא מַעֲשֶׂה לְקַמֵּיהּ. [10]אֲמַר לֵיהּ רֵישׁ לָקִישׁ: "רְאִיתִיו שֶׁחִילֵּק עַל הַגּוֹרֶן"? [11]אֲמַר לֵיהּ רַבִּי יוֹחָנָן: [12]"וְאִם אֵין שָׁם גּוֹרֶן, בָּטְלָה כְּהוּנָּה"? [13]הֲדַר חַזְיֵיהּ לְרַבִּי אֶלְעָזָר בִּישׁוּת.

LITERAL TRANSLATION

[1]There was a certain man who came before Resh Lakish. [2]He said to him: "I am sure about this [man] that he is a priest." [3]He said to him: "What did you see?" [4]He said to him: "That he read first in the synagogue." [5]He said to him: "Did you see that he was distributed [a share] at the threshing floors?" [6]Rabbi Elazar said to him: [7]"And if there is no threshing floor there, is the priesthood abolished?" [8]On [another] occasion, they sat before Rabbi Yoḥanan. [9]A case like this came before him. [10]Resh Lakish said to him: "Did you see that he was distributed [a share] at the threshing floor?" [11]Rabbi Yoḥanan said to him: [12]"And if there is no threshing floor there, is the priesthood abolished?" [13]He turned and looked at Rabbi Elazar with displeasure (lit., "badly").

TRANSLATION AND COMMENTARY

הַהוּא דַּאֲתָא [1]The Gemara now relates another, similar story. **There was a certain man who came before Resh Lakish** to give testimony. [2]The man **said to** Resh Lakish: **"I am sure that this** other **man is a priest."** [3]Resh Lakish **said to** the witness: **"What did you see?"** [4]The witness **said to him:** "I saw **that** this man **read first** from the Torah **in the synagogue,** and a known Levite read after him." [5]But Resh Lakish queried further. **He said to** the witness: "Granted that he acted as a priest in the synagogue, but **did you** also **see that he received a share** of terumah **at the threshing floors?"** This implies that as long as we do not know that he was given terumah to eat, we cannot presume that he is a priest. [6]Resh Lakish's colleague, **Rabbi Elazar,** was present when Resh Lakish issued his ruling. He **said to** Resh Lakish: "I disagree with your ruling. We can rely on the status given to the man in the synagogue. [7]For according to you, **if** the man lives in a place where **there is no threshing floor** (e.g., an area where there is no agriculture), **shall** the possibility of accepting him into **the priesthood be abolished?** We cannot be so selective, and must accept all convincing evidence." [8]The Gemara relates that, **on a subsequent occasion,** Resh Lakish and Rabbi Elazar **sat before Rabbi Yoḥanan** bar Nappaḥa, their teacher. [9]**A case like this came before him** for decision. A man testified that another man was a priest, citing as evidence the fact that the other man was called to the first section of the Torah reading in the synagogue. [10]Again, **Resh Lakish said to** the witness: "Granted that he acted as a priest in the synagogue, but **did you also see that he received a share** of terumah **at the threshing floors?"** As long as we do not know that he was given terumah to eat, we cannot presume that he is a priest. [11]At this point, **Rabbi Yoḥanan said to** Resh Lakish: "I disagree with your ruling. We can rely on the status given to the man in the synagogue. [12]For according to you, **if** the man lives in a place where **there is no threshing floor, shall** the possibility of accepting him into **the priesthood be abolished?** We cannot be so selective, and must accept all convincing evidence." Resh Lakish realized at once that the similarity of the comments was too great to be a coincidence. [13]**He turned and looked at Rabbi Elazar with**

RASHI

ואם אין שם גורן — אם אין שם זורעי תבואה במקומו. **זימנין** — פעם אחרת. **הדר** — ריש לקיש. **חזייה לרבי אלעזר בישות** — החזיר פניו, ונסתכל ברבי אלעזר בעין רעה. שהבין שמפי רבי יוחנן שמע לשון זה, וכשאמר לשון זה לא אמרה בשם רבי יוחנן, לפיכך לא קיבלה הימנו.

NOTES

Levites — even though first tithe may be eaten by anyone — so as to fulfill the Torah's commandment to give the tithe to a Levite. Thus, the Gemara is ruling that being called up to the Torah as a Levite is sufficient proof for this purpose.

וְאִם אֵין שָׁם גּוֹרֶן And if there is no threshing floor there. Our commentary follows *Rashi*, who explains that Rabbi Elazar and Rabbi Yoḥanan objected to using the threshing floor as a proof because this would disqualify priests living in non-agricultural areas. *Ḥatam Sofer* explains that this priest did not come from such an area, but refrained from claiming his share of terumah for reasons of modesty. Resh Lakish maintained that a true priest should make an effort to take his share of terumah at least once a year, even if he is a very modest person and finds it embarrassing to assert his rights. But Rabbi Yoḥanan was of the opinion that since there are some priests living in non-agricultural areas who would find this almost impossible, other priests are also permitted to forego their share of terumah, if they wish.

Ritva notes that even in non-agricultural areas there are other ways to establish that a person is a presumed priest, such as giving the Priestly Benediction and receiving a share in the priestly gifts (see above, 25a). However, these methods do not apply universally. Thus the Gemara cited a Baraita which ruled that giving the Priestly

SAGES

רַבִּי אֶלְעָזָר (בֶּן פְּדָת) Rabbi Elazar (ben Pedat). One of the greatest of the Palestinian Amoraim, he came originally from Babylonia and studied there with Rav and Shmuel. But it seems that he immigrated to Eretz Israel as a young man, married, and became the main disciple of Rabbi Yoḥanan. The spiritual affinity between Rabbi Elazar and Rabbi Yoḥanan was so great that occasionally an objection is raised to an argument presented in the name of one of them because it conflicts with the other's teachings, since they are assumed to have adopted the same approach to Halakhah. Rabbi Elazar venerated his teacher, and in time the bond between them grew so strong that Rabbi Yoḥanan said of him: "Have you seen the son of Pedat, who sits and expounds the Torah like Moses from the very mouth of the Almighty?" Rabbi Elazar was a priest. He was very poor for most of his life, and his material situation apparently did not improve until his later years, when he was one of the leaders of the nation.

After Rabbi Yoḥanan's death, Rabbi Elazar was one of the most important scholars in Eretz Israel. He was also one of the Sages who participated in setting the Hebrew calendar, and he would send Halakhic rulings from Eretz Israel to Babylonia, where they were regarded as authoritative and binding.

Many stories are told of Rabbi Elazar's great love for the Torah, and he is presented as the model of a person entirely immersed in its study.

Because of his greatness, he was known as מָרָא דְאַרְעָא דְיִשְׂרָאֵל — "Master of Eretz Israel." Almost all the Amoraim of the third generation in Eretz Israel were his students. His son, Rabbi Pedat, was also a Sage.

BACKGROUND

בִּישׁוּת Displeasure. This is an abstract noun derived from the word בִּישׁ, meaning "bad." Its root is באש, meaning "to putrefy." It is used in the Bible to describe bad relationships between people, as

[1]אֲמַר: ״שָׁמְעַתְּ מִילֵּי דְּבַר נַפָּחָא, וְלָא אָמְרַתְּ לָן מִשְּׁמֵיהּ״?! [2]רַבִּי וְרַבִּי חִיָּיא, [3]חַד הֶעֱלָה בֵּן עַל פִּי אָבִיו לִכְהוּנָּה, [4]וְחַד הֶעֱלָה אָח עַל פִּי אָחִיו לִלְוִיָּה. [5]תִּסְתַּיֵּים דְּרַבִּי הֶעֱלָה בֵּן עַל פִּי אָבִיו לִכְהוּנָּה, [6]דְּתַנְיָא: ״הֲרֵי שֶׁבָּא וְאָמַר: ׳בְּנִי זֶה, וְכֹהֵן הוּא׳, [7]נֶאֱמָן לְהַאֲכִילוֹ בִּתְרוּמָה,

LITERAL TRANSLATION

[1]He said: "You heard the words of Bar Nappaha, and you did not say [them] to us in his name?!" [2][Concerning] Rabbi [Yehudah HaNasi] and Rabbi Ḥiyya, [3]one elevated a son to the priesthood on the evidence of his father, [4]and one elevated a brother to the status of Levite on the evidence of his brother. [5]Conclude that Rabbi [Yehudah HaNasi] elevated a son to the priesthood on the evidence of his father, [6]for it was taught: "If someone came and said: 'This is my son, and he is a priest,' [7]he is believed to feed him terumah,

TRANSLATION AND COMMENTARY

displeasure, [1]and **said** to him: **"You heard the words of** Rabbi Yoḥanan **bar Nappaḥa, and you did not tell us that you were speaking in his name?!** When you criticized my ruling, you should have told me that you had heard this viewpoint from Rabbi Yoḥanan, for if you had done so, I would have changed my ruling."

רַבִּי וְרַבִּי חִיָּיא [2]The Gemara now relates another story on the subject of presumed priesthood on the basis of testimony. There were two similar incidents, one **concerning Rabbi Yehudah HaNasi and** the other concerning **Rabbi Ḥiyya.** [3]In one case, **one** of these Rabbis **elevated a man to the priesthood on the** uncorroborated **evidence of his father,** [4]**and** in the other case, **the other** Rabbi **elevated a man to the status of Levite on the** uncorroborated **evidence of his brother.**

תִּסְתַּיֵּים [5]The Gemara observes: We do not have explicit information as to which Rabbi was involved in each case, but we may reasonably **conclude that** it was **Rabbi Yehudah HaNasi** who **elevated a man to the priesthood on the evidence of his father,** because we know that Rabbi Ḥiyya was opposed to doing this. [6]**For** the following **was taught** in a Baraita: **"If** a man known to be a priest **comes** forward **and says: 'This is my son, and he is a priest,'** [7]**he is believed** and the son is entitled **to be given terumah** (i.e., he is given

NOTES

Benediction applies only where there is a permanent court, such as existed in Babylonia and in Syria, and that the distribution of priestly gifts applies only in big cities. Hence it is possible that a would-be priest would have no way of proving his priesthood except by being called up first to the Torah. Thus, by insisting that the would-be priest must be given a share at the threshing floor, Resh Lakish was in effect disqualifying such people unfairly. *Ḥatam Sofer* notes that a priest also officiates at the ceremony of the redemption of the firstborn, but since this is an infrequent occurrence and is done privately, it cannot serve as a proof one way or the other.

וְלָא אָמְרַתְּ לָן מִשְּׁמֵיהּ And you did not say them to us in his name?! A very similar incident is described in tractate *Makkot* (5b). Our commentary follows *Rashi* here, who explains that Resh Lakish would have considered the argument more favorably if he had heard it in the name of Rabbi Yoḥanan. For Resh Lakish was Rabbi Yoḥanan's most outstanding disciple and was also his equal in scholarship (*Bava Metzia* 84a). *Rabbenu Ḥananel* (commenting on *Makkot*) explains that Resh Lakish would not have ruled against Rabbi Yoḥanan in his presence had he known that Rabbi Yoḥanan had issued a ruling on the matter.

It seems that Rabbi Elazar often issued rulings without mentioning that they were in fact Rabbi Yoḥanan's. In tractate *Yevamot* (96b), the Gemara relates that on one such occasion Rabbi Yoḥanan was very upset about this, but that Rabbi Ya'akov consoled him by explaining that Rabbi Elazar was so faithful to Rabbi Yoḥanan's tradition that people assumed that everything he said derived from Rabbi Yoḥanan, even when he did not mention it explicitly. *Ritva* explains that this was not just a flattering excuse, but was the real reason why Rabbi Elazar frequently failed to cite Rabbi Yoḥanan.

בְּנִי זֶה, וְכֹהֵן הוּא "This is my son, and he is a priest." It is not entirely clear if the Baraita is referring to a case where a priest produces an unknown child and claims that the child is his son and is qualified for the priesthood, or if it is referring to a case where the child was known to be the priest's son, and the father's sole claim is that the child was born of a woman who was qualified to marry a priest. *Tosafot* points out that the conjunction "and" in the father's statement ("this is my son *and* he is a priest") suggests that the father made two claims, and that we are dealing with an unknown child. *Rambam*, however, removes the conjunction when he cites this Baraita, suggesting that we are dealing with a child who was known to be the son of the priest.

This question is of crucial importance in understanding the reasoning underlying this passage. According to *Ramban*'s explanation of this passage (see following notes), we can only be referring to a case where the child is unknown to us. In such a case, the father is believed about his son being a priest on the basis of a *miggo*, since he could have said that the boy was a priest but was not his son. But if the boy were known to be the priest's son, the father would not be believed, because a relative is not

HALAKHAH

״בְּנִי זֶה, וְכֹהֵן הוּא״ "This is my son, and he is a priest." "If a priest says: 'This is my son, and he is a priest,' we presume the son to be a priest, and we permit him to eat terumah. The father need not prove his relationship to his

in I Samuel 13:4, and elsewhere.

In the context here, it is known that Resh Lakish was extremely stringent both with himself and with others, being strict in matters about which others were forgiving, to the extent that it was said of him that a person to whom Resh Lakish spoke in public was so trustworthy that one could lend him money without witnesses.

SAGES

בַּר נַפָּחָא Bar Nappaḥa. In many places in the Talmud, Rabbi Yoḥanan is referred to as "Bar Nappaḥa," or "Ben HaNappaḥ" in Hebrew (mainly in the Jerusalem Talmud). While little is known about the family of Rabbi Yoḥanan (who was orphaned at an early age), some scholars maintain that he was called "Ben HaNappaḥ" (lit., "the blacksmith's son") because his father was a blacksmith. Others explain that Rabbi Yoḥanan was described in this way because he was so handsome, the term "blacksmith's son" being used as a kind of euphemism.

רַבִּי חִיָּיא Rabbi Ḥiyya. Originating from the town of Kafri in Babylonia, Rabbi Ḥiyya was one of the last of the Tannaim, and a student and colleague of Rabbi Yehudah HaNasi.

Rabbi Ḥiyya came from a distinguished family that was descended from King David and produced many Sages. While he still lived in Babylonia he was already considered a great Torah scholar, and when he left Babylonia with the members of his family to settle in Eretz Israel, there were those who said, in exaggeration, that the Torah would have been forgotten in Eretz Israel had he not arrived from Babylonia to reestablish it. Upon his arrival in Eretz Israel, he became the student and colleague of Rabbi Yehudah HaNasi. He became a close friend of Rabbi Yehudah HaNasi and in particular of his son, Rabbi Shimon, who was also Rabbi Ḥiyya's business partner. Rabbi Ḥiyya was one of the greatest Sages of his generation. Not only was he a great Torah scholar, he was

also very pious, as is related in many places in the Talmud. His great achievement was the editing of collections of Baraitot, as a kind of supplement to the Mishnah edited by Rabbi Yehudah HaNasi. These collections, which he seems to have edited in collaboration with his colleague and student, Rabbi Oshaya, were considered extremely reliable, so much so that it was said that any Baraitot not reported by them were not worthy of being cited in the House of Study.

It seems that, upon his arrival in Eretz Israel, he received some financial support from the House of the Nasi, but he mainly earned his living from international trade on a large scale, especially in silk. He had twin daughters, Pazi and Tavi, from whom important families of Sages were descended. He also had twin sons, Yehudah (Rabbi Yannai's son-in-law) and Ḥizkiyah, who were important scholars during the transitional generation between the Tannaim and the Amoraim. They apparently took their father's place at the head of his yeshivah in Tiberias, where he lived. All of Rabbi Yehudah HaNasi's students were Rabbi Ḥiyya's colleagues, and he was also on close terms with the Tanna Rabbi Shimon ben Ḥalafta. Rabbi Yehudah HaNasi's younger students (Rabbi Ḥanina, Rabbi Oshaya, Rabbi Yannai, and others) all studied under Rabbi Ḥiyya as well, and to some degree were considered his disciples. Rabbi Ḥiyya's nephews, Rabbah bar Ḥanah, and, above all, the great Amora Rav, were his outstanding disciples. He also appears as one of the central figures in the *Zohar*. Rabbi Ḥiyya was buried in Tiberias, and his two sons were later buried at his side.

[1] וְאֵינוֹ נֶאֱמָן לְהַשִּׂיאוֹ אִשָּׁה. [2] דִּבְרֵי רַבִּי. [3] אָמַר לוֹ רַבִּי חִיָּיא: [4] 'אִם אַתָּה מַאֲמִינוֹ לְהַאֲכִילוֹ בִּתְרוּמָה, [5] תַּאֲמִינוֹ לְהַשִּׂיאוֹ

LITERAL TRANSLATION

[1] but he is not believed to marry him to a woman. [2] [These are] the words of Rabbi [Yehudah HaNasi]. [3] Rabbi Ḥiyya said to him: [4] 'If you believe him to feed him terumah, [5] believe him to marry him

RASHI

להשיאו אשה — שמא ממזר או נתין הוא.

TRANSLATION AND COMMENTARY

the status of a presumed priest), since it is clear that he is indeed the son of a priest. [1] **But** the father **is not believed** if the purpose is **to marry him to a woman** of unblemished lineage, because for that purpose two qualified witnesses are needed. It is possible that the man in question is indeed the son of a priest, but has been disqualified from the priesthood because of some problem concerning his mother's status. [2] **These are the words of Rabbi Yehudah HaNasi.** [3] **Rabbi Ḥiyya said to** Rabbi Yehudah HaNasi: 'Your rulings here are inconsistent. The laws regarding terumah and lineage are the same. Only a man whose mother is qualified to marry a priest is considered a priest. [4] So **if you believe** the father's testimony that the boy's mother was qualified, **and the boy is therefore entitled to eat terumah,** [5] you should also **believe** the father when he comes **to marry** the son **to a woman**.

NOTES

believed on questions of priesthood. According to *Rashba*'s interpretation, by contrast (see following notes), we are referring to a case where the child was known to be the priest's son. *Rashba* explains that the reasoning underlying this passage is based on the special credibility of a father when it comes to determining the status of his children, and on the father's ability to establish his children's presumptive status by giving them terumah to eat.

נֶאֱמָן לְהַאֲכִילוֹ בִּתְרוּמָה He is believed to feed him terumah. *Tosafot* asks: How can Rabbi Yehudah HaNasi rule that it is in the father's power to feed his son terumah? In tractate *Kiddushin* (79b), the Mishnah rules that a priest from Eretz Israel who has spent an extended period abroad, and returns with children born abroad, is not believed when he claims that his children are priests, unless he can prove that their mother was eligible to marry into the priesthood. Thus we see that it is not in a father's power to feed his sons terumah, unless he first establishes their mother's lineage.

Tosafot and *Rambam* explain that the Mishnah in *Kiddushin* was not referring to terumah, but rather to questions of lineage. According to this explanation, a father's testimony renders his sons presumed priests, since he can feed them terumah from his home, as Rabbi Yehudah HaNasi ruled in our Gemara, but a father's testimony cannot give his sons full priestly status, unless he can prove their mother's qualifications, in accordance with the passage in *Kiddushin*. This explanation is difficult, because the Gemara in *Kiddushin* specifically mentions eating terumah as one of the things that the sons may not do unless the father brings proof. But *Tosafot* explains that the Gemara may have been referring to Torah terumah, and may be reflecting the view of Rabbi Yehudah, who maintains that only priests of unblemished lineage may eat Torah terumah (see also *Maggid Mishneh*).

Alternatively, *Tosafot* notes that the Mishnah in *Kiddushin* explicitly refers to a case where the woman presumed to be the children's mother has died, or where the priest married abroad and we do not know if his second wife was eligible to marry into the priesthood. But if the man claims that the boys are the children of his original, qualified wife, and the wife is still with him, and the boys behave in the manner of children with their mother, the Mishnah rules that we do not require the father to prove that his sons are her children. Thus, in our Gemara as well, Rabbi Yehudah HaNasi may be referring to a case where the priest's wife is alive, and the children recognize her as their mother. Other resolutions of this problem are offered by *Ritva* and other Rishonim.

According to *Ramban*'s explanation of our passage (see previous and following notes), this question is not difficult. According to his explanation, our Gemara is specifically referring to a case where we do not know that the boy is the priest's son. Hence the priest has a *miggo*, since he could have said that the boy was not his son, and he would then have been believed when he testified that the boy was a priest. The Mishnah in *Kiddushin*, by contrast, refers to a case where we know that the children are the priest's, and the only question concerns their mother. Hence even Rabbi Yehudah HaNasi would agree that it is not permissible to feed the son terumah on the basis of his father's word, with no further proof, because the testimony of a witness about the priestly status of one of his relatives is inadmissible, unless he has a *miggo*.

אִם אַתָּה מַאֲמִינוֹ If you believe him. It is possible to explain this passage in two ways. (1) The father testified alone, and Rabbi Yehudah HaNasi accepted his uncorroborated testimony for terumah but not for lineage. (2) The father brought another witness to corroborate his claim, and wished to serve as one of the two witnesses for his son, but though Rabbi Yehudah HaNasi accepted him as one of the witnesses for terumah, he disqualified him for lineage. Both of these explanations pose serious difficulties.

If we assume that the father testified alone, and Rabbi Yehudah HaNasi accepted his testimony without corroboration for terumah but not for lineage, why did Rabbi Ḥiyya accuse Rabbi Yehudah HaNasi of inconsistency in rejecting the father as a relative for lineage while overlooking this fact for terumah? For even if we overlook the fact that the father is a relative, he is still at best one witness, and the Sages maintain that one witness is sufficient for terumah but not for lineage! Thus Rabbi Yehudah HaNasi was right

HALAKHAH

son, nor that the son's mother was qualified to marry a priest. But we do not give the son the full status of a priest — even if the father has that status — unless two qualified witnesses testify to the son's status." (*Rambam, Sefer Kedushah, Hilkhot Issurei Bi'ah* 20:5,10; *Shulḥan Arukh, Even HaEzer* 3:2.)

TRANSLATION AND COMMENTARY

[1]**And if you do not believe** the father's testimony that the son's mother was qualified, and you do not give permission **to marry him to a woman,** [2]**you should** also **not believe** the father if the effect is **to let** the son **eat terumah!** The only reason you have for assuming that the son is a priest is his father's testimony, and while the father is believed when he says that the boy is his son, an unrelated witness is needed to establish the status of the boy's mother.' [3]Rabbi Yehudah HaNasi **said to** Rabbi Ḥiyya: **'I believe** the known priest **to** the extent of **giving his** son **terumah,** not because I believe a father who testifies about his son's qualifications, but because the father's claim is supported by a *miggo* argument, [4]**because it is in his power to give** his son **terumah to eat** without

אִשָּׁה, [1]וְאִם אִי אַתָּה מַאֲמִינוֹ לְהַשִּׂיאוֹ אִשָּׁה, [2]לֹא תַּאֲמִינוֹ לֶאֱכוֹל בִּתְרוּמָה׳! [3]אָמַר לוֹ: ׳אֲנִי מַאֲמִינוֹ לְהַאֲכִילוֹ בִּתְרוּמָה, [4]שֶׁבְּיָדוֹ לְהַאֲכִילוֹ

LITERAL TRANSLATION

to a woman, [1]and if you do not believe him to marry him to a woman, [2]do not believe him to [let him] eat terumah!' [3]He said to him: 'I believe him to feed him terumah, [4]because it is in his power (lit., "hand") to feed him

RASHI

שיש בידו להאכילו תרומה — שהרי הוא כהן, והכל חולקין לו תרומה.

NOTES

in rejecting the father's testimony for lineage, even if he had some grounds for accepting his testimony for terumah! And if Rabbi Ḥiyya's objection was based on the viewpoint of Rabbi Yehudah (bar Il'ai), who is of the opinion that two witnesses are required for terumah just as they are for lineage, he should have rejected the ruling of Rabbi Yehudah HaNasi outright, on the grounds that the father was only one witness, rather than accuse Rabbi Yehudah HaNasi of inconsistency, and enter into a discussion about relatives!

If, on the other hand, we assume that there was another witness to corroborate the father's story, and Rabbi Yehudah HaNasi accepted the father as one of the witnesses for terumah but disqualified him for lineage, why did Rabbi Yehudah HaNasi need to explain that the father is believed about terumah because his claim is supported by a *miggo*? If there was another independent witness supporting his story, the father would have been believed without any *miggo*, because the Sages maintain that a single unrelated witness is believed concerning terumah, even without the father's support! And if the argument of Rabbi Yehudah HaNasi was based on the viewpoint of Rabbi Yehudah, who is of the opinion that two witnesses are required for terumah, how could Rabbi Yehudah HaNasi distinguish between terumah and lineage? For Rabbi Yehudah maintains that we elevate from terumah to lineage. Hence, even if the father has a *miggo* for terumah and not for lineage, the moment we accept the son as a priest regarding terumah we automatically elevate him to lineage as well!

The Rishonim offer two basic interpretations of this matter. These are based on the assumption that both Rabbi Yehudah HaNasi and Rabbi Ḥiyya agree with the Sages that one witness is believed for terumah, but two witnesses are required for lineage, and that we do not elevate from terumah to lineage.

Tosafot and *Ramban* explain that the father's testimony in the case of terumah is different from his testimony in the case of lineage. In the case of terumah the father is testifying alone, but in the case of lineage, he produces an independent witness to corroborate his story. The dispute between Rabbi Yehudah HaNasi and Rabbi Ḥiyya is about whether we accept a relative as a witness as a single witness for terumah or as one of a pair of witnesses for lineage. Rabbi Ḥiyya argues that a father should either be acceptable as a witness in both cases or be unacceptable in both. But Rabbi Yehudah HaNasi rules that the father can serve as a single witness for terumah, because he has a *miggo* regarding terumah, but not as one of a pair of witnesses for lineage, because he has no *miggo* regarding lineage.

Our commentary follows *Rashba*, who explains that the father testified alone in both cases, and the dispute between Rabbi Ḥiyya and Rabbi Yehudah HaNasi is based on a passage in tractate *Bava Batra* (127b). There, the Gemara considers a verse (Deuteronomy 21:17) which says that the father must "acknowledge his firstborn son by giving him a double portion of all that he has." The Gemara cites a Baraita which explains that the verse teaches us that a father is believed when he declares which of his sons was his firstborn, so that the son receives the double portion. Two opinions are cited in the Baraita. According to Rabbi Yehudah, the Torah believes the father absolutely, even if people are under the impression that a different son was the firstborn, and the father is also believed when he declares his son qualified for the priesthood or disqualified from it, and the like. According to the Sages, however, the Torah relies on the father's designation of his firstborn son only when the court is in doubt as to which son is the firstborn; hence, the father has no special credibility about his son, and is not believed at all regarding his qualifications for the priesthood and the like.

Rashba explains: Rabbi Ḥiyya thought that the reasoning of Rabbi Yehudah HaNasi in accepting the father's testimony about terumah was based on Rabbi Yehudah's reasoning in *Bava Batra* — that the Torah believes the father, without proof, when he declares his son to be qualified, or disqualified, for the priesthood. Therefore, Rabbi Ḥiyya accused Rabbi Yehudah HaNasi of inconsistency. For according to the view that the Torah believes a father about his son regarding priesthood, he is believed regarding lineage as well as terumah. But Rabbi Yehudah HaNasi responded that his reasoning was not based on the view of Rabbi Yehudah in *Bava Batra* at all. Rabbi Yehudah HaNasi did not believe the father in our passage merely because he was the father, but rather because he had a *miggo*, and this *miggo* applied only to terumah and not to lineage (see also *Ritva*).

שֶׁבְּיָדוֹ לְהַאֲכִילוֹ בִּתְרוּמָה Because it is in his power to feed him terumah. Rabbi Yehudah HaNasi explains that the father is believed when he claims that his son has the right to eat terumah, because he has a *miggo*, since he could have fed his son terumah in a simpler way. Our commentary follows *Rashi* and *Tosafot*, who explain that

בִּתְרוּמָה, [1] וְאֵינִי מַאֲמִינוֹ לְהַשִּׂיאוֹ אִשָּׁה, [2] שֶׁאֵין בְּיָדוֹ לְהַשִּׂיאוֹ אִשָּׁה״. [3] תִּסְתַּיֵּים.

LITERAL TRANSLATION

terumah, [1] but I do not believe him to marry him to a woman, [2] because it is not in his power to marry him to a woman.'" [3] Conclude [that this is so].

TRANSLATION AND COMMENTARY

asking our permission.' The priest has terumah home and can easily give it to his son, thereby establishing a presumption that the boy is indeed a priest. And the rule is that if someone testifies about the status of something, and it is in his power to make it so even if we do not believe him, we believe him without further corroboration, because of the *miggo* argument. [1] 'On the other hand,' continued Rabbi Yehudah HaNasi, **'I do not believe** the priest's testimony that his son is a priest, **to** the extent of allowing him **to marry a woman** of unblemished lineage, [2] **because it is not in** the father's **power to marry him to a woman** of unblemished lineage, until the court confirms his status. Hence we are left with the father's testimony alone, and that, as you rightly pointed out, is not acceptable in court because the father is a relative.'" [3] Having quoted this Baraita, the Gemara says that we may indeed **conclude** from it that Rabbi Ḥiyya could not have been the Rabbi who accepted the testimony of the father on a question of priestly status. The Rabbi who did so must have been Rabbi Yehudah HaNasi.

TERMINOLOGY

תִּסְתַּיֵּים Conclude. Sometimes the Talmud notes that there was a controversy between two Sages concerning a certain issue, but it is not clear which Sage took what position. In such cases, the Talmud's initial attempt to attribute the views correctly is often introduced by the expression תִּסְתַּיֵּים דְּרַבִּי פְּלוֹנִי הוּא דְּאָמַר — "Conclude that it was Rabbi A who said ... [and that Rabbi B holds the other view]." If this suggestion is confirmed later in the discussion, the Talmud may close the discussion with the remark תִּסְתַּיֵּים — "Conclude [that the suggested identification was indeed correct]."

NOTES

the father could have fed his son terumah without going to court at all. The father is a known priest, and it is in his power to give his son a share of the terumah he has in his home, without asking anybody's permission.

The Rishonim note that this explanation is difficult in the light of the passage in tractate *Bava Batra* (127b), which explains that the Torah believes the father when he declares which of his sons is his firstborn, and that son receives a double portion of his inheritance. Two opinions are cited in that passage. According to Rabbi Yehudah, the father is believed absolutely, whereas according to the Sages, the father has no special credibility regarding his son; the Torah believes him only when it comes to determining which of his sons is the firstborn, when we ourselves are in doubt. The Gemara there objects to the Sages' view: Why do the Sages need a verse to teach us that the father is believed in such a case? Surely the father has a *miggo*, for it is in his power to give the favored son any part of his estate that he wishes, by making him a deed of gift, even if we do not accept his statement! The Gemara answers that the father's *miggo* extends only to the property in the father's possession at the time of his statement, but for property that he has not yet acquired he has no *miggo*, because he cannot make a gift of it in advance. Hence we need a verse to inform us that when the father states which of his sons is the firstborn, he is believed, even regarding property he has not yet acquired.

Accordingly, the Rishonim ask: According to *Rashi* and *Tosafot*, Rabbi Yehudah HaNasi believed the father with a *miggo*, because it is in his power to give his son terumah as a gift. But surely the father's *miggo* covers only the period while the father is alive and living in close proximity to the son, whereas the father wishes us to believe that his son and his descendants are permitted to eat terumah for all time! How, then, is this *miggo* any better than the flawed *miggo* in *Bava Batra*?

Rosh adds that the *miggo* used by Rabbi Yehudah HaNasi is flawed for another reason. A *miggo* is valid only if the alternative route is at least as advantageous as the one actually taken. But while it is in the father's power to give his son a share of the terumah he has in his home, without asking anyone's permission, it is not in his power to persuade farmers to give him a double share of terumah to give to his son. But if we believe the father, the son will henceforth receive a share of terumah in his own right, and in effect, the income of this family will double. It is thus in the father's interest to go to court and claim that his son is a priest, rather than feed him from his own private stock.

Tosafot answers that it seemed reasonable to Rabbi Yehudah HaNasi that if the father is believed when it comes to feeding his son terumah under some circumstances, we accept that the son is a priest, even when the *miggo* does not apply. *Rashba* explains along similar lines that once the son is seen eating terumah, a presumption is established that he is permitted to eat terumah, and this applies even where the *miggo* itself does not. (Our commentary follows this explanation.)

Ramban has an entirely different explanation of the *miggo* in our Gemara. He explains that the father is believed when he testifies that his son is a priest, because, had he wanted to lie, he could have omitted the part about the boy being his son, and then he would definitely have been believed when he testified that the boy was a priest. *Ramban* explains: One witness is sufficient to testify that a person is a priest and permitted to eat terumah; the only problem in our case is that the witness happens to be a relative, who is thus not qualified to testify. Our Gemara, however, is dealing with a case where we do not know that the boy is the priest's son. Hence the priest is believed when he testifies that the boy is his son and a priest, since he could have said that the boy was a priest, but not his son. But this *miggo* is effective only regarding terumah. Regarding lineage, the father is not qualified to serve as one of a pair of witnesses, even though he has the same *miggo*, since he could have said that the boy enjoyed full priestly status and was not his son, because lineage requires two qualified witnesses, and the rule is that the testimony of two qualified witnesses is believed absolutely, and cannot be enhanced or affected by a mere *miggo*.

The Rishonim note that in the version of this passage in the Jerusalem Talmud (*Ketubot* 2:7), the positions of Rabbi Yehudah HaNasi and Rabbi Ḥiyya are reversed, with Rabbi Ḥiyya accepting the father's testimony and Rabbi Yehudah HaNasi rejecting it. Allowing for that one important difference, however, the Jerusalem Talmud explains this passage as does *Ramban* (see also *Ra'ah*).

TRANSLATION AND COMMENTARY

וּמִדְּרַבִּי [1] **And**, continues the Gemara, since we have established that Rabbi Yehudah HaNasi and Rabbi Ḥiyya were each involved in one of the two cases, and it was **Rabbi Yehudah HaNasi** who **elevated a son to the priesthood on the evidence of his father** in the first case, [2] **Rabbi Ḥiyya** must have been the Rabbi who **elevated a brother to the status of Levite on the evidence of his brother**, in the other **case**.

וְרַבִּי חִיָּיא [3] **But**, the Gemara objects, we have seen that **according to Rabbi Ḥiyya** we cannot rely on a priest who testifies about his son, but we can rely on a Levite who testifies about his brother. [4] But **what is** so **different about** the case of a son, that Rabbi Ḥiyya maintains that **he is not elevated** to the priesthood on the evidence of his father? Why does Rabbi Ḥiyya not accept the father's testimony? [5] Clearly, it is because the father is the only witness, the son **is related to his father**, and the rules of evidence require that the witness be unrelated. [6] But **a brother, too, is a relative of his brother!** How, then, could Rabbi Ḥiyya accept the testimony of a Levite about his brother? If he does not rely on relatives, he should reject the testimony in both cases!

בְּמֵסִיחַ לְפִי תוּמּוֹ [26A] [7] The Gemara answers: Rabbi Ḥiyya accepted the testimony of one brother about another in a case **where** the brother who was known to be a Levite did not come to court to testify, but **made a casual**, unguarded **remark** without being aware that his words had legal significance. When a person who for some reason is disqualified from being a witness tells a story without any intention of testifying, he is generally believed. [8] The Gemara now illustrates how a person can make a casual remark of legal significance by quoting the following **story that Rav Yehudah related in the name of Shmuel:** [9] **An incident** once **occurred in which a certain man made a casual**, unguarded **remark and said:** [10] **"I remember when I was a child and riding on my father's shoulder**, that one day **they took me out of school and took off my shirt**, [11] **and they immersed me** in a *mikveh* [ritual bath] to purify me of ritual impurity, so that I could **eat terumah**

[1] וּמִדְּרַבִּי הֶעֱלָה בֵּן עַל פִּי אָבִיו לִכְהוּנָּה, [2] רַבִּי חִיָּיא הֶעֱלָה אָח עַל פִּי אָחִיו לִלְוִיָּה.
[3] וְרַבִּי חִיָּיא, [4] מַאי שְׁנָא בֵּן דְּלָא? [5] דְּקָרוֹב הוּא אֵצֶל אָבִיו? [6] אָח נַמִי קָרוֹב הוּא אֵצֶל אָחִיו!
[26A] [7] בְּמֵסִיחַ לְפִי תוּמּוֹ, [8] כִּי הָא דְּאָמַר רַב יְהוּדָה אָמַר שְׁמוּאֵל: [9] מַעֲשֶׂה בְּאָדָם אֶחָד שֶׁהָיָה מֵסִיחַ לְפִי תוּמּוֹ וְאָמַר: [10] "זָכוּרְנִי כְּשֶׁאֲנִי תִינוֹק וּמוּרְכָּב עַל כְּתֵיפוֹ שֶׁל אַבָּא, וְהוֹצִיאוּנִי מִבֵּית הַסֵּפֶר וְהִפְשִׁיטוּנִי אֶת כּוּתָּנְתִּי, [11] וְהִטְבִּילוּנִי לֶאֱכוֹל

LITERAL TRANSLATION

[1] And since Rabbi [Yehudah HaNasi] elevated a son to the priesthood on the evidence of his father, [2] Rabbi Ḥiyya elevated a brother to the status of Levite on the evidence of his brother.

[3] But [according to] Rabbi Ḥiyya,[4] what is different about a son that he is not [elevated]? [5] Because he is a relative of his father? [6] A brother, too, is a relative of his brother!

[26A] [7] When he is talking innocently, [8] as [in] this [story] that Rav Yehudah related in the name of Shmuel: [9] An incident [occurred] concerning a certain man who was talking innocently and said: [10] "I remember when I was a child and riding on my father's shoulder, and they took me out from the school and stripped me of my shirt, [11] and they immersed me to eat

RASHI

והטבילוני — מפני שסתם תינוק מטפח באשפות, ושרצים מצויין שם.

CONCEPTS

בְּמֵסִיחַ לְפִי תוּמּוֹ When he is talking innocently. Since, in Jewish law, testimony is regarded as critical for proving any matter, a system of formal regulations governing testimony was developed, both with respect to how it must be given (specifically, orally), and, even more so, regarding the qualifications necessary for giving valid testimony. For testimony to be accepted by a court, there must be two witnesses, and they must be Jewish men who are at least thirteen years old. They must not be related either to the litigants or to each other. Although unqualified witnesses are not permitted to testify except in special circumstances, such as to testify that a woman's husband has died, there are instances in which a court may glean information from unqualified witnesses when they are not formally testifying.

A person who "talks innocently" is simply recounting something that happened. He has no intention of testifying; he is just telling a story. Occasionally a court accepts information revealed in this fashion as a significant proof. Hence, in various cases, if a person intends to testify, his remarks may not be accepted as evidence because he is not a qualified witness, or because he has an interest in the litigation. But if his remarks are not intended as evidence, they may be accepted and considered by the court.

NOTES

וְהִטְבִּילוּנִי And they immersed me. A person who is ritually impure may not eat terumah. To purify himself, he must undergo a purification ritual which varies in severity depending on the type of ritual impurity involved. For all forms of ritual impurity, however, it is necessary to immerse oneself in a ritual bath, called a *mikveh*, and to wait until nightfall. Except in the case of the most severe forms of ritual impurity, these two procedures are all that are required. Most common types of ritual impurity are not applicable to young children (e.g., menstruation for girls, or seminal emissions for boys). Our commentary follows *Rashi*, who explains that we are afraid that the child may have come into contact with the carcass of an animal while playing outdoors. In particular, the carcasses of certain lizards and small mammals, such as mice, impart ritual impurity.

Ritva rejects *Rashi*'s explanation. He notes that our Gemara can best be understood in the light of a Tosefta

HALAKHAH

בְּמֵסִיחַ לְפִי תוּמּוֹ When he is talking innocently. "If a man claims to be a priest but can bring no proof, he is not believed. But if, while telling a story, he makes a casual remark from which we can infer that he is a priest, he is believed. We presume him to be a priest and permit him to eat Rabbinic terumah," following our Gemara. (*Rambam, Sefer Kedushah, Hilkhot Issurei Bi'ah* 20:14; *Shulḥan Arukh, Even HaEzer* 3:1.)

בִּתְרוּמָה לָעֶרֶב״. [1]וְרַבִּי חִיָּיא מְסַיֵּים בָּהּ: [2]״וַחֲבֵירַי בְּדֵילִין מִמֶּנִּי, וְהָיוּ קוֹרִין אוֹתִי ׳יוֹחָנָן אוֹכֵל חַלּוֹת׳״. [3]וְהֶעֱלָהוּ רַבִּי לִכְהוּנָּה עַל פִּיו.

[4]תַּנְיָא: [5]״רַבִּי שִׁמְעוֹן בֶּן אֶלְעָזָר אוֹמֵר: כְּשֵׁם שֶׁתְּרוּמָה חֲזָקָה לִכְהוּנָּה, [6]כָּךְ מַעֲשֵׂר רִאשׁוֹן חֲזָקָה לִכְהוּנָּה. [7]וְהַחוֹלֵק בְּבֵית דִּין, אֵינָהּ חֲזָקָה״.

[8]מַעֲשֵׂר רִאשׁוֹן דְּלֵוִי הוּא!

LITERAL TRANSLATION

terumah in the evening." [1]And Rabbi Ḥiyya concludes this [story]: [2]"And my friends kept away from me, and they would call me 'Yoḥanan [the] eater of *ḥallot.*'" [3]And Rabbi [Yehudah HaNasi] raised him to the priesthood on [the basis of] his words (lit., "mouth").

[4]It was taught: [5]"Rabbi Shimon ben Elazar says: Just as terumah is a presumption for the priesthood, [6]so too is first tithe a presumption for the priesthood. [7]But [if] someone receives a share [of terumah] in court, it is not a presumption."

[8][But] first tithe belongs to the Levite!

TRANSLATION AND COMMENTARY

that evening." A person who touches the carcass of certain small mammals (such as mice or lizards) becomes ritually impure. The ritual impurity is removed when he has immersed in a *mikveh* and waited till nightfall of that day. Children of priestly families are assumed to have touched such objects in the course of play, and are permitted to eat terumah only after they have been purified and supervised till evening. This man was telling a story about his childhood for entertainment, not as legal testimony in court. Hence his remark was regarded as casual and unguarded, and when it was reported in court by witnesses, it was believed. [1]The Gemara goes on to relate that in **Rabbi Ḥiyya's** version of **this story,** the man **concluded** his story thus: [2]**"And my schoolmates kept away from me, and would call me 'Yoḥanan the eater of *ḥallot*.'"** Only a priest is permitted to eat *ḥallah*, as we have seen above. As a child, Yoḥanan was given *ḥallah* to eat, and was told not to share it with his non-priestly friends, and this led to jealousy among the children. [3]**And,** the story concludes, **Rabbi Yehudah HaNasi elevated** Yoḥanan **to the priesthood on the basis of this story,** without any corroborating testimony. Presumably, Yoḥanan's father died while Yoḥanan was a child, and this was the only evidence that he was a priest. Thus we see that Rabbi Yehudah HaNasi and Rabbi Ḥiyya agree that a person who makes a casual remark is believed even about himself. Hence it follows that if a man who is known to be a Levite mentions in the course of conversation that someone is his brother and is thus also a Levite, he is believed even according to Rabbi Ḥiyya, who does not normally accept the testimony of relatives in such matters.

תַּנְיָא [4]The Gemara now cites a Tosefta on a related topic (*Pe'ah* 4:5 and *Ketubot* 3:1). **It was taught:** [5]**"Rabbi Shimon ben Elazar says: Just as** eating **terumah is presumptive proof that the man** eating the terumah **is a priest,** [6]**so too is** eating **first tithe** — which the Torah [Numbers 18:21-24] states must be given to a Levite — **presumptive proof that the man is a priest.** [7]**But if someone receives a share of terumah in court, it is not a presumptive proof** that he is a priest."

מַעֲשֵׂר רִאשׁוֹן דְּלֵוִי הוּא [8]The Gemara begins its analysis of this Tosefta by considering Rabbi Shimon ben Elazar's first statement — that eating first tithe is a sign of priesthood. **But** surely, asks the Gemara, **first tithe belongs to the Levite,** not to a priest. How, then, can eating first tithe serve as an indication that the person eating it is a priest?

RASHI

לערב — דצריך הערב שמש. **והחולק בבית דין** — קא סלקא דעתך שעל פי בית דין הקבוע בעיר היו חולקין לו תרומה בבית הגרנות. ולקמיה פריך: אי בבית דין לא הוי חזקה — היכא הויא חזקה?

NOTES

(*Teharot* 3:5), from which it appears that every unsupervised child is considered ritually impure, because children are often embraced by passing women, and it is possible that this child was touched by a menstruating woman.

וְרַבִּי חִיָּיא מְסַיֵּים בָּהּ **And Rabbi Ḥiyya concludes this story.** Since Rabbi Ḥiyya took the trouble to add details to the story, it is clear that all the elements recorded in it are of Halakhic significance. It was important to make the point that the boy was taken out of school, because a priest's slave is also permitted to eat terumah. Hence we might have suspected that the boy was the priest's slave, rather than his son, were it not for the fact that he attended school, which was a privilege denied to slave children (*Tosafot*). *Taz* adds that it was important to mention that the child was carried on his father's shoulders for the same reason. *Bet Ya'akov* explains that Rabbi Ḥiyya added the detail about the child's jealous friends because he maintained that a father is not believed if he testifies that his son is a priest, even though it is in his power to feed him terumah. Hence we must be told that everyone, and not just Yoḥanan's father, considered the child to be an eater of *ḥallot*.

BACKGROUND

יוֹחָנָן אוֹכֵל חַלּוֹת **Yoḥanan the eater of *ḥallot*.** This story provides a vivid picture of life in Mishnaic times. The narrator, who is an adult at the time he tells the story, recalls something that happened when he was a child, maybe four or five years old, so small that he still rode on his father's shoulders. The fact that he was little is also shown by his wearing only a cotton tunic, and not the other clothes worn by adults. The final passage about his friends who kept away from him is also a description of the sad surprise of a small child who has to part from his friends. They called him "*ḥallot*-eater" because the portion set aside for priests which children commonly see is not the large quantities of terumah given in the field, but rather the *ḥallah* which is removed from dough. Little children were warned not to touch it, and certainly not to eat it. Thus they were astonished, and perhaps angry, that their friend could now eat what they were forbidden.

וְהַחוֹלֵק בְּבֵית דִּין **But if someone receives a share of terumah in court.** Generally a court is not needed to divide an inheritance. No matter whether the deceased has left a will or whether there are disputes among the heirs, according to law they may divide the inheritance among themselves. However, the division of an inheritance sometimes raises problems. For example, the double portion given to the firstborn is not taken from all the property of the deceased, but only from what was actually in his possession when he died. Sometimes a claim may be lodged by the widow or the daughters, and sometimes there may be a dispute among the heirs as to how to divide the legacy. In such cases, the heirs bring their problem before the court and the court allots each one the portion to which he is entitled. Because this division is done in court, we assume that the court has considered all aspects of the case to make sure that every detail

TRANSLATION AND COMMENTARY

כְּרַבִּי אֶלְעָזָר בֶּן עֲזַרְיָה [1]The Gemara answers: The ruling of Rabbi Shimon ben Elazar **is in accordance with** the opinion of **Rabbi Elazar ben Azaryah,** [2]**which was taught** in the following Baraita: **"Terumah is for the priest,** [3]and **first tithe is for the Levite,** as the Torah commands. [4]**These are the words of Rabbi Akiva.** Just as terumah may be given only to the priest, so too may the first tithe be given only to the Levite. [5]**Rabbi Elazar ben Azaryah says: First tithe** may **also** be given to **the priest."** Priests, like Levites, are members of the tribe of Levi, and are entitled to receive the Levitical portions (see note). Thus, when Rabbi Shimon ben Elazar said that eating first tithe could serve as presumptive proof of priesthood, he was following the opinion of Rabbi Elazar ben Azaryah, who said that first tithe is given to priests.

אֵימוּר [6]But, the Gemara objects, **granted that** the Baraita **said that Rabbi Elazar ben Azaryah said** that first tithe may ***"also*** be given **to the priest,"** i.e., it may be given to either a priest or a Levite. [7]But **did** Rabbi Elazar ben Azaryah say that first tithe must be given *only* **"to the priest and *not* to the Levite"**? But how, then, can the eating of first tithe be a presumptive proof of priesthood? How do we know that this man is a priest and not a Levite?

[1]כְּרַבִּי אֶלְעָזָר בֶּן עֲזַרְיָה, [2]דְּתַנְיָא: "תְּרוּמָה לְכֹהֵן; [3]מַעֲשֵׂר רִאשׁוֹן לְלֵוִי. [4]דִּבְרֵי רַבִּי עֲקִיבָא. [5]רַבִּי אֶלְעָזָר בֶּן עֲזַרְיָה אוֹמֵר: מַעֲשֵׂר רִאשׁוֹן אַף לְכֹהֵן".

[6]אֵימוּר דְּאָמַר רַבִּי אֶלְעָזָר בֶּן עֲזַרְיָה: "אַף לְכֹהֵן". [7]"לְכֹהֵן וְלֹא לְלֵוִי" מִי אֲמַר?

LITERAL TRANSLATION

[1][It is] in accordance with Rabbi Elazar ben Azaryah, [2]for it was taught: "Terumah is for the priest; [3]first tithe is for the Levite. [4][These are] the words of Rabbi Akiva. [5]Rabbi Elazar ben Azaryah says: First tithe is also for the priest."

[6]Granted (lit., "say") that Rabbi Elazar ben Azaryah said: "Also for the priest." [7]Did he say: "For the priest and not for the Levite"?

NOTES

מַעֲשֵׂר רִאשׁוֹן אַף לְכֹהֵן **First tithe is also for the priest.** The Gemara in tractate *Yevamot* (86b) explains that Rabbi Elazar ben Azaryah derives his ruling from the fact that Scripture frequently describes priests as members of the tribe of Levi (e.g., Ezekiel 44:15). Rabbi Akiva counters with another verse (Numbers 18:31), from which we learn that the tithe may be eaten anywhere, even in a place where a priest is not permitted to go, such as a graveyard. From this it follows that first tithe was intended for Levites, but not for priests.

The Rishonim note that in several places in the Talmud we are told that first tithe was given to Levites in Talmudic times. Moreover, the Gemara (*Sotah* 47b) explains that the "tithe declaration" (וידוי מַעֲשֵׂר) recited once every three years — stating that all of one's agricultural obligations regarding tithes have been fulfilled (Deuteronomy 26:12-15) — must not be recited if the tithe was given to a priest rather than to a Levite. All of this indicates that the Halakhah follows Rabbi Akiva, who maintains that by Torah law first tithe is given only to Levites, and not to priests.

The Rishonim offer many different explanations of this dispute and its relationship with Ezra's penalty (see following note). According to one view, attributed to *Rashi* but not found in our editions of the Talmud, Rabbi Akiva and Rabbi Elazar ben Azaryah do not disagree about Torah law at all. Their disagreement is confined to the scope of Ezra's penalty. It is difficult to reconcile this view with the exegetical dispute in tractate *Yevamot*, and it is accordingly rejected by the Rishonim.

Our commentary follows *Tosafot*, who explains that the Tannaim disagree about the situation that prevailed both before and after Ezra's penalty. Rabbi Akiva maintains that by Torah law first tithe may be given only to Levites and not to priests, but after Ezra's penalty it was permitted to give it either to Levites or to priests (or to poor people, according to one Amora; see following note). Rabbi Elazar ben Azaryah, on the other hand, maintains that by Torah law first tithe may be given either to Levites or to priests, but after the penalty, it could be given only to priests, and not to Levites at all.

Ritva explains that all Talmudic references to the fact that Ezra awarded first tithe to the priests (or the poor) follow Rabbi Elazar ben Azaryah, who is of the opinion that first tithe may be given to priests by Torah law. But according to Rabbi Akiva, who maintains that first tithe may be given only to Levites, Ezra's penalty did not concern Torah law; rather, he imposed some other penalty on the Levites, unconnected with tithing (in *Yevamot*,

HALAKHAH

תְּרוּמָה לְכֹהֵן **Terumah is for the priest.** "Terumah — both the initial portion removed from the crops, and the tithe given by the Levite to the priest from the first tithe that the Levite receives from the owner — may be eaten only by priests and members of their households. All members of a priestly household may eat terumah — adults and children, male and female, including the priest's wife, but not a daughter who has married a non-priest. Even the priest's slaves and his livestock may eat terumah. Even a wife or a slave who has run away may continue to eat terumah, so long as she or he is legally part of the priest's household." (*Rambam, Sefer Zeraim, Hilkhot Terumot* 6:1.)

מַעֲשֵׂר רִאשׁוֹן **First tithe.** "After the initial portion (terumah) is removed from the crops to be given to the priest, one-tenth of the remainder must be set aside as first

of the division is carried out properly. Hence the share of each heir is ratified by the court. In the present case, it is clear that the court ratified the rights of the brother concerning whom there was doubt as to the inheritance. However, Rabbi Shimon ben Elazar explains that although this establishes his right as an heir, it does not confirm his status as a priest.

SAGES

רַבִּי אֶלְעָזָר בֶּן עֲזַרְיָה **Rabbi Elazar ben Azaryah.** One of the most important Tannaim of the generation following the destruction of the Second Temple, Rabbi Elazar ben Azaryah came from a highly learned family, and one of distinguished lineage. His father, Azaryah, was also a scholar and a very wealthy man, who supported his brother, the Sage Shimon, known for that reason as "Shimon the brother of Azaryah." Rabbi Elazar ben Azaryah's family was a priestly one, descended from Ezra the Scribe, and the story is told that there was a physical resemblance between them.

Rabbi Elazar ben Azaryah took part in the dispute in which Rabban Gamliel II was dismissed from his position as president of the Sanhedrin. Although Rabbi Elazar was very young (only sixteen or eighteen) at the time, he was declared the worthiest candidate for the post because of the virtues the Sages found in him, and because he maintained good relations with everyone. Even after he became a kind of deputy president, he remained very active in community affairs, and traveled to Rome at the head of a delegation of Jewish Sages, as a representative of his people.

Despite his youth, the greatest Sages of his generation regarded him as an equal, and he expressed his opinions about them with vigor. Nevertheless he refrained from implementing his own decisions when he disagreed with his colleagues, and once fasted for a long period to atone for having misled his neighbors into committing a transgression (even though

TRANSLATION AND COMMENTARY

אִין [1] **Yes**, answers the Gemara, Rabbi Elazar ben Azaryah did indeed say that first tithe must be given only to priests and not to Levites, for this was the situation **after Ezra penalized them.** The Gemara (*Yevamot* 86b) explains that Ezra punished the Levites for their reluctance to return to Eretz Israel by taking away their right to first tithe and giving it to the priests instead. According to Rabbi Akiva, Ezra *permitted* farmers to give the first tithe to priests instead of to Levites; but according to Rabbi Elazar ben Azaryah, who maintains that priests are entitled to a share of the tithe by Torah law, Ezra *ordered* farmers to give their first tithe to priests and not to Levites. Thus, when Rabbi Shimon ben Elazar said that first tithe could serve as presumptive proof of priesthood, he was following the opinion of Rabbi Elazar ben Azaryah, who ruled that first tithe is given to priests but not to Levites.

[1]אִין, בָּתַר דְּקָנְסִינְהוּ עֶזְרָא.

LITERAL TRANSLATION

[1] Yes, after Ezra penalized them.

RASHI

בתר דקנסינהו עזרא – ללוים, דלא ליתבו להו. כדאמרינן ביבמות בפרק "יש מותרות" (פו,ב).

NOTES

however, *Ritva* gives a different explanation; see following note).

Rambam has a unique view on this matter. In *Hilkhot Ma'aser* (1:1), he rules that first tithe is given to the Levites alone by Torah law, following Rabbi Akiva. Later (ibid., 1:4), however, he rules that Ezra penalized the Levites and ordered that the tithe should not be given to them at all, but only to the priests, apparently following Rabbi Elazar ben Azaryah. *Kesef Mishneh* notes that *Rambam* says that Ezra penalized the Levites *in his time. Kesef Mishneh* explains that *Rambam* maintains that Rabbi Akiva agrees with Rabbi Elazar ben Azaryah that Ezra penalized the Levites of his generation by ordering that first tithe be given to priests and not to Levites. But Rabbi Elazar ben Azaryah, who maintains that priests may receive the tithe by Torah law, is of the opinion that the penalty applies even to later generations, whereas Rabbi Akiva, who maintains that priests may not receive the tithe by Torah law, is of the opinion that the penalty was a suspension of Torah law, which was intended to last only one generation, and that afterwards the tithe was once again given to Levites. It is not clear, according to this explanation, whether Ezra's penalty still had some residual effect even in later generations (see *Ḥatam Sofer, Minḥat Ḥinnukh*).

בָּתַר דְּקָנְסִינְהוּ עֶזְרָא After Ezra penalized them. In several places in the Talmud we are told that Ezra penalized the Levites by taking away their right to receive first tithe. The Gemara in tractate *Yevamot* (86b) explains that this was because the Levites were less responsive than the other tribes to Ezra's call to return to Eretz Israel (Ezra 8:15-19). In tractate *Sotah* (47a), the Mishnah relates that Yoḥanan the High Priest (one of the early Hasmonean kings) decreed that people should no longer recite the "tithe declaration" which is recited once every three years and states that all one's agricultural obligations regarding tithes have been fulfilled (Deuteronomy 26:12-15). The Gemara explains that this was because the tithes were no longer being given to the Levites, as commanded by the Torah, but rather to the priests, as ordained by Ezra.

The Rishonim try to explain how Ezra could have uprooted a law of the Torah, particularly according to Rabbi Akiva, who maintains that by Torah law first tithe is not given to the priests at all (see previous note). *Ritva*, commenting on the passage in *Yevamot*, explains that Ezra's penalty was based on the Rabbis' power to expropriate property (הֶפְקֵר בֵּית דִּין הֶפְקֵר). According to this explanation, the Rabbis did not change the Halakhah whereby the tithe is supposed to be given to a Levite, but rather gave the priest the right to collect it for him, as it were, as though he were the Levite's creditor (in *Ketubot*, however, *Ritva* retracted this explanation; see preceding note). *Meiri* explains that Ezra decreed that the priest should go with the Levite to the farmer, and they should collect the tithe together; then the priest should take as much as he wants, and leave the rest to the Levite.

The Gemara in *Yevamot* cites an Amoraic dispute as to whether the penalty was in favor of the priests or in favor of the poor. The Rishonim discuss the relationship between this dispute and the dispute between Rabbi Akiva and Rabbi Elazar ben Azaryah (see *Tosafot, Ritva, Shittah Mekubbetzet*).

The penalty imposed by Ezra is not mentioned explicitly anywhere in the Book of Ezra, and the references to it in the Talmud are presumably based on oral tradition. But the Rishonim suggest that a hint of it may be found in the following verse (Nehemiah 10:39): "And the priest the son of Aaron shall be with the Levites when the Levites take tithes." *Tosafot* notes, however, that this verse is a satisfactory source only if we say that the penalty was to permit priests — or poor people — to take a share of first tithe together with the Levites. But if we say that the Levites lost their share entirely, it is not a valid source (see previous note). Accordingly, *Tosafot* suggests another verse

HALAKHAH

tithe. First tithe is given to Levites, both male and female, but not to priests, following Rabbi Akiva. Yet if a priest has first tithe in his possession, he need not give it to a Levite. Ezra penalized the Levites of his generation because they did not return to Eretz Israel with him, and he decreed that first tithe should be given to the priests rather than to the Levites. *Kesef Mishneh* notes that this ruling appears to follow Rabbi Elazar ben Azaryah, in contradiction to *Rambam*'s previous ruling in favor of Rabbi Akiva. He explains that *Rambam* consistently follows Rabbi Akiva; however, according to *Rambam*, Ezra's penalty applied only to that generation, but in later generations the tithe was given both to Levites and to priests." (*Rambam, Sefer Zeraim, Hilkhot Ma'aser* 1:1,4.)

he himself believed that the act in question was permitted).

Rabbi Elazar ben Azaryah was one of the greatest preachers of his generation, and even Rabbi Yehoshua marveled at his talent, saying: "No generation is orphaned if Rabbi Elazar ben Azaryah is one of its members."

SAGES

רַבִּי עֲקִיבָא Rabbi Akiva. The greatest of the Tannaim, Rabbi Akiva (ben Yosef) belonged to the fourth generation. He began his Torah education when already an adult, and studied under Rabbi Eliezer and Rabbi Yehoshua for many years. Many stories are told in Rabbinic literature of his devotion to Torah study, of the loyalty of his wife, and of the financial difficulties they had to overcome.

Rabbi Akiva was responsible for the first systematic arrangement and division of the Oral Law. This work was carried on by his disciple Rabbi Meir, and formed the basis of the Mishnah as finally edited by Rabbi Yehudah HaNasi. Rabbi Akiva was also the founder of a new school of Biblical interpretation, according to which almost all the regulations of the Oral Law are found to have their basis in the text of the Bible. Rabbi Akiva was active in the period between the destruction of the Second Temple and the Bar Kokhba revolt, in the preparations for which he took an active part. He met his death as a martyr at the hands of the Romans.

LITERAL TRANSLATION

[1] But perhaps they happened to give it to him? [2] Rav Ḥisda said: With what are we dealing here? [3] For example, where we are sure about the father of this man that he is a priest, [4] and a rumor went out about him [the son] that he is the son of a divorcee or the son of a woman who received *ḥalitzah*, [5] and they distributed a share of tithe to him at the threshing floor. [6] [As for being] a Levite, he is not a Levite. [7] What is there to say? [8] [That] he is the son of a divorcee or the son of a woman who received *ḥalitzah*? [9] There is no need [to ask] according to the one who says [that] first tithe is forbidden to strangers, [10] that they would not have given [it] to him.

[1] וְדִלְמָא אִיקְרוּ וְיָהֲבוּ לֵיהּ? [2] אָמַר רַב חִסְדָּא: הָכָא בְּמַאי עָסְקִינַן? [3] כְּגוֹן דְּמוּחְזָק לָן בַּאֲבוּהּ דְּהַאי דְּכֹהֵן הוּא, [4] וּנְפַק עֲלֵיהּ קָלָא דְּבֶן גְּרוּשָׁה וּבֶן חֲלוּצָה הוּא, [5] וְחָלְקוּ לֵיהּ לְדִידֵיהּ מַעֲשֵׂר בְּבֵית הַגְּרָנוֹת. [6] לֵוִי, דְּלָאו לֵוִי הוּא. [7] מַאי אִיכָּא לְמֵימַר? [8] בֶּן גְּרוּשָׁה אוֹ בֶּן חֲלוּצָה הוּא? [9] לָא מִיבַּעְיָא לְמַאן דְּאָמַר מַעֲשֵׂר רִאשׁוֹן אָסוּר לְזָרִים, [10] דְּלָא הֲווּ יָהֲבִי

TRANSLATION AND COMMENTARY

וְדִלְמָא [1] **But**, asks the Gemara, **perhaps they happened to give it to this man by chance?** For Ezra only gave the priests preference over the Levites; and even after he penalized the Levites, if there were no priests available, the farmer had to give the first tithe to a Levite rather than not give it at all. But if so, how can eating first tithe be a presumptive proof of priesthood? How do we know that this man is a priest and not a Levite?

אָמַר רַב חִסְדָּא [2] **Rav Ḥisda said in reply: With what are we dealing here?** With a case in which there can be no question of the man being a Levite. He can only be a priest or neither a priest nor a Levite. [3] Such a situation can arise, **for example, where we know** for certain **that the father of the man** in question **is a priest.** [4] **But** then **a rumor spreads that** although the man in question is indeed the son of a priest, he is not a priest himself because **he is the son of a divorcee or the son of a woman who received *ḥalitzah***, and these are women whom a priest is not permitted to marry (see note). According to the rumor, the father of the man in question was illegally married to a woman who was not permitted to marry a priest, and his son was therefore disqualified from the priesthood. [5] The court ordered the rumor investigated, **and** discovered that people were accustomed **to give a share of** first **tithe to** this man **at the threshing floor.** The question arose: Why was he being given a share? There are only two possible answers: Either he was a Levite, or he was a priest (in accordance with the view of Rabbi Elazar ben Azaryah, above). [6] **As for** his **being a Levite,** we know that **he is not a Levite,** as his father was a priest. Clearly, then, he could only have been a priest. [7] **What is there to say** in such a situation? Can we say that, although he received a share of first tithe, he was not a qualified priest [8] because **he was the son of a divorcee or the son of a woman who had received *ḥalitzah***? This is surely impossible, because a disqualified son of a priest has the same status as that of an ordinary Jew — neither a priest nor a Levite — and would never be given a share of first tithe! [9] The Gemara explains further: **There is no need to ask** this question **according to** Rabbi Meir, **who says** (*Yevamot* 86b) **that first tithe is forbidden to ordinary Jews** who are neither priests nor Levites. [10] Clearly, according to Rabbi Meir, **people would not give** first tithe to a disqualified priest, who is considered by the Halakhah to

RASHI

לוי דלאו לוי הוא — כלומר, בלוי ליכא לספוקי — דהא אביו כהן. **למאן דאמר כו׳** — פלוגתא היא ביבמות (שם).

TERMINOLOGY

הָכָא בְּמַאי עָסְקִינַן With what are we dealing here? I.e., the case we are referring to here is.... This expression is used by the Gemara to introduce an אוֹקִימְתָּא — an explanation whose purpose is usually to answer a previous objection, and to limit the application of the Mishnah or the Baraita under discussion to one particular set of circumstances.

NOTES

(Malachi 3:10): "Bring all the tithes into the storehouse," and argues that from Nehemiah 10:38 it is clear that the storehouse in the Temple treasury was the place where terumah was kept for the priests.

וְדִלְמָא אִיקְרוּ וְיָהֲבוּ לֵיהּ But perhaps they happened to give it to him? The Gemara (*Ḥullin* 131b) rules that even after Ezra's penalty, and even according to Rabbi Elazar ben Azaryah, if a Levite happens to come into possession of first tithe, he is entitled to keep it and need not give it to a priest. Our commentary follows *Meiri*, who takes this idea even further, arguing that when there are no priests available the farmer is required to give the tithe to a Levite, even after Ezra's penalty was instituted. A similar idea is suggested by *Radbaz* (*Hilkhot Ma'aser* 1:4).

בֶּן גְּרוּשָׁה אוֹ בֶּן חֲלוּצָה The son of a divorcee or the son of a woman who received *ḥalitzah*. The Torah (Leviticus 21:7) forbids priests from marrying certain categories of women — among them divorcees. From the Torah's commandment regarding the High Priest (ibid., verse 15), we infer that if a priest violates this commandment, his sons are disqualified from the priesthood, and his daughters become *ḥallalot*, who are listed among the women forbidden to marry priests (*Kiddushin* 77a).

The Torah (Deuteronomy 25:5-10) commands a widow whose husband died childless to marry her late husband's brother. If her brother-in-law does not wish to marry her, she may not marry anyone else until her brother-in-law formally releases her through a ceremony called *ḥalitzah*.

TRANSLATION AND COMMENTARY

be neither a priest nor a Levite. [1]**But even according to** the Sages, **who say that first tithe is permitted to ordinary Jews** who are neither priests nor Levites, a disqualified priest would still not be given a share of first tithe. [2]For the Sages' ruling **applies only to feeding** non-priests and non-Levites with the tithe. According to the Sages, the Levite may give first tithe to whomever he wishes, after he receives it. [3]**But** until the Levite receives his share, the owner has an obligation to give it to a Levite (or to a priest) and to no one else. Hence an ordinary Jew would not benefit **by right from distribution** of first tithe, as would a Levite or a priest, and a farmer **would not have given it to him.** We can therefore prove from the fact that this son of a priest was given first tithe that he was not disqualified from the priesthood and that the rumor was false.

לֵיהּ. [1]אֶלָּא אֲפִילּוּ לְמַאן דְּאָמַר מַעֲשֵׂר רִאשׁוֹן מוּתָּר לְזָרִים, [2]הָנֵי מִילֵּי לְמִיסְפַּק לְהוּ, [3]אֲבָל בְּתוֹרַת חֲלוּקָּה לָא יָהֲבֵי לֵיהּ. [4]״וְהַחוֹלֵק בְּבֵית דִּין, אֵינָהּ חֲזָקָה״. [5]אִי בְּבֵית דִּין לָא הָוְיָא חֲזָקָה, [6]הֵיכָא הָוְיָא חֲזָקָה? [7]אָמַר רַב שֵׁשֶׁת: [8]הָכִי קָאָמַר:

LITERAL TRANSLATION

[1]But even according to the one who says [that] first tithe is permitted to strangers, [2]these words [apply only] to feeding them, [3]but as (lit., "in the form of") a distribution [by right] they do not give [it] to him.

[4]"But [if] someone receives a share [of terumah] in court, it is not a presumption." [5]If in court it is not a presumption, [6]where is it a presumption?

[7]Rav Sheshet said: [8]This is what it is saying:

וְהַחוֹלֵק [4]The Gemara now considers Rabbi Shimon ben Elazar's second statement, that **"if someone receives a share of terumah in court, it is not presumptive proof** that he is a priest." At first glance, Rabbi Shimon appears to be saying that if the would-be priest went to court and the court ruled that he was a priest and therefore he was entitled to a share of terumah, this is not presumptive proof. But surely this is impossible! [5]**If** terumah awarded **in court is not presumptive proof,** [6]then **where is** terumah **presumptive proof?** Surely the court is precisely the place where such questions are determined!

אָמַר רַב שֵׁשֶׁת [7]**Rav Sheshet said in reply:** Our previous understanding of this Tosefta was incorrect. Here, too, Rabbi Shimon ben Elazar was referring in his statement to the problem of a priest's son who was rumored to be disqualified from the priesthood, [8]**and this is what** Rabbi Shimon ben Elazar **is saying:**

NOTES

Ḥalitzah is thus similar to divorce, in that it is a procedure whereby a man releases a woman from a marital relationship, leaving her free to marry another man. Accordingly, the Rabbis instituted a number of regulations for *ḥalitzah* that were borrowed from the laws of divorce. In particular, they decreed that a woman who has received *ḥalitzah* is considered like a divorcee, and is therefore forbidden to marry a priest. If she does marry a priest, her children are disqualified from the priesthood (*Yevamot* 24a).

מַעֲשֵׂר רִאשׁוֹן מוּתָּר לְזָרִים **First tithe is permitted to strangers.** In tractate *Yevamot* (85b), the Mishnah rules that a woman who is not the daughter of a priest or a Levite may not eat first tithe unless she is married to a Levite. The Gemara objects that the accepted Halakhah is that the first tithe may be eaten by anyone. And the Gemara answers that this question is a dispute between Rabbi Meir and the Sages, and cites a Baraita to that effect.

The Gemara explains that Rabbi Meir derives this law from a verse (Numbers 18:24) in which first tithe is called "terumah" — implying that, like terumah, it is forbidden to unauthorized persons. The Rishonim agree that the source for the position of the Sages who disagree with Rabbi Meir is found in *Sifrei* (*Koraḥ* 70-71), part of which is cited in the passage in *Yevamot*. *Sifrei* notes that the Torah (Numbers 18:30) declares that after the Levite has given the priest his share of the tithe, he may treat the remainder like an Israelite treats his crops after he has given all the tithes. From this we learn that the remainder of the tithe is treated like an ordinary crop, without special sanctity. Similarly, in the following verse, the Torah permits the Levite to eat the tithe anywhere, implying that there are no rules of ritual purity associated with it.

Although the Gemara never explicitly rules on this matter, and the Mishnah in *Yevamot* clearly follows the view of Rabbi Meir, the Rishonim all agree that the Halakhah follows the Sages and that first tithe may be eaten by anyone. *Maggid Mishneh* explains that this is because the Gemara's language in its objection to the Mishnah in *Yevamot* indicates that the Halakhah follows the Sages. *Mishneh LeMelekh* adds that this appears to be the position of the Gemara in another passage as well (*Yevamot* 91a).

HALAKHAH

מַעֲשֵׂר רִאשׁוֹן מוּתָּר לְזָרִים **First tithe is permitted to strangers.** "First tithe has no sanctity attached to it. It may be eaten by non-Levites, and also eaten by a person while he is ritually impure. Even the daughter of a Levite who was taken captive and raped may eat first tithe. *Kesef Mishneh* notes that although there is a Tannaitic dispute as to whether first tithe may be eaten by non-Levites, the Halakhah follows the Sages, who rule that this is permitted." (*Rambam, Sefer Zeraim, Hilkhot Ma'aser* 1:2.)

TRANSLATION AND COMMENTARY

If the son of a priest **receives a share of terumah from his father's property** together **with his brothers, in court,** [1]**it is not presumptive proof** that he himself is a priest. Although the court was clearly satisfied that he was the son of the priest, we have no evidence that the rumors of his disqualification were not true.

פְּשִׁיטָא [2]But, the Gemara objects, surely **this is obvious!** The fact that the man is the son and heir of a priest tells us nothing about his personal status. Why would Rabbi Shimon ben Elazar need to tell us this?

מַהוּ דְּתֵימָא [3]The Gemara answers: If Rabbi Shimon ben Elazar had not taught us this law, **you might have said** the following: The court awarded this purported priest a share of his father's terumah together with his brothers, who are definitely priests, without any attempt to distinguish between the shares or to give the terumah to the other brothers and compensate him with some other part of the estate. [4]And **since** the terumah **these** other brothers received **was** intended **for eating,** for they are definitely priests, [5]we can assume that the terumah this man received **was also** intended **for eating**. Hence the court was in effect quashing the rumors about this man. [6]**Therefore** Rabbi Shimon ben Elazar **informs us** that we cannot read such an intention into the court decision. The court decided the ownership of the terumah on the basis of the laws of inheritance, without taking into consideration the use to which the terumah would be put. In fact, the terumah received by **these** other brothers **was** intended **for** their own **consumption,** [7]whereas the terumah received by this man **was meant to be sold** to qualified priests.

הַחוֹלֵק תְּרוּמָה בְּנִכְסֵי אָבִיו עִם אֶחָיו בְּבֵית דִּין, [1]אֵינָהּ חֲזָקָה.
[2]פְּשִׁיטָא!
[3]מַהוּ דְּתֵימָא: [4]מִדְּהָנָךְ לַאֲכִילָה, [5]הַאי נַמִי לַאֲכִילָה. [6]קָא מַשְׁמַע לָן: הָנָךְ לַאֲכִילָה; [7]הַאי לְזַבּוּנֵי.

LITERAL TRANSLATION

[If] someone receives a share of terumah in the property of his father with his brothers in court, [1]it is not a presumption.

[2]It is obvious!

[3]You might have said: [4]Since these are for eating, [5]this is also for eating. [6][Therefore] it tells us: These are for eating; [7]this is for selling.

RASHI

בנכסי אביו כו׳ אינה חזקה — להשבית מעליו קול היוצא על אמו שהיא גרושה, והוא חלל. **פשיטא** — דהא אפילו הוא חלל יורש את אביו.

NOTES

הַחוֹלֵק תְּרוּמָה בְּנִכְסֵי אָבִיו If someone receives a share of terumah in the property of his father. The Rishonim ask: In the previous case, the Gemara explained that we were referring to a situation in which the father of the man in question was known to be a priest, but there was a rumor that his mother was a divorcee. By implication, where there is no rumor, we are permitted to rely on the father's status and to give the son terumah. Why, then, does the son who receives a share of terumah from his father's estate need to prove that he is entitled to eat terumah?

Our commentary follows *Rashi* and *Ra'avad*, who explain that here too we are referring to a case where the dead man was known to be a priest, and the brothers were known to be his sons, but there was a rumor that one of the sons was the son of a divorcee. Hence the Baraita informs us that, although the would-be priest's brothers permitted him to take a share of the terumah from his father's estate, this is not in itself proof of priestly status and is not sufficient to quell the rumor.

Rashba and *Ritva* suggest that it is possible to construct a case without introducing the factor of a rumor — for example, where the father went abroad for several years with several sons, and returned with an additional son. The Mishnah (*Kiddushin* 79b) rules that if the father's wife returns with him, and is known to be qualified to marry a priest, he does not need to prove that she was the boy's mother; but if the mother died abroad, the father must prove that the boy was the son of a mother whose status was not in doubt. Thus the Baraita is teaching us that the fact that the doubtful priest's brothers permitted him to take a share of the terumah from his father's estate is not a substitute for the proof of priestly status demanded by the Mishnah in *Kiddushin*.

Rambam (*Hilkhot Issurei Bi'ah* 20:15) rules that if two witnesses testify that a man was a priest, his sons are presumed to be priests as well, without proof; but if the father was presumed to be a priest on the basis of a single witness, the sons must prove that their mother was qualified to marry a priest. Accordingly, *Maggid Mishneh* explains that in the previous case of the Gemara the father had two witnesses, and the son would have been presumed to be a priest without proof had it not been for the rumor, but in the case of the terumah from the father's estate, the father had only one witness, and the son could not be presumed to be a priest without proof.

מִדְּהָנָךְ לַאֲכִילָה Since these are for eating. *Ritva* explains that if the court believed the rumor, it would give the late priest's terumah to his other sons and give the son of doubtful status other property in place of it, rather than giving him terumah and directing him to sell it. But Rabbi Shimon ben Elazar teaches us that we cannot prove anything from the court's action, because the late priest

HALAKHAH

הַחוֹלֵק תְּרוּמָה בְּנִכְסֵי אָבִיו עִם אֶחָיו בְּבֵית דִּין If someone receives a share of terumah in the property of his father with his brothers in court. "If witnesses testify that the sons of a priest divided up their father's estate in court, and they divided up terumah as well, we do not consider this to be proof of presumptive priesthood, because it is possible that one of the sons was the son of a divorcee, and was thus disqualified from the priesthood, and he plans to sell his share of the terumah." (*Rambam, Sefer Kedushah, Hilkhot Issurei Bi'ah* 20:12.)

[1]"Rabbi Yehudah says: "We do not elevate to the priesthood on the evidence of one witness, etc." [2]Rabban Shimon ben Gamliel is the same as Rabbi Eliezer!

[3]And if you say [that] they differ about (lit., "there is between them") an objection by one, [4]in that Rabbi Eliezer maintains [that] an objection [may be made] by one, [5]and Rabban Shimon ben Gamliel maintains [that] an objection [must be made] by two,

[1]"רַבִּי יְהוּדָה אוֹמֵר: אֵין מַעֲלִין לִכְהוּנָּה עַל פִּי עֵד אֶחָד, וכו'". [2]רַבָּן שִׁמְעוֹן בֶּן גַּמְלִיאֵל הַיְינוּ רַבִּי אֱלִיעֶזֶר!

[3]וְכִי תֵּימָא עַרְעָר חַד אִיכָּא בֵּינַיְיהוּ, [4]דְּרַבִּי אֱלִיעֶזֶר סָבַר עַרְעָר חַד, [5]וְרַבָּן שִׁמְעוֹן בֶּן גַּמְלִיאֵל סָבַר עַרְעָר תְּרֵי,

RASHI

רבן שמעון היינו רבי אליעזר — דהא ודאי במקום שיש עוררין לא אמר רבן שמעון דליהוי חד נאמן. **וכי אמר מעלין** — מקום שאין עוררין קאמר. **דרבי אליעזר סבר ערער חד** — הוי ערער, ואין אחד נאמן עליו להכשירו.

TRANSLATION AND COMMENTARY

רַבִּי יְהוּדָה אוֹמֵר [1]The Gemara now returns to the Tannaitic dispute in our Mishnah (above, 23b). **"Rabbi Yehudah says: We do not elevate to the priesthood on the testimony of one witness,"** whereas Rabbi Elazar says that this is true only when there are objectors, and Rabban Shimon ben Gamliel says that we do elevate to the priesthood on the evidence of one witness. [2]The Gemara objects: Surely the viewpoint of **Rabban Shimon ben Gamliel is the same as that of Rabbi Eliezer!** (This is the reading found in the Gemara here, although in the Mishnah this viewpoint is attributed to Rabbi Elazar rather than to Rabbi Eliezer.) Ostensibly, Rabbi Elazar and Rabban Shimon ben Gamliel disagree as to whether we elevate to the priesthood on the evidence of one witness when there are objectors. But this is untenable, because the term "objectors" always means two unfavorable witnesses, and it is inconceivable that Rabban Shimon ben Gamliel would accept the testimony of one favorable witness over the objections of two unfavorable witnesses. So if Rabban Shimon ben Gamliel accepts that we do not elevate to the priesthood on the evidence of one witness when there are objectors, and Rabbi Elazar accepts that we do elevate to the priesthood on the evidence of one witness when there are no objectors, what is the difference between them?

וְכִי תֵּימָא [3]The Gemara first considers an obvious solution to this problem: **If you say** that the term "objectors" used here means one unfavorable witness, not two, and that Rabbi Elazar and Rabban Shimon ben Gamliel **differ about** the law when the single favorable witness is opposed by **one objector**, there is a simple explanation of their dispute. [4]**Rabbi Eliezer maintains that an objection can be raised by one** unfavorable witness, and once this happens we do not accept the testimony of the favorable witness, because Rabbi Elazar said that we do not elevate to the priesthood on the evidence of one witness when there are objectors. [5]**Rabban Shimon ben Gamliel**, on the other hand, **maintains that an objection can only**

NOTES

may have left a great deal of terumah and little else, so that it was not practicable to give all the terumah to the brothers whose status as priests was not in doubt.

רַבָּן שִׁמְעוֹן בֶּן גַּמְלִיאֵל הַיְינוּ רַבִּי אֱלִיעֶזֶר **Rabban Shimon ben Gamliel is the same as Rabbi Eliezer.** Slightly different versions of this passage are presented by the various Rishonim. Our translation and commentary follow *Rashi*, who explains that the Gemara has difficulty in distinguishing between the view of Rabbi Elazar and that of Rabban Shimon ben Gamliel. For Rabbi Elazar (who appears in general to be less willing to accept one witness) expressly accepts the testimony of one witness when there are no objectors, and it is inconceivable that Rabban Shimon ben Gamliel (who appears in general to be more willing to accept one witness) would accept the testimony of one witness against two objectors. Hence the Gemara seeks a possible difference between them regarding the definition of the term "objectors."

Some Rishonim follow the reading of *Rabbenu Ḥananel*, according to which the Gemara is seeking to make a distinction between Rabban Shimon ben Gamliel and the first Tanna, rather than between Rabban Shimon ben Gamliel and Rabbi Elazar. *Ritva* suggests that even according to this reading the reference is to Rabbi Elazar, and the Gemara calls him "the first Tanna" because he appears before Rabban Shimon ben Gamliel. *Yad Ramah*, however, explains that the reference is to the first Tanna in our Mishnah, who dealt with the case of the two purported priests who testify about each other (see also *Ramban*). This question is closely connected to that of whether there is a difference of opinion between Rabbi Elazar and Rabban Shimon ben Gamliel, on the one hand, and the first Tanna on the other, when there are grounds to suspect a conspiracy between the two purported priests.

Later in this passage, when the Gemara explains the Tannaitic dispute, the one disagreeing with Rabban Shimon ben Gamliel is described as the first Tanna, even in *Rashi's* text of the Talmud (although in the parallel passage in *Bava Batra* [31b], Rabbi Elazar's name appears).

It should also be noted that there is an apparent scribal error in the standard texts of the Talmud. In our Mishnah and in *Bava Batra* the Tanna appearing before Rabban Shimon ben Gamliel is called "Rabbi Elazar," and this is also the reading found in the Rishonim here. But in this

TRANSLATION AND COMMENTARY

be raised by two, but in a case of one against one we rely on the single favorable witness and elevate to the priesthood. [1]But the Gemara immediately dismisses this solution: **Surely** there is an authoritative statement by **Rabbi Yoḥanan**, who **said**: [2]**According to all** opinions, **there can be no objection by less than two!** We do not accept testimony by one witness disqualifying a person or a document, and there is no dispute about this matter. Whenever the term "objectors" appears in the Mishnah, the reference is always to two witnesses or to a person who has special credibility for some reason (such as a husband who denies writing a bill of divorce), but never to one witness. Thus, when Rabbi Elazar ruled that a single favorable witness is believed concerning priesthood, except where there are objectors, he was implying that we reject the testimony of a single favorable witness only where there are objectors; but when there is only one unfavorable witness opposing the single favorable witness, we rely on the favorable testimony and elevate to the priesthood on the basis of that testimony. What, then, is the dispute between Rabbi Elazar and Rabban Shimon ben Gamliel?

אֶלָּא [3]**Rather,** answers the Gemara, we must explain the dispute as follows: Rabbi Elazar is of the opinion that there is never a case in which we elevate to the priesthood on the evidence of one witness when there are objectors (i.e., two unfavorable witnesses), because one witness cannot prevail over two. Rabban Shimon ben Gamliel, by contrast, is of the opinion that there is a case — which Rabbi Elazar would describe as one witness against two objectors — in which the testimony of the single witness is accepted, because it can be viewed as a case of two against two, rather than one against two. [4]The Gemara explains: **With what are we dealing here?** [5]With a case **where we know** for certain **that the father of the man** in question

[1]הָאָמַר רַבִּי יוֹחָנָן: [2]דִּבְרֵי הַכֹּל, אֵין עַרְעָר פָּחוֹת מִשְּׁנַיִם! [3]אֶלָּא, [4]הָכָא בְּמַאי עָסְקִינַן? [5]דְּמוּחְזָק לָן בְּאָבוּהּ דְּהַאי

LITERAL TRANSLATION

[1]surely Rabbi Yoḥanan said: [2]According to (lit., "the words of") all, there is no objection [by] less than two!

[3]Rather, [4]with what are we dealing here? [5]Where we are sure about the father of this

NOTES

one place — in the text of the Talmud itself and in *Rashi's* comment — this view is attributed to Rabbi Eliezer (*Rashash*). We have followed the standard text of the Talmud in our translation, and have noted the problem in the commentary.

וְרַבָּן שִׁמְעוֹן בֶּן גַּמְלִיאֵל סָבַר עַרְעָר תְּרֵי **And Rabban Shimon ben Gamliel maintains that an objection must be made by two.** Neither Rabbi Elazar nor Rabban Shimon ben Gamliel says anything explicit about a single objector, but the Gemara assumes that Rabban Shimon ben Gamliel is the Tanna who rejects the objection of a single objector, and Rabbi Elazar is the Tanna who accepts it. In tractate *Bava Batra* (93b), the Gemara explains that whenever we have a situation like this one, in which two Tannaim differ over a case and it is not clear which one is saying what, we may assume that the Tanna cited last in the Mishnah was the one who added a case. Hence, at first glance it would seem that we should have said that it was Rabban Shimon ben Gamliel who recognizes the objection of a single objector, and Rabbi Elazar who takes the more conventional position that two objectors are required.

Shittah Mekubbetzet explains that the rule in *Bava Batra* applies only where there is no indication in the language of the Mishnah as to which Tanna held which position. But here Rabbi Elazar's language ("in a place where there are no objectors") implies that if there was even one objector the testimony of the single witness would be rejected.

Ritva explains that our Mishnah in fact follows the rule expressed in *Bava Batra*. For by rejecting the objection of a single objector, Rabban Shimon ben Gamliel is in effect saying that we accept the testimony of a single favorable witness in an additional instance, whereas Rabbi Elazar, who maintains that a single objector is effective, is of the opinion that a single favorable witness is not accepted in such a case.

דִּבְרֵי הַכֹּל, אֵין עַרְעָר פָּחוֹת מִשְּׁנַיִם **According to all, there is no objection by less than two.** According to Rabbi Yoḥanan's authoritative statement, the word "objectors" never refers to just one witness. *Ritva* points out that the word "objectors," although in the plural, does not necessarily imply two objectors, as the use of the plural in this way is a standard convention of Talmudic legal language. Indeed, in tractate *Gittin* (2a), the word "objectors" appears in connection with the validity of a bill of divorce, and the Gemara (9a) explains that the reference is to the husband.

Rabbi Yoḥanan's statement appears in several places in the Talmud. Everywhere it is cited as a well-known dictum, but we are never told in what context it was originally made. *Ramban* suggests that Rabbi Yoḥanan may have been referring to the general concept of objectors, and not to any specific Halakhah. Most Rishonim, however, including *Tosafot*, explain that Rabbi Yoḥanan was referring to our Mishnah. According to this explanation, Rabbi Yoḥanan had a tradition that the dispute between the Tannaim in our Mishnah did not revolve around this question, and that Rabbi Elazar and Rabban Shimon ben Gamliel agree that one witness would be acceptable as evidence of priestly status if there was only one objector (*Ramban*). Presumably Rabbi Yoḥanan's statement was borrowed in other passages, because it stands to reason that if the Tannaim in our Mishnah agree that a single objector would not prevail over a single witness, a single objector would also not be effective in other contexts. Support for this explanation can also be found in the parallel passage in the Jerusalem Talmud.

TRANSLATION AND COMMENTARY

is a priest. [1] **But** then **a rumor spreads that** although the man in question is indeed the son of a priest, he is not a priest himself, because **he is the son of a divorcee or the son of a woman who received *ḥalitzah***, whom a priest is not permitted to marry. According to the rumor, the father of the man in question illegally married a woman who was not permitted to marry a priest, and his son was therefore disqualified from the priesthood. [2] When the court heard the rumor, it ordered the man temporarily **demoted** from the priesthood, pending investigation of the matter. Although rumor has no legal status, we are very scrupulous about priestly lineage, and when doubts are raised we do not dismiss them without investigation. [3] The court then looked into the matter of the status of the man's mother, **and one witness came forward and said: "I know that** this man **is a priest.** His father was a priest and there was no impediment in his mother's status to prevent her from marrying a priest." [26B] When the court heard the witness, it **elevated** the man to the priesthood, and considered the matter closed and the rumor dismissed. [4] But then **two witnesses came** forward **and** substantiated the rumor, **saying:** "This man **is** indeed **the son of a divorcee or the son of a woman who received *ḥalitzah*.**" [5] When the court heard this testimony, it ordered the man **demoted** from the priesthood, since the favorable testimony of the first witness and our initial favorable presumption are without value when they are contradicted by two qualified witnesses. [6] The matter might have rested there, but at this point another **individual witness came forward and said: "I know that** this man **is a priest,** because his mother was not in any way disqualified from marrying a priest." There were now two witnesses on both sides. Had the two favorable witnesses come at the same time, this would have been considered a case of two witnesses against two witnesses, and the doubt would have been resolved on the basis of our initial presumption in the man's favor. But since the two favorable witnesses came separately, there are grounds for treating each of them as a single witness who is confronted by two unfavorable witnesses.

דְּכֹהֵן הוּא, [1] וּנְפַק עֲלֵיהּ קָלָא דְּבֶן גְּרוּשָׁה אוֹ בֶּן חֲלוּצָה הוּא, [2] וְאַחְתִּינֵיהּ, [3] וַאֲתָא עֵד אֶחָד וַאֲמַר: ״יָדַעְנָא בֵּיהּ דְּכֹהֵן הוּא״, [26B] וְאַסְקִינֵיהּ, [4] וַאֲתוּ בֵּי תְּרֵי וְאָמְרִי: ״בֶּן גְּרוּשָׁה וּבֶן חֲלוּצָה הוּא״, [5] וְאַחְתִּינֵיהּ, [6] וַאֲתָא עֵד אֶחָד וַאֲמַר: ״יָדַעְנָא בֵּיהּ דְּכֹהֵן הוּא״.

LITERAL TRANSLATION

man that he is a priest, [1] and a rumor went out about him [the son] that he is the son of a divorcee or the son of a woman who received *ḥalitzah*, [2] and we demoted him, [3] and one witness came and said: "I know about him that he is a priest," [26B] and we elevated him, [4] and two [witnesses] came and said: "He is the son of a divorcee or the son of a woman who received *ḥalitzah*," [5] and we demoted him, [6] and one witness came and said: "I know about him that he is a priest."

RASHI

ונפק עליה קלא – קול בעלמא, ולא עדות. **ואחתיניה** – מן הכהונה עד שיבדקו את הדבר, שמעלה הוא לכהונה. **ואסקיניה** – דבמקום קול הוי חד מהימן.

NOTES

וּנְפַק עֲלֵיהּ קָלָא And a rumor went out about him. The Rishonim ask: The Gemara (*Gittin* 89b) rules that any rumor that has not been investigated by a court is of no consequence. In his commentary there, *Rashi* explains (on the basis of a previous statement of the Gemara) that the Gemara means that a court takes a rumor into consideration only if it can establish its source and determine exactly how it came to be spread. Why, then, did the court in our Gemara order the man demoted from the priesthood because of the rumor?

Tosafot (*Bava Batra* 32a) explains that the court did not order the man demoted; rather, people paid attention to the rumor and ceased to treat him as a priest. *Ritva* explains that in our passage we are, in fact, referring to a rumor that has been investigated by the court.

Some Rishonim, however, explain that the rumor in our passage was not substantiated at all, and that the court ordered the man demoted as a precautionary measure until the rumor could be investigated. *Rashba* explains that the Gemara in *Gittin* means that unsubstantiated rumors are not taken seriously as a basis to overturn an established legal presumption. In our case, however, the legal presumption supporting the man's claim is very weak. For although this man's father was known to be a priest, we know nothing about the man himself. Hence the court was bound to take into consideration the rumor about his

HALAKHAH

וְאַסְקִינֵיהּ And we elevated him. "If a man's father is known to be a priest, and there is a rumor that the man's mother was disqualified from marrying a priest, we take the rumor into account and demote the man from the priesthood. If one witness then comes and testifies that the man's mother was qualified, we accept his testimony and dismiss the rumor, and we restore the man to the priesthood. If two witnesses subsequently come forward and testify that the man's mother was disqualified, we demote him again, as two witnesses are believed against one. If another individual favorable witness then comes forward, we combine his testimony with that of the other

TRANSLATION AND COMMENTARY

וּדְכוּלֵּי עָלְמָא [1]The Gemara explains: **According to** both Rabbi Elazar and Rabban Shimon ben Gamliel, the two favorable witnesses can be **combined** into a pair **for testimony**. In other words, they are considered to be a pair of witnesses whose standing is equal to that of the unfavorable witnesses, since the fact that they came separately has no legal significance. [2]**But Rabbi Elazar and Rabban Shimon ben Gamliel disagree about whether** we should accept these two favorable witnesses, **since** accepting them **might lead to disrespect for the court.** Observers are likely to have a poor opinion of the court for changing its mind so often — first announcing that the priest was found qualified on the basis of the testimony of one witness, then reversing itself after hearing the testimony of two witnesses, and then reversing itself yet again. [3]According to this explanation, **the first Tanna** (i.e., Rabbi Elazar) **maintains** that **since we** have already **demoted** this man, [4]**we cannot elevate him** again, **since we are anxious not to bring the court into disrepute.**

[1]וּדְכוּלֵּי עָלְמָא, מִצְטָרְפִין לְעֵדוּת, [2]וְהָכָא בְּמֵיחָשׁ לְזִילוּתָא דְּבֵי דִינָא קָמִיפַּלְגִי. [3]תַּנָּא קַמָּא סָבַר: כֵּיוָן דְּאַחְתִּינֵיהּ, [4]לָא מַסְּקִינַן לֵיהּ, חָיְישִׁינַן לְזִילוּתָא דְּבֵי דִינָא.

LITERAL TRANSLATION

[1]And according to all, they combine for testimony, [2]but here they disagree about whether we are concerned about disrespect for the court. [3]The first Tanna maintains: Since we demoted him, [4]we do not elevate him, [for] we are concerned about disrespect for the court.

RASHI

ודכולי עלמא — בין לרבי אלעזר בין לרבי שמעון. **מצטרפין** — שני עדים המעידים זה שלא בפני זה כשאר עדיות. **דחיישינן לזילותא דבי דינא** — שהורידוהו שני פעמים, ועכשיו יעלוהו, ויבטלו דבריהם. והיינו דקאמר רבי אלעזר: דמאחר שהורדנוהו על פי העוררין — אין מעלין על פי עד זה השני, אף על פי שיש לצרפו עם האחר.

BACKGROUND

לְזִילוּתָא דְּבֵי דִינָא **About disrespect for the court.** When a court frequently reverses its decisions, people may become contemptuous of it, thinking that it does not know what it is doing, since its actions appear ridiculous and unreliable. Disrespect for a court can have grave consequences, for if the honor of the judges is reduced, people may not heed their rulings on other matters. Therefore, there is reason for arguing that even though, according to law, a man is a fit priest, it is preferable to have him remain in his status of unfitness so as not to have people lose respect for the court. However, the Sage who maintains that we need not be concerned about this argues that it is the duty of the court to act solely according to the law, and it need not fear public reaction of any sort. Just as judges are forbidden to reverse a ruling because of threats, so too they should not refrain from ruling properly, even if it places them, in the eyes of those who do not know the facts, in a ridiculous position.

NOTES

mother, until it could investigate the matter. However, once a single witness has come forward to support the legal presumption, we no longer concern ourselves about the rumor.

Our commentary follows *Rashi*, who explains that the court was empowered to demote the man from the priesthood temporarily, as a special stringency because of the reverence with which we regard priestly lineage. However, once the first witness came forward, the rumor ceased to be of any consequence, because it had been investigated and found groundless.

לְזִילוּתָא דְּבֵי דִינָא **About disrespect for the court.** The Rishonim ask: According to this explanation, we demoted and elevated the man to the priesthood twice. We demoted him the first time because of the rumor, and we then elevated him because of the first favorable witness; we demoted him a second time because of the two unfavorable witnesses, and we elevated him again because of the second favorable witness. Why, then, does Rabbi Elazar argue that only the second elevation brings the court into disrepute? Why did he not reject the first elevation as well?

Rashi explains that the disrespect for the court arises because the court demoted and elevated the man twice. The Rishonim understand *Rashi* as saying that we are concerned about bringing the court into disrepute only if the court changes its mind twice, whereas a single change of mind will not raise doubts in the minds of people. Most Rishonim, including *Tosafot*, reject this explanation, because the Gemara in tractate *Bava Batra* (31b) compares the dispute in our Mishnah with an Amoraic dispute about bringing a court into disrepute, and the Amoraic dispute concerns a case where the court changed its mind only once. Indeed, *Ramban* goes so far as to question whether *Rashi* really meant his comment to be understood this way, since *Rashi* is of the opinion that the first demotion was not considered a court decision at all, so that there was really only one instance of demotion and elevation.

Tosafot explains that when the man was demoted and then elevated to the priesthood the first time, the court was not brought into disrepute because everyone understood that the initial demotion was not a court decision but rather a temporary measure, in force while the court investigated the rumor. Thus it was only the second instance of demotion and elevation which raised questions in people's minds.

Ritva explains that a court is not brought into disrepute when it reverses a ruling on the basis of new evidence. On the contrary, everyone understands that a court must decide on the basis of the best evidence before it. Hence the court's first decision on the basis of a rumor was legitimately overturned by the superior evidence of the single favorable witness, and the testimony of the single witness was legitimately refuted by the conflicting testimony of the two unfavorable witnesses. And if the pair of witnesses had been conclusively refuted (for example, through *hazamah*), this would also be legitimate. But in our case the unfavorable witnesses were not refuted. They

HALAKHAH

favorable witness, so that we now have two against two. As a result, we dismiss both sets of witnesses as well as the rumor, and return to the initial presumption about the man, which was that he was qualified for the priesthood, following Rabban Shimon ben Gamliel, according to Rav Ashi's authoritative explanation. *Bet Shmuel* notes that all this applies to men presumed to be priests, who are permitted to eat Rabbinic terumah, but we would not be so lenient regarding Torah terumah (*Rambam, Sefer Kedushah, Hilkhot Issurei Bi'ah* 20:16; *Shulḥan Arukh, Even HaEzer* 3:7.)

[1] וְרַבָּן שִׁמְעוֹן בֶּן גַּמְלִיאֵל סָבַר: אֲנַן אַחְתִּינַן לֵיהּ, [2] וַאֲנַן מַסְּקִינַן לֵיהּ, וּלְזִילוּתָא דְּבֵי דִינָא לָא חָיְישִׁינַן.

LITERAL TRANSLATION

[1] And Rabban Shimon ben Gamliel maintains: We demoted him and we elevate him, [2] and we are not concerned about disrespect for the court.

TRANSLATION AND COMMENTARY

[1] **And Rabban Shimon ben Gamliel maintains** that the court must uphold the law, regardless of the appearance created by its decisions. [2] **We demoted** its man when that was the proper course of action, **and we elevate him** once again when that is what the law demands, **and it is not our concern if this brings the court into disrepute**.

RASHI

ואנן מסקינן ליה — ואי קשיא: תרי ותרי נינהו! אוקי תרי לגבהדי תרי, ואוקמינן אחזקיה קמייתא, דאסקיניה על פי עד הראשון, שהוא נאמן, דהא אכתי אין עוררין. דקול לאו עוררין הוא.

NOTES

were contradicted by other witnesses of equal status. Hence most people will not understand that the court is now in a position of doubt, which it must resolve in accordance with a legal presumption. Rather, they will see the court as arbitrarily rejecting the pair of witnesses it previously accepted in favor of a new pair, and this is liable to bring the court into disrepute.

אֲנַן אַחְתִּינַן לֵיהּ, וַאֲנַן מַסְּקִינַן לֵיהּ We demoted him, and we elevate him. According to this explanation, Rabban Shimon ben Gamliel maintains that a court is permitted to reverse itself, in spite of the danger of incurring disrespect. Therefore, although we originally considered the favorable testimony of the first witness to be that of one witness against two, we must now treat it as a regular case of two against two, since a second witness has come forward with favorable testimony. Likewise, according to Rav Ashi's explanation below, Rabban Shimon ben Gamliel accepts the two favorable witnesses as a true pair, even though they did not testify at the same time, and he treats this as an ordinary case of two against two. Rabbi Elazar, by contrast, treats this as a case of one against two, either because of the concern about bringing the court into disrepute, or because the two favorable witnesses cannot be combined to form a pair. The Rishonim ask: The assumption underlying both explanations is that in a case of two against two, we can be lenient and elevate the man to the priesthood. But surely, if it is a case of two against two, we remain in doubt and should be strict!

Rashi explains that we elevate the man to the priesthood in a case of two against two because the first ruling that the court made was favorable, and this established a favorable presumption. Therefore, since we cannot resolve our doubt, we return to our original ruling, and restore the man to the priesthood. This explanation is difficult, because the first ruling the court made was to demote the man as a result of the rumor. But *Rashi* explains that that decision did not establish a negative presumption, since it was merely a provisional measure, pending investigation of the rumor. Rather, the first true ruling was the one issued in response to the first favorable witness.

Most Rishonim reject *Rashi*'s explanation. *Rashba* points out that *Rashi* seems to be arguing that if two pairs of witnesses contradict each other, we should rule in accordance with the first pair that came before us, and yet it is clear from several places in the Talmud that this is not the case (see also *Ramban* and *Ra'ah*).

Most Rishonim explain that since this man's father was known to be a priest, there is an initial presumption in his favor, unless there is evidence that his mother was disqualified. Hence we decide the dispute between the two pairs of witnesses in his favor, relying on the legal presumption (our commentary follows this explanation). This explanation is a little difficult, since we have seen above (e.g., in the case of Rabbi Yehudah HaNasi and Rabbi Ḥiyya) that even where the father was known to be a priest, the son needs some sort of proof that his mother was qualified to marry a priest. *Rambam* (*Hilkhot Issurei Bi'ah* 20:15), however, rules that proof must be brought only where the father himself was presumed to be a priest on the basis of one witness; but where there were two witnesses to establish the father's status, the son does not need to bring proof about his mother.

Rosh objects to this argument: How can we return to the initial presumption that the father was a priest? The court rejected this presumption when it heard the rumor and ordered the priest demoted the first time! *Rosh* explains that the man was demoted in order to investigate the source of the rumor, but now the source of the rumor has been traced to the two unfavorable witnesses. Hence the rumor itself is of no further consequence, and the case must be decided on the basis of the conflicting testimony alone. *Rambam* explains that a rumor is no better than another witness. But the law is that additional witnesses cannot increase the credibility of a pair of witnesses, since 100 witnesses are no better than two. Hence the rumor cannot tip the balance between the two pairs of conflicting witnesses, and we must decide the case on the basis of the legal presumption, without taking the rumor into consideration.

וּלְזִילוּתָא דְּבֵי דִינָא לָא חָיְישִׁינַן And we are not concerned about disrespect for the court. The Rishonim explain that since we are not concerned about bringing the court into disrepute, we treat this as an ordinary case of two against two, and decide it in the would-be priest's favor on the basis of a legal presumption (see previous note). The Rishonim ask: Even if we assume that the would-be priest's claim is supported by a favorable legal presumption, this passage is still difficult. For the Gemara (*Yevamot* 31a) rules that in every case of two against two we are required to take the strict position, and not rely on a legal presumption. According to one opinion in the Gemara (followed by some Rishonim, such as *Rid*), this is a Torah requirement, but even according to the other opinion (followed by most Rishonim), it is still a requirement, albeit Rabbinic.

Tosafot explains that the passage in *Yevamot* was referring to conflicting evidence about serious Torah offenses, involving such matters as marriage and divorce, in which a mistaken decision can lead to adultery. But regarding Rabbinic offenses, the Rabbis were lenient in resolving conflicting testimony on the basis of legal presumptions. Hence it is possible that this passage follows the opinion that terumah nowadays is Rabbinic, and that the Rabbis were lenient for that reason.

TRANSLATION AND COMMENTARY

מַתְקִיף לַהּ רַב אַשִׁי [1]**Rav Ashi objected** to this explanation: Rabbi Elazar's ruling in the Mishnah specifically referred to a single favorable witness not being accepted when there are objectors, and we have just explained that he was referring to a single favorable witness who testified after another single favorable witness and two unfavorable witnesses. [2]But **if** the motive behind Rabbi Elazar's ruling is to protect the court from being brought into disrepute, the same law should apply **as well, even** where there is a direct confrontation between **two** unfavorable witnesses **and two** favorable witnesses! If at the last stage two favorable witnesses were to come forward instead of one, and we were to restore the man to the priesthood on the basis of their evidence, observers would still not be able to understand why we disregarded the two unfavorable witnesses. For the unfavorable testimony has not been refuted, since the *three* favorable witnesses (the one at the beginning and the two at the end) are no more effective than the *two* unfavorable witnesses. But Rabbi Elazar said in the Mishnah that *one* witness is not accepted where there are objectors. Clearly, then, he was referring to a case where two witnesses *would* be accepted.

אֶלָּא אָמַר רַב אַשִׁי [3]**Rather, Rav Ashi said,** the facts in the case in dispute between Rabbi Elazar and Rabban Shimon ben Gamliel are as we described, but the reasoning behind the dispute is different. [4]In fact, **they disagree about** whether the two favorable witnesses can be **combined** into a pair **for testimony**. Rabbi Elazar is of the opinion that two witnesses who do not testify at the same time are separate, individual witnesses, and they cannot contradict a true pair, whereas Rabban Shimon ben Gamliel maintains that the two favorable witnesses are considered a true pair, on a par with the unfavorable witnesses, even though they did not testify at the same time, and the fact that they came separately has no legal significance. [5]Rav Ashi explains: The dispute between Rabbi Elazar and Rabban Shimon ben Gamliel is the same as **the following dispute between Tannaim.** Rav Ashi now cites a Tosefta (*Sanhedrin* 5:5) which includes two Tannaitic disputes on related subjects. The first does not directly concern us, but the second

[1]מַתְקִיף לַהּ רַב אַשִׁי: [2]אִי הָכִי, אֲפִילּוּ תְּרֵי וּתְרֵי נַמִי!
[3]אֶלָּא אָמַר רַב אַשִׁי: [4]בְּמִצְטָרְפִין לְעֵדוּת קָמִיפַּלְגִי, [5]וּבִפְלוּגְתָּא דְּהָנֵי תַּנָּאֵי,

LITERAL TRANSLATION

[1]Rav Ashi objected: [2]If so, even two and two as well!

[3]Rather, Rav Ashi said: [4]They disagree about combining for testimony, [5]and about the dispute between these Tannaim,

RASHI

אפילו תרי — אתו בהדי הדדי נמי בפעם שניה, לרבי אלעזר לא מסקינן ליה.

NOTES

אִי הָכִי אֲפִילּוּ תְּרֵי וּתְרֵי נַמִי If so, even two and two as well! Our commentary follows *Rashi*, who explains that Rav Ashi is suggesting that the Mishnah should have illustrated the dispute about bringing the court into disrepute with a case where there were three favorable witnesses — one who came first, and two more who came after the unfavorable witnesses. It is essential to explain Rav Ashi this way, according to *Rashi*, because the legal presumption is established by the first witness. Moreover, the problem about bringing the court into disrepute arises only when the court changes its mind twice.

Most Rishonim, however, explain that Rav Ashi is suggesting that the Mishnah should have selected a case where the two unfavorable witnesses came first, followed by the two favorable witnesses (*Tosafot*, *Ritva*, and others). *Ra'ah* notes that, according to *Rashi*, Rav Ashi's objection is hard to understand. Granted that the Mishnah could have constructed a case in which two favorable witnesses came at the end, rather than one — but why introduce an additional witness if the dispute can be presented without him? According to the Rishonim, however, Rav Ashi is objecting to the Mishnah's division of the favorable testimony when it could have been presented as a straightforward case of two against two. From here we see, argues Rav Ashi, that the division of the testimony was the essence of the dispute in the Mishnah. Hence we must explain that the Tannaim disagree about combining testimony given at different times (see also following note).

בְּמִצְטָרְפִין לְעֵדוּת קָמִיפַּלְגִי They disagree about combining for testimony. *Rashba* asks: If the dispute between Rabbi Elazar and Rabban Shimon ben Gamliel concerns all cases in which two witnesses testify at separate times, why do we need to construct a case in which one of the favorable witnesses testified first, followed by the two unfavorable witnesses, followed by the other favorable witness? We could just as easily construct a case in which the two unfavorable witnesses testified first, followed by one of the favorable witnesses, followed somewhat later by the other favorable witness. What is important is that the two favorable witnesses did not testify together. Why, then, do we need to construct a case in which the favorable testimony was split by the unfavorable testimony?

Rashba answers that if the unfavorable testimony was given first, Rabbi Elazar's ruling rejecting the subsequent favorable testimony on the grounds that it was not given by two witnesses at the same time would appear reasonable, since the unfavorable testimony had the advantage of being given at the same time, and the favorable testimony was in no way superior to the unfavorable. But in a case where one of the favorable witnesses had come forward first, and the court had already issued a ruling on the basis of his testimony, we might have thought that Rabbi Elazar

LITERAL TRANSLATION

[1] for it was taught: "Their testimony is not combined unless both of them see together. [2] Rabbi Yehoshua ben Korḥah said: Even when [they see] one after the other. [3] And their testimony is not valid in court unless both of them testify together. [4] Rabbi Natan says: We hear the words of this one

[1] דְּתַנְיָא: ״אֵין עֵדוּתָן מִצְטָרֶפֶת עַד שֶׁיִּרְאוּ שְׁנֵיהֶם כְּאֶחָד. [2] רַבִּי יְהוֹשֻׁעַ בֶּן קָרְחָה אָמַר: אֲפִילּוּ בְּזֶה אַחַר זֶה. [3] וְאֵין עֵדוּתָן מִתְקַיֶּימֶת בְּבֵית דִּין עַד שֶׁיָּעִידוּ שְׁנֵיהֶם כְּאֶחָד. [4] רַבִּי נָתָן אוֹמֵר: שׁוֹמְעִין דְּבָרָיו שֶׁל זֶה הַיּוֹם,

RASHI

עד שיראו שניהם כאחד – את העדות. לאפוקי אחד אומר: בפני הלווהו, ואחד אומר: בפני הודה לו עליו. **ואין עדותן מתקיימת** – להתקבל בבית דין, ואפילו ראו שניהן כאחד. ופלוגתא אחריתי היא, ולאו רבי יהושע בן קרחה קאמר לה. ורבי אלעזר ורבן שמעון בפלוגתא דרבי נתן ורבנן פליגי.

TRANSLATION AND COMMENTARY

is the basis of the dispute in our Mishnah. [1] For **it was taught: "The testimony** of two witnesses concerning monetary matters **cannot be combined unless both of them witnessed together** the event they described. If the two witnesses viewed different stages of the event, they are considered individual witnesses, even though they may tend to confirm each other's testimony (for example, if one witness says he saw a loan being transacted, and the other says that he heard the alleged debtor admit the debt). [2] But **Rabbi Yehoshua ben Korḥah** disagreed and **said: Even if they saw** the event **one after the other** (i.e., even if the witnesses viewed different stages of the event they describe), they are still considered a valid pair of witnesses, provided that their testimonies clearly refer to the same financial obligation." (This dispute has no bearing on the dispute between Rabbi Elazar and Rabban Shimon.) [3] The Tosefta goes on to cite a second Tannaitic dispute: **"And their testimony is not valid in court unless both of them testify together**, but if the two witnesses come to court separately, they are not a valid pair, and are treated as individual witnesses. [4] But **Rabbi Natan** disagrees and **says: We accept**

BACKGROUND

עַד שֶׁיִּרְאוּ שְׁנֵיהֶם כְּאֶחָד Unless both of them see together. In capital trials it is essential that both witnesses see the act at the same time, so much so that if one witness saw it through one window and the other saw it through another window, their testimony is not taken together (*Makkot* 6b). The logical reason for this strict attitude is that if the witnesses have not seen exactly the same thing, they are in fact testifying about two separate things. However, in civil suits testimony is given not about an act that took place but rather about a legal obligation. Therefore, Rabbi Yehoshua ben Korḥah concludes that even if the two testimonies relate to different aspects of the matter, since the testimony essentially refers to a legal obligation, and not to an event, the two witnesses are in fact testifying about the same matter.

NOTES

would agree that we should treat the favorable testimony as at least equal to the unfavorable. Hence this case was selected to teach us that Rabbi Elazar rejects testimony that was not given by two witnesses at the same time, even in a case where it was heard first.

Our commentary follows *Ran*, who explains that the Gemara was forced to adopt this distinction because of the language of the Mishnah, which states that Rabbi Elazar and Rabban Shimon ben Gamliel disagree about the credibility of an individual favorable witness. According to this explanation, the dispute really has nothing to do with the credibility of a single witness; rather, we are dealing with a case of two against two, and the question in dispute is whether the favorable witnesses can be combined into a valid pair. But when the favorable testimony was split by the unfavorable, the situation can superficially be perceived as one in which Rabban Shimon ben Gamliel accepts the testimony of the second favorable witness over the two unfavorable objectors, even though technically he accepts it only because he combines it with that of the other favorable witness, who testified earlier.

אֵין עֵדוּתָן מִצְטָרֶפֶת Their testimony is not combined. The Gemara (*Sanhedrin* 30a) explains that the reasoning in each of the two disputes in this Tosefta is based on a combination of logic and Scriptural exegesis.

In the first clause, there is a dispute as to whether we can combine testimony submitted from different perspectives. The first Tanna is of the opinion that if one witness testifies that he saw a loan transaction and another witness testifies that he heard the alleged debtor admit the loan, it is like a case where one witness testifies to one loan and another witness testifies to another, and in such a case we clearly cannot combine the two testimonies. Rabbi Yehoshua ben Korḥah, however, maintains that, as long as it is clear that the two witnesses are in fact testifying about the same loan, we can combine their testimony.

The first Tanna and Rabbi Yehoshua ben Korḥah also differ in their interpretation of a Biblical verse (Leviticus 5:1): "And he was a witness, or he saw or he knew; if he does not tell, he will bear his iniquity." The first Tanna infers from the use of the singular "witness," even though two witnesses are always required, that the Torah requires that the two witnesses must see the event as one, whereas Rabbi Yehoshua ben Korḥah infers from the words "or he saw or he knew" that the two witnesses may view the same event from different perspectives.

In the second clause, there is a dispute as to whether we can combine testimony given at different times. The first Tanna argues that when a single witness testifies by himself, his testimony can compel a defendant to take an oath, whereas a pair of witnesses can compel a defendant to pay money. Thus we see that a pair of witnesses are more than the sum of their parts; hence two individual witnesses cannot be combined to form a pair. Rabbi Natan, however, maintains that this argument must be rejected, because if followed to its logical conclusion, it would lead

HALAKHAH

עַד שֶׁיִּרְאוּ שְׁנֵיהֶם כְּאֶחָד Unless both of them see together. In capital cases, the witnesses must have observed the event together, and must testify together. But in monetary cases, this is not necessary. Rather, if one witness testifies that he witnessed the loan transaction, and another witness testifies that he did not see the loan transaction itself but heard the borrower admit that he owed the money, the evidence of the two witnesses is combined, and the borrower must pay, following Rabbi Yehoshua ben Korḥah, in accordance with the ruling of the Gemara in tractate *Sanhedrin*." (*Rambam, Sefer Shofetim, Hilkhot Edut* 4:1,3; *Shulḥan Arukh, Ḥoshen Mishpat* 30:6.)

עַד שֶׁיָּעִידוּ שְׁנֵיהֶם כְּאֶחָד Unless both of them testify as one. "If one witness testifies on one day and goes away,

TRANSLATION AND COMMENTARY

the testimony of this witness today, [1] **and when his colleague comes tomorrow, we accept his testimony."** Thus, according to Rabbi Natan, the fact that the two witnesses came separately has no legal significance.

According to Rav Ashi, our Mishnah is to be explained as follows: Rabbi Elazar agrees with the first Tanna in the Tosefta. He is of the opinion that if a single favorable witness comes forward, followed by two unfavorable witnesses testifying together, followed by another favorable witness, we do not combine the evidence of the two favorable witnesses. Rather, we consider the second favorable witness to be a single witness testifying against a pair of objectors, and we reject his testimony. By contrast, Rabban Shimon ben Gamliel agrees with Rabbi Natan in the Tosefta. He maintains that we combine the evidence of the two favorable witnesses — even though they came forward at different times — and we consider it to be a case of two against two. Accordingly, he rules that we follow the normal procedure for cases of two against two, and we elevate the man to the priesthood on the basis of the initial presumption. Thus we are in effect elevating a man to the priesthood on the evidence of the last favorable witness, even though Rabbi Elazar considers him to be one individual witness against a pair of objectors.

MISHNAH **הָאִשָּׁה שֶׁנֶּחְבְּשָׁה בִּידֵי גוֹיִם** This Mishnah returns to the subject of a captive woman who is disqualified from marrying into the priesthood because we fear that her captors violated her. Until now we have dealt with cases where the woman was kidnapped by roving bandits. The Mishnah now considers a situation in which a woman was imprisoned by a hostile government. In Talmudic times, the situation in government prisons was so appalling that if the wife of a priest had the misfortune of being imprisoned for some reason, there was good reason to suspect that she was raped there and thus forbidden to return to her husband. Nevertheless, the Mishnah tells us that the law applying to a government prison is not quite as strict as that applying to roving bandits. [2] **If a woman was imprisoned at the hands of a non-Jewish** government, her status depends on the reason for her imprisonment. If it was [3] **because of a monetary offense,**

[1] וּכְשֶׁיָּבֹא חֲבֵירוֹ לְמָחָר, שׁוֹמְעִין דְּבָרָיו.

משנה [2] הָאִשָּׁה שֶׁנֶּחְבְּשָׁה בִּידֵי גוֹיִם, [3] עַל יְדֵי מָמוֹן,

LITERAL TRANSLATION

today, [1] and when his fellow comes tomorrow, we hear his words."

MISHNAH [2] [If] a woman was imprisoned by the hands of non-Jews, [3] because of money,

RASHI

משנה **על ידי ממון** מותרת לבעלה — דמרתתי להפסיד ממונן, ולאין מפקירין אותה.

NOTES

to the disqualification of all testimony. For two witnesses are still individuals, and even when they come to court at the same time, they do not speak at the same moment.

The first Tanna and Rabbi Natan also differ in their interpretations of the verse from Leviticus. The first Tanna, following the view of the first Tanna in the first clause, argues that the verse disqualifies testimony submitted from different perspectives, and further argues that the juxtaposition of the phrase "if he does not tell" with the phrase "or he saw or he knew" teaches us that "telling" must also be done together, just like "seeing." Rabbi Natan, however, either interprets the verse as did Rabbi Yehoshua ben Korḥah, or else argues that nothing can be learned from the juxtaposition of the phrases.

The Gemara explains that the two disputes in this Tosefta are connected. Rabbi Yehoshua ben Korḥah follows the view of Rabbi Natan, and the Tanna who disagrees with Rabbi Natan follows the view of the Tanna who disagrees with Rabbi Yehoshua ben Korḥah. This is clear both from the exegetical argument described above and from a logical argument: If Rabbi Yehoshua ben Korḥah accepts testimony, even when the witnesses did not see the same thing, it stands to reason that he will accept testimony even if the witnesses do not say the same thing or speak at the same time.

The Gemara concludes that the Halakhah follows Rabbi Yehoshua ben Korḥah. The Gemara never rules explicitly on the dispute between Rabbi Natan and the first Tanna, but since Rabbi Yehoshua ben Korḥah's view is inconsistent with that of the Tanna who disagrees with Rabbi Natan, the Rishonim agree that the Halakhah follows Rabbi Natan as well. Support for this ruling can be found in our Gemara, in which Rabbi Natan's view is linked to Rabban Shimon ben Gamliel, and the view of the first Tanna is linked to Rabbi Elazar, since the Gemara (*Ketubot* 77a, *Bava Metzia* 38b) rules that (with three exceptions) the Halakhah follows Rabban Shimon ben Gamliel whenever he is mentioned in the Mishnah (*Kesef Mishneh*).

עַל יְדֵי מָמוֹן Because of a monetary offense. Our commentary follows *Rashi*'s comment on the parallel passage in tractate *Avodah Zarah* (23a), where he explains that the woman herself was guilty of some monetary

HALAKHAH

and another witness testifies the next day, we combine their testimony, and the borrower must pay the debt, following Rabbi Natan. *Kesef Mishneh* explains that the Gemara in *Sanhedrin* declares that Rabbi Yehoshua ben Korḥah follows the view of Rabbi Natan. Hence, since we rule in favor of Rabbi Yehoshua ben Korḥah, we must also rule in favor of Rabbi Natan." (*Rambam, Sefer Shofetim, Hilkhot Edut* 4:4; *Shulḥan Arukh, Ḥoshen Mishpat* 30:9.)

הָאִשָּׁה שֶׁנֶּחְבְּשָׁה If a woman was imprisoned. "If the wife of a priest was imprisoned by non-Jews in a place where Jews are powerful and the non-Jews are afraid of them, and if she was imprisoned for a monetary offense, she is

מוּתֶּרֶת לְבַעֲלָהּ; [1]עַל יְדֵי נְפָשׁוֹת, אֲסוּרָה לְבַעֲלָהּ.

LITERAL TRANSLATION

she is permitted to her husband; [1]because of a capital [offense], she is forbidden to her husband.

TRANSLATION AND COMMENTARY

a charge that could be settled by payment of a fine, and the woman was being held pending payment, then the woman **is permitted to her husband,** the priest, upon her release, because in such cases the government protects female prisoners lest their families be discouraged from paying the fine and ransoming them. [1]On the other hand, if the woman was held **because of a capital offense,** she **is forbidden to her husband** in the event that she is released, because the government does not protect prisoners of this type, since it does not expect them to be ransomed.

RASHI

על ידי נפשות — היתה נידונת למות.
אסורה לבעלה — דהואיל ונוהגין בה הפקר — חוששין שמא נתרצתה באחד מהן.

NOTES

offense (for example, she was unable to pay a debt). *Rabbenu Yehonatan* explains that it was her husband who owed the money, and the government imprisoned his wife in order to force him to pay. *Meiri* (commenting on *Avodah Zarah*) explains that the Mishnah is referring to both cases.

According to each of these interpretations, it is clear why the prison authorities would be careful with the woman in a place where Jewish influence was great. For the authorities were trying to pressure her husband into paying a debt, and clearly they were more likely to achieve their aim if the husband had a chance of receiving her back unharmed than if they defiled her and rendered her forbidden to him.

It is not entirely clear what the law would be if the couple were not guilty of any offense, but the woman was simply being held for ransom. *Rosh* (in *Avodah Zarah*) argues that in such a case the captors would have no compunction about violating her. Indeed, this might make the need to ransom her all the more acute. On the other hand, *Meiri* points out that even in such a case the captors might have thought that they would get a higher ransom if they did not defile her.

אֲסוּרָה לְבַעֲלָהּ She is forbidden to her husband. Our commentary follows *Rabbenu Ḥananel* and most of the Rishonim, who explain that the law of our Mishnah is a special case of the law of a captive woman who is disqualified from marrying into the priesthood because we suspect that she was raped. According to this explanation, the law of our Mishnah — that the woman is forbidden to her husband — applies only to the wife of a priest. This is because a priest whose wife was raped must divorce her, whereas an ordinary Jew is permitted (and even required) to remain married to his wife if she was raped, unless she voluntarily committed adultery (see below, 51b). Although the Mishnah does not explicitly say that we are referring to the wife of a priest, *Ramban* explains that this Mishnah should be viewed in the context of the previous Mishnayot in this chapter and those that follow, which refer to priests and their wives.

Rashi and *Tosafot* explain that the law of our Mishnah applies to all married women, regardless of whether they are married to priests or to non-priests. For although a non-priest is permitted to remain with his wife if she has been raped, he is forbidden to do so if she committed adultery willingly, even out of fear for her life. Hence we suspect that under the inhumane conditions of ancient prisons this woman may have submitted to her tormentors in an effort to win favor, and thus to save her life. The wording of the Mishnah supports this explanation, because the Mishnah says that the woman is "forbidden to her husband," rather than the usual "disqualified from marrying into the priesthood." *Ritva*, however, explains that the

HALAKHAH

permitted to return to her husband, because we do not suspect that she was raped. But if she was imprisoned for a capital offense, she must not return to her husband, because we suspect that she was raped, unless witnesses testify that she was not defiled. However, in a place where Jews are powerless and oppressed, we draw no distinction between monetary and capital offenses, and in both cases the wife of a priest is forbidden to return to her husband, following Rav's statement. *Ba'er Hetev* and *Pitḥei Teshuvah* cite an opinion that countries with an orderly system of government are treated like countries where Jews are powerful, but they reject this opinion.

"Regarding the definition of a monetary offense, *Rema* cites *Rosh*, who rules that we are lenient only when the non-Jews are owed money, because they are afraid to violate the woman lest they lose their money. But if the non-Jews simply seized the woman and held her for ransom, the law is the same as for a capital offense. *Ḥelkat Meḥokek,* however, notes that *Rosh* also cites a more lenient opinion.

"If the wife of a non-priest was imprisoned by non-Jews, *Rambam* and *Shulḥan Arukh* rule that she may return to her husband in all cases, because we do not suspect her of willingly submitting to her captors. *Rema* cites *Tosafot* and *Tur*, who rule that if she was imprisoned for a capital offense, she is forbidden to her husband, even if he is not a priest, because we suspect her of seducing her captors to persuade them to spare her. If she was imprisoned for a monetary offense, however, she is permitted to her husband, even in a place where Jews are powerless. Moreover, for this purpose, a woman who was held for ransom is governed by the same law as a woman held for a monetary offense, since she would not resort to seduction if she thought that there was a chance of buying her freedom with money (see *Ḥelkat Meḥokek* and *Bet Shmuel*). *Rema* notes that in practice the custom during the periods of medieval persecution was to be lenient, following *Rambam*. *Bet Shmuel* explains that this was because during this time experience showed that women could not save themselves from death by resorting to seduction." (*Rambam, Sefer Kedushah, Hilkhot Issurei Bi'ah* 18:30; *Shulḥan Arukh, Even HaEzer* 7:11.)

גמרא ¹אָמַר רַב שְׁמוּאֵל בַּר רַב יִצְחָק אָמַר רַב: ²לֹא שָׁנוּ אֶלָּא שֶׁיַּד יִשְׂרָאֵל תַּקִּיפָה עַל אוּמּוֹת הָעוֹלָם. ³אֲבָל יַד אוּמּוֹת הָעוֹלָם תַּקִּיפָה עַל עַצְמָן, ⁴אֲפִילּוּ עַל יְדֵי מָמוֹן אֲסוּרָה לְבַעֲלָהּ.

⁵מְתִיב רָבָא: ⁶״הֵעִיד רַבִּי יוֹסֵי הַכֹּהֵן וְרַבִּי זְכַרְיָה בֶּן הַקַּצָּב עַל בַּת יִשְׂרָאֵל שֶׁהוּרְהֲנָה

LITERAL TRANSLATION

GEMARA ¹Rav Shmuel the son of Rav Yitzḥak said in the name of Rav: ²They only taught [this] when the hand of Israel is strong over the nations of the world. ³But [when] the hand of the nations of the world is strong over themselves, ⁴even because of money, she is forbidden to her husband.

⁵Rava objected: ⁶"Rabbi Yose the priest and Rabbi Zekharyah ben HaKatzav testified about a Jewish girl (lit., "a daughter of Israel") who was taken as a

TRANSLATION AND COMMENTARY

GEMARA אָמַר רַב שְׁמוּאֵל בַּר רַב יִצְחָק ¹The Mishnah ruled that if the woman was held for a monetary offense, she is not treated as a captive, because the government is careful not to harm prisoners of this type, in order to encourage their families to ransom them. **Rav Shmuel the son of Rav Yitzḥak said in the name of Rav:** ²The law **taught by this** Mishnah applies **only when Israel has power over the nations of the world.** In a situation where Jews are powerful and influential, the non-Jewish authorities are careful to protect their Jewish prisoners, for fear of the consequences. ³**But** in a situation **where the nations of the world have power over themselves** — i.e., where Jews are powerless and without influence, and the government persecutes them without compunction (properly speaking, this is a situation where the non-Jews have power over the Jews rather than over "themselves," but the convention in the Talmud is to employ a euphemism when describing a distasteful situation) — then the law of the Mishnah does not apply. Rather, every imprisoned woman is assumed to have been raped, ⁴and **even** if she was imprisoned **because of a monetary offense, she is forbidden to her husband** upon her release.

מְתִיב רָבָא ⁵**Rava raised an objection** from a Mishnah (*Eduyyot* 8:2). Tractate *Eduyyot* (lit., "testimonies") is devoted to rulings issued by various Tannaim in the course of deciding difficult questions that actually came before the courts. These rulings are called "testimonies" (whence the name of the tractate), and are always authoritative. ⁶The Mishnah states: **"Rabbi Yose the priest and Rabbi Zekharyah ben HaKatzav testified about a Jewish girl who was taken as a pledge** by the non-Jewish government and was imprisoned

RASHI

גמרא לא שנו – דעל ידי ממון מותרת לבעלה. **אלא שיד ישראל תקיפה על אומות העולם** – ויראים לעשות שלא כדין, שמא יפסידו ממונם. **שהורהנה** = נתמשכנה.

NOTES

Mishnah may be stressing that not only is she disqualified from marrying a priest in the future, but she must even leave her present husband, if he is a priest. (Other explanations are given by *Ramban* and *Ran*.)

Most Rishonim reject *Rashi's* explanation. *Rashba*, *Ritva*, and *Ramban* cite numerous sources which prove that we do not suspect a woman of committing adultery willingly, even under the worst conditions.

Meiri notes that the clause of the Mishnah that permits a woman imprisoned for a monetary offense to return to her husband clearly refers to the problem of a priest's wife who was raped. Likewise, the Mishnah from tractate *Eduyyot*, which is cited by the Gemara below, clearly refers to the wife of a priest, even though this point is not made explicitly. All this lends support to the idea that this entire Mishnah is referring to the case of the wife of a priest.

אֲבָל יַד אוּמּוֹת הָעוֹלָם תַּקִּיפָה But when the hand of the nations of the world is strong. *Meiri* explains that this Mishnah applies only to savage, corrupt regimes, where the prison authorities behave like bandits and have almost unlimited powers. But a woman who is held in an official prison under the authority of a court in a law-abiding country is not forbidden to return to her husband, since the prison authorities fear the government and this restrains their behavior even in capital cases. Similarly, *Haggahot Mordekhai* (*Ketubot* 286) rules that if the government has an orderly system of courts and competent judges, we do not suspect that the woman was raped, even where Jews are not influential. *Bet Yosef* (*Even HaEzer* 7) notes, however, that this distinction was not made by the other authorities.

בַּת יִשְׂרָאֵל שֶׁהוּרְהֲנָה A Jewish girl who was taken as a pledge. *Rashi* explains that the Gemara is referring to a case where a man owed money to powerful non-Jews, and the creditors demanded that his wife serve as collateral. Later, when the debt came due and the husband did not pay, the creditors seized his wife. Below, our Gemara suggests that the law in this case is more severe than in the case of a woman imprisoned for a monetary offense. *Rashi* explains that the non-Jews interpret their contract with the husband as granting them the right to do whatever they please with his wife. The Jerusalem Talmud explains that the situation of a woman taken as a pledge is worse than that of an imprisoned woman, because she is treated like a prostitute.

Ritva adds that even according to the Gemara's suggestion that there is a difference between a woman who was taken as a pledge and a woman who was imprisoned, the difference applies only if the debt fell due and was not paid. But if the creditors seized the woman before the debt fell due, she would be considered a prisoner rather than a pledge.

BACKGROUND

שֶׁיַּד יִשְׂרָאֵל תַּקִּיפָה When the hand of Israel is strong. Where Jews wield power, non-Jews do not attempt to molest Jewish women in prison, for fear of punishment or revenge at the hands of the Jews. But where non-Jews wield power, and the Jews are unable to respond effectively, there are grounds for suspicion that the prison authorities will not be strict with guards who molest Jewish women in their custody.

SAGES

רַבִּי יוֹסֵי הַכֹּהֵן Rabbi Yose the priest. A Tanna of the second generation, Rabbi Yose was a student of Rabban Yoḥanan ben Zakkai, and lived during the period when the Second Temple was destroyed. Little remains of his Torah teachings, nor is much known of the events of his life. However, Rabban Yoḥanan ben Zakkai called him "pious," and elsewhere he is called "the most pious of his generation." He was a colleague of Rabbi Yehoshua, and they studied mysticism together.

רַבִּי זְכַרְיָה בֶּן הַקַּצָּב Rabbi Zekharyah ben HaKatzav. Rabbi Zekharyah ben HaKatzav was a priest and a Tanna who lived in the generation when the Second Temple was destroyed. He was one of Rabban Yoḥanan ben Zakkai's most senior students, and accordingly we find them citing his teachings and joining him to give testimony. Several of his teachings are cited in the Mishnah, the Tosefta, and the Talmud.

LANGUAGE

שֶׁהוּרְהֲנָה Who was taken as a pledge. The root of this word (רהן) is cognate to the Arabic رهن, and means "to give something as a pledge."

BACKGROUND

אַשְׁקְלוֹן **Ashkelon.** A Philistine city in Biblical times, Ashkelon became influenced by Greek culture during the Hellenistic period (even though its residents continued to adhere to some of their ancient religious practices). Even at the height of Hasmonean expansion, the Jews failed to conquer Ashkelon, and it was a "free city" under Roman rule. Although some Jews lived there, it was undoubtedly a place "where the hand of the nations of the world is strong," as the Gemara relates here.

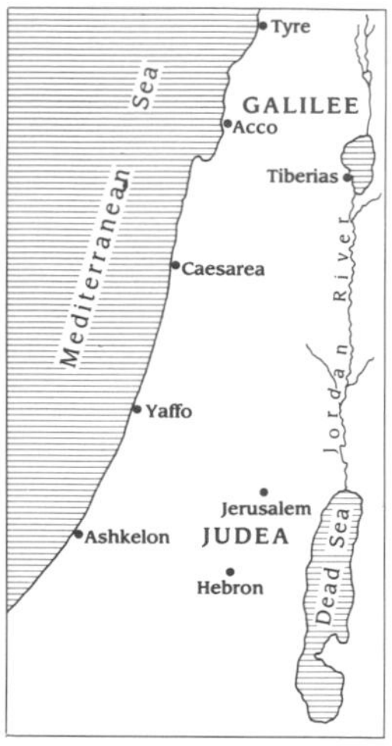

בְּאַשְׁקְלוֹן, [1]וְרִיחֲקוּהָ בְּנֵי מִשְׁפַּחְתָּהּ, [2]וְעֵדֶיהָ מְעִידִים אוֹתָהּ שֶׁלֹּא נִסְתְּרָה וְשֶׁלֹּא נִטְמְאָה. [3]וְאָמְרוּ לָהֶם חֲכָמִים: אִם אַתֶּם מַאֲמִינִים שֶׁהוּרְהֲנָה, [4]הַאֲמִינוּ שֶׁלֹּא נִסְתְּרָה וְשֶׁלֹּא נִטְמְאָה. [5]וְאִם אִי אַתֶּם מַאֲמִינִים שֶׁלֹּא נִסְתְּרָה וְשֶׁלֹּא נִטְמְאָה, [6]אַל תַּאֲמִינוּ שֶׁהוּרְהֲנָה״. [7]וְהָא אַשְׁקְלוֹן דְּיַד אוּמּוֹת הָעוֹלָם תַּקִּיפָה עַל עַצְמָן, [8]וְקָתָנֵי: [27A] ״הוּרְהֲנָה״ — אִין; [9]״נֶחְבְּשָׁה״ — לָא!

LITERAL TRANSLATION

pledge in Ashkelon, [1]and the members of her family rejected her, [2]but her witnesses testified about her that she had not been secluded and that she had not been defiled. [3]And the Sages said to them: If you believe that she was taken as a pledge, [4]believe that she was not secluded and that she was not defiled. [5]And if you do not believe that she was not secluded and that she was not defiled, [6]do not believe that she was taken as a pledge."

[7]But surely Ashkelon [is a place] where the hand of the nations of the world is strong over themselves, [8]and it teaches: [27A] "Taken as a pledge" — yes; [9]"imprisoned" — no!

RASHI

ועדיה — אותן שהעידו שהורהנה. והא אשקלון — דארץ פלשתים היא, ועוד: כבר גלו ישראל. הורהנה — דמדעת. וכיון דהגיע זמן ולא נפדית — הרי היא של נכרים בדיניהם, משום הכי בעינן עדים מעידין אותה שלא נסתרה. נחבשה — דאינה נחלטת להם — לא בעינן עדים, הואיל ועל ידי ממון הוא.

TRANSLATION AND COMMENTARY

in Ashkelon, because her family had failed to pay a debt to the local authorities. [1]When she was released, **the members of her family rejected her**, treating her as a captive woman. [2]**But** the same **witnesses** who testified that she had been taken by the government as a pledge and imprisoned, **testified that** while she was in the hands of the non-Jews **she had not** once **been in seclusion** with a man (so that it would have been impossible for her to have been raped in private) **and that she had not been defiled** by being raped in public. [3]**The Sages said to** her family: You have no right to shun this girl. **If you believe** the witnesses when they testify **that she was taken as a pledge,** [4]you must also **believe that she was never in seclusion and that she was not defiled,** because the testimony was given by the same witnesses, and the mouth that forbade is the mouth that permitted. [5]**And if you do not believe** the witnesses when they testify **that she was never in seclusion and that she was not defiled,** [6]**do not believe that she was taken as a pledge,** since the sole evidence of her captivity is the testimony of these same witnesses." Thus, the authoritative ruling of the Mishnah in *Eduyyot* is that a woman who was imprisoned by the government is permitted to her husband if witnesses testify that she was not defiled. This implies that if there are no such witnesses, she is forbidden.

וְהָא אַשְׁקְלוֹן [7]Rava now explains how this Mishnah contradicts our Mishnah as explained by Rav Shmuel the son of Rav Yitzḥak in the name of Rav: **But surely Ashkelon is a place where the nations of the world have power over themselves** (i.e., where Jews are powerless), and according to Rav's explanation of our Mishnah, even a woman imprisoned by the government for a monetary offense is forbidden to her husband in such a place. [8]**And** yet **the Mishnah** in *Eduyyot* **teaches** that this law applies [27A] when the woman was **taken as a pledge** [9]but **not** when she was **imprisoned!** When a man's wife is seized by non-Jewish authorities to enforce payment of a debt, they do whatever they please with her. Hence the situation is much worse than in a case of imprisonment. Admittedly, the government is lax in its care of prisoners, but

NOTES

אִם אַתֶּם מַאֲמִינִים **If you believe.** Since the Sages argued that the witnesses should be believed, the Gemara infers that a woman who was taken as a pledge is forbidden to her husband unless she can prove that she was not violated. The Rishonim ask: Why did the Sages need to persuade the family to believe the witnesses, and why did they need to argue that the witnesses' testimony was supported by the "mouth that forbade" argument, since they were the only witnesses who testified that she was taken prisoner? Surely it is obvious that witnesses who testify that a woman was not defiled should be believed, even if they are not the same witnesses who testified that she was taken prisoner?

Rashba and *Ritva* explain that the witnesses in this case happened to be people who were disqualified from giving testimony, such as relatives or slaves. *Rashba* adds that we know from the next Mishnah (below, 27a) that such witnesses are believed regarding a captive woman, even if their testimony is not supported by a *miggo*. But in this case the family argued that a woman who was taken as

HALAKHAH

נֶחְבְּשָׁה **Imprisoned.** "If the wife of a priest was imprisoned by non-Jews for a capital offense, we suspect that she was raped, and we do not permit her to return to her husband unless witnesses testify that she was not defiled. If the wife

TRANSLATION AND COMMENTARY

there is still a good chance that the woman will be released undefiled. So if the Mishnah in *Eduyyot* had wished to teach us that in a place like Ashkelon all imprisoned women are considered to have been raped, it should have mentioned a case where a woman was imprisoned for an ordinary monetary offense, and should have ruled that she is presumed to have been raped unless it is proved otherwise. But in fact it selected a case where a woman was taken as a pledge. Thus, by implication, a woman who was imprisoned for a monetary offense would not be presumed to have been raped, even in a place like Ashkelon where the non-Jewish authorities have no fear of the Jews. It would therefore seem that the Mishnah's ruling permitting women imprisoned for monetary offenses to return to their priestly husbands applies even to Ashkelon, and not just to places where the Jews have power. And this contradicts Rav's explanation.

[1]הוּא הַדִּין אֲפִילּוּ נֶחְבְּשָׁה, [2]וּמַעֲשֶׂה שֶׁהָיָה, כָּךְ הָיָה.

[3]אִיכָּא דְּאָמְרִי: [4]אֲמַר רָבָא: אַף אֲנַן נַמִי תְּנֵינָא:

LITERAL TRANSLATION

[1]The law is the same even if she was imprisoned, [2]and the case that happened, happened that way.

[3]There are [some] who say: [4]Rava said: We too have also learned thus:

הוּא הַדִּין אֲפִילּוּ נֶחְבְּשָׁה [1]The Gemara answers: **The law would be the same even if she were imprisoned** for a monetary offense, since Ashkelon is a place where Jews are powerless, and Rav ruled that in such places even imprisonment for a monetary offense places a woman in the Halakhic category of a captive. In fact, the Mishnah in *Eduyyot* mentioned the case of a woman who was taken as a pledge to illustrate this law, because tractate *Eduyyot* lists rulings that were actually issued in difficult cases, [2]**and the case that happened, happened that way.** No proof can therefore be brought from that Mishnah.

The Gemara now presents two other versions of the contradiction between our Mishnah, as explained by Rav Shmuel the son of Rav Yitzḥak in the name of Rav, and the Mishnah in *Eduyyot*. There is no substantial difference in the reasoning of each of these versions, but the question is put in a different form in each.

אִיכָּא דְּאָמְרִי [3]**There are some who say** that Rav Shmuel the son of Rav Yitzḥak explained in the name of Rav that our Mishnah is referring specifically to situations in which Jews are powerful and influential; but when Jews are powerless, all imprisoned women have the status of captives. [4]**Rava said:** This explanation is not original. **We have already learned this** in a Mishnah in tractate *Eduyyot*, which clearly rules that in

NOTES

a pledge is more likely to have been violated than an ordinary female captive (as the Gemara explains below). Hence they thought that disqualified witnesses should not be accepted. But the Sages explained to them that, even according to their reasoning, the disqualified witnesses' testimony should be accepted in this case, since it was supported by a *miggo*. *Pnei Yehoshua* points out that support for this explanation can be found in the language of the Mishnah, which describes the witnesses as "her witnesses" rather than simply as "witnesses," suggesting that there was something unusual about them.

HALAKHAH

of a non-priest was imprisoned by non-Jews for a capital offense, *Rambam* and *Shulḥan Arukh* rule that she may return to her husband, because we do not suspect her of willingly submitting to her captors' sexual assaults. *Rema* cites *Tosafot* and *Tur*, who rule that she is forbidden to her husband, even if he is not a priest, because we suspect her of seducing her captors to persuade them to spare her life.

"The above law applies in a case where the woman herself is guilty of a capital offense. If her husband was guilty of a capital offense, *Shulḥan Arukh* follows *Rambam* in omitting this case. *Maggid Mishneh* explains that, according to this view, the woman is disqualified from the priesthood only if she herself was guilty of a capital offense, or she was at least implicated in her husband's crimes to the extent of facing a possible death penalty. But if the woman's life had not been in danger, she is not disqualified from the priesthood (in a place where Jews are powerful). According to this view, *Rambam* rules in favor of Rav (who maintains that all capital offenses are included in this law), and against Levi (who maintains below that it applies only to murderers' wives). Moreover, *Rambam* does not mention that this law applies only after sentence has been passed, implying that he follows Rabbi Yoḥanan against Ḥizkiyah (below). *Tur*, however, rules that this law also applies to a woman who was imprisoned because of her husband, but only if her husband had committed murder and had already been sentenced to death — following Levi against Rav, and Ḥizkiyah against Rabbi Yoḥanan.

Rema explains that *Tur* ruled in favor of Levi and Ḥizkiyah only in the case where the husband was guilty. But if the woman herself was guilty of a capital offense, *Tur* would agree that she is forbidden to her husband, even before she is sentenced, even if she was guilty of nothing more than theft. On the other hand, this law does not apply if there is a possibility that she will be ransomed, even where she herself was guilty of a capital offense. *Ḥelkat Meḥokek* and *Bet Shmuel* explain that *Rema* is referring to the wife of a non priest, but he would agree with *Rambam* and *Shulḥan Arukh* that the wife of a priest is always forbidden, unless she was arrested for only a monetary misdeed, in a place where Jews are powerful." (*Rambam, Sefer Kedushah, Hilkhot Issurei Bi'ah* 18:30; *Shulḥan Arukh, Even HaEzer* 7:11.)

BACKGROUND

וּמַעֲשֶׂה שֶׁהָיָה, כָּךְ הָיָה **And the case that happened, happened that way.** The details mentioned in a Mishnah are generally scrutinized carefully in the Gemara, since statements are made in a certain form in order to teach us not only what was stated but also what was not stated. However, when reference is made not to a hypothetical case but to something that actually happened, conclusions cannot be drawn from the details of the event. For the story may have been told in this form for the sake of descriptive accuracy, and not for the purpose of drawing Halakhic conclusions.

The Halakhic authorities make similar distinctions with respect to later sources. A book that deals with questions that were actually asked is not to be scrutinized regarding the details of the cases, in contrast to a book of Halakhic decisions, or a book discussing questions of principle that were not actually asked. In the latter instance, every detail is likely to be significant.

TERMINOLOGY

אַף אֲנַן נַמִי תְּנֵינָא **We too have also learned thus.** This expression is used in the Gemara when proof is adduced for the ruling of an Amora from the words of a Mishnah or a Baraita. In general, the Tannaitic quotation does not deal directly with the subject at hand (for it would be surprising to have an Amora make a Halakhic ruling that had already appeared in a Mishnah), but the proof is usually more complex, stating that if one examined the matter closely one would reach the conclusion reached by the Amora, although he did not base his ruling on the Mishnah.

TRANSLATION AND COMMENTARY

a place where Jews are powerless, all imprisoned women have the status of captives: [1]**"Rabbi Yose the priest and Rabbi Zekharyah ben HaKatzav testified about a Jewish girl who was taken as a pledge** by the government and imprisoned **in Ashkelon**, because her family had failed to pay a debt to the local authorities. [2]When she was released, **the members of her family rejected her** and considered her to have the status of a captive woman. [3]**But** the **witnesses** who testified that she had been taken by the government as a pledge and imprisoned, **also testified that** while she was in the hands of the non-Jews **she had not** once **been in seclusion** with a man (so that it would have been impossible for her to have been raped in private) **and that she had not been defiled** by being raped in public. [4]**And the Sages said to** her family: You have no right to shun this girl. **If you believe** the witnesses when they testify **that she was taken as a pledge,** [5]you must also **believe that she was never in seclusion and that she was not defiled,** because both parts of the testimony were given by the same witnesses, and the mouth that forbade is the mouth that permitted. [6]**And if you do not believe** the witnesses when they testify **that she was never in seclusion and that she was not defiled,** [7]**do not believe that she was taken as a pledge,** since the sole evidence of her captivity is the testimony of these same witnesses." Thus, the authoritative ruling of the Mishnah in *Eduyyot* is that a woman who was imprisoned as a pledge in a place like Ashkelon is permitted to her husband only if she has witnesses who testify that she was not defiled.

וְהָא אַשְׁקְלוֹן [8]**But surely,** the Gemara continues, in **the case in Ashkelon** the woman was seized because of a **monetary** matter — the failure to pay a debt — and in such cases, according to the plain meaning of our Mishnah (before it was explained by Rav Shmuel the son of Rav Yitzḥak in the name of Rav), the woman should have been permitted to her husband without proof. [9]Yet **the reason** why the Mishnah in *Eduyyot* permitted the woman **was because witnesses testified in her** favor, [10]**but if witnesses had not testified in her** favor, she would **not** have been permitted. Thus we see that the Mishnah in *Eduyyot* was more stringent in its ruling than our Mishnah. [11]**Is it not** true **that there is no difference between** the case of a woman who is **taken as a pledge** to secure repayment of a debt, **and** the case of a woman who is **imprisoned** for a monetary offense? The same law should apply in both cases. Yet we see that the lenient ruling of our Mishnah was not applied in Ashkelon! Surely the only possible explanation is the one given by Rav Shmuel the son of Rav Yitzḥak in the name of Rav — that our Mishnah refers to places where Jews have power, whereas the Mishnah in *Eduyyot* refers to Ashkelon, where Jews were powerless. The Mishnah in *Eduyyot* explicitly ruled that in a place like Ashkelon all imprisoned women have the status of captives. Hence Rav's explanation is not original.

לָא [12]The Gemara replies: **No,** without Rav's statement we might have said that **if** a woman **was taken as a pledge**, the law is **different** from that described in our Mishnah, which deals with a woman who was

[1]"הֵעִיד רַבִּי יוֹסֵי הַכֹּהֵן וְרַבִּי זְכַרְיָה בֶּן הַקַּצָּב עַל בַּת יִשְׂרָאֵל שֶׁהוּרְהֲנָה בְּאַשְׁקְלוֹן, [2]וְרִיחֲקוּהָ בְּנֵי מִשְׁפַּחְתָּהּ, [3]וְעֵדֶיהָ מְעִידִים עָלֶיהָ שֶׁלֹּא נִסְתְּרָה וְשֶׁלֹּא נִטְמְאָה. [4]וְאָמְרוּ חֲכָמִים: אִם אַתֶּם מַאֲמִינִים שֶׁהוּרְהֲנָה, [5]הַאֲמִינוּ שֶׁלֹּא נִסְתְּרָה וְשֶׁלֹּא נִטְמְאָה. [6]וְאִם אֵין אַתֶּם מַאֲמִינִים שֶׁלֹּא נִסְתְּרָה וְשֶׁלֹּא נִטְמְאָה, [7]אַל תַּאֲמִינוּ שֶׁהוּרְהֲנָה."

[8]וְהָא אַשְׁקְלוֹן דְּעַל יְדֵי מָמוֹן הֲוָה, [9]וְטַעְמָא דְּעֵדִים מְעִידִין אוֹתָהּ, [10]הָא אֵין עֵדִים מְעִידִין אוֹתָהּ, לָא! [11]מַאי לָאו לָא שְׁנָא הוּרְהֲנָה וְלָא שְׁנָא נֶחְבְּשָׁה?

[12]לָא, הוּרְהֲנָה שָׁאנֵי.

LITERAL TRANSLATION

[1]"Rabbi Yose the priest and Rabbi Zekharyah ben HaKatzav testified about a Jewish girl who was taken as a pledge in Ashkelon, [2]and the members of her family rejected her, [3]but her witnesses testified about her that she had not been secluded and that she had not been defiled. [4]And the Sages said: If you believe that she was taken as a pledge, [5]believe that she was not secluded and that she was not defiled. [6]And if you do not believe that she was not secluded and that she was not defiled, [7]do not believe that she was taken as a pledge."

[8]But surely [the case in] Ashkelon was because of money, [9]and the reason was that witnesses were testifying about her, [10]but if witnesses were not testifying about her, no! [11]Is it not [that] there is no difference [if] she was taken as a pledge and there is no difference [if] she was imprisoned?

[12]No, [if] she was taken as a pledge, it is different.

NOTES

הוּרְהֲנָה שָׁאנֵי **If she was taken as a pledge, it is different.** According to all three versions of the discussion in our Gemara, the conclusion is that there is no difference between a woman taken as a pledge and an imprisoned

TRANSLATION AND COMMENTARY

imprisoned. We would not have attributed significance to the fact that the Mishnah in *Eduyyot* refers to Ashkelon, and we would have said that a woman taken as a pledge requires testimony (in Ashkelon and elsewhere) that she was not defiled, whereas a woman imprisoned for a monetary offense is permitted, in accordance with the plain meaning of our Mishnah, even in a place like Ashkelon, where the Jews are powerless. Therefore Rav needed to explain that this is not so, and that in a place like Ashkelon even a woman imprisoned for a monetary offense is forbidden, whereas in a place where Jews are powerful even a woman taken as a pledge is permitted.

אִיכָּא דְּרָמֵי לָהּ מֵירְמָא [1]The Gemara now presents a third version of the contradiction between our Mishnah and the Mishnah in *Eduyyot*. **There are some who put** the question **in the form of a** direct **contradiction** between two Mishnayot. [2]**We learned** in our Mishnah: "If a woman was imprisoned **because of a monetary offense, she is permitted to her husband."** [3]But, continues the Gemara, let us **consider the following contradiction** from the Mishnah in *Eduyyot*: [4]**"Rabbi Yose testified, etc."** From a comparison of these two Mishnayot we see that the authoritative ruling of the Mishnah in *Eduyyot* is that a woman who was taken as a pledge to enforce payment of a debt is considered undefiled only if she has witnesses to testify that she was not defiled, whereas our Mishnah ruled that a woman who was imprisoned for a monetary offense is permitted without proof.

וְהָא אַשְׁקְלוֹן [5]**But**, continues the Gemara, **surely** in **the case** that took place **in Ashkelon** the woman **was** seized **over** a matter of **money**, and in such a case, according to the plain meaning of our Mishnah, the woman should have been permitted to her husband without proof. [6]Yet **the Mishnah** in *Eduyyot* **teaches us that the reason** the woman was permitted **was because witnesses testified in her** favor, [7]**but if witnesses had not testified in her** favor, she would **not** have been permitted. Thus we see that the Mishnah in *Eduyyot* contradicts our Mishnah, and forbids all imprisoned women, even those imprisoned for monetary offenses.

וּמְשַׁנֵּי [8]According to this version, those who posed this contradiction **answered** as follows: **Rav Shmuel the son of Rav Yitzḥak said in the name of Rav:** [9]**There is no difficulty** in reconciling the two Mishnayot. Here, in our Mishnah, we are dealing with a situation **in which Israel has power over the nations of the world,** so that the non-Jewish authorities are careful to protect Jews imprisoned because of monetary matters, and the law of our Mishnah applies. In tractate *Eduyyot*, by contrast, we are dealing with Ashkelon, [10]which is a place **where the nations of the world have power over themselves** (i.e., over the Jews).

[1]אִיכָּא דְּרָמֵי לָהּ מֵירְמָא. [2]תְּנַן: "עַל יְדֵי מָמוֹן, מוּתֶּרֶת לְבַעְלָהּ". [3]וּרְמִינְהוּ: [4]"הֵעִיד רַבִּי יוֹסֵי, כו'".

[5]וְהָא אַשְׁקְלוֹן דְּעַל יְדֵי מָמוֹן, [6]וְקָתָנֵי טַעְמָא דְּעֵדִים מְעִידִים אוֹתָהּ, [7]הָא אֵין עֵדִים מְעִידִין אוֹתָהּ, לָא!

[8]וּמְשַׁנֵּי: אָמַר רַב שְׁמוּאֵל בַּר רַב יִצְחָק: [9]לָא קַשְׁיָא. כָּאן שֶׁיַּד יִשְׂרָאֵל תַּקִּיפָה עַל אוּמּוֹת הָעוֹלָם; [10]כָּאן, שֶׁיַּד אוּמּוֹת הָעוֹלָם תַּקִּיפָה עַל עַצְמָן.

LITERAL TRANSLATION

[1]There are [some] who put it [in the form of] a contradiction. [2]We learned: "Because of money, she is permitted to her husband." [3]But consider [the following] contradiction: [4]"Rabbi Yose testified, etc."

[5]But surely [the case in] Ashkelon was because of money, [6]and it teaches [that] the reason was that witnesses were testifying about her, [7]but [if] witnesses were not testifying about her, no!

[8]And they answer: Rav Shmuel the son of Rav Yitzḥak said: [9]There is no difficulty. Here, it is when the hand of Israel is strong over the nations of the world; [10]here, it is when the hand of the nations of the world is strong over themselves.

RASHI

ואיכא דרמי לה מרמא — לא מתני לה להא דרב שמואל בר רב יצחק אפירושא דמתניתין בלשון לא שנו, אלא רמי מירמא מתניתין וברייתא אהדדי, ועלה שני רב שמואל חילוק בין יד ישראל תקיפה ליד אומות העולם תקיפה.

TERMINOLOGY

אִיכָּא דְּרָמֵי לָהּ מֵירְמָא There are [some] who put it [in the form of] a contradiction. This term introduces a variant of a previous discussion, in which the discussion is organized in the form of a contradiction between two Tannaitic sources, followed by an Amoraic statement resolving the contradiction.

NOTES

woman; rather, our Mishnah is referring to a place where Jews are powerful, whereas the Mishnah in *Eduyyot* is referring to a place where Jews are powerless. The Jerusalem Talmud also cites this apparent contradiction between the two Mishnayot, but concludes that the Mishnah in *Eduyyot* is referring to a woman taken as a pledge, whereas our Mishnah is referring to an imprisoned woman. No mention is made in the Jerusalem Talmud of any distinction between places where Jews are powerful and places where they are powerless. The Rishonim agree, however, that the Halakhah follows the Babylonian Talmud. Hence the strict law of the Mishnah in *Eduyyot* applies to imprisoned women as well as to women taken as a pledge, and the lenient law of our Mishnah applies only in places where Jews are powerful.

LITERAL TRANSLATION

[1]"Because of a capital [offense], she is forbidden, etc." [2]Rav said: For example, the wives of thieves. [3]But Levi said: For example, the wife of Ben Dunai.

[1]"עַל יְדֵי נְפָשׁוֹת, אֲסוּרָה וכו׳". [2]אָמַר רַב: כְּגוֹן נְשֵׁי גַנָּבֵי. [3]וְלֵוִי אָמַר: כְּגוֹן אִשְׁתּוֹ שֶׁל בֶּן דּוּנַאי.

RASHI

הני נשי דגנבי — שבעליהן ניתלין, ודרך המלכות להפקיר ביתם ונשיהן. **בן דונאי** — רוצח היה ואלעזר שמו. כדאמרינן בפרק "עגלה ערופה" (סוטה מז,א). אבל נשי דגנבי הגונבים ממון — לא מפקרי.

TRANSLATION AND COMMENTARY

Where Jews are powerless and without influence, and the non-Jewish government persecutes them without compunction, then the law described in the Mishnah in *Eduyyot* applies, and every imprisoned woman is assumed to have been raped, even if she was imprisoned because of a monetary matter.

עַל יְדֵי נְפָשׁוֹת [1]The Gemara now considers the next clause of our Mishnah: "If the woman was imprisoned **because of a capital offense, she is forbidden** to her husband in the event that she is released, because the government does not try to protect its capital prisoners from sexual assault, since it does not expect them to be ransomed." Analyzing this clause, the Gemara looks for an instance in which a woman was seized for a capital offense and was later released. [2]**Rav said:** Such a situation can arise, **for example,** in the case of a thief's wife. In Talmudic times, thieves were hanged and their property was seized. Typically, the government would also seize the thief's wife and deny her protection against rapists. Thus, says Rav, the law of our Mishnah also applies where the woman's husband was executed in this way, even if the wife was innocent. [3]**But Levi said:** The situation described in our Mishnah could arise, **for example**, in the case of the wife of Ben Dunai, a notorious murderer. Only the wives of murderers were treated in this way, whereas the wives of thieves were treated like women seized because of a monetary matter, and held for ransom.

SAGES

לֵוִי Levi. Levi ben Sisi was a Palestinian Sage of the transitional generation between the Tannaitic and Amoraic periods. He was the outstanding student of Rabbi Yehudah HaNasi, editor of the Mishnah. He would sit before Rabbi Yehudah HaNasi and discuss the Halakhah with his other great students. Rabbi Yehudah HaNasi held him in great esteem, and sent him to be chief judge and preacher in the town of Simonia. He said of him that he was "a man like myself." In several sources it is told that he acquired a limp while trying to show Rabbi Yehudah HaNasi how the High Priest used to prostrate himself on Yom Kippur. It is also explained that this was a punishment for having reproached the Almighty in his prayers.

Toward the end of his life he went to Babylonia. There he renewed his close bonds with Rav — with whom he had studied under Rabbi Yehudah HaNasi — and he also became a close friend of Abba bar Abba, Shmuel's father. Shmuel was his student and colleague.

Rambam decided Halakhic rulings in accordance with Levi, against Rav and Shmuel, for in his opinion Levi was their superior. It is not clear whether Levi had sons or who they were. Some authorities believe that Bar Liva'i, who is mentioned in the Talmud, was his son. Others believe that Rabbi Yehoshua ben Levi, the famous Amora, was his son. These conjectures, however, have not been proven.

BACKGROUND

בֶּן דּוּנַאי Ben Dunai. Ben Dunai (or Dinai), a well-known murderer, is also mentioned in tractate *Sotah* (47a), where it is stated that his full name was Elazar ben Dinai (he was also known by the nickname of Teḥinah ben Perishah).

Ben Dunai is also mentioned by his contemporary, Josephus, who relates that Ben Dunai was the leader of a group of armed robbers and murderers in the Galilee for approximately twenty years, until he was finally captured

NOTES

כְּגוֹן נְשֵׁי גַנָּבֵי For example, the wives of thieves. Our commentary follows *Rashi*, *Rashba*, and most Rishonim, who explain that the Gemara is specifically referring to a case where the woman herself was innocent, but her husband was guilty of a capital offense. *Rashi* explains that in antiquity the authorities confiscated the property of people they executed, and in many cases their wives would be seized as well. In his comment on our Mishnah, however, *Rashi* explains that it refers to a case where the woman herself was sentenced to death. *Rashi* explains that if the woman's captors intend to execute her, they have no financial incentive to protect her from violation.

Shittah Mekubbetzet explains that the Mishnah does indeed refer to a case where the woman herself committed a capital crime, and that the Gemara is not explaining the Mishnah but rather adding additional cases. *Rema* notes that the disputes between Rav and Levi, and between Rabbi Yoḥanan and Ḥizkiyah, apply only when it was the husband who was guilty. In such a case, Levi and Ḥizkiyah maintain that the wife is forbidden only in the more severe cases, whereas Rav and Rabbi Yoḥanan maintain that she is forbidden whenever her husband is subject to execution. When she herself is guilty of a capital crime, however, she is forbidden to her husband in all cases, regardless of the nature of the crime or of the stage of the judicial process (see following note).

Meiri explains that the law does not distinguish between a woman who was herself sentenced to death and a woman whose husband was sentenced to death. According to this explanation, the Mishnah and the Gemara are both referring to both cases. *Meiri* argues that Levi is of the opinion that a woman who was herself sentenced to death is not forbidden to her husband unless she was guilty of murder, but not if she was guilty of theft. Likewise, Ḥizkiyah is of the opinion that she is forbidden only if sentence has already been passed.

Rambam cites the case where it was the woman who was guilty of a capital offense, and makes no mention of the case where it was her husband who was guilty. *Maggid Mishneh* explains that, according to *Rambam*, an innocent woman who was imprisoned because her husband was guilty of a crime is not forbidden to her husband. Rather, our Gemara, like the Mishnah, is referring to a case where the woman herself was guilty. The reason our Gemara mentioned the wives of thieves and murderers is because these women are usually accessories to their husbands' crimes, and have reason to fear for their own lives.

In the version of this passage found in the Jerusalem Talmud, this question is presented as part of the Amoraic dispute. Ḥizkiyah says that the law of the Mishnah applies only when the woman has been sentenced to death. But Rabbi Yoḥanan replies that it applies even before she is sentenced to death, and that the wife of a bandit is treated like a bandit for this purpose.

כְּגוֹן אִשְׁתּוֹ שֶׁל בֶּן דּוּנַאי For example, the wife of Ben Dunai. In ancient times, theft was a capital offense. Thus it is difficult to understand how Levi could distinguish between the wives of murderers and the wives of thieves. One would think that the law of the Mishnah should apply to any capital offense, so long as the authorities are not trying to pressure the husband into repaying a debt. The Rishonim give differing explanations of the Amoraic dispute in our Gemara, depending on their explanation of the Gemara itself (see previous note) and of the Mishnah.

Most Rishonim explain that our Gemara is referring to a case where the woman's husband was guilty of a capital offense, and the woman was seized together with her husband's property, even though she herself was innocent. *Rashi* explains that the government does not protect such prisoners, even in a place where Jews are powerful enough to compel the government to protect prisoners accused of monetary offenses. Rav and Levi disagree as to whether the

TRANSLATION AND COMMENTARY

אָמַר חִזְקִיָּה [1]The Gemara cites another Amoraic dispute about this clause of the Mishnah. **Ḥizkiyah said:** The law of our Mishnah applies, **when** the woman's husband, the thief (or the murderer), **has** already **been sentenced to death;** but until sentence is passed the law is the same as for monetary offenses, because the government protects its prisoners until sentence has been passed. [2]**But Rabbi Yoḥanan said: Even though** the woman's husband **has not** yet **been sentenced to death,** she is still forbidden, provided he was guilty of a capital offense such as theft (according to Rav) or murder (according to Levi).

MISHNAH עִיר שֶׁכְּבָשׁוּהָ כַּרְכּוֹם [3]Continuing the theme of the captive woman, the Mishnah rules: **If a city was conquered by siege troops,** [4]**all the priestesses** (the wives or daughters of priests) **who were found**

[1]אָמַר חִזְקִיָּה: וְהוּא שֶׁנִּגְמַר דִּינָן לַהֲרִיגָה. [2]וְרַבִּי יוֹחָנָן אָמַר: אַף עַל פִּי שֶׁלֹּא נִגְמַר דִּינָן לַהֲרִיגָה.

משנה [3]עִיר שֶׁכְּבָשׁוּהָ כַּרְכּוֹם, [4]כָּל כֹּהֲנוֹת שֶׁנִּמְצְאוּ

LITERAL TRANSLATION

[1]Ḥizkiyah said: And that is when they have been condemned (lit., "their judgment is concluded") to death. [2]But Rabbi Yoḥanan said: Even though they have not been condemned to death.

MISHNAH [3][If] a city was conquered by siege troops, [4]all the priestesses who were found

RASHI

משנה כרכום — ״מצור״ מתרגמינן כרכומא (דברים כ).

NOTES

government abandons interest in the wives of all its capital offenders, or only in the most serious cases; likewise, Rabbi Yoḥanan and Ḥizkiyah disagree as to whether the government loses interest before sentence is passed, or only afterwards.

According to *Rashi* and *Tosafot*, the law of the Mishnah applies even to the wife of a non-priest, because we suspect her of seducing her captors to induce them to spare her life. According to this explanation, if the woman was herself guilty of a capital crime, she would certainly be forbidden, regardless of the nature of the crime or of the stage in the judicial proceedings. However, if the husband was guilty of a capital crime, and his wife was seized together with his property, Rav maintains that we still suspect her of seducing her captors. Levi, however, maintains that this is the case only when her husband was guilty of murder; but when her husband was executed for theft, her chances of being released are good, and she does not resort to seduction.

Ramban, *Rashba*, and *Ritva* agree with *Rashi*'s explanation of the Gemara. But they argue that we are concerned about rape, not seduction, and that the law of our Mishnah applies only to the wives of priests. Accordingly, they explain that Rav is of the opinion that the wives of all capital prisoners are liable to be raped, even in a place where Jews are powerful and the government protects its monetary prisoners, whereas Levi is of the opinion that the wife of a capital prisoner can still complain to the authorities if she is mistreated, and this acts as a deterrent against rape, unless the husband was a criminal as vile as Ben Dunai, whose wife the government would not protect.

According to *Rambam*, as explained by *Maggid Mishneh*, the Gemara is referring to a priest's wife who was an accessory to her husband's capital crime and thus has reason to fear for her own life. Rav maintains that in such a case we suspect that she was raped, whatever capital crime was involved, whereas Levi maintains that we suspect this only if she was an accessory to murder; but if she was an accessory to theft, the government protects her from rape. Likewise, Rabbi Yoḥanan is of the opinion that she is forbidden at any stage of the judicial process, whereas Ḥizkiyah is of the opinion that she is forbidden only when a death sentence has already been passed.

The Rishonim had difficulty in deciding the Halakhah in this dispute. On the one hand, the Halakhah normally follows Rav (*Ritva*); on the other hand, Levi was Rav's superior in the Talmudic Academy (*Bet Yosef*). Likewise, the Halakhah normally follows Ḥizkiyah against Rabbi Yoḥanan, who was his disciple (*Ritva*), but in this case Rabbi Yoḥanan's explanation appears to fit the language of the Mishnah better (*Meiri*). *Ritva* cites an opinion that there is really only one dispute here, and that Ḥizkiyah's view is logically dependent on Rav's, and Rabbi Yoḥanan's on Levi's; but this explanation is not accepted by any of the authorities. In practice, *Rambam* rules in favor of Rav and Rabbi Yoḥanan, *Tur* rules in favor of Levi and Ḥizkiyah, and *Ritva* rules in favor of Rav and Ḥizkiyah.

כָּל כֹּהֲנוֹת All the priestesses. The Mishnah is referring to the law that a priest's wife who was raped is forbidden to her husband and must be divorced. *Rosh* notes, however, that the law of this Mishnah has wider ramifications. Thus a priest's daughter who was raped is forbidden to eat terumah, even if she was not married; and any woman who was raped — even if she was in no way connected to the priesthood — is forbidden to marry a priest in the future. *Rosh* explains that the Mishnah selected this language, instead of the more usual "all women are disqualified from the priesthood," because it wished to introduce the case of the next Mishnah (below, 27b), which specifically deals with the wife of a priest.

HALAKHAH

עִיר שֶׁכְּבָשׁוּהָ כַּרְכּוֹם If a city was conquered by siege troops. "If a city is besieged and sacked, all the women in the city are disqualified from the priesthood, like captive women. The women are forbidden only if the besiegers surrounded the city from all sides, so that not one woman could escape, but if even one woman could have escaped without being seen, none of them is disqualified on the basis of suspicion alone. *Rambam* rules that this law

---

by the Roman governor and taken to Rome.

Ben Dunai's activities apparently had political overtones, and his band of men were probably a partisan group that fought against the Roman authorities, though the sources do not explicitly state this. This would also explain why Ben Dunai was tried in Rome, and not in Eretz Israel. According to contemporary Roman law, political criminals who rebelled against the Roman authorities had all their property confiscated, including their wives, and this would explain why Ben Dunai's wife was forbidden, according to Levi.

LANGUAGE

כַּרְכּוֹם Siege troops. This word seems to derive ultimately from the Sanskrit *kunkuma*, and it was subsequently absorbed by other languages. The letter *n* was interchanged with the letter *r*, as a result of which it took on the Latin form *crocus*.

BACKGROUND

שֶׁנִּגְמַר דִּינָן לַהֲרִיגָה When they have been condemned to death. Since these thieves were accused of a crime punishable by death, and since the authorities tended not to defend the accused, it could be said that even though they had not yet been sentenced, they were already treated as condemned men. However, Ḥizkiyah maintains that since there is some chance that the suspect will be found innocent, his wife is not left unprotected so long as he has not been sentenced.

SAGES

חִזְקִיָּה Ḥizkiyah. The son of Rabbi Ḥiyya, Ḥizkiyah was a first-generation Amora. He and his twin brother, Yehudah, immigrated to Eretz Israel from Babylonia while they were still young. In Eretz Israel they studied with Rabbi Yehudah HaNasi, even though they were already considered important scholars in their own right. Rabbi Yehudah HaNasi held Rabbi Ḥiyya and his sons in high esteem, and maintained a warm relationship with them because of his high regard for their learning and piety.

Ḥizkiyah's brother, Yehudah, died young. Ḥizkiyah edited collections of Baraitot (as his father, Rabbi Ḥiyya, had done before him), and these are often cited by the Gemara as "the teachings of the School of Ḥizkiyah" (תַּנָּא דְּבֵי חִזְקִיָּה). Ḥizkiyah engaged in Halakhic discussions with other leading disciples of Rabbi Yehudah HaNasi. His own students included the noted Sage Rabbi Yoḥanan, as well as other Amoraim of that generation. Ḥizkiyah and his brother apparently earned their livelihood from commerce and from their extensive real-estate holdings. Ḥizkiyah lived in Tiberias and was buried there, near his father's grave.

BACKGROUND

בַּלֶּשֶׁת **A searching troop.** This term refers to a military unit sent to search an area, usually to collect taxes which the local residents sought to avoid paying. Such a military unit, though it did not carry out specific punitive action, was known to act arbitrarily within the city to which it was sent, since the soldiers had the right to enter any place they wished, to search it, and to strike out against anyone standing in their way.

TRANSLATION AND COMMENTARY

in it are disqualified. When a besieged city falls, the conquerors rape the women at will. Hence all the women in the city are assumed to have been raped, and are disqualified from the priesthood. As a result, wives of priests must be divorced, and daughters of priests are no longer permitted to eat terumah. [1] **But if** a priestess **has witnesses** to testify that she was not molested — **even** if she has only one witness and that witness would normally be disqualified from testifying, such as where the witness is **a male or a female slave** — [2] the favorable witness **is believed** and the priestess is presumed not to have been defiled, in accordance with the general practice of the Sages to show leniency in the case of captive women. [3] **But,** continues the Mishnah, **a person is not believed about himself.** Hence a priestess who, without producing proof, insists that she was not defiled, is not believed. Likewise, the priest who is the woman's husband is not believed when he claims, without proof, that he knows that his wife was not violated.

GEMARA וּרְמִינְהוּ [4] The Gemara **presents a contradiction** to the ruling of our Mishnah from another Mishnah (*Avodah Zarah* 70b), one dealing with the laws of wine used for pagan libations (*nesekh*). Wine used as a libation in an idolatrous ceremony is forbidden by Torah law, and the Rabbis extended this prohibition to include any wine owned by non-Jews, or handled by non-Jews in an open container (see note). The Mishnah deals with a band of non-Jewish troops who sacked a city. In the Mishnaic and Talmudic periods, roving bands of semi-official privateers would live off the land, raiding cities in their path. In time of war, these men might be hired by the government to attack enemy cities, and in time of peace they would extort supplies and money from unprotected cities. When such a band sacked a city, there was no way of preventing them from violating the women, or from taking anything they pleased. [5] The Mishnah declares: **"If** a band of non-Jewish **search troops come to a city,** any wine they may have handled there must be considered '*nesekh* wine,' in accordance with the decree of the Rabbis. [6] If the raid takes place **in a time of peace,** when the troops are extorting supplies from the city before going on their way, only the

LITERAL TRANSLATION

in it are disqualified. [1] But if they have witnesses, even a slave, even a maidservant, [2] they are believed. [3] But a man is not believed about himself. **GEMARA** [4] But consider [the following] contradiction: [5] "If a searching troop came to a city, [6] in time of peace,

בְּתוֹכָהּ פְּסוּלוֹת. וְאִם יֵשׁ לָהֶן עֵדִים, אֲפִילוּ עֶבֶד, אֲפִילוּ שִׁפְחָה, [2] הֲרֵי אֵלּוּ נֶאֱמָנִין. [3] וְאֵין נֶאֱמָן אָדָם עַל יְדֵי עַצְמוֹ. **גמרא** [4] וּרְמִינְהוּ: [5] "בַּלֶּשֶׁת שֶׁבָּאָה לָעִיר, [6] בִּשְׁעַת שָׁלוֹם,

RASHI

פסולות — אסורות לבעליהן, דאשת כהן אסורה באונס.
גמרא בלשת — חיל. על שם שמחפשים כל המטמונים.

NOTES

בִּשְׁעַת שָׁלוֹם **In time of peace.** The Mishnah rules that in peacetime open barrels of wine are forbidden, but sealed barrels are permitted. *Ran* explains that we may assume that a sealed barrel has not been opened, for if the troops had opened it, they would not have troubled to reseal it. He notes, however, that where the barrel was not sealed, but merely plugged with a cork, the normal practice of someone drinking from it is automatically to replug it. Hence, even plugged barrels are forbidden in peacetime, because we suspect that the troops opened them and replugged them.

HALAKHAH

applies only if the city was sacked by soldiers of the same country, who have nothing to fear from opposing forces, and thus have plenty of opportunity to rape and plunder at will. But if the city is sacked by a foreign army on the move, the women are permitted, because the soldiers do not have time to rape them, following the statement of Rabbi Yitzḥak bar Elazar in the name of Ḥizkiyah, as explained by *Rabbenu Ḥananel*. Some authorities (*Rif, Ramban, Rashba, Rosh*) say, however, that the law applies even if the city was sacked by a foreign army, because the soldiers will always find time to rape, following the opinion of Rav Mari. *Bet Shmuel* adds that, even according to *Rambam*, this law does apply to a foreign army if it has completed its victory and has no more to fear from its enemies." (*Rambam, Sefer Kedushah, Hilkhot Issurei Bi'ah* 18:26,27,29; *Shulḥan Arukh, Even HaEzer* 7:10.)

וְאִם יֵשׁ לָהֶן עֵדִים **But if they have witnesses.** "A woman who was in a city that was besieged and sacked has the status of a captive woman. If she was at least three years old, we assume that she was raped, and she is disqualified from the priesthood. Any captive woman who has a witness who can testify that she was never secluded with a non-Jew is permitted. Even a male or a female slave or a relative is believed for this purpose, because the prohibition of a captive woman is of Rabbinic status, and the Rabbis were lenient in such cases. Her husband, however, cannot testify in her favor, since a person cannot testify on his own behalf." (*Rambam, Sefer Kedushah, Hilkhot Issurei Bi'ah* 18:17,19,26; *Shulḥan Arukh, Even HaEzer* 7:1,2,10.)

בַּלֶּשֶׁת שֶׁבָּאָה לָעִיר **If a searching troop came to a city.** "If a company of soldiers enters a city in time of peace, all

חָבִיּוֹת פְּתוּחוֹת אֲסוּרוֹת, [1]סְתוּמוֹת מוּתָּרוֹת. [2]בִּשְׁעַת מִלְחָמָה, אֵלּוּ וְאֵלּוּ מוּתָּרוֹת, [3]לְפִי שֶׁאֵין פְּנַאי לְנַסֵּךְ״. [4]אָמַר רַב מָרִי: לִבְעוֹל יֵשׁ פְּנַאי. [5]לְנַסֵּךְ אֵין פְּנַאי.

LITERAL TRANSLATION

open barrels are forbidden, [1][and] closed [barrels] are permitted. [2]In time of war, these and those are permitted, [3]because there is no time to make wine forbidden."

[4]Rav Mari said: To have intercourse there is time. [5]To make wine forbidden there is no time.

RASHI

לבעול יש פנאי – דתקיף להו יצרייהו.

TRANSLATION AND COMMENTARY

open barrels of wine in the city **are forbidden,** because we fear that the troops may have drunk from them. [1]**Sealed barrels,** on the other hand, **are permitted,** for if the troops had opened the barrels, they would not have taken the trouble to seal them again. [2]**In time of war,** however, all the wine **is permitted,** even that in open barrels, [3]**because** the troops have **no time to make wine forbidden."** When the troops are attacking a town by order of the king, they plunder it and do not have time to stop to drink. Thus we see that when a town is taken by besiegers in time of war, we assume that they have no time for anything but plunder. Why, then, does our Mishnah rule that we assume that the women in such a town have been violated?

אָמַר רַב מָרִי [4]**Rav Mari said** in reply: There is no contradiction between the rulings. When a town is besieged and sacked, the invaders have **time to rape** the women, [5]but they do **not** have **time to make wine forbidden.** The urge to rape is so great that military discipline cannot control it.

SAGES

רַב מָרִי Rav Mari. The reference here is probably to the Rav Mari who was a Babylonian Amora of the third generation (another Rav Mari was a fifth-generation Amora), and who became a disciple of Rabbi Yoḥanan in Eretz Israel. Rav Mari is regarded as a highly important Torah authority, and the Amoraim of the following generation regarded his Halakhic rulings and Aggadic teachings with great respect.

NOTES

בִּשְׁעַת מִלְחָמָה In time of war. This Mishnah from *Avodah Zarah* (70b) distinguishes between peacetime, when the troops have time to drink the town's wine, and wartime, when they do not. *Meiri* explains that in peacetime the troops do not attack the city, but take whatever food and drink they want before going on their way. *Rashi* and *Tosafot* explain that during wartime the troops are too busy plundering the city to spare the time to drink wine, whereas during peacetime they do not systematically plunder the city, and so have time to seize all the food and drink they please. *Rambam* reads here "peacefully" rather than "in peacetime," and states that only the wine in the taverns is assumed to have been touched by the troops. Presumably he would explain that we are referring to orderly troops who billet in a town before going on their way.

Rashi explains that the Mishnah's leniency in wartime is based on the reasoning of the Gemara in another passage on the same page in *Avodah Zarah*. The Gemara rules there that if a gang of armed robbers plunders a city and opens all the wine barrels, the wine is permitted, because we assume that they opened the barrels to see if there was money in them, and as soon as they saw the wine, they left the barrels alone without touching the wine. Similarly, troops in wartime are too busy looking for money to trouble themselves with wine. According to this explanation, the Mishnah would permit the wine, even when the troops themselves opened the barrels, so long as they were looking for money. *Ran*, however, rules that the Mishnah permits only barrels that were already open when the troops raided the city in wartime, because we assume that they did not have time to touch them; but if the barrels were opened by the troops, we do not permit the wine merely because we assume that they were looking for money. *Taz* explains that in practice the law depends on the circumstances of the raid. He notes that the troops who raided towns in his day (the mid-seventeenth century) found time both for pillage and for wine.

אֵלּוּ וְאֵלּוּ מוּתָּרוֹת These and those are permitted. The following is a brief outline of the laws of *nesekh* wine. By Torah law, anything that is offered as a sacrifice or as a libation to an idol is forbidden; it may not be eaten or drunk, nor may any benefit be derived from it. The Rabbis extended this prohibition to include any wine owned or handled by non-Jews. In some cases the Rabbis forbade deriving benefit from the wine, but in others (e.g., where the non-Jew was known to be a strict monotheist who never worshipped idols), they only forbade drinking the wine.

The formal reason behind the Rabbinic prohibition was the possibility that the non-Jew might have used the wine in some idolatrous way. However, the Rabbis were strict about this law, beyond any reasonable suspicion of actual idolatrous practice, because they sought to make it difficult for Jews to drink wine in the company of non-Jews, so as to interfere with social intercourse, as a measure to combat intermarriage (*Avodah Zarah* 36b).

As a result, the laws of *nesekh* wine are a combination of these two concerns. On the one hand, wine is forbidden as *nesekh*, even where there is no reason to suspect that it was used for an idolatrous purpose. On the other hand, wine that has been boiled is permitted, even if it is subsequently handled by a non-Jew (*Avodah Zarah* 30a). The Rishonim explain that this is because boiled wine may

HALAKHAH

the open barrels of wine are forbidden, but the sealed ones are permitted. For this purpose, a barrel that is merely plugged is not considered sealed. If the company passes through a town in time of war, even the open barrels are permitted, because the soldiers have no time for wine, but barrels that were opened by the soldiers are forbidden, following the Mishnah. *Shakh* adds that this law applies irrespective of whether the soldiers who attacked the city came from the same country or from a foreign country." (*Rambam, Sefer Kedushah, Hilkhot Ma'akhalot Asurot* 12:24; *Shulḥan Arukh, Yoreh De'ah* 129:12.)

TRANSLATION AND COMMENTARY

רַבִּי יִצְחָק בַּר אֶלְעָזָר [1] **Rabbi Yitzḥak bar Elazar said in the name of Ḥizkiyah:** Although it is true that troops generally find time for rape, even in wartime, there are circumstances in which they are not in a position to commit rape, and in such a case the women are permitted. [2] Rabbi Yitzḥak's statement is **dealing with siege troops from the same kingdom** as that to which the city owes allegiance. When the king orders a city in his own kingdom sacked, in order, for example, to quell a rebellion, he takes care to prevent it from being completely plundered, so that he can continue to rule over it. In such a case, we do not fear that the wine in the city was drunk by the attacking troops, nor do we fear that the women of the city were violated. [3] In our Mishnah, by contrast, we are dealing **with siege troops from another kingdom.** When the king's army sacks a foreign city, the king has no interest in protecting it from plunder. Hence, the invading troops take all the property, and although they do not generally have time to render the wine forbidden, the women in the city are all assumed to have been raped.

[1] רַבִּי יִצְחָק בַּר אֶלְעָזָר מִשְּׁמֵיהּ דְּחִזְקִיָּה אָמַר: [2] כָּאן בְּכַרְכּוֹם שֶׁל אוֹתָהּ מַלְכוּת; [3] כָּאן בְּכַרְכּוֹם שֶׁל מַלְכוּת אַחֶרֶת.

LITERAL TRANSLATION

[1] Rabbi Yitzḥak bar Elazar said in the name of Ḥizkiyah: [2] Here [we are dealing] with siege troops of that kingdom; [3] here [we are dealing] with siege troops of another kingdom.

RASHI

רבי יצחק בן אלעזר אמר — אף בבעילה פעמים שהן מותרות. ברכום של אותה מלכות — אינו רוצה להשחית את בני העיר, וכשכובש עיר הסמוך לממשלתו — שומרה, והיא לו למס עובד.

SAGES

רַבִּי יִצְחָק בַּר אֶלְעָזָר **Rabbi Yitzḥak bar Elazar.** A Palestinian Amora of the second and third generations, Rabbi Yitzḥak bar Elazar was apparently a disciple of Rabbi Yoḥanan. He is mentioned as debating with the other great Sages of his time.

NOTES

not be used as a libation in our own Temple, and hence we assume that the non-Jews would not use it for an idolatrous libation either. *Rambam* cites a tradition that this same exemption applies to all wine rendered unfit for use in the Temple (e.g., if honey was added to sweeten it). *Rosh*, however, maintains that the Gemara's dispensation permitting the use of boiled wine should not be extended to other cases, since the primary reason for the prohibition is the danger of intermarriage, and this has nothing to do with the quality of the wine.

כָּאן בְּכַרְכּוֹם שֶׁל אוֹתָהּ מַלְכוּת **Here we are dealing with siege troops of that kingdom.** Our translation and commentary follow the standard Vilna edition of the Talmud and *Rashi*'s commentary. According to this view, the statement of Rabbi Yitzḥak bar Elazar has no bearing on the Mishnah in *Avodah Zarah*. Rather, he accepts Rav Mari's solution to the contradiction between the two Mishnayot — that in wartime, troops have time to rape (as implied by our Mishnah), but do not have time to make libations (as implied by the Mishnah in *Avodah Zarah*) — and he makes an independent statement that even though our Mishnah rules that the troops have enough time to rape the women, there are circumstances in which we do not assume that this happened, namely, where the besiegers came from the same kingdom as the inhabitants of the city. In such a case, not only do we presume that they did not touch the wine, but we even assume that the women were not defiled.

According to this explanation, the Gemara objects to the statement of Rabbi Yitzḥak bar Elazar, arguing that even if the king ordered the troops to be merciful, one of the soldiers may have attacked the women in defiance of orders. And the Gemara answers that Rabbi Yitzḥak bar Elazar is referring to a case where the king set up watchtowers to discipline his forces, and took elaborate precautions, including chains and dogs and geese, to prevent insubordinate soldiers from entering the town. According to this explanation, the clause, "it is impossible that not one of them will run away," refers to the soldiers, and must be written in the masculine.

Most Rishonim reject this explanation. First, if the king ordered the soldiers not to violate the women, the situation is similar to the case of imprisonment for a monetary offense in a place where Jews are powerful, and in such cases we do not suspect that the women were raped (*Rashba*). Second, Rabbi Yirmeyah proposes (below) that in a case of doubt, if one of the women had a chance to escape the troops, we can be lenient and permit all the women. Why, then, should we forbid all the women because one soldier may have attacked the women against orders (*Tosafot*)? Third, the expression used by Rabbi Yitzḥak bar Elazar ("here it is the same kingdom, here it is another kingdom") suggests that he is trying to resolve the contradiction between our Mishnah and the Mishnah in *Avodah Zarah*, implying that he does not accept Rav Mari's solution (*Ramban*). In addition, the idea that the king would show more mercy to a rebellious city than to a foreign city is contrary to all experience (*Rashbatz*).

Accordingly, most Rishonim follow *Rabbenu Ḥananel*'s text of the Talmud, according to which the clause "it is impossible that not one of them will run away" refers to the women, and must be written in the feminine. According to this explanation, Rabbi Yitzḥak bar Elazar disagrees with Rav Mari's resolution of the contradiction between the two Mishnayot. He explains that the Mishnah in *Avodah Zarah* is referring to a foreign army, which neither takes wine nor rapes women, because it must maintain discipline, for fear that its enemies will attack it at any moment. °But our Mishnah is referring to a local army, which plunders and rapes at will. According to this explanation, the Gemara objects to the solution proposed by Rabbi Yitzḥak bar Elazar, arguing that even under the assault of a local army bent on plunder, some of the women might have escaped and hidden, and if even one of the women could have hidden, they should all be permitted (as Rabbi Yirmeyah proposes below). The Gemara answers that we are dealing with a king who took elaborate precautions, including the use of dogs and geese, to prevent the escape of rebels from the city.

Tosafot notes that *Rabbenu Ḥananel*'s explanation is supported by the version of this passage found in the Jerusalem Talmud. There, the Gemara says that our

LITERAL TRANSLATION

[1] Of that kingdom, too, [2] it is impossible that not one of them will run away!

[3] Rav Yehudah said in the name of Shmuel: When the watches can see each other.

[4] It is impossible that they will not sleep a little!

[5] Rabbi Levi said: For example, when they surround the town [with] chains, [6] and dogs, and branches, and geese.

[7] Rabbi Abba bar Zavda said: Rabbi Yehudah Nesi'ah and the Rabbis disagree about this: [8] One said: Here [we are dealing] with siege troops of that kingdom, [9] here [we are dealing] with siege troops of another kingdom, [10] and he had no difficulty at all [with these

[1] שֶׁל אוֹתָהּ מַלְכוּת נַמִּי, [2] אִי אֶפְשָׁר דְּלָא עָרַק חַד מִינַּיְיהוּ! [3] אֲמַר רַב יְהוּדָה אֲמַר שְׁמוּאֵל: כְּשֶׁמִּשְׁמָרוֹת רוֹאוֹת זוֹ אֶת זוֹ. [4] אִי אֶפְשָׁר דְּלָא נָיְימָא פּוּרְתָּא! [5] אֲמַר רַבִּי לֵוִי: כְּגוֹן דְּמַהֲדַר לָהּ לְמָתָא שׁוֹשִׁילְתָּא, [6] וְכַלְבָּא, וְגַוְוזָא, וְאַוְוזָא.

[7] אֲמַר רַבִּי אַבָּא בַּר זַבְדָּא: פְּלִיגִי בָּהּ רַבִּי יְהוּדָה נְשִׂיאָה וְרַבָּנַן: [8] חַד אֲמַר: כָּאן בְּכַרְכּוֹם שֶׁל אוֹתָהּ מַלְכוּת, [9] כָּאן בְּכַרְכּוֹם שֶׁל מַלְכוּת אַחֶרֶת, [10] וְלָא קַשְׁיָא לֵיהּ וְלָא מִידֵי.

TRANSLATION AND COMMENTARY

שֶׁל אוֹתָהּ מַלְכוּת נַמִּי [1] The Gemara objects: But even if the besiegers are **from the** same **kingdom** as the inhabitants of the city, the women in the city should still not be permitted. [2] For **it is impossible that not one of** the siege troops **will desert his post!** Military discipline in these matters is far from reliable, and it is virtually certain that rape will take place.

אֲמַר רַב יְהוּדָה אֲמַר שְׁמוּאֵל [3] **Rav Yehudah said in the name of Shmuel:** Rabbi Yitzḥak bar Elazar is referring to a case **where the** king set up watches to enforce military discipline over his soldiers, and the **watches could see each other,** so that there was no way to escape their surveillance.

אִי אֶפְשָׁר [4] But, the Gemara objects again, surely it **is impossible that** one of the watchmen **will not sleep a little!** No army is ever completely successful in imposing discipline.

אֲמַר רַבִּי לֵוִי [5] **Rabbi Levi said:** The situation is one **where, for example, the city is surrounded with chains** that rattle on contact, [6] **and dogs** that bark, **and** barriers of **branches, and geese** that cackle. If the government made a major effort to enforce discipline, we may indeed rely on this to permit the women and the wine.

אֲמַר רַבִּי אַבָּא בַּר זַבְדָּא [7] **Rabbi Abba bar Zavda said: Rabbi Yehudah Nesi'ah** (an early Amora, whose grandfather, Rabbi Yehudah HaNasi, was the editor of the Mishnah) **and the** other **Rabbis** of his generation **disagreed about this** statement of Rabbi Yitzḥak bar Elazar, and we are not certain which party took which position. [8] **One** party **said:** The women in the city are permitted when **we are dealing with siege troops from the** same **kingdom** as the inhabitants of the city. In such a case, we do not fear that the women were violated, because the king protects them. [9] In our Mishnah, by contrast, **we are dealing with siege troops from another kingdom.** In that case, all the women in the city are forbidden, although the wine is permitted. [10] Moreover, the Rabbi who explained the contradiction in this way **had no difficulty at all** in dealing with the Gemara's objections. According to his interpretation, governmental supervision was sufficient to reduce the risk of rape considerably, and we do not forbid all the women in a city because of a possible

RASHI

משמרות – מקום מעמד השומרים שהעמיד המלך שלא יחבל אדם באנשי העיר. **דמהדר למתא כו'** – שמו סביבות העיר שלשלות ברזל שישמיעו קול בהכשל איש רץ עליהם, וכלבים ואווזים זועקין. **וגווזא** – מקלות וקיסמין להכשל בהן. **ולא קשיא ליה מידי** – לא חייש למיעקר אינש יחידאה ולבעול, הואיל ואין הדבר הפקר.

NOTES

Mishnah, which rules that the priestesses are forbidden, is referring to a case in which besiegers surrounded the city with dogs and geese, and that it applies only if the besiegers come from the same kingdom; but if the besiegers come from a different kingdom, they are treated like ordinary bandits, and the women are permitted. On the other hand, *Rashi*'s explanation is supported by the parallel passage in *Avodah Zarah* (70b), where the Gemara is dealing with *nesekh* wine. There, the Gemara raises the contradiction from our Mishnah, and cites Rav Mari's answer alone, without that of Rabbi Yitzḥak bar Elazar. This suggests that Rabbi Yitzḥak bar Elazar accepted Rav Mari's explanation of the Mishnah in *Avodah Zarah*, and was merely making an independent comment regarding the law of our Mishnah, with no bearing on the laws of *nesekh* wine (see also following note).

פְּלִיגִי בָּהּ רַבִּי יְהוּדָה נְשִׂיאָה וְרַבָּנַן Rabbi Yehudah Nesi'ah and the Rabbis disagree about this. Our translation and commentary follow *Rashi* and other Rishonim (*Ritva, Meiri, Ran*). According to this view, in the dispute between Rabbi Yehudah Nesi'ah and the other Rabbis, one party held that the distinction made by Rabbi Yitzḥak bar Elazar between local armies and foreign armies applies only if the city was sealed off with watchtowers and dogs and geese. But the other party held that the distinction applies even without such elaborate precautions, because we are not concerned

SAGES

רַבִּי לֵוִי Rabbi Levi. A Palestinian Amora of the third generation, Rabbi Levi was particularly noted for his Aggadic statements and homiletical insights. He preached in the academy of Rabbi Yoḥanan for over twenty years, and Rabbi Yoḥanan praised his sermons highly.

רַבִּי יְהוּדָה נְשִׂיאָה Rabbi Yehudah Nesi'ah. He was the son of Rabban Gamliel, the son of Rabbi Yehudah HaNasi, and he was called "Nesi'ah" to distinguish him from his eminent grandfather, the editor of the Mishnah. Rabbi Yehudah Nesi'ah was among the foremost Palestinian Amoraim, and the greatest disciples of Rabbi Yehudah HaNasi were his colleagues, including Rabbi Yoḥanan and Resh Lakish.
The court of Rabbi Yehudah Nesi'ah introduced various ordinances, and was regarded as the greatest Torah center in the Jewish world, to the degree that even Rav, the great Amora, revised his opinions to agree with that court.
Rabbi Yehudah Nesi'ah served for many years as Nasi, and he seems to have been the last Nasi who was a great Torah scholar and served as head of the Sanhedrin. His place as Nasi, though not as head of the Sanhedrin, was taken by his son, Rabban Gamliel.

LANGUAGE

וְגַוְוזָא And branches. This word is apparently derived from the Persian *gavaz,* meaning "stick," "rod," or "branch," and is used in Rabbinic literature in the sense of rods or cut branches.

REALIA

וְאַוְוזָא And geese. Geese, particular male geese, jealously guard the areas where they live, making loud noises and attacking outsiders who attempt to enter their territory. Hence geese were used instead of watchdogs, to prevent people from trespassing.

[1]וְחַד קַשְׁיָא לֵיהּ כָּל הָנֵי, וּמְשַׁנֵּי: [2]כְּגוֹן דְּמַהֲדַר לֵיהּ לְמָתָא שׁוֹשִׁילְתָּא, [3]וְכַלְבָּא, וְגַוְוזָא, וְאַוְוזָא.

[4]אָמַר רַב אִידִי בַּר אָבִין אָמַר רַב יִצְחָק בַּר אַשְׁיָאן: [5]אִם יֵשׁ שָׁם מַחֲבוֹאָה אַחַת, [6]מַצֶּלֶת עַל הַכֹּהֲנוֹת כּוּלָּן.

LITERAL TRANSLATION

questions]. [1]And one had difficulty with all these [questions], and he answered: [2]"For example, when they surrounded the town [with] chains, [3]and dogs, and branches, and geese.

[4]Rav Idi bar Avin said in the name of Rav Yitzḥak bar Ashyan: [5]If there is one hiding-place there, [6]it protects all the priestesses.

TRANSLATION AND COMMENTARY

infringement of discipline by one or two soldiers. [1]On the other hand, the other Rabbi **had difficulty with all of** the Gemara's objections to this explanation, **and he answered** them as we did before: [2]The women are permitted only **if the city was surrounded with chains** that rattle on contact, [3]**and dogs** that bark, **and** barriers of **branches, and geese** that cackle. Only if the government made an extreme effort to impose order do we permit the women. But in other cases the law of the Mishnah applies, and the women are forbidden, even where the siege troops were from the same kingdom.

אָמַר רַב אִידִי בַּר אָבִין [4]Our Mishnah ruled that all the priestesses in the city must be presumed to have been raped, unless it is proved otherwise. Commenting on this, **Rav Idi bar Avin said in the name of Rav Yitzḥak bar Ashyan:** [5]**If there is one hiding-place there** in the city, where the women could have escaped the notice of the besiegers, [6]**it** is considered to have **protected all the priestesses,** and it saves them from disqualification from the priesthood, even though we do not know whether they in fact hid there. We assume that all the women hid there and were not raped, unless the contrary is proved, and we do not disqualify them because of doubt.

NOTES

about the possibility of an individual soldier raiding the city (according to *Rashi*) or of an individual woman escaping (according to *Rabbenu Ḥananel*; see previous note).

Shittah Mekubbetzet cites another reading, in the name of *Ra'avad*, in which there is a totally different version of the dispute between Rabbi Yehudah Nesi'ah and the Rabbis. According to this view, one party agreed with Rav Mari and maintained that there is no distinction between local armies and foreign armies, and that every army has time to rape but not to drink. This party explained the contradiction between the two Mishnayot without difficulty. The other party agreed with Rabbi Yitzḥak bar Elazar, and maintained that there is no distinction between rape and wine, and that the Mishnah in *Avodah Zarah* is dealing with a foreign army, and our Mishnah with a local army. This party can explain the Mishnah only by introducing dogs, chains, and geese.

Ramban, *Rashba*, and *Rosh* rule in favor of Rav Mari, since the Gemara in *Avodah Zarah* raises the contradiction from our Mishnah, and cites Rav Mari's answer alone, without that of Rabbi Yitzḥak bar Elazar (see previous note). The Rishonim interpret *Rif* as ruling in a similar way. *Ran*, *Ritva*, and *Maggid Mishneh* object to this view, however, since our Gemara deals at far greater length with Rabbi Yitzḥak bar Elazar than with Rav Mari. It is possible, however, that the Rishonim follow the reading of *Ra'avad*, according to which the conclusion of our Gemara is that there was an Amoraic dispute whether to rule in favor of Rav Mari or in favor of Rabbi Yitzḥak bar Elazar, and the opinion ruling in favor of Rav Mari entailed fewer problems in explaining the Mishnah.

All these Rishonim follow *Rabbenu Ḥananel*'s explanation of the Gemara, according to which a local army is more likely than a foreign army to rape the women. According to *Rashi*, there is no question that the Halakhah follows Rav Mari, because Rabbi Yitzḥak bar Elazar does not disagree with his explanation (see previous note).

Rambam (*Hilkhot Issurei Bi'ah* 18:26,29) rules that the women in the besieged city are forbidden only if the attackers were from the same kingdom and took elaborate precautions to prevent anyone escaping, following Rabbi Yitzḥak bar Elazar, as explained by *Rabbenu Ḥananel*. On the other hand, he also rules (*Hilkhot Ma'akhalot Asurot* 12:24) that the city's wine is permitted regardless of the identity of the attackers, following Rav Mari. *Ritva* explains that it is possible to say that Rabbi Yitzḥak bar Elazar and Rav Mari do not disagree (as stated by *Rashi*), and still maintain that a local army is more likely than a foreign army to rape the women (as stated by *Rabbenu Ḥananel*).

אִם יֵשׁ שָׁם מַחֲבוֹאָה אַחַת If there is one hiding-place there. *Ramban* reads: "Even if there is only one hiding-place" (אֵין שָׁם אֶלָּא וכו׳), and he asks: Why the emphasis on *one* hiding-place? If there is room for all the women in it, what difference does it make if there is only one place? And if Rav Idi bar Avin means that there are not enough hiding-places for all the women, how is his statement different from Rabbi Yirmeyah's problem below, about a hiding-place with only enough room in it for one woman?

Ramban answers that Rav Idi bar Avin may be referring to a place that had enough room for all the women. Nevertheless, it was important to mention that all the women, including the women who did not hide there, are permitted where there was one hiding-place, even though

HALAKHAH

אִם יֵשׁ שָׁם מַחֲבוֹאָה אַחַת If there is one hiding-place there. "If there was a hiding-place in the sacked city, all the priestesses are spared, following Rabbi Yitzḥak bar Ashyan. Even if there was only one hiding-place with barely

SAGES

רַב אִידִי בַּר אָבִין Rav Idi bar Avin. Rav Idi bar Avin belonged to the third and fourth generations of Babylonian Amoraim. Of Rav Idi's father, Rav Avin Nagara ("the carpenter"), it is told that he was especially punctilious in the ceremony of lighting the Sabbath candles, and Rav Huna predicted that Rav Avin would be privileged to have sons who were eminent scholars. Indeed, his sons were Rav Ḥiyya bar Avin and Rav Idi bar Avin.

Rav Idi bar Avin was a student of Rav Ḥisda, but he also quotes other Sages of the second generation of Babylonian Amoraim. He was one of the greatest authorities of his generation, and many of his Halakhic discussions with Abaye are recorded in the Talmud. Rav Idi was the chief Rabbinic authority in his city, Shekanzib, where he apparently had a yeshivah. Rav Idi lived to a great age, and the most eminent scholars of the next generation — Rav Pappa and Rav Huna the son of Rav Yehoshua — were his students. In his old age he called his students דַּרְדְּקֵי — "infants."

We know little of his deeds or the story of his life, except that he had two sons who were Sages.

רַב יִצְחָק בַּר אַשְׁיָאן Rav Yitzḥak bar Ashyan. A Babylonian Amora of the third generation, Rav Yitzḥak bar Ashyan was the teacher of Rav Idi bar Avin.

TRANSLATION AND COMMENTARY

בָּעֵי רַבִּי יִרְמְיָה ¹**Rabbi Yirmeyah asked: If** there was only a single, small hiding-place in the city, which **could hold only one** woman, ²**what is the law?** Presumably, one of the women is considered to have been protected, but the others must be considered to have been raped, and we have no way of knowing which one. There are two ways of dealing with this question. ³**We can say about each and every** priestess: "**This is the one** who hid in the hiding-place," and in this way we can give them all the benefit of the doubt. ⁴**Or perhaps we do not say this,** and we assume instead that all of them were raped, until we can determine which woman, if any, actually hid in the hiding-place.

וּמַאי שְׁנָא ⁵The Gemara now compares Rabbi Yirmeyah's problem with another well-known case, one dealing with the laws of ritual impurity. **But what is the difference between this case** and that described in the following Mishnah (*Teharot* 5:5): "**There are two paths** linking one place to another, ⁶and we know that **one** path **is ritually impure** [i.e., because a body was buried there] **and one is ritually pure,** but we do not

LITERAL TRANSLATION

¹Rabbi Yirmeyah asked: [If] it can hold only one, ²what is [the law]? ³Do we say [about] each and every one: "This is the one," ⁴or do we perhaps not say [this]?

⁵But what is the difference from [the following case: "There were] two paths, ⁶one ritually impure and one ritually pure,

בָּעֵי רַבִּי יִרְמְיָה: אֵינָה מַחֲזֶקֶת אֶלָּא אַחַת, ²מַהוּ? ³מִי אָמְרִינַן כָּל חֲדָא וַחֲדָא: "הַיְינוּ הָא", ⁴אוֹ דִּלְמָא לָא אָמְרִינַן? ⁵וּמַאי שְׁנָא מִ"שְּׁנֵי שְׁבִילִין, ⁶אֶחָד טָמֵא וְאֶחָד טָהוֹר,

RASHI

וּמאי שנא משני שבילין — דכיון דבא לשאול עליו ועל חבירו — אמר רבי יוסי טמאין, הכא נמי — לכולהו שרינן כי הדדי. אחד טמא — שיש בו קברות מפסיק כל רחבו, ואין ידוע איזהו הטמא, אבל כך מוחזקים באחד מהן.

TERMINOLOGY

בָּעֵי **He asked.** Generally a בָּעֵיָא — "problem" — arises from a given Halakhic ruling and raises a specific case of possibility which cannot be resolved by the existing ruling. A problem generally has two sides: i.e., someone asks a question (or the Gemara explains the questioner's position) showing that, in the given situation, two different solutions are possible. Frequently a problem (בָּעֵיָא) is raised with the purpose of sharpening the definitions and distinctions used in formulating the existing Halakhic decision.
The Jerusalem Talmud uses this term in a different sense.

SAGES

רַבִּי יִרְמְיָה **Rabbi Yirmeyah.** Born in Babylonia, Rabbi Yirmeyah was one of the leading Amoraim of the third and fourth generations. He studied in Babylonia in his youth, but soon thereafter immigrated to Eretz Israel. There, he was a disciple of the greatest Sages of the generation — the students of Rabbi Yoḥanan (Rabbi Zera and Rabbi Abbahu). Rabbi Yirmeyah had a special dialectical method of great acuity, and he used to ask provocative questions of his teachers and colleagues. Since these questions may have given the impression that Rabbi Yirmeyah was seeking to undermine the accepted rules of Halakhic dialectic, he was punished and removed from the House of Study for a limited period. Rabbi Yirmeyah's teachings are quoted extensively in both the Babylonian and the Jerusalem Talmud, so much so that in Babylonia his teachings are often simply referred to as "They say in the West" (i.e., in Eretz Israel).

NOTES

there was nowhere else to hide. Moreover, if there was only one hiding-place, the danger of discovery was great; nevertheless, the women are all permitted. Alternatively, *Ramban* suggests that Rav Idi bar Avin may have meant that there was only one hiding-place, and it did not have enough space for all the women. Nevertheless, Rabbi Yirmeyah asked about a hiding-place with only enough space in it for one woman, since the idea of permitting all the women because one of them had hidden appears less probable than permitting them when an indeterminate number had hidden, even if there was not enough room for them all.

שְׁנֵי שְׁבִילִין **Two paths.** This Mishnah is an application of the law that doubtful ritual impurity in a public place is treated leniently (*Rambam, Hilkhot Avot HaTumah* 14:1). *Rambam* explains (ibid., 15:8) that if a corpse is buried in a private place, and a person walks by in such a way that he does not know if he walked over it, we must be strict and consider the person ritually impure. But if the corpse was buried in a public place, the walker is considered pure. For this purpose, any place where three people congregate is considered a public place (ibid., 16:2).

Tosafot explains that even when we declare doubtful impurity in a public place to be pure, the doubtful impurity remains potentially capable of conveying ritual impurity. Thus, in the case of the two paths, it would be forbidden for one person to eat both items of food, because one of

them is definitely ritually impure. Likewise, if the man who walked along one path subsequently walked along the other, he is considered definitely impure. Moreover, *Tosafot* rules that even in a case where we declare both items of food to be ritually pure, the walkers themselves should purify themselves, even though they are legally pure, lest they subsequently walk along the other path and become definitely impure.

Tosafot brings support for his position from a passage in tractate *Shevuot* (19a). The Gemara rules there that if a person walks along one path and then along the other, and then enters the Temple without purifying himself, he must bring a sin-offering to atone for his transgression, even though a sin-offering may be brought only when a person is definitely impure by Torah law. Further support can be brought from another Mishnah in tractate *Teharot* (5:3). The Mishnah there rules that if a single person walks along one path and then touches food, and subsequently walks along the other path and then touches the same food, the food is definitely impure and must be burned. On the other hand, if he walks along one path and then touches food and then purifies himself, and then walks along the other path and touches a different piece of food, if he has already eaten the first piece of food, the second is considered pure, but if he has not yet eaten the first piece of food, both items of food must be treated as being of doubtful impurity, and should neither be eaten nor burned.

HALAKHAH

enough room in it for one woman, they are all spared, following the lenient side of Rabbi Yirmeyah's problem. *Bet Shmuel* notes that, although Rabbi Yirmeyah's problem is not resolved by the Gemara, *Ran* explains that we take a lenient view because the prohibition of a captive woman is of Rabbinic status." (*Rambam, Sefer Kedushah, Hilkhot Issurei Bi'ah* 18:27; *Shulḥan Arukh, Even HaEzer* 7:10.)

שְׁנֵי שְׁבִילִין **Two paths.** "If there are two paths, one ritually pure and one ritually impure, and one person walks along

one path and a second person walks along the other, and each of them then handles food that is supposed to be kept ritually pure, the law is as follows: If each of them comes separately to ask about his food, we tell each one that his food is ritually pure. If they come together to ask about both items of food, we tell them that both items of food are ritually impure, and in some cases (e.g., terumah), we order the food to be burned, following Rava's authoritative explanation of the Mishnah in *Teharot*, according to

[1]וְהָלַךְ בְּאֶחָד מֵהֶן וְעָשָׂה טְהָרוֹת, [2]וּבָא חֲבֵירוֹ וְהָלַךְ בַּשֵּׁנִי וְעָשָׂה טְהָרוֹת. [3]רַבִּי יְהוּדָה אוֹמֵר: אִם נִשְׁאַל זֶה בִּפְנֵי עַצְמוֹ וְזֶה בִּפְנֵי עַצְמוֹ, טְהוֹרוֹת. [4]שְׁנֵיהֶם כְּאַחַת, טְמֵאוֹת. [5]רַבִּי יוֹסֵי אוֹמֵר: בֵּין כָּךְ וּבֵין כָּךְ, טְמֵאִין״.

LITERAL TRANSLATION

[1]and [someone] walked along one of them and [then] dealt with (lit., 'did') ritually pure things, [2]and his fellow came and walked along the second [path] and [then] dealt with ritually pure things. [3]Rabbi Yehudah says: If this one comes to ask by himself and that one by himself, [the things] are ritually pure. [4]Both of them as one, they are ritually impure. [5]Rabbi Yose says: Whichever way, they are ritually impure."

RASHI

ועשה טהרות – נגע בטהרות. **טהורים** – דכל חד כי אתי לקמן תלינן ליה למימר בטהור הלך, דהוה ליה ספק טומאה ברשות הרבים – וספיקו טהור. **טמאין** – דהיכי נימא להו טהורים אתם? חד מינייהו ודאי בטמא אזל.

TRANSLATION AND COMMENTARY

know which was which. Two people went from the one place to the other. [1]**One walked along one of** the paths **and** then **handled ritually pure things**, i.e., he handled food that was supposed to be kept ritually pure, [2]**and his colleague came and walked along the second path, and then handled ritually pure things."** It is thus clear that one of the two people has become ritually impure, and has rendered the food he touched ritually impure, but we have no way of determining which one. There are two ways of dealing with this question. We can either say that each man was the one who walked down the ritually pure path, and in this way both pieces of food can be considered ritually pure, or we assume that both pieces are ritually impure, until we determine which of the paths was actually ritually pure. The Mishnah goes on to tell us that this question was the subject of a Tannaitic dispute: [3]**Rabbi Yehudah says: If** each **one** of the two people who walked along the paths comes **by himself** and **asks** a Rabbi whether his food is still ritually pure, the Rabbi should rule that **they are** both **ritually pure.** For both pieces of food are of doubtful ritual purity, and the rule is that doubtful ritual impurity in a public place is considered pure (see note). [4]But if **both of** the men come to the Rabbi **together** and ask about both pieces of food at the same time, the Rabbi should rule that **they are** both ritually impure, because it is impossible for both of them to be considered pure at the same time. [5]**Rabbi Yose says: Either way**, whether they come individually or together, the Rabbi should rule that both pieces of food **are ritually impure,** because it is impossible for both of them to be ritually pure."

NOTES

וּבָא חֲבֵירוֹ וְהָלַךְ בַּשֵּׁנִי And his fellow came and walked along the second. This Mishnah is an application of the law that doubtful ritual impurity in a public place is treated leniently (see previous note). Accordingly, both of the walkers are technically pure, since the doubts about their status relate to a public place. *Tosafot* (*Pesaḥim* 10a) explains that by Torah law this is true even if they both come to ask at the same time. Nevertheless, Rabbi Yehudah and Rabbi Yose agree that in such a case we declare both of them impure, because the questioners will not understand how we can declare both of them pure when one of them definitely had contact with a corpse.

Shittah Mekubbetzet brings support for *Tosafot*'s argument from a passage in tractate *Nazir* (57a) dealing with a Nazirite, who must bring a sacrifice if he becomes impure (Numbers 6:9-12). The Gemara declares that if two Nazirites walk along two different paths in a private place, they bring one sacrifice between them, and declare that it is to atone for the one who became impure. But if the paths are in a public place, they do not bring a sacrifice at all, because they are both completely pure. *Shittah Mekubbetzet* notes that the Gemara makes no distinction between a case where they came to ask at the same time and a case where they came separately, suggesting that this distinction is merely a Rabbinic consideration and does not affect the laws of sacrifices.

Rashi (*Pesaḥim* 10a) explains that this same Rabbinic consideration underlies the dispute between Rabbi Yehudah and Rabbi Yose. Rabbi Yehudah maintains that when one of the walkers asks about himself and his colleague, we can avoid confusion by simply answering his question about himself and ignoring his question about his colleague. Rabbi Yose, however, does not accept this argument. *Ran* explains that Rabbi Yose maintains that since the questioner knows full well that his colleague is in precisely the same situation as he is, the kind of response proposed by Rabbi Yehudah would appear specious to him.

HALAKHAH

which everyone agrees about these cases. Likewise, if one of the men comes to us to ask about his own food and that of his colleague, we tell him that both items of food are ritually impure and must be burned, following Rabbi Yose against Rabbi Yehudah." (*Rambam, Sefer Tohorah, Hilkhot Avot HaTumah* 19:2.)

TRANSLATION AND COMMENTARY

וַאֲמַר רָבָא [1]The Gemara now cites an authoritative explanation of this Mishnah. **Rava — and some say, Rabbi Yoḥanan — said:** Although Rabbi Yose appears to disagree with Rabbi Yehudah about the case where the two people came to the Rabbi separately, in fact this is not the case. [2]Rather, **both** Rabbi Yehudah and Rabbi Yose **agree that** if the men come to ask the Rabbi **at the same time,** he should rule that both items of food **are ritually impure.** [3]Moreover, they also **agree that** if the men come to ask the Rabbi **one after the other,** he should rule that both items of food **are ritually pure.** [4]**They disagree only** about a case **where one** of the men **comes** to the Rabbi and **asks about himself and about the other man.** [5]**One Sage** (Rabbi Yose) **compares it to asking at the same time,** [6]and forbids both items of food, **and one Sage** (Rabbi Yehudah) **compares it to asking one** after the other, and permits both items of food.

וְהָכָא נַמִי [7]The Gemara now explains how this Mishnah sheds light on Rabbi Yirmeyah's problem: **Here too,** in the case of the small hiding-place, **since all** the priestesses in the town **are being permitted** at once, [8]**it is like** asking at **the same time.** Even though the priestesses come before us separately to ask their questions, the issue clearly involves all of them equally, and it is as though each priestess is asking about herself and about all the other priestesses. Hence Rabbi Yirmeyah's problem is in fact the issue in dispute between Rabbi Yehudah and Rabbi Yose — and according to the Halakhah, which follows Rabbi Yose, the women should be forbidden.

הָכִי הַשְׁתָּא [9]But the Gemara rejects this comparison: **Now is this so?** Is this comparison valid? [10]**There,** in the Mishnah in tractate *Teharot,* **ritual impurity is definitely present,** and the only question is which food was rendered impure. In such a case, we cannot apply those lenient rules of doubt that we apply when all the cases are considered at once. [11]But **here,** in the case of the priestesses, even if we do not assume that this particular woman actually hid in the hiding-place, **who says that she was defiled?** The entire situation is marked by uncertainty, since it is always possible that the besiegers did not rape any of the women. Hence, the Mishnah from *Teharot* is not relevant here, and we can assume that each woman hid in the hiding-place, and we can permit her.

LITERAL TRANSLATION

[1]And Rava, and some say Rabbi Yoḥanan, said: At the same time, [2]all agree [that] they are ritually impure. [3]One after the other, all agree [that] they are ritually pure. [4]They disagree only if one comes to ask about himself and about his fellow. [5]One Sage compares it to [asking] at the same time, [6]and one Sage compares it to [asking] one after the other.

[7]And here too, since they are all being permitted, [8]it is like the same time! [9]Now is this so? [10]There, there is definitely ritual impurity. [11]Here, who says that [any of them] was defiled?

וַאֲמַר רָבָא, וְאִיתֵּימָא רַבִּי יוֹחָנָן: בְּבַת אַחַת, [2]דִּבְרֵי הַכֹּל טְמֵאִין. [3]בָּזֶה אַחַר זֶה, דִּבְרֵי הַכֹּל טְהוֹרִים. [4]לֹא נֶחְלְקוּ אֶלָּא בְּבָא לִישָׁאֵל עָלָיו וְעַל חֲבֵירוֹ. [5]מַר מְדַמֵּי לֵיהּ לִבְבַת אַחַת, [6]וּמַר מְדַמֵּי לֵיהּ לְבָזֶה אַחַר זֶה. [7]וְהָכָא נַמִי, כֵּיוָן דְּשָׁרֵי לְהוּ לְכוּלְּהוּ, [8]כְּבַת אַחַת דָּמֵי! [9]הָכִי הַשְׁתָּא? [10]הָתָם, וַדַּאי אִיכָּא טוּמְאָה. [11]הָכָא, מִי יֵימָר דְּאִיטַמֵּי?

RASHI

בבת אחת — באו לשאול בבת אחת.

הכא נמי כו' — ורבי יהודה ורבי יוסי הלכה כרבי יוסי.

NOTES

לִישָׁאֵל עָלָיו וְעַל חֲבֵירוֹ To ask about himself and about his fellow. There is a dispute among the Rishonim about this case. All agree that Rabbi Yirmeyah's problem is similar to a case where one of the walkers came to ask about his own food and about that of his colleague, at the same time. For even if only one of the women comes forward to ask about her status, and does not mention anyone else, it is clear that her question concerns all the other women in town as well.

Our commentary follows *Rashi,* who explains that the dispute between Rabbi Yose and Rabbi Yehudah concerns precisely this case, where one of the walkers asked about his own food and about that of his colleague, at the same time. According to this explanation, the Gemara was objecting that Rabbi Yirmeyah's problem was in fact the subject of a Tannaitic dispute in the Mishnah in *Teharot.*

Since we know that the Halakhah always follows Rabbi Yose in his disputes with Rabbi Yehudah (*Eruvin* 46b), we should follow Rabbi Yose's reasoning here too, and consider all the women defiled. *Ran* explains that in both cases — the case of the women in the city and the case of the walkers — we know that it appears illogical to declare everyone pure. Nevertheless, Rabbi Yehudah maintains that we do not argue along these lines as long as the question was asked by one party alone. Thus it is clear that Rabbi Yehudah would permit the women in the city, and the Gemara's objection is based on Rabbi Yose alone.

Tosafot explains that Rabbi Yose and Rabbi Yehudah agree about the case where one of the walkers came to ask about his own food and about that of his colleague, at the same time. He argues that it should not make any difference if the two questions were posed at the same

BACKGROUND

נְהַר פְּקוֹד, נֶרֶשׁ Nehar Pekod, Neresh. Nehar Pekod was a city situated near the Tigris River, north of Ctesiphon, whereas Neresh was located on the Euphrates, south of Sura. Nehar Pekod and Neresh were important commercial centers, and their residents were known to be particularly shrewd (see *Bava Metzia* 68a). Different roads led to these two centers, for Nehar Pekod was in the north, and Neresh was in the south.

LITERAL TRANSLATION

[1] Rav Ashi asked: [2] [If] she said: "I did not hide and I was not defiled," [3] what is [the law]? [4] Do we say: [27B] [5] "Why should I lie?"? [6] Or do we perhaps not say [this]?

[7] But what is the difference between [this and] the following case, [8] where a certain man who hired out an ass to his fellow said to him: [9] "Do not go on the Nehar Pekod road, where there is water. [10] Go on the Neresh road, where there is no water." [11] But he went on the Nehar Pekod road, [12] and the ass died. [13] He came before Rava. [14] He said to him: "Yes, I did go on the Nehar Pekod road, [15] but there was no water." [16] Rava said: Why should he (lit., "I") lie? [17] If he had wanted to, he could have said to him: [18] "I went on the Neresh road."

[1] בָּעֵי רַב אַשִׁי: [2] אָמְרָה: "לֹא נֶחְבֵּאתִי וְלֹא נִטְמֵאתִי", [3] מַהוּ? [4] מִי אָמְרִינַן: [27B] [5] "מַה לִּי לְשַׁקֵּר?" [6] אוֹ דִּלְמָא לָא אָמְרִינַן?

[7] וּמַאי שְׁנָא מֵהַהוּא מַעֲשֶׂה, [8] דְּהַהוּא גַּבְרָא דַּאֲגַר לֵיהּ חֲמָרָא לְחַבְרֵיהּ אֲמַר לֵיהּ: [9] "לָא תֵּיזִיל בְּאוֹרְחָא דִּנְהַר פְּקוֹד, דְּאִיכָּא מַיָּא. [10] זִיל בְּאוֹרְחָא דְּנֶרֶשׁ, דְּלֵיכָּא מַיָּא". [11] וַאֲזֵיל אִיהוּ בְּאוֹרְחָא דִּנְהַר פְּקוֹד, [12] וּמִית חֲמָרָא. [13] אֲתָא לְקַמֵּיהּ דְּרָבָא. [14] אֲמַר לֵיהּ: "אִין, בְּאוֹרְחָא דִּנְהַר פְּקוֹד אֲזַלִי, [15] מִידהוּ לָא הֲווּ מַיָּא". [16] אֲמַר רָבָא: מַה לִּי לְשַׁקֵּר? [17] אִי בָּעֵי, אֲמַר לֵיהּ: [18] "בְּאוֹרְחָא דְּנֶרֶשׁ אֲזַלִי".

RASHI

מה לי לשקר – אי בעיא אמרה נחבאתי.

TRANSLATION AND COMMENTARY

בָּעֵי רַב אַשִׁי [1] The Gemara now considers another problem arising from Rav Idi bar Avin's statement. **Rav Ashi asked: If** there was a hiding-place in the town, so that all the women can be considered protected by it, [2] but one of the women comes forward and **says: "I did not hide** in the hiding-place, **but I was not defiled,"** [3] **what is the law?** In this case, the woman admits that she did not hide, so we cannot permit her on that basis, and her claim not to have been defiled is not normally believed without proof. She does, however, have a *miggo* argument, because she could have claimed that she had hidden, and she would then have been believed. [4] Thus the question arises: **Do we say:** [27B] [5] **"Why should she lie?"?** In other words, do we accept a *miggo* argument and, without proof, believe her claim that she was not defiled, since if she had wanted to lie she could easily have claimed that she hid? [6] **Or do we perhaps not say this,** since the woman's claim that she escaped rape without hiding is hard to believe?

וּמַאי שְׁנָא [7] The Gemara now compares the problem raised by Rav Ashi with a well-known case of an implausible *miggo*: **But what is the difference between** Rav Ashi's problem **and the following case** (*Bava Metzia* 81a)? [8] **A certain man hired out an ass to someone else** and **instructed him** as follows: [9] **"Do not travel on the Nehar Pekod road, where there is** a great deal of **water,** and the animal may meet with an accident. [10] **Use the Neresh road** instead, **where there is no water."** [11] **But** the hirer disregarded the owner's instructions, and **took the Nehar Pekod road,** [12] **and the ass died** on the journey. There were no witnesses as to the route the hirer took, nor as to how the ass died. The hirer admitted that he took the Nehar Pekod road, but insisted that the ass died from some natural cause that could in no way be attributed to the route taken. [13] The parties **came before Rava,** and the owner demanded that the hirer pay for the loss of the ass, because he had disobeyed his instructions. [14] The hirer **said to** the owner: **"Yes, I did use the Nehar Pekod** road, [15] **but there was no water** there, and the animal's death had nothing to do with my disobeying your instructions." [16] **Rava said:** We can assume that the hirer is telling the truth when he says that the Nehar Pekod road was not flooded, because it can be argued that **he had no reason to lie** about the condition of the road. [17] **If he had wanted** to lie, he could have presented a claim more advantageous to himself, for **he could have said to** the owner: [18] **"I used the Neresh road,** as you instructed me, and the animal died of natural causes. Since he would have been believed had he made such a claim, and since no witnesses have come

NOTES

time by one walker or by the two walkers appearing together. Rather, the dispute between Rabbi Yehudah and Rabbi Yose concerns a case where one of the walkers asked about his own food, and then returned later and asked about his colleague's. In such a case, Rabbi Yehudah permits the food, since the questions were asked separately, whereas Rabbi Yose forbids it, since the questions were asked by the same person. According to this explanation, the Gemara was objecting that even Rabbi Yehudah would rule strictly on Rabbi Yirmeyah's problem. *Ritva* notes that this explanation fits the language of the Gemara better, since no mention is made in the Gemara that the objection was based on the principle that the Halakhah follows Rabbi Yose against Rabbi Yehudah.

TRANSLATION AND COMMENTARY

forward to testify otherwise, we should also believe him when he makes a claim less advantageous to himself — that he violated the rental agreement but that this did not cause the animal's death. Thus the hirer is not liable for the loss of the ass, and need not compensate the owner. [1]**But Abaye said to** Rava: The argument "Why should he lie?" is not effective here, [2]because **we do not use the argument of "Why should he lie?" where there are witnesses** who contradict the litigant's claim. Here the hirer's claim is contradicted not by the testimony of individual witnesses, but by the universal testimony of all who know the condition of the roads in the area. Everyone knows that there is always water on the Nehar Pekod road. Thus the hirer is liable for the death of the animal because he violated the owner's instructions and as a result the animal died. Rava accepted Abaye's argument, and ordered the hirer to pay damages. From here we see that an implausible *miggo* is not believed. This would seem to resolve Rav Ashi's problem. For there is a powerful presumption that captive women who do not hide are raped, and this woman wishes us to believe that she did not hide but was spared.

הָכִי הָשְׁתָּא [3]The Gemara rejects this proof: **Now is this so?** How can the cases be compared? [4]**There,** in the case of the ass, **there are definitely witnesses that there was water** on the Nehar Pekod road, and the hirer's claim to the contrary is extremely implausible. [5]**Here,** by contrast, do we know that the captive woman **was definitely defiled?** [6]**It is** merely **an apprehension, and** although we normally assume that captive women are raped, nevertheless **where there is** no more than **an apprehension** that rape may have occurred, [7]**we accept** the statement of a person whose claim is supported by a *miggo* argument. The woman's claim that she was not defiled is believed if she could have claimed that she hid.

[1]וְאָמַר לֵיהּ אַבַּיֵי: ״מַה לִּי לְשַׁקֵּר?״ [2]בִּמְקוֹם עֵדִים לָא אָמְרִינַן.

[3]הָכִי הָשְׁתָּא? [4]הָתָם, וַדַּאי אִיכָּא עֵדִים דְּאִיכָּא מַיָּא. [5]הָכָא, וַדַּאי אִיטַּמֵּי? [6]חֲשָׁשָׁא הוּא, וּבִמְקוֹם חֲשָׁשָׁא, [7]אָמְרִינַן.

LITERAL TRANSLATION

[1]But Abaye said to him: We do not say "Why should I lie?" [2]where there are witnesses.

[3]Now is this so? [4]There, there are definitely witnesses that there was water. [5]Here, was she definitely defiled? [6]It is an apprehension, and where there is an apprehension, [7]we say [this].

RASHI

במקום עדים – דלקן סהדי דכל שעתא איכא מיא. **ודאי אוטמו** – בתמיה.

BACKGROUND

״מַה לִּי לְשַׁקֵּר?״ בִּמְקוֹם עֵדִים לָא אָמְרִינַן We do not say "Why should I lie?" where there are witnesses. Some authorities have stated, on the basis of other examples of this principle, that we never accept a *miggo* when there are witnesses. This applies not only when the witnesses deny the claim advanced by the defendant or challenge its trustworthiness, but also when there are witnesses who support his claim. This is because the *miggo* argument is valid only when we have no other evidence. But when there is concrete evidence, we no longer need to depend upon a supposition, and the decision is made on the basis of the quality and reliability of the evidence.

NOTES

מַה לִּי לְשַׁקֵּר? בִּמְקוֹם עֵדִים לָא אָמְרִינַן We do not say "Why should I lie?" where there are witnesses. A similar dispute between Abaye and Rava about the validity of a *miggo* where there are witnesses appears in tractate *Bava Batra* (31a). All authorities agree that the Halakhah follows Abaye, who rules that a *miggo* argument is worthless when it is contradicted by witnesses. A *miggo* is a logical argument, not a proof, whereas witnesses are the strongest proof possible. A *miggo* strengthens a person's claim, so that we give greater weight to it than to that of his opponent, since we can see no reason for him to lie, because he could have won his case by making a different claim. But if we are convinced that the claim is false, the *miggo* is worthless.

Ritva explains that everyone — even Rava — agrees with the principle that a *miggo* is worthless when it is flatly contradicted by witnesses. But Rava maintains that when it is possible to reconcile the testimony of the witnesses with the claim of the litigant, we accept the *miggo*, even where the reconciliation is farfetched. Thus in our case Rava would have agreed that the *miggo* was unacceptable if witnesses had come forward and testified that the Nehar Pekod road was in fact flooded when the man traveled on it with the ass. But here the witnesses said that the Nehar Pekod road was generally flooded, so that it was possible but unlikely that there was no flooding at the time of the hirer's journey. *Rambam* also appears to interpret this passage in the same way.

וּבִמְקוֹם חֲשָׁשָׁא, אָמְרִינַן And where there is an apprehension, we say this. The Gemara's comparison of Rav Ashi's *miggo* with a case of *miggo* where there are witnesses, and the Gemara's solution of this problem, are both difficult to understand. The Gemara knows full well that the prohibition of captive women is based on doubt, and that some of the women may not have been raped. How, then, could the Gemara have said that a woman who claims to have been spared without hiding is considered to be contradicting witnesses? And if the Gemara is referring to a case in which we are certain that the woman was defiled, what does the Gemara mean when it answers that the case of

HALAKHAH

מַה לִּי לְשַׁקֵּר? בִּמְקוֹם עֵדִים לָא אָמְרִינַן We do not say "Why should I lie?" where there are witnesses. "If a person hires out an ass to somebody, warning him not to take a certain route because it is flooded, and after the animal has died on the journey the hirer admits that he took that route but he claims that there was no water there, the hirer is liable to pay for the damage, because he deviated from the owner's instructions. The hirer's claim that he did not cause the animal's death is rejected, because there are witnesses testifying that the road he took was flooded, and the argument 'Why should he lie' is not accepted when the litigant's claim is contradicted by the testimony of witnesses." (*Rambam, Sefer Mishpatim, Hilkhot Sekhirut* 4:3.)

וּבִמְקוֹם חֲשָׁשָׁא, אָמְרִינַן And where there is an apprehension, we say this. "If there was a hiding-place in the city,

LITERAL TRANSLATION

[1]"If there are witnesses, [2]even a slave, and even a maidservant, [3]they are believed."

[4]And is even her own maidservant believed? [5]But consider [the following] contradiction: "She must not be alone with him

[1]״אִם יֵשׁ עֵדִים, [2]אֲפִילּוּ עֶבֶד, וַאֲפִילּוּ שִׁפְחָה, [3]נֶאֱמָנִין״.
[4]וַאֲפִילּוּ שִׁפְחָה דִּידָהּ מְהֵימְנָא? [5]וּרְמִינְהִי: ״לֹא תִתְיַיחֵד עִמּוֹ

RASHI

לא תתייחד עמו — במסכת גיטין היא, שכיב מרע שכתב ומסר גט לאשתו על מנת שאם מת יהא גט למפרע ולא תיזקק לחליצה — לא תתייחד עמו שמא יבא עליה, והוה ליה גט ישן. ותנן: בית הלל אוסרין לפטור בגט ישן. ואיזהו גט ישן — כל שנתייחד עמה מאחר שכתבו לה וטעמא: גזירה שמא יאמרו גיטה קודם לבנה.

TRANSLATION AND COMMENTARY

אִם יֵשׁ עֵדִים [1]The Gemara now considers the next clause of the Mishnah: "**If** one of the priestesses in the besieged city has **witnesses** who will testify that she was spared by the conquerors — [2]**even** if she has only one witness, and that witness would normally be disqualified from testifying, because that person is **a slave or a maidservant** — [3]the favorable witness **is believed,** and the priestess is presumed not to have been defiled, in accordance with the general policy of leniency toward captive women. Only the priestess herself and her husband are excluded from testifying."

וַאֲפִילּוּ [4]The Gemara asks: The Mishnah made a general statement about accepting testimony relating to a captive woman from anyone — even a maidservant — except for the priestess herself. It would appear, therefore, that **even** if the only witness is the priestess's **own maidservant,** she is still **believed.** But is this so? [5]**Consider the contradiction** presented by the **following** Mishnah (*Gittin* 73a). That Mishnah rules that "if a husband has given his wife a conditional bill of divorce, and the condition has not yet been fulfilled, **she must not be alone with him unless there are witnesses** present, lest he have intercourse with her and

NOTES

the water on the Nehar Pekod road was certain, whereas the case of the captive woman was doubtful?

Our commentary follows *Shittah Mekubbetzet*, who explains that the Gemara initially thought that the claim that the woman was spared without hiding was not impossible but highly unlikely, because there is a strong presumption that all captive women are raped. The case is therefore similar to that of the ass, in which the hirer made a highly implausible claim that the flooding on the Nehar Pekod road had subsided when he traveled along it. (This explanation is also followed by *Rashi* in the parallel passage in tractate *Bekhorot* 36a.) The Gemara answers that the doubt in the case of the captive woman is greater than the doubt in the case of the water on the Nehar Pekod road. According to this explanation, the Gemara has not resolved Rav Ashi's question completely, but has merely made a distinction between this case and the case of *miggo* where there are witnesses.

Ritva has a different explanation of this matter, according to which the Gemara resolves Rav Ashi's problem completely. *Ritva* explains that Rav Ashi was referring to the case of Rabbi Yirmeyah (above, 27a), where there was only one hiding-place in the town, and this hiding-place had room in it for only one woman. We have seen that if a woman claims to have hidden there, she is believed. Rav Ashi was asking whether a woman who admitted that she did not hide there is believed on the basis of a *miggo* — since she could have claimed to have hidden there — or whether we reject the *miggo*, since the woman might have found it difficult to claim that she hid in the one hiding-place in town, and might have preferred to claim that she was not raped and did not hide. For a *miggo* is valid only if the person could easily have made the better claim but refrained from doing so out of honesty; but where the better claim is implausible, the principle of *miggo* does not apply.

According to this explanation, the analogy between the case of the captive woman and the case of the water on the Nehar Pekod road is not very convincing. For in the case of the Nehar Pekod road, it was the defendant's actual claim that was implausible, whereas in our case the better claim that the woman did not make was problematic. *Ritva* explains, however, that the Gemara wishes to prove from Abaye's ruling in the case of the ass that a *miggo* is generally not accepted when it involves an implausibility. But the Gemara answers that Abaye's ruling in the case of the Nehar Pekod road applies only if the defendant's claim conflicts with known facts; but if the claim itself is plausible, as in our case, the *miggo* is accepted, even if the better claim is somewhat problematic.

לֹא תִתְיַיחֵד עִמּוֹ She must not be alone with him. The Mishnah in *Gittin* refers to a husband who gave his wife a conditional bill of divorce, and then was alone with her between the time the bill of divorce was delivered and the time when the condition was fulfilled. Our commentary follows *Rabbenu Tam*, whose view is followed by *Rashi* here. They explain that when the couple are alone together, the problem of an "old bill of divorce" (גֵּט יָשָׁן) arises. There is a dispute between Bet Shammai and Bet Hillel as to the law if a man was alone with his wife between the time he drew up a bill of divorce and the time he delivered it (*Gittin* 79b). According to Bet Shammai, the bill of divorce is

HALAKHAH

every woman who claims that she was not defiled is believed on the basis of a *miggo* argument, even if she says that she did not hide. For the woman could have claimed that she hid," following the Gemara's conclusion that in a doubtful situation we do accept a *miggo* argument, even where it appears implausible. (*Rambam, Sefer Kedushah, Hilkhot Issurei Bi'ah* 18:28; *Shulḥan Arukh, Even HaEzer* 7:10.)

לֹא תִתְיַיחֵד עִמּוֹ She must not be alone with him. "If a husband gives his wife a conditional bill of divorce and the

TRANSLATION AND COMMENTARY

thereby invalidate the bill of divorce." For the Rabbis decreed (*Gittin* 79b) that if a husband and wife are alone together between the time that a bill of divorce is drawn up and the time that it takes effect, the bill must be discarded and a new one drawn up. But the Mishnah rules that, for this purpose, "it is sufficient if one witness testifies that he was with them, [1]**even** if the witness is **a slave or a maidservant.** [2]**The only exception is** the wife's own **maidservant, because** her mistress **behaves in a familiar manner with her maidservant,** and may not be embarrassed to have intercourse in her presence." Thus we see that if a woman's own maidservant testifies that she did not leave her mistress unaccompanied, she is not believed. How, then, can our Mishnah rule that we believe a captive woman's maidservant when she testifies that her mistress was not raped?

אָמַר רַב פַּפִּי [3]The Gemara gives three answers to this question: (1) **Rav Pappi said: Concerning a captive woman** the Sages **were lenient.** Even though a maidservant is not ordinarily believed when she testifies about her mistress, the Rabbis were lenient in the case of a captive woman. They accepted her maidservant's testimony to avoid disqualifying her for the priesthood because of a mere doubt.

אֶלָּא עַל פִּי עֵדִים, [1]וַאֲפִילוּ עַל פִּי עֶבֶד וְעַל פִּי שִׁפְחָה, [2]חוּץ מִשִּׁפְחָתָהּ, מִפְּנֵי שֶׁלִּבָּהּ גַּס בְּשִׁפְחָתָהּ".

[3]אָמַר רַב פַּפִּי: בִּשְׁבוּיָה הֵקִילוּ.

LITERAL TRANSLATION

unless there are (lit., 'by the mouth of') witnesses, [1]and even a slave or a maidservant, except for her maidservant, [2]because she is familiar (lit., 'her heart is large') with her maidservant."

[3]Rav Pappi said: Concerning a captive woman they were lenient.

RASHI

ואפילו על פי עבד — דייה בעבד שהיה עמה. **שלבה גס בשפחתה** — ותשמש בפניה.

NOTES

completely valid, since the couple were still fully married at the time. Bet Hillel, however, rules that the bill of divorce may not be used, because it was drawn up before the time they were alone together, and if the couple had intercourse and a child was born nine months later, people would think that the child was born out of wedlock. Rather, a new bill of divorce should be drawn up. (This is one of the rare instances in which Bet Hillel are stricter than Bet Shammai.)

The Halakhah follows Bet Hillel, and an "old bill of divorce" may not be used. The Gemara rules, however, that even Bet Hillel required that a new bill of divorce be drawn up only as a precautionary measure, but they did not invalidate the old bill. Thus, if the husband did divorce his wife with the old bill, the divorce would be valid and the woman could remarry.

According to *Rashi*'s explanation in *Gittin* (73a), the Mishnah is not concerned there about the problem of an "old bill of divorce"; rather, the concern is that the conditional bill of divorce may eventually take retroactive effect, and the couple may discover that they were not married at the time they were alone together. Indeed, according to one opinion cited in the Gemara there, in such a situation we would consider the divorced couple as having remarried, and they would require a second bill of divorce.

The dispute revolves around the Mishnah immediately preceding this one (*Gittin* 72a). In Talmudic times, it was customary for a man who was seriously ill to write his wife a bill of divorce, conditional upon his death. The purpose of this bill of divorce was to give his wife the legal status of a divorcee rather than a widow, in order to avoid the problems associated with levirate marriage. The Mishnah lists several ways of wording such a condition. Some of these conditions apply retroactively if the husband does in fact die; some apply moments before his death; and some are invalid altogether, because they theoretically apply only after his death, when it is too late to effect a divorce.

מִפְּנֵי שֶׁלִּבָּהּ גַּס בְּשִׁפְחָתָהּ Because she is familiar with her maidservant. The Gemara argues that just as a maidservant is not believed if she testifies that her mistress did not have intercourse with her husband, so too she is not believed if she testifies (in other circumstances) that her mistress was not raped. *Rashba* asks: The Mishnah in *Gittin* rejects the wife's maidservant's testimony because her mistress is not embarrassed to have intercourse in her presence. But how does this prove that the maidservant's testimony is not acceptable if she testifies that her mistress did *not* have intercourse? *Rashba* answers that the Gemara assumes that if the mistress is not afraid to have intercourse in her maidservant's presence, this implies that she trusts her not to talk about it to anyone. Hence it follows that if the maidservant testifies that her mistress did not have intercourse, she is not to be believed. According to *Rashba*, this argument is the basis of the dispute between Rav Pappi and Rav Ashi below.

HALAKHAH

condition has not yet been fulfilled, he must not remain alone with his wife unless there is another person in the room with them. The other person need not be a qualified witness. Even a relative, a slave, or a maidservant is acceptable. Her own maidservant or her minor child is not acceptable, however because the wife may not be embarrassed to have sexual intercourse with her husband in their presence." (*Rambam, Sefer Nashim, Hilkhot Gerushin* 8:2; *Shulḥan Arukh, Even HaEzer* 148:2.)

CONCEPTS

אֵין אָדָם מֵעִיד עַל עַצְמוֹ A man may not testify about himself. The principle that one may not testify about oneself is explained in various sources on the basis of the axiom that "a man is considered his own relative." Since one may not testify about one's relatives, even more so one may not testify about oneself. In general, any statement a person makes about himself does not belong to the legal category of testimony, but is a claim or a confession.

According to a general Halakhic principle which also applies in laws of testimony, a man's wife is like his own body (אִשְׁתּוֹ כְּגוּפוֹ), meaning that just as a man may not testify about himself, so too he may not testify about his wife, who is regarded as though she were part of him; by the same token, she may not testify about him.

LITERAL TRANSLATION

[1]Rav Pappa said: This [refers] to her maidservant; that [refers] to his maidservant.

[2]But is her maidservant not believed? [3]Surely it teaches: "A man may not testify about himself." [4]But her own maidservant is believed!

[5]Her maidservant is also considered as herself.

[6]Rav Ashi said: This and that [refer] to her maidservant, [7]but a maidservant sees and is silent. [8]There,

[1]רַב פַּפָּא אֲמַר: הָא בְּשִׁפְחָה דִּידָהּ; הָא בְּשִׁפְחָה דִּידֵיהּ. [2]וְשִׁפְחָה דִּידָהּ לָא מְהֵימְנָא? [3]הָא קָתָנֵי: "אֵין אָדָם מֵעִיד עַל עַצְמוֹ". [4]הָא שִׁפְחָה דִּידָהּ מְהֵימְנָא! [5]שִׁפְחָתָהּ נַמִי כְּעַצְמָהּ דָּמֵי. [6]רַב אַשִׁי אֲמַר: הָא וְהָא בְּשִׁפְחָה דִּידָהּ, [7]וְשִׁפְחָה מִיחֲזָא חַזְיָא וְשָׁתְקָה. [8]הָתָם,

RASHI

רב אשי אמר הא והא בשפחה דידה — והיינו טעמא דמתניתין מהימנא והתם לא מהימנא. דשפחה דידה מיחזא חזיא בקילקול גבירתה, ושתקה. **התם** — גבי גט.

TRANSLATION AND COMMENTARY

רַב פַּפָּא אֲמַר [1](2) **Rav Pappa said:** The Mishnah in tractate *Gittin* **refers specifically to** the woman's maidservant, whereas our Mishnah simply said "a maidservant" and **was referring to** her husband's or to someone else's **maidservant,** but not to her own. The mistress's own maidservant is not believed at all regarding her mistress, even if her mistress was a captive woman. But her husband's maidservant is believed, both in the case of the conditional divorce and in the case of the captive woman.

וְשִׁפְחָה דִּידָהּ לָא מְהֵימְנָא [2]But, the Gemara objects, is Rav Pappa saying that the captive woman's **maidservant is not believed** in the case of our Mishnah? [3]**Surely** the Mishnah **teaches** that any witness is believed, even a slave or a maidservant. The only exception is that **"a person is not permitted to testify about himself,"** which excludes herself (and her husband), but no one else. [4]**But** this implies that **her own maidservant is believed!**

שִׁפְחָתָהּ נַמִי כְּעַצְמָהּ דָּמֵי [5]The Gemara answers: **Her maidservant,** like her husband, **is also considered like herself.** The Mishnah is saying that in general a maidservant is believed. The only exception is if her testimony is tantamount to that of a person testifying about himself, such as when the maidservant belongs to the priestess in question.

רַב אַשִׁי אֲמַר [6](3) **Rav Ashi said:** Both Mishnayot **refer to her maidservant.** [7]**But** we suspect that **a maidservant** who **sees** her mistress doing something embarrassing **will remain silent** about it. Rav Ashi goes on to explain: [8]In the Mishnah in *Gittin*, **where** the **silence** of the witness **permits** the wife and makes the

NOTES

הָא בְּשִׁפְחָה דִּידָהּ; הָא בְּשִׁפְחָה דִּידֵיהּ This refers to her maidservant; that refers to his maidservant. *Shittah Mekubbetzet* asks: Why is his maidservant believed? Surely his maidservant would lie to protect her master, just as her maidservant would lie to protect her mistress! *Shittah Mekubbetzet* notes that it is not possible to explain that this is because the wife is closer to her maidservant than he is to his, because they are both women, since the Gemara later cites a Baraita which specifically disqualifies her manservant as well as her maidservant.

Accordingly, *Shittah Mekubbetzet* explains that even though his servants are just as loyal as hers, we are not afraid that his maidservant will lie to protect him. It is in the husband's best interest not to have relations with his wife if she is forbidden to him, and although the husband himself may be willing to sin rather than lose his wife, his servant will be more objective and will show genuine loyalty to him by telling the truth. In the wife's case, however, her servants may feel that there is an overriding consideration to protect her reputation, even if it means doing something forbidden; hence we are afraid that they will testify that she was not defiled, even if it is not true.

וְשִׁפְחָה מִיחֲזָא חַזְיָא וְשָׁתְקָה But a maidservant sees and is silent. Our commentary follows *Ritva*, who explains that the woman's maidservant is not suspected of lying to the court to protect her mistress, but she is suspected of misleading the court by telling only part of what she knows. Now, in the case of the conditional divorce, the maidservant need only say that she was in the room with the couple at all times for the bill of divorce to be valid. Hence the testimony of the wife's maidservant is not accepted, because we are afraid that if the couple did have intercourse in her presence, she would suppress the information and simply say that she was in the room. In the case of the captive woman, by contrast, the witness must expressly testify in court that the captive was not raped. Only such testimony is effective to make the captive woman permitted. In this case the wife's maidservant can serve as a witness, since there is no way for her to mislead the court without telling an outright lie.

HALAKHAH

הָא בְּשִׁפְחָה דִּידָהּ This refers to her maidservant. "A maidservant is believed if she testifies that a captive woman was not raped. The captive's own maidservant, however, is not believed, following Rav Pappa. But if her maidservant was speaking casually, she is believed," following Rav Pappa's explanation of the second Baraita. (*Rambam, Sefer Kedushah, Hilkhot Issurei Bi'ah* 18:19; *Shulḥan Arukh, Even HaEzer* 7:1,2.)

TRANSLATION AND COMMENTARY

bill of divorce valid, [1]the wife's maidservant **is not believed.** The witness only has to testify that he or she was present in the room whenever the husband and wife were there together, and this satisfies us that they did not have intercourse. But if the wife's maidservant was the witness, and the couple had intercourse (because they would not have been embarrassed to do so in the maidservant's presence), the maidservant would not tell us about it. Therefore the maidservant cannot serve as a witness in such a case. [2]**Here,** by contrast, in our Mishnah, **where** the witness's **silence forbids** the captive woman and disqualifies her from the priesthood, [3]the wife's maidservant **is believed.** A woman who was taken captive or was in a city when it was taken by storm is presumed to have been raped, unless a witness explicitly testifies that she was spared. Hence, even if the wife's maidservant was the witness, we have nothing to fear. For if the maidservant is silent in order to protect her mistress, we will still presume that her mistress was raped; but if she speaks out and explicitly says that her mistress was not violated, she is believed.

הָשְׁתָּא נַמִּי אָתְיָא וּמְשַׁקְּרָא [4]But, the Gemara objects, if Rav Ashi is correct, and the maidservant will attempt to protect her mistress by not telling us what happened, **now, too, she may come** forward **and lie** by telling us that her captive mistress was not violated, when in fact she was.

תַּרְתֵּי לָא עָבְדָה [5]The Gemara answers: **Two things she will not do.** The maidservant may be willing to conceal the truth for the sake of her mistress, but she will not be willing to give false testimony in court. [6]The Gemara brings support for the distinction between concealing the truth and testifying falsely from **the following story about Mari bar Isak,** [7]**and some say** that the story involved **Ḥana bar Isak.** [8]A stranger **came to him from Bei Ḥoza'ah** — a distant region — and claimed to be his **brother.** [9]The stranger **said to** Mari:

דִּשְׁתִיקָתָהּ מַתִּירָתָהּ, [1]לָא מְהֵימְנָא. [2]הָכָא, דִּשְׁתִיקָתָהּ אוֹסַרְתָּהּ, [3]מְהֵימְנָא.
[4]הָשְׁתָּא נַמִּי אָתְיָא וּמְשַׁקְּרָא!
[5]תַּרְתֵּי לָא עָבְדָה, [6]כִּי הָא דְּמָרִי בַּר אִיסַק, [7]וְאָמְרִי לָהּ: חָנָא בַּר אִיסַק. [8]אֲתָא לֵיהּ אַחָא מִבֵּי חוֹזָאָה. [9]אֲמַר לֵיהּ:

LITERAL TRANSLATION

where her silence permits her, [1]she is not believed. [2]Here, where her silence forbids her, [3]she is believed.

[4]Now too she may come and lie!

[5]Two [things] she will not do, [6]as [in] the following [story] about Mari bar Isak, [7]and some say: Ḥana bar Isak. [8]A brother came to him from Bei Ḥoza'ah. [9]He said to him:

RASHI

דשתיקותה מתירתה — שאינה צריכה שתעיד לומר לא שמשה, אלא שתאמר: אני הייתי עמה. **לא מהימנא** — להיות זו מותרת על ידה. דאי נמי חזיא — לא מסהדא. **הכא** — גבי שבויה. **דשתיקותה** — דשפחה. **אוסרתה** — לגבירתה, דכל כמה שאינה מעידה לומר טהורה היא — מחזקינן לה בטמאה. כי מסהדא ואמרה טהורה היא — מהימנא, דלשקורי לאו אורחא, אלא למשתק. **השתא נמי** — כיון דרחמא לה לגבירתה, או דדחלה מינה — אתיא ומשקרא, ואמרה: טהורה היא. **תרתי לא עבדא** — חדא למשתק בקלקולה, ועוד דתיתי ותשקר. **אחא מבי חוזאה** — שהלך אביו שם והוליכו עמו וגדלו שם, ומת אביו, וחזר לעירו ותבע חלקו בנכסי אביו.

BACKGROUND

מָרִי בַּר אִיסַק **Mari bar Isak.** He is mentioned in several places in the Talmud. Some authorities claim that there were two people of this name. However, it is possible that there was only one man, and that he lived to a great age.

Mari bar Isak was wealthy, and various Sages used to frequent his home. Nonetheless, the Sages believed that he misused his wealth, and for that reason they reversed the laws of evidence to his disadvantage. They also regarded his generosity with suspicion.

בֵּי חוֹזָאָה **Bei Ḥoza'ah** (this is a variant of the more commonly used place-name Bei Ḥoza'i). During the Talmudic period, the Persian kingdom was ruled by the Sassanid dynasty, and it was divided into large units similar to independent states. Bei Ḥoza'i refers to the area near the Persian Gulf, far from the centers of Jewish settlement in Babylonia. This area is known to this day as Huzistan — the Persian form of the Aramaic name Bei Ḥoza'i.

NOTES

תַּרְתֵּי לָא עָבְדָה **Two things she will not do.** *Ritva* asks: In the case of Mari bar Isak, the witnesses are prepared to commit one transgression (suppressing their evidence), but not a second one (testifying falsely). But in the case of the captive woman, if the maidservant saw that her mistress was raped and suppressed her evidence, she would not be committing any transgression at all, since we assume in any case that she was raped unless she can prove otherwise. Hence, testifying falsely would be the maidservant's first transgression, not her second. How, then, can the Gemara compare the cases?

Ritva answers that the number of transgressions is not significant. What the Gemara means is that a maidservant is prepared to suppress evidence to protect her mistress, but not to testify falsely. Hence, in the case of the conditional divorce, she is not believed, because she is capable of misleading the court by suppressing evidence, but in the case of the captive woman she is believed, since she cannot mislead the court without testifying falsely (see previous note).

Alternatively, *Ritva* suggests that the case may be one in which the captive comes with her servant to court and says, "I was not defiled," and the servant stands there saying nothing. In such a case, we would ordinarily interpret the silence as affirmation of the captive's story. But Rav Ashi maintains that a silent maidservant is not believed in this situation, because we suspect that she is remaining silent in court to protect her mistress. But if we asked the maidservant and she expressly confirmed her mistress's story, she would be believed, because a maidservant is willing to commit one transgression (misleading the court through silence) but not a second one (testifying falsely).

אֲתָא לֵיהּ אַחָא **A brother came to him.** The story of Mari bar Isak's brother presents a number of difficulties. The Rishonim agree that it is obvious that a stranger who suddenly appears and claims to be a rich man's brother is not believed without conclusive proof, and even if the rich man is known to be violent, his fundamental right to protection against baseless claims is inalienable. Why, then, did Rav Ḥisda need to seek Scriptural justification for Mari's denial? Even if his brother had had a beard, Mari

TRANSLATION AND COMMENTARY

"Divide the estate you inherited from **our father with me,** since I am your brother." [1] Mari **said to him** in reply: **"I do not know you!** Why should I accept your claim that you are my brother?" [2] The case **came before Rav Ḥisda** for judgment, [3] and **he said to** the claimant: **"What** Mari **said to you was reasonable.** It is quite likely that he does not recognize you because, even according to your own story, a very long time has passed since you were together. I can illustrate this from an incident in the Torah (Genesis 42:8), [4] where a similar situation **is recounted**: **'And Joseph recognized his brothers, but they did not recognize him.'"** [5] Rav Ḥisda then quoted the traditional explanation of this verse: **"This** verse **teaches** us **that** Joseph **departed without** any **sign of a beard,** as he was only seventeen (Genesis 37:2) when he was sold by his brothers into slavery, [6] **and he came** before his brothers as the viceroy of Egypt at the age of thirty-nine **with the signs of a beard.** On the other hand, the other brothers were older, and were already bearded when Joseph was sold. Therefore, Joseph had no difficulty in recognizing them, but they did not recognize him. Thus we see that it is possible that your brother may not recognize you with the passage of time, particularly if he last saw you, as you claim, when you were a child." [7] Rav Ḥisda then **said to** the claimant: **"Go and bring witnesses that you are his brother."** [8] **He said to** Rav Ḥisda in reply: **"I have witnesses,** [9] **but they are afraid** that Mari may harm them if they testify on my behalf, **because he is a violent man."**

"פְּלוֹג לִי בְּנִכְסֵי דְּאַבָּא". [1] אֲמַר לֵיהּ: "לָא יָדַעְנָא לָךְ". [2] אֲתָא לְקַמֵּיהּ דְּרַב חִסְדָּא. [3] אֲמַר לֵיהּ: "שַׁפִּיר קָאָמַר לָךְ, [4] דִּכְתִיב: 'וַיַּכֵּר יוֹסֵף אֶת אֶחָיו, וְהֵם לֹא הִכִּירֻהוּ'. [5] מְלַמֵּד שֶׁיָּצָא בְּלֹא חֲתִימַת זָקָן, [6] וּבָא בַּחֲתִימַת זָקָן". [7] אֲמַר לֵיהּ: "זִיל, אַיְיתֵי סָהֲדֵי דַּאֲחוּהּ אַתְּ". [8] אֲמַר לֵיהּ: "אִית לִי סָהֲדֵי, [9] וּמִסְתְּפִינוּ מִינֵּיהּ, דְּגַבְרָא אַלָּמָא הוּא".

LITERAL TRANSLATION

"Divide [our] father's estate with me." [1] He said to him: "I do not know you." [2] He came before Rav Ḥisda. [3] He said to him: "He spoke well to you, [4] for it is written: 'And Joseph knew his brothers, but they did not know him.' [5] [This] teaches that he departed without the sign (lit., 'signature') of a beard, [6] and he came with the sign of a beard." [7] He said to him: "Go, bring witnesses that you are his brother." [8] He said to him: "I have witnesses, [9] but they are afraid of him, because he is a violent man."

RASHI

אמר ליה — רב חסדא לההוא אחא. **שפיר קאמר לך** — שאינו מכירך, לפי שיצאת בלא חתימת זקן [ובאת בחתימת זקן]. **ויכר יוסף את אחיו** — שכשפירש מהן כבר היו חתומי זקן.

NOTES

should still have been believed if he claimed not to know him, as the burden of proof was on his brother.

The Rishonim offer two principal explanations. *Tosafot*, and apparently *Rashi*, explain that Mari did not deny the claimant's story. On the contrary, he tended to believe it, as he knew that he indeed had a long-lost brother. *Rashi* and *Tosafot* both suggest here that the brother may have been born in Babylonia and was taken by his father to Bei Ḥoza'ah while still an infant. In the parallel passage in *Bava Metzia* (39b), *Rashi* suggests that the entire family may have moved to Bei Ḥoza'ah, where the father married a second wife and had this infant son. Mari returned home after his father's death, whereas the infant brother remained with his mother, and only reappeared in Babylonia after many years. According to both suggestions, Mari knew he had a brother in Bei Ḥoza'ah. Nevertheless, he claimed that he was unable to recognize him, and demanded proof. Now, ordinarily, Mari's claim would raise suspicion: If the stranger was not his brother, why did Mari not say so directly? Nevertheless, Rav Ḥisda ruled that Mari's claim was reasonable, as he had last seen his brother when he was an infant, and could not be expected to recognize him now (see following note).

Ritva in *Bava Metzia* explains that Mari was indeed denying the brother's claim entirely, and his denial was acceptable even without Scriptural justification. Rav Ḥisda was not trying to justify Mari, but was trying to reassure his brother by explaining to him that Mari might have made an honest mistake. Either of these explanations would fit the story of Mari as told here; but the full version of the story of Mari in *Bava Metzia* presents difficulties for both explanations.

שֶׁיָּצָא בְּלֹא חֲתִימַת זָקָן That he departed without the sign of a beard. According to *Rashi* and *Tosafot*, Mari for fully aware that he had a long-lost brother in Bei Ḥoza'ah, but he insisted that he did not recognize this claimant. The brother argued that this was suspicious. If Mari was denying that he was his brother, why did he not say so directly? Nevertheless, Rav Ḥisda ruled that Mari's claim was reasonable, as he had last seen his brother when he was an infant, and could not be expected to recognize him now (see previous note).

The Rishonim disagree as to what the law is in a case where the brother lost contact after he was already an adult. *Ritva* argues that if a man admits the existence of a long-lost brother, but says that he does not recognize a particular claimant, his claim is rejected unless he expressly denies that the claimant is his brother. *Or Zarua*, however, rules that the claim is not rejected, although it appears dubious. He rules that even in a case where there are several brothers, and all of them admit that there is a long-lost brother, and a stranger comes forward, and one of the brothers recognizes him, and the other brothers say that they do not recognize him, even in such a case the other brothers are within their rights in demanding proof, even though their refusal to deny the stranger's claim outright is suspicious.

LITERAL TRANSLATION

[1] He said to [Mari] himself: "You go [and] bring them [to testify] that he is not your brother." [2] He said to him: "Is this the law? [3] Whoever seeks to take [something] away from his fellow, upon him is the [burden of] proof!" [4] He said to him: "This is how I judge you and all your violent friends."

[5] Now too they may come and lie!

[6] Two [things] they will not do.

[1] אֲמַר לֵיהּ לְדִידֵיהּ: "זִיל אַיְיתִינְהוּ אַתְּ דְּלָאו אֲחוּךְ הוּא". [2] אֲמַר לֵיהּ: "דִּינָא הָכִי? [3] הַמּוֹצִיא מֵחֲבֵירוֹ עָלָיו הָרְאָיָה!" [4] אֲמַר לֵיהּ: "הָכִי דָּאֵינְנָא לָךְ וּלְכוּלְּהוּ אַלָּמֵי חַבְרָךְ".

[5] הַשְׁתָּא נַמִי אָתוּ וּמְשַׁקְּרֵי!

[6] תַּרְתֵּי לָא עָבְדֵי.

RASHI

אמר ליה — רב חסדא למרי. **זיל אייתינהו את** — להנהו סהדי המכירין אותו, ויעידון שאינו בן אביך. **השתא נמי** — כיון דדחלי מיניה אתו ומשקרי. **תרתי לא עבדי** — חדא דשתקי מלהעיד אמת, וחדא דמסהדי שיקרא.

TRANSLATION AND COMMENTARY

[1] Rav Ḥisda then turned **to Mari himself** and **said: "You go and bring** the witnesses that the man claiming to be your brother has named, and we will see if they **testify that he is not your brother.** Or bring other witnesses of your own." [2] Mari then **said to** Rav Ḥisda: **"Is this the law?** [3] Surely the law is that whenever **anyone seeks to take something away from another person, the burden of proof falls upon** the plaintiff! Thus the burden of proof should fall upon the claimant, not upon me!" [4] Rav Ḥisda **said to him** in reply: **"This is the way** I propose to **judge you and all your violent friends.** Since you are known to be violent, I am ordering *you* to bring the witnesses."

הַשְׁתָּא נַמִי אָתוּ וּמְשַׁקְּרֵי [5] The Gemara objects to Rav Ḥisda's ruling: If Rav Ḥisda was so concerned about the witnesses being too frightened to testify on behalf of the claimant, what good would it do if Mari were to bring them? **Now, too, they may come and lie**, rather than risk Mari's violent reaction!

תַּרְתֵּי לָא עָבְדֵי [6] The Gemara answers that Rav Ḥisda was not afraid that Mari would influence the witnesses to lie in court, as witnesses may do one forbidden thing out of fear, such as refusing to give evidence, but **they will not do two things**, such as refraining from telling the truth and testifying falsely. Thus we see that even if a person is suspected of withholding evidence in order to protect someone, he is not suspected of actively lying for him. Hence, the woman's maidservant is not believed in the case of the conditional divorce, because she may be misleading us by withholding part of her testimony; but she is believed in the case of the captive woman, because in that case she must testify positively that her mistress was not violated.

The Gemara has now quoted three explanations of the apparent contradiction between our Mishnah and the Mishnah in *Gittin*. According to Rav Pappi, a captive woman's maidservant is believed when she testifies that her mistress was not defiled, whereas a woman's maidservant is not believed in the case of a conditional divorce because the Rabbis were lenient concerning captive women. Likewise, according to Rav Ashi, the captive woman's maidservant is believed when she testifies that her mistress was not defiled, whereas a woman's maidservant is not believed in the case of a conditional divorce because we believe the maidservant when she testifies positively, but not when she is silent. According to Rav Pappa, however, there is no difference between the case of the captive woman and the case of the conditional divorce. In both cases, the priestess's own maidservant is not believed, and our Mishnah is referring to other maidservants.

NOTES

זִיל אַיְיתִינְהוּ אַתְּ **You go and bring them.** The Rishonim agree that even a violent person is not considered guilty without proof, so Rav Ḥisda could not have been ordering Mari to disprove his brother's uncorroborated assertion. *Tosafot* explains that we are referring to a case where the brother's witnesses gave a clear indication that they were afraid to testify.

Tosafot also says that Rav Ḥisda did not order Mari to bring witnesses of his own; rather, Mari was ordered to bring the witnesses named by his purported brother, who were allegedly afraid to come forward on their own. This is the position adopted by most Rishonim, including *Rashi* here. In *Bava Metzia*, however, *Rashi* explains that Rav Ḥisda told Mari that if he could not bring his brother's witnesses, he would have to bring witnesses of his own to prove that the stranger was not his brother. *Rashba* and *Ritva* reject this explanation, arguing that even a violent man has rights, and such a demand is unreasonable.

HALAKHAH

הָכִי דָּאֵינְנָא לָךְ וּלְכוּלְּהוּ אַלָּמֵי חַבְרָךְ **This is how I judge you and all your violent friends.** "If the court knows (based on positive proof — *Rema*; and see *Sma*) that one of the litigants is a violent person, and the other litigant maintains that he has witnesses to support his claim but says that they are afraid of the violent litigant, the court compels the violent litigant to bring the witnesses himself," following Rav Ḥisda's ruling here. (*Rambam, Sefer Shofetim, Hilkhot Edut* 3:12; *Shulḥan Arukh, Ḥoshen Mishpat* 28:5.)

TERMINOLOGY

לֵימָא כְּתַנָּאֵי Shall we say that this is like the following dispute between Tannaim? Sometimes, in an attempt to understand an Amoraic controversy, the Gemara may suggest that each of the Amoraic viewpoints parallels a corresponding Tannaitic viewpoint. This suggestion is usually rejected by the Gemara, which proceeds to show that the Amoraim are in fact discussing a previously unconsidered aspect of law. The expression לֵימָא — "shall we say" — generally introduces a proposition which is rejected at the end of the discussion.

TRANSLATION AND COMMENTARY

לֵימָא כְּתַנָּאֵי [1] The Gemara asks: **Shall we say that this** Amoraic dispute as to whether a captive woman's maidservant can testify on her behalf **is like the following Tannaitic dispute**, and that Rav Pappa takes one side in the Tannaitic dispute and Rav Pappi and Rav Ashi the other? For one Baraita says: [2] "Testimony permitting a captive woman **is testimony that may be given by a man or a woman** (even though women are not normally accepted as witnesses), [3] **by a boy or a girl** (even though they are minors), by the captive woman's **father or her mother, or her brother or her sister** (even though they are relatives), [4] **but not by her son or her daughter, and not by her slave or her maidservant,** since we suspect that these people may testify falsely on her behalf." [5] **And another Baraita** (Tosefta, *Ketubot* 3:2) teaches: **"All are believed when they testify** about a captive woman, **except for herself and her husband."** The second Baraita implies that a captive woman's son or daughter, or slave or maidservant, *would* be believed. Thus, suggests the Gemara, the first Baraita reflects the viewpoint of Rav Pappa, and the second the viewpoint of Rav Pappi and Rav Ashi.

דְּרַב פַּפִּי [6] The Gemara answers: **The explanations of Rav Pappi and of Rav Ashi are** indeed the subject of **dispute between Tannaim.** For Rav Pappi and Rav Ashi say that the priestess's maidservant is believed, and the first Baraita explicitly says that she is not. Thus their explanations must be in accordance with the ruling of the second Baraita, and they must concede that the first Baraita explains the Mishnah in the way Rav Pappa did. [7] But **shall we say that the explanation** given **by Rav Pappa is** also the subject of **a dispute between Tannaim,** or could his explanation be in accordance with either Baraita? Rav Pappa said that the captive woman's maidservant is not believed, and this appears to be inconsistent with the second Baraita, which says that everyone is believed except the captive woman herself and her husband. Can Rav Pappa explain the second Baraita, or must he concede that it explains the Mishnah in the way Rav Pappi or Rav Ashi did?

[1] לֵימָא כְּתַנָּאֵי: [2] ״זוֹ עֵדוּת אִישׁ וְאִשָּׁה, [3] תִּינוֹק וְתִינוֹקֶת, אָבִיהָ וְאִמָּהּ, וְאָחִיהָ וַאֲחוֹתָהּ, [4] אֲבָל לֹא בְּנָהּ וּבִתָּהּ, לֹא עַבְדָּהּ וְשִׁפְחָתָהּ״. [5] וְתַנְיָא אִידָךְ: ״הַכֹּל נֶאֱמָנִין לְהָעִיד, חוּץ מֵהֵימֶנָּה וּבַעְלָהּ״.

[6] דְּרַב פַּפִּי וּדְרַב אַשִׁי תַּנָּאֵי הִיא. [7] דְּרַב פַּפָּא מִי לֵימָא תַּנָּאֵי הִיא?

LITERAL TRANSLATION

[1] Shall we say that this is like the [following dispute between] Tannaim: [2] "This is testimony [that may be given by] a man or a woman, [3] a boy or a girl, her father or her mother, or her brother or her sister, [4] but not [by] her son or her daughter, [and] not [by] her manservant or her maidservant." [5] And it was taught [in] another [Baraita]: "All are believed to testify, except for herself and her husband."

[6] [The explanations] of Rav Pappi and of Rav Ashi are [disputes between] Tannaim. [7] Shall we say that [the explanation] of Rav Pappa is [a dispute between] Tannaim?

RASHI

לימא כתנאי — שפחתה אי מהימנא אי לא. **זו עדות** — עדות זו של שבויה הכל כשרים בה, איש ואשה תינוק ותינוקת. **חוץ מהימנה** — היא עצמה. **דרב פפי ורב אשי** — דאמרו לעיל שפחה דידה מהימנא. **ודאי תנאי היא** — על כרחך יאמרו: אנן דאמרינן — כי מתניתא בתרייתא, מדקשיא להו קמייתא. **דרב פפא** — דאמר: לא מהימנא. **מילימא תנאי היא** — כלומר, דחוק הוא לומר: אנא דאמרי כי מתניתא קמייתא, או יוכל לתרץ מתניתא בתרייתא נמי כוותיה, למימר: שפחתה כעצמה דמי, והרי היא בכלל חוץ מהימנה דקתני בה, או תירוצא אחרינא.

NOTES

דְּרַב פַּפִּי וּדְרַב אַשִׁי תַּנָּאֵי הִיא The explanations of Rav Pappi and of Rav Ashi are disputes between Tannaim. The Rishonim disagree about how to rule on the dispute between Rav Pappi, Rav Pappa, and Rav Ashi. *Ra'avad* rules in favor of Rav Ashi, because the Halakhah normally follows Rav Ashi. Hence he rules that the captive's own maidservant is believed when she testifies that her mistress was not defiled. *Rif* and *Rambam* rule in favor of Rav Pappa, because the Gemara declares that his explanation is consistent with either Baraita, whereas Rav Pappi's and

HALAKHAH

אֲבָל לֹא בְּנָהּ וּבִתָּהּ But not by her son or her daughter. "If a captive woman's relatives, even including her father or her mother, testify that she was not defiled, they are believed. According to *Rambam*, even the captive's son or daughter is believed. But *Ḥelkat Meḥokek* cites *Rosh* and *Ran*, who rule that they are not believed, following the first Baraita, which the Gemara states supports Rav Pappa. But even these authorities agree that her son or her daughter is believed when they are talking unguardedly, following Rav Pappa's explanation of the second Baraita. According to *Ran*, a minor who is not a son or a daughter of the captive woman is believed, even when he is aware that he is testifying. According to *Rambam*, however, a minor is believed only when he is talking unguardedly." (*Rambam, Sefer Kedushah, Hilkhot Issurei Bi'ah* 18:18; *Shulḥan Arukh, Even HaEzer* 7:1.)

[1]אָמַר לָךְ רַב פַּפָּא: [2]כִּי תַּנְיָא הַהִיא, בִּמְסִיחָה לְפִי תוּמָּהּ. [3]כִּי הָא דְּכִי אֲתָא רַב דִּימִי אֲמַר: [4]רַב חָנָן קַרְטִיגְנָאָה מִשְׁתָּעֵי: [5]מַעֲשֶׂה בָּא לִפְנֵי רַבִּי יְהוֹשֻׁעַ בֶּן לֵוִי — וְאָמְרִי לָהּ: רַבִּי יְהוֹשֻׁעַ בֶּן לֵוִי מִישְׁתָּעֵי: [6]מַעֲשֶׂה בָּא לִפְנֵי רַבִּי — בְּאָדָם אֶחָד שֶׁהָיָה מֵסִיחַ לְפִי תוּמּוֹ, וְאָמַר: [7]״אֲנִי וְאִמִּי נִשְׁבֵּינוּ לְבֵין הַנָּכְרִים. [8]יָצָאתִי לִשְׁאוֹב מַיִם, דַּעְתִּי עַל אִמִּי. [9]לְלַקֵּט עֵצִים, דַּעְתִּי עַל אִמִּי״. [10]וְהִשִּׂיאָהּ רַבִּי לִכְהוּנָּה עַל פִּיו.

LITERAL TRANSLATION

[1]Rav Pappa can say to you: [2]When that [Baraita] was taught, it was when she was talking innocently. [3]As in the following [case] that Rav Dimi said when he came: [4]Rav Ḥanan of Carthage related: [5]A case came before Rabbi Yehoshua ben Levi — and some say: Rabbi Yehoshua ben Levi related: [6]A case came before Rabbi [Yehudah HaNasi] — about one man who was talking innocently, and said: [7]"I and my mother were taken captive among the non-Jews. [8][When] I went out to draw water, my mind was on my mother. [9]To gather wood, my mind was on my mother." [10]And Rabbi [Yehudah HaNasi] married her into the priesthood by his words (lit., "mouth").

RASHI

אמר לך רב פפא כי תניא ההיא — דקתני הכל נאמנים ואפילו שפחה דידה — במסיחה לפי תומה. **רב חנא קרטיגנאה משתעי** — רב חנן דמן קרטיגי היה מספר מעשה זה.

TRANSLATION AND COMMENTARY

אָמַר לָךְ רַב פַּפָּא [1]The Gemara answers: **Rav Pappa can say to you:** My explanation can also be reconciled with the second Baraita, and I can explain both Baraitot in such a way that they do not contradict each other. The first Baraita refers to formal testimony, and in such a case the wife's son, daughter, slave, and maidservant are not believed, as I explained. [2]But the second **Baraita is teaching** us about a case **where** the witness **was** not giving formal testimony but was **speaking unguardedly.** We have already seen (above, 26a) that when a person is heard telling a story that has legal implications of which he is oblivious, his story has greater credibility than if he were giving formal testimony. Hence the second Baraita is informing us that if the captive woman's witness did not testify formally, but provided unsolicited information that the woman was not violated, the witness is believed — even if the witness was the woman's own maidservant — unless the information was provided by the captive woman herself or by her husband, in which case we do not accept it as evidence.

כִּי הָא [3]The Gemara now cites an example of a case where a witness whose testimony would not normally be admissible in deciding the status of a captive woman — in this case, a son — was believed when he spoke casually. The situation occurred **in the following case that Rav Dimi related** to the Sages **when he came** to Babylonia from Eretz Israel: [4]**Rav Ḥanan of Carthage related:** [5]**A case came before Rabbi Yehoshua ben Levi — and some say** that **Rabbi Yehoshua ben Levi related:** [6]**A case came before Rabbi Yehudah HaNasi — about a man who was speaking casually and said:** [7]**"My mother and I were taken captive among the non-Jews,** but I protected her from them. [8]When **I went out to draw water** at my captors' command, **my mind was on my mother**, and I did not let her out of my sight. [9]When I was told **to** go out and **gather wood, my mind was** also **on my mother,** and I did not leave her alone and unprotected." [10]**And,** concluded Rav Ḥanan, even though the information was provided by the captive woman's son, and the first Baraita above ruled that in such a case the witness is not believed, nevertheless **Rabbi Yehudah HaNasi married her into the priesthood on the basis of his statement,** because a son's casual remark about his mother is believed. Thus, Rav Pappa can argue, there is no contradiction between the two Baraitot. A maidservant — or a son or a daughter — is not believed if giving formal testimony, but everyone is believed when making an unconsidered remark, except the woman herself and her husband. Thus, Rav Pappa's explanation of our Mishnah, unlike Rav Pappi's and Rav Ashi's, is consistent with both Baraitot.

NOTES

Rav Ashi's are consistent only with the second Baraita. Hence they rule that the captive's own maidservant is not believed when she testifies that her mistress was not defiled (see *Ran*). *Ramban* cites an early version of *Rif*, in which *Rif* ruled in favor of Rav Ashi. *Ramban* notes, however, that *Rif* crossed out the ruling, and wrote in his own handwriting that the Halakhah follows Rav Pappa.

כִּי תַּנְיָא הַהִיא, בִּמְסִיחָה לְפִי תוּמָּהּ When that Baraita was taught, it was when she was talking innocently. *Rashi* explains that Rav Pappa could, in fact, have explained the second Baraita in the same way as he explained the Mishnah itself, for the Mishnah also said that everyone is believed except for the captive herself; yet Rav Pappa was able to explain that the captive's own servant is like herself. However, Rav Pappa preferred to find a literal interpretation of the Baraita. Hence he explained that it was

TERMINOLOGY

כִּי תַּנְיָא הַהִיא When that Baraita was taught.... Sometimes an objection based on a Baraita is directed against the opinion of an Amora. The Talmud may resolve such an objection by arguing that the Baraita applies only in certain cases. This expression is one of a number of terms used when the Talmud seeks to limit the application of a certain law to specific circumstances.

BACKGROUND

דַּעְתִּי עַל אִמִּי My mind was on my mother. In other words, even when he was occupied with other matters, he was never distracted from keeping watch over his mother. In this story, nothing is said of her remaining pure, but we understand from the context that the man was telling the story because he had watched over his mother so well that no harm befell her. Hence Rabbi Yehudah HaNasi concluded that she had remained pure.

SAGES

רַב חָנָן קַרְטִיגְנָאָה Rav Ḥanan of Carthage. He seems to be the same person as Rav Ḥinena of Carthage, who is mentioned in the Jerusalem Talmud. From the little that we know of him, it seems that he was a second-generation Amora who was born in the North African city of Carthage, a region where Jews had lived as early as Second Temple times. Others believe he was from the city of Carthage in Spain.

רַב דִּימִי Rav Dimi. An Amora of the third and fourth generations, Rav Dimi lived both in Babylonia and in Eretz Israel. He seems to have been a Babylonian who moved to Eretz Israel in his youth. He returned to Babylonia several times, taking with him the teachings of Eretz Israel. Rav Dimi was responsible for the transmission of these teachings, and in the Jerusalem Talmud he is called Rav Avdimi (or Avduma) Naḥota. He was one of the Sages who were given the title רַבָּנַן נָחוֹתֵי — "the emigrant Rabbis" — because they carried

the teachings of Eretz Israel to Babylonia, mainly the teachings of Rabbi Yoḥanan, Resh Lakish, and Rabbi Elazar. Others who shared in this task were Rabbah bar Bar Ḥanah and Ulla, and later Ravin, Rav Shmuel bar Yehudah, and others. The Talmud reports dozens of Halakhic decisions that Rav Dimi took from one Torah center to the other, and he debated with the greatest Sages of his generation about them. At the end of his life he seems to have returned to Babylonia, where he died.

LITERAL TRANSLATION

MISHNAH [1] Rabbi Zekharyah ben HaKatzav said: [2] [By] this Abode! Her hand did not move from within my hand, from the time that the non-Jews entered Jerusalem until they left. [3] They said to him: [4] A man may not testify about himself.

משנה [1] אָמַר רַבִּי זְכַרְיָה בֶּן הַקַּצָּב: [2] הַמָּעוֹן הַזֶּה! לֹא זָזָה יָדָהּ מִתּוֹךְ יָדִי, מִשָּׁעָה שֶׁנִּכְנְסוּ נָכְרִים לִירוּשָׁלַיִם וְעַד שֶׁיָּצְאוּ. [3] אָמְרוּ לוֹ: [4] אֵין אָדָם מֵעִיד עַל עַצְמוֹ.

RASHI

משנה המעון הזה – שבועה היא.

TRANSLATION AND COMMENTARY

MISHNAH אָמַר רַבִּי זְכַרְיָה בֶּן הַקַּצָּב [1] The previous Mishnah (27a) ruled that a woman in a conquered city is permitted to remain married to a priest if she can produce a single witness — even a slave or a maidservant — to testify that she was not defiled. She is not believed, however, if she testifies about herself. The present Mishnah illustrates this ruling with a story about Rabbi Zekharyah ben HaKatzav, a priest who lived through the capture of Jerusalem and the destruction of the Second Temple at the hands of the Romans (70 C.E.). When Jerusalem fell, all the women in the city were disqualified for the priesthood as captives, in accordance with the previous Mishnah's ruling, and all the priests were required to divorce their wives, unless they could prove that their wives had not been raped. **Rabbi Zekharyah ben HaKatzav** could not find any independent proof about his wife, but he **said:** [2] I swear **by** the sanctity of **this Temple** that my wife's **hand did not leave my hand from the time that the non-Jews entered Jerusalem until they left,** and she was not raped. [3] But the Rabbis **said to him:** Your wife is forbidden to you, for a woman in a conquered city is assumed to have been raped unless she can produce evidence that she was spared. In this case the only evidence is your own testimony, [4] and **a person cannot testify about himself,** for a man's wife is considered like his own person for this purpose. Therefore, even though we do not doubt the truth of your statement, we cannot accept your testimony, and unless you can find an independent witness, your wife is forbidden to you.

NOTES

referring to a case where the maidservant was speaking casually.

Rashba, *Ritva*, and *Ramban* cite *Shmuel HaNagid*, who explains that Rav Pappa could not have interpreted the second Baraita as he did the Mishnah. For the Mishnah says only that a man is not believed when he testifies about himself, yet it clearly means to exclude not only the captive herself but also her husband. Hence Rav Pappa could say that the maidservant is also considered like the captive herself. The second Baraita, by contrast, specifies that the only people who are not believed are the captive herself and her husband. Hence it was not possible for Rav Pappa to interpret it as excluding the maidservant as well, and he was forced to explain that the Baraita was referring to a case where the witness was speaking casually. It should be noted, however, that the Gemara rules (*Eruvin* 27a) that when a Mishnah or a Baraita makes a general statement like this, even when it lists the exceptions, we cannot rule out the possibility of additional exceptions, since the authors of the Mishnah never intended to limit their statements in such an arbitrary way (see also *Maharsha*).

הַמָּעוֹן הַזֶּה By this Abode! *Rashi* explains that Rabbi Zekharyah was uttering some kind of oath, and similar oaths "by the Temple" do indeed appear in many places in the Talmud (e.g., *Kiddushin* 71a). Nevertheless, *Shulḥan Arukh* (*Yoreh De'ah* 237:6) rules that such oaths do not have the legal status of an oath, even when it is clear that the speaker meant to swear by the One who dwells in the Temple, and not by the Temple itself. *Tosefot Yom Tov* points out that Rabbi Zekharyah had no need for a legal oath here. If his testimony was to be accepted, it would be accepted without an oath, and if it was to be rejected, it would be rejected anyway, in spite of the oath. Rather, Rabbi Zekharyah was making an emphatic statement in the form of an oath, and not uttering a genuine oath.

In our commentary we have followed *Rav Tzemaḥ Gaon*, who explains that the oath was inspired by the sight of the destruction of the Temple, and Rabbi Zekharyah's choice of the term מָעוֹן (lit., "home") for the Temple refers to Psalm 90:1, where God is described as the Eternal Home. *Tosefot Yomtov*, however, notes that מָעוֹן was used as a pseudo-oath by Rabbi Bava ben Buta, about a century before the destruction (*Keritot* 25a), and by Rabban Shimon ben Gamliel in connection with a ruling issued well before the destruction (ibid., 8a).

מִשָּׁעָה שֶׁנִּכְנְסוּ נָכְרִים לִירוּשָׁלַיִם From the time that the non-Jews entered Jerusalem. From the Mishnah's ruling in the case of Rabbi Zekharyah, it is clear that when the Romans conquered Jerusalem all the women there were

HALAKHAH

אֵין אָדָם מֵעִיד עַל עַצְמוֹ A man may not testify about himself. "A captive woman's husband is not believed if he testifies that she was not defiled, because a person cannot testify about himself. *Bet Shmuel* adds that this law applies even if the husband was speaking casually, following the Gemara's explanation of the second Baraita. But this law applies only if his testimony was legally required to permit her; but if the husband was the only one who knew that his wife was taken captive, and he is certain that she was not violated, she is permitted to him, because he is permitted to rely on his own knowledge where it does not involve testimony." (*Rambam, Sefer Kedushah, Hilkhot Issurei Bi'ah* 18:19; *Shulḥan Arukh, Even HaEzer* 7:2.)

TRANSLATION AND COMMENTARY

GEMARA תָּנָא [1]Additional information about the incident involving Rabbi Zekharyah ben HaKatzav **is provided** in the following Tosefta (*Ketubot* 3:2): "Although the Rabbis forbade Rabbi Zekharyah ben HaKatzav to have conjugal relations with his wife, nevertheless he did not divorce her. [2]Rather, **he set aside a house in his courtyard for her** to live separately from him, and provided for her needs there. [3]**And** in order to prevent them from being secluded together, he arranged that his children were always there when he and his wife were both in the courtyard. Accordingly, **whenever she left** the courtyard, **she would leave before her children**, who would remain in the courtyard with their father until she had left, [4]**and whenever she entered** the courtyard, **she would enter after her children**, who would enter the courtyard first."

גמרא [1]תָּנָא: [2]"וְאַף עַל פִּי כֵן יִיחֵד לָהּ בַּיִת בַּחֲצֵרוֹ, [3]וּכְשֶׁהִיא יוֹצְאָה, יוֹצְאָה בְּרֹאשׁ בָּנֶיהָ, [4]וּכְשֶׁהִיא נִכְנֶסֶת, נִכְנֶסֶת בְּסוֹף בָּנֶיהָ". [5]בָּעֵי אַבַּיֵי: מַהוּ לַעֲשׂוֹת בִּגְרוּשָׁה כֵּן? [6]הָתָם הוּא, דִּבִשְׁבוּיָה הֵקִילוּ, [7]אֲבָל הָכָא לָא? [8]אוֹ דִּלְמָא לָא שְׁנָא?

LITERAL TRANSLATION

GEMARA [1]It was taught: [2]"And nevertheless he set aside a house in his courtyard for her, [3]and when she went out, she would go out ahead of her children, [4]and when she came in, she would come in after her children."

[5]Abaye asked: What is [the law about] doing the same with a divorcee? [6]Is this [the law] there, because they were lenient about a captive woman, [7]but not here? [8]Or is there perhaps no difference?

RASHI

גמרא ואף על פי כן – שאסרו עליו, לפי שכהן היה. **כשהיא יוצאה יוצאה בראש בניה** – והוא בחצר. – שיהו הבנים עמהם, שלא יתייחדו. **וכשהיא נכנסת, נכנסת בסוף בניה** – כדי שלא יהא הוא והיא בחצר, והבנים מבחוץ. **בגרושה** – כהן שגירש את אשתו, מהו לדור עמו בחצר?

בָּעֵי אַבַּיֵי [5]**Abaye asked: What is the law about doing the same with a divorcee?** A priest who divorces his wife is forbidden by Torah law to remarry her. But is he permitted to live near her in the same courtyard, and to arrange with his children never to leave their parents alone together? [6]Abaye explains: Was the arrangement made by Rabbi Zekharyah HaKatzav permitted by the Rabbis **because they were lenient about a captive woman,** [7]**but not** regarding a divorcee? Rabbi Zekharyah ben HaKatzav was permitted by Torah law to retain his wife, and it was only as a Rabbinic stringency that she was forbidden to him; hence this may have been why the Rabbis permitted the arrangement described in the Tosefta. [8]**Or is there perhaps no difference** between the cases, and if a divorced priestly couple wish, they are permitted to live near each other and to share the same courtyard?

NOTES

considered defiled, and were thus forbidden unless they could prove that they had not been raped. *Tosafot Ḥadashim* asks: In its explanation of the previous Mishnah, the Gemara ruled that if there was one hiding-place in the city, with room in it for one woman, none of the women are considered captives, even if they admit that they did not hide in it. Surely Jerusalem had hiding-places in it. Moreover, according to most Rishonim, this law applies only if it was impossible for anyone to escape the siege, but otherwise the women are permitted. Why, then, should the women of Jerusalem have been forbidden?

Tiferet Yisrael notes that in tractate *Yoma* (53b-54a) the Gemara interprets a verse from Lamentations (1:6) as teaching us that the conquerors searched through all the secret chambers in Jerusalem and found everything. Thus there were no hiding-places, and everyone was captured.

וְאַף עַל פִּי כֵן יִיחֵד And nevertheless he set aside. It is not entirely clear to what exactly the words וְאַף עַל פִּי כֵן — "and nevertheless" — refer. Our commentary follows *Rashi* and *Ritva*, who explain that although Rabbi Zekharyah's wife was forbidden to him, he *nevertheless* refused to divorce her, and instead made an arrangement with his children not to leave him alone with his former wife. *Shittah Mekubbetzet* cites an explanation in the name of the Geonim, that although Rabbi Zekharyah knew that his wife was really permitted to him, he *nevertheless* accepted the ruling of the Rabbis, and made elaborate arrangements to ensure that he would never be alone with her.

מַהוּ לַעֲשׂוֹת בִּגְרוּשָׁה כֵּן What is the law about doing the same with a divorcee? Our commentary follows *Rashi* and *Ritva*, who explain that Abaye's question refers specifically to a priest, who is forbidden to remarry his divorced wife, and not to non-priests who divorce their wives. We have seen that a priest whose wife was taken captive is permitted to live in the same courtyard with her, provided that their children do not leave them alone together. Hence, the question arises: Does this dispensation apply to any case where a priest's wife becomes disqualified for the priesthood, or only to a captive woman, where

HALAKHAH

יִיחֵד לָהּ בַּיִת בַּחֲצֵרוֹ He set aside a house in his courtyard for her. "The entire prohibition of captive women is a stringency based on doubt. Therefore, if a priest's wife has become forbidden to him as a captive, she is permitted to continue living in the same courtyard with him, provided that their children are present whenever he is together with his wife, so that they are never alone together," following the story of Rabbi Zekharyah ben HaKatzav. (*Rambam, Sefer Kedushah, Hilkhot Issurei Bi'ah* 18:25; *Shulḥan Arukh, Even HaEzer* 7:9.)

BACKGROUND

מָבוֹי **Alley.** This was a kind of small street, which usually had entrances into courtyards. Each courtyard opening onto the alley might contain a few houses. In certain areas of Halakhah a distinction is made between a "closed alley" (מָבוֹי סָתוּם) and an "open alley" (מָבוֹי מְפוּלָּשׁ). In our context, however, the alley spoken of is a housing unit — a place where dozens of families lived. A neighborhood (שְׁכוּנָה) is generally defined as a small unit containing three houses and a small number of families.

כְּפָר קָטָן נִידּוֹן כִּשְׁכוּנָה **A small village is considered as a neighborhood.** A small village usually contains more people than a neighborhood. Because a village is a unit in itself — and occasionally an isolated one — the residents of a village naturally have more contact among themselves than people living in an alley, who have businesses and friends in other places in the city.

TRANSLATION AND COMMENTARY

תָּא שְׁמַע [1]The Gemara answers: **Come and hear** a solution to Abaye's problem **from the following statement** made in a Baraita: [2]**"If** a non-priest **divorces his wife** and she **remarries, she is not permitted to live in his neighborhood.** We are afraid that if the couple live too near each other they may have an adulterous relationship, as they know each other so well. Until she remarries, however, she is permitted to live in the same neighborhood as her ex-husband, because the couple are permitted — and indeed encouraged — to settle their differences and remarry, if they wish. [28A] [3]Moreover, **if** the first husband **is a priest, she must not live in the same street** (a larger area than 'the same neighborhood') as he does, even if she has not remarried, since a priest is forbidden to marry a divorcee, including his own divorced wife. But a non-priest's divorced wife is permitted to live on the same street as her ex-husband, even after she has remarried, but not in close proximity in the same neighborhood. [4]**If** they live in **a small village — such a case actually occurred,** [5]**and** the Rabbis **said: A small village is considered as a neighborhood."** Hence even a non-priest is not permitted to live in the same village with his divorced and remarried wife. In conclusion, a priest is forbidden to live on the same street as his divorced wife, and he may certainly not live in the same courtyard, even if their children are able to ensure that they are never left alone together. Thus the Tosefta's dispensation (above, 27a) applies only to captive women, toward whom the Rabbis were lenient, and the problem raised by Abaye is solved.

[1]תָּא שְׁמַע, דְּתַנְיָא: [2]"הַמְגָרֵשׁ אֶת אִשְׁתּוֹ, לֹא תִּנָּשֵׂא בִּשְׁכוּנָתוֹ. [28A] [3]וְאִם הָיָה כֹּהֵן, לֹא תָּדוּר עִמּוֹ בְּמָבוֹי. [4]אִם הָיָה כְּפָר קָטָן, זֶה הָיָה מַעֲשֶׂה, [5]וְאָמְרוּ: כְּפָר קָטָן נִידּוֹן כִּשְׁכוּנָה".

LITERAL TRANSLATION

[1]Come [and] hear, for it was taught: [2]"[If] someone divorces his wife, she may not marry [and live] in his neighborhood. [28A] [3]And if he was a priest, she may not live with him in [the same] alley. [4]If it was a small village, there was such a case, [5]and they said: A small village is considered as a neighborhood."

RASHI

לא תנשא בשכונתו — לפי שמכירה ברמיזותיו וקרילותיו, שמא יבואו לידי עבירה. **ואם היה כהן** — אפילו לא ניסת. **לא תדור עמו במבוי** — שמא יבא עליה, וכהן אסור בגרושה. אבל ישראל, כל זמן שלא ניסת — תדור בשכונתו. ואמר רב גרס, ומהאי קרא שמעינן לה.

NOTES

the Rabbis were generally lenient? But if a non-priest divorces his wife, there is no prohibition at all against them living in the same courtyard, since the couple are permitted — indeed encouraged — to become reconciled and to remarry, and we need not take any special precautions against their being secluded together, beyond the laws applying to any unmarried man and woman.

Likkutei Geonim cites an opinion that Abaye's question applies even to a non-priest whose wife has remarried. According to this view, we are afraid that the couple may have an affair if we allow them to live in the same courtyard. But even this opinion agrees that an unmarried divorcee may live in the same neighborhood with her ex-husband (if he is not a priest), as we wish to encourage them to become reconciled and to remarry. *Rambam* and *Shulḥan Arukh* rule in favor of this opinion.

Ran takes an intermediate position. He agrees with *Rashi* that Abaye's question refers specifically to a priest. Thus a non-priest may live in the same courtyard with his ex-wife, provided that they have arranged for their children not to leave them alone together. But he agrees with the Geonim that they may not live without restriction in the same courtyard, even if the husband is not a priest, for fear of an affair. *Ḥelkat Meḥokek* suggests that *Rambam* and *Ran* may agree in practice that a non-priest may live in the same courtyard with his ex-wife if they have arranged for their children not to leave them alone together. For the prohibition against unmarried people having an affair is no more severe than the prohibition against a priest marrying a captive woman. *Bet Shmuel*, however, disagrees. But if a man has been required to divorce his wife (e.g., where she was suspected of adultery), *Or Zarua* rules that the couple must follow the same law that applies to a priest and a divorcee, even before the wife remarries.

לֹא תָּדוּר עִמּוֹ בְּמָבוֹי **She may not live with him in the same alley.** Our commentary follows *Tosafot*, who explains that an alley (or street) is a larger area than a neighborhood. This explanation finds support in tractate *Avodah Zarah* (21a), where the Gemara states that a neighborhood is a place where at least three families live. According to

HALAKHAH

וְאִם הָיָה כֹּהֵן **And if he was a priest.** "A non-priest who divorces his wife after marriage (but not after betrothal) may not live in the same courtyard with her, lest they have an illicit relationship. If the former husband was a priest, he may not even live on the same street as his divorced wife. In this context a small village has the same status as a street. *Maggid Mishneh* notes that this ruling of *Rambam* is based on *Rambam*'s text of our Gemara, which differs from that appearing in the standard editions.

Rema adds that *Rambam*'s distinction between priests and non-priests applies only if the ex-wife has not remarried; but if she has remarried, she must not live on

TRANSLATION AND COMMENTARY

מִי נִדְחֶה מִפְּנֵי מִי [1] Continuing the same theme, the Gemara notes: We have already established that if a priest divorces his wife, or if a non-priest's divorced wife remarries, the previously married couple may not continue to live in the same courtyard, or even in the same neighborhood or street. Thus either the ex-husband or the ex-wife must move out. **Who**, asks the Gemara, **gives way to whom?** If both parties wish to remain, which one is forced to move?

תָּא שְׁמַע [2] The Gemara answers: **Come and hear, for** the answer to our question **was taught** in the following Baraita: [3] "In normal circumstances, **she must give way to him, and he need not give way to her** (i.e., it is the ex-wife who must move). [4] **But if** the place where they were living **was her courtyard,** which she had inherited from her family, **he must give way to her** (i.e., it is the ex-husband who must move)."

[1] מִי נִדְחֶה מִפְּנֵי מִי? [2] תָּא שְׁמַע, דְּתַנְיָא: [3] "הִיא נִדְחֵית מִפָּנָיו, וְאֵין הוּא נִדְחֶה מִפָּנֶיהָ. [4] וְאִם הָיְתָה חָצֵר שֶׁלָּהּ, הוּא נִדְחֶה מִפָּנֶיהָ".

LITERAL TRANSLATION

[1] Who gives way to (lit., "is pushed away from before") whom?

[2] Come [and] hear, for it was taught: [3] "She gives way to him, and he does not give way to her. [4] But if it was her courtyard, he gives way to her."

NOTES

this explanation, a small village is considered a neighborhood, and therefore it is forbidden for a divorced couple to live in the same small village — both when the wife has remarried, even if her husband is not a priest, and also if the husband is a priest, even if the wife has not remarried.

Ran explains that an alley is a smaller area than a neighborhood. *Ran* argues that the Gemara compares a village to a neighborhood, and it is not reasonable to imagine that a village, however small, should be considered smaller than an alley. *Tosafot*, however, explains that the Gemara is referring to a very small and isolated village; but a somewhat larger village would not be regarded as a neighborhood. According to *Ran*'s explanation, a small village is forbidden only to a man and his remarried wife, but not to a priest and his ex-wife who has not remarried.

According to *Ran*'s explanation, a priest is permitted to live in the same neighborhood as his unmarried ex-wife, though not in the same alley. The restrictions on a priest are thus milder than those imposed on a remarried ex-wife, who is forbidden to live in the same neighborhood as her ex-husband, even if he is not a priest. *Ran* argues that the restrictions increase with the severity of the prohibition. For although a priest is forbidden to remarry his divorced wife even if she has not remarried, the prohibition is relatively light, but if the wife has remarried, any further contact with her ex-husband could entail the grave sin of adultery.

According to *Tosafot*'s explanation, a non-priest is permitted to live in the same alley as his remarried ex-wife, though not in the same neighborhood. The restrictions on a priest are thus stricter than those imposed on a remarried ex-wife, since the priest is forbidden to live in the same alley as his ex-wife, even if she has not remarried. *Tosafot* explains that since the sin of adultery is so severe, people show restraint and can be trusted to live in the same alley, but they are more likely to be lax regarding the relatively less severe prohibitions of priesthood. *Ramakh* adds that if the woman has remarried, her new husband can be relied upon to keep her at a distance from her ex-husband; but if she is still single, there is need for an additional safeguard.

Rambam has a different reading in this Baraita, according to which a non-priest who divorces his wife *after marriage* (rather than a non-priest whose divorced wife remarries) may not live with her in the same *courtyard* (rather than in the same neighborhood), and a priest may not live in the same alley, and a small village has the status of an *alley* (rather than a neighborhood). But if the couple divorced after betrothal, they may continue living in the same courtyard. *Rambam* does not explicitly discuss the case of the ex-wife who has remarried. *Taz* explains that, according to *Rambam*, the law in such a case would be the same as for the priest, and the remarried ex-wife and her ex-husband would be forbidden to live in the same alley (see also *Ḥelkat Meḥokek*).

הִיא נִדְחֵית מִפָּנָיו, וְאֵין הוּא נִדְחֶה מִפָּנֶיהָ **She gives way to him, and he does not give way to her.** *Ritva* explains that the Baraita employed this emphatic, double language to teach us that this law applies even when it would be much more difficult for her to move than for him, such as when he has another place to move to nearby but she would have to go far away.

HALAKHAH

the same street as her first husband, even if he is not a priest. *Bet Shmuel* notes that, according to *Rosh* and *Tur*, if she has remarried, she may not live even in the same neighborhood as her first husband — a larger area than the same street. *Bet Shmuel* suggests that *Rema*'s relatively lenient ruling applies only to a woman who has remarried and then divorced again; but if she is still married, *Rema* would agree that she may not live even in the same neighborhood. *Ḥelkat Meḥokek* suggests, however, that *Rema* is following the viewpoint of *Rambam*, who maintains that there are no restrictions on areas larger than a street." (*Rambam, Sefer Kedushah, Hilkhot Issurei Bi'ah* 21:27; *Shulḥan Arukh, Even HaEzer* 119:7.)

מִי נִדְחֶה מִפְּנֵי מִי **Who gives way to whom?** "If a man has divorced his wife, and they are forbidden to live together in the same courtyard (or on the same street), and neither wishes to move, the law is as follows: If the courtyard belongs to the wife, the husband must move. But if the courtyard belongs to the husband, or even if it belongs to neither of them and is rented, or even if it belongs to both of them jointly, the wife must move out and allow her ex-husband to remain," following our Gemara. (*Rambam, Sefer Kedushah, Hilkhot Issurei Bi'ah* 21:27; *Shulḥan Arukh, Even HaEzer* 119:7.)

TERMINOLOGY

מַאי הָוֵי עֲלַהּ **What happened about it?** I.e., what conclusion was reached about the matter? Or: What was the final Halakhic ruling in this case? This question is usually asked at the end of a lengthy discussion of a problem, in which different opinions have been expressed without being either proved or dismissed.

TRANSLATION AND COMMENTARY

אִיבַּעְיָא לְהוּ [1]The Gemara observes that the following question **was asked of** the Rabbis in the academy: **What is the law if** the couple had been living in a **courtyard** that belonged to **both of them** (in other words, it was not inherited from either family, but was bought with money from both families)? Is she compelled to move in this case as well, or does the law forcing her to give way not apply when she must surrender her property rights by doing so?

תָּא שְׁמַע [2]The Gemara replies: **Come and hear,** for the answer to this question is implicit in the Baraita we have just quoted, which ruled that "in normal circumstances **she must give way to him.**" [3]Now, **with what** situation **are we dealing** in this clause of the Baraita? [4]**If we say** that we are dealing **with** a case in which they were living in a **courtyard** belonging to **him,** surely **it is obvious** that it is she who must move, [5]so we have no need for a ruling. **On the other hand, if** you say that we are dealing **with** a case in which they were living in a **courtyard** belonging to **her,** [6]**surely the Baraita** specifically **teaches** that **"if it was her courtyard, he must give way to her"!** Clearly, then, the case referred to in the first clause describes a situation in which the courtyard was neither completely his nor completely hers. [7]**Is it not, then,** referring to **a case like this,** in which the courtyard belonged to both of them?

דִּלְמָא דַּאֲגִיר מֵיגָר [8]The Gemara answers: Not necessarily. The Baraita may **perhaps** be referring to a case **where** the courtyard belonged to neither of them and **they** had **rented it** from someone else. In such a situation, we would apply the rule that the husband takes precedence, since in any case the courtyard does not belong to either of them. But if the wife actually owns a share in the courtyard, it is possible that we would not force her to move. We cannot, therefore, resolve our problem from this Baraita.

מַאי הָוֵי עֲלַהּ [9]The Gemara asks: **What was the outcome of this?** If the problem cannot be resolved from the Baraita, how was it ultimately resolved?

תָּא שְׁמַע [10]The Gemara answers: **Come and hear**: There is a Biblical verse (Isaiah 22:17) which says: **"Behold, the Lord will move you about with the movement of a man."** [11]**And Rav** made an authoritative comment on this verse, **saying:** Since Isaiah emphasized that he was threatening to move a man forcibly from his present place, [12]we see that **moving for a man is more difficult than for a woman.** A woman is accustomed to move when she gets married, whereas a man does not normally move. Thus, everything else being equal, we prefer to make the woman move rather than the man, even if the ex-wife is forced to sell her share in her own courtyard as a result.

[1]אִיבַּעְיָא לְהוּ: הָיְתָה חָצֵר שֶׁל שְׁנֵיהֶם, מַהוּ? [2]תָּא שְׁמַע: "הִיא נִדְחֵית מִפָּנָיו". [3]בְּמַאי עָסְקִינַן? [4]אִילֵימָא: בְּחָצֵר שֶׁלּוֹ, פְּשִׁיטָא! [5]וְאֶלָּא בְּחָצֵר שֶׁלָּהּ, [6]וְהָתַנְיָא: "אִם הָיְתָה חָצֵר שֶׁלָּהּ, הוּא נִדְחֶה מִפָּנֶיהָ"! [7]אֶלָּא לָאו כִּי הַאי גַּוְונָא? [8]דִּלְמָא דַּאֲגִיר מֵיגָר. [9]מַאי הָוֵי עֲלַהּ? [10]תָּא שְׁמַע: "הִנֵּה ה׳ מְטַלְטֶלְךָ טַלְטֵלָה גָּבֶר". [11]וְאָמַר רַב: [12]טַלְטוּלֵי דְּגַבְרָא קָשִׁין מִדְּאִיתְּתָא.

LITERAL TRANSLATION

[1]It was asked of them: [If] it was the courtyard of both of them, what is [the law]?

[2]Come [and] hear: "She gives way to him." [3]With what are we dealing? [4]If we say: With his courtyard, it is obvious! [5]And [if] rather with her courtyard, [6]but surely it was taught: "If it was her courtyard, he gives way to her"! [7]Rather, is it not like this case?

[8]Perhaps it is where he rented it.

[9]What happened about it?

[10]Come [and] hear: "Behold, the Lord will move you about with the movement of a man." [11]And Rav said: [12]Moving about for a man is more difficult than for a woman.

NOTES

טַלְטוּלֵי דְּגַבְרָא **Moving about for a man.** The verse quoted here is part of an exhortation by the Prophet Isaiah to Shebna, an important figure in the court of King Hezekiah, who had committed a grievous sin. According to the account in *Sanhedrin* 26a, Shebna conspired with Sennacherib, King of Assyria, to betray the city of Jerusalem, in exchange for which Shebna was to be made king. Shebna apparently selected a burial plot for himself in the cemetery reserved for royalty, but Isaiah warned him that God would punish him by making him move from there with "the movement of a man." *Radak* explains that the phrase should be translated as "movement fit for a man" — in other words, a very powerful movement. Rav made a play on the words of the verse, as though it meant that Shebna was being cursed with "the movement of a man," as opposed to that of a woman, implying that movement involves greater effort and is more difficult for a man than for a woman.

It is not entirely clear why the Sages considered that moving house was so much more difficult for men than for women. *Maharsha* (in his comment on the parallel passage in *Sanhedrin* 26a) explains that a woman who is forced into exile can expect people to have pity on her and help her through her difficulties, whereas a man often gets no sympathy. *Maharsha* notes, however, that it is difficult to apply this explanation to our Gemara, which is referring

TRANSLATION AND COMMENTARY

תָּנוּ רַבָּנַן [1]**Our Rabbis taught** the following Baraita: "**If**, while the priest and his wife were still married, the husband **borrowed from property** his wife had inherited **from her father,** and before the debt fell due the couple divorced, [2]the ex-wife **may exact payment** from her ex-husband **only through another person.**" She must send a representative to speak to her ex-husband, and must not approach him directly, in accordance with the law mentioned above — that a priest who has divorced his wife may not live on the same street as she does, for fear of contact.

אָמַר רַב שֵׁשֶׁת [3]**Rav Sheshet said: If** the divorced couple do not follow this procedure, but deal with each other directly and are unable to resolve the dispute about the debt, and **they** then **come before us for judgment,** [4]**we do not deal with their** case, in order to show our disapproval of their behavior. [5]**Rav Pappa said:** Not only do we not hear their case, but **we** also **excommunicate them** for violating the law. [6]**Rav Huna the son of Rav Yehoshua said:** Not only do we excommunicate them, but **we also punish them with lashes.**

אָמַר רַב נַחְמָן [7]**Rav Naḥman said: It was taught in** tractate *Evel Rabbati* (2:14): [8]**"In what circumstances does this ruling apply,** that the ex-wife is not permitted to collect a debt directly from her ex-husband?

[1]תָּנוּ רַבָּנַן: "לָוָה הֵימֶנָּה בְּנִכְסֵי אָבִיהָ, [2]אֵינָהּ נִפְרַעַת אֶלָּא עַל יְדֵי אַחֵר".

[3]אֲמַר רַב שֵׁשֶׁת: וְאִי אָתוּ לְקַמָּן לְדִינָא, [4]לָא מִזַּדַּקְקִינַן לְהוּ. [5]רַב פַּפָּא אֲמַר: שַׁמּוּתֵי מְשַׁמְּתִינַן לְהוּ. [6]רַב הוּנָא בְּרֵיהּ דְּרַב יְהוֹשֻׁעַ אֲמַר: נַגּוּדֵי נַמִי מְנַגְּדִינַן לְהוּ.

[7]אֲמַר רַב נַחְמָן: תָּנָא בְּאֵבֶל רַבָּתִי: [8]"בַּמֶּה דְּבָרִים אֲמוּרִים?

LITERAL TRANSLATION

[1]Our Rabbis taught: "[If] he borrowed from her from the property of her father, [2]she may only be paid through another [person]."

[3]Rav Sheshet said: And if they came before us for judgment, [4]we do not attend to them. [5]Rav Pappa said: We excommunicate them. [6]Rav Huna the son of Rav Yehoshua said: We also flog them.

[7]Rav Naḥman said: It was taught in *Evel Rabbati*: [8]"In what [case] are these things

RASHI

לוה הימנה — כשהיתה תחתיו. **בנכסי אביה** — שהיו בידה נכסי מלוג, וככהן שגירש את אשתו קא מיירי. **אינה נפרעת** — הימנו על ידי עצמה, שלא יקרבו בדברים. **באבל רבתי** — מסכתא היא, וקורין אותה שמחות, וזו היא משנה ראשונה שלה: הגוסס הרי הוא כחי לכל דבריו.

NOTES

in principle to a limited move from one street to another in a town. Our commentary follows *Rashbatz*, who explains that it is customary for a woman to move into her husband's home when she marries. It is thus not unusual for a woman to leave her home and move to another; moreover, the inconvenience for her is likely to be of limited duration, since she will probably remarry and move into her new husband's home.

נַגּוּדֵי נַמִי מְנַגְּדִינַן We also flog them. *Tosafot* explains that the rulings of the Amoraim are listed in order of increasing severity: Rav Sheshet rules that we refuse to deal with their case; Rav Pappa rules that we excommunicate them; and Rav Huna the son of Rav Yehoshua rules that we flog them. *Tosafot* notes that it appears from tractate *Mo'ed Katan* (17a) that excommunication is a more severe punishment than lashes. He therefore explains that Rav Huna the son of Rav Yehoshua agrees with Rav Pappa that we excommunicate them, but maintains that we flog them as well. Support for this explanation can be found in *Ritva*'s text of the Talmud, followed by the standard Vilna text (and by our tradition), in which the word "also" appears in Rav Huna's statement.

Rambam rules that the court has the option of applying any one of the sanctions suggested in our Gemara. *Maggid Mishneh* explains that *Rambam* could not decide whether the Halakhah follows Rav Pappa or Rav Huna the son of Rav Yehoshua, and left the matter to the court's discretion. *Bayit Ḥadash* explains that *Rambam* is of the opinion that the Amoraim in our Gemara are not disagreeing with each other. Rather, Rav Pappa is referring to a case where the ex-wife has remarried, and we prefer to excommunicate them rather than flog them, lest people imagine that the woman and her ex-husband have committed adultery, and are being punished with lashes. And Rav Huna the son of Rav Yehoshua is referring to a case where the ex-husband is a priest and the ex-wife has not remarried, and in these circumstances we prefer to flog them rather than excommunicate them, since lashes are the lesser punishment.

תָּנָא בְּאֵבֶל רַבָּתִי It was taught in *Evel Rabbati*. *Evel Rabbati* (lit., "great mourning") is one of the so-called "small tractates," which are collections of Baraitot on specific subjects that were not fully covered in the Mishnah. In the standard editions of the Talmud, they are printed at the

HALAKHAH

לָוָה הֵימֶנָּה בְּנִכְסֵי אָבִיהָ If he borrowed from her from the property of her father. "If a man has divorced his wife and owes her money from the time of their marriage, she must not approach him directly for her money but must send a representative, following the Baraita. *Ḥelkat Meḥokek* adds that the same law applies in reverse if she owes him money. If they violate this law, and then come before us for judgment, we excommunicate them or flog them. *Bet Shmuel* adds that the same rule applies if they violate the law by living in the same courtyard. *Bet Shmuel* also notes that, according to *Rosh*, we excommunicate them only if the ex-husband is a priest or if the ex-wife

SAGES

רַב אַדָּא בַּר מַתְנָא **Rav Adda bar Matena.** A Babylonian Amora of the fourth and fifth generations, Rav Adda bar Matena is quoted frequently in the Talmud. He discussed Halakhic matters with Abaye and Rava, and was a colleague of Rav Pappa and of Ravina. Little is known of his personal life apart from the fact that he was very poor and his family had great difficulty in finding subsistence.

LANGUAGE (RASHI)

פריווי״ץ* From the Old French *privez*, meaning "uninhibited."

LITERAL TRANSLATION

said? [1]When she was divorced after marriage. [2]But when she was divorced after betrothal, she may be paid by herself, for he is not familiar (lit., 'his heart is not large') with her."

[3]A certain betrothed man and his [former] betrothed bride came before Rava. [4]Rav Adda bar Matena sat before him. [5]Rava put a messenger between them. [6]Rav Adda bar Matena said to him: But surely Rav Naḥman said: [7]"It was taught in *Evel Rabbati*, etc."! [8]He said to him: We see that they are familiar with each other.

[9]There are [some] who say: [10]Rava did not put a messenger between them. [11]Rav Adda bar

[1]שֶׁנִּתְגָּרְשָׁה מִן הַנִּשּׂוּאִין. [2]אֲבָל כְּשֶׁנִּתְגָּרְשָׁה מִן הָאֵירוּסִין, נִפְרַעַת עַל יְדֵי עַצְמָהּ, שֶׁאֵין לִבּוֹ גַּס בָּהּ".

[3]הַהוּא אָרוּס וַאֲרוּסָתוֹ דְּאָתוּ לְקַמֵּיהּ דְּרָבָא. [4]יְתֵיב רַב אַדָּא בַּר מַתְנָא קַמֵּיהּ. [5]אוֹקֵי רָבָא שְׁלוּחָא בֵּינָתַיְיהוּ. [6]אֲמַר לֵיהּ רַב אַדָּא בַּר מַתְנָא: וְהָאָמַר רַב נַחְמָן: [7]"תָּנָא בְּאֵבֶל רַבָּתִי כו׳"! [8]אֲמַר לֵיהּ: קָא חָזֵינַן דְּקָא גָּיְיסִי בַּהֲדָדֵי.

[9]אִיכָּא דְּאָמְרִי: [10]לָא אוֹקֵי רָבָא שָׁלִיחַ בֵּינָתַיְיהוּ. [11]אֲמַר לֵיהּ

RASHI

ארוס וארוסתו – כהן היה. **והאמר רב נחמן תנא באבל רבתי** – דמן האירוסין נפרעת על ידי עצמה. **דגייסי בהדדי** – מכירין זה את זה ברמיזות וקריצות. בלעז *פריווי״ץ.

TRANSLATION AND COMMENTARY

[1]**If she was divorced after marriage.** [2]**But if she was divorced after betrothal, she may exact payment by herself, since he does not** behave in a **familiar** way **with her."** In Jewish law, marriage takes place in two stages. After the first stage — called *erusin* or *kiddushin* (usually translated as "betrothal") — the couple are legally married, but they do not live together and the marriage is not consummated until the second stage — called *nissu'in* (translated as "marriage"). The laws restricting contact between a priest and his divorced wife apply only if they divorced after *nissu'in*, when they had already become intimate; but if they divorced after *erusin* — even though the divorce is fully effective by Torah law and the woman is strictly forbidden to remarry her ex-husband or any other priest — we are nevertheless not concerned about their having contact, because they have not had a chance to become familiar with each other. In such a case, the ordinary laws regarding relationships between unmarried men and unmarried women apply, with no additional restrictions.

הַהוּא אָרוּס [3]The Gemara relates that **a certain betrothed** priest **and his former betrothed bride,** who had divorced and had a dispute about a debt, **came before Rava** for adjudication. [4]Rava's disciple, **Rav Adda bar Matena, sat before** Rava, observing the conduct of the case. [5]**Rava put a representative between** the divorced couple, and did not allow them to address each other or to appear together in court, in accordance with the Gemara's ruling forbidding a divorced couple to appear together in court. [6]**Rav Adda bar Matena said to** Rava: **But surely Rav Naḥman said:** [7]**"It was taught in** ***Evel Rabbati*** that all these restrictions apply only after marriage," and this couple were only betrothed! [8]**Rava said to** Rav Adda bar Matena in reply: **I can see** by their behavior **that** although they were never married, **they are familiar with each other.** Therefore the ordinary laws apply.

אִיכָּא דְּאָמְרִי [9]**There are some who transmit a** slightly **different version** of this story: [10]When the couple came to Rava for adjudication, **Rava did not put a representative between them,** but permitted them to address each other directly. [11]**Rav Adda bar Matena said to** Rava: **Sir, you should put a representative between them,**

NOTES

end of *Nezikin*, after tractates *Horayot*, *Eduyyot*, and *Avot*. *Evel Rabbati* deals with the subjects of death and mourning, beginning with the proper behavior toward a dying person, and continuing with funeral arrangements, the laws of mourning, and the laws regarding suicide. It is often designated by the euphemistic title *Semaḥot*, which means "happy occasions," in accordance with the Talmudic custom of using a euphemism when referring to distressing matters. *Evel Rabbati* is called "great mourning" to distinguish it from *Evel Zutrati*, "lesser mourning," which is a second, shorter collection of Baraitot on the same topic. *Evel Zutrati* was lost for a long period, but manuscripts of it have been rediscovered and published in modern times.

HALAKHAH

has remarried, but according to *Rambam*, this law applies even if he is not a priest and she has not remarried." (*Rambam, Sefer Kedushah, Hilkhot Issurei Bi'ah* 21:27; *Shulḥan Arukh, Even HaEzer* 119:8,9.)

כְּשֶׁנִּתְגָּרְשָׁה מִן הָאֵירוּסִין **When she was divorced after betrothal.** "The law forbidding a divorced couple to live in the same courtyard, or to approach each other directly to settle a debt, applies only if they divorced after marriage. But if a man divorces his betrothed bride, they are permitted to live in the same courtyard or to sue each

TRANSLATION AND COMMENTARY

in accordance with the Gemara's ruling that forbids a divorced couple from appearing together in court! [1]Rava **said to** Rav Adda bar Matena in reply: **But surely Rav Naḥman said: "It was taught in** ***Evel Rabbati*** that all these restrictions apply only after marriage," and this couple were only betrothed! [2]Rav Adda bar Matena **said to** Rava in reply: **This ruling applies** only in an ordinary situation, **where** the couple **are not familiar with each other.** [3]**But I can see that this couple are familiar with each other**, as if they were already married. Rava accepted this argument, and ordered the couple to address each other through an intermediary.

רַב אַדָּא בַּר מַתְנָא: נֵיקוּם מָר שְׁלוּחָא בֵּינָתַיְיהוּ. [1]אֲמַר לֵיהּ: וְהָא אָמַר רַב נַחְמָן: "תָּנָא בְּאֵבֶל רַבָּתִי כו'"! [2]אֲמַר לֵיהּ: הָנֵי מִילֵּי הֵיכָא דְּלָא גָּיְיסֵי בַּהֲדָדֵי. [3]אֲבָל הָנֵי, קָא חָזֵינָא לְהוּ דְּגָיְיסֵי בַּהֲדָדֵי.

מִשְׁנָה [4]וְאֵלּוּ נֶאֱמָנִין לְהָעִיד בְּגוֹדְלָן מַה שֶּׁרָאוּ בְּקוֹטְנָן.

LITERAL TRANSLATION

Matena said to him: Sir, you should put a messenger between them. [1]He said to him: But surely Rav Naḥman said: "It was taught in *Evel Rabbati* etc."! [2]He said to him: These words [apply] where they are not familiar with each other. [3]But [as for] these, I see that they are familiar with each other.

MISHNAH [4]And these are believed to testify when they are grown up [about] what they saw while they were minors.

MISHNAH וְאֵלּוּ נֶאֱמָנִין לְהָעִיד [4]The previous Mishnayot ruled that someone who testifies that a captive woman was not raped is believed, even if the witness is not ordinarily qualified to testify. This Mishnah describes additional cases in which a disqualified witness is believed. Ordinarily, the testimony of a minor is not accepted. Moreover, the testimony of an adult about events he observed while he was a minor is also not accepted, in accordance with the general Talmudic principle that a witness must have been qualified to testify both when he witnessed the events and when he actually testified. In **the following** cases, however, evidence is not required by Torah law, and although the Rabbis insisted that testimony be given (in some cases by one witness, and in others by two), they relaxed their requirements in these cases and **believed** a witness who **testified when he was grown up about** something **that he saw while he was a minor.**

NOTES

וְאֵלּוּ נֶאֱמָנִין לְהָעִיד בְּגוֹדְלָן מַה שֶּׁרָאוּ בְּקוֹטְנָן **And these are believed to testify when they are grown up about what they saw while they were minors.** A minor is not permitted to testify. This is both a logical requirement and a formal Scriptural law. The Gemara (*Bava Batra* 155b) rules that even an intelligent child, who is competent to buy and sell small movable items, is nevertheless not permitted to testify, because the law that a witness must be an adult is derived from a Biblical verse (Deuteronomy 19:17), and it applies even where we might logically have accepted his testimony. *Rambam* (*Hilkhot Edut* 9:7,8) rules that even the most intelligent of minors is not permitted to testify until he reaches the age of legal majority (13 for a boy and 12 for a girl), and even a child who has reached the age of legal majority is permitted to testify only about what he understands. Testimony about more complicated matters must wait until he reaches fuller maturity.

From our Mishnah, it is clear that the testimony of an adult who is fully qualified to give evidence is not acceped about something he saw when he was a minor, even if he insists that he is certain about what he saw. *Rambam* (ibid., 14:2) and other Rishonim explain that this is a special case of the rule (*Bava Batra* 128a) that a witness must have been qualified to testify when he saw the event, as well as when he actually testified. But *Shittah Mekubbetzet* notes that there is a logical consideration here as well, since it is possible that the witness was not precise in his observations when he was a child, and although he is certain now, his memory of such events cannot be trusted.

The Gemara explains that although the testimony of an adult is not normally accepted about something he saw when he was a minor, he is permitted to testify about the cases listed in the Mishnah, because they are all Rabbinic matters, about which the Rabbis were lenient. *Tosefot Rid* explains that the Mishnah did not permit a child to testify in these cases, because we cannot expect a child to be a reliable witness, but this consideration does not apply to an adult who is testifying about something he saw as a child.

Tosafot asks: In the cases listed in our Mishnah, the Rabbis are willing to accept such testimony from an adult regarding Rabbinic matters, but not from someone who is a minor. In tractate *Pesaḥim* (4b), however, the Gemara rules that a minor who testifies that he inspected a house and removed all the leaven from it is believed. And the Gemara explains that this is because the inspection is a Rabbinic requirement; hence the Rabbis were lenient and believed a minor. But why were the Rabbis more lenient about Rabbinic matters there than here?

Tosafot answers that in the cases in our Mishnah the witness is testifying about something that happened to someone else. But in the case of the inspection for leaven in tractate *Pesaḥim*, the minor claims to have inspected

HALAKHAH

other in the usual manner, following Rav Naḥman. But if it is clear from their behavior that they are familiar with each other, they must not do so, following Rava and Rav Adda bar Matena (*Rambam, Sefer Kedushah, Hilkhot Issurei Bi'ah* 21:27; *Shulhan Arukh, Even HaEzer* 119:10.)

LITERAL TRANSLATION

[1] A man is believed to say: "This is my father's handwriting," or "This is my teacher's handwriting," or "This is my brother's handwriting."

[2] "I remember about So-and-so, that she went out with a *hinuma* and [the hair of] her head was loose."

[1] נֶאֱמָן אָדָם לוֹמַר: "זֶה כְּתַב יָדוֹ שֶׁל אַבָּא", וְ"זֶה כְּתַב יָדוֹ שֶׁל רַבִּי", וְ"זֶה כְּתַב יָדוֹ שֶׁל אָחִי".

[2] "זָכוּר הָיִיתִי בִּפְלוֹנִית, שֶׁיָּצְאָה בְּהִינוּמָא וְרֹאשָׁהּ פָּרוּעַ".

RASHI

משנה זה כתב ידו של אבא — ומקיימין השטר על פיו, אף על פי שמת אביו בעוד זה קטן. שיוצאת בהינומא — והוא סימן שניסת בתולה וכתובתה מאתים, כדאמרינן בריש פירקין.

TRANSLATION AND COMMENTARY

נֶאֱמָן אָדָם לוֹמַר [1] The first case described by the Mishnah in which the testimony of an adult is accepted about something he saw as a child is as follows: **A man is believed** when he says: **"This is my father's handwriting," or "This is my teacher's handwriting," or "This is my brother's handwriting."** An earlier Mishnah (above, 20b) ruled that when the authenticity of a document is in doubt, the two witnesses who signed the document must come forward and authenticate their signatures, or two independent witnesses must authenticate each of the signatures. Our Mishnah rules that the son (or brother or student) of the witness who signed the document may serve as one of the independent witnesses who authenticates the witness's signature, even if the father (or brother or teacher) died while the son (or brother or student) was still a child. Although the independent witness is a relative, and his testimony about the signature would not normally be accepted at all, and although the testimony of an adult about something he saw as a child would not normally be accepted, nevertheless the Mishnah rules that testimony of this kind is admissible.

זָכוּר הָיִיתִי בִּפְלוֹנִית [2] The second case in which the testimony of an adult about something he saw as a child is accepted is as follows: If an adult says: **"I remember** that when **So-and-so** was married, and I was a child at the time, **she went out** to the wedding ceremony with a ***hinuma*, and the hair of her head was loose,"** the witness is believed. An earlier Mishnah (above, 15b) ruled that if a woman has been widowed or divorced, and she comes to court to demand her ketubah, and she demands the full 200 zuz to which a virgin is entitled, while her husband or his heirs claim that she was already a widow when he married her, and is therefore entitled to only 100 zuz, the burden of proof falls on the wife, as she is the plaintiff. But to prove her claim she need not bring proof that she was a virgin when she married. It is sufficient for her to demonstrate that at her wedding ceremony she was treated in the manner customary for virgins. Thus, if she can produce witnesses that she went out to the wedding with an adornment called a *hinuma* on her head and with her hair hanging loose (as was customary in Talmudic times when virgins married), she is considered to have proved her case, and is entitled to the full 200 zuz. Our Mishnah rules that for this purpose someone who attended the wedding as a child may serve as one of the witnesses.

NOTES

the house himself, and this gives his testimony additional credibility. *Rashba* notes that this explanation fits well with one reading of the text in *Pesaḥim*, which states that the child is believed only if he says that he inspected the house himself; but according to other readings, he is believed even if he says that someone else inspected it.

Rashba explains that inspecting a house for leaven is a family event that takes place every year, and children understand its significance well; hence a child is believed about it. In the cases in our Mishnah, by contrast, a child may not have a proper grasp of the situation, and may testify incorrectly.

HALAKHAH

זֶה כְּתַב יָדוֹ שֶׁל אַבָּא **"This is my father's handwriting."** "An adult is believed when he authenticates the signature of his father, his teacher, or his brother, even if he last saw the signatures as a child. But he may serve only as one of the witnesses who authenticate the signature. The other witness must have been familiar with it as an adult, following Rav Huna the son of Rav Yehoshua. *Shulḥan Arukh* cites *Rosh*, who rules that this law applies only to signatures with which the child was somewhat familiar, such as his father's, brother's, or teacher's, but not to other signatures. *Sma* insists that *Rosh*'s position is correct, as it is supported by the Jerusalem Talmud, but *Shakh* notes that many Rishonim disagree, and that *Bet Yosef* explained that *Rosh*'s proof from the Jerusalem Talmud is not conclusive." (*Rambam, Sefer Shofetim, Hilkhot Edut* 7:1 and 14:3; *Shulḥan Arukh, Ḥoshen Mishpat* 35:4 and 46:17.)

שֶׁיָּצְאָה בְּהִינוּמָא **That she went out with a *hinuma*.** "An adult is believed if he testifies that as a child he attended a wedding and saw that the bride was treated as a virgin, in accordance with local customs. If the woman is then divorced, she is entitled to the full ketubah of a virgin, provided that another witness corroborates the first witness's testimony. *Ḥelkat Meḥokek* explains that, according to *Rambam*, the adult testifying to what he saw as a child is believed by himself. But *Kesef Mishneh* cites *Rivash*, who explains that two witnesses are required, although both may be adults testifying to what they saw as children. *Maggid Mishneh* notes that, according to many authorities, the second witness must be an adult testifying to what he saw as an adult." (*Rambam, Sefer Nashim, Hilkhot Ishut* 16:25 and *Sefer Shofetim, Hilkhot Edut* 14:3; *Shulḥan Arukh, Even HaEzer* 96:15 and *Ḥoshen Mishpat* 35:5.)

TRANSLATION AND COMMENTARY

וְשֶׁהָיָה אִישׁ פְּלוֹנִי [1]The third case in which the testimony of an adult is accepted regarding something he saw as a child is as follows: If an adult says: "I remember from my childhood that **So-and-so used to go out of school to immerse** himself **in order to eat terumah,"** or: [2]"I remember from my childhood **that** So-and-so **received a share of terumah with us at the threshing floor,"** the witness is believed. An earlier Mishnah (above, 23b) ruled that a stranger who claims to be a priest is not believed without proof, but if he can produce one witness to support his claim, he is believed, even if that witness is an interested party. The Gemara rules that other forms of proof are also sufficient, such as the testimony of witnesses that the purported priest was called first to the Torah reading (above, 25b). Another acceptable form of proof is evidence that the man claiming to be a priest received a share of terumah at the threshing floor (above, 25a), or evidence that he was taken out of school as a child to eat terumah (above, 26a). Our Mishnah rules that the testimony of a witness who saw such an incident while he was a child is believed.

וְהַמָּקוֹם הַזֶּה בֵּית הַפְּרָס [3]The fourth case in which the testimony of an adult is accepted regarding something he saw as a child is as follows: If an adult says: "I remember from my childhood that **this place is a *bet haperas*,"** the witness is believed. A *bet haperas* is a field in which a human corpse was buried, and which was subsequently plowed over. We assume that, in the plowing, the pieces of bone were scattered all over the field to a distance of 100 cubits in each direction. To prevent people from accidentally touching a bone and becoming ritually impure, the Rabbis decreed that all the earth in such a field is ritually impure. If it is known that one field in a valley is a *bet haperas*, but it is not known which field, and a witness testifies that when he was a child his father would not allow him to go into one of the fields there but allowed him to go into the others, and the witness identifies the field, we accept this testimony and declare that the other fields are ritually pure.

וְעַד כָּאן הָיִינוּ בָּאִין בְּשַׁבָּת [4]The fifth case is as follows: If an adult says: "I remember from my childhood that **we used to walk up to here on Shabbat,"** he is believed. On Shabbat it is permitted to walk anywhere in the town in which one lives, and a further 2,000 cubits in any direction away from the town, but it is forbidden to walk beyond this limit. It is not always obvious where the 2,000-cubit limit is, and person

[1]וְשֶׁ"הָיָה אִישׁ פְּלוֹנִי יוֹצֵא מִבֵּית הַסֵּפֶר לִטְבּוֹל לֶאֱכוֹל בִּתְרוּמָה", [2]וְשֶׁ"הָיָה חוֹלֵק עִמָּנוּ עַל הַגּוֹרֶן".
[3]וְ"הַמָּקוֹם הַזֶּה בֵּית הַפְּרָס".
[4]וְ"עַד כָּאן הָיִינוּ בָּאִין בְּשַׁבָּת".

LITERAL TRANSLATION

[1]Or that "So-and-so used to go out of school to immerse in order to eat terumah," [2]or that "He used to receive a share with us at the threshing floor." [3]Or: "This place is a *bet haperas*." [4]Or: "Up to here we used to come on Shabbat."

RASHI

יוצא מבית הספר – כשהיינו למידין תינוקות בבית רבן. וכולהו מפרש טעמא בגמרא.

NOTES

עַד כָּאן הָיִינוּ בָּאִין בְּשַׁבָּת "Up to here we used to come on Shabbat." The law is that a person may not walk more than 2,000 cubits (approximately one kilometer) out of town on Shabbat (*Eruvin* 49b). The Gemara (*Eruvin* 17b) derives this law from a Biblical verse (Exodus 16:29): "Let no man go out of his place on the seventh day." In tractate *Sotah* (27b and 30b) the Gemara cites a Tannaitic dispute as to whether this is a Torah law or a Rabbinic law. According to *Tosafot* (*Eruvin* 17b), the opinion that this law is Rabbinic maintains that by Torah law there is no prohibition at all against walking out of town, provided nothing is carried (we have followed this opinion in our commentary). However, according to many authorities, including *Rambam* (*Hilkhot Shabbat* 27:1), the Tannaitic dispute concerns only the 2000-cubit limit; but everyone agrees that, by Torah law, it is forbidden to go more than 24,000 cubits out of town.

The procedure for measuring the 2,000 cubits is quite complicated, and may be done only by experts. Thus, in general, we rely on tradition, and do not attempt periodic remeasurement. For this purpose, the tradition may be transmitted by a person who is not qualified to testify, even a slave or a maidservant, since the 2,000 cubits are in any case Rabbinic (*Eruvin* 59a). For the same reason, our Mishnah permits us to rely on information transmitted by a person who last saw the boundary when he was a child.

HALAKHAH

לִטְבּוֹל לֶאֱכוֹל בִּתְרוּמָה "To immerse in order to eat terumah." "An adult is believed if he testifies that as a child he saw a certain person immerse himself in order to eat terumah, and we consider that person to have the status of the presumed priests of today, who are permitted to eat Rabbinic terumah." (*Rambam, Sefer Kedushah, Hilkhot Issurei Bi'ah* 20.15; *Shulḥan Arukh, Even HaEzer* 3:5 and *Ḥoshen Mishpat* 35:6.)

LITERAL TRANSLATION

[1] But a man is not believed to say: "So-and-so had a path in this place," [2] [or] "So-and-so had a standing area and a lamentation area in this place."

GEMARA [3] Rav Huna the son of Rav Yehoshua said: And provided that there is an adult with him.

[1] אֲבָל אֵין אָדָם נֶאֱמָן לוֹמַר: ״דֶּרֶךְ הָיָה לִפְלוֹנִי בְּמָקוֹם הַזֶּה״, [2] ״מַעֲמָד וּמִסְפֵּד הָיָה לִפְלוֹנִי בְּמָקוֹם הַזֶּה״.

גמרא [3] אָמַר רַב הוּנָא בְּרֵיהּ דְּרַב יְהוֹשֻׁעַ: וְהוּא שֶׁיֵּשׁ גָּדוֹל עִמּוֹ.

RASHI

אבל אין נאמנין כו׳ – דלאפוקי ממונא הוא, ובעינן עדות מעלייתא. וכתובה היינו טעמא – דרוב נשים בתולות נישאות. **מעמד ומספד** – מקום היה לו כאן להספיד מתיו כשמוליכן לבית קברות שלו, ולעשות שם מעמדות ומושבות שהיו עושין שבעה למת. **רבי יוחנן בן ברוקא אומר נאמנים** – לא גרסינן ליה במתניתין, אלא בברייתא, ולא אדרך מעמד ומספד קאי.

TRANSLATION AND COMMENTARY

is permitted to ask another and to trust his information. Our Mishnah teaches us that, for this purpose, a person whose information is based on childhood memories is believed, since in any case the prohibition against walking beyond the Shabbat limit is of Rabbinic origin.

אֲבָל אֵין אָדָם נֶאֱמָן לוֹמַר [1] Having given a series of examples of cases in which the testimony of a witness about something he saw as a child is accepted, the Mishnah now gives two examples in which such testimony is not accepted. **A man is not believed** if he says: "I remember as a child that **So-and-so had a path in this place."** If a man claims a right-of-way in his neighbor's field, and he and his neighbor have a disagreement about its location, the man claiming the right-of-way must produce qualified witnesses to testify to its exact location, and the testimony of a witness who saw the path as a child is not accepted. [2] Likewise, if the witness testifies that as a child he saw that **So-and-so had a standing area and a lamentation area in this place,** he is not believed. It was customary to set aside an area near the cemetery where mourners gathered and where eulogies were delivered. If a person had a private cemetery near a neighbor's field, and he claimed that part of his neighbor's field was in fact the area where mourners were entitled to stand or the area where eulogies were delivered, he is not believed unless he can produce qualified witnesses to support his claim. Our Mishnah rules that, for this purpose, testimony based on childhood memories is not believed.

GEMARA אָמַר רַב הוּנָא בְּרֵיהּ דְּרַב יְהוֹשֻׁעַ [3] The Gemara begins its analysis of the Mishnah by considering the first clause, which ruled that the testimony of a son about his father's signature is believed, even if the son last saw the signature as a child. **Rav Huna the son of Rav Yehoshua said:** The Mishnah's ruling applies **provided that there is an adult with** the son when he testifies. The Gemara ruled above (21a) that if the original witnesses who signed a document are not available to authenticate their signatures, two independent witnesses must authenticate each signature. Our Mishnah ruled that the son (or the brother or the student) of one of the witnesses who signed the document can serve as one of the independent

NOTES

וְהוּא שֶׁיֵּשׁ גָּדוֹל עִמּוֹ And provided that there is an adult with him. From the expression used by Rav Huna the son of Rav Yehoshua, it is not entirely clear if this restriction applies only to documents or to all the cases of the Mishnah. Our commentary follows *Ran*, *Tosafot*, *Meiri*, and most other Rishonim, who agree that the Mishnah is not discussing how many witnesses are required for each case. Rather, the Mishnah is telling us that the witness who is testifying to what he saw as a child may serve as the sole witness in cases where one witness is sufficient (e.g., the Shabbat limit and the *bet haperas*), and as one of a pair of witnesses in cases where two witnesses are required (e.g., with regard to the signatures of the witnesses on the document, and the case of the bride who wore a *hinuma*). According to *Ran* and *Tosafot*, whenever two witnesses are required, the restrictive ruling of Rav Huna the son of Rav Yehoshua applies, and the second witness must be an adult. According to *Meiri*, however, the restrictive ruling of Rav Huna the son of Rav Yehoshua applies only in the case of the document, whereas in the case of the bride who wore a *hinuma*, two witnesses are required, but both of them may be adults testifying to what they saw as children.

The case of terumah is somewhat problematic. *Ran* explains that here, too, two witnesses are required (and the restrictive ruling of Rav Huna the son of Rav Yehoshua applies to the second witness), but *Tosafot* argues that the Gemara rules (below, 28b) that we believe the witness who is testifying to what he saw as a child only regarding Rabbinic terumah, and according to the Gemara's conclusion above (25a), one witness is sufficient for Rabbinic terumah.

According to these Rishonim, the restrictive ruling of Rav Huna the son of Rav Yehoshua does not apply to the cases of the Shabbat limit and the *bet haperas*, because a single witness is sufficient for these, and if the adult testifying to what he saw as a child were believed only together with an adult, we would not need him at all, since the adult could testify alone (*Ran*).

גָּדוֹל An adult. Rav Huna the son of Rav Yehoshua rules that the son of a witness who signed a document may serve as one of the witnesses who authenticates his father's signature, even if the father died while his son was a child; but the son may not authenticate it by himself. It

[1] וּצְרִיכָא. [2] דְּאִי אַשְׁמַעִינַן אָבִיו, מִשּׁוּם דִּשְׁכִיחַ גַּבֵּיהּ, [3] אֲבָל רַבּוֹ, לָא. [4] וְאִי אַשְׁמַעִינַן רַבּוֹ, מִשּׁוּם דְּאִית לֵיהּ אֵימְתֵיהּ דְּרַבֵּיהּ, [5] אֲבָל אָבִיו, לָא. [6] וְאִי אַשְׁמַעִינַן הָנֵי תַּרְתֵּי, [7] אָבִיו, דִּשְׁכִיחַ גַּבֵּיהּ, וְרַבּוֹ, דְּאִית לֵיהּ אֵימְתֵיהּ. [8] אֲבָל אָחִיו, דְּלֵית לֵיהּ לָא הָא וְלָא הָא, [9] אֵימָא לָא.

LITERAL TRANSLATION

[1] And [it is] necessary. [2] For if [the Mishnah] had informed us [about] his father, [we would say that it is] because he was frequently with him, [3] but [regarding] his teacher, he is not [believed]. [4] And if it had informed us [about] his teacher, [we would say that it is] because awe for his teacher was upon him, [5] but [regarding] his father, he is not [believed]. [6] And if it had informed us [about] these two, [7] [we would say that it applies to] his father, because he was frequently with him, and [to] his teacher, because his awe was upon him. [8] But [regarding] his brother, for whom he has neither this nor that, [9] [we would] say he is not

TRANSLATION AND COMMENTARY

witnesses to authenticate his signature, even if the witness was a child when he saw his father sign his name. Rav Huna the son of Rav Yehoshua rules that only one of the independent witnesses may be an adult testifying about what he saw as a child. The second independent witness must be an adult testifying about what he saw as an adult.

וּצְרִיכָא [1] The Gemara now explains that **it was necessary** for the Mishnah to illustrate this law with three cases — the father, the teacher, and the brother. [2] **For if** the Mishnah **had informed us** only **about the witness's father, we would have said** that the son is believed in such a case **because he was frequently with** his father as a child, and even though his father may have died while the son was still a child, his father's signature remains etched in his memory. [3] **But regarding the witness's teacher,** we might have thought that the former student **should not be** believed unless he saw the signature when he was already an adult. [4] **And if** the Mishnah **had informed us** only **about the witness's teacher, we would have said** that the former student is believed in such a case **because he had** a feeling of **awe for his teacher,** and therefore paid close attention to his handwriting, [5] **but regarding his** own **father,** we might have thought that the son **is not** believed unless he saw the signature when he was already an adult. [6] **And if** the Mishnah **had informed us** only **about these two** cases, but not about the brother, [7] **we would have said that** the Mishnah's ruling **applies to his father, because he was frequently with him, and to his teacher, because he had** a feeling of **awe for him**, as explained above. [8] **But** regarding **his brother, for whom he** may have **felt neither** a close affinity **nor** great reverence, [9] **we would have said** that the brother **is not believed** unless

RASHI

גמרא דשכיח גביה — ונתן עיניו בקטנותו בכתב יד אביו.

NOTES

is clear from the language used by Rav Huna the son of Rav Yehoshua that the other witness must not be another adult testifying to what he saw as a child. It is not clear, however, if he must be completely qualified, or if two relatives are believed when it comes to authenticating a signature, provided that one of them saw it as an adult. *Ritva* cites an opinion that at least one of the witnesses must be qualified. Most authorities, however, agree with an opinion cited by *Ran* in the name of *Ba'al HaMa'or*, who says that the other witness may also be a relative, although he must be an adult. *Ritva* notes that *Ran*'s explanation is supported by the language used by Rav Huna the son of Rav Yehoshua. For if a relative cannot serve as the second witness, Rav Huna the son of Rav Yehoshua should have said that the other witness must be qualified, instead of saying that he must be an adult. But *Ritva* concedes that Rav Huna the son of Rav Yehoshua may have been focusing on the main point of the Mishnah, which is that the testimony of an adult about what he saw as a child is believed.

Mordekhai agrees with the other Rishonim that relatives of the witnesses to a document may authenticate their signatures. But he cites a ruling of *Rabbenu Ḥananel* that it is only the relatives of these witnesses who are permitted to testify in this way, but not relatives of the borrower or the lender. For if a lender could authenticate a document by producing his own relatives as witnesses, it would become quite easy to forge a document. Nevertheless, *Meiri* permits this.

Ran adds that although the witnesses who authenticate the signatures may be related to the witnesses to the document, they may not be related to each other, as this disqualifies them from serving as witnesses.

אֲבָל אָחִיו... אֵימָא לָא But regarding his brother... we would say he is not believed. The Gemara explains that the Mishnah illustrated this law by means of three different cases, to teach us that it applies even if the witness was not unusually familiar with or awed by the signatory. *Rosh* and *Meiri* note, however, that the Jerusalem Talmud rules that the witness is believed only if he is somewhat familiar with the signature, as in the case of a brother, but if he claims to have seen the signature only once or twice, and only when he was a child, he is not believed. Other Rishonim, however, rule that the witness is believed about any signature of which he is certain (*Ittur*, *Ra'ah*, *Ritva*). *Bet Yosef* explains that these Rishonim rely on our Gemara, which does not make any distinction between signatures with which the witness is familiar and other signatures. *Bet Yosef* says that these Rishonim either explain the Jerusalem Talmud differently, or reject its ruling in favor of that of the Babylonian Talmud.

TRANSLATION AND COMMENTARY

he saw the signature when he was already an adult. [1]**Therefore** the Mishnah cites all three illustrations of this law **to inform us** that a man may serve as a witness to authenticate a signature he last saw as a child, even if during his childhood he was not in intimate contact with the person who signed the document. [2]The Gemara explains: **Since the authentication of documents is** a **Rabbinic** requirement, **the Rabbis believed** the witness **about Rabbinic matters**. The Gemara explained above (21a) that the Rabbis were lenient regarding the authentication of documents, since such authentication is in any case only a Rabbinic requirement. By Torah law, a document signed by witnesses is considered the equivalent of oral testimony that has been investigated and confirmed by the court (above, 18b), and a lender can use the document as proof of a loan, without having to prove that the witnesses' signatures are authentic. Accordingly, the Rabbis were lenient here as well, and they accepted the testimony of an adult about what he saw as a child as that of one of the independent witnesses who certifies the signatures on the document.

זָכוּר הָיִיתִי בִּפְלוֹנִית [3]The Gemara now considers the next clause of the Mishnah, which ruled that "a man who attended a wedding as a child is believed when he testifies as an adult that **he remembers that** when **So-and-so** was married, she **went out with a *hinuma* and the hair of her head was loose.**" [4]The Gemara asks: **What is the reason** that the witness is believed? Why is the woman not required to produce qualified witnesses to testify that she was a virgin when she married, in accordance with the general principle that the burden of proof always falls on the plaintiff? For the Gemara explains below (28b) that an adult is not accepted as a witness to what he saw as a child, if his testimony is needed to effect a transfer of property or to compel a defendant to pay money.

כֵּיוָן דְּרוֹב נָשִׁים [5]The Gemara answers: **Since most women are married as virgins,** the witness's testimony **merely reveals a matter.** The Gemara explained above (16a) that the wife's claim is far more credible than the husband's because most women do in fact marry as virgins. Indeed, later on the same page, the Gemara goes so far as to suggest that the wife's claim should be believed without proof, since it is statistically much more likely than the husband's. The Gemara answers that she would in fact be believed without proof were we not concerned that so few people seem to remember this woman's wedding, and the weddings of virgins usually attract notice. Therefore we require some evidence, but not necessarily full-fledged testimony. Evidence of this sort is called "revealing a matter," and the Gemara declares (above, 22a) that when this is all that is required, the normal rules of testimony are relaxed. Accordingly, our Mishnah rules that the testimony of an adult about what he saw as a child is sufficient for this purpose.

[1]קָא מַשְׁמַע לָן: [2]כֵּיוָן דְּקִיּוּם שְׁטָרוֹת מִדְּרַבָּנַן, הֵימְנוּהוּ רַבָּנַן בִּדְרַבָּנַן.

[3]"זָכוּר הָיִיתִי בִּפְלוֹנִית, שֶׁיָּצְאָה בְּהִינוּמָא וְרֹאשָׁהּ פָּרוּעַ". [4]מַאי טַעְמָא?

[5]כֵּיוָן דְּרוֹב נָשִׁים בְּתוּלוֹת נִישָּׂאוֹת, גִּלּוּי מִלְּתָא בְּעָלְמָא הוּא.

LITERAL TRANSLATION

[believed. [1]Therefore] it tells us: [2]Since the authentication of documents is Rabbinic, the Rabbis believed him about Rabbinic [matters].

[3]"I remember about So-and-so, that she went out with a *hinuma* and [the hair of] her head was loose." [4]What is the reason?

[5]Since most women are married [as] virgins, it is merely the revealing of a matter.

RASHI

קיום שטרות מדרבנן — דמדאורייתא לא בעינן קיום, דאמר ריש לקיש (כתובות יח,ב): עדים החתומים על השטר נעשה כמי שנחקרה עדותן בבית דין. **הימנוהו רבנן בדרבנן** — בדבר שהוא מדבריהם האמינו, ואין זה עוקר דבר מן התורה, הם אמרו והם אמרו. הם הצריכו קיום העדות, והם הכשירו בו את אלו. **גלוי מלתא בעלמא הוא** — כלומר, אין הדבר צריך עדות, אלא לפרסם שיצא הדין לאור בלא גמגום.

NOTES

כֵּיוָן דְּקִיּוּם שְׁטָרוֹת מִדְּרַבָּנַן **Since the authentication of documents is Rabbinic.** In several places (e.g., above, 21b) the Gemara notes that the Rabbis were lenient about certain procedural regulations governing the authentication of documents, since authentication is in any case only required by Rabbinic decree. In tractate *Gittin* (3a), the Gemara connects this idea with Resh Lakish's maxim (above, 18b) that witnesses who have signed a document have the status of oral witnesses who have already been examined in court. Since the witnesses' signatures on the document are considered the equivalent of testimony that has been examined, no further objections can be raised against them. Accordingly, most Rishonim explain that by Torah law the lender can use the document as proof of the loan, without having to prove that the witnesses' signatures are authentic. It is only by Rabbinic decree that the lender must prove the authenticity of the signatures when challenged, in order to close the obvious opening this law presents to forgers.

גִּלּוּי מִלְּתָא בְּעָלְמָא הוּא **It is merely the revealing of a matter.** It is clear from our Gemara that the woman does not need the testimony of witnesses to support her claim. It is not clear, however, what the Gemara means here by "merely the revealing of a matter." Our commentary

TRANSLATION AND COMMENTARY

וְשֶׁהָיָה אִישׁ פְּלוֹנִי [1]The Gemara now considers the next clause of the Mishnah, which ruled that a person is believed if he testifies that a childhood friend of his **"used to go out of school to immerse in order to eat terumah."** [2]**But,** the Gemara asks, even if we believe the witness's testimony that his friend ate terumah as a child, how does this prove that his friend is a priest? **Perhaps he was the slave of a priest?** For the Torah (Leviticus 22:11) specifically permits a priest's slave to eat terumah, together with the other members of the priest's household.

[1]״וְשֶׁהָיָה אִישׁ פְּלוֹנִי יוֹצֵא מִבֵּית הַסֵּפֶר לִטְבּוֹל לֶאֱכוֹל בִּתְרוּמָה״. [2]וְדִלְמָא עֶבֶד כֹּהֵן הוּא? [3]מְסַיֵּיעַ לֵיהּ לְרַבִּי יְהוֹשֻׁעַ בֶּן לֵוִי. [4]דְּאָמַר רַבִּי יְהוֹשֻׁעַ בֶּן לֵוִי: אָסוּר לְאָדָם שֶׁיְּלַמֵּד אֶת עַבְדּוֹ תּוֹרָה. [5]וְלָא? [6]וְהָתַנְיָא: ״לָוָה הֵימֶנּוּ רַבּוֹ, אוֹ שֶׁעֲשָׂאוֹ רַבּוֹ

LITERAL TRANSLATION

[1]"Or that 'So-and-so used to go out of school to immerse in order to eat terumah.'" [2]But perhaps he was the slave of a priest?

[3]This supports Rabbi Yehoshua ben Levi, [4]for Rabbi Yehoshua ben Levi said: It is forbidden for a man to teach his slave Torah.

[5]But is it not [permitted]? [6]But surely it was taught: "[If] his master borrowed [money] from him, or if his master made him

מְסַיֵּיעַ לֵיהּ [3]The Gemara answers: **This** Mishnah **supports** the following statement of **Rabbi Yehoshua ben Levi.** [4]**For Rabbi Yehoshua ben Levi said: It is forbidden for a person to teach his slave Torah.** Accordingly, a child who was taken out of school to immerse himself in order to eat terumah could not have been a slave, and must have been the son of a priest. The Mishnah's ruling is thus best explained in the light of Rabbi Yehoshua ben Levi's statement, and indeed supports it.

וְלָא [5]The Gemara asks: **But is it not permitted** to teach a slave Torah? [6]**Surely it was taught** in a Baraita: **"If** a slave's master behaves toward his slave as though the slave were a free man, this is no proof that he has been freed. If, for example, the slave's **master borrows money from him, or if his master makes him**

NOTES

follows *Tosafot* (above, 16b), who explains that "merely revealing a matter" is a term for weak evidence that is valid only in conjunction with other arguments. Since the woman's claim is supported by a strong statistical majority, we need only a little concrete evidence to overcome our doubts about the lack of a public rumor. The same term appears above (22a), in a passage in which the Gemara declares that when we are "merely revealing a matter," we accept one pair of witnesses over another, and do not say that they are two against two. *Ritva* explains the term there in the same way as *Tosafot* explains it here.

Rashi gives a nonidiomatic interpretation of the phrase here, as though it meant "publicizing the court's decision." *Rashi* explains that the court is ready to rule in the woman's favor, but prefers to have some firm evidence to support its ruling.

וְדִלְמָא עֶבֶד כֹּהֵן הוּא But perhaps he was the slave of a priest? *Ritva* asks: What difference does it make if the schoolmate was a slave or a priest? The Gemara explains, below, that we allow this person to eat only Rabbinic terumah, and everyone agrees that we do not elevate from Rabbinic terumah to lineage, and that a slave is permitted to eat terumah. So what difference does it make if we give him the terumah as a slave or as a priest?

Tosafot answers that our concern here is that the schoolmate may have been the slave of a priest at the time and subsequently may have been freed. Thus, by accepting the witness's testimony, we would be permitting a freed slave to eat terumah. *Ritva* rejects this explanation, because it is forbidden to free a slave except under unusual circumstances, and if this slave's master had done so, people would have known about it. *Ritva* also points out that the Gemara above (25a) ruled that receiving a share of terumah at the threshing floor is proof of priesthood. But if we are concerned about the possibility that the person receiving the terumah may have been a slave who was subsequently freed, why did the Gemara not raise this objection there?

Ritva explains that the Gemara's concern here is not that the slave will eat terumah now, but that he may give terumah to the members of his household and establish a precedent for all his descendants. *Ritva* explains that this concern does not apply above (25a), because the Gemara there is referring to a witness who explained that the would-be priest was given terumah regularly, in the manner of a priest, and not on an occasional basis, in the manner of a slave collecting terumah for his master. Here, however, where the witness saw the events as a child, he may be confused about crucial details that would enable him to distinguish between a priest's son and his slave.

Rashba explains that the Gemara above (25a) is referring to a case where it was clear that the would-be priest was the son of a priest and not his slave; but doubts arose as to whether his mother was qualified for the priesthood. Here, by contrast, it is clear from the fact that the school was mentioned in the story that we suspect that the would-be priest may have been a slave.

HALAKHAH

אָסוּר לְאָדָם שֶׁיְּלַמֵּד אֶת עַבְדּוֹ תּוֹרָה It is forbidden for a man to teach his slave Torah. "A master may not teach his slave Torah, but if he does so, the slave does not thereby go free, following Rabbi Yehoshua ben Levi." (*Rambam, Sefer Kinyan, Hilkhot Avadim* 8:18; *Shulḥan Arukh, Yoreh De'ah* 267:71.)

TRANSLATION AND COMMENTARY

[28B] **guardian** of his property, [1]**or if** the slave **put on tefillin in the presence of his master, or if** the slave was called up to **read three verses in the synagogue** (i.e., was called to the reading of the law), [2]in all these cases he does not **have the status of a free man,** even though his master is allowing him to behave like one." This Baraita shows us that it is possible for a slave to study Torah, for otherwise how was he able to take an active part in the synagogue service?

הָתָם [3]The Gemara answers: **There,** in the Baraita, **it is** referring to a case **where the slave** learned to **read of his own** volition. It is not unheard of for a slave to become learned in Torah, if he makes a point of studying on his own. [4]**When we say** that a master must not teach his slave Torah, we are referring to a situation in which **he treated him like a son.** It is forbidden to send a slave to school and to treat him like a free man, but a slave who decides to study on his own is permitted to do so.

[28B] אַפּוֹטְרוֹפּוֹס, [1]אוֹ שֶׁהִנִּיחַ תְּפִילִּין בִּפְנֵי רַבּוֹ, אוֹ שֶׁקָּרָא שְׁלֹשָׁה פְּסוּקִים בְּבֵית הַכְּנֶסֶת, [2]הֲרֵי זֶה לֹא יָצָא לְחֵירוּת״! [3]הָתָם, דְּאִיקְרִי עֶבֶד מִדַּעְתּוֹ. [4]כִּי קָאָמְרִינַן, דְּקָא נָהֵיג בֵּיהּ מִנְהַג בָּנִים.

LITERAL TRANSLATION

[28B] a guardian, [1]or if he put on tefillin in front of his master, or if he read three verses in the synagogue, [2]he has not gone out to freedom"!

[3]There, it is when the slave read of his own volition.

[4]When we say [this], it is when he treated him like a son (lit., "the custom of sons").

RASHI

אפוטרופוס — מסר נכסיו בידו להכניס ולהוציא לסחורה. **הרי זה לא יצא לחירות** — ולא אמרינן: אי לאו דשחרריה לא הוה יזיף מיניה ולא הוה שביק ליה לנהוג מנהג בן חורין. ושמעינן מינה דיש עבד שלומד תורה.

LANGUAGE

אַפּוֹטְרוֹפּוֹס Guardian. This word is derived from the Greek ἐπίτροπος, *epitropos*, meaning "guardian" or "trustee."

BACKGROUND

אַפּוֹטְרוֹפּוֹס Guardian. Although this term sometimes refers to an official who is appointed to administer property, and receives a salary for doing so, in this case the term refers to someone who takes it upon himself to look after someone else's property without receiving any fee. Occasionally a guardian was appointed by the court, or by the father of orphaned children in his will. Although it was an honor to be appointed guardian, and a guardian had broad discretionary powers over the property entrusted to him, it was unlikely that someone would assume this responsibility without some special reason, either friendship with the orphans' late father or respect for the court. There was great reluctance to accept a guardianship for an extended period, or without some particular reason for doing so.

NOTES

אוֹ שֶׁהִנִּיחַ תְּפִילִּין Or if he put on tefillin. In four places in the Torah (Exodus 13:9 and 13:16; Deuteronomy 6:8 and 11:18) Jews are commanded to place certain verses of the Torah upon the hand and between the eyes. The traditional interpretation of this commandment is that pieces of parchment with these verses written on them are to be placed inside two specially designed black leather boxes, and tied with black leather straps to the left arm and to the head above the forehead. These two boxes with their contents are called tefillin (often translated as "phylacteries"). They may be worn at any time during the day on weekdays, but customarily they are worn during the morning prayers only.

Women and slaves are exempt from wearing tefillin, and the Rabbis disapproved of their putting them on voluntarily (*Shulḥan Arukh, Oraḥ Ḥayyim* 38:3). Nevertheless, it is not technically forbidden for them to put on tefillin, and if they do so, they may even recite the blessing, according to many authorities. Since it was not customary for slaves to wear tefillin, if a man thought to be a slave did so, it suggested that he had been freed.

לֹא יָצָא לְחֵירוּת He has not gone out to freedom. In the parallel passage in tractate *Gittin* (40a), the Gemara cites our Baraita, which rules that a slave does not gain his freedom merely by behaving like a free man. However, the Gemara concludes that if his master participated in the slave's actions — such as by helping the slave put on tefillin — the slave does go free.

The language of the Baraita and of the Gemara in *Gittin* appears to imply that if the slave acts in this way, it is the behavior itself that gives him his freedom. But the Rishonim maintain that a slave cannot be freed on the basis of his behavior alone, unless the master gives him a formal bill of emancipation. Our commentary follows *Rashi*, who explains that the slave's behavior is treated as proof that the master has already freed him, provided that the master played an active role in preparing the slave for freedom. But if the slave studied Torah or put on tefillin on his own initiative, we do not assume that he has already been freed, because although it is not proper for the slave to behave in this way, it is possible that this particular master was liberal in these matters.

Rif has a variant reading, followed by *Rambam* and *Rosh*, that if the master plays an active role in his slave's behavior, the master is required to draw up a bill of emancipation for him and set him free. *Rosh* notes that this reading is difficult to reconcile with *Rashi*, because *Rashi*'s explanation is based on the assumption that the master has already freed the slave. *Rosh* explains that in fact we believe that the slave has already been freed, and so a bill of emancipation is not strictly necessary, but we insist on its being drawn up as an added precaution. *Rambam* follows *Rif*'s reading and explains it literally: Whenever the master declares verbally or indicates by his actions that he wishes his slave to go free, the slave is automatically freed, and the master is compelled to write a formal bill of emancipation.

HALAKHAH

לֹא יָצָא לְחֵירוּת He has not gone out to freedom. "If a master marries his slave to a free woman, or places tefillin on his head, or tells him to read from the Torah before the congregation (and similarly with other matters that characterize free people) the slave goes free, and we force the master to write him a bill of emancipation. But if the master borrows money from the slave, or makes him guardian of his property, or if the slave puts on tefillin or reads from the Torah before his master, and his master does not protest, the slave does not go free," following the Baraita. (*Rambam, Hilkhot Avadim* 8:17; *Shulḥan Arukh, Yoreh De'ah* 267:70.)

TRANSLATION AND COMMENTARY

לְטְבּוֹל לֶאֱכוֹל בִּתְרוּמָה [1]The Gemara now returns to the clause of the Mishnah which ruled that the testimony of a man that he was present as a child when his schoolmate was taken out of school **"to immerse in order to eat terumah"** is accepted to elevate his friend to the priesthood. [2]The Gemara explains: **This clause in the Mishnah refers to Rabbinic terumah.** To be given permission to eat Rabbinic terumah, it is not necessary to produce qualified witnesses. Hence the Rabbis were lenient and permitted the would-be priest to eat Rabbinic terumah on the basis of the testimony of his former schoolmate. But they would not allow him to eat Torah terumah, nor would they elevate him to full priestly lineage, on the basis of such testimony, even if the witness testified as an adult that he remembered from his childhood that his schoolmate ate Torah terumah or engaged in some behavior indicating that he was a fully qualified priest.

[1]״לִטְבּוֹל לֶאֱכוֹל בִּתְרוּמָה״. [2]בִּתְרוּמָה דְּרַבָּנַן.
[3]״וְשֶׁהָיָה חוֹלֵק עִמָּנוּ עַל הַגּוֹרֶן״. [4]וְדִלְמָא עֶבֶד כֹּהֵן הוּא?
[5]תְּנַן כְּמַאן דְּאָמַר: אֵין חוֹלְקִין תְּרוּמָה לְעֶבֶד אֶלָּא אִם כֵּן רַבּוֹ עִמּוֹ. [6]דְּתַנְיָא: ״אֵין חוֹלְקִין תְּרוּמָה לְעֶבֶד אֶלָּא אִם כֵּן רַבּוֹ עִמּוֹ. [7]דִּבְרֵי רַבִּי יְהוּדָה. [8]רַבִּי יוֹסֵי אוֹמֵר: יָכוֹל הוּא שֶׁיֹּאמַר:

LITERAL TRANSLATION

[1]"To immerse in order to eat terumah." [2][This refers] to Rabbinic terumah.

[3]"Or that he used to receive [a share] with us at the threshing floor." [4]But perhaps he was the slave of a priest?

[5][The Mishnah] is teaching in accordance with the one who says: We do not distribute terumah to a slave unless his master is with him. [6]For it was taught: "We do not distribute terumah to a slave unless his master is with him. [7][These are] the words of Rabbi Yehudah. [8]Rabbi Yose says: He can say:

RASHI

בתרומה דרבנן — כגון תרומת חוצה לארץ, או פירות — המניניהו להני להאכילו על פיהם. הכי גרסינן: **דתניא שאין חולקין תרומה לעבד כו׳** — ורישא דברייתא: כהנת שנתערב וולדה בוולד שפחתה שניהן יוצאין לגורן ונוטלין חלק אחד, שאין חולקין תרומה לעבד כו׳. הלכך, אי אזיל חד מינייהו לא פלגינן ליה, דלמא אתי לאחזוקי בכהן, ודלמא האי ניהו העבד.

וְשֶׁהָיָה חוֹלֵק עִמָּנוּ [3]The Mishnah also ruled that if an adult priest recalls that his childhood friend **"used to receive a share** of terumah **with us at the threshing floor,"** he is believed, and his friend is elevated to the priesthood on the basis of an adult's testimony as to what he saw as a child. [4]**But**, the Gemara objects, even if we believe the witness that his friend was given terumah to eat as a child, how does this prove that his friend is a priest? **Perhaps** his friend **was the slave of a priest,** who is also permitted to eat terumah?

תְּנַן כְּמַאן דְּאָמַר [5]The Gemara answers: The law that **the Mishnah is teaching** us is in accordance with the viewpoint of Rabbi Yehudah, **who says:** Even though a priest's slave is permitted to eat terumah, **we do not distribute terumah to a** priest's **slave unless his master is with him** at the time. According to Rabbi Yehudah, if someone receives a share of terumah at the threshing floor, it is conclusive proof that he is a priest, because a priest's slave is not given a share unless his master is with him. Therefore, there is no danger of error, and to the extent that we believe the witness that his childhood friend was given terumah, we can be confident that his friend is a priest. The Gemara now cites the source of Rabbi Yehudah's view, which is recorded in a Tosefta (*Yevamot* 12:4). This Tosefta considers a case in which the wife of a priest and his female slave gave birth to sons at the same time, and the sons got mixed up. Thus one son is a priest, and the other is a slave, but it is impossible to tell which is which. [6]The Tosefta **teaches** that even though a priest's slave is permitted to eat terumah, we must not give either son a share of terumah unless they come together to collect it, because **"we do not distribute terumah to a** priest's **slave unless his master is with him.** [7]**This is the opinion of Rabbi Yehudah.** [8]But **Rabbi Yose says:** Each of the sons **can** come on his

NOTES

דִּבְרֵי רַבִּי יְהוּדָה **These are the words of Rabbi Yehudah.** This dispute has already appeared in this chapter. The Mishnah (above, 23b) ruled that, according to the Sages, if an unknown person claims to be a priest and produces one witness to support his claim, he is believed, even if that witness is another would-be priest with an obvious interest in his testimony. Rabbi Yehudah, by contrast, insists on two qualified witnesses. The Gemara (above, 24b) cites a Baraita elaborating on the dispute between Rabbi Yehudah and the Sages in the Mishnah. In the Baraita, the Sages rule that the testimony of one other would-be priest is believed to the extent of allowing the stranger to eat

HALAKHAH

אֵין חוֹלְקִין תְּרוּמָה לְעֶבֶד **We do not distribute terumah to a slave.** "Although a priest's slave is permitted to eat terumah, we must not distribute terumah to a slave at the threshing floor, lest people mistakenly think that he is a priest." (*Rambam, Sefer Zeraim, Hilkhot Terumot* 12:22.)

BACKGROUND

בְּמְקוֹמוֹ שֶׁל רַבִּי יְהוּדָה In Rabbi Yehudah's place. If no Halakhic ruling has yet been issued on a given subject, local custom is followed. Where there is no fixed custom on a certain matter, the decision of the local Rabbinic authority (מָרָא דְּאַתְרָא) is followed. This situation led to the creation of customs based on the approaches of the Sages of various places. Consequently, the custom of one place might remain different from that of other places on subjects regarding which no obligatory Halakhic ruling had been issued.

We know that Rabbi Yose lived in Sepphoris in Upper Galilee, and in that region people apparently followed his approach. However, Rabbi Yehudah lived in Usha in Lower Galilee.

TRANSLATION AND COMMENTARY

own, and **say** to the farmer: [1] **'If I am** the son of the **priest, give me** terumah **for my own sake, and if I am the priest's slave, give me terumah for my master's sake.** For although my lineage is in doubt, there is no question that I am entitled to eat terumah.'" [2] The Tosefta goes on to explain (this explanation does not appear in our editions of the Tosefta) that **"in Rabbi Yehudah's place they used to elevate from terumah to lineage.** Therefore Rabbi Yehudah did not permit the distribution of terumah to a slave in his master's absence, lest the slave one day use this as proof of priestly lineage. [3] **In Rabbi Yose's place,** by contrast, **the practice was not to elevate from terumah to lineage."** Therefore Rabbi Yose saw no reason to forbid the distribution of terumah to a priest's slave, since in any case this could not serve as proof of priestly lineage. It follows that in Rabbi Yose's place — where terumah was not restricted to priests of established lineage — the fact that a person was given terumah to eat was not proof of anything, because it was possible that he was merely a priest's slave. But in Rabbi Yehudah's place — where only priests of established lineage were given terumah — the fact that someone was given terumah was conclusive proof that he was a priest and not a slave. Therefore, to the extent that we believe the witness's childhood recollection that his friend was given terumah, we can be confident that his friend is a priest.

[1] ׳אִם כֹּהֵן אֲנִי, תְּנוּ לִי בִּשְׁבִיל עַצְמִי, וְאִם עֶבֶד כֹּהֵן אֲנִי, תְּנוּ לִי בִּשְׁבִיל רַבִּי׳. [2] בִּמְקוֹמוֹ שֶׁל רַבִּי יְהוּדָה הָיוּ מַעֲלִין מִתְּרוּמָה לְיוֹחֲסִין. [3] בִּמְקוֹמוֹ שֶׁל רַבִּי יוֹסֵי לֹא הָיוּ מַעֲלִין מִתְּרוּמָה לְיוֹחֲסִין״.

LITERAL TRANSLATION

[1] 'If I am a priest, give me for my own sake, and if I am the slave of a priest, give me for my master's sake.' [2] In Rabbi Yehudah's place they used to elevate from terumah to lineage. [3] In Rabbi Yose's place they used not to elevate from terumah to lineage."

RASHI

במקומו של רבי יהודה – משום הכי אמר: אין חולקין.

NOTES

terumah, but not to the extent of permitting him to marry a woman of unblemished lineage. By contrast, Rabbi Yehudah rules that the witness is not even believed if the effect is to feed the stranger terumah. All agree, however, that we do not believe a single witness if the effect is to permit an unknown man to marry a woman of unblemished lineage.

Based on this Baraita, the Gemara explains that Rabbi Yehudah does not accept the testimony of a single witness for terumah because he disagrees with the Rabbis about elevating from terumah to lineage. Rabbi Yehudah maintains that if a man was given a share of terumah, we may assume that his lineage was definitely established, and that he is permitted to marry a woman of unblemished lineage, whereas the Sages — Rabbi Yose in our passage — maintain that eating terumah is not a sign of lineage. Hence Rabbi Yehudah requires two witnesses for terumah, just as for lineage, for if we were to accept one witness for terumah, we would indirectly be accepting a single witness for lineage as well. But the Sages follow Rabbi Yose, who maintains that eating terumah is not a sign of lineage. Hence they do not require two witnesses, but rather treat this as an ordinary case where we question the permissibility of an item of food; in such cases one witness is sufficient, even if the witness has an interest in his testimony.

According to the conclusion of the Gemara (above, 25a), Rabbi Yehudah elevates only from Torah terumah to lineage, but does not elevate from Rabbinic terumah to lineage, or even to Torah terumah. The Sages, by contrast, do not distinguish between Rabbinic and Torah terumah. Any testimony that is acceptable for the one is acceptable for the other, but we do not elevate to lineage from either.

בִּמְקוֹמוֹ שֶׁל רַבִּי יוֹסֵי לֹא הָיוּ מַעֲלִין In Rabbi Yose's place they used not to elevate. Rabbi Yehudah may have had other reasons for not giving a slave terumah, and as a result he felt free to elevate from terumah to lineage (see *Shittah Mekubbetzet*). But the simple meaning of this Baraita is that Rabbi Yehudah forbade the slave to receive terumah because he elevated from terumah to lineage. *Tosafot* points out that in the parallel passage in tractate *Yevamot* (100a), the Gemara explicitly interprets the Baraita in this way. It thus follows that Rabbi Yose felt free to permit the slave to receive terumah because he did not elevate from terumah to lineage.

The Rishonim ask: How could Rabbi Yose have allowed himself to distribute terumah to a slave? Even if there is no danger of the slave being elevated to lineage, there is still a danger that the slave may one day be freed or sold to a non-priest, and may continue to eat terumah by pretending to be a priest.

Tosafot explains that we are not concerned that a freed slave will continue to ask for terumah, since this is liable to remind people that he was a slave — something he would presumably prefer to be forgotten. *Ramban* and *Ritva* explain that we are not concerned that the slave will be freed and continue to ask for terumah, because it is unusual for a master to free his slaves and whenever this happens, it is public knowledge. *Ramban* adds that the former slave may be tempted to pretend to be a priest in order to marry a woman of unblemished lineage, but we are not worried that a freed slave would deliberately deceive us just in order to eat terumah.

Regarding the possibility that the slave may be sold to a non-priest, *Tosafot* explains that we are not concerned that he will continue to eat terumah, because his new master will maintain him, and the slave has no interest in eating terumah illegally just to save his master some money.

TRANSLATION AND COMMENTARY

תַּנְיָא [1]The Gemara relates that the following incident **was described** in a Baraita: **"Rabbi Elazar the son of Rabbi Yose said: In all my days, I have never** been called upon to **testify.** [2]Only **on one occasion did I testify, and** my testimony had disastrous consequences because it was misunderstood, and **on my evidence they elevated a slave to the priesthood.** My testimony resulted in a slave being mistakenly declared a priest, with all the consequences that entails."

הֶעֱלוּ [3]Before explaining this Baraita, the Gemara raises a question: Rabbi Elazar the son of Rabbi Yose said that **"they elevated"** a slave to the priesthood. In other words, his misunderstood testimony was accepted, and the slave was declared to be a priest. But **can it enter your mind** that, through an unfortunate error, a righteous man like Rabbi Elazar the son of Rabbi Yose could have been the cause of such a mistake? [4]We have a tradition that **the Holy One, blessed be He, does not bring about a stumbling block** even **through the animals of the righteous** (i.e., God's providence will prevent unfortunate accidents leading to sin, even when the sin involves only the animal of a righteous person). [5]**How much more so does He not do** such a thing **through the righteous themselves!** Surely God would not have allowed such a serious mistake to occur!

אֶלָּא [6]**Rather,** the Gemara answers, Rabbi Elazar the son of Rabbi Yose **meant to say** that the court misunderstood his testimony, and as a result **it wished to elevate a slave to the priesthood on** the basis of **his evidence**; but Rabbi Elazar the son of Rabbi Yose realized the error in time and explained the situation to the court, and as a result the erroneous ruling was not issued.

חֲזָא בְּאַתְרֵיהּ דְּרַבִּי יוֹסֵי [7]The Gemara now explains how the testimony of Rabbi Elazar the son of Rabbi Yose came to be misunderstood: **He saw** a slave receiving a share of terumah **in Rabbi Yose's place,** in accordance with Rabbi Yose's ruling that a priest's slave may be given a share of terumah, since we do not elevate from terumah to lineage. Later, the slave went to Rabbi Yehudah's place, and claimed to be a priest. He then called on Rabbi Elazar the son of Rabbi Yose to testify that he saw him receiving terumah, [8]**and** Rabbi Elazar the son of Rabbi Yose **went as requested and testified in Rabbi Yehudah's place,** not realizing that being given terumah was proof of lineage there. The court was about to declare that the slave was a priest, when the mistake was discovered.

[1]תַּנְיָא: ״אָמַר רַבִּי אֶלְעָזָר בְּרַבִּי יוֹסֵי: מִיָּמַי, לֹא הֵעַדְתִּי. [2]פַּעַם אַחַת הֵעַדְתִּי, וְהֶעֱלוּ עֶבֶד לִכְהוּנָּה עַל פִּי״.
[3]״הֶעֱלוּ״. סָלְקָא דַּעְתָּךְ? [4]הַשְׁתָּא, וּמַה בְּהֶמְתָּן שֶׁל צַדִּיקִים אֵין הַקָּדוֹשׁ בָּרוּךְ הוּא מֵבִיא תַּקָּלָה עַל יָדָם, [5]צַדִּיקִים עַצְמָם לֹא כָּל שֶׁכֵּן!
[6]אֶלָּא: ״בִּקְּשׁוּ לְהַעֲלוֹת עֶבֶד לִכְהוּנָּה עַל פִּי״.
[7]חֲזָא בְּאַתְרֵיהּ דְּרַבִּי יוֹסֵי, [8]וַאֲזַל וְאַסְהֵיד בְּאַתְרֵיהּ דְּרַבִּי יְהוּדָה.

LITERAL TRANSLATION

[1]It was taught: "Rabbi Elazar the son of Rabbi Yose said: In [all] my days, I have never testified. [2]Once I did testify, and they elevated a slave to the priesthood on my evidence (lit., 'mouth')."
[3]"They elevated." Can [this] enter your mind? [4]Now, if the Holy One, blessed be He, does not bring [about] a stumbling block through the animals of the righteous, [5]how much more so [through] the righteous themselves!
[6]Rather, [he said:] "They wished to elevate a slave to the priesthood on my evidence."
[7]He saw [him] in Rabbi Yose's place, [8]and he went and testified in Rabbi Yehudah's place.

RASHI

בהמתן של צדיקים – חמורו של רבי פנחס בן יאיר, ב״הכל שוחטין״ (חולין ז,א). **חזא באתריה דרבי יוסי** – שחלקו לו תרומה בגורן. **ואסהיד באתריה דרבי יהודה** – ושם לא היו חולקין תרומה לעבדי כהנים.

NOTES

בְּהֶמְתָּן שֶׁל צַדִּיקִים **The animals of the righteous.** This remark of the Gemara, which is mentioned in several places in the Talmud, is based on a story in tractate *Hullin* (7a). The Gemara relates that Rabbi Pineḥas ben Yair came to an inn. The innkeeper gave Rabbi Pineḥas's donkey barley to eat, but the donkey would not touch it. The innkeeper cleaned the barley, but the donkey still would not eat. Rabbi Pineḥas said to the innkeeper: "Is it possible that you have not tithed the barley?" The embarrassed innkeeper quickly tithed the barley, and the donkey ate. Rabbi Pinchas said: "This poor donkey is doing the will of its Creator, and you would feed it untithed produce?"

Tosafot (*Gittin* 7a) notes that disastrous errors have been committed by righteous people. *Tosafot* explains that the divine providence mentioned by our Gemara refers only to questions of food, about which the righteous person will have a premonition and refuse to eat something that is not kosher. Errors unconnected with food, however, sometimes do occur, and they may be very serious. According to this explanation, it is hard to understand our Gemara's objection, since Rabbi Elazar the son of Rabbi Yose did not eat

TRANSLATION AND COMMENTARY

וְשֶׁהַמָּקוֹם הַזֶּה [1] The Gemara now considers the next clause of the Mishnah, which ruled that an adult testifying about what he saw as a child is believed if he says **"that this place is a *bet haperas*,"** and we regard the other fields in the valley as ritually pure. [2] The Gemara asks: **What is the reason** that the evidence of this witness is accepted?

בֵּית הַפְּרָס דְּרַבָּנַן [3] The Gemara answers: The law regarding **a *bet haperas* is Rabbinic.** By Torah law, a person need not be concerned about coming into contact with a corpse if he walks through a field in which a grave was previously plowed over, because the danger that he will tread on a bone is remote. [4] Since the law regarding a *bet haperas* is of Rabbinic origin, the Rabbis were lenient about it, **for Rav Yehudah**

[1] "וְשֶׁהַמָּקוֹם הַזֶּה בֵּית הַפְּרָס הוּא". [2] מַאי טַעֲמָא? [3] בֵּית הַפְּרָס דְּרַבָּנַן. [4] דְּאָמַר רַב יְהוּדָה אָמַר שְׁמוּאֵל:

LITERAL TRANSLATION

[1] "Or that this place is a *bet haperas*." [2] What is the reason?

[3] A *bet haperas* is Rabbinic. [4] For Rav Yehudah said in the name of Shmuel:

RASHI

בית הפרס — החורש את הקבר — הרי זה עושה בית הפרס מאה אמה, שכך שיערו שהמחרישה מולכת את עצמות המת, ודלמא נגע או הסיט המהלך בו את עצם כשעורה, שמטמאה במגע ובמשא.

LANGUAGE

בֵּית הַפְּרָס ***Bet haperas.*** The commentators disagree about the etymology of this expression. *Rashi* and *Tosafot* derive the word פְּרָס from the Hebrew root פרס, meaning "to shatter" or "to break," since a *bet haperas* is an area where bones were broken (because they were plowed). *Rambam*, however, seems to associate פְּרָס with the word פְּרִיסָה, meaning "spreading," since ritual impurity is "spread" throughout a *bet haperas*. Others derive the expression from the Greek φάρος, *pharos*, meaning "a plough," while others derive it from the Greek ἄπορος, *aporos*, meaning "an area where it is forbidden to pass."

NOTES

anything non-kosher, but nearly caused a slave to be declared a priest. *Ritva* explains that the Gemara was objecting because Rabbi Elazar the son of Rabbi Yose allowed the slave's family to eat terumah illegally. But *Tosafot* insists that divine providence protects only the righteous person himself from eating something that is not kosher, and does not extend to cases like ours. Indeed, in tractate *Pesaḥim* (106b) *Tosafot* explains that divine providence does not even extend to food that is itself permitted, when the righteous person is forbidden to eat it for some other reason. Accordingly, *Tosafot* amends our passage to remove the Gemara's question about the animals of the righteous, noting that it does not appear in many texts of the Talmud.

בֵּית הַפְּרָס ***Bet haperas.*** By Torah law, a person who has come into contact with a dead body, or even is present with it under the same tent, is ritually impure (Numbers 19:14-16). "Being under the same tent" also describes a person who stands over a dead body, so that he himself is the tent (*Rambam, Hilkhot Tumat Met* 1:10). If the body is not intact, and the person has contact with a part of it, he becomes impure only if the part was at least the size of a barleycorn. But a person cannot become impure by being under the same tent with a part of a body unless there is a substantial part (*Ohalot* 2:2,3).

Bet haperas is a term used for a field that is ritually impure by Rabbinic decree. There are three kinds of fields that are sometimes called *bet haperas* (*Ohalot* 18:2). The first is a field that was used as a gathering place for mourners. The Rabbis imposed certain restrictions on such a field, even though it was not known to have been used for burial, in case someone chose to bury his dead there (*Ohalot* 18:4). The second case is a field in which a body was buried and the precise location of the grave has been forgotten. The third case is the *bet haperas* proper — a field in which a grave was plowed over (or obliterated in some other way) and the bones were scattered throughout the field. In such a case, the entire section that was plowed is considered ritually impure, up to an area of 100 cubits square around the grave (*Ohalot* 17:1). This is the case discussed by our Gemara.

A field in which a grave was lost is considered ritually impure for two reasons: (1) We do not know if the grave is intact, and (2) if the grave is intact, we do not know where it is. Accordingly, the entire field imparts ritual impurity, both to a person who touches or moves its earth, and to a person who stands on it. For if the grave is intact, it is possible that the person standing in the field is standing over the grave itself, and has become ritually impure by being "under the same tent" as a substantial part of the body. And if the grave was obliterated, it is possible that the bones were spread around the field and the person who touched the earth had contact with a bone the size of a barleycorn (*Ohalot* 18:3).

The law in the case of a field in which a grave is known to have been obliterated is less severe than in the case of a field in which a grave was lost, because we know that the grave is not intact. Therefore, a person who stands in the field but does not touch or move its earth (i.e., when he is riding on an animal; *Ohalot* 18:6) is not ritually impure, because there is no danger of being in the same tent with a large enough piece of the body to impart ritual impurity. If he touches or moves the earth, however, he is ritually impure, because we are concerned that he may have had contact with a bone the size of a barleycorn (*Ohalot* 18:2). Accordingly, it is possible to purify a *bet haperas* of this type by ensuring that contact with surface bones is impossible (e.g., by paving it over [*Ohalot* 18:5], or by one of the methods described in our Gemara).

It is not entirely clear why a *bet haperas* is forbidden by Rabbinic decree. *Rashi* explains that the danger of contact with a bone is remote, and is considered to be of Rabbinic status. *Tosafot* explains that this is an example of the law that doubtful ritual impurity in the public domain is considered ritually pure (see above, 27a). *Tosafot* explains that since it is doubtful whether the person will touch a bone, he is considered completely ritually pure by Torah law. But the Rabbis decreed that he should be considered ritually impure, since the impurity is not localized but spread throughout the field.

בֵּית הַפְּרָס דְּרַבָּנַן ***Bet haperas* is Rabbinic.** The Mishnah is dealing with cases where the testimony of an adult about

HALAKHAH

בֵּית הַפְּרָס דְּרַבָּנַן **A *bet haperas* is Rabbinic.** "A man is believed if he testifies that when he was a child he saw that a certain place was a *bet haperas*, since the impurity of a *bet haperas* is Rabbinic." (*Rambam, Sefer Shofetim, Hilkhot Edut* 14:3; *Shulḥan Arukh, Ḥoshen Mishpat* 35:5.)

TRANSLATION AND COMMENTARY

said in the name of Shmuel: One may blow on the earth of a *bet haperas* and walk there. If a person is confident that he has not come into contact with a bone, because he examined the earth carefully before walking on it, he may presume that he is still ritually pure. The only problem with a *bet haperas* is the danger of becoming ritually impure by touching a human bone. [1]**And Rav Yehudah bar Ammi said in the name of Rav Yehudah: A *bet haperas*** that has been trodden by many feet (as when a road goes through the field) **is** completely **ritually pure** and requires no inspection, because a person walking through the field can be confident that he will not touch any bones the size of a barleycorn (the minimum size at which a bone imparts ritual impurity by touch). [2]**What is the reason?** [3]**It is impossible for a bone the size of a barleycorn not to have been trodden down by the feet** of the many people who have walked along the road. We may assume that all the larger bones were crushed into such small pieces that they would not impart ritual impurity if touched. Thus we see that the Rabbis were lenient regarding the danger of touching a small bone in a *bet haperas*. It is clear that a *bet haperas* is a Rabbinic concern, about which an adult is believed when he testifies to what he saw as a child.

וְעַד כָּאן [4]The Gemara now considers the next clause of the Mishnah, which ruled that the testimony of an adult that he remembers as a child that **"we used to walk as far as here on Shabbat," is believed.** [5]The Gemara explains: The author of this Mishnah **maintains that the Shabbat limits are Rabbinic.** Although there is a Tannaitic dispute on this matter, and one opinion bases the prohibition against walking beyond the Shabbat limits on a verse (Exodus 16:29), the Halakhah is that the prohibition is Rabbinic.

מְנַפֵּחַ אָדָם בֵּית הַפְּרָס וְהוֹלֵךְ. [1]וְרַב יְהוּדָה בַּר אַמִּי מִשְּׁמֵיהּ דְּרַב יְהוּדָה אָמַר: בֵּית הַפְּרָס שֶׁנִּידַּשׁ טָהוֹר. [2]מַאי טַעְמָא? [3]אִי אֶפְשָׁר לְעֶצֶם כִּשְׂעוֹרָה שֶׁלֹּא נִידַּשׁ בָּרֶגֶל.

[4]"וְ'עַד כָּאן הָיִינוּ בָּאִין בְּשַׁבָּת'". [5]קָסָבַר: תְּחוּמִין דְּרַבָּנַן.

LITERAL TRANSLATION

A man may blow [on the earth of] a *bet haperas* and walk [there]. [1]And Rav Yehudah bar Ammi said in the name of Rav Yehudah: A *bet haperas* that has been trodden is ritually pure. [2]What is the reason? [3]It is impossible for a bone [the size] of a barleycorn not to be trodden down by the foot.

[4]"Or: 'Up to here we used to come on Shabbat.'" [5]He maintains [that the Shabbat] limits are Rabbinic.

RASHI

מנפח אדם בית הפרס — וסומך על כך, שאם יש עצם — רואהו. ואף על גב דמאהיל — לא חיישינן, דאין עצם כשעורה מטמא באהל עד דאיכא שדרה או גולגלת שלמה, או רוב בנין, או רוב מנין. **שנידש** — דישה רבה, ברגלים הרבה. **טהור** — דתלינן לקולא, ואמרינן: כל העצמות נכתתו לפחות מכשיעור. אלמא, חששא דרבנן בעלמא הוא.

SAGES

רַב יְהוּדָה בַּר אַמִּי **Rav Yehudah bar Ammi.** An Amora of the third generation, Rav Yehudah bar Ammi is quoted in the Jerusalem Talmud as transmitting a teaching in the name of Resh Lakish, and here in the Babylonian Talmud as transmitting a teaching in the name of Rav Yehudah. Few details of his personal life are known, though some authorities are of the opinion that he was a son of the famous Amora, Rabbi Ammi.

NOTES

what he saw as a child is believed to the extent that matters that would otherwise be forbidden by Rabbinic decree are permitted. Thus it would appear that the Mishnah is ruling that the testimony of the witness that a field which was presumed to be a *bet haperas* is in fact ritually pure is accepted. *Ra'ah* points out, however, that it is inconceivable that the testimony of a single witness about what he saw as a child could override an established legal presumption. Rather, *Ra'ah* explains that we are referring to a case where the adult testifies that a certain field which we thought was ritually pure is in fact a *bet haperas.*

Other Rishonim reject this explanation, because it is clear throughout this passage that we are dealing with cases in which the testimony of the witness is believed to the extent of permitting matters that would otherwise be forbidden by Rabbinic decree. Our commentary follows *Ran*, who explains that we are dealing with a case where we knew that one of the fields in a valley is a *bet haperas*, but we are not certain which. In such a case, the witness is believed and clarifies the matter for us, so that we can permit those fields that are not a *bet haperas. Tosefot Rid* explains along similar lines that a *bet haperas* is forbidden for 100 cubits square around the site of the grave; hence, it is important to know exactly where the grave originally was, and for this the testimony of an adult about what he saw as a child is believed (see also *Tosafot*).

Ra'avad has a very different explanation, according to which we are referring to a case where a field is known to be a *bet haperas*, but an adult testifies that he remembers from his childhood that it was purified, by careful examination of the earth (as suggested by Rav Yehudah in the name of Shmuel), or by being thoroughly trodden down (as suggested by Rav Yehudah bar Ammi in the name of Rav Yehudah). Thus the Mishnah is ruling that the adult is believed about this, since the impurity of a *bet haperas* is in any case Rabbinic.

HALAKHAH

מְנַפֵּחַ אָדָם בֵּית הַפְּרָס **A man may blow on the earth of a *bet haperas*.** "If a man finds himself in a *bet haperas* when on his way to the Temple to bring the Paschal sacrifice, he may blow on the earth, and if he does not find any bones, he may offer the sacrifice. Likewise, if the *bet haperas* was thoroughly trodden down, he may offer the sacrifice. For the impurity of *bet haperas* is Rabbinic, and the Rabbis relaxed their restrictions for the sake of the Paschal sacrifice, which is a very serious obligation." (*Rambam, Sefer Korbanot, Hilkhot Korban Pesaḥ* 6:8.)

תְּחוּמִין דְּרַבָּנַן **The Shabbat limits are Rabbinic.** "An adult is believed if he testifies that when he was a child he was

TRANSLATION AND COMMENTARY

וְאֵין נֶאֱמָן לוֹמַר [1]The Gemara now considers the next clause of the Mishnah, which ruled that the testimony of an adult that he remembers as a child that **"So-and-so had a path in this place,"** or that **"So-and-so had a standing area or a lamentation area in this place," is not believed** even if this witness's testimony is corroborated by one qualified witness. [2]The Gemara asks: **What is the reason** that the adult testifying about what he saw as a child is not believed in this matter?

אַפּוּקֵי מָמוֹנָא לָא מַפְּקִינַן [3]The Gemara answers: He is not believed because if his testimony were accepted, we would be **taking money away** from the neighbor, and **money may not be taken away** from one person by the court and given to another, except as a result of the testimony of two qualified witnesses. The cases of the Mishnah, by contrast, were all cases of ritual law with no monetary ramifications, except for the cases of the signatures on the document and the bride who wore a *hinuma*, where proper testimony is not required, as the Gemara explained above.

תָּנוּ רַבָּנַן [4]**Our Rabbis taught** the following Baraita: **"A child** who later gives evidence as an adult about what he saw as a child **is believed if he says:** [5]When I was still a child, **my father said to me: 'This family is** ritually **pure** and **that family is** ritually **impure.'"**

טְהוֹרָה וּטְמֵאָה [6]The Gemara interjects: "Ritually **pure and** ritually **impure**"? [7]**Is it conceivable** that a family can be ritually pure or impure? An individual can become ritually impure (for example, by contact with a dead body) or ritually pure (for example, by immersing himself in a ritual bath), but such terms cannot be applied to a family.

אֶלָּא [8]**Rather,** answers the Gemara, we must amend the Baraita as follows: The man testifies that his father told him when he was a child that **a certain** priestly **family was fit** (i.e., all its members had married women who were permitted to marry priests), [9]**and another** priestly **family was disqualified,** because one of its ancestors had married a divorcee or a woman who was otherwise disqualified from the priesthood.

[1]״וְאֵין נֶאֱמָן לוֹמַר: ׳דֶּרֶךְ הָיָה לִפְלוֹנִי בַּמָּקוֹם הַזֶּה׳, ׳מַעֲמָד וּמִסְפֵּד הָיָה לִפְלוֹנִי בַּמָּקוֹם הַזֶּה׳״. [2]מַאי טַעְמָא? [3]אַפּוּקֵי מָמוֹנָא לָא מַפְּקִינַן.
[4]תָּנוּ רַבָּנַן: ״נֶאֱמָן הַתִּינוֹק לוֹמַר: [5]כָּךְ אָמַר לִי אַבָּא: ׳מִשְׁפָּחָה זוֹ טְהוֹרָה; מִשְׁפָּחָה זוֹ טְמֵאָה׳״.
[6]״טְהוֹרָה וּטְמֵאָה״. [7]סָלְקָא דַּעְתָּךְ?
[8]אֶלָּא: ״מִשְׁפָּחָה זוֹ כְּשֵׁרָה, [9]וּמִשְׁפָּחָה זוֹ פְּסוּלָה״.

LITERAL TRANSLATION

[1]"But [a man] is not believed to say: 'So-and-so had a path in this place,' [2][or] 'So-and-so had a standing area and a lamentation area in this place.'" What is the reason?

[3]We do not take away money [on such evidence].

[4]Our Rabbis taught: "A child is believed to say: [5]My father said to me thus: 'This family is pure; that family is impure.'"

[6]"Pure and impure." [7]Can [this] enter your mind?

[8]Rather [he said]: "This family is fit, [9]and that family is disqualified."

RASHI

נאמן התינוק – להעיד כגודלו מה שראה בקוטנו. **טמאה וטהורה סלקא דעתך** – מה טומאה וטהרה יש לומר במשפחות?

NOTES

אַפּוּקֵי מָמוֹנָא לָא מַפְּקִינַן **We do not take away money on such evidence.** The Gemara explains that an adult testifying about what he saw as a child may not serve as a witness on a monetary question. The Jerusalem Talmud discusses a case where such a witness testified about a ritual question with monetary ramifications. For example, if qualified witnesses testify that the boundary between two neighbors' fields is the Shabbat limit of a town, and an adult testifies that he remembers from his childhood that the Shabbat limit was in a certain place, is he believed regarding the boundary or not? The Jerusalem Talmud does not resolve this question. The Jerusalem Talmud also discusses a related case, where such a witness testified about a Rabbinic ritual question with ramifications connecting it to a matter of Torah ritual. Here, too, the Jerusalem Talmud leaves the matter unresolved. But one further question is resolved: In a case where the witness's testimony from childhood has financial implications, as in the case of the bride who wore a *hinuma*, if his testimony was subsequently refuted through the *hazamah* process, he and his fellow witness are not punished by being forced to pay the husband the sum that they tried to make him pay his wife (see Deuteronomy 19:19), because the laws of *hazamah* apply only where both witnesses are completely qualified.

מִשְׁפָּחָה זוֹ כְּשֵׁרָה **This family is fit.** Our commentary follows *Rambam*, who explains that the Baraita is referring to a

HALAKHAH

told not to walk past a certain point on Shabbat. Even a slave or a maidservant is believed about this, but not a witness who is a minor. The reason we rely on this testimony is because the laws of the Shabbat limit are Rabbinic. *Shulḥan Arukh* adds that the same applies to other Rabbinic laws." (*Rambam, Sefer Zemanim, Hilkhot Shabbat* 28:19 and *Sefer Shofetim, Hilkhot Edut* 14:3; *Shulḥan Arukh, Oraḥ Ḥayyim* 399:11 and *Ḥoshen Mishpat* 35:6.)

מִשְׁפָּחָה זוֹ כְּשֵׁרָה **This family is fit.** "If an adult testifies that his father told him when he was a child that one family

TRANSLATION AND COMMENTARY

וְשֶׁאָכַלְנוּ בְּקְצָצָה [1] The Gemara returns to the Baraita: "An adult is believed if he testifies that when he was a child, **he ate at the cutting-off ceremony** when **So-and-so's daughter** married **So-and-so.**" (The Gemara explains this below.)

וְשֶׁהָיִינוּ מוֹלִיכִים [2] The Baraita continues: "An adult is believed if he testifies that when he was still a child his family **used to bring** *ḥallah* **and priestly gifts to So-and-so the priest.**" The man's statement implies that So-and-so was indeed a priest. But the Baraita restricts this rule, saying: [3] "The adult is believed **only** if he says that he **personally took** the *ḥallah* to the priest, **but not** if he says that his family sent the *ḥallah* to the priest **through someone else,** because we cannot rely on his childhood recollections if he was not personally involved."

LITERAL TRANSLATION

[1] "Or that 'we ate at the cutting-off ceremony of So-and-so's daughter to So-and-so.'"

[2] "Or that 'we used to bring *ḥallah* and [priestly] gifts to So-and-so the priest.'
[3] [But only] by himself, but not through someone else."

"[1]וְשֶׁאָכַלְנוּ בְּקְצָצָה שֶׁל בַּת פְּלוֹנִי לִפְלוֹנִי".

"[2]וְשֶׁהָיִינוּ מוֹלִיכִים חַלָּה וּמַתָּנוֹת לִפְלוֹנִי כֹּהֵן". [3]עַל יְדֵי עַצְמוֹ, אֲבָל לֹא עַל יְדֵי אַחֵר".

RASHI

בקצצה — לקמן מפרש לה. של בת פלוני לפלוני — כשנשא פלוני את בת פלוני. ושהיינו מוליכין כו' על ידי עצמו — אם כך העיד התינוק: על ידי היה אבא שולח לו חלה ומתנות.

NOTES

priestly family which intermarried with women who were forbidden to marry priests. Similarly, below, in the case of the cutting-off ceremony, we are referring to a priest who married a woman who was forbidden to marry a priest. *Bet Shmuel* explains that a similar law would apply if a non-priest married a woman who was a *mamzeret*.

The Rishonim ask: Ostensibly we are referring to a case in which a family was presumed to be fit, and the witness declared it unfit (or vice versa). But how can an adult be believed, and a fit family be declared unfit, on the basis of something the witness heard from his father? Even if the father himself had come forward and testified, he would not have been believed, because we require two qualified witnesses to change a person's or a family's presumed status.

Ra'avad explains that the Baraita is teaching us that the testimony of an adult as to what he heard as a child is the equivalent of the testimony of a qualified witness for this purpose, since the fitness of a family is a matter of public knowledge. Hence, if two witnesses were to testify in this way, we would accept their testimony and reverse the family's presumed status. When there is only one

witness, however — regardless of whether he is qualified or an adult testifying about a childhood memory — we do not reverse the family's presumed status, but we note that it has been called into question, and we seek a second witness to confirm the testimony (cf. above, 26a).

Ran, however, argues that we cannot alter a family's presumed status on the testimony of less than two qualified witnesses. *Ran* explains that the Baraita is referring to a case in which we know that a member of the family married a woman who was forbidden to him, but we have forgotten who it was. In such a case, the witness is believed when he says that he knows from childhood that this branch of the family is fit and that branch unfit, just as he is believed when he says that this field is a *bet haperas* and that one is not. According to this view, the two halves of this clause ("this family is fit; that family is unfit") refer to the same cases, and the witness is believed when he declares one family unfit only if he simultaneously declares another family to be fit. *Ran* notes that *Rambam* (*Hilkhot Edut* 14:3) appears to support his view (see *Kesef Mishneh*).

HALAKHAH

was fit and another one not, he is believed. Likewise, an adult is believed if he testifies that as a child he ate the fruit at a cutting-off ceremony held by a certain family to announce publicly that one of its members had married a woman who was not fit for him. *Rema* adds that the witness is also believed regarding any other public demonstration that a member of the family married a woman who was not fit for him. *Kesef Mishneh* and *Sma* note that there is a dispute between *Ra'avad* and *Ran* about this matter. *Ra'avad* rules that the witness is believed in these matters like a fully qualified witness. Hence, if there are two adults testifying to what they saw as children, we accept their testimony absolutely, even if it conflicts with an established legal presumption; and if there is only one adult witness testifying to what he saw as a child, we take the matter into consideration but do not render a final decision. *Ran,* however, maintains that the witness is not

believed if his testimony conflicts with an established legal presumption, but only if it determines which person or family is unfit when we are already certain that one member of the family married a woman unfit for him." (*Rambam, Sefer Shofetim, Hilkhot Edut* 14:3; *Shulḥan Arukh, Ḥoshen Mishpat* 35:6.)

שֶׁהָיִינוּ מוֹלִיכִים חַלָּה **That we used to bring** *ḥallah.* "If an adult testifies that when he was a child he would personally deliver the *ḥallah* and priestly gifts to a certain priest, we believe him and we presume the man to be a priest. *Sma* adds that if the adult testifies that when he was a child he saw the *ḥallah* delivered by someone else, he is not believed, because we fear that he may have been mistaken in his observations if he was not personally involved." (*Rambam, Sefer Shofetim, Hilkhot Edut* 14:3; *Shulḥan Arukh, Ḥoshen Mishpat* 35:6.)

[1]״וְכוּלָּן, אִם הָיָה נָכְרִי וְנִתְגַּיֵּיר, עֶבֶד וְנִשְׁתַּחְרֵר, [2]אֵין נֶאֱמָנִים״. [3]״וְאֵין נֶאֱמָן לוֹמַר: ׳דֶּרֶךְ הָיָה לִפְלוֹנִי בַּמָּקוֹם הַזֶּה׳, [4]׳מַעֲמָד וּמִסְפֵּד הָיָה לִפְלוֹנִי בַּמָּקוֹם הַזֶּה׳״.

[5]״רַבִּי יוֹחָנָן בֶּן בְּרוֹקָא אוֹמֵר: נֶאֱמָנִים״.

[6]רַבִּי יוֹחָנָן בֶּן בְּרוֹקָא אַהֵיָּיא? [7]אִילֵימָא: אַסֵּיפָא, אַפּוּקֵי מָמוֹנָא הוּא! [8]אֶלָּא, אַרֵישָׁא: [9]״וְכוּלָּם, אִם הָיָה גּוֹי וְנִתְגַּיֵּיר, עֶבֶד וְנִשְׁתַּחְרֵר, [10]אֵין נֶאֱמָנִין. [11]רַבִּי יוֹחָנָן בֶּן בְּרוֹקָא אוֹמֵר: נֶאֱמָנִין״.

[12]בְּמַאי קָמִיפַּלְגִי?

LITERAL TRANSLATION

[1]"And [in] all these [cases], if he was a non-Jew and he converted, [or] a slave and he was freed, [2]they are not believed."

[3]"And he is not believed to say: 'So-and-so had a path in this place,' [4][or] 'So-and-so had a standing area or a lamentation area in this place.'"

[5]"Rabbi Yoḥanan ben Beroka says: They are believed."

[6]To which [case does] Rabbi Yoḥanan ben Beroka [refer]? [7]If you say: [he refers] to the last clause, it is taking away money! [8]Rather, to the first clause: [9]"And [in] all these [cases], if he was a non-Jew and he converted, [or] a slave and he was freed, [10]they are not believed. [11]Rabbi Yoḥanan ben Beroka says: They are believed."

[12]About what do they disagree?

TRANSLATION AND COMMENTARY

וְכוּלָּן [1]The Baraita continues: "The leniency of the Rabbis in this context is shown only with regard to an adult testifying to what he saw as a child. Even though the witness would have been disqualified from testifying at the time he observed the event, the Rabbis believe his adult recollections about his childhood, since he is qualified to testify now. But **in all of these cases, if** the witness is **a non-Jew who converted** to Judaism, **or a slave who was freed,** [2]**such a witness is not believed** when testifies about something he saw before his conversion or before he was freed."

וְאֵין נֶאֱמָן לוֹמַר [3]The Baraita continues: "Even in the case of the adult testifying to what he saw as a child, **he is not believed if he says: 'So-and-so had a path in this place,'** [4]**or 'So-and-so had a standing area or a lamentation area in this place,'** because we require two qualified witnesses to effect a transfer of money."

רַבִּי יוֹחָנָן בֶּן בְּרוֹקָא אוֹמֵר [5]The Baraita concludes: **"Rabbi Yoḥanan ben Beroka says: They are believed."**

רַבִּי יוֹחָנָן בֶּן בְּרוֹקָא אַהֵיָּיא [6]The Gemara begins its analysis of this Baraita by explaining this last clause: It is clear that Rabbi Yoḥanan ben Beroka is referring to a case where the first Tanna is of the opinion that the witness is *not* believed. But **to which case was Rabbi Yoḥanan ben Beroka referring?** There are only two cases in which the first Tanna says that the witness is not believed: (1) If he was a non-Jew or a slave, and (2) if he was testifying about a monetary matter. [7]Now, **if you say** that Rabbi Yoḥanan ben Beroka was referring **to the last clause,** and was ruling that an adult *is* believed if he testifies on the basis of what he saw as a child that one man owns a part of another man's field, such testimony has the effect of **taking away money!** Surely Rabbi Yoḥanan ben Beroka agrees that we cannot effect a transfer of property without two qualified witnesses. [8]**Rather, says the Gemara,** he must have been referring **to the earlier clause.** [9]In that clause the first Tanna said that **in all these cases, if** the witness was not an adult testifying about what he saw as a child, but rather **a non-Jew who converted** and is now testifying about something he saw before his conversion, **or a slave who was freed** and is testifying about something he saw before he was freed, [10]such a witness **is not believed.** [11]And we are now informed that **Rabbi Yoḥanan ben Beroka says: Such a witness is believed,** because there is no difference between a child who has grown up, a non-Jew who has converted to Judaism, or a slave who has been freed. In all these cases, the witness was not qualified when he observed the event, but is qualified now; and since he claims that he remembers the events well, he should be believed.

בְּמַאי קָמִיפַּלְגִי [12]The Gemara asks: Now that we have established that Rabbi Yoḥanan ben Beroka was referring to the clause in the Baraita about the non-Jew and the slave, **about what** principle of law **do** Rabbi Yoḥanan ben Beroka and the first Tanna **disagree?**

RASHI

אם היה נכרי ונתגייר — והעיד משנתגייר שראה את אלה בגויותו — אינו נאמן.

HALAKHAH

וְכוּלָּן And in all. "Even in a situation in which an adult is believed regarding what he saw as a child, the evidence of a convert is not believed about something he saw while he was a non-Jew, and the evidence of a freed slave is not believed about something he saw while he was still a slave," following the anonymous first opinion in the Baraita. (*Rambam, Sefer Shofetim, Hilkhot Edut* 14:4; *Shulḥan Arukh, Ḥoshen Mishpat* 35:7.)

TRANSLATION AND COMMENTARY

תַּנָּא קַמָּא סָבַר [1]The Gemara answers: **The first Tanna maintains** that there is an additional problem in the case of the non-Jew who converted, beyond the technical problem that he was not qualified at the time of the observation to be a witness. [2]**Since** the witness **was a non-Jew** when he observed the event, **he may not have been precise** in his observation, and although he thinks he remembers it now, he may be mistaken. He did not attach any special significance to his observations at the time, because he did not know then that he would eventually convert to Judaism and would testify about them. A child, on the other hand, realizes the significance of his observations, and within the limits of his maturity he does his best to be precise. Therefore, an adult testifying about what he saw as a child is disqualified only for technical reasons, and the Rabbis were willing to be lenient regarding certain Rabbinic matters, whereas a convert to Judaism is disqualified for substantial reasons, and the Rabbis were not lenient in such a case. [3]**Rabbi Yoḥanan ben Beroka**, on the other hand, **maintains** that the first Tanna's argument may be valid for most non-Jews, [4]but **since** this particular non-Jew already **intended to convert** at the time he witnessed the events about which he is now testifying, **he was precise** in his observations and is disqualified only for technical reasons. Therefore, in those cases where we believe an adult's testimony about what he saw as a child, we also believe a convert to Judaism about what he saw before his conversion.

מַאי קְצָצָה [5]The Gemara now considers the next clause of the Baraita, which ruled that an adult is believed if he testifies that while he was a child he ate at the cutting-off ceremony when So-and-so's daughter married So-and-so. The Gemara asks: **What is a cutting-off ceremony?**

[1]תַּנָּא קַמָּא סָבַר: [2]כֵּיוָן דְּגוֹי הוּא, לָא הֲוָה דָּיֵיק. [3]וְרַבִּי יוֹחָנָן בֶּן בְּרוֹקָא סָבַר: [4]כֵּיוָן דְּדַעְתֵּיהּ לְאִיגַּיּוּרֵי, מֵידַק הֲוָה דָּיֵיק.
[5]מַאי קְצָצָה?

LITERAL TRANSLATION

[1]The first Tanna maintains: [2]Since he was a non-Jew, he did not pay attention. [3]And Rabbi Yoḥanan ben Beroka maintains: [4]Since his intention was to convert, he did pay attention.
[5]What is a cutting-off ceremony?

NOTES

כֵּיוָן דְּדַעְתֵּיהּ לְאִיגַּיּוּרֵי **Since his intention was to convert.** The Gemara explains that even Rabbi Yoḥanan ben Beroka agrees that a non-Jew or a slave would not have paid close attention to the events, and we cannot rely on their testimony later, even if they claim to be certain. But Rabbi Yoḥanan ben Beroka maintains that a non-Jew who is planning to convert is an exception, because he anticipates being called upon to testify after his conversion.

Ritva asks: Under Jewish law, it is not up to the potential convert to decide to convert. He must apply to the court, and the court decides whether or not to accept him. For this reason, the Gemara (*Kiddushin* 62b) rules that a non-Jew cannot be considered to have it within his power to decide to convert. How, then, can Rabbi Yoḥanan ben Beroka argue that the non-Jew plans to become a convert? Moreover, Rabbi Yoḥanan ben Beroka and the first Tanna also disagree about the case of a slave, and presumably they are referring to a case where the slave was "planning to be freed." But how can a slave "plan to be freed"? Surely, it is entirely up to his master whether or not he is freed!

Ritva answers that non-Jews generally do not know Jewish law, and assume that they can convert whenever they please. Hence, the non-Jew who planned to convert was careful in his observations as though it was in his power to carry out his plans. Likewise, the dispute about the slave concerns a case where the master told the slave that he was planning to free him, and the slave had such complete confidence that it was as though he was "planning" to be freed.

Ayelet Ahavim has a different explanation for the case of the slave. He explains that Rabbi Yoḥanan ben Beroka maintains that every slave is accurate in his observations, even if he is not "planning to be freed," since he is obliged to perform most commandments of the Torah. According to this explanation, there are two separate and distinct disputes between Rabbi Yoḥanan ben Beroka and the first Tanna, and it is not clear why the Gemara mentioned only one.

קְצָצָה **The cutting-off ceremony.** Our translation of the term קְצָצָה as "cutting-off ceremony" follows the Jerusalem Talmud, which explains that it refers to a person being cut off from his family. *Maharsha* suggests that it is a term of insult, and refers to the unfit woman who is marrying into the family.

The Jerusalem Talmud has a longer version of this Baraita, which reads: "When a man sold a field inherited

HALAKHAH

מַאי קְצָצָה **What is a cutting-off ceremony?** "A man must never marry a woman who is unfit for him. *Bet Shmuel* explains that this refers to a woman who is suspected of being a *mamzeret*, or of being forbidden to the priesthood where the potential husband is a priest. If a man decides to marry a woman who is unfit for him, his family should take action to indicate their disapproval. If this does not succeed, they should make a public demonstration of some kind, so that people will distinguish between this man and the rest of his family, along the lines of the cutting-off ceremony mentioned by the Talmud." (*Shulḥan Arukh, Even HaEzer* 2:1.)

BACKGROUND

אִשָּׁה שֶׁאֵינָהּ הוֹגֶנֶת לוֹ **A woman who is not fit for him.** Literally this expression can be interpreted in several ways — with respect to social status, education, or personality. But all these traits are a matter of subjective judgment, which is an area in which the Sages do not intervene or institute ordinances. Here, and in other passages, a woman who is not "fit" is one who is not fit for that specific man, such as a divorcee, who may not marry a priest, though she may well be entirely fit for someone else, since any other Jew is permitted to marry her.

TRANSLATION AND COMMENTARY

דְּתָנוּ רַבָּנַן [1]The Gemara answers: **It is** the ceremony **mentioned** to us by **our Rabbis** in the following Baraita: **"How does a cutting-off ceremony take place?** [2]**If one of the brothers** in a priestly family **has married a woman who is not fit for him** (i.e., a woman who was forbidden to marry a priest), [3]**the members of the family come and bring a barrel full of fruit, and break it in the middle of the open space** near the brother's home, in order to attract public attention. [4]**And they say: 'Our brothers, the House of Israel, hear! Our brother, So-and-so, has married a woman who is not fit for him, and we are afraid lest his seed become mingled with our seed** (i.e., that with the passage of time, people will not remember which brother married the unfit woman, and the entire family will lose its reputation of unblemished lineage). [5]**Come and take** heed, and let this ceremony serve as **a sign for future generations**. Let the memory of this ceremony ensure that people will remember the details of the marriage, [6]so **that his seed will not become mingled with our seed,** and the rest of our family will retain its reputation.' The entire town will be attracted by the ceremony, the children will run to pick up the fruit, and the memory of the event will be etched in public memory. [7]**And** [the Baraita concludes] **this is the cutting-off ceremony about which** the other Baraita ruled that an adult who **testifies** to what he saw as a **child is believed."**

[1]דְּתָנוּ רַבָּנַן: ״כֵּיצַד קְצָצָה? [2]אֶחָד מִן הָאַחִין שֶׁנָּשָׂא אִשָּׁה שֶׁאֵינָהּ הוֹגֶנֶת לוֹ, [3]בָּאִין בְּנֵי מִשְׁפָּחָה וּמְבִיאִין חָבִית מְלֵיאָה פֵּירוֹת, וְשׁוֹבְרִין אוֹתָהּ בְּאֶמְצַע רְחָבָה, [4]וְאוֹמְרִים: ׳אַחֵינוּ, בֵּית יִשְׂרָאֵל, שְׁמְעוּ! אָחִינוּ, פְּלוֹנִי, נָשָׂא אִשָּׁה שֶׁאֵינָהּ הוֹגֶנֶת לוֹ, וּמִתְיָירְאִים אָנוּ שֶׁמָּא יִתְעָרֵב זַרְעוֹ בְּזַרְעֵינוּ. [5]בּוֹאוּ וּקְחוּ לָכֶם דּוּגְמָא לְדוֹרוֹת, [6]שֶׁלֹּא יִתְעָרֵב זַרְעוֹ בְּזַרְעֵינוּ׳. [7]וְזוֹ הִיא קְצָצָה שֶׁהַתִּינוֹק נֶאֱמָן לְהָעִיד עָלֶיהָ״.

הדרן עלך האשה שנתארמלה

LITERAL TRANSLATION

[1][It is] as our Rabbis taught: "How [does] a cutting-off ceremony [take place]? [2][If] one of the brothers has married a woman who is not fit for him, [3]the members of the family come and bring a barrel full of fruit, and break it in the middle of the open space, [4]and they say: 'Our brothers, the House of Israel, hear! Our brother, So-and-so, has married a woman who is not fit for him, and we are afraid lest his seed be mingled with our seed. [5]Come and take for yourselves a sign for [future] generations, [6]that his seed not be mingled with our seed.' [7]And this is the cutting-off ceremony about which a child is believed to testify."

RASHI

דוגמא — אות וסימן, זכרון לדורות הבאים.

הדרן עלך האשה שנתארמלה

NOTES

from his family, his relatives would fill barrels with grains and nuts and break the barrels in front of the town's children, and the children would gather the nuts and say: 'So-and-so has been cut off from his inheritance.' When someone bought back his family field, they would do the same thing, and the children would say: 'So-and-so has returned to his inheritance.' Rabbi Yose the son of Rabbi Boon said: Similarly, if someone married a woman who was not fit for him, his relatives would fill barrels with grains and nuts and break the barrels in front of the town's children, and the children would gather the nuts and say: 'So-and-so has been cut off from his family.' And when he divorced her, they would do the same thing, and the children would say: 'So-and-so has returned to his family.'"

Maharsha explains that the barrel of nuts was meant to attract the children's attention. Since these matters need to be remembered for a long time, it is important for the children to be involved. *Rashbatz* adds that in all the cases in which an adult is believed about what he saw as a child, the witness played an active role of some kind as a child, but if he was completely passive (for example, where he testifies that other people used to bring terumah to a certain priest), he is not believed.

Conclusion to Chapter Two

One major topic discussed in this chapter is the rule that "the mouth that forbade is the mouth that permitted." Whenever we rely on someone's statement, we must believe it in its entirety, if we believe it at all. Therefore, when someone testifies about a fact (whether it concerns himself or others) and adds details which limit or annul the testimony's Halakhic significance, we accept and believe the entire statement. This principle applies to laws of personal status (for example, if a woman claims that she was taken captive but was not raped, or that she was married and then divorced), and to monetary matters (for example, if someone living in a field admits that it originally belonged to someone else's father, but claims that he bought it from the father; or if witnesses admit the authenticity of their signatures, but insist that they signed under duress).

The reliability of such testimony has two restrictions: First, we use the argument that "the mouth that forbade is the mouth that permitted" only when there is no other source for the facts of the case. Second, we do not use this argument if the person making the statement is incriminating himself.

An argument similar to that of "the mouth that forbade" applies if someone makes a statement that causes something to be forbidden to him (for example, if an apparently unmarried woman declares that she was married) and then adds details that limit or annul its Halakhic significance (for example, if she continues: "But I was divorced"). But if the person retracts the statement altogether, we believe him only if he gives a plausible reason for having made the statement in the first place.

Two very important Halakhic topics are discussed in detail in this chapter, after being mentioned in connection with the "mouth that forbade" argument: (1) the laws for authenticating documents, and (2) the laws of the captive woman.

The Gemara's conclusion regarding the authentication of documents is as follows: If a borrower challenges the validity of a document (on the grounds that it was forged, or the like), the document is presented to the court, and the court determines whether the signatures of the witnesses who signed the document are in fact genuine (by considering testimony, or by comparing the signatures on the document with the signatures on other documents known to have been signed by these witnesses). It is sufficient for us to prove that the witnesses did sign the document. We do not investigate the content of the document, for we assume that the witnesses did this before signing. If the witnesses who signed the document authenticate their own signatures, they are considered to be testifying about the content of the document, and not about the signatures; but if independent witnesses authenticate the signatures, they are considered to be testifying about the signatures and not about the content of the document.

The law of the captive woman is as follows: If a woman was kidnapped, or was in a city conquered by an enemy army, or was imprisoned, the Sages rule that we must assume that she was raped, unless there is proof to the contrary. Therefore, such women are disqualified from marrying or remaining married to a priest, since a woman who has had intercourse with a non-Jew is disqualified from the priesthood, even if she was raped. Nevertheless, since there is only a suspicion that she was raped, the Rabbis were lenient and agreed to rely on the testimony of witnesses who would not ordinarily be considered acceptable in court (a single witness, a woman, a relative, etc.), if they testify that she was not raped. Only the testimony of the woman herself or that of her husband — who is deemed to be like herself; and, according to some views, the testimony of her children and her slaves — is not accepted. But her testimony is accepted if she gives it immediately after her release, before we know that she was taken captive at all.

In a similar vein, the Sages relied on the testimony of a single witness, or of a relative, or of an adult who testified about something he saw as a child, for several matters that are Rabbinic in essence (such as testimony by a man claiming to be a priest, who wishes to eat Rabbinic terumah, and testimony about the Shabbat boundary, etc.). We also accept such testimony relating to certain matters about which we are fairly certain in any case, so that full testimony is not required — such as determining which family is of pure lineage and which is of blemished lineage, and whether or not a bride was treated as a virgin at her wedding ceremony.

List of Sources

Aḥaronim, lit., "the last," meaning Rabbinical authorities from the time of the publication of Rabbi Yosef Caro's code of Halakhah, *Shulḥan Arukh* (1555).

Arba'ah Turim, code of Halakhah by Rabbi Ya'akov ben Asher, b. Germany, active in Spain (c. 1270–1343).

Arukh, first Talmudic dictionary, by Rabbi Natan of Rome, 11th century.

Arukh HaShulḥan, commentary on *Shulḥan Arukh* by Rabbi Yeḥiel Mikhel Epstein, Byelorussia (1829–1908).

Ayelet Ahavim, novellae on *Ketubot* by Rabbi Aryeh Leib Zuenz, Poland, 19th century.

Ba'al HaMa'or, Rabbi Zeraḥyah ben Yitzḥak HaLevi, Spain, 12th century. *HaMa'or*, Halakhic commentary on *Hilkhot HaRif*.

Ba'al HaIttur, see *Ittur*.

Ba'er Hetev, commentary on *Shulḥan Arukh, Ḥoshen Mishpat*, by Rabbi Zeḥaryah Mendel of Belz, Poland (18th century).

Bahag, Ba'al Halakhot Gedolot. See *Halakhot Gedolot*.

Bayit Ḥadash, commentary on *Arba'ah Turim* by Rabbi Yoel Sirkes, Poland (1561–1640).

Bedek HaBayit, additions to *Shulḥan Arukh* by Rabbi Yosef Karo. See *Shulḥan Arukh*.

Bereshit Rabbah, Midrash on the Book of Genesis.

Bet HaLevi, responsa and novellae by Rabbi Yosef Dov Soloveichik of Brisk, Poland (1820–1892).

Bet Shmuel, commentary on *Shulḥan Arukh, Even HaEzer*, by Rabbi Shmuel ben Uri Shraga, Poland, second half of the 17th century.

Bet Ya'akov, novellae on *Ketubot*, by Rabbi Ya'akov Lorberboim of Lissa, Poland (1760–1832).

Bet Yosef, Halakhic commentary on the *Arba'ah Turim* by Rabbi Yosef Caro (1488–1575), which is the basis of his authoritative Halakhic code, the *Shulḥan Arukh*.

Derishah and *Perishah*, commentaries on *Tur* by Rabbi Yehoshua Falk Katz, Poland (c. 1555–1614).

Ein Ya'akov, collection of Aggadot from the Babylonian Talmud by Rabbi Ya'akov ben Shlomo Ḥabib, Spain and Salonika (c. 1445–1515).

Etz Yosef, commentary on *Ein Ya'akov* by Rabbi Ḥanokh Zundel ben Yosef, Russia (d. 1867).

Even HaEzer, section of *Shulḥan Arukh* dealing with marriage, divorce, and related topics.

Geonim, heads of the academies of Sura and Pumbedita in Babylonia from the late 6th century to the mid-11th century.

Gilyon Efraim, commentary on the Jerusalem Talmud by Rabbi Efraim Dov HaKohen Lapp, Jaroslaw, Poland (late 19th century).

Gra, Rabbi Eliyahu ben Shlomo Zalman (1720–1797), the Gaon of Vilna. Novellae on the Talmud and *Shulḥan Arukh*.

Hafla'ah, novellae on *Ketubot*, by Rabbi Pinḥas HaLevi Horowitz, Poland and Germany (1731–1805).

Haggahot Mordekhai, glosses on the *Mordekhai*, by Rabbi Shmuel ben Aharon of Schlettstadt, Germany, late 14th century.

Halakhot Gedolot, a code of Halakhic decisions written in the Geonic period. This work has been ascribed to Rav Yehudai Gaon and Rabbi Shimon Kayyara.

Hashlamah, see *Sefer HaHashlamah*.

Ḥatam Sofer, responsa literature and novellae on the Talmud by Rabbi Moshe Sofer (Schreiber), Pressburg, Hungary and Germany (1763–1839).

Ḥelkat Meḥokek, commentary on *Shulḥan Arukh, Even HaEzer*, by Rabbi Moshe Lima, Lithuania (1605–1658).

Ḥoshen Mishpat, section of *Shulḥan Arukh* dealing with civil and criminal law.

Ittur, Halakhic work by Rabbi Yitzḥak Abba Mari, Provence (1122–1193).

Kesef Mishneh, commentary on *Mishneh Torah* by Rabbi Yosef Caro, author of the *Shulḥan Arukh*.

Ketzot HaḤoshen, novellae on *Shulḥan Arukh, Ḥoshen Mishpat*, by Rabbi Arieh Leib Heller, Galicia (1754?–1813).

Kikayon DeYonah, novellae on the Talmud by Rabbi Yonah Te'omim, Bohemia and Germany, 19th century.

Korban HaEdah, commentary on the Jerusalem Talmud by Rabbi David ben Naftali Frankel, Germany (1707–1762).

Kovetz Shiurim, novellae on the Talmud by Rabbi Elḥanan Wasserman, Lithuania (1875–1941).

Leḥem Mishneh, commentary on *Mishneh Torah* by Rabbi Avraham di Boton, Salonica (1560–1609).

Likkutei Geonim, collection of Geonic material from *Shittah Mekubbetzet.* See *Shittah Mekubbetzet.*

Magen Avraham, commentary on *Shulḥan Arukh, Oraḥ Ḥayyim,* by Rabbi Avraham HaLevi Gombiner, Poland (d. 1683).

Maggid Mishneh, commentary on *Mishneh Torah* by Rabbi Vidal de Tolosa, Spain, 14th century.

Maharal, Rabbi Yehudah Loew ben Betzalel of Prague (1525–1609). Novellae on the Talmud.

Maharam Schiff, novellae on the Talmud by Rabbi Meir ben Ya'akov HaKohen Schiff (1605–1641), Frankfurt, Germany.

Maharik, Rabbi Yosef Kolon, France and Italy (c. 1420–1480). Responsa literature.

Maharsha, Rabbi Shmuel Eliezer ben Yehudah HaLevi Edels, Poland (1555–1631). Novellae on the Talmud.

Maharshal, Rabbi Shlomo ben Yeḥiel Luria, Poland (1510–1573). Novellae on the Talmud.

Meiri, commentary on the Talmud (called *Bet HaBeḥirah*) by Rabbi Menaḥem ben Shlomo, Provence (1249–1316).

Melekhet Shlomo, commentary on the Mishnah by Rabbi Shlomo Adeni, Eretz Israel (1567–1626).

Minḥat Ḥinnukh, commentary on *Sefer HaḤinnukh* by Rabbi Yosef Babad, Poland (1800–1874/5).

Mishneh LeMelekh, commentary on *Mishneh Torah* by Rabbi Yehudah ben Shmuel Rosanes, Turkey (1657–1727).

Mordekhai, compendium of Halakhic decisions by Rabbi Mordekhai ben Hillel HaKohen, Germany (1240?–1298).

Or Zarua, collection of Halakhic rulings of German and French Rabbis by Rabbi Yitzḥak ben Moshe of Vienna (c. 1180–1250).

Oraḥ Ḥayyim, section of *Shulḥan Arukh* dealing with daily religious observances, prayers, and the laws of the Sabbath and Festivals.

Perishah, see *Derishah.*

Pitḥei Teshuvah, compilation of responsa literature on the *Shulḥan Arukh* by Rabbi Avraham Tzvi Eisenstadt, Russia (1812–1868).

Pnei Moshe, commentary on the Jerusalem Talmud by Rabbi Moshe ben Shimon Margoliyot, Lithuania (c. 1710–1781).

Pnei Yehoshua, novellae on the Talmud by Rabbi Ya'akov Yehoshua Falk, Poland and Germany (1680–1756).

Ra'ah, see *Rabbi Aharon Halevi.*

Ra'avad, Rabbi Avraham ben David, commentator and Halakhic authority. Wrote comments on *Mishneh Torah.* Provence (c. 1125–1198?).

Rabbenu Ḥananel (ben Ḥushiel), commentator on Talmud, North Africa (990–1055).

Rabbenu Nissim Gaon, Egypt, first half of 11th century. Talmudist.

Rabbenu Shlomo Min HaHar, Talmudist, France (12th–13th centuries).

Rabbenu Tam, commentator on Talmud, Tosafist, France (1100–1171).

Rabbenu Yeḥiel, French Tosafist (d. 1268).

Rabbenu Yehonatan, Yehonatan ben David HaKohen of Lunel, Provence, Talmudic scholar (c. 1135–after 1210).

Rabbenu Yonah, see *Talmidei Rabbenu Yonah.*

Rabbenu Yeruḥam, Rabbi Yeruḥam ben Meshullam, Halakhist, Spain, 14th century. Author of *Toledot Adam VeḤavah.*

Rabbi Aharon HaLevi, Spain, 13th century. Novellae on the Talmud.

Rabbi Akiva Eger, Talmudist and Halakhic authority, Posen, Germany (1761–1837).

Rabbi Avigdor HaKohen, Tosafist, Austria (1180–1255).

Rabbi Ya'akov Emden, Talmudist and Halakhic authority, Germany (1697–1776).

Radak, Rabbi David Kimḥi, grammarian and Bible commentator, Narbonne, Provence (1160?–1235?)

Radbaz, Rabbi David ben Shlomo Avi Zimra, Spain, Egypt, Eretz Israel and North Africa (1479–1589). Commentary of *Mishneh Torah.*

Ramakh, Rabbi Meir HaKohen of Rothenburg, Germany (14th century). Author of *Haggahot Maimoniyot* (commentary on *Mishneh Torah*).

Rambam, Rabbi Moshe ben Maimon, Rabbi and philosopher, known also as Maimonides. Author of *Mishneh Torah*, Spain and Egypt (1135–1204).

Ramban, Rabbi Moshe ben Naḥman, commentator on Bible and Talmud, known also as Naḥmanides, Spain and Eretz Israel (1194–1270).

Ran, Rabbi Nissim ben Reuven Gerondi, Spanish Talmudist (1310?–1375?).

Rashash, Rabbi Shmuel ben Yosef Shtrashun, Lithuanian Talmud scholar (1794–1872).

Rashba, Rabbi Shlomo ben Avraham Adret, Spanish Rabbi famous for his commentaries on the Talmud and his responsa (c. 1235–c. 1314).

Rashbam, Rabbi Shmuel ben Meir, commentator on the Talmud, France (1085–1158).

Rashbatz, Rabbi Shimon ben Tzemaḥ Duran, known for his book of responsa, *Tashbatz,* Spain and Algeria (1361–1444).

Rashi, Rabbi Shlomo ben Yitzḥak, the paramount commentator on the Bible and the Talmud, France (1040–1105).

Rav Aḥa (Aḥai) Gaon, author of *She'iltot.* Pumbedita, Babylonia and Eretz Israel, 8th century. See *She'iltot.*

Rav Hai Gaon, Babylonian Rabbi, head of Pumbedita Yeshivah, 10th century.

Rav Sa'adyah Gaon, scholar and author, Egypt and Sura, Babylonia (882–942).

Rav Tzemaḥ Gaon, Tzemaḥ ben Ḥayyim, Gaon of Sura from 889 to 895.

Rema, Rabbi Moshe ben Yisrael Isserles, Halakhic authority, Cracow, Poland (1525–1572).

Remah, novellae on the Talmud by Rabbi Meir ben Todros HaLevi Abulafiya, Spain (c. 1170–1244). See *Yad Ramah.*

Ri Migash, Rabbi Yosef Ibn Migash, commentator on the Talmud, Spain (1077–1141).

Rid, see *Tosefot Rid.*

Rif, Rabbi Yitzḥak Alfasi, Halakhist, author of *Hilkhot HaRif,* North Africa (1013–1103).

Rishonim, lit., "the first," meaning Rabbinical authorities active between the end of the Geonic period (mid-11th century) and the publication of the *Shulḥan Arukh* (1555).

Ritva, novellae and commentary on the Talmud by Rabbi Yom Tov ben Avraham Ishbili, Spain (c. 1250–1330).

Rivash, Rabbi Yitzḥak ben Sheshet, Spain and North Africa (1326–1408). Novellae on the Talmud mentioned in *Shittah Mekubbetzet.*

Rosh, Rabbi Asher ben Yeḥiel, also known as Asheri, commentator and Halakhist, Germany and Spain (c. 1250–1327).

Sefer HaHashlamah, supplement to *Hilkhot HaRif* by Rabbi Meshullam ben Moshe, Provence, early 13th century.

Sefer HaḤinnukh, anonymous work on the 613 Biblical precepts, 14th century.

Sefer HaTerumot, Halakhic work by Rabbi Shmuel ben Yitzḥak Sardi, Spain (1185/90–1255/56)

Sefer VeHizhir, midrash on the Book of Exodus, author unknown, 10th century.

Shakh (Siftei Kohen), commentary on *Shulḥan Arukh* by Rabbi Shabbetai ben Meir HaKohen, Lithuania and Germany (1621–1662).

She'iltot, by Aḥa (Aḥai) of the Pumbedita Yeshivah, 8th century. One of the first books of Halakhah arranged by subjects.

Shev Shemateta, essays on Halakhic concepts by Rabbi Aryeh Leib Heller, Galicia (1754?–1813).

Shiltei HaGibborim, glosses on *Rif* and *Mordekhai* by Rabbi Yehoshua Boaz ben Shimon Barukh, Italy, 16th century.

Shittah Mekubbetzet, a collection of commentaries on the Talmud by Rabbi Betzalel ben Avraham Ashkenazi of Egypt (c. 1520–1591).

Shmuel HaNagid, Spain (993–1055 or 1056). Novellae on the Talmud found in *Shittah Mikubbetzet.*

Shoel Umeshiv, responsa literature by Rabbi Yosef Shaul Nathanson, Brody, Poland (1810–1875).

Shulḥan Arukh, code of Halakhah by Rabbi Yosef Caro, b. Spain, active in Eretz Israel (1488–1575).

Sifra (also known as *Torat Kohanim*), Halakhic Midrash on the Book of Leviticus.

Sifrei, Halakhic Midrash on the Books of Numbers and Deuteronomy.

Sma (Sefer Meirat Einayim), commentary on *Shulḥan Arukh, Ḥoshen Mishpat*, by Rabbi Yehoshua Falk Katz, Poland (c. 1555–1614).

Smag (Sefer Mitzvot Gadol), an extensive work on the positive and negative commandments by Rabbi Moshe ben Ya'akov of Coucy, 13th century.

Talmid Rabbenu Peretz, commentary on *Ketubot* by the school of the Tosafist Rabbi Peretz of Corbeil, France (13th century).

Talmidei Rabbenu Yonah, commentary on *Hilkhot HaRif,* by the school of Rabbi Yonah of Gerondi, Spain (1190–1263).

Taz, abbreviation for *Turei Zahav.* See *Turei Zahav.*

Tiferet Yisrael, commentary on the Mishnah by Rabbi Yisrael Lipshitz, Germany (1782–1860).

Tosafot, collection of commentaries and novellae on the Talmud, expanding on Rashi's commentary, by the French-German Tosafists (12th–13th centuries).

Tosafot Ḥadashim, commentary on the Mishnah, by Rabbi Shimshon Bloch, Hamburg, Germany (d. 1737).

Tosefot Rid, commentary on the Talmud by Rabbi Yeshayahu ben Mali di Trani, Italian Halakhist (c. 1200–before 1260).

Tosefot Yom Tov, commentary on the Mishnah by Rabbi Yom Tov Lipman HaLevi Heller, Prague and Poland (1579–1654).

Tur, abbreviation of *Arba'ah Turim,* Halakhic code by Rabbi Ya'akov ben Asher, b. Germany, active in Spain (c. 1270–1343).

Turei Zahav, commentary on *Shulḥan Arukh* by Rabbi David ben Shmuel HaLevi, Poland (c. 1586–1667).

Yad Ramah, novellae on the Talmud by Rabbi Meir ben Todros HaLevi Abulafiya, Spain (c. 1170–1244).

Yoreh De'ah, section of *Shulḥan Arukh* dealing with dietary laws, interest, ritual purity, and mourning.

About the Type

This book was set in Leawood, a contemporary typeface designed by Leslie Usherwood. His staff completed the design upon Usherwood's death in 1984. It is a friendly, inviting face that goes particularly well with sans serif type.